The Sociology of Health

Other Wadsworth Titles of Related Interest in Sociology

The cover and text opening pages include the cylix and serpent of Hygeia, the Greek goddess and personification of health. It was Hygeia's philosophy that men and women were entitled to health, provided they governed their lives wisely. For Hygeia and her philosophical heirs, the fundamental function of medicine was first to discover and then to teach the natural laws that would ensure a healthy mind and a healthy body— what today we would call a preventive and maintenance-oriented philosophy. (See page 4.)

The Sociology of Health

Principles,
Practitioners,
and Issues

SECOND EDITION

Fredric D. Wolinsky

Texas A&M University

Wadsworth Publishing Company
Belmont, California
A Division of Wadsworth, Inc.

Sociology Editor: Sheryl Fullerton
Editorial Associate: Cynthia Haus
Print Buyer: Karen Hunt
Text and Cover Design: Seventeenth Street Studios
Technical Illustrator: Valerie Felts
Compositor: G & S Typesetters, Inc.
Signing Representative: Ragu Raghaven

Library of Congress Cataloging-in-Publication Data

Wolinsky, Fredric D.
    The sociology of health.

    Bibliography: p.
.   Includes index.
    1. Social medicine.   2. Social medicine—
United States.   I. Title.   [DNLM: 1. Social Medicine.
WA 31 W861s]
RA418.W64   1988   306′.4   87-18862
ISBN 0-534-08701-9

Printed in the United States of America   19
1 2 3 4 5 6 7 8 9 10——92 91 90 89 88

P. 13: Table from Lisa Berkman and Lester Breslow, *Health and Ways of Living: The Alameda County Study.* © 1983 by Oxford University Press, Inc. Reprinted by permission.

Pp. 29, 30, 32: Excerpts from George Foster, "Medical Anthropology: Some Contrasts With Medical Sociology," from *Social Science and Medicine,* Volume 9, 1975. Reprinted by permission of Pergamon Journals, Ltd. and the author.

Pp. 75, 80, 269, 305, 306, 308: Excerpts from Robert N. Wilson, *The Sociology of Health,* Copyright © 1970 by Random House, Inc. Reprinted by permission of the publisher.

Pp. 108–9: Excerpts from Talcott Parsons, "The Sick Role and the Role of the Physician Reconsidered," from *Milbank Memorial Fund Quarterly,* Volume 53, 1975. Reprinted by permission of the publisher.

Pp. 112, 113, 114, 218, 222, 223, 226, 227, 228, 265: Excerpts from Eliot Freidson, *Profession of Medicine: A Study in the Sociology of Applied Knowledge,* 1970. Reprinted by permission.

Pp. 118–19: Excerpts from David Mechanic, *Medical Sociology: A Comprehensive Text,* Second Edition. Copyright © 1978 by The Free Press, a Division of Macmillan, Inc. Reprinted by permission of the publisher.

P. 130: Figure 6.3 from Irwin Rosenstock, "Historical Origins of the Health Belief Model," from *Health Education Monographs,* Volume 2, 1974. Reprinted by permission of Charles B. Slack, Inc.

Pp. 133–35: Excerpts from LuAnn Aday and Ronald Andersen, *Access to Medical Care,* 1975. Reprinted by permission of the Pluribus Press, Chicago.

P. 158: Figure 7.1 from David Hayes-Bautista, "Modifying the Treatment: Patient Compliance, Patient Control, and Medical Care," from *Social Science and Medicine,* Volume 10, 1976. Reprinted by permission of Pergamon Journals, Ltd. and the author.

Pp. 181–82: Excerpts from William R. Thomson, *Black's Medical Dictionary,* Twenty-fourth Edition. Reprinted by permission of A & C Black (Publishers) Ltd.

P. 211: Excerpts from Logan Clendening, *Sourcebook of Medical History.* Reprinted by permission of Dover Publications, Inc.

Pp. 229–30: Excerpts from Eliot Freidson, "The Changing Nature of Professional Control," from *Annual Review of Sociology,*

Volume 10, 1984, © 1984 by Annual Reviews Inc. Reprinted by permission of the author and publisher.

P. 241: Excerpts from Rue Bucher and Joan Stelling, *Becoming Professional,* Copyright © 1977 by Sage Publications, Inc. Reprinted by permission of the publisher.

Pp. 259, 260, 261: Excerpts from Daniel J. Benor, "Psychic Healing," in J. W. Salmon, ed., *Alternative Medicines.* Reprinted by permission of Tavistock Publications.

Pp. 260, 262: Excerpts from Warren E. Schaller and Charles R. Carroll, *Health, Quackery and the Consumer.* Reprinted by permission of CBS College Publishing.

Pp. 270, 272, 275, 677–78: Excerpts from Hans O. Mauksch, "Nursing: Churning for Change?" in *Handbook of Medical Sociology,* Second Edition, edited by Freeman, Levine and Reeder, © 1972, pp. 208, 211–212, 215. Reprinted by permission of Prentice-Hall, Inc., Englewood Cliffs, New Jersey.

Pp. 321–22: Excerpts from Paul J. Feldstein, *Health Care Economics,* Second Edition, © 1983 by John Wiley & Sons, Inc. Reprinted by permission of the publisher.

Pp. 341, 342–43: Excerpts from Ivan Illich, *Medical Nemesis: The Expropriation of Our Health,* Copyright © 1975 by Ivan Illich. Copyright © 1976 by Random House, Inc. Reprinted by permission of Pantheon Books, a Division of Random House, Inc. and Marion Boyars Publishers Ltd.

Pp. 341–42, 343: Excerpts from Renee C. Fox, "Doing Better and Feeling Worse: Health in the United States," Volume 106, No. 1, Winter 1977. Reprinted by permission of *Daedalus,* Journal of the American Academy of Arts and Sciences.

Pp. 343, 344: Excerpts from Peter Conrad, *Identifying Hyperactive Children,* 1976. Reprinted by permission of Lexington Books, a Division of D. C. Health and Company.

Pp. 340, 341: Excerpts from Leon Wyszewianski, John Wheeler and Avedis Donabedian, "Market-oriented Cost-containment Strategies and the Quality of Care," in *Milbank Memorial Fund Quarterly,* Volume 60, 1982. Reprinted by permission of the publisher.

Pp. 345, 346, 348, 354–55: Excerpts from William Rushing, *Journal of Health and Social Behavior,* Volume 26, 1985, pp. 297–311. Reprinted by permission of the American Sociological Association and the author.

For Rodney M. Coe

Mentor,

Colleague,

and

Friend

Contents

Part Two
Principles

Preface

MEDICAL SOCIOLOGY is the largest and most vibrant specialization in the discipline. The health care industry, which has been big business for some time, has become even more pervasive in our society. In so doing, it has changed the way we live. In the process, both the public and policymakers have become increasingly concerned about equitable access and the cost of health care. As a result, the demand for courses on the sociology of health is increasing once again.

Faculty and students alike are searching for a text that will make the most of their classroom experience. Such a book should have four main features:

—it must be readable,

—it must be comprehensive,

—it must have a guiding framework that interrelates all the pieces of the health care delivery puzzle, and

—it must address the crucial issues of the next ten years.

This book has those features, and more.

The rationale for writing this book is to provide a coherent and in-depth understanding of the sociology of health and the health care delivery system. To do so, the book is divided into four sections. The first is an overview of social factors and health, the development of medical sociology, and the health care delivery system. This provides a description of where things are today, and the historical context from which they evolved.

It is against this backdrop that the next two sections comprehensively and systematically identify and interrelate each of the principles and practitioners involved in the delivery of health care. This is a conceptual approach that incorporates the most up-to-date facts and examples. The focus is on three crucial questions: (a) why do people behave the way they do when they are sick, (b) how do patients and their practitioners interact with each other under a variety of circumstances, and (c) how did the profession of medicine achieve its dominant position in both the health care industry and our society? The answers are found by carefully examining the conceptual issues that underpin the questions, reviewing what has been done to study them, and showing how they are interrelated by use of the systems perspective.

Having identified and interrelated the various pieces of the health care delivery puzzle, the fourth section of the book focuses on crucial issues for the coming decade. Because money drives the system, an entire chapter is devoted to health care economics. It raises the issue of whether traditional economic principles are applicable to the medical marketplace, and reviews the effect of different methods of health insurance and financing, highlighting Medicare's newest cost-containment effort, Diagnostic Related Groups. The book concludes with a thorough discussion of three pressing issues: quality care assessment, the medicalization of life, and the coming of the physician surplus.

Acknowledgements

The first edition of this book was used in hundreds of courses taken by thousands of students. Many of them have let me know how much they enjoyed it, and how well it worked. That makes all the effort it takes to write a book worthwhile. More gratifying, however, have been the suggestions for making the book even better. Among the more frequent have been adding an overview of the health care delivery system, separate chapters on alternative practitioners and health care economics, more comprehensive coverage of competing theoretical perspectives, and the implications of the physician surplus. Old friends will find all of these have been included in this edition.

Just as no man is an island, neither is any book. This edition is no exception. A number of colleagues have read and commented on part or all of the manuscript at one stage or another. For this my heartfelt thanks go out to Bebe Lavin, Peter Conrad, Karen Peterson, Donald Metz, Thomas Sullivan,

and Michael Kleiman. Jackie Sandles helped prepare the tables, which was no mean feat. The folks at Wadsworth were just great. Sheryl Fullerton, Hal Humphrey, Bob Kauser, and Ragu Raghaven are truly an author's best co-workers.

But no one has been more helpful than Sally Wolinsky. She is my best friend, my best critic, and my partner in life. Sally read each and every chapter, made numerous suggestions, and then scrutinized the changes. Her perspective as a nurse-sociologist was invaluable. And her patience with my many hours on the word processor was extraordinary.

Fredric D. Wolinsky
College Station, Texas
October 1987

I. Introduction

1. Social Factors and Health: Is There a Relationship?

A TEXTBOOK SHOULD begin with a rationale for studying the subject at hand. Justification for the study of the sociology of health can be made by demonstrating the relationship between social factors and health, health-related behavior, and health institutions. The purpose of this chapter is to document that relationship by showing how social factors influence our health.

This chapter has three major sections. In the first section, we trace the development of medicine by briefly examining the eight crucial periods in the shaping of the world view of medicine. Four important dualities in modern medicine are also identified and discussed. In the second section, we explore the field of social epidemiology, whose purpose is to identify the distribution of health and illness across different social groupings. After defining social epidemiology and discussing its procedure, we review the classic contributions of Sir Percival Pott and Sir John Snow. We then turn to more contemporary examples of social epidemiology, such as the research on smoking and lung cancer, legionnaires' disease, myocardial infarction, health habits and mortality rates, and AIDS. We present next the basic tools of the social epidemiologist and define their relationship to the principal variables of the discipline. In the final section, we use health and social data from two adjacent states within the United States to demonstrate and clarify the relationship between social factors and health.

The Emergence of Modern Medicine

Eight Crucial Periods in the World View of Medicine

Modern medicine is just that—*modern* medicine. It has evolved, over the centuries, out of the interplay of several elements including medical science, the social orientation of the day, the religious orientation of the day, humanity's struggle to master the environment, and the biological adaptation of the human body. These elements did not produce modern medicine overnight. Rather, there has been a long and surprisingly clear history to its evolution. The most influential components of this history should become clear as we review the eight periods that mark the most significant changes in the world view of modern medicine.

THE PHILOSOPHY OF HYGEIA. Hygeia appears in ancient Greek legends by about the fifteenth century B.C. Hygeia is generally portrayed as a goddess who represented probably the earliest philosophical orientation toward health. It was Hygeia's philosophy that, in the natural order of things, health was to be considered a positive attribute to which men were entitled, provided they governed their lives wisely. For Hygeia and her philosophical heirs, the fundamental function of medicine was first to discover and then to teach the natural laws that would ensure man a healthy mind and a healthy body (i.e., a preventive and maintenance-oriented philosophy). The Hygeian philosophy held that health referred to both body and mind. Hygeia's philosophy on the nature and role of medicine was dominant until the twelfth century B.C. (The cover and text opening pages of this book include the cylix and serpent of Hygeia.)

THE CULT OF ASCLEPIUS. The erosion of Hygeia's popularity was due to the emergence of the cult of Asclepius. According to legend, Asclepius was the first Greek physician, appearing around 1200 B.C. Asclepius' rise to fame and the formation of his cult were based on his mastery in the use of the knife and his knowledge of the curative power of plants in restoring the physical body to its original state of health. In contrast to Hygeia, Asclepius believed that the primary role of the physician was to treat disease, and by so doing to restore health (i.e., a corrective or interventionist philosophy). The restoration of health was accom-

plished by correcting the imperfections in the human body that were caused by the accidents of birth or life. Because of Asclepius' dramatic successes, and his training of others in the use of the knife and herbs, his philosophical orientation to health remained in vogue for centuries.

THE AGE OF HIPPOCRATES. Hippocrates was a Greek physician who lived in the fifth century B.C. While we credit many things to Hippocrates, we actually know very little about him as an individual. Most of what we do know is based on a series of books that bear his name (although it is not certain that he actually wrote them). Hippocrates is most famous for the Hippocratic oath, which stands as the cornerstone of contemporary medical ethics. In brief, by taking the oath the physician swears: (1) to help the sick, (2) to refrain from intentional wrongdoing or harm to the patient, and (3) to keep sacred the patient-practitioner relationship. While we know of and applaud the Hippocratic oath, Hippocrates should be remembered for two more important contributions. First, he demanded a rational and systematic approach to patient care, rejecting the effects of supernatural phenomena. In essence, Hippocrates urged the adoption of a scientific medicine rather than one that appealed to the supernatural, practiced divination, or haphazardly applied curative techniques. Second, Hippocrates maintained that the mind and the body affect each other: they cannot be considered as independent entities. Hippocrates believed in treating the whole person. He also recognized the importance of the social environment in understanding illness. A new era of medical history had clearly arrived, an era guided by a scientific and holistic medical philosophy.

THE CONSTRAINTS OF THE CHURCH. Unfortunately for medical history, the Age of Hippocrates was followed by the rise and fall of Rome, and then by the Dark Ages. It was during this chaotic and tumultuous period that much of the existing knowledge of medicine was lost. This was a mixed blessing, in that the Church assumed control of and responsibility for the general areas of the mind and of the social problems of the day. Medicine was relegated to considering only the problems of the physical body. As a result, medicine was forced to return to treating the physical ailments of the individual, apart from mental disorders or adverse social factors. The whole-person approach of Hippocrates came to an abrupt end.

DESCARTES AND SEVENTEENTH-CENTURY RATIONALISM. By the 1600s, the constraints on medicine imposed by the Church were still in existence, but the dogmatic separation of mind and body appeared to be weakening. Then, like the cavalry rushing onto the scene at the last moment, René Descartes and several other seventeenth-century rationalist philosophers came to the rescue. They reinforced the Church's position by arguing that a mind-body dichotomy did indeed exist and that each was independent of the other. Further, Descartes philosophized that medicine should concentrate its efforts on the physical functioning of the body. The mind, according to Descartes, was to be left in the hands of God and his agents (the Church). There is little wonder that Descartes's position was readily accepted by the Church.

THE AGE OF ADVANCES IN PUBLIC HEALTH. Perhaps the greatest shift in the orientation of medicine from that of Descartes to a more humanistic philosophy came, ironically, at the time of the Industrial Revolution. The shift was accompanied by a change in emphasis from the health of the individual in isolation to medicine in the context of society. In particular, the efforts of such Utopians as Robert Owen and Saint-Simon brought a strong sense of humanitarianism to the emerging field of public health. The Utopians, many of whom were industrialists, studied the link between lifestyle and health that the Industrial Revolution had made so obvious. Pressing for uncontaminated food, air, water, and sanitary living conditions, they hoped to improve public health. Whether the motivation of the Utopians was humanitarian—to better the plight of mankind—or economic—to increase the productivity of their workers by keeping them healthy—doesn't really

matter. The end result was that substantial improvement was made in public hygiene (from the same root as *Hygeia*) and sanitation. As a result, many epidemic diseases quickly disappeared. In fact, Dubos (1959) states that "the most effective techniques to avoid disease came out of the attempts to correct by *social* measures the injustices and the ugliness brought about by industrialization."

PASTEUR, KOCH, SPECIFIC ETIOLOGY, AND GERMS. During the 1800s, medicine once again became more concerned with technological advancement than with social reform. In particular, based on the pioneering work of Louis Pasteur, Robert Koch, and others, bacteriological research flourished. This research resulted in the postulation of a *germ theory of disease*, accompanied by marked advances in clinical medicine, especially anesthesiology, pathology, immunology, and surgery. The basic premise of the germ theory is that for every disease there is a specific pathogenic cause (subsequently expanded to include multiple pathogenic causes). The best method of treating the disease was to remove or control the cause within a biomedical framework. One result of the germ theory was a view of medicine dominated, in physicians' thinking, by the search for what Dubos (1959) calls "magic bullets." Magic bullets are used to shoot down and kill the disease. This view is still widely accepted: witness the extensive use of pharmaceuticals in the treatment of disease by modern medical workers. Another result of the germ theory is that the patient often comes to be identified by his or her disease rather than as a person. For example, the contemporary physician might talk about the diseased kidney in room 321, rather than talking about its owner. This aspect is referred to as the old scientific fragmentation method, which, in tandem with "medical uncertainty," allows physicians to become body mechanics or tradesmen.

WHOLE-PERSON HEALTH: AN EMERGING SYSTEMATIC APPROACH. In the latter half of this century, there is a trend to return our conception of medicine and health to the study of the whole person. At the forefront of this movement is the World Health Organization (1958), which identifies three major dimensions on which health must be addressed: (1) the physiological dimension of health, (2) the psychological dimension of health, and (3) the social dimension of health. Dubos (1959) not only recognizes these three dimensions of health but takes WHO's argument one step further, writing that the pursuit of health is an ongoing, adaptive process and not a static state that can always be achieved or purchased. In other words, health means constant adaptation to ever-changing biological and social environments.

At the core of this new trend is the fundamental concept that health must be defined in terms of the whole person. Further, treatment must be directed toward the whole person, which can include family members and significant others, not just toward the particular physiological pathology in the patient. This new philosophy of medicine and health, however, is only just beginning: whether it will ever become the dominant orientation—and when—is not yet known. The issue is still much in doubt (see Elinson, 1985). One alternative open to the medical profession would be to ignore the changing times and restrict the definitions of disease (and its concomitant research and treatment) to purely physiological phenomena. The systematic whole-person approach to health, on the other hand, requires a change in the general orientation and training of physicians, and calls for a close association between medicine and the behavioral sciences (especially sociology, anthropology, economics, psychology, and epidemiology). One indication of the acceptance of the whole-person approach is the large-scale recruitment of behavioral science faculty by medical schools over the past two decades. In fact, some graduates in the behavioral sciences are now being admitted to medical schools. This new alliance between medicine and the behavioral sciences, however, is still uneasy.

Four Dualities in Modern Medicine

As we have mentioned, the world view of modern medicine has been affected by the world view of medicine in prior periods. As a result, there are four dualities in modern medicine (Carlson, 1975). The first duality concerns the simultaneous reliance on magic and science, a duality that has always existed in medicine. During the Neolithic Age, the medicine men of the eastern Mediterranean and North Africa practiced a very interesting surgical procedure called trepanation. Believing that illness was caused by evil spirits invading the body, these primitive surgeons bored holes in the skulls of sick people to let the evil spirits escape. Judging from the anthropological evidence, including skulls with more than one hole, this procedure was not always fatal. This indicates some competence in surgical technique, coupled with a belief in supernatural spirits. Somewhat less gruesome was the practice of drawing "bad" blood from sick people, surgically or with leeches, on through the early 1800s. This mixture of science and the supernatural resulted in many deaths, including the wife of United States President Andrew Jackson. The duality continues today: note the emotional, public debate that flourished in the early 1980s over the pharmaceutical known as laetrile. At issue was whether laetrile was an active anticarcinogen or a placebo, or, in fact, a toxic substance.

A second duality in modern medicine is the distinction between individual-oriented medicine and population-oriented medicine. Carlson (1975) notes that individual-oriented medicine has been the domain of medical schools for some time. The basic approach of individual-oriented medicine is curative and restorative. On the other hand, population-oriented medicine has been the domain of schools of public health, where the basic approach is preventive. As we shall see in later chapters, although population-oriented medicine has the greater impact on health levels, most of our health money is spent on individual-oriented medicine (McKinlay and McKinlay, 1977).

The third duality in modern medicine is between those who consider the body and mind as separate entities and those who would treat them as a unity. Perhaps the most convincing support for the latter comes from the growing body of scientific knowledge linking social and emotional stress directly to physiological tissue change (Cohen and Syme, 1985; Kaplan, 1984a). On the one hand, modern medicine continues to treat the mind and the body as if they were separate entities; on the other hand, modern medical research continues to compile a substantial body of data linking psychological and social stress to actual changes in body conditions.

Linked closely to the above is the fourth duality. The technical advances of modern medicine have resulted in the technical treatment of disease rather than the anthropological (or holistic) treatment of the whole person (Carlson, 1975). This is a refinement of the scientific fragmentation method in which the disease, and not the whole person, becomes the subject to be treated. Thus, although it is the whole person who walks into the physician's office, it is only the identifiable disease process that is treated by the technocratic physician. Accordingly, the anthropological qualities of the patient-practitioner relationship of the Hippocratic oath appear to be in conflict with the technical training of the modern physician. Taken together, then, the four dualities represent a significant internal dilemma for modern medicine.

Social Epidemiology

So far, we have been concerned with the variety of world views and general orientations that medicine has reflected in history. Each of these general orientations was intertwined with the social tradition of its day. Each has influenced the orientation of modern medicine. We now turn our attention to social epidemiology, the study of the ways in which social factors are intertwined with the distribution of disease within the general population. (For a comprehensive sur-

vey of the fundamental principles of epidemiology, see Lilienfeld [1980].)

The Nature of Social Epidemiology

Social epidemiology is the study of the distribution of disease, impairment, and general health status across various social groups within the same population (Ibrahim, 1983). It originated as the scientific study of epidemics (how they got started, how disease was transferred from one area to another, and so forth). Since then, contemporary social epidemiology has broadened its scope of interest considerably. Social epidemiologists are now concerned with nonepidemic disease and injuries, including cancer, coronary heart disease, automobile accidents, drug addiction (including alcoholism), and suicide.

According to the epidemiologist, social epidemiology is primarily concerned with finding out under what circumstances diseases occur, and when and where diseases flourish or die (Paul, 1966). Most medical sociologists, however, consider social epidemiology to be more than merely a particular topical area of interest within the sociology of health. According to David Mechanic (1978), social epidemiology is the dominant analytic perspective employed by medical sociologists. The social epidemiological perspective views disease "in its larger socioecological context in which disease agents (such as viral or bacterial agents, noxious environmental substances, and dangerous technologies) have differential effects depending on the characteristics of the host (biological, genetic, psychological, and social capabilities and characteristics) and on the larger sociocultural and physical environment."

The job of the social epidemiologist, then, is to try to determine the common social characteristics of the people in a given population who are more likely to be stricken by the disease or ailment. Accomplishing this task, the social epidemiologist gains a better understanding of the disease. This sense of understanding helps the medical scientist focus his or her search on the cause of the disease, which is generally not yet known. Accordingly, the major concern of the social epidemiologist is not with the health of the individual but with the health problems of the social group or social aggregate (in which all individuals share the same social characteristics). In essence, the role of the social epidemiologist is very similar to the role of the detective. He or she investigates the scene of the crime (the incidence of the disease), looking for clues (common social characteristics among the people stricken with the disease). Then, mostly by inference, the social epidemiologist logically constructs the chain of events that explains why people with those common social characteristics are more likely than other people to be stricken with the disease.

The History of Social Epidemiology

The roots of social epidemiology may be traced far back in history. In fact, the eminent medical historian Henry Sigerist (1960) informs us that even in ancient Greece and Egypt there were documents indicating a relationship between specific diseases or illnesses and particular occupations. Over the centuries, the interest in relating social factors to disease became an increasingly popular topic, and many studies have examined this relationship. Of particular interest and importance in establishing social epidemiology as a systematic and accepted mode of scientific inquiry were the studies of Sir Percival Pott and Sir John Snow.

SIR PERCIVAL POTT. Sir Percival Pott (1775) is most noted for his investigation of the increase in scrotal cancer in England in 1775. Enthusiastically playing the role of the detective, Pott was able to identify the specific etiological (causal) chain of events that resulted in an unusually high rate of scrotal cancer among lower class, urban whites. He found that many homes in Britain were heated by space heaters. The fuel for these space heaters, coal, did not burn completely,

and one resulting by-product was a considerable amount of soot. This soot accumulated in the chimneys of the space heaters, and as a result, the chimneys needed periodic cleaning. This produced a new occupation, chimney sweeping. The process of cleaning soot from chimneys, however, was not very pleasant. It was relegated, therefore, to members of the lower social class, who were forced to take whatever employment they could get. The chimney sweep came into frequent contact with soot, in which there is a (still) unknown agent that causes scrotal cancer in susceptible organisms. Accordingly, the incidence of scrotal cancer was bound to increase among lower-class, urban whites.

In establishing the chain of events leading to high rates of scrotal cancer among lower-class, urban whites in England, Pott made two major contributions to social epidemiology. The first contribution was in establishing the strategy of disease causation used in investigating the differential distribution of disease in society. This strategy is portrayed in Figure 1-1, in which the stages of the general procedure are set in the links, and the particular processes Pott identified, in studying scrotal cancer, are set in parentheses. Figure 1-1 shows that the etiological chain of events may begin with a given occupation (chimney sweep) into which a certain social group (lower-class, urban white Britons) is typically recruited. Next, there is usually some characteristic behavioral pattern of this occupation that brings its workers into contact with the vehicle of the disease (soot). Within the frequently contacted vehicle is some agent, usually unknown, that causes the tissue change (scrotal cancer) to occur in the susceptible host (the chimney sweep).

Pott's second contribution was equally important. He demonstrated that, having identified the etiological chain of events producing the disease, the practitioner could break the chain at any of its links, even if the actual agent remained unknown. Pott successfully broke the scrotal cancer chain by prescribing daily baths for chimney sweeps (in 1775, daily bathing was not a common practice).

Figure 1-1. The Etiological Chain of Events Producing Disease.

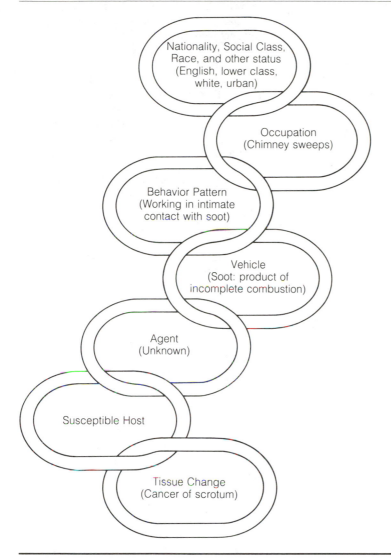

SOURCE: Ronald Andersen and Odin Anderson, "Trends in the Use of Health Services" in Howard E. Freeman, Sol Levine, and Leo G. Reeder, eds., *Handbook of Medical Sociology,* 3rd ed. New York: Prentice-Hall. Adapted by permission of Prentice-Hall, Inc., Englewood Cliffs, New Jersey.

SIR JOHN SNOW. Although Sir Percival Pott made two major contributions to social epidemiology, the systematic and scientific analysis that we now know of as social epidemiology did not develop until the mid 1800s. The primary force behind this development was Sir John Snow (1855). Snow was concerned with the outbreak of cholera in London in 1854, which resulted in the deaths of over 8,000 Londoners. In an attempt to find the cause of cholera, or at least to alleviate its devastating effect, Snow first marked on maps of London the location of all reported cases of cholera. Armed with this information, he set out to interview the surviving family members and neighbors in order to gather information about the victims' daily lives, from what they ate to where they worked and where they played. After collecting an enormous amount of information, he began to see a pattern. All the victims for whom he had data got their drinking water from the Broad Street water pump. Based on this pattern, he inferred that cholera was a waterborne disease. Further, he hypothesized that the Broad Street water pump was providing Londoners with contaminated—cholera-infested—water. Accordingly, he had the Broad Street water pump shut down. In so doing, Snow stopped the cholera epidemic.

As in the case of Sir Percival Pott, Sir John Snow made two major contributions to social epidemiology. First, he established a systematic method of social epidemiology: the tracing back from the disease (cholera) to the common social characteristics (use of the Broad Street water pump) that brought the victims to the disease's agent (the cholera bacterium). Unlike Pott's discovery of the link between soot and scrotal cancer, the cause of cholera (waterborne bacteria) was not readily associable with any social characteristics, such as the occupation of chimney sweep. Snow's second contribution was the confirmation of Pott's discovery that the etiological chain of disease could be broken by intervention at any link. He chose to intervene by shutting down the Broad Street water pump.

Contemporary Social Epidemiology

Sir Percival Pott and Sir John Snow made lasting contributions to the development of social epidemiology. There are five examples, however, from more recent literature that may also be used to demonstrate both the importance of social epidemiology and the relationship between social factors and health: (1) the relationship of lung cancer to smoking, (2) the interesting case of legionnaires' disease, (3) the relationship of myocardial infarction to occupational stress and behavioral patterns, (4) health habits and mortality, and (5) AIDS.

SMOKING AND LUNG CANCER. The possibility of a relationship between smoking and

lung cancer has been under investigation for more than fifty years. It was not until the late 1950s, however, that the relationship received heavy publicity. About that time, lung cancer had become a major cause of death in the United States and other countries. This resulted in accelerated research into the lung cancer–smoking relationship. Following Graham (1972), the data that has emerged from this research may be placed into four basic categories: (1) animal studies, in which tar, the suspected cancer agent, from cigarettes is applied to the shaven skin of mice or hamsters; (2) retrospective studies, in which lung cancer victims and nonvictims are asked about their prior smoking or nonsmoking behavior; (3) prospective studies, in which groups of initially well individuals, smokers and nonsmokers, are identified, examined, and periodically reexamined, or their death certificates are reviewed, in order to compute the incidence rates of lung cancer in both groups; and (4) studies of cellular changes in the respiratory tissue of smokers and nonsmokers. Findings from all four types of studies show that the incidence of cancer increases with increased exposure to cigarette tar (Dorn, 1959; The Surgeon General's Report, 1984).

The relationship between lung cancer and smoking is strong, as is shown in Table 1-1. The data in Table 1-1 are taken from the classic prospective study of 1,078,894 people conducted by Hammond (see Hammond and Horn, 1958). These data clearly show that death from lung cancer is nine times as great among cigarette smokers as it is among those who have never smoked. In a related and interesting study, Graham and his associates (Graham, Crouch, Levin, and Back, 1963) simulated "puffing patterns" on smoking machines and were able to show that frequent puffing at the end of a cigarette increased the level of tar retrieved (1.73 grams). Increased puffing at the beginning of the cigarette followed by a tapering-off pattern decreased the level of tar received (1.43 grams). Thus, smoking is not the only component in lung cancer rates: how one smokes is also important.

Table 1-1. *Deaths from lung cancer by smoking status.*

Smoking status	Mortality rates of smokers compared to nonsmokers, expressed in ratios
Never smoked regularly	1.00
Pipe only	2.24
Pipe and cigar	0.90
Cigar only	1.85
Cigarette and other	7.39
Cigarette only	9.20

SOURCE: E. Cuyler Hammond. 1966. *Smoking in Relation to the Death Rates of One Million Men and Women.* Washington, D.C.: National Cancer Institute, U.S. Government Printing Office.

LEGIONNAIRES' DISEASE. In July 1976, a mysterious disease appeared without warning in Pennsylvania (Cockerham, 1986). At first, physicians thought it was a form of typhoid. To avoid an epidemic of new typhoid cases, social epidemiologists were brought in to track down the unknown source. That part was easy. All 29 individuals who died, and the 200 or so who became seriously ill, had a very recognizable common social trait. They had attended either the American Legion convention (hence, the "legionnaires' disease") or the Eucharistic Congress of the Roman Catholic Church earlier that month. Both conventions were held at the same Philadelphia hotel, the Bellevue-Stratford. Having identified the Bellevue-Stratford Hotel as the vehicle in the etiological chain of the legionnaires' disease, the social epidemiologists concentrated their efforts on identifying the particular agent that caused the disease.

Laboratory tests demonstrated that the disease was not typhoid. Further tests showed that it wasn't caused by a virus. Other tests eventually ruled out all other known possibilities, including food poisoning. With all tests turning up negative results, the social epidemiologists turned once more to the reconstruction of the social activities of the disease-stricken individuals. Again, no answer was found. Eventually, in January 1977, clinical epidemiologists working for the federal government's Center for Disease Control in Atlanta, Georgia, were able to isolate new bacterialike organisms in the lung tissue of the victims. Further test-

ing revealed bacteria larger than rickettsia but smaller than other known bacteria. This new strain was called legionellosis. What this new disease is, how and why people contract it, and how it kills them are still unknowns. Fortunately, the antibiotic erythromycin is an effective treatment for the legionellosis bacteria, thus providing a mechanism for breaking the disease's etiological chain. Social epidemiologists continue to study legionnaires' disease, however, hoping that someday they will be able to solve this intriguing epidemiological mystery.

MYOCARDIAL INFARCTION. Coronary heart disease is the leading cause of death today in the United States (National Center for Health Statistics, 1985b). One of the more common forms of heart disease is myocardial infarction, or the heart attack. From the classic Framingham study, which prospectively followed and kept detailed health records on some 5,000 residents of that Massachusetts community over a 20-year period (see Dawber, Meadors, and Moore, 1951), it is well known that a variety of physiological factors, often resulting from lifestyle patterns, increase the risk of heart attacks. Among these risk factors are high levels of cigarette smoking, obesity, blood sugar, blood pressure, and cholesterol (Epstein, 1965; Moriyama, Krueger, and Stamler, 1971). What is less well known is that the risk of heart attack is also related to decidedly more social factors, especially occupational stress. For example, in another study, House (1974) found that the risk of heart attack is far more concentrated during the peak occupational years (i.e., ages 25 to 64). House found that the rates for white men ranged from 2.75 to 6.50 times the rates for white women, who, at the time his study was conducted, were much less likely to work. Moreover, the rates for heart attacks among white men vary considerably across occupational categories, with higher rates occurring among the more stressful occupations.

In addition to occupational stress, another social factor that affects heart attack rates is the way in which people behave. Based on a long series of prospective studies involving some 3,400 men, Friedman, Rosenman, and Jenkins (see Jenkins, Rosenman, and Friedman, 1967) have identified two behavioral patterns: Type A and Type B. On the one hand, the Type A behavioral pattern is characterized by "excessive drive, aggressiveness, ambition, involvement in competitive activities, frequent vocational deadlines, [and] an enhanced sense of urgency." On the other hand, the Type B behavioral pattern is characterized by "the relative absence of this interplay of psychological traits and situational pressures." A checklist for detecting Type A behavior includes vocal explosiveness, constant motion, impatience, thinking or doing two or more things at once, dominating conversations, feeling guilty when relaxing, a preoccupation with having rather than being, scheduling more and more in less and less time, feeling compelled to challenge others, nervous tics or gestures, fear of slowing down, and an attachment to the numbers game.

The evidence for differential risk of heart attack associated with the behavioral patterns is marked. Men with Type A behavior have been shown to have from 1.4 to 6.5 times greater risk for having heart attacks than men with Type B behavior. Moreover, the risk of recurrent and fatal heart attacks is also greater in Type A men than in Type B men (Jenkins, 1971; Sales, 1969). Caplan (1971) has suggested that the markedly higher risk rates for Type A men is in part a function of their being in high stress occu-

pations at the same time. In those situations, the external stress of the job and the internal stress of the behavior pattern seem to feed on one another.

HEALTH HABITS AND MORTALITY. For quite some time popular wisdom and public health authorities have suggested that certain routine practices (such as smoking, drinking, and exercise) are involved in the development of various diseases, especially chronic ones. To scientifically address this issue, the Human Population Laboratory in Berkeley, California, was established in 1965 with funds from the National Institutes of Health. For the next nine years, epidemiologists followed some 4,700 residents of Alameda County (hence, the frequent reference to the "Alameda County" study), tracking both their health and their ways of living. The results have been most influential in planning for the public health of the nation.

One of the major findings of the Alameda County study was that certain health habits were strongly related to mortality risks among adults 30 to 69 years old. Five good health habits were found to be especially good predictors of life expectancy rates for these individuals, including never having smoked, engaging in exercise activities on a regular basis, having less than five drinks at one sitting, being of average weight for height, and getting seven or eight hours of sleep a day. A summary index, created by giving one point for each good health habit, was found to be remarkably well correlated with mortality rates for several diseases, including heart disease, cerebrovascular disease, and cancer (Berkman and Breslow, 1983). As shown in Table 1-2, individuals with a greater number of good health habits had considerably lower mortality rates. Indeed, men with the least healthy habits (none, one, or two) had about three times the mortality rate of men with the most healthy habits (four or five). The same was true for women. Moreover, these marked differences continued to exist even after adjusting the data for confounding factors, such as perceived health status, socioeconomic status, and a variety of psychologi-

Table 1-2. *Age-adjusted cause-specific mortality rates (per 100) by the number of good health practices for men and women aged 30–69 in the 1965–1974 Alameda County study.*

Cause of death	Number of good health practices		
	0–2	3	4–5
Men (number of cases)	(404)	(748)	(1,077)
Ischemic heart disease	5.2	4.4	2.2
Cerebrovascular or circulatory disease	2.2	1.5	0.5
Cancer	2.6	1.9	1.5
Other diseases	5.7	3.1	1.6
All causes combined	16.0	10.9	5.8
Women (number of cases)	(426)	(809)	(1,261)
Ischemic heart disease	4.2	1.4	0.7
Cerebrovascular or circulatory disease	1.4	1.1	0.6
Cancer	2.6	2.0	1.4
Other diseases	3.8	2.6	1.1
All causes combined	11.9	7.1	3.9

SOURCE: Lisa F. Berkman and Lester Breslow. 1983. *Health and Ways of Living: The Alameda County Study.* New York: Oxford University Press.

cal traits. These results clearly show that healthy lifestyles, which are often shaped by social forces, are quite important in whether we live or die, and if we live, how long we live. Government estimates show that widespread adoption of these and other healthy habits could save billions of dollars in annual health care costs (Office of Health Research, Statistics, and Technology, 1981).

AIDS. The first cases of acquired immune deficiency syndrome (AIDS) were identified in 1981. By 1985 more than 13,000 cases of AIDS had been reported to the Centers for Disease Control, with half of these being new cases diagnosed that year. Using sophisticated projection procedures, Curran, Morgan, Hardy, Jaffe, Darrow, and Dowdle (1985) estimated that 12,500 new cases of AIDS would be reported in 1986, with the apparent exponential growth rate suggesting a doubling of new cases each year thereafter. Coupled with the facts that this infectious disease is almost always fatal and is not well understood, the rapid spread of AIDS has set off a "second epidemic" of fear, both in the lay community (see Peabody, 1986) and in the health care delivery system itself (see Cecchi, 1986).

Initially, AIDS appeared among homosexual men and users of intravenous drugs,

suggesting some transmissible agent as the cause. Subsequent identification of the syndrome among hemophiliacs and recipients of blood transfusions led to the isolation of human T-lymphotropic virus type III (HTLV-III) as the cause of AIDS. To date, the HTLV-III has been isolated in peripheral blood, semen, saliva, and tears (Curran et al., 1985). About 73 percent of AIDS patients are homosexual or bisexual men, 17 percent are heterosexual men or women who use intravenous drugs, 1.5 percent have no other risk factors except having received a blood transfusion, less than 1 percent are hemophiliacs who receive clotting factor treatments, and about 1 percent are heterosexual partners of either AIDS patients or persons at risk for AIDS. The remaining 6.4 percent of AIDS patients cannot be classified by recognized risk factors, although the majority of them were born outside the United States, in countries were AIDS cases are unassociated with known risk factors.

Reviewing the available evidence, epidemiologists have been able to identify two major links in the etiological chain of events for AIDS that suggest intervention. The first involves safeguarding the donated blood supply. In September 1985 the American Red Cross Association (1985) adopted important new procedures for screening potential donors for AIDS. They now exclude from blood donorship: (1) AIDS victims or anyone having AIDS symptoms (e.g., unexplained weight loss, night sweats, blue or purple spots under the skin or on mucous membranes, swollen lymph glands lasting for more than a month, persistent white spots in the mouth, fever above 99 degrees Fahrenheit for 10 days or more, persistent cough or shortness of breath, and persistent diarrhea); (2) past or present users of intravenous drugs; (3) males who have had sex with more than one male since 1979 (and males whose male partner has had sex with more than one male since 1979); (4) Haitians who entered the United States after 1977; (5) hemophiliacs; and (6) sexual partners of any of the above. In addition, before being put into use, each blood donation is screened for HTLV-III antibodies, although this test is not perfectly accurate (it gives both false positives and false negatives, especially during the latency period of the AIDS virus, which can be as long as five years). Essentially, this approach attempts to prevent individuals who are at risk for AIDS from donating blood that may be contaminated.

The second point in the etiological chain of AIDS involves breaking the point of contact with the known risk factors. As you might imagine, intervention of this sort is more difficult inasmuch as it involves the personal sexual habits of (primarily) homosexual and heterosexual men. In 1986 the state of Texas Board of Health tried to implement procedures that would permit the quarantine of promiscuous AIDS patients. This proposal met with considerable outcry from the gay community, who threatened to no longer cooperate with the Board of Health in the control of AIDS if the quarantine procedure was approved. At issue were First Amendment rights. Recognizing that the loss of cooperation from the gay community in controlling AIDS would be far more harmful in the long run than a procedure aimed at a few promiscuous individuals with AIDS, the Board of Health withdrew its request.

As unsettling as the public controversy surrounding AIDS has been, it has also had a positive impact. Efforts by gay groups to provide information on ways to avoid contracting AIDS has significantly altered the sexual practices of homosexual men. For example, there seems to be less promiscuity, smaller crowds at gay baths and bars, and an increased use of condoms. The intense media publicity about AIDS also appears to have affected the sexual practices of heterosexual men and women. Indeed, the prevalence of casual and recreational sex appears to be on the decline. As these changes in sexual behavior evolve, epidemiologists worldwide continue to search for better AIDS screening tests, as well as a cure.

The Basic Social Epidemiological Measures

INCIDENCE AND PREVALENCE. In the practical work of the social epidemiologist, two concepts are used extensively to demonstrate the social and ecological distribution of disease, impairment, and accident. These two concepts are incidence and prevalence. The *incidence* of disease, impairment, or accident is the number of times the event occurs among a given social group within a given time period. For example, the incidence of the A-Victoria strain of influenza in Chicago during February 1988 would be the number of new A-Victoria influenza cases reported in Chicago during that month. Incidence figures, then, allow us to measure the epidemic proportions of a disease, because they indicate how many new cases have appeared within a specified period of time. This information is especially useful in looking for the cause of a disease.

There are many situations, however, in which both the social epidemiologist and the public are interested in knowing more than just how many new cases of the disease have been identified. Sometimes we are more concerned with the extent to which the disease has affected the population. To measure this, social epidemiologists use *prevalence*, which refers to the total number of people in which a disease, impairment, or accident occurs. The prevalence figure tells us how many *total* cases of A-Victoria influenza existed in Chicago during February

1988, while the incidence figure tells us how many *new* cases of A-Victoria influenza occurred in Chicago during that month. That information is especially relevant to health policy decisions. These two concepts, incidence and prevalence, are widely used by the social epidemiologist.

CONSTRUCTING RATES. Social epidemiologists are concerned with comparing the distribution of disease in different populations or social groups. These groups are not usually of the same size. Therefore, a direct comparison of prevalence or incidence figures between the Chicago metropolitan area (with 6 million people) and New Orleans (with 600,000 people) would not be very meaningful. Accordingly, most of the figures that social epidemiologists calculate are normed, or adjusted, to the size of the social group. This process results in *ratios*, where the number of cases of the disease (the prevalence or incidence figure) is divided by the number of people in the population. Because computation of ratios results in very small numbers, usually fractions, that may appear unimportant, the ratio is usually multiplied by 1,000. This has the effect of producing a *rate*, which indicates how many cases of the disease exist per 1,000 persons. The general formula for calculating the rate per 1,000 persons is:

$$\frac{\text{number of people with the disease in the population}}{\text{number of people in the population}} \times 1,000$$

In addition to calculating the rate per 1,000 persons in the general population, social epidemiologists usually find it beneficial to calculate the rate for specific subgroups within the population. Information contained in general rates is usually too gross to be of much value to social epidemiologists; therefore, a *specific* rate for various subgroups of the population is calculated. The most frequent specific rates are *age-specific* and *sex-specific*, although other specific rates (such as *occupation-specific*, *region-specific*, and *disease-specific*) are calculated when needed. To calculate a specific rate, the general formula for the rate per 1,000 persons is modified thus:

$$\frac{\text{number of people with the disease in the specific population}}{\text{number of people in the specific population}} \times 1,000$$

MORTALITY AND MORBIDITY RATES. Two of the more commonly used specific rates in social epidemiology are the infant mortality (death) rate and the life expectancy rate. The *infant mortality rate* is traditionally used as a measure of the medical care and sanitary conditions present in a given society, one indicator of a country's health or illness (morbidity) status. For example, the infant mortality rate during the 1980s in the United States was approximately 11.5 deaths per 1,000 live births—the fifteenth lowest infant mortality rate internationally. (Sweden, with the lowest rate, recorded less than 8 deaths per 1,000 live births.) This indicates that while the United States has the highest per capita income in the world, it does not have the highest health level (National Center for Health Statistics, 1985b), where infant mortality is concerned.

A more accurate reflection of morbidity levels may be gained when one divides the infant mortality rate into two components, neonatal and postneonatal. On the one hand, neonatal mortality rates measure the mortality rate among infants from birth through their first 28 days of life. During this period, nearly three fourths of all infant deaths occur, deaths which are generally attributed to biological problems arising out of the birthing process. On the other hand, postneonatal mortality rates reflect the age-specific mortality rate for infants between 29 days and one year old. Most postneonatal deaths may be attributed to social and environmental conditions. Thus, by comparing neonatal and postneonatal mortality rates, we can make a clear distinction between the relative differences in medical care systems and social and environmental characteristics.

For example, in both 1968 and 1982, the infant mortality rate for blacks in the United States was about two times the rate for whites. If the neonatal and postneonatal rates are examined, however, another distinction becomes apparent. On the one hand, the neonatal mortality rate of blacks in the United States was only 1.59 times as large as the white rate in 1968, but by 1982 it was about two times the white rate (note that the rates for both groups actually declined; the rate for whites simply declined faster). On the other hand, the postneonatal mortality rate for blacks in 1968 was 2.5 times as large as that for whites, but by 1982 it was only about twice as large. When taken together, these data tend to show that since 1968: (1) access to medical care in the United States has become less equitable (as evidenced by larger racial differences in neonatal mortality rates), but that (2) basic socioeconomic and environmental inequities (as evidenced by differences in postneonatal mortality rates) have relatively declined somewhat (National Center for Health Statistics, 1985b).

Life expectancy rates, the second of the most commonly used specific rates in social epidemiology, reflect the average number of years that a person with certain social characteristics can expect to live. The social characteristics that are usually used in calculating life expectancy rates are age, sex, and race. Life expectancy rates are usually presented in the form of current life tables, calculated on the basis of age-sex-race–specific mortality data for the current calendar year. The social epidemiologist assumes that these hypothetical (current) mortality rates will be similar to the actual (subsequent) mortality rates for this specific population, though some age-sex-race specific factors may change over time. Table 1-3 is an example of a current life table, showing the average life expectancy for specific age-sex-race groups in the United States, based on mortality rates in 1982. From Table 1-3 we can see that whites can expect to live longer than nonwhites (except among males 70 or older, and there is considerable debate as to whether this exception is real or artifact [see Wing, Manton, Stallard, Hames, and Tyroler, 1985]), while females of all ages can expect to live longer than males. Current life tables are used extensively by insurance companies in determining the premium rates, based on risk rates, for life insurance.

The Basic Variables in Social Epidemiology

As one can see from the current life table, there are several characteristics of the individual that are related to health and death rates. The four basic variables that social epidemiologists use in illustrating the distribution of mortality (death) and morbidity (illness) in a given population are age, sex, race, and socioeconomic status. Let us now turn our attention to each of these four.

Table 1-3. *A current life table for the United States: Average number of remaining years based on age-sex-race–specific mortality rates in 1982.*

Age	Male		Female	
	White	Nonwhite	White	Nonwhite
0 (at birth)	71.5	66.8	78.8	75.0
5 years	67.5	63.3	74.6	71.4
20 years	53.0	48.8	59.9	56.8
30 years	43.8	39.9	50.2	47.2
40 years	34.5	31.3	40.6	37.9
50 years	25.6	23.4	31.3	29.2
60 years	17.9	16.8	22.8	21.5
70 years	11.6	11.7	15.3	15.0

SOURCE: National Center for Health Statistics. 1985. *Vital Statistics of the United States, 1982 Life Tables.* Washington, D.C.: National Center for Health Statistics, U.S. Government Printing Office.

Table 1-4. *Death rates (per 1,000) in the United States for all causes by age, for selected years,*
1940–1983.

Age	Year					
	1940	1950	1960	1970	1980	1983
Under 1 year	55.1	33.0	27.0	21.4	12.9	10.8
1–4 years	3.0	1.4	1.1	0.8	0.6	0.5
5–14 years	1.1	0.6	0.5	0.4	0.3	0.3
15–24 years	2.1	1.3	1.1	1.3	1.2	1.0
25–34 years	3.1	1.8	1.5	1.6	1.4	1.2
35–44 years	5.2	3.6	3.0	3.1	2.3	2.0
45–54 years	10.5	8.5	7.6	7.3	5.8	5.4
55–64 years	21.9	19.1	17.4	16.6	13.5	13.0
65–74 years	47.5	40.7	38.2	35.8	29.9	28.8
75–84 years	109.7	93.3	87.5	80.0	66.9	63.1
85 years or more	229.3	202.0	198.6	175.4	159.8	154.2

SOURCE: National Center for Health Statistics. 1985. *Health, United States, 1984*. Washington, D.C.: National Center for Health Statistics, U.S. Government Printing Office.

AGE. There are two very important and striking facts about the relationship between age and mortality in the United States. The first fact is that the average life expectancy of Americans has increased markedly in the twentieth century. In 1900, the average life expectancy for an American was only 49 years. By the mid 1980s, the average life expectancy had risen to 75 years, an increase of 26 years. This dramatic increase in life expectancy, or the dramatic decrease in mortality, may be attributed to two major factors. First and foremost, as a result of the increasing industrialization of American society, public health measures, especially sanitation, and the control of infectious diseases have improved markedly. This improvement in living and working conditions has been accompanied by improved nutrition and expanded leisure time. The second factor behind the improved life expectancy in the United States (although not nearly as effective) has been the increasing quantity, quality, and availability of health services. Americans now live much longer, and when they die today, it is not from infectious epidemics typical of the Dark Ages. Rather, today most Americans die from the physiological deterioration of the body (Rice and Feldman, 1983).

The second important and striking fact about the relationship between age and mortality is the stability of the mortality rate between the ages of 1 and 54. As shown in Table 1-4, the age-specific mortality rate for the United States is high among infants, even in 1983. However, the rate drops dramatically among those who achieve their first birthday and remains low (never exceeding the rate of 6 deaths per 1,000 persons) into their fourth and fifth decades. The mortality rate climbs markedly for those over 55, reflecting the physiological deterioration of the body. We also see that age-specific mortality rates have been decreasing over the last 40 years. For example, between 1940 and 1983 the infant mortality rate dropped from 55 to less than 11 deaths per 1,000 live births. What one can deduce from these data is that if an individual survives the birthing process and the first year of life, he or she is likely to reach old age.

As a result of having more Americans live longer, aging and the aged present new social problems in the United States because of two related factors (see Binstock, 1985; Butler, 1975, 1983; Fischer, 1978; Rice and Feldman, 1983; Suzman and Riley, 1985). First, in American society the role of the elderly individual has gradually been devalued: once in a position of esteem and central to the family, the elderly individual now occupies a position of imputed incompetence, disrespect, and isolation. The attendant devaluations of the social role of the elderly has resulted in the second factor, the increasing development of feelings of uselessness, life dissatisfaction, and anomie. While society has been influential in expanding the ranks of the elderly (through better public health and medical care), it has contributed very little toward understanding the new social and psychological problems related to the aging process. In chapter 8, the processes of aging and death and dying will be taken up in greater detail.

SEX. Sex differences in mortality data are marked in the United States. In Table 1-3, we saw that at every age males have higher mortality rates than females. This situation does not change when mortality rates between males and females are compared for specific causes of death (except for diabetes). The end result of lower mortality rates for females is that on the average, white females may expect to live 78.8 years while white males may expect to live 71.5 years, a difference of 7.3 years. Similarly, on the average, nonwhite females may expect to live 75.0 years while nonwhite males may expect to live 66.8 years, a difference of 8.2 years. In addition to the existing gap between male and female life expectancy, the mortality rate among American males has been rising during the last three decades (especially during the 1960s), even after adjustment for war-related military deaths. At the same time, female mortality rates have remained the same. As a result of this and of the general mortality trends of the twentieth century, the excess of males to females that existed during the early 1900s (approximately 106 men for every 100 women) has disappeared, and instead there is now an excess of females to males (100 women for every 95 men). The excess of females to males is accentuated among the elderly, where increasing numbers of elderly widows, with an insufficient supply of males for friendship and remarriage, present a growing social problem.

There are two major reasons why males have a higher mortality rate than females (Waldron, 1976). The first reason is biological. The human male is simply weaker than the human female. Evidence of this comes, in part, from the fact that prenatal or fetal death rates for males are about 12 percent higher than for females. After birth, the difference becomes even greater, as reflected in the neonatal mortality statistics for the first month of life. The neonatal death rates of males is 130 percent higher than that of females. These differences in prenatal and neonatal mortality clearly establish the biological superiority of females, because there can be little effect of nonbiological factors before birth or during the first four weeks of life.

The second reason for the higher mortality rate of males is linked to social and social-psychological factors (Waldron, 1976). The social factors involved are related to the sex role distinctions that exist in American society. Males are expected to be more aggressive than females, both in work and leisure activities, and to be the major breadwinners. As a result, males tend to dominate the high-risk occupations, such as coal mining, high-steel construction, and law enforcement. Therefore, when fatalities occur in these occupations, the victim is likely to be a male. In addition to these social factors, the competition and pressure associated with being the breadwinner produces social-psychological tensions or stress, which we have already shown to be related to higher incidence of heart disease. The relationship between stress and mortality has become so clear that middle-aged males engaged in professional work are often considered to be high risks by life insurance companies. A contributing factor here is that these middle-aged professionals tend to be overweight, to smoke, and to overwork, a combination that we have also already shown results in high morbidity and ultimately, high mortality levels. To combat this problem, health insurance companies, such as Blue Cross and Blue Shield, launched mass-media campaigns during the 1980s to the effect that people with high-risk lifestyles are the ones responsible for the high cost of health insurance.

Sex differences in morbidity rates are

also marked, although here it is the men who are at an advantage. While women live longer than men, men tend to be healthier than women. In explaining this apparent anomaly, Verbrugge (1985) writes that "sex differences in health are principally the outcome of differential risks acquired from roles, stress, life styles, and preventive health practices." Far less important here are other factors, such as biological risks, prior health care, symptom reporting, and care-taker effects. The fundamental cause of the observed differences in morbidity levels, then, is related to gender (i.e., social as opposed to biological) differences in the perception, evaluation, and treatment of mild chronic conditions.

RACE. Table 1-3, used to demonstrate age and sex differences in mortality rates, may also serve to demonstrate differences in life expectancy between whites and nonwhites. For both sexes and at all ages (with the exception, already noted, of males over age 70 [see Wing et al., 1985]), whites may expect to live longer lives than nonwhites. In other words, the mortality rate is higher for non-whites than for whites, even when adjustments are made for age and sex. While the difference in life expectancy reflected in Table 1-3 is marked, the difference is shocking where infant mortality is concerned. The difference in the infant mortality rates for white and nonwhite infants from 1940 to 1982, cited in Table 1-5, shows that historically the nonwhite infant mortality rate has been about twice as high as the white infant mortality rate, even though the absolute level of infant mortality rates has declined significantly for both groups.

To better understand the effects of race on mortality and morbidity patterns in the general population, it would be beneficial to know the makeup of the nonwhite group. In almost all the data gathered in the United States on the topic of mortality and morbidity, the nonwhite category consists primarily of black Americans. While other nonwhite groups are incorporated into the nonwhite category, their inclusion is minimal (usually less than 10 percent of the

Table 1-5. *Infant mortality rates (deaths per 1,000 live births) by race for the United States: 1940, 1950, 1960–1975, and 1982.*

| | Infant mortality rate | | |
Year	Total	White	Nonwhite
1940	47.0	43.2	73.8
1950	29.2	26.8	44.5
1960	26.0	22.9	43.2
1961	25.3	22.4	40.7
1962	25.3	22.3	41.4
1963	25.2	22.2	41.5
1964	24.8	21.6	41.1
1965	24.7	21.5	40.3
1966	23.7	20.6	38.8
1967	22.4	19.7	35.9
1968	21.8	19.2	34.5
1969	20.9	18.4	32.9
1970	20.0	17.8	30.9
1971	19.1	17.1	28.5
1972	18.5	16.4	27.7
1973	17.7	15.8	26.2
1974	16.7	14.8	24.9
1975	16.1	14.4	22.9
1982	11.5	10.1	18.9

SOURCE: National Center for Health Statistics. 1985. *Charting the Nation's Health: Trends Since 1960.* Washington, D.C.: National Center for Health Statistics, U.S. Government Printing Office.

nonwhites are nonblacks [see Secretary's Task Force, 1985]). In essence, then, the nonwhite mortality and morbidity rates refer to blacks.

This does not in itself explain the disparity in rates, of course, but awareness of the composition of the nonwhite group has facilitated etiological research. In a recent review of the literature on the incidence and prevalence of hypertension, Cockerham (1986) has identified the major theoretical schemes used to explain the disparity between black and white rates. Although blacks represent only 10 percent of the general population, they represent more than 20 percent of all cases of hypertension. Even more marked than these differences are the age- and sex-adjusted rates. Black males aged 25 to 44 years have 15.5 times the hypertension-mortality rate of white males of the same age. The six major theoretical schemes, according to Cockerham, that seek to explain the disparity in the incidence of hypertension, are: (1) the genetic theory, which suggests that blacks are genetically predisposed toward hypertension; (2) the manual-labor theory, which suggests that blacks are more likely to engage in physically strenuous occupations, which lead to a higher incidence of hypertension; (3) the associated-disorder theory, which suggests that blacks are more predisposed to other diseases to which hypertension is a typical secondary condition; (4) the strain theory, which suggests that, as a result of racial discrimination, a higher level of repressed aggression produces more hypertension; (5) the dietary theory, which suggests that the dietary lifestyle of blacks increases their susceptibility to hypertension; and, (6) the medical-care-access theory, which suggests that blacks receive less medical care—and of poorer quality—resulting in higher mortality rates from hypertension (as well as other diseases, of course).

To date, none of these theories has been conclusively confirmed—or refuted—by any reliable authority. Given the complex nature of social and biological phenomena, it seems likely that the ultimate answer will draw on several of the separate theories rather than any single one. Social and social psychological factors are likely to be at the core of our future understanding of racial differences in mortality and morbidity. The reason for this is that the information we have on nonwhite, nonblack mortality and morbidity rates (such as those related to Mexican Americans and American Indians) seems to focus on poverty-related issues, as it often does in relation to blacks. We note that social factors, such as minority and disadvantaged socioeconomic status, are rather constant across these nonwhite, nonblack groups, while genetic composition is not. Therefore, even if the nonsocial and nonsocial psychological factors were among the causes of racial differences in mortality and morbidity, it would appear that in the end the social and social psychological factors would carry more weight.

SOCIOECONOMIC STATUS. In discussing the effect of minority racial status on mortality

and morbidity, we have observed that a common characteristic of racial minorities is their disadvantaged socioeconomic status, which social epidemiologists equate with social class. There appears to be a correlation, then, between racial status and socioeconomic status in the United States. However, each has a significant independent effect on mortality and morbidity; within racial categories there is a significant difference in health levels according to socioeconomic status, and within socioeconomic status levels there is a significant difference according to racial status.

In a classic review of the literature relating socioeconomic status to mortality, Antonovsky (1972) revealed a very important pattern. He found that by every available measure, socioeconomic status clearly affects one's life expectancy. The higher your socioeconomic status, the longer you may expect to live. In fact, the pattern in the data was so clear that Antonovsky reached the "inescapable conclusion" that higher socioeconomic status was a major causal factor in staying alive longer.

Data bearing more directly on the distribution of morbidity across socioeconomic status groups reflect a similar pattern. The data in Table 1-6 show that the incidence of cancer in various parts of the body varies according to socioeconomic status. In these data, gathered in Buffalo, New York, between 1948 and 1952, we can see that socioeconomic status and the incidence of cancer are clearly related. For tracheal, stomach, and esophageal cancer among men there is, with minor exceptions, an inverse relationship between socioeconomic status and the incidence of cancer; the higher the socioeconomic status, the lower the incidence of cancer. Among women, however, the relationship between socioeconomic status and breast cancer is direct: the higher the socioeconomic status, the higher the incidence of breast cancer. This may reflect more on preventive health behavior, breast screening examinations, and higher subsequent detection rates rather than on true differences in the prevalence of breast cancer. In any event, these and other data corroborate the existence of a relationship

Table 1-6. *Average annual age-standardized incidence rates (per 100,000) of cancer in various parts of the body by social-class quartile in Buffalo, New York, 1948–1952.*

Bodily site	Social-class quartile			
	I (highest)	II	III	IV (lowest)
Trachea, bronchus, and lung (males only)	35.8	31.1	44.8	57.9
Stomach (males only)	19.6	24.9	28.0	38.0
Esophagus (males only)	6.7	10.5	9.0	18.7
Breast (females only)	115.8	86.9	74.2	51.6

SOURCE: Saxon Graham, M. Levin, and Abraham Lilienfeld. 1960. "The Socioeconomic Distribution of Cancer at Various Sites in Buffalo, N.Y.: 1948–1952." *Cancer* 13:180. Reprinted by permission.

between socioeconomic status and morbidity (see Office of Health Research, Statistics, and Technology, 1985).

A common assumption has been that the underlying reason for the significant correlation between low socioeconomic status, low life expectancy, and high morbidity is that the socioeconomically disadvantaged do not have sufficient access to medical care. Thus, it would seem to follow that if access to medical care were equalized among various socioeconomic groups, the differences in the mortality and morbidity rates would decrease and eventually disappear. One of the goals of the National Health Service in Britain was to establish a more equitable access system producing more equitable rates of mortality and morbidity. In a survey of National Health Service data, however, Forsyth (1973) concludes that the hoped-for effect has not been realized. Although access was equalized, environmental conditions and social lifestyles were not; therefore, the roots of the problem—poverty and its correlates—remained intact.

While the relationship between socioeconomic status and morbidity has been well documented, there are two competing causal explanations for the link. The first is the "social class explanation." It was most clearly presented by Antonovsky (1972), in his review of the data bearing on the relationship between social class and life expectancy. He believed that socioeconomic status produces health status because of socioeconomic status's intermediate effects on sanitation, preventive health behavior, and

access to medical care. Lawrence (1958), on the other hand, has suggested the "drift hypothesis" to explain this relationship, arguing that those who contract disabling diseases drift downward in socioeconomic status during their lifetime. The disabilities of the chronically ill keep them from getting better jobs reflecting their former illness-free capability, or even from maintaining their present jobs. Thus, according to the drift hypothesis, the chronically ill have a marked tendency to move down the socioeconomic ladder, as time goes by.

In bringing seemingly appropriate data to bear on this controversy, Harkey and his colleagues (Harkey, Miles, and Rushing, 1976) found support for the drift hypothesis. Using a measure of social role dysfunction as an indicator of chronic disability, they found a larger percentage of social role dysfunction among the lower income groups than among the higher income groups. This relationship held for all people aged 25 years or older. Among those younger than 25, only minor differences between socioeconomic groups were found. This was to be expected, according to the drift hypothesis, because those younger than 25 come under the financial umbrella of their parents. Harkey and his associates used these data to support the drift hypothesis.

Wolinsky (1980a; Wolinsky and Wolinsky, 1981a) suggests that a closer examination of the competing explanations is in order. He argues that, on the one hand, the social class explanation does not appear to explain very well the effect of *chronic* illness on downward social mobility. On the other hand, it does appear to explain the differential incidence of *acute* disease. Better sanitation, preventive health measures, and greater access to medical care should help reduce the incidence of acute disease and its limiting effect on the individual. At the same time, while the drift hypothesis does not apply very well to acute disease, it does explain the long-term effect of chronic illness on downward socioeconomic mobility. Therefore, it would seem that a comprehensive explanation of the relationship between socioeconomic status and morbidity would incorporate both the social class and drift hypotheses into a composite theory. Such a composite theory would explain the effects of socioeconomic status on acute disease, and the effect of chronic illness on socioeconomic status. In addition, it would tend to shed light on a suspected relationship between acute and chronic illness among the disadvantaged, who are caught in a vicious downward socioeconomic cycle. Their socioeconomic status leads to a high incidence of acute disease, which in turn makes them more susceptible to chronic illness, which in turn leads to still further downward drifting socioeconomic status.

A Tale of Two States

In the previous section we have shown that health is related to various sociodemographic characteristics, such as age, sex, race, and socioeconomic status. We presented convincing evidence of the relationship, yet we omitted a clear picture of the causal process as well as the intriguing story of the effect of social factors on our health. We will present these now, expanding on Fuchs's (1974) theme and using the provocative data compiled by Clark (1977) on the effect of purely social factors on our health. We will compare social and health data from two adjacent states within the United States. For the time being, we will call these states State A and State B, giving you an opportunity to try out the investigative skills of social epidemiology to guess the real names of the two states.

Differential Health Levels

The first step in demonstrating the effect of social factors on health is to point out that State A and State B have different health levels. First of all, there is a wide disparity in life expectancy between the two states, as the data in Table 1-7 clearly indicate. Males in State B can expect to live 3.9 years longer than males in State A; females in State B can expect to live 3.3 years longer than females in State A. At first glance, this might not seem like much of a difference, but when we examine the states' ranking in life expectancy among all of the United States, we note that State B ranks third best, while State A ranks fifth worst.

Another measurement for comparing the health levels of the two states is their age- and sex-adjusted mortality rates. This has been done in Table 1-8. The figures indicate by what percentage the death rate is greater

Table 1-7. *Life expectancy for States A and B (1969–1971).*

Sex	State A	State B
Male	65.6	69.5
Female	73.3	76.6
Rank among U.S. states	46th	3rd

SOURCE: Leon E. Clark. 1977. *Mortality American Style: A Tale of Two States.* Washington, D.C.: Population Reference Bureau. Reprinted by permission.

Table 1-8. *Death rates expressed as the percentage greater in State A than in State B (average for 1959–1961 and 1966–1968).*

Age	Males	Females
Under 1 year	42%	35%
1–19 years	16%	26%
20–29 years	44%	42%
30–39 years	37%	42%
40–49 years	54%	69%
50–59 years	38%	28%
60–69 years	26%	17%
70–79 years	20%	6%

SOURCE: Leon E. Clark. 1977. *Mortality American Style: A Tale of Two States.* Washington, D.C.: Population Reference Bureau. Reprinted by permission.

in State A than in State B, within each age-sex group. These data clearly show that for both sexes and at all ages the death rate is considerably higher in State A than in State B. These data also particularize the life expectancy data in Table 1-7.

Comparable Sociodemographic Characteristics

The second step in demonstrating the effect of social factors on health is to point out that the sociodemographic characteristics of the population in both states are similar. If these characteristics differed markedly between State A and State B, the difference in health levels might be attributed to the differences in the characteristics. Table 1-9 presents a wide array of sociodemographic data by which we can compare State A with State B. State B has a larger population than State A, for example, but the two states have almost identical levels of urbanization, eliminating this as a reliable explanation of the disparity in health levels. The age, sex, and race makeup of the population in the two states is rather interesting. State B has a higher percentage of elderly persons, who are more prone to illness, but it also has a lower percentage of blacks and males, who usually have lower

life expectancy rates. These differences would seem to offset each other, in terms of overall health levels.

The indicators of social status also provide some interesting comparisons. The education levels in both states are nearly identical. The per capita income, however, which is usually related to better health, is lower in State B than in State A (although both are clearly well above the poverty level). This anomaly, however, may be offset by the fact that there is greater access to medical care (more physicians per person) in State B than in State A. Because the two states are adjacent, we would expect that their environmental conditions are virtually identical, which is in fact true. From these data we may conclude that although there are some differences in the sociodemographic characteristics between State A and State B, the differences are neither of sufficient magnitude nor consistently weighted in the same direction to be relied on to explain the difference in health levels.

Focusing on the Cause

If the sociodemographic characteristics cannot be used to explain why people in State B are healthier than people in State A, then what can be used? A clue may be

Table 1-9. Sociodemographic characteristics of States A and B.

Sociodemographic characteristics	State A	State B
Total population (1970)	489,000	1,059,000
Per capita income (1973)	$5,560	$4,005
Percent urbanized (1970)	80.9%	80.4%
Physicians per 100,000	119	144
Average years of school completed (1971)	12.4	12.0
Age structure (1971)		
65 and over	6.8%	7.4%
21 and over	61.0%	54.0%
Racial composition (1970)		
White	91.7%	97.4%
Black	5.7%	0.6%
Males per 100 females (1970)	102.6	97.6
Environmental conditions	Virtually identical: the states are contiguous	

SOURCE: Leon E. Clark. 1977. *Mortality American Style: A Tale of Two States*. Washington, D.C.: Population Reference Bureau. Reprinted by permission.

Table 1-10. *Deaths from cirrhosis of the liver and cancer of the respiratory system, expressed as the percentage greater in State A than in State B (average for 1966–1968).*

Age	Males	Females
30–39 years	590%	443%
40–49 years	111%	296%
50–59 years	206%	205%
60–69 years	117%	227%

SOURCE: Leon E. Clark. 1977. *Mortality American Style: A Tale of Two States.* Washington, D.C.: Population Reference Bureau. Reprinted by permission.

Table 1-11. *Alcohol and cigarette consumption in States A and B.*

Alcohol consumption (gallons per person)			
Year	United States	State A	State B	Percentage greater in State A than in State B
1961	17	29	9	322
1965	18	29	10	290
1970	22	36	13	277
1975	25	45	16	281
Rank among U.S. states		1st	50th	

Cigarette consumption (packs per person)			
Year	United States	State A	State B	Percentage greater in State A than in State B
1950	120	176	72	244
1955	116	185	62	298
1960	132	199	69	288
1965	135	193	65	297
1970	127	190	66	288
1975	134	205	76	270
Rank among U.S. states		4th	50th	

SOURCE: Leon E. Clark. 1977. *Mortality American Style: A Tale of Two States.* Washington, D.C.: Population Reference Bureau. Reprinted by permission.

found by reviewing the causes of death. Heart disease, cancer, stroke, and accidents, in that order, are the primary causes of death in both states. After these causes, the leading causes in State A include suicide, cirrhosis of the liver, infant mortality, and lung disease, while in State B the list after the first four includes influenza, infant mortality, diabetes, and suicide. There is an obvious disparity, then, in the pattern of the causes of death for the two states. Cirrhosis of the liver and respiratory cancer are not among the leading causes of death in State B, as they are in State A. Table 1-10 demonstrates the dramatic difference in the death

rate from cancer of the respiratory system or cirrhosis of the liver between the two states. The percentages indicate how much higher the death rate from these causes is in State A than in State B. These data clearly show that for all age-sex groups, people in State A are from 111 to 590 percent more likely to die from these causes than are people in State B.

Cirrhosis of the liver and cancer of the respiratory system are, as is well known, linked directly to the consumption of alcohol and tobacco. Therefore, the comparison between State A and State B in Table 1-11, with respect to alcohol and cigarette consumption, should not be surprising. State B has the lowest rate of cigarette and alcohol consumption of any state in the United States. State A has the highest rate of alcohol consumption and the fourth highest rate of cigarette consumption of any state in the United States.

There are three factors that possibly could explain these different levels of alcohol and tobacco consumption, which in turn might explain the different health levels in States A and B. The first factor is the cost of alcohol and tobacco, but in States A and B alcohol and tobacco cost about the same. The second factor is the availability of alcohol and tobacco, but again, in States A and B the availability of tobacco and alcohol is about the same. Moreover, the legal drinking age is identical. The third factor is the attitude toward the consumption of alcohol and tobacco, and there is an important difference in this regard. While the religious composition of both states is predominantly Christian, in State B about 75 percent of the people are Mormons. In State A only about 10 percent of the people are Mormons. The correlation, of course, lies in the fact that Mormonism forbids the consumption of alcohol and tobacco.

We have traced the cause for the disparity in levels of health in States A and B, which were alike in every other detail, to differing lifestyles based on social—namely, religious—norms. As we shall see in greater detail in the following chapters, social factors, along with the environment, play perhaps the major role in determining our health behavior—and thus, our health itself. By the way, State A is Nevada, and State B is Utah.

Summary

In this chapter we have introduced you to the existence of a relationship between social factors and health, establishing in the process a case for the study of the sociology of health as a distinct subdiscipline. To demonstrate this relationship we first examined the world view of modern medicine in its historical perspective, reviewing eight major periods in the development of medicine: (1) the philosophy of Hygeia; (2) the cult of Asclepius; (3) the age of Hippocrates; (4) the constraints of the Church; (5) Descartes and seventeenth-century rationalism; (6) the age of advances in public health; (7) Pasteur, Koch, specific etiology, and germ theory; and (8) the emerging systematic approach to whole-person health. Then we discussed the existence and impact of four dualities in modern medicine: (1) the simultaneous reliance on magic and science; (2) the distinction between individual-oriented and population-oriented medicine; (3) the dichotomy between mind and body as independently treatable entities; and (4) the contrast between the technical treatment of disease and the anthropological treatment of the whole person.

In the second section we shifted our attention to the science of social epidemiology, the study of the differential distribution of disease, impairment, and general health status across various social groups within the same population. Although studies of a social epidemiological nature are documented in ancient Greece and Egypt, the etiological chain-of-events model was first presented by Sir Percival Pott in 1775. In 1854, Sir John Snow systematized and formalized the method of social epidemiology in his study of the London cholera epidemic. The tradition of Pott and Snow has been carried on by contemporary social epidemiologists who have been concerned with the social correlates of cancer, legionnaires' disease, myocardial infarction, health habits and mortality rates, and AIDS, among other topics. The basic concepts of the social epidemiologist are incidence and prevalence. They indicate the number of new and the total number of cases per 1,000 people and are frequently calculated for specific subgroups of the population so that the differential distribution of disease and death across the subgroups can be identified. Incidence and prevalence rates are most valuable when calculated for various combinations of the social characteristics of special interest to the social epidemiologist: (1) age, (2) sex, (3) race, and (4) socioeconomic status.

In the final section of this chapter, we presented social and health data from two adjacent states within the United States, along with the enigmatic, empirical conclusion that the people in one state were healthier than the people in the other. Gradually the mystery was unraveled, as we learned that the strong social (i.e., religious) affiliations among the people in one state led to a lifestyle in which the deleterious consumption of alcohol and tobacco were rejected. The health of the other state was markedly worse by comparison, and it is clear that purely social factors (in this case, religious preference) can have very strong effects on our health.

2. The Sociology of Health: Its Origin, Nature, Present, and Future

*I*N CHAPTER 1, we first chronicled the sociophilosophical development of medicine and its relationship to the general social system. We then explored the relationship between certain sociodemographic characteristics (such as age, sex, race, and socioeconomic status) and morbidity and mortality rates, which are part of the science known as social epidemiology. Finally, we demonstrated ways in which health is affected by social factors such as lifestyle. In this chapter, we shall focus on the origins of medical sociology.

We have divided chapter 2 into five major sections. In the first section, we shall examine how the subdivision called medical sociology came to be, showing that it is both similar and dissimilar to medical anthropology, its "first cousin." In the second section, we shall present and modernize Straus's distinction between two orientations to medical sociology, which he labeled the sociologies *of* and *in* medicine. We will examine the historical efforts in both of these orientations, as well as their respective contributions to medical sociology and to the parent discipline of sociology. In the third section, we will survey the wide range of work that has been done by medical sociologists, presenting a short summary of the more popular topics. In the fourth section, we will present an outline of what medical sociologists are most likely to concentrate on in the future, and why. The final section will present an overview of the relevancy to and contributions of economics, political science, demography, law, and ethics to the sociology of health.

The Development of Medical Sociology: A Recent Phenomenon

As we have seen in chapter 1, the relationship between social phenomena and medicine has been coming more clearly into focus within the last two centuries or so. In 1854, Sir John Snow (1855) introduced the fundamental principles of social epidemiology when he traced London's horrendous outbreak of cholera to a contaminated public water pump. In 1879, Billings explicitly linked the study of hygiene with sociology. And in 1894, McIntire presented a formal definition of medical sociology: "The science of the social phenomena of the physicians themselves as a class apart and separate; and the science which investigates the laws regulating the relations between the medical profession and human society as a whole; treating of the structure of both, how the present conditions came about, what progress civilization has affected and indeed everything relating to the subject." Since that time, articles and monographs have frequently appeared in which some portion of the work reflected McIntire's (1894) definition of medical sociology. At the time of their appearance, however, these works were not identified with medical sociology per se.

In fact, it was not until the mid 1950s that medical sociology became a legitimate intellectual activity in its own right, even in the United States. Since then, however, it has become one of the six specialty areas in which sociologists can be certified by the American Sociological Association. According to the all-encompassing definition adopted by the Committee on Certification in Medical Sociology (1986), it is

the subfield of sociology which applies the perspectives, conceptualizations, theories, and methodologies of sociology to phenomena having to do with human health and disease. As a specialization, medical sociology encompasses a body of knowledge which places health and disease in a social, cultural and behavioral context. Included within its subject matter are descriptions and explanations or theories relating to the distribution of diseases among various population groups; the behaviors or actions taken by individuals to maintain, enhance, or restore health or cope with illness, disease or disability; people's attitudes and beliefs about health, disease, disability and medical care providers and organizations; medical occupations or professions and the organization, financing, and delivery of medical care services; medicine as a social institution and its relationship to other social institutions; cultural values and societal responses with respect to health, illness, and disability; and the role of social factors in the etiology of disease, especially functional and emotion-related disorders and what are now being called stress-related diseases.

The Origin of Medical Sociology in America

To a large degree, contemporary medical sociology is an American phenomenon. Indeed, in 1974 the German medical sociologist Pflanz flatly stated that most publication and research in medical sociology comes from the United States. The same can be said today (see Elinson, 1985; Fox, 1985; Wardwell, 1983), although the contributions from England and western Europe are growing (see Claus, 1983). Consequently, in tracing the origins of medical sociology, we will focus primarily on the American medical sociology tradition.

In an enlightening article, Olesen (1975) has identified at least six major factors in the history of the growth and legitimacy of American medical sociology. First, during the 1920s and 1930s a variety of intellectual endeavors and movements gradually evolved into a coherent group, focusing on the topic of social medicine. The impact of this concern about social medicine was a broad-based inquiry into problem areas that are common to the social and medical sciences. In fact, it appeared almost as if the public health movement produced by the Industrial Revolution (discussed in chapter 1) would spawn a second-generation movement.

This did not happen, but the stage was set for the second major factor in the origin of medical sociology. During the 1940s and 1950s, there was a considerable increase in the frequency and intensity of social epidemiological studies. The support for many of these studies, according to Olesen (1975), can be traced to "sociology's longstanding concerns with social amelioration of human problems." American sociology had been traditionally associated with policy-oriented social problems, and by the 1940s and 1950s it was evident that health and health care were to be considered as social problems, and treated accordingly.

Following this development came the third major factor in the emergence of medical sociology: sociologists began to be employed on a regular basis in medical schools (Olesen, 1975). In 1949 the first full-time sociologist was appointed to the faculty of the Department of Psychiatry and Preventive Medicine at the University of Ontario. Soon after this initial appointment, sociologists began to appear in medical and nursing schools with regularity. This trend was accelerated in the 1950s, when Robert Straus, a medical sociologist, was invited to set up a Department of Behavioral Science as an integral part of the new medical school being established at the University of Kentucky (Straus, 1959, 1963). Straus's efforts at the University of Kentucky served as a landmark in opening up medical schools to medical sociologists.

A fourth factor in the origin of medical sociology was the influence and interest of several private foundations (Olesen, 1975). These foundations began to support individual research efforts, training programs, and demonstration projects concerned primarily with public health and medical education. Among the more influential of these were the Russell Sage Foundation, the Milbank Memorial Fund, and the Commonwealth Fund. With the moral and financial support of these philanthropies, the sociologists' concern with health problems grew in both scope and depth.

A sense of permanence was added to this specialty area in 1955, when an informal Committee on Medical Sociology was formed within the American Sociological Association. This informal committee soon led to the formal recognition and chartering of the Section on Medical Sociology of the American Sociological Association in 1959. This was the fifth major factor in the origin and growth of medical sociology, and this recognition effectively established medical sociology as a legitimate discipline within sociology (Olesen, 1975).

The sixth factor in the growth and legiti-

mation of medical sociology came in 1965 when the *Journal of Health and Human Behavior*, an interdisciplinary journal first established in 1960, was taken over by the American Sociological Association (Olesen, 1975). The journal was renamed the *Journal of Health and Social Behavior* and became the official journal of medical sociology. It emphasized its formal purpose with the statement that it would be "distinctive for a sociological approach to the definition and analysis of problems bearing on human health and welfare." The establishment of this journal provided medical sociologists with an official forum in which to publish the results of their research and communicate their theories more readily among themselves and others. In addition to the *Journal of Health and Social Behavior*, the Section on Medical Sociology also publishes the *Medical Sociology Newsletter*, which serves as the major information conduit for medical sociologists. Since the founding of the Section on Medical Sociology in 1959, membership grew to nearly one thousand medical sociologists in 1986, making it the largest and most active of the official sections of the American Sociological Association.

Medical Anthropology: A First Cousin

As medical sociology was developing into a legitimate specialty area within sociology, medical anthropology was emerging in a similar way within anthropology. There are two factors that make the origin of medical anthropology especially pertinent to our discussion of the origin of medical sociology. First, medical sociologists and anthropologists investigate many of the same topics, including, according to Foster (1975), "definitions of health and disease, social and cultural factors in the cause and incidence of disease epidemiology, the training of medical personnel, medical bureaucracies, hospitals, communication problems between doctors and patients, innovation and change in medical beliefs and practices, mental health, and drug addiction." Clearly, medical sociology and medical anthropology have common research interests. This should not come as much of a surprise, given that the distinction between anthropology and sociology has been perceived by some as a fabricated disciplinary struggle rather than as a "real distinction" (Wax, 1970).

In addition to similarities in research interests, a second factor makes the development of medical anthropology relevant to the development of medical sociology; that is, the training of anthropologists and sociologists. Foster (1975) has summarized these similarities with the statement that "anthropologists and sociologists (including those whose chief interests lie in the health field) have been exposed to essentially the same formal and informal training and socialization processes, they share common bodies of theory and conceptualization and they know how and often use each other's research methodologies." Except for formal disciplinary ties, then, medical sociologists and medical anthropologists are interested in the same subject matter for research purposes and have received very similar formal and informal training. There is, however, one notable exception. Medical sociology has yet to develop an analog of medical anthropology's long-standing interest in the study of physical adaptations to environments and pathogens. That difference notwithstanding, the historical influences in the development of medical anthropology should have had some influence in the development of medical sociology as well, and it stands to reason that our understanding of the origin of medical sociology will be enhanced by examining the development of medical anthropology.

The Origin of Medical Anthropology

While the six major influences in the development of medical sociology have also affected the development of medical anthropology, there are some additional factors that were much more salient to medical anthropology's development. Foster (1975) traces these factors to three sources. First, contemporary medical anthropology may be seen as a "lineal descendant" of anthropology, in its long-standing interest in the

medical institutions of non-Western societies. In particular, anthropologists have always been interested in the medical beliefs and practices (including witchcraft and magic) of primitive peoples. This interest has been especially keen with regard to the way in which medical beliefs form a part of the entire cultural systems of such peoples. Anthropological studies of medical beliefs are now referred to as "ethnomedical" studies, rather than studies in traditional cultural anthropology.

The second source of medical anthropology's development may be found in the culture and personality studies that blossomed into a major movement within anthropology in the 1930s and 1940s (Foster, 1975). These studies concentrated on the ethnographic documentation of psychological and psychiatric phenomena from which certain "patterns of behavior" or "cultural response sets" were generalized (for a classic example, see Benedict, 1934). Although most of these studies were concerned primarily with psychiatric or mental health (and discussions of the sociocultural context of health behavior were rare), they provided a significant impetus for early endeavors in medical anthropology. This was especially true of conjoint research between psychiatry and anthropology.

The third source in the development of medical anthropology was the growth of the *international* public health movement after World War II. While the public health movement and the national concern for curing social problems were major factors in medical sociology's development, the international public health concern was a special impetus for medical anthropology (Foster, 1975). Anthropology was an obvious resource for international policy planners, because of the usefulness of anthropological research techniques in underdeveloped countries. How else could public health personnel determine what aspects of non-Western beliefs were the most resistant to change from external sources? That somewhat typical topic was clearly recognized as lying within the domain of anthropology. Therefore, when international public health concerns were raised, it was the anthropologists who received the call.

Differences Between Medical Anthropology and Medical Sociology

While the historical development of medical sociology and medical anthropology have been of quite a similar and complementary nature, there are three important differences to be noted, according to Foster (1975). First, medical sociologists traditionally identify with and view health problems from the medical perspective. In examining patient-practitioner relationships, medical sociologists tend to focus their attention on the physician, not on the patient. In essence, this amounts to identifying with management. On the other hand, medical anthropologists tend to focus their attention on the patient, not on the physician. Thus, medical anthropologists take on a role similar to that of the consumer advocate. This difference in perspective is very important. Gold (1977) has argued that medical sociology suffers from a "crisis in identity," in that medical sociologists play handmaiden to physicians (i.e., medical sociologists take on a subordinate role). To the extent that medical sociologists as handmaidens adopt existing medical value assumptions, "medical bias" minimizes the theoretical and political integrity of medical sociology. Although it is important to recognize that cooperation between the various disciplines is necessary in any research effort, this does not give one discipline license to dominate another. This domination, however, has been waning rapidly during the past decade as medical sociologists have become far more critical of the medical enterprise.

The second major difference, says Foster (1975), between medical sociology and medical anthropology is a difference in methodology. By and large, medical sociologists rely upon social survey techniques, in which respondents are asked by an interviewer to recall their health-related behavior, as the principal data collection technique. (Of course there are exceptions: see especially the studies of medical education conducted by Merton, Reader, and Kendall, 1957; Becker, Geer, Hughes, and Strauss, 1961; the studies of death and dying conducted by Glaser and Strauss, 1965; and the studies of women physicians' careers conducted by Lorber, 1984.) The data gathered in these surveys, often supplemented by aggregate characteristics of the health care delivery system, are then submitted to statistical analysis. In contrast, the major research technique used in medical anthropology is participant observation, in which the researcher "goes native" and as unobtrusively as possible participates in the life of the subject group in order to gather data. Participant observation emphasizes a holistic or systems approach, in which health and illness behavior are examined within the context of the total cultural system. This is a much more qualitative orientation, although the resulting data may still be submitted to extensive statistical analysis (see Young, 1981).

The third major difference between medical anthropology and medical sociology, according to Foster (1975), is one of mutually exclusive cultural interest. Medical sociologists almost always are concerned with the medical care system in the United States, other English-speaking countries, and western Europe. This is probably a function of the social problems orientation involved in medical sociology's development, in that health problems are seen in the context of social problems to be corrected. Since Western medical care systems are the most similar to the American medical care system (especially those in English-speaking England, Canada, and Australia; see Bates, 1983, and Stevens, 1983), it is natural for these societies to maintain an interchange of information in order to glean further insights into and solutions for our similar, if not common, problems. On the other hand, medical anthropologists are primarily concerned with non-Western cultures. This is not only for the intrinsic interest of such cultures but also because knowing more about their medical beliefs helps us to better understand the medical beliefs of all societies.

The Value of Cross-Disciplinary Cooperation

Foster (1975) summarized the similarities and differences between medical sociology and medical anthropology quite well, noting that

the basic concepts of the sister disciplines culture and society hold the key. The anthropologist . . . sees problems and data in a cultural context, while the sociologist sees them in a social context. A systems approach, a holistic view . . . underlies medical anthropological research. . . . The sociologist thinks first of social and class differences, of economic levels and standard of living, of role and status, of professions and professionalization, of dependent and independent variables. . . . Both approaches are valid, both are important . . . This . . . is the rationale for separate but allied medical behavioral science specializations. . . . We are in complementary and not competitive lines of work. We learn from each other and teach each other. Our society needs both of us.

Olesen (1975) extended this reasoning in her comment that "if [these] disciplines are to make genuine contributions to the understanding of health and the contexts of health, cross-disciplinary communication and cooperation are highly desirable." We find Olesen's and Foster's statements to be quite valid and important commentaries. Therefore, while this text is designed to introduce you to the sociology of health, we shall not confine ourselves within rigid disciplinary boundaries. When it is appropriate and beneficial for us to borrow or gain insight from medical anthropology—or any of the other social sciences—we shall do so. This will be especially evident in chapters 6 and 10, where we present extended discussions of ethnomedical approaches to health care and the use of nonmedical healers as alternatives to physicians. It will also be more evident toward the end of this chapter where we shall briefly overview the relevance to and contributions of economics, political science, demography, law, and ethics to the sociology of health.

The Sociologies *of* and *in* Health

Having examined the origins and the influential factors in the development of medical sociology, we shall now turn to an examination of the nature of medical sociology and the contributions of medical sociologists. In order to examine the development of any scientific discipline, it is necessary to have a framework within which to organize the contributions to knowledge made by that discipline. An examination of the foundations of the sociology of health is no exception. About thirty years ago, when medical sociology was beginning to become an acceptable specialty area within sociology, Straus (1955) proposed just such a framework for use in overviewing medical sociology. Straus's framework was neither elaborate nor revolutionary. It was readily accepted, however, and most would agree that with some relatively minor changes it has stood the test of time (see Levine and Sorenson, 1983). In this section, we shall trace the development of Straus's framework and then use it to evaluate the present status of the sociology of health.

Straus's Sociologies *of* and *in* Medicine

Straus (1955, 1957) suggested two categories into which all efforts in medical sociology could be logically divided. These categories were the sociologies *of* and *in* medicine. He said (1957) that the subject matter of the sociology *of* medicine is "concerned with studying such factors as the organizational structure, role relationships, value systems, rituals and functions of medicine as a system of behavior and that this type of activity can best be carried out by persons operating from independent positions outside the formal medical setting." In other words, Straus saw the sociology *of* medicine as the sociological study of medicine. These sociological studies should be conducted by professional sociologists whose employment is outside of the medical realm, such as academic sociologists housed in departments of sociology in universities.

At the heart of Straus's concept of the sociology *of* medicine is the notion that it can provide an opportunity to apply, refine, and test sociological principles and theories. The particular arena or laboratory of medicine is not fundamentally important. The important point is the opportunity to submit existing sociological principles to empirical testing and to use this new proving ground for the clarification of those principles.

The sociology *in* medicine category is quite different, according to Straus (1957), who stated it "consists of collaborative research or teaching often involving the integration of concepts, techniques and personnel from many disciplines." Under this category, Straus placed all those efforts in which sociologists and other social scientists ply their skills within the realm of medicine. Those skills include the teaching of medical students, identifying differences in the definitions and reactions to health and illness, and social epidemiology. The primary concern of studies in this category is the introduction and use of sociological concepts, principles, and research in medicine.

At the heart of Straus's concept of the sociology *in* medicine is the opportunity it provides for sociologists to work within the medical world, as applied sociologists. In contrast to the sociology *of* health, the important point here is the specification of the actual arena of medicine. Thus, the purpose of the sociology *in* health is to make the medical world aware of the utility of sociological principles and concepts concerning social behavior, and the ability of sociologists to provide certain types of research within the realm of social medicine.

In addition to describing the two categories of the sociologies *of* and *in* medicine, Straus also identified their interrelationship. He suggested (1957) that the roles played by these two types of medical sociologists are incompatible: "The sociologist of medicine may lose objectivity if he identifies too closely with medical teaching or clinical research while the sociologist in medicine risks a good relationship if he tries to study his colleagues." In this passage, Straus identified dilemmas that exist for both the soci-

ologist *of* medicine and the sociologist *in* medicine. According to Straus, the sociologist *of* medicine experiences difficulty gaining access to medical research sites, because the profession of medicine is not interested in being subjected to sociological scrutiny. This disinterest is especially salient when such scrutiny raises serious questions about the medical community, because these questions may tend to diminish its power and prestige.

At the same time, the sociologist *in* medicine also faces a perplexing dilemma. Using sociological skills in an applied fashion, the sociologist *in* medicine easily gains access to valuable information and other resources. However, in the process of serving the medical interests, he or she may find himself divested of his or her unique sociological perspective. This may occur primarily as a result of the secondary status accorded to the sociologist in medicine (or for that matter, to any nonclinical non-M.D.) by most of the medical professionals with whom he or she works.

The noncompatability between the roles of the sociologist *in* medicine and the sociologist *of* medicine may be abstracted to the more general level. There it can be recast in the form of the question that has interested many scientists in modern history. In order to advance the general discipline (in this case, sociology), which is more valuable, applied research or basic research? There are prestigious sociologists who would support the role of applied research, and there are prestigious sociologists who would support the role of basic research. Indeed, this very issue has recently been rather hotly debated within the sociological community (see Huber, 1984). We shall withhold our support for either of these roles until the latter portions of this section. There, the ramifications of each of these roles will be discussed in terms of the future of medical sociology.

Elaborating on Straus's Distinctions

Straus's (1957) distinction between the sociologies *of* and *in* medicine was immediately recognized as a major contribution toward understanding not only this new specialty area but also the directions in which it might develop. As medical sociology began to emerge as a legitimate area within American sociology, however, the number of studies in this new specialty area increased exponentially. In a short period of time the growing literature in medical sociology began to tax the simple distinction that Straus originally described, and a number of refinements were suggested that elaborated on Straus's basic dichotomy (Kendall and Merton, 1958; Kendall, 1963; Suchman, 1967).

These refinements have been reviewed and summarized by Kendall and Reader (1972) at some length. According to them, the sociology *of* medicine deals with "questions which belong within the traditions of the sociology of the professions and organizational sociology. Relevant topics include recruitment into and training for the profession, the organization of the profession, and finally, its relations to external pressures and agencies." They describe sociology *in* medicine as "the application of sociological concepts, knowledge, and techniques in efforts to clarify medical and social-psychological problems in which the medical profession and its allied workers are interested. In this instance, sociological knowledge supplements medical knowledge, in order to find solutions to what are essentially medical problems." Thus, although Kendall and Reader had elaborated upon the categorical nature of Straus's distinction, the basic decision criteria for the classification of studies remained the same. Studies that were conducted along the lines of traditional sociology belonged to the sociology *of* medicine. Studies that were conducted as an applied venture belonged to the sociology *in* medicine.

A Little Modernization

One might consider Kendall and Reader's (1972) framework suitable for evaluating existing contributions to medical sociology. But there is something missing, and that something is the scope of the framework

and its concepts. Developing rather slowly at first, a new way of looking at health and health care has been emerging in the United States since the 1960s. There are at least two major factors that have stimulated this development.

The first major factor has been the increasing role of the government, at the local, state, and federal levels, in providing health care to the population. Beginning with local governments in the early 1950s, the trend toward third-party payment or provision of health care has increased markedly. With the provision of Medicare and Medicaid in 1965, as well as other programs, an ever growing portion of the population comes under the umbrella of health services provided by the government. This umbrella will certainly have wider coverage if some form of mandatory national health insurance is adopted.

As this umbrella of provided care expands, the nature of medicine becomes more social. This is particularly evident in the increasingly national nature of the health care delivery system. As the various levels of government become more and more involved in the health care enterprise, research addressing the many-faceted problems of comprehensive health care policy and planning becomes more and more important to them. Consequently, the various levels of government make available more and more financial and other support for research. As a result, medical sociologists find, and are drawn to, new and nonmedical health research topics.

The second and somewhat related factor has been the growing redefinition of health and illness. Beginning with a classic essay by Dubos (1959), a new orientation toward health has developed. (This topic is taken up extensively in chapters 3 and 4.) Dubos argued that the traditional image of health as the absence of disease was merely a mirage. The conception of the established germ theory (discussed in chapter 1) held that germs cause disease and that medicine's job was to eliminate germs, thus eliminating disease. Dubos argued that it is impossible to completely eliminate disease, especially in modern industrialized nations, where the process of living itself constantly modifies the environment. For people, health consists of a relative state of adaptation to the environment. Because people constantly modify the environment, they are constantly in a relative state of maladaptation to it. Therefore, for Dubos and those who rallied to his position, the simplistic assumption that disease was something that could be totally eliminated by medical science became inappropriate. Rather, it was argued that medicine should change its concentration of effort from strictly the elimination of disease to a more balanced approach, including the care and treatment of the sick. In so doing, not only would physiological concerns be considered and treated, so would social and psychological concerns. (A more detailed discussion of this point may be found in chapter 4.)

As a result of the changing scope of medicine and the increasingly social nature of its delivery, sociological interest and research has gone beyond the general domain of medical personnel and their work. Sociological studies now regularly report on a wide variety of health and health related issues. While *medicine* proper remains one of the major topics of theoretical and research interest, the allied fields and the general nature of *health*—broadly defined as consisting of physiological, social, and psychological adaptation—are being studied by many medical sociologists.

In order to modernize the original distinction between the sociologies *of* and *in* medicine, a number of medical sociologists have suggested that the distinction be changed to the sociologies *of* and *in health* (although some view this as more of a semantic than substantive modification; see Levine and Sorenson, 1983). Wilson (1970) has succinctly captured the meaning of this modernized distinction in writing that most sociological concerns with health may be characterized either as "(1) detached observation and analysis, motivated primarily by a sense of *sociological* problem, or (2) more intimate, applied and conjoint research and teaching, motivated primarily by a sense of

health problem." Studies that fall under the first category belong to the sociology *of* health, while those falling under the second category belong to the sociology *in* health.

The Current Status of the Sociology of Health

So far, we have developed and expanded Straus's (1957) initial concepts into the sociologies *of* and *in health*. It is now time to assess the current state of affairs in the sociology of health. The question of interest may be stated as follows: What is the current distribution of research efforts in the sociology of health in terms of the dichotomous distinction? In other words, what portion of the research currently being done may be classified as belonging to the sociology *of* health, and what portion may be classified as belonging to the sociology *in* health? We also want to know whether this proportion represents a change from the distribution of work done in this area during earlier periods.

To answer these questions, we must do two things. First, we must establish some benchmark for the distribution of work in medical sociology during its formative years. Second, we must survey current research efforts in the sociology of health. The first task, establishing a benchmark for purposes of comparison, is the easier of the two. Wilson (1970) has argued that in its formative years (approximately 1955 to 1964), most of the work done in medical sociology was clearly classifiable as sociology *of* medicine. In the years following this formative period (approximately 1965 to 1970), Wilson contends that efforts in medical sociology became rather evenly distributed. A review of the literature published during these periods provides a considerable amount of support for Wilson's evaluation.

A review of the state of medicine in these periods may provide an explanation for the changing distribution that Wilson (1970) describes. During the formative years of medical sociology, the invincible autonomy and private nature of medicine was reaching its peak. The rather rapid decline that medicine is currently experiencing began after 1970 (see Starr, 1982). This decline highly correlates with the increasing social nature of medicine, which was dramatically thrust upon the nation with the advent of Medicare in 1965. As the social nature of medicine increased, the need for applied studies in the distribution and utilization of health services for use in planning new social programs and health care delivery systems also increased. The need for such applied studies was recognized, and research funds began to be earmarked more and more for them (see Flook and Sanazaro, 1973). In addition to the social interest in health services studies, this helped to stimulate an increasing interest among sociologists for applied research. As a result of all this, research in the sociology *in* health soon became as common as research in the sociology *of* health.

Since 1970, popular and government interest in health and the health care system have become even more keen (see Starr, 1982; Wolinsky and Marder, 1985). It would seem reasonable to assume, therefore, that the distribution of research in medical sociology has continued to reflect the pattern that Wilson (1970) described. Our assumption is that this trend has continued to the point where most research in medical sociology may now be classified as sociology *in* health.

In order to test this assumption (the second task), we must survey the recent literature in the sociology of health. We can facilitate this survey by dividing the literature into the more or less natural categories of books and articles, addressing the latter first. Let us further limit our examination of articles to those published between 1981 and 1985 in the *Journal of Health and Social Behavior*, the official medical sociology journal of the American Sociological Association. This should provide us with a rather representative example of the nature and distribution of articles published by sociologists of health.

The *Journal of Health and Social Behavior* published 149 articles during this period. We reviewed these articles using Wilson's (1970) distinction between the sociologies

of and *in* health. Using what we consider to be a reasonable understanding of the *sense of health problem* versus the *sense of sociological problem* (and when in doubt, erring on the sociology *of* health side), we found that the trend identified earlier by Wilson had indeed continued. About 36 percent of the articles could be classified as belonging to the sociology *of* health. The remaining 64 percent seemed rather clearly to belong to the sociology *in* health. Even more astonishing is the fact that this lopsided distribution may reflect a conservative bias favoring the sociology *of* health. This is because sociologists *in* health may seek (or be forced) to have their work published in journals that are more clearly oriented toward health services research. This would result in an underrepresentation of studies in the sociology *in* health appearing in the *Journal of Health and Social Behavior* (see Gold, 1977, for an elaboration on this point).

An examination of books published during this period is somewhat more difficult. This is primarily due to the problem of deciding which books fall into the general area of the sociology of health. In order to circumvent this problem, we limited our examination to the 125 books listed as being in medical sociology and reviewed by the American Sociological Association's official book review journal, *Contemporary Sociology*, between 1981 and 1985. This may also result in a bias favoring the sociology *of* health, because applied books are less likely to be reviewed in *Contemporary Sociology*.

The results reveal a slightly more pronounced pattern than that found for articles. Nearly three quarters of the books listed and reviewed could be classified as belonging to the sociology *in* health. There were, of course, several exceptions, including a number of new textbooks and handbooks (Cockerham, 1986; Mechanic, 1983), and several excellent books clearly in the sociology *of* health (Lorber, 1984; Schneider and Conrad, 1983; Starr, 1982; and Strauss, Fagerhaugh, Suczek, and Wiener, 1985). Nonetheless, the pattern seems fairly clear. The majority of work published by medical sociologists (whether in article or book form) appears to be motivated by a sense of health problem rather than by a sense of socio-logical problem.

Ramifications of This Lopsided Distribution

What effect does this current concentration of research efforts in the sociology *in* health have upon the general development of the sociology of health? Has the lopsided distribution of efforts aided or hindered the growth of the sociology of health? This subject has been addressed in detail by Gibson (1972), Pflanz (1974, 1975), Johnson (1975), Frankenberg (1974), and Cockerham (1983). With the exception of Cockerham, these authors believe that the dominance of the studies in the sociology *in* health has served to cultivate and perpetuate the atheoretical nature of the sociology of health. In all fairness to these authors, we must point out that our primary concern is not to debunk the work of sociologists *in* health. Indeed, the quality and applicability of their research are not in question here. Our primary concern is with the adverse effect that the dominance of the sociology *in* health has had upon the development of the sociology of health as a *sociological enterprise*, and with the elimination of the adverse effects of what appears to be theoretical stagnation.

Much of the substance of Gibson's (1972), Pflanz's (1974, 1975), Johnson's (1975), and Frankenberg's (1974) critiques must be taken with a grain of salt. Johnson, however, presents a realistic picture of the causes of the atheoretical nature of the sociology of health, noting that the stunted theoretical growth of the sociology of health may be traced to four causal factors: "[its] relative youth, financial and professional constraints and pressures on research, the apparent inability to challenge the fundamental precepts of society's dependence on medicine, and academic isolationism." These four factors, which can be seen as a result of the historical development of medicine and sociology discussed in this chapter and in chapter 1, have resulted in the present concentration on the sociology *in* health rather than the sociology *of* health. Being quite

concerned that the stunted nature of theoretical development in the sociology of health would continue, Johnson proposed the following strategy:

There must be an accommodation between the sociologies *of* and *in* medicine, which allows their different perspectives to fertilize rather than antagonize each other. . . . It is suggested that a general pathway . . . is through the rediscovery of sociology as outlined earlier, and this can be divided into: (i) the widening of the sociological perspective in health and illness; (ii) becoming aware of and increasingly avoiding constraints on research; (iii) seeking firmer roots in mainstream sociology and (iv) re-excavating the theoretical tradition.

Of these four routes to a sociology of health, the latter two are the most important. It is only through the medical sociologist's return to sociological training, especially its reliance upon the theoretical tradition, that a truly viable and useful sociology *of* health can be developed. This return to mainstream sociology within the sociology of health must not, however, ignore the contributions of sociologists *in* health. It should bring the distribution of efforts within the sociology of health back to the point where a more productive balance exists.

Cockerham (1983) takes a rather different and refreshing perspective. Basically, he argues that most medical sociological research today focuses on practical health problems, regardless of whether that research is conducted in sociology departments or medical centers. The reason for this is that over the past ten years governmental and philanthropic support has been directed primarily toward research relevant to medicine and health care policy. As a result, it has been necessary for medical sociologists to focus on health problems (as opposed to sociological problems) in order to receive research funding.

Despite this focus on applied research, Cockerham is not worried about medical sociologists being too close to medicine or becoming handmaidens to physicians. He (1986) argues that what makes contemporary medical sociology so different is that it "has achieved a state of development that allows it to investigate even medical problems from an independent sociological perspective. Contemporary medical sociologists are less concerned with whether or not a piece of work is in the sociology of medicine or sociology in medicine, but rather with how much it increases our understanding of the complex relationship between social factors and health."

We could not agree more with Cockerham; medical sociology has certainly matured over the past ten years. The principal concern of medical sociologists today lies in understanding the relationship between social factors and health. Where the research comes from that leads to this understanding is irrelevant. For sociology in general, however, this is not yet the case (see Huber, 1984). Moreover, some of the traditional tension between sociologists *of* and *in* medicine still remains. Perhaps these final growing pains will come to an end during the 1990s.

A Survey of Medical Sociology

In the previous sections, we have been concerned with two questions: (1) how medical sociology came to be, and (2) the major perspectives or orientations with which medical sociologists identify. We now turn our attention to the topic of what it is that medical sociologists are doing these days. Since its earliest days, medical sociology has been periodically surveyed, reviewed, and overviewed. Various of these "state-of-the-field" pieces have been concerned with mapping out the early literature (Freeman and Reeder, 1957; Pearsall, 1963), the early research interests and priorities (Mangus, 1955; Jaco, 1958; Anderson and Seacat, 1958; Roemer and Elling, 1963; Medalia, 1964), the developing viewpoints (Bloom, 1965; Mechanic, 1966b), or the developing literature (Simmons and Berkanovic, 1972; Freeman, Levine, and Reeder, 1972; Susser, 1974b, 1974c; Badgley, 1976). Others have concentrated on a specific topical area within medical sociology (McKinlay, 1972; Lorber, 1975b) or shown the relevance of medical sociology for a particular health profession (Levine and Sorenson,

1983). There are also two excellent, all-encompassing annotated bibliographies of the medical sociological literature (Litman, 1976; Bruhn, Phillips, and Levine, 1985). In addition to these and other individual efforts, the Medical Sociology Section of the American Sociological Association has prepared two monographs (Mechanic and Levine, 1977; Aiken and Mechanic, 1986); one contains a series of state of the field papers for the major interest areas within medical sociology, and the other documents the relevance of medical sociology for the health care field.

Rather than present yet another state-of-the-field section at this point, we shall briefly describe what medical sociologists are doing in the twelve special interest areas within which most contemporary medical sociology may be categorized. If, after reading the brief descriptions that follow, you find yourself developing an appetite for further information in any specific area, or for looking at the research literature in medical sociology firsthand, we suggest that you turn first to the *Journal of Health and Social Behavior*. It is the richest resource in all of medical sociology. Afterward, to find articles focusing on special topics you may want to thumb through the tables of contents in the more recent issues of these related journals that frequently publish the work of medical sociologists: *Social Science and Medicine*, *Medical Care*, *Health Services Research*, the *American Journal of Public Health*, the *Milbank Memorial Fund Quarterly*, the *International Journal of Health Services*, the *Journal of Chronic Diseases*, the *Journal of Medical Education*, the *Journal of Human Stress*, *Sociology of Health and Illness*, and the *Journal of Behavioral Medicine*. Somewhat less frequently, the work of medical sociologists may also be found in the *British Journal of Preventive and Social Medicine*, the *New England Journal of Medicine*, the *Journal of the American Medical Association*, the *American Sociological Review*, the *American Journal of Sociology*, and *Social Forces*. Finally, for a thoroughly enjoyable personal glimpse at how the careers of two distinguished medical sociologists developed, turn to the autobiographical articles of Fox (1985) and Elinson (1985).

Social Epidemiology

Social epidemiology is the first category of special interest within medical sociology. As defined in chapter 1, social epidemiology involves studying the incidence, prevalence, and pattern of disease, disability, or mortality across a particular population. The social epidemiologist wants to: (1) determine on what basis a disease is distributed within the population, and (2) identify the social factors that may be among the causes of that disease. While social epidemiologists have traditionally been concerned with the social factors of age, sex, race, and social class, contemporary interest in the effects of attitudes and beliefs on the distribution of disease is increasing. Two examples of studies in social epidemiology are those studies that link social factors (such as the lifestyle trait of smoking) to the distribution of cancer and coronary heart disease. In these studies, higher incidence and prevalence rates for cancer and coronary heart disease are linked to cigarette smoking (showing how the disease is differentially distributed in the population). Then, the etiological or causal relationship is identified through controlled, longitudinal experiments. The most outstanding characteristic of social epidemiology is that it involves the application of the scientific method of investigation to trace the disease process. This investigation flows backwards from the end result or dependent variable (disease) through time to the social factors or independent variable (smoking) that occurred earlier in the patient's life. In essence, the social epidemiologist attempts to discover, much like a detective, what social factors are different in the life history of the disease-stricken individual from the life history of the general population.

Sociocultural Responses to Health and Illness

Studies that fall into this category of medical sociology are concerned with how people from different sociocultural heritages view their health, especially how their different sociocultural traditions affect their attitudes, beliefs, and behavior concerning health, illness, and death. At the moment, medical sociologists are especially interested in how and why people from different social groups respond differently to the same symptoms, such as pain, fever, and general malaise. The underlying assumption here is that each sociocultural group has its own world view or philosophy. This world view is then manifest in the various typical behavior patterns that its members exhibit.

Patient-Practitioner Relationships

Studies in this category of medical sociology are primarily concerned with examining the social interactions that take place between the patient and the physician. Of special interest is the changing relationship between patient and physician in which the patient is becoming less dependent and more of an equal in these social interactions. This change from the traditionally physician-dominated patient-practitioner relationship may be traced to: (1) the rise of the consumer advocacy ethic, (2) the growth of the women's equal rights movement in American society, and (3) the increasing competition among physicians. Contemporary studies of the patient-practitioner relationships are showing much more of a negotiated-order process in medical care than ever before. The effects of this negotiated-order process on the traditional role of the patient and the physician are also of considerable interest. In fact, these effects serve as the motivation for several studies currently in progress.

The Sociology of the Hospital

In this area of medical sociology, the central theme concerns the organizational analysis of the hospital as a major component in the health care system. The most popular concepts or topics that are examined include the bureaucratic structure of the hospital; intraprofessional relationships within the hospital; authority, power, and decision-making lines within the hospital; the growth of multihospital systems; and the relationship of the hospital to the larger community within which it exists. One particularly interesting phenomenon has been the changing nature of the hospital emergency room. In the past it was used mainly for the intake of trauma or accident victims. Emergency rooms are now, however, regularly used as the main source of medical care by the lower and lower-middle socioeconomic groups because of financial and other access barriers to more traditional sources of primary care. Another particularly interesting issue is the increasing vertical and horizontal integration of hospitals. In recent years several hospital corporations have emerged, some of which operate hundreds of hospitals nationwide. The impact of these hospital corporations on the health care delivery system is fascinating.

The Organization of Medical Care

Studies in this area of medical sociology are concerned with how differences in the organization of medical practice affect the practice of medicine. These studies typically examine the effects of differences in the delivery system, such as method of payment (fee-for-service versus prepaid) and type of practice setting (solo versus group), on outcome characteristics, such as consumer satisfaction, surgical and hospital utilization, and the use of paraprofessionals. Most of these studies involve comparing these outcomes for similar individuals in one type of health care delivery system with the outcomes for individuals in a different type of health care delivery system. It was in these studies that the prepaid, group practice plans (health maintenance organizations) were shown to result in lower hospitalization rates, which meant a reduction in health care costs.

Health Services Utilization

Studies in health services utilization are concerned with finding out who uses, or does not use, health services (i.e., physicians, dentists, hospitals, clinics, and pharmaceuticals), how, when, where, and why. Most of these studies have emphasized two sets of individual characteristics, in addition to the nature and severity of the individual's illness, as the major causal factors. In the first set of characteristics are sociodemographic variables, such as age, sex, ethnicity, marital status, occupation, income, and education. In the second set of characteristics are the social psychological variables such as the individual's attitudes, beliefs, and orientation toward scientific medicine, and his or her perception of the marginal utility of health services to alleviate or prevent illness. To some extent, the social psychological characteristics are considered to be shaped by the sociodemographic characteristics. Health services utilization studies are concerned with the use of services for both restorative and preventive purposes.

The Sociology of Medical Education

The sociology of medical education has traditionally been one of the most popular areas in medical sociology. Most of the studies in this area have been concerned with how physicians are trained, how they come to be socialized into their role, and how they select a medical specialty. With the increasing societal concern about the overproduction of physicians (Graduate Medical Education National Advisory Committee, 1983), studies concerned with the process of selecting a medical specialty, and a practice location, have become especially salient. The major components in the causal process of medical specialty selection have been identified as the personal characteristics of the medical student (past and present experiences and personality), the cognitive conception by the medical student of his or her environment, and the educational environment of the medical school attended (including self-images, and refracted faculty images).

The Sociology of Health Occupations

Interests in this area of medical sociology arise out of the general sociological concern about the study of occupations and professions. Studies of health occupations may be roughly divided into three groups. In the first group of studies the central concern is with the profession of medicine, its development, growth, and continued autonomy as a true profession. Of particular interest here are the ramifications of the independence, autonomy, and dominance of physicians for the entire health care system. In the second group of studies the general concern is with the development of the newer health occupations or the paraprofessionals (nurse practitioners, physicians' assistants, medical technologists). Of particular sociological interest here is the push for professional recognition by these occupations as evidenced in their increasing unionization, militancy toward physicians and health care administrators, and the changing nature of the assignments of health care tasks. The third group of studies is concerned with the relationships between the various health occupations and how these relationships are changing. Of special interest here is the "pyramid" effect, in which, as the new health occupations are introduced at the patient contact level, the existing health occupations are pushed further away from the patient into bureaucratic, administrative, or consulting roles.

The Medicalization of American Society

In this area of medical sociology the major concern is with illness behavior as a form of deviance, generally studied using the theoretical perspective known as labeling or societal reaction. The particular sociological question that has been formulated is: How does deviant behavior become defined as a medical problem? The most widely know socially deviant behavior to be viewed in the context of medical problems have been, of course, certain forms of mental illness and homosexuality. Perhaps a less value-laden example of socially deviant behavior as an outcome of a medical problem would be hyperactivity (hyperkinesis). Although hyperactivity is recognized as a common medical illness among contemporary children, it did not exist a generation ago. In fact, the "hyperkinetic impulse disorder" was not recognized until 1957. While it is now a recognized disorder, no direct, organic causes of hyperactivity have yet been established. In essence, the medicalization of American society is concerned with

how social control over socially deviant behavior is being transferred to the medical sector.

The Sociology of Stress and Coping Behavior

This area of medical sociology is concerned with studying (1) how social, organizational, and structural factors produce stress in our daily lives; (2) how social stress is related to illness; and (3) how individuals cope or adapt to their stressful environment. The major approaches in studying stress have their roots in social psychology. Some studies are concerned with how specific changes in our regular life events result in stress. Other studies are concerned with how these life change events are accumulated and increase the likelihood of illness and specific diseases, such as coronary heart disease, stomach ulcers, and schizophrenia. Some researchers now focus more on the production of social stress from the daily hassles of life, rather than on major life crises. Researchers appear to be divided on the issue of whether it is the life change events themselves, the individual's perceptions of these events, or the processes that produce the life change events that are the true causes of the social stress. Medical sociologists are also working on models that explain how an individual copes with or adapts to social stress. A particular concern in this regard is whether or not the socialization process has provided the individual with the appropriate coping mechanisms or routines.

Social Psychiatry and Mental Health

One major result of research in this area of medical sociology has been the recognition that social factors affect the development, diagnosis, treatment, and duration of mental illness in the community. Much of this recognition has been the direct result of the earlier community psychiatry studies that were concerned with identifying the nature and prevalence of psychiatric impairment in the noninstitutionalized population. In these studies, the distribution of psychiatric disorders was found to be correlated with several social factors, especially social class position. Social class position was also found to play an important role in the differential treatment of psychiatric disorders. Of particular interest in recent years have been the social, legal, and ethical issues involved in defining mental illness and in the treatment of the mentally ill. In some respects, this concern with the treatment of the mentally ill has ceased to remain within the value-free orientation of sociology and has taken on an ideological tone.

Social Policy and Health Care

Interest in this area of medical sociology is motivated by a desire to provide a better, or at least an equitable, health care delivery system. Accordingly, most of the studies that fall into this category suggest methods by which the alleged "crisis" in health care may be resolved. These studies and their proponents may be placed into three general groups. In the first group are those who suggest that the crisis in the health care system may be fixed-up or healed by minor adjustments to the existing delivery system. The second group of critics suggest that equitable and humane health care is just not feasible within a capitalistic system. They suggest that for the crisis in the health care system to be alleviated, we must adopt a socialized medical subsystem within a larger socialized social system. The suggestions from the third group of critics are more devastating. They argue that we have misconceived the notions of health and illness, and in so doing have allowed our health to be expropriated by the established medical system. Their position is that we should increase self-care, assume more individual responsibility for our own health, and demystify medical care. These and more of the interesting issues involved in social policy concerning health care will be taken up extensively in chapters 3 and 14.

What the Future Holds for Medical Sociology

In presenting the above summaries of the major areas of interest in medical sociology, we have tried to paint you a picture of where medical sociology stands today. Now we shall turn to a prediction of where medical sociology is likely to be in the future. To be more specific, we shall look into our crystal ball to see where medical sociology will be in the late 1980s and beyond. In outlining medical sociology's future, we shall briefly discuss seven factors that we feel will be important in the molding process.

The first factor is the continued expansion of the scope of interest in medical sociology. Earlier in this chapter we commented that medical sociologists had at first been primarily interested in studying *medical* phenomena, or more specifically, those phenomena that were directly related to physicians. As medical sociology progressed, the focus on physicians began to widen so as to include other medical professionals. Later, medical sociology went beyond the realm of medical care and expanded into the larger domain of health care. As medical sociology moves into the 1990s, it will become much more diversified and the metamorphosis to the sociology of health will be more complete. The areas of new or increasing interest will include (1) a greatly expanded concern with nonmedical or alternative health care providers, (2) an intensification of research correlating social lifestyles with the occurrence of social stress and its relation to disease and impairment, (3) a shift in emphasis from the study of restorative health services utilization to preventive health behavior, and (4) the development of research aimed at identifying the most healthy combinations of social activities and characteristics.

A second factor that will help shape medical sociology in the future is the continued, growing concentration on applied studies in the sociology *in* health. Earlier in this chapter we noted that both the social problems orientation and the lure of governmental research funding had attracted medical sociologists into applied research. With the increasing governmental involvement in the financing and delivery of health care (see chapters 3 and 13 for further details), the concentration of studies belonging to the sociology *in* health domain will be intensified by the early 1990s. This will, of course, result from the need for a considerable amount of research to facilitate rational health care policy planning decisions by the various levels of government, especially by the federal government, which is rapidly becoming the principal payer for health services. Even after such policies have been implemented, still more research will be required in order to make the necessary adjustments for a smoothly operating system. The nature of much of this research will bring medical sociologists into closer contact and cooperation with health professionals and administrators at all levels.

As a result of this close contact with health professionals, a third factor will emerge and have considerable influence on medical sociology's future. This factor is the establishment and maintenance of an appropriate distance between the medical sociologist and the health professional. This reflects an updating of Straus's (1957) perplexing dilemma in which (1) sociologists *in* health are likely to get expropriated into the health field, and thus lose their sociological perspective (which is their most important contribution to the study of health); and (2) sociologists *of* health are likely to become too far removed from health care so that their subject matter becomes foreign to them, and they propose health care policies that would either be unrealistic or do grievous damage to the health care system's ability to function. There are at present no warning signals to indicate when a sociologist *in* health has come too close to the health professional's perspective or to indicate when a sociologist *of* health has gone too far away from the health professional's perspective. What remains to be seen is whether or not medical sociologists will be able to keep their balance in an atmosphere of increasing emphasis on applied research.

A fourth factor in medical sociology's future is the growing concern for taking into consideration the perspective of the consumer in analyzing the health care system. As we discussed earlier in this chapter, the medical sociologist has traditionally taken the view of the health professional in analyzing provider-consumer relationships, while the medical anthropologist has taken the consumer's perspective. Partially because of the chiding from within (see Gold, 1977), but mainly because of the increasing popularity of the consumer advocacy movement coupled with the growing surplus of physicians, the medical sociologist will begin to view health care from the patient's perspective to some extent. This change in orientation will bring about a considerable rethinking of the basic principles of medical sociology, including the sick role concept, health status indicators, health services utilization, the role of the patient, the role of the practitioner, and the patient-practitioner encounter.

A fifth factor influencing the future direction of medical sociology will be the employment opportunities for medical sociologists. While medical sociology is one of the most open and opportune of all specialty areas within sociology, the academic or university market for Ph.D. medical sociologists will continue to shrink during the 1990s. This does not mean that medical sociology is just a passing fad. Rather, it is indicative of the general cutbacks in academic employment brought about by hard times, tight money, and declining student enrollments. Ph.D. medical sociologists will not go unemployed. They will, however, be pushed more extensively into applied research and administrative settings in the health care field. This push movement will be complemented by a pulling movement derived from the increased governmental role in the financing and delivery of health care. Doctorally trained medical sociologists will be able to make important contributions in the planning and design of these new health care policies. As these policies are being implemented, there will be a growing need for a new breed of health services planners and administrators to take over the daily operation of the health care system at the local and regional level. These positions will be filled by behavioral scientists with specializations in health care studies. These men and women will have concentrated training at the bachelor's or master's degree level in medical sociology (or medical anthropology, or medical economics, or medical psychology) and will have the necessary practical skills in research methodology (especially in evaluation research design and applied statistical analysis). These skills will enable them to make the necessary planning decisions and adjustments in the new health care delivery and financing systems.

Closely associated with the factors already mentioned will be the growing realization that the scientific study of health, whether in an applied or basic research setting, must become an interdisciplinary endeavor. The major reason behind this sixth factor in medical sociology's future is the recognition that the subsystem of health care penetrates almost all of the other subsystems in society. Among the most important of the other subsystems that are affected are the family subsystem, the economic subsystem, the educational subsystem, the legal subsystem, the political subsystem, and the religious subsystem. In order to clearly understand the extremely complex subject of health-related behavior, it will be necessary to increase interdisciplinary collaboration and conjoint research endeavors. Such cooperation will mean that the contributions of the individual medical behavioral social science disciplines will be increased, and the end result will be greater than the sum of the individual disciplinary accomplishments.

Finally, as a result of the factors mentioned above, especially the increasing employment of medical sociologists in planning and administrative positions in the health care system, and because of the increasing quality of their research, medical sociologists will find an increase in the attention paid them by policymakers and the public. This may be considered a mixed blessing. On the one hand, to the extent that policymakers and the public begin to listen to

medical sociologists or to take their recommendations more seriously, there will be more research areas and support made available. On the other hand, to the extent that policymakers and the public listen to or take medical sociologists seriously, medical sociologists must be sure that their work is as accurate and complete as possible. If, based on the recommendations of medical sociologists, new policies are implemented that fare poorly or fall completely apart, it is unlikely that medical sociologists will be asked again for recommendations. Part of this pressure on medical sociologists stems from the fact that even now the crisis in the health care system is almost intolerable. If an alternative system is designed and fails, it may be too much for people to cope with. Therefore, someone will be marked with the infamy of the scapegoat.

Other Social Science Approaches to Studying Health

As we indicated earlier in this chapter, medical sociology is not the only subdiscipline that examines the relationship between social factors and health. Indeed, we discussed at some length how medical anthropology has developed and how it may be viewed as medical sociology's first cousin. There are some other members of the social science family that you should meet as well. Although their overlap with medical sociology is not as large as that of medical anthropology, the increasingly interdisciplinary nature of health care policy suggests that you should become at least somewhat familiar with them. Accordingly, in this section we shall briefly overview the relevance for and contributions to the sociology of health of its second cousins: economics, political science, demography, law, and ethics.

Health Economics

As a discipline, economics is fundamentally concerned with the production and distribution of goods and services. It should come as no surprise, then, that the dominant themes in the health economics literature relate to the intertwined questions of what health services will be produced, how will they be produced, and where they will be distributed (Berry and Feldman, 1983). The laws of economics suggest that the answer to these questions may be found at the intersection of supply and demand in the health care marketplace.

Unfortunately, it's not quite that simple. The problem is that medical care does not conform to the economist's notion of the ideal marketplace. Three reasons are generally cited in explanations of why the health care industry is so different (AMA National Commission on the Cost of Medical Care, 1978). First, there is the perverse effect of health insurance on the consumer, or what health economists call moral hazard. Moral hazard refers to the fact that when consumers pay virtually nothing for health care when they receive it (because of third-party payers, such as private or public insurance), they tend to use more than they need or to use more than they would if they had to pay for the health services out of their own pockets. As a result, the effective price (as economists would say) approaches zero. Second, there is a dearth of consumer and provider knowledge regarding the cost, efficacy, or necessity of specific medical procedures. In essence, both patient and practitioner are relatively poorly informed about the services under consideration. Third, given the first two factors (i.e., health insurance to pay the bills and the trust placed in physicians by patients because of their medical ignorance), health care providers have the potential ability to affect the demand for their own services. Health economists refer to this as supplier-induced demand. An additional problem is that classic economic theories assume that people are rational. This is clearly not always the case when it comes to health care.

What, then, is the relevance of economics for the sociology of health? We believe the answer lies in economic's focus on incentive structures. Specifically, by understanding how atypical the marketplace incentives are for providers, consumers, and third-party payers, we can obtain a better understanding of both how and why the

health care delivery system has gotten to its present state, as well as what changes are necessary if we are to achieve a more rational, cost-effective system.

Political Science and Health

The fundamental concern of political science is how people are governed. Ultimately, this comes down to decisions about the distribution of benefits and burdens within society. The politics of health considers health care to be one of the benefits and its associated costs to be one of the burdens that society must distribute (Marmor and Dunham, 1983). There is little agreement, however, on how that distribution should be made. Indeed, perhaps the most common thread in the literature on the politics of health is that health policy is ultimately forged from the coming together of a myriad of competing factors (or a "multipolitics" of strange bedfellows), rather than from a more permanent coalition of related interest groups.

Perhaps the most relevant aspect of political science for the sociology of health is its focus on how political policies are developed and maintained. As Ehrenreich and Ehrenreich (1970) and Krause (1977) point out, there really is no single, unified health care policy with identifiable goals in the United States. Rather, what exists is a hodgepodge of particularistic entitlements and promises won over the years by a variety of special interest groups and their lobbyists (Alford, 1975). As a result, there is an uneasy tension in general between the public and the private sectors (Anderson, 1985), and specifically between the various competing players (i.e., patients, providers, and payers). Clearly, a good grasp of the politics of health care facilitates understanding the relationship between social factors and health care.

Demography and Health Care

The principal concern of demography is the structure and dynamics of the population (Verbrugge, 1983). As we have already seen, this is very important for the sociology of health; demographic trends and projections suggest the nature and size of the health care delivery system that will be needed in the future. For example, recall (from chapter 1) the remarkable effect that the increases in life expectancy experienced during the first half of the twentieth century will have on health care planning for the second half. Never before has the health care delivery system been faced with so many elderly individuals who are likely to suffer from multiple chronic conditions requiring a considerable amount of institutional care.

In addition to the traditional value of demography for health planning, the newly emerging subdiscipline of health demography holds great promise for enhancing our understanding of the relationship between demographic factors and health status. Unlike social epidemiologists, who look at the effects of demographic factors on health status, health demographers go one step further by examining the subsequent effect of health status on demographic factors (Verbrugge, 1983). Examples of health demography include studies of how women's nutritional intake affects their fertility, how changes in health status affect family stability, and how decreases in infant mortality rates in developing countries encourage families to have fewer children. By examining the effect of health status on demographic characteristics, health demographers are able to provide more accurate, long-term projections of the demand for health care.

Health Law

The role of law in health care has been to establish rules and regulations governing what can be done and under what circumstances it can be done. According to Schramm (1983), the presence of law in the health care system was given a considerable boost during the mid 1970s when the federal government began taking a more regulatory posture. This approach put in place a labyrinth of codes and regulations to be followed whenever major expenditures of capital were to be made. Although these actions

were designed to instill some degree of cost containment in the health care delivery system, adherence to the strict legal procedures proved to be both frustrating and expensive. Therefore, although Schramm clearly recognizes the need for rules and regulations in the health care industry, he argues that "the proper legal perspective on health policy making should be respect for the goals of the legal system, both the preservation of individual rights and the procedural system used in their protection, but with an awareness that the law exists to serve and not to be served."

There are three major issues under discussion in health law that have considerable relevance for the sociology of health. The first concerns malpractice litigation and the current crisis in the malpractice insurance industry. More and more malpractice law suits are being filed, and the amounts awarded by juries are also rising (up to an average of nearly two-thirds of a million dollars in 1984). In response, companies that offer malpractice insurance to physicians have either raised their rates (as much as 40 percent a year) or simply refused to offer policies to high-risk medical specialists, especially obstetrician-gynecologists. The result has been an increasing antagonism between the medical and legal professions, each of which blames the other for the problem, which ultimately is changing the nature of the patient-practitioner relationship.

The second major issue under discussion in health law concerns the application of antitrust legislation to the emerging nationally based health care corporations. Of principal interest here is whether the larger hospital chains will be able to extract such advantageous rates from the suppliers of their goods and services that unaffiliated hospitals will no longer be able to compete.

The third health law issue of considerable relevance to the sociology of health concerns the traditional legal debate over the rights of the individual versus the rights of the state. This issue becomes especially salient whenever discussions of the future of the health care delivery system focus on zero-sum alternatives, because it raises the question of whether society will allow any individual to spend more than a fixed amount on their health care, regardless of their personal resources.

Health Care Ethics

If the principal role of law is to determine what *can* be done, to whom, and by whom, the principal role of ethics is to determine what *should* be done, to whom, and by whom. In essence, the role of ethics in health care is to be the conscience of the health care delivery system. At present, there are three pressing ethical questions that have considerable relevance for the sociology of health. The first is rather well known. It concerns establishing and safeguarding the nature of informed and proxy consent. As alluded to in the discussion of health economics, patients (or their proxies) are oftentimes not as informed as they need to be when faced with major medical decisions. Therefore, they depend extensively on the advice of and information provided by their physicians. The doctrine of informed consent helps to ensure that patients get to make their own decisions, based on their personal values and perceptions of the situation. This is especially important in cases of the terminally ill, when a request for a DNR (do not resuscitate) order is made.

The second ethical question of considerable relevance for the sociology of health is also rather well known. It concerns the increasing use of high technology medical experimentation. Perhaps the most controversial example during the 1980s has been the use of the Jarvik-7 artificial heart. At issue is whether benefits to the patient and/or to future patients outweigh not so much the risk (because Barney Clark and those who followed him were dying anyway) but the emotional and monetary costs involved (see Fox, 1984; Shaw, 1984).

The third issue in contemporary health ethics that has considerable ramifications for the sociology of health concerns who will provide health care for those who cannot afford to pay for it themselves. Although this is not a new issue, recent changes in the financing and delivery of medical care have made it more pressing. More and more, proprietary (for-profit) and nongovernmental not-for-profit hospitals are becoming increasingly reluctant to provide charity care. As a result, the demand on city- and county-owned hospitals is overwhelming their capacity, and individuals in need are being turned away. The ethical issue is who is responsible for caring for these individuals.

Summary

In this chapter we have discussed the origin, nature, present, and future of medical sociology. In the first section, we saw that medical sociology was a recent development within sociology and that six factors helped to establish it as a legitimate specialty: (1) the social medicine movement of the 1920s and 1930s; (2) the social epidemiology studies resulting from sociology's social problems orientation in the 1940s and 1950s; (3) the employment of full-time sociologists by medical and nursing schools, beginning in 1949; (4) the moral and financial support of several private foundations in the 1950s and 1960s; (5) the chartering of the Section on Medical Sociology of the American Sociological Association in 1959; and (6) the publication by the American Sociological Association, in 1965, of the *Journal of Health and Social Behavior* as its official journal.

We then examined the origin of medical anthropology and found that while it had a similar history and interests, there were three distinctions between it and medical sociology: (1) the medical sociologist takes the perspective of the health professional, while the medical anthropologist takes the perspective of the patient; (2) the medical sociologist relies primarily on the survey method for data collection, while the medical anthropologist relies primarily on participant observation; and (3) the medical sociologist is interested mainly in the medical care systems of the United States and western Europe, while the medical anthropologist is interested in the health care systems of all societies.

In the second section, we presented Straus's (1955) original distinction between studies in the sociology *in* medicine—concerned with applying sociological principles and methods to applied problems of interest to the medical community—and studies in the sociology *of* medicine—concerned with applying, refining, and testing sociological principles and theories in the health care setting. We considered the dilemma of how the sociologist *in* medicine can become too close to medicine and lose the sociological perspective, and how the sociologist *of* medicine can get too far removed from the subject matter and miss the nuances in the data or even misunderstand them entirely. Elaborations of this basic *of* and *in* distinction were then presented, and the case was made for substituting the word *health* for the word *medicine* in order to reflect sociology's expanded interests in the entire health field. We then examined the historical distribution of efforts in medical sociology, and their ramifications.

In the third section, we turned to summarizing the twelve most popular research areas in medical sociology: (1) social epidemiology, (2) sociocultural responses to health and illness, (3) patient-practitioner relationships, (4) the sociology of the hospital, (5) the organization of medical care, (6) health services utilization, (7) the sociology of medical education, (8) the sociology of health occupations, (9) the medicalization of American society, (10) the sociology of stress and coping behavior, (11) social psychiatry, and (12) social policy and health care.

In the fourth section, we turned to a forecast of medical sociology's future in the 1990s and beyond, as reflected by seven influential factors: (1) a continued expansion of interest in the health care field; (2) a growing concern with applied research; (3) a balance increasingly difficult to maintain between getting too close to or too far from health professionals; (4) a growing interest in the consumer's perspective in analyzing health care interactions; (5) a shift from academic employment of medical sociologist to employment in more practical settings, organizations, and agencies; (6) a more integrated interdisciplinary approach to the study of health care; and (7) a greater recognition of medical sociologists and attention to their suggestions by policy planners and the public. In the final section we presented an overview of the relevancy to and contributions of economics, political science, demography, law, and ethics for the sociology of health.

3. An Overview of the Health Care System

IN CHAPTER 1 we examined the relationship between social factors and health; in chapter 2 we reviewed the development of the sociology of health as an academic subdiscipline. In this concluding introductory chapter, we turn to a brief overview of the American health care delivery system. The reason for doing this now is to set the stage for the subsequent discussion of the principles, practitioners, and issues involved in the sociology of health. Having an overview of the health care delivery system, including how it has radically changed during the twentieth century, provides the context with which to gain a sense of perspective on the sociology of health.

Chapter 3 is divided into six sections. The first focuses on changes in the disease burden and current health practices; special attention is paid to the implications that these changes have for the health care delivery system. The second section documents the remarkable growth of the health care industry in the twentieth century. In the third section we consider changes in the way that medicine is practiced and the impact that this has had on certain medical procedures. Next, we examine data on current health services utilization patterns, paying special attention to the most common reasons for going to see the doctor or being hospitalized. The fifth section focuses on how the health care delivery system is controlled, and by whom. In the final section we present the views of two distinguished medical sociologists on the social history of the American health care delivery system.

Changes in the Disease Burden

To understand the sociology of health, one must first have some knowledge of the disease burden (i.e., the distribution of diseases, especially "killer" diseases) that the health care delivery system faces and how

changes in that disease burden have brought about changes in the health care delivery system. Torrens (1978) identifies four fundamentally different periods. During the first period, from 1850 to 1900, most of the health conditions facing the American people were epidemics of acute infections, such as influenza and tuberculosis. There was little that the health care technology of the 1800s could do to stem these epidemics. Physicians and nurses were poorly trained, and hospitals were where the sick and poor, who could not afford to be treated at home, went as a last resort. As a result, hospital patients and staff actually suffered the highest mortality rates of any group whenever epidemics broke out, because of the ease of disease communication and the lack of knowledge of prevention. Moreover, even for those who could afford not to be hospitalized, the health care delivery system, as we know it today, did not exist. Individuals were left to fend for themselves, without any major form of social or public services for assistance.

During Torrens's (1978) second period, the first half of the twentieth century, the illness burden shifted from epidemics of infectious disease affecting large groups of Americans to more acute events, trauma, and infections that affected individual Americans. Thus, we see a shift from population-based medicine to individual-based medicine. Coupled with the change in the illness burden was a considerable expansion of basic medical science and technology. Medicine was beginning to be more capable of helping cure Americans of their acute conditions. Medical discoveries—such as vitamins in 1912, insulin in 1921, and penicillin in 1928—and their implications for the successful treatment of diseases considerably increased the prestige of medicine. The training of physicians (see chapter 9) and nurses (see chapter 11) was drastically modified, creating an emphasis on science as well as practice. Hospitals, too, began to change, becoming centers of health care technology that no private physician's office could rival. As a result, hospitals became the place of first choice for Americans who needed health care. At the societal level,

both public and private sector efforts to help those who could not help themselves began to emerge, marking the beginning of the social welfare approach to health care in the United States.

The third period that Torrens (1978) describes runs from the end of World War II to the present. During this period the disease burden facing the American health care delivery system changed radically; chronic diseases, such as heart disease, cancer, and stroke became the leading causes of death. In an attempt to overcome these new chronic killers, public and private agencies made enormous sums of money available for medical science and medical technology research. Indeed, an official war on cancer was declared. It is important to note, however, that the war on cancer, as well as those on other targeted conditions like heart disease, focused primarily on curing rather than on prevention. That is, the dominant paradigm in medical science, and in the funding of medical science, remained the search for those "magic bullets" (Dubos, 1959) that would cure cancer, heart disease, and stroke after they occurred, rather than preventing their occurrence in the first place.

Nonetheless, the end result was that the spirit of technology captured the health care delivery system. Physicians and nurses came to believe that the best quality medical care could only be provided if the latest available technology were used. The public also began to idolize health care technology. As a result, hospitals were most eager to acquire the latest in health care technology, and an ever-increasing upward pressure was placed on the cost of health care. As health care became more and more expensive, there was an increased pressure to define health care as a basic right for all Americans. Otherwise, less fortunate individuals would be denied health care merely because of its high-technology–based costs.

This lead to an expanded notion of social and governmental responsibility for organizing and providing health care. Indeed, it marked the beginning of the "entitlement era," a period during which the social and political philosophy toward health care viewed it as an inalienable right of all Americans. Two of the most significant legislative steps in this direction were the implementation of the Medicare and Medicaid programs in the 1960s. In addition, several federal agencies were charged with the responsibility to monitor the health of and health care received by all Americans in order to ensure that these new programs were being successful in eliminating existing social and economic differentials in access to health care.

The last major period in Torrens's (1978) review of the development of health care in America focuses on the future. Here he predicts an important shift from chronic physiologically based conditions to chronic emotionally and behaviorally based conditions. As a result, although the health care technology industry will continue to grow, Torrens believes that there will be marked attempts to *repersonalize* that technology and make it more amenable to the treatment of individuals rather than clinical entities. He also expects there to be more centralization of responsibility for and control over

the health care delivery system by the federal government. The principal reason for this lies in the increasing proportion of health care expenditures paid for by the federal government as a result of the growth of the entitlement programs. Given the highly volatile nature of the health care delivery system today, it is, of course, difficult to speculate about the future.

The crucial point to remember from Torrens's (1978) discussion is how changes in the illness burden affect the health care delivery system, especially during the twentieth century. This can best be seen by examining more specific data on the conditions facing the health care delivery system. Table 3-1 contains death rates for the 10 leading causes of death at the turn of the twentieth century and in 1985. There are two important points worth noting in this table. The first is the most obvious and concerns remarkable changes in the illness burden just discussed. In 1900 the three leading causes of death were influenza, tuberculosis, and diarrhea; in 1985 the three leading causes of

Table 3-1. *Death rates for the ten leading causes of death, 1900 and 1985.*

1900		1985	
Causes of death	Death rate (per 100,000)	Causes of death	Death rate (per 100,000)
All causes	1,719.0	*All causes*	876.6
Pneumonia and influenza	202.2	Diseases of the heart	324.2
Tuberculosis	194.4	Malignancies	193.2
Diarrhea, enteritis, and ulceration of the intestine	142.7	Cerebrovascular disease	64.3
Diseases of the heart	137.4	Accidents	38.3
Senility, ill-defined or unknown	117.5	Influenza and pneumonia	27.8
Intracranial lesions of vascular origin	106.9	Suicide and homicide	19.8
Nephritis	88.6	Diabetes mellitus	15.8
All accidents	72.3	Cirrhosis of the liver	11.3
Cancer and other malignant tumors	64.0	Arteriosclerosis	10.0
Diphtheria	40.3	Bronchitis, emphysema, and asthma	9.1
		Certain diseases of early infancy	7.9

SOURCE: National Center for Health Statistics. 1986. "Births, Marriages, Divorces, and Deaths for 1985." *Monthly Vital Statistics Report* 34(12):1–12.

death were heart disease, cancer, and stroke. Thus, in just 85 years the targets of the health care system shifted from epidemics of acute, infectious diseases to chronic, non-infectious conditions affecting individuals.

The second important point worth noting in Table 3-1 is somewhat less obvious. It concerns the remarkable decline in the overall death rate. In 1900 the death rate per 100,000 individuals for all causes was 1,719.0; by 1985 it had fallen to 876.6, representing a 50 percent decline. As a result, average life expectancy for Americans rose from 49 to 75, an impressive gain of 26 years. As Americans lived longer, their exposure to chronic conditions increased; these chronic conditions required continued management, as opposed to the one-shot cures available for acute conditions.

When taken together, these two points suggest the need for a health care delivery system in the 1980s that is organized around the treatment of chronic conditions. Unfortunately, today's health care delivery system is not like that. It is fundamentally organized as an acute care system, with an insufficient amount of long-term and other chronic care facilities available. The reason for this is that most of the "bricks-and-mortar" aspects of the system were built in response to the illness burden faced during the first half of the twentieth century. Moreover, despite the changing nature of the illness burden, most health care facility modernization and renovation projects since 1950 have continued to emphasize the acute care philosophy. As a result, America finds itself in the 1980s with a health care delivery system designed for acute care, but a disease burden that is fundamentally chronic in nature.

As if the mismatch between the illness burden we face and the health care delivery system we have wasn't bad enough, we must note that the length of time individuals are affected by chronic conditions is ever-increasing. Although the data in Table 3-1 showed the three leading causes of death in 1985 (heart disease, cancer, and stroke) accounted for more than two thirds of all deaths in the United States, they do not indicate the progress made in treating these

Figure 3-1. Death Rates for Heart Disease, Cancer and Stroke for Persons 55 to 64 Years of Age, 1960–1982.

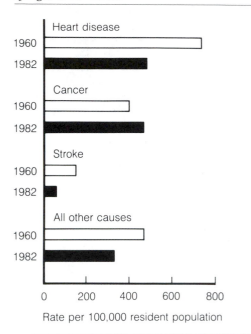

Rate per 100,000 resident population

SOURCE: National Center for Health Statistics. 1985. *Charting the Nation's Health: Trends Since 1960.* DHHS Publication 85-1251. Washington, D.C.: Government Printing Office.

killers. Figure 3-1 shows the death rates for these conditions between 1960 and 1982. As indicated, there has been a 36 percent decline in mortality due to heart disease, and a 60 percent decline in mortality due to stroke; when combined, the increased success in treating heart disease and stroke accounts for most of the overall decline in mortality. (The 11 percent increase in mortality from cancer is largely due to the marked increase in smoking among women.) As medicine becomes more successful in treating these conditions, it alters the nature of the illness burden itself, creating an ever-increasing need for follow-up treatment and long-term monitoring for recurrent episodes. Thus, the "good news" is that these killer chronic diseases are now much less likely to kill; the "bad news" is that this medical success has brought new meaning to the chronicity of these diseases.

It is only recently that the health care industry, health care policymakers, and the public have begun to see the potential for avoiding these chronic diseases in the first place by increasing preventive health behavior. In chapter 1 we examined data from the Alameda County study (see Berkman and Breslow, 1983), which convincingly demonstrated the ability of good health practices to reduce both mortality and morbidity rates. It would seem logical that Americans would rush to adopt such preventive health practices; but alas, Americans have not begun to exhibit healthy lifestyles until recently. Just as chronic conditions (such as lung cancer or emphysema from smoking) takes years to develop, it takes time for preventive health behavior to reduce the risk of chronic diseases. Thus, although healthy lifestyles may be rather popular during the 1980s, their long-term effects will not be felt by the health care delivery system for some time to come.

But how much healthy behavior do Americans actually engage in today? This is a difficult question to answer, because there is little agreement on the best way to collect such data. One method is to conduct a public opinion survey and simply ask people. In 1986 the Prevention Research Center (1986) did just that, asking about 1,256 adults to indicate which of 21 health-seeking behaviors they engaged in. Table 3-2 shows what they found. It is important to note that 70 percent of all adults do not smoke, and 73 percent try to control their daily stress levels; both of these are primary risk factors for the three leading causes of death. At the same time, however, it is distressing to note that only two out of every five adults restrict their cholesterol intake, less than a third exercise regularly, and only about a fifth maintain a healthy weight; these three behaviors are also primary risk factors for the three leading causes of death. Thus, it would appear that the healthy behavior of Americans is rather spotty; we seem to do the easier things but avoid doing the tougher ones. Moreover, although progress has been made during the 1980s in some

Table 3-2. *Percent of adults engaging in twenty-one health-seeking behaviors, 1986.*

Health-seeking behaviors	Adult's practice of health-seeking behavior (percent)
Avoid smoking in bed	91
Moderate alcohol consumption	87
Socialize regularly	85
Do not smoke	70
Avoid home accidents	80
Avoid driving while drinking	75
Have their blood pressure checked	86
Have a smoke detector in the home	76
Control stress	73
Have an annual dental exam	74
Restrict fatty food intake	56
Obey speed limits	56
Consume high fiber content foods	59
Gets 7–8 hours of sleep	64
Take adequate vitamins and minerals	63
Restrict sodium intake	54
Restrict sugar intake	50
Restrict cholesterol intake	42
Exercise regularly	30
Wear seat belts	41
Maintain a healthy weight	21

SOURCE: Adapted from Prevention Research Center. 1986. *The Prevention Index '86.* Emmaus, Pennsylvania: Rodale Press. Reprinted by permission of Prevention Magazine.

areas (notably in stress reduction, accident prevention, and seat belt use), retrogression has also occurred (notably in obeying the speed limit and taking enough vitamins and minerals). In sum, we simply don't seem to be helping ourselves all that much.

The Growth of the Health Care Delivery System

Do We Actually Have a System?

One of the most frustrating aspects of describing the health care delivery system is that we simply do not have one. According to most definitions, a system consists of a combination of things or parts that form a unitary whole (see Barnhart, 1965; Salloway, 1982). A good example is a heating and air conditioning system. It contains a regulating device (the thermostat) that oversees the output of the production devices (the furnace and the air conditioner) and their resource inputs. All of the parts of a heating and air conditioning system work together to achieve the system's goal of maintaining a desired temperature. If the thermostat determines that the room temperature is warmer than desired, it calls on the air conditioner to lower the temperature. Similarly, if the room temperature is colder than desired, the thermostat calls on the furnace to raise the temperature.

The health care delivery system in the United States isn't like that. There is no analog of the thermostat, and the various components of the health care industry do not work together toward a common goal. As a result, it is somewhat misleading to talk about the American health care delivery *system*, because a real system doesn't exist. There are, however, a number of subsystems that serve different populations in different ways. Torrens (1978) identifies four: (1) the private practice, fee-for-service system; (2) local government health care; (3) the military medical care system; and (4) the Veterans Administration health care system. The private practice, fee-for-service system is what most middle-class Americans are familiar with. This is actually the least systematic of any of the subsystems, because

each family is responsible for putting together its own informal network of health care services. As a result, neighbors in the same suburban subdivision may receive their health care from markedly different "systems." The most popular aspect of the middle-class health care system is the freedom of choice available to the individual (or family) to pick and choose from available health care providers and services. That is, individuals in this health care subsystem can have whatever health services they want, from whomever they choose, as long as they (or their insurance) can pay for them.

For those who cannot afford to pay for their health care and are not eligible for any special entitlements, there is the local government health care subsystem (or what Salloway [1982] refers to as "residual" institutions). The principal clients of this subsystem are generally poor, live in the inner-city areas, and are more likely to be members of minority groups (Torrens, 1978). Like the middle-class subsystem, the subsystem of health care for the poor is not formally organized, with individuals and families having to make their own arrangements. There is, however, a major difference between these two subsystems. In the local government system there is very little opportunity for choice; the poor must take what is offered and make up their system out of what is available. The majority of services available are provided through city and county hospitals, and local health departments. One of the most significant shortcomings of this subsystem is the lack of continuity. Unlike those in the middle-class health care subsystem, the poor seldom have the equivalent of a family physician, often seeing a seemingly endless stream of different practitioners with each illness episode. This is a considerable disadvantage for the treatment of chronic conditions and also serves to decrease compliance with treatment regimens.

The military medical system, in contrast to those for the middle class and the poor, is truly a system (Torrens, 1978). It is all-inclusive and omnipresent in the lives of military personnel. Indeed, the military medical care system is charged with the responsibility for protecting and maintaining the health of all military personnel. Because of this responsibility, the military health care subsystem takes an aggressive posture in providing health care and reaches out to its clients, rather than passively waiting for its clients to come in for services (as in the two previous subsystems). Because it serves only those on active military duty, the services provided by this subsystem are very different; they are predominantly preventive and acute restorative services. Long-term care treatment of chronic conditions is rare, because individuals with disabilities are discharged from military service and thus become ineligible for health care.

The last subsystem identified by Torrens (1978) is the Veterans Administration health care system. Operating 174 medical centers nationwide, the Veterans Administration subsystem serves retired, disabled, and otherwise eligible veterans of previous military service. Most of the health care provided by the Veterans Administration is long-term institutional-based care, either in hospitals or nursing homes. The typical Veterans Administration patient is an older male with multiple chronic conditions, both physical and emotional. Unlike the military health care system, the Veterans Administration health care system is relatively uncoordinated and not very aggressive in caring for its patients. As a result, most veterans appear to use the Veterans Administration health care system only when they have no other option.

Another way of looking at the nonsystem of health care in the United States is to place the subsystems described above, and the federal entitlement programs, into a hierarchy based on desirability. Figure 3-2 does this, assuming four levels or tiers in the health care delivery system. The most desirable tier contains the middle-class subsystem, wherein individual choice of health care practitioners is paramount. The second tier consists of the five major federal entitlement programs: the Indian Health Service, the Veterans Administration system, the military health care system, the Medicare program, and the Medicaid program. It is notable that rather than having one coordi-

nated health care subsystem, the federal government has pursued a path of creating categorical programs for each special interest group for which it has assumed responsibility. The lack of coordination between these entitlement programs has resulted in considerable inefficiencies. Less desirable than the entitlement programs, which often allow at least a limited amount of practitioner choice by means of voucher programs, are the local government programs. Worse yet is the situation of those in the fourth tier. These individuals have fallen through the "safety nets" (i.e., the floors of the three upper tiers) and receive no health care. Clearly, it requires a stretch of the imagination to consider such an array of health services a "system." Nonetheless, it is common parlance to refer to the totality of the health care industry in the United States as its health care delivery system. Therefore, although it is somewhat misleading, we shall not break with established tradition.

How the System Grew

There are a variety of ways to show how dramatically the American health care delivery system has grown during the twentieth century. Perhaps the most straightforward way to begin is to simply examine the number of persons employed in the health care delivery system. Table 3-3 does just that. It is astonishing to note that the actual number of persons employed in the health care sector has increased more than tenfold between 1910 and 1980. Moreover, even after adjusting for the growth in the population in general, these data show a 400 percent increase in the relative number (proportion) of health care workers to the overall labor force. There are now 2,209 health care workers for every 100,000 Americans. The health care industry is one of the three largest in the country.

Perhaps the most central component of the health care delivery system is the hospital. Although hospitals will be discussed in detail in chapter 12, some mention of how they have grown during the twentieth century is in order at this point. In 1930 there were about 6,700 hospitals in the United

Figure 3-2. *An Overview of the Multi-Tiered American Health Care Delivery System.*

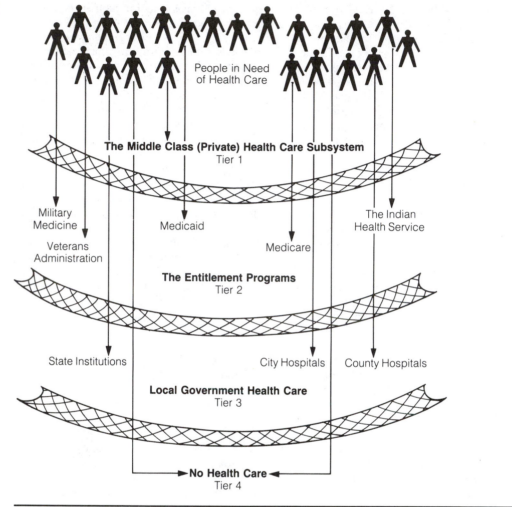

States, having a total of about 956,000 beds. About 45 percent of these hospitals were of the non-governmental not-for-profit variety, which is the kind of "community" hospital most of us envision when we think of a hospital.

Over the next 50 years, the situation had changed in some ways and remained much the same in others. By 1980 there were about 6,900 hospitals in the United States, having a total of about 1,362,000 beds. Thus, although the number of hospitals remained about the same, the combined number of hospital beds increased by about

42 percent. The mix of hospital ownership also remained much the same, with about 57 percent of hospitals in 1980 being of the nongovernmental not-for-profit variety. (The 12 percent increase here is due primarily to changes in the definition of proprietary hospitals over the past 50 years.) When combined with the information in Table 3-3, these data suggest that health care delivery became very labor-intensive during the twentieth century.

The most expensive component of the health care labor force, of course, is the physician. In addition to receiving about

Table 3-3. *Persons employed in the health care delivery system, 1910 to 1980.*

Characteristics	1910	1920	1930	1940	1950	1960	1970	1980
Total number of persons employed (1,000s)	38,167	41,614	48,829	44,888	56,225	64,639	78,627	97,270
Number of persons employed in the health sector (1,000s)	479	624	859	972	1,394	1,966	3,130	5,030
Health sector as a proportion of all occupations (percent)	1.3	1.5	1.8	2.2	2.5	3.0	4.0	5.2
Total U.S. population (1,000,000s)	92.4	106.5	123.1	132.6	152.3	180.7	205.1	227.7
Rate of health personnel per 100,000 population	518	586	698	733	915	1,088	1,428	2,209

SOURCE: Adapted from Stephen S. Mick. 1977. "Understanding the Problems of Human Resources in Health, 1925–77: Recommendations from the Commission on the Cost of Medical Care and Current Realities." Unpublished manuscript. Reprinted by permission of the author.

Table 3-4. *The number of physicians actively engaged in the practice of medicine, 1965 to 1985.*

Health occupation	1965		1970		1975	
	Number	Personnel per 100,000 population	Number	Personnel per 100,000 population	Number	Personnel per 100,000 population
Physicians	288,700	145.5	323,200	154.5	377,400	176.8
MDs	277,600	139.9	311,200	148.7	363,300	170.2
DOs	11,100	5.7	12,000	6.0	14,100	6.6

Health occupation	1980		1985		Percent increase, 1965–1985
	Number	Personnel per 100,000 population	Number	Personnel per 100,000 population	
Physicians	449,500	202.3	519,100	216.9	79.8
MDs	432,400	194.6	499,440	208.7	79.9
DOs	17,100	7.7	19,660	8.2	77.1

SOURCE: Department of Health and Human Services. 1982. *Third Report to the President and Congress on the Status of Health Professions Personnel in the United States.* DHHS Publication No. 82–2. Washington, DC: U.S. Government Printing Office. Department of Health, Education and Welfare. 1974. *The Supply of Health Manpower: 1970 Profiles and Projections to 1990.* DHEW Publication No. 75–38. Washington, DC: U.S. Government Printing Office.

20 percent of all monies spent on health care, physicians exercise considerable control over how the remainder is spent. (For a more detailed discussion of the role of the physician in the health care delivery system, see chapter 9.) Therefore, any discussion of the growth of the health care delivery system would be incomplete without looking at trends in the supply of physicians. Table 3-4 contains data on the number of physicians actively practicing medicine in the United States from 1965 to 1985. In 1965 there were 145.5 physicians per 100,000 population; by 1985 there were 216.9 physicians per 100,000 population. That represents an increase in the relative supply of physicians of nearly 50 percent in only 20 years.

Under ideal economic market situations,

such an increase in the relative supply of physicians would generally be considered good news. However, as indicated in chapter 2, the market for physicians' services appears not to be subject to the normal market forces of supply and demand. Rather, physicians have the opportunity to generate demand for their own services, as well as for other health care services. Thus, the more physicians we have, the higher the nation's health care bill. As a result, there has been a growing concern over the increasing supply of physicians.

The fundamental problem, of course, lies

Table 3-5. *The ratio of the projected supply of physicians to the estimated requirements, by medical specialty, 1990.*

	Ratio (percent)	Requirements	Surplus (shortage)
Shortages			
Child psychiatry	45	9,000	(4,900)
Emergency medicine	70	13,500	(4,250)
Preventive medicine	75	7,300	(1,750)
General psychiatry	80	38,500	(8,000)
Near Balance			
Hematology/oncology-internal medicine	90	9,000	(700)
Dermatology	105	6,950	400
Gastroenterology-internal medicine	105	6,500	400
Osteopathic general practice	105	22,000	1,150
Family practice	105	61,300	3,100
General internal medicine	105	70,250	3,550
Otolaryngology	105	8,000	500
General pediatrics and subspecialties	115	36,400	4,950
Surpluses			
Urology	120	7,700	1,650
Orthopedic surgery	135	15,100	5,000
Ophthalmology	140	11,600	4,700
Thoracic surgery	140	2,050	850
Infectious diseases-internal medicine	145	2,250	1,000
Obstetrics gynecology	145	24,000	10,450
Plastic surgery	145	2,700	1,200
Allergy immunology-internal medicine	150	2,050	1,000
General surgery	150	23,500	11,800
Nephrology-internal medicine	175	2,750	2,100
Rheumatology-internal medicine	175	1,700	1,300
Cardiology-internal medicine	190	7,750	7,150
Endocrinology-internal medicine	190	2,050	1,800
Neurosurgery	190	2,650	2,450
Pulmonary-internal medicine	195	3,600	3,350
Others *			
Physical medicine and rehabilitation	75	3,200	(800)
Anesthesiology	95	21,000	(1,550)
Nuclear medicine	N/A	4,000	N/A
Pathology	125	13,500	3,350
Radiology	155	18,000	9,800
Neurology	160	5,500	3,150

*The requirements in these six specialties were estimated crudely after a review of the literature. The full GMENAC modelling methodology was not applied to them.

SOURCE: Department of Health and Human Services. 1981. *Summary Report of the Graduate Medical Education National Advisory Committee.* DHHS Publication No. 81–651. Washington, DC: U.S. Government Printing Office.

in determining how many physicians are enough. In the late 1970s, when policy-makers at various levels began to foresee a potential "surplus" of physicians, the federal government established the Graduate Medical Education National Advisory Committee (GMENAC). Its purpose was to conduct an extensive examination of the physician supply issue, determine how many physicians would be needed in each medical specialty by 1990, and project whether there would be shortages, near balance, or surpluses of physicians. Using a complicated set of econometric projection techniques and input from a number of "blue-ribbon" panels of medical and policy specialists, the GMENAC came up with the results shown in Table 3-5. Shortages were expected to exist for only four medical specialties (child psychiatry, emergency medicine, preventive medicine, and general psychiatry); by 1990 it was estimated that there would be a need for 18,900 *more* physicians in these specialties. For 15 other medical specialties, however, considerable surpluses were expected. It was estimated that by 1990 there would be 55,800 physicians too many in these specialties. The two largest surpluses were projected for obstetrics-gynecology (10,450) and general surgery (11,800); for these two specialties the excess was nearly half again as much as the total need.

There are two important points to note from the data in Table 3-5. First, the surplus in the supply of physicians underscores the fact that the health care delivery system is not a real system. A real system would have had an effective regulation device (like a thermostat) to control the mix of inputs to the production of health services so that overproduction would not occur. Second, because of the surplus in the supply of physicians, we can expect the health care delivery system to undergo marked changes in the 1980s and 1990s. Indeed, the health care delivery system is currently in a highly volatile state, and no one is quite sure of what the future holds. That is one of the reasons why the sociology of health is so interesting.

Before leaving the discussion of the growth of the health care delivery system,

Table 3-6. *The number of dentists actively engaged in the practice of dentistry, and the dentist-to-population ratio, 1950 to 1985.*

Year	Number of dentists	Dentists per 100,000 population
1950	79,190	51.5
1955	84,370	50.4
1960	90,120	49.4
1965	95,990	49.0
1970	102,220	49.6
1975	112,020	52.2
1980	126,240	56.4
1985	140,950	58.9

SOURCE: Department of Health and Human Services. 1982. *Third Report to the President and Congress on the Status of Health Professions Personnel in the United States.* DHHS Publication No. 82–2. Washington, DC: U.S. Government Printing Office. Department of Health, Education and Welfare. 1974. *The Supply of Health Manpower: 1970 Profiles and Projections to 1990.* DHEW Publication No. 75–38. Washington, DC: U.S. Government Printing Office.

we should consider the special case of dentistry. As the data in Table 3-6 indicate, the relative supply of dentists to the population has not changed much. In 1950 there were 51.5 dentists per 100,000 population. The comparable number in 1985 was 58.9, representing about a 14 percent increase. Thus, relative to the increase in the supply of physicians, the growth in the supply of dentists seems modest.

The situation, however, is somewhat more complex. Two additional factors must be considered. First, because of significant advances in water and toothpaste fluoridation, as well as personal dental hygiene, the incidence of dental caries has been markedly reduced. This has served to reduce the demand for restorative dental services. Second, the employment of dental hygienists by dentists has increased fourfold. As a result, it is increasingly rare that dentists (as opposed to their hygienists) provide prophylaxis to their patients, which also decreases the demand for dentist's services. Thus, despite stability in the relative supply of dentists, competition within the dental industry has become intense. The reason for this is twofold: (1) it is not as easy for dentists (as it is for physicians) to generate demand for their services; and (2) because the prevalence of dental insurance is relatively low, the demand for dental services is quite sensitive to the health of the economy.

Changes in the Practice of Medicine

So far we have seen how the disease burden has changed and how the health care delivery system has grown during the twentieth century. It is important to note too that the way health care is practiced may vary independently of these changes. That is, just as with any other social institution, there are normative expectations concerning how medicine is to be practiced, and these are subject to changing popularity. To illustrate this point, we shall briefly consider changes in the incidence of three surgical procedures: tonsillectomies, hysterectomies, and cesarean sections.

In the 1940s and 1950s, it was quite common for any children under the age of 16 years old to have their tonsils (and adenoids) surgically removed if there was any history of their having more than their fair share of colds. Indeed, the popularity of tonsillectomies was so great, despite any evidence that the procedure effectively reduced the risk of catching colds, that a number of medical professionals became quite concerned. The reason for their concern is that the surgical mortality rate for tonsillectomies is relatively high (for a procedure whose benefits have not been demonstrated), with about 1 child in 1,000 dying from complications. Therefore, at the rate that tonsillectomies were being performed in the 1940s and 1950s, more than 300 children would unnecessarily die annually from this unproven procedure.

To determine exactly what the normative expectation among physicians was for recommending a tonsillectomy, Bakwin (1945) conducted an intriguing experiment. He began by examining a random sample of 1,000 schoolchildren, 611 of whom had already had their tonsils surgically removed. Then Bakwin arranged for two panels of physicians to examine the 389 remaining chil-

dren with intact tonsils. These physicians did not know the true nature of the experiment and believed that they would be participating in an epidemiological study to determine the incidence of tonsillitis. After examining the children, the first panel of physicians indicated that 174 of them needed to have tonsillectomies. Bakwin then took the 205 remaining children, whom the first panel of physicians (and their own family physicians) had already judged not to need tonsillectomies, to the second panel of doctors. After examining these children, the second panel of doctors recommended that 99 of them needed to have their tonsils surgically removed. Thus, if these physicians had had their way, 894 out of 1,000 schoolchildren would have had their tonsils surgically removed.

The point of the tonsillectomy experiment was to document the normative expectations held by physicians concerning the need for surgical intervention. In the 1940s and 1950s, it appears that the medical profession believed that it was normal to recommend tonsillectomies for 50 to 60 percent of all children. These normative expectations are subject to change over time, due to a variety of factors. This is evident from Figure 3-3, which graphs the incidence of tonsillectomies per 100,000 children under the age of 16 from 1965 to 1983. As these data indicate, the rate dropped by nearly 63 percent, going from more than 1,600 to less than 600 per 100,000 (or less than 1 percent of all children). Although it is difficult to determine precisely the reasons for this massive decline, it is likely that most of it resulted from the recognition that the surgical removal of tonsils was an ineffective method for reducing the number of colds in 97 percent of children.

The tonsillectomy example exemplifies changes in the practice of medicine brought about primarily by physicians. This, however, is not always the way in which the norms of medical practice are changed. Sometimes the demand for change is generated by patients, in an attempt to be fashionable. Let us consider the issue of hysterectomies for women. Between 1970 and 1983, hysterectomies were the most common major surgical procedure performed in

Figure 3-3. *Tonsillectomy Rates for Persons Under 16 Years of Age, 1965 to 1983.*

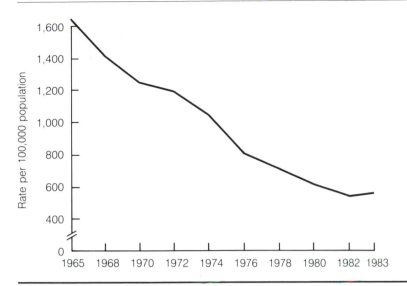

SOURCE: National Center for Health Statistics. 1985. *Charting the Nation's Health: Trends Since 1960.* DHHS Publication 85-1251. Washington, D.C.: Government Printing Office.

Figure 3-4. *Hysterectomy Rates for Women 15 Years of Age and Over, 1970 to 1983.*

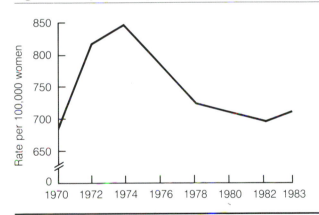

SOURCE: National Center for Health Statistics. 1985. *Charting the Nation's Health: Trends Since 1960.* DHHS Publication 85-1251. Washington, D.C.: Government Printing Office.

community hospitals. The incidence of hysterectomies, however, was not constant during this period, as the data in Figure 3-4 indicate. What accounted for the considerable increase in hysterectomy rates during the early 1970s? Again, although it is difficult to know for sure, it is possible that some of the increase was due to the desire of middle-class women to identify with this rather serious, midlife crisis marker. That is, in deciding to have a hysterectomy, some middle-class women may have been underscoring the severity of their trauma with the intent of generating additional support during this traumatic transitional period. The decline and subsequent stabilization of hysterectomy rates during the late 1970s and early 1980s may reflect the increase in alternative modes of additional supports that emerged concomitant with the women's liberation movement.

We now turn to the matter of cesarean section delivery rates. In 1965 less than 5 percent of all newborn children were delivered by cesarean section. Today, however, more than 20 percent of all newborn deliveries are by cesarean section. And this explosive growth is expected to continue. The reason for this is that after having delivered one child by cesarean section, most of a woman's subsequent deliveries will be by the same technique. Unlike the incidence of tonsillectomies, which could primarily be attributed to supply-side factors, or the increase in the incidence of hysterectomies, which could primarily be attributed to demand-side factors, the reasons behind the rapid increase in the incidence of cesarean sections are somewhat mixed (National Center for Health Statistics, 1985). On the supply side, there has been a remarkable increase in specialization among physicians (such as subspecialties like pediatric cardiology), as well as a remarkable increase in the availability of health care technology (such as fetal heart monitors). These factors have contributed to the increase in all surgical procedure rates. On the demand side, there has been a change in our cultural values that has generally lowered our pain tolerance levels. As a result, women may be more willing to opt for cesarean sections when the delivery process appears to be long and painful. In any event, the end result is that cesarean delivery, a rather expensive and once a relatively rare practice, is now fairly common.

Current Patterns of Health Services Use

Having considered how health, health care, and the health care delivery system have all changed during the twentieth century, we now turn to a brief review of current patterns of health services use. We begin with visits to physicians in their offices, which is the most common form of health services utilization. Table 3-7 shows the number of visits to the doctor's office per year for various age groups, and for both sexes. Although the overall average was 2.6 office visits per person, there are marked differences by age and sex. Elderly men and women go to the doctor more often than any other age-sex group, averaging 4.1 and 4.5 visits, respectively. Men and women between 45 and 64 years of age have the next highest rates, with women going about one more time a year than men. Boys and girls both average about 2.1 visits annually. The largest sex difference occurs between the reproductive years, with women having nearly twice the rate of office visits of men.

Table 3-8 contains data on the 20 most common reasons given by patients for going to the doctor's office. There are three interesting points to note here. First, we go to see the doctor for a wide variety of reasons. Indeed, the most common reason, to have a general medical examination, is given only about 5 percent of the time. Moreover, nearly 60 percent of all office visits are for reasons given by less than 1 percent of all people. Second, a substantial proportion of all office visits are basically of a preventive nature; general medical, prenatal, progress, and well-baby examinations account for 13.9 percent of all office visits. Third, 6 percent of all office visits are due to colds and coldlike symptoms. When taken together, this means that nearly 25 percent of all office visits occur for reasons no more serious than the common cold.

Table 3-9 contains data on the 20 most common diagnoses made by physicians during these same office visits. Note that although the list of diagnoses appears different from the list of reasons, that difference is more apparent than real. Patients describe their reasons in terms of symptoms, while physicians translate the symptoms into specific diagnostic terminology. As a result, cold symptoms become suppurative and unspecified otitis media, acute upper respiratory infections, acute pharyngitis, and bronchitis. In general, the three patterns described for patients' reports of symptoms are replicated in their physicians' reports of diagnoses; most office visits tend to be for preventive purposes, common colds, or other relatively minor ailments.

Nonetheless, a number of office visits oc-

Table 3-7. *The number, percent distribution, and annual rate of office visits by sex and age, 1981.*

Sex and age	Number of visits (1,000s)	Percent distribution of visits	Number of visits per person per year
Both sexes			
All ages	585,177	100.0	2.6
Under 15 years	106,773	18.3	2.1
15–24 years	79,234	13.5	2.0
25–44 years	155,689	26.6	2.4
45–64 years	136,055	23.3	3.1
65 years and over	107,426	18.4	4.3
Female			
All ages	353,612	60.4	3.1
Under 15 years	52,130	8.9	2.1
15–24 years	52,397	9.0	2.6
25–44 years	102,838	17.6	3.1
45–64 years	80,646	13.8	3.5
65 years and over	65,606	11.2	4.5
Male			
All ages	231,565	39.6	2.1
Under 15 years	54,643	9.3	2.1
15–24 years	26,837	4.6	1.3
25–44 years	52,856	9.0	1.7
45–64 years	55,408	9.5	2.7
65 years and over	41,820	7.1	4.1

SOURCE: National Center for Health Statistics. 1983. "1981 Summary: National Ambulatory Medical Care Survey." In *Advance Data*. DHHS Publication No. 83–1250. Washington, DC: U.S. Government Printing Office.

Table 3-8. *The number and percent of office visits for the twenty most common principal reasons, 1981.*

Most common principal reason for visit	Number of visits (1,000s)	Percent
General medical examination	30,222	5.2
Prenatal examination	23,501	4.0
Postoperative visit	18,071	3.1
Symptoms referable to the throat	15,098	2.6
Progress visit not otherwise specified	14,864	2.5
Well-baby examination	12,922	2.2
Cough	12,783	2.2
Blood pressure test	10,662	1.8
Back symptoms	10,318	1.8
Head cold, upper respiratory infection	9,185	1.6
Fever	9,160	1.6
Skin rash	8,882	1.5
Earache, or ear infection	8,745	1.5
Headache, pain in head	8,436	1.4
Chest pain and related symptoms	8,368	1.4
Abdominal pain, cramps, spasms	8,240	1.4
Eye examination	7,790	1.3
Hypertension	7,531	1.3
Knee symptoms	7,102	1.2
Vision dysfunctions	6,834	1.2
All other reasons	346,463	59.2

SOURCE: National Center for Health Statistics. 1983. "1981 Summary: National Ambulatory Medical Care Survey." In *Advance Data*. DHHS Publication No. 83–1250. Washington, DC: U.S. Government Printing Office.

Table 3-9. *The number and percent of office visits for the twenty most common principal diagnoses, 1981.*

Most common principal diagnosis	Number of visits (1,000s)	Percent
Essential hypertension	28,765	4.9
Normal pregnancy	25,051	4.3
Health supervision of infant or child	18,583	3.2
Acute upper respiratory infections of multiple or unspecified sites	14,853	2.5
General medical examination	14,132	2.4
Suppurative and unspecified otitis media	13,106	2.2
Diabetes mellitus	10,772	1.8
Special investigations and examinations	10,548	1.8
Follow-up examinations	10,207	1.7
Diseases of sebaceous glands	9,661	1.7
Neurotic disorders	9,590	1.6
Acute pharyngitis	8,473	1.4
Allergic rhinitis	8,441	1.4
Disorders of refraction and accommodation	8,216	1.4
Bronchitis, not specified as acute or chronic	6,731	1.2
Other forms of chronic ischemic heart disease	6,498	1.1
Osteoarthrosis and allied disorders	5,691	1.0
Contact dermatitis and other eczema	5,228	0.9
Acute tonsillitis	5,148	0.9
Asthma	5,024	0.9
All other diagnoses	360,460	61.6

SOURCE: National Center for Health Statistics. 1983. "1981 Summary: National Ambulatory Medical Care Survey." In *Advance Data.* DHHS Publication No. 83–1250. Washington, DC: U.S. Government Printing Office.

Figure 3-5. *Average Length of Stay in Short-Stay Hospitals, 1966 to 1983.*

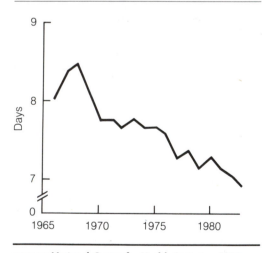

SOURCE: National Center for Health Statistics. 1985. *Charting the Nation's Health: Trends Since 1960.* DHHS Publication 85-1251. Washington, D.C.: Government Printing Office.

Figure 3-6. *Hospital Discharge Rates per 1,000 Persons, 1965 to 1983.*

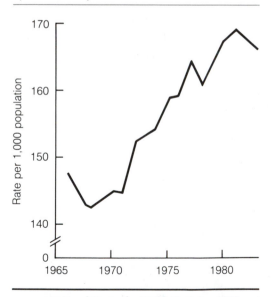

SOURCE: National Center for Health Statistics. 1985. *Charting the Nation's Health: Trends Since 1960.* DHHS Publication 85-1251. Washington, D.C.: Government Printing Office.

cur for more serious conditions that ultimately require hospitalization. As indicated in Figure 3-5, the length of hospitalization has been changing rapidly over the past two decades. In the mid 1960s the average length of stay was about 8.5 days per hospital episode. By the mid 1980s that figure had fallen to about 6.9 days. Although a 1.6-day decline may not seem like much, in this case it represents almost a 19 percent drop. Knowing that the number of hospital beds increased during this same period, one must assume that the decline in the average length of stay was accompanied by an increase in the number of people admitted to

hospitals. The data in Figure 3-6 support this, showing a 10 percent increase in the number of hospital discharges (an outcome measure of hospital admissions), from 152 per 1,000 persons in 1972 to 167 per 1,000 persons in 1983. Thus, there has been a notable change in the nature of hospitalization during the past ten years; more people are being hospitalized, but they are having shorter stays.

Table 3-10 contains data on the conditions and surgical procedures for which people were hospitalized in 1981, as well as the number of people hospitalized with that condition and their average length of stay.

Table 3-10. Number of persons under age 65 with selected conditions and operative procedures requiring hospitalization, and average number of days hospitalized, 1981.

Conditions and operative procedures	Number (1,000s)	Average number of days hospitalized per person in 1981
Condition		
Malignant neoplasms	406	14.0
Diabetes mellitus	241	14.5
Disease of the heart	751	12.6
Cerebrovascular disease	115	20.9
Upper respiratory conditions	700	2.8
Other respiratory system conditions	1,268	7.9
Ulcer of stomach and duodenum	250	9.6
Hernia of abdominal cavity	484	5.2
Diseases of the gallbladder	390	9.6
Male genital disorders	155	6.1
Female genital disorders	862	5.1
Complications of pregnancy and the puerperium	495	4.2
Diseases of the skin and cellular tissue, (not elsewhere classified)	251	6.5
Arthritis and other conditions of bones and joints	634	11.2
Fractures and dislocations	951	10.1
Operative procedure		
Operations on the eye	244	4.5
Operations on the ear	156	2.9
Operations on tonsils and adenoids	438	2.1
Other operations on nose, mouth, and pharynx	501	4.3
Operations on the respiratory system	163	13.5
Operations on the cardiovascular system	374	12.6
Operations on gallbladder and biliary tract	330	10.0
Repair of hernia	422	5.4
Other operations on the digestive system	963	9.4
Operations on the urinary system	387	8.7
Operations on male genital organs	270	5.1
Operations on the female genital organs	1,662	5.1
Cesarean section and removal of fetus	511	6.1

SOURCE: National Center for Health Statistics. 1985. *Hospitalization of Persons Under 65 Years of Age, United States, 1980–81.* DHHS Publication No. 85–1580. Washington, DC: U.S. Government Printing Office.

The most frequent operative procedures involved women's genital organs (nearly 1.7 million operations), correction of the digestive tract (about a million operations), and cesarean sections (about a half million operations). The most common conditions not requiring surgery were respiratory ailments (nearly 2.0 million admissions), and fractures and dislocations (about a million admissions). Cerebrovascular conditions, such as stroke, required the longest hospital stays, averaging about 21 days. Length of stay for other conditions varied from two days to two weeks.

Controlling the Health Care Delivery System

Strictly speaking, there is no health care delivery system, because what exists lacks the formal properties of a system. The most glaringly absent feature of what does exist is a control mechanism. Using the earlier analogy of the heating and air conditioning system, the health care delivery system lacks a thermostat. Accordingly, many choose to discuss the health care delivery system as being out of control.

Although there is no centralized control mechanism for the health care delivery system, the federal government has been moving in that direction, with ever-increasing speed. Three decades ago the health care delivery system was significantly smaller than it is today. Indeed, during the early 1950s the role of the federal government's Department of Health, Education, and Welfare was primarily limited to research and development activities, and to the approval of new drugs and other medical devices. This situation had changed markedly by 1987, including the nominal change to the Department of Health and Human Services. The federal government is now additionally responsible, either directly or indirectly, for the Medicare and Medicaid programs, as well as for most health care quality assurance programs. Moreover, it now pays for more than 40 percent of all health care expenditures.

To begin to understand how the health care delivery system is controlled, whether by the federal government or other concerns, it is important to note the differences between planning and regulation. There are four stages or steps in the *planning* process: (1) setting goals or defining the problem, (2) formulating alternative means to achieve those goals, (3) implementing those means, and (4) evaluating the progress made. As such, planning is an ongoing process, often involving multiyear plans in order to venture far enough into the future to provide stability, while being responsive enough to short-term changes in the environment. The key elements in planning, then, involve the establishment of a mission or philosophy, setting goals or the desired end points to be achieved, and the meeting of objectives or measurable milestones along the way to the goals. It is important to note that planning implies rationality and a self-directed nature. Usually when we think of health care planning, we think of the health care delivery system planning for its own future. Because there has never really been a health care delivery system, there has never really been much health care planning.

In contrast, *regulation* occurs when an external party either pushes or pulls you to do something, using various incentive structures to influence your behavior. Regulation is the method that the federal government is using to control the health care delivery system. Over the years, a number of different programs have been used by the federal government in an attempt to regulate health care delivery, including the Hill-Burton Hospital Construction Act, the Regional Medical Programs, the Comprehensive Health Planning Program, the National Health Planning and Resources Development Act, and the newest of them all, the Prospective Payment System (for an excellent review of these specific programs, and the planning and regulation process in general, see Bice, 1984).

Figure 3-7 contains a typology of the various regulatory instruments currently in use in the health care delivery system. Basically, there are four types of instruments— subsidies, entry restrictions, rate controls, and quality controls—that may be imposed on either individuals or institutions. The object of these regulatory instruments, of

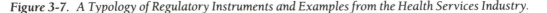

Figure 3-7. A Typology of Regulatory Instruments and Examples from the Health Services Industry.

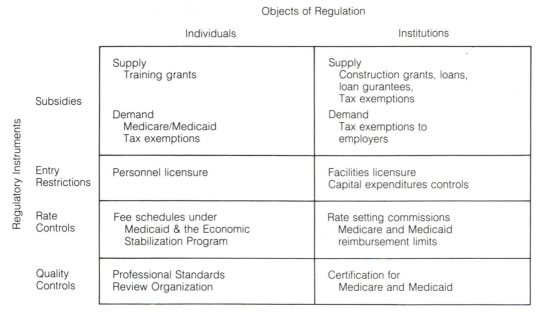

	Objects of Regulation	
Regulatory Instruments	Individuals	Institutions
Subsidies	Supply 　Training grants Demand 　Medicare/Medicaid 　Tax exemptions	Supply 　Construction grants, loans, 　loan gurantees, 　Tax exemptions Demand 　Tax exemptions to 　employers
Entry Restrictions	Personnel licensure	Facilities licensure Capital expenditures controls
Rate Controls	Fee schedules under 　Medicaid & the Economic 　Stabilization Program	Rate setting commissions 　Medicare and Medicaid 　reimbursement limits
Quality Controls	Professional Standards Review Organization	Certification for 　Medicare and Medicaid

SOURCE: Thomas W. Bice. "Health services planning and regulation." In Stephen Williams and Paul Torrens, eds., *Introduction to Health Services,* 2d ed. New York: Wiley and Sons. Reprinted by permission of the publisher.

course, is to either induce or compel behavior consistent with the goals of the regulator, which in most cases is the federal government. Consider the example of subsidies used to alter the number of students enrolled in medical schools. Because of the coming surplus of physicians, and the associated increased costs of health care that the federal government must pay, the number of training grants (scholarships) available to medical students and residents (as individuals) has been markedly reduced. So, too, has the number of construction grants to medical schools and teaching hospitals, not only for expansion projects but also for replacement facilities. The other regulatory instruments are used for similar purposes.

It should be becoming clear that the way to control the health care delivery system is to regulate the flow of money into and within the system. Salloway (1982) has succinctly described this process by writing that "money makes the system go 'round." Therefore, if you want to control the system, you must control the purse strings. Until recently, not even the federal government paid

a large enough share of total health care expenditures to exert much control. Now that the federal government has become the principal payer for health care services and pays for nearly half of all the health care that is delivered, however, it has achieved what the economists call a monopsonist position, in which the power of the principal buyer of goods and services dictates terms to suppliers. The remarkable changes occurring during the late 1980s as a result of the implementation of the Prospective Payment System for Medicare patients exemplifies the potential impact of this newly achieved ability to regulate the health care delivery system.

Two Views on the Social History of the American Health Care Delivery System

We conclude this chapter with a brief review of two very important social histories of the American health care delivery system. In his Pulitzer Prize–winning book *The So-*

cial Transformation of American Medicine,
Paul Starr (1982) has presented perhaps the
most comprehensive and thoughtful examination of medicine's rise to become a sovereign profession and the vast industry that it
has spawned. In his remarkably insightful
Health Services in the United States, Odin
Anderson (1985) focuses primarily on the
health care delivery system as a growth enterprise, especially during the twentieth
century. No course in the sociology of
health would be complete without a discussion of these two books. We do so now to
help bring closure to this overview of the
American health care delivery system.

The Social Transformation
of American Medicine

Trying to distill Starr's (1982) lucid and
copiously referenced tome into but a few
paragraphs is a most difficult task that shall
not be attempted here. Rather, we shall
focus on three aspects of the book that have
particular relevance for an overview of the
health care delivery system: Starr's theoretical framework, the structural changes
that led to the emergence of the sovereign
profession of medicine, and the ongoing
struggle for medical care.

There are four basic tenets in the theoretical framework that Starr (1982) uses to
approach the emergence of the American
health care delivery system, all of which
cluster around issues of dependency and
cultural authority. The first tenet is that the
dominance of the medical profession goes
well beyond the rational foundations of its
authority. Indeed, there is something mystical, if not sacred, about the authority medicine has achieved in American society. The
second tenet is that medicine's legitimacy is
based not on individual doctors but on the
strength of the professional community.
This implies a charismatic quality to the
profession, not to the individual practitioner; it is only as a member of the profession that the individual physician gains
access to the legitimacy of the institutionalized role-set of being a doctor.

In part as a result of the first two, the
third tenet is that what has evolved for

medicine is cultural authority. This cultural
authority includes the construction of reality, in which the medical profession redefines the realities presented to it by its
clients. The final tenet in Starr's (1982)
theoretical framework is the role of the
client's dependency in solidifying and maintaining the previous tenets. This dependency is manifest at several levels of gate-
keeping, including access to health care
(such as hospitalization), validation of the
sick role, and the verification of reality
(such as certifying an injured worker as disabled). In essence, Starr argues that during
the twentieth century medicine was transformed into an unrivaled and incredibly
powerful social institution in the United
States.

American medicine did not achieve this
sovereignty overnight. Rather, Starr (1982)
argues that it gradually developed over the
last half of the nineteenth and first third of
the twentieth centuries. At the root of the
transformation of American medicine are
five major structural changes. The first was
the emergence of an informal control system
in medical practice. This resulted from the
explosive growth of specialization within
medicine, and of hospitals. With this emphasis on specialization came a shift from client-
dependency to colleague-dependency, as specialists received more and more of their
patients on referral from other doctors
rather than directly off the street. This also
caused the emergence of a corporate orientation that rapidly replaced the previous
competitive atmosphere.

The second major structural change involved medicine's gaining control over the
labor markets involved in the provision of
medical care (Starr, 1982). This control not
only involved the exercise of authority over
the lower-level health occupations, such as
nursing, but also over the supply of physicians themselves. The latter was accomplished by organized medicine's gaining
control of medical education. By controlling
the educational process, organized medicine
was able to effectively chart its own destiny.

The third structural change involved the
elimination of commercialism from medicine (Starr, 1982). This was brought about

by the emergence of community hospitals. Investment in community hospitals was provided by the public, not by physicians. As a result, hospitals were viewed not as profit-making entities for physicians but rather as community resources where physicians provided services in the public interest.

The fourth structural change that Starr (1982) identifies is the elimination of countervailing power from the state, other corporations, or voluntary associations. This evolved from the granting of professional autonomy to physicians. Essentially, a "great trade" took place in which organized medicine, in the image of the American Medical Association (AMA), was effectively granted monopolistic control over the health care delivery system in exchange for a promise to develop and maintain the best-quality health care possible. (The role of the AMA in the "great trade" will be discussed in detail in chapter 9.)

The final structural change that Starr (1982) describes involves the establishment of specific spheres of professional authority. These included the boundaries of the profession's domain, which had the effect of establishing that no changes in the health care delivery system would be considered acceptable, unless they respected the professional sovereignty of physicians. As a result, medicine became insulated against any changes that it did not desire to make.

Based on these five structural changes, the profession of medicine was well entrenched as a sovereign institution (perhaps the only one) in American society by 1920. Between 1920 and 1970 this sovereignty served American medicine well, allowing the profession of medicine to prosper and grow into an extraordinarily vast industry. At the same time, however, Starr (1982) notes that this sovereignty proved to be the major factor leading to the downfall of medicine, which began in the 1970s. Indeed, Starr views the current struggle within the health care delivery system as the inevitable result of the insularity of medicine and its insensitivity to changes in the social environment. As a result, in the 1980s we have seen what he calls the re-

privatization of the public household, or the transfer of what had previously been public services to the administration and control (or ownership) of private corporations.

This reprivatization of the public household has remarkable implications for medicine in general, but especially for physicians (Starr, 1982). For them it connotes the loss of autonomy in the new corporate work setting. Although this decline in autonomy will take many forms, it will fundamentally mean increased regulation, not by peers or government agencies but by the corporation. It will also move the locus of control outside of the setting in which health care is provided to the home office of the investors. With this will come corporate influence over rules and standards of work, or corporate socialization. In the end, Starr anticipates that the most important distinction between and among physicians will be if they are independent practitioners, employees, managers, or owners of medical corporations.

Although there is some question as to the degree of accuracy of Starr's (1982) predictions for the future course of American medicine, there is general agreement that he is looking in the right direction. That direction involves a marked growth in corporate medicine. Among the specific changes that Starr expects during the 1980s and 1990s are: (1) changes in the type of ownership and control of health services settings, going from a predominance of nonprofit to profit organizations; (2) an increase in the horizontal integration of health care facilities, such as several hospitals forming limited partnerships to share services; (3) the diversification and restructuring of health care facilities, such as the polycorporatization of freestanding hospitals; (4) the vertical integration of health care organizations, such as the growth of health maintenance organizations; and (5) industry concentration, in which several hospital (or other health service industry) chains will gain regional or even national market consolidation.

In the end, Starr (1982) concludes that American medicine's current fall from grace was the inevitable result of its ascent to sovereignty in the first place:

The failure to rationalize medical services under public control meant that sooner or later they would be rationalized under private control. Instead of public regulation, there will be private regulation; instead of public planning, there will be corporate planning. Instead of public financing for prepaid plans that might be managed by subscribers' chosen representatives, there will be corporate financing for private plans controlled by conglomerates whose interests will be determined by the rate of return on investments.

There are, of course, other ways of looking at these same events. It may be that what we are seeing today is federal intervention, but simply *not* by traditional regulation methods (see Wolinsky and Marder, 1985). Rather, the new federal approach focuses on the manipulation of the incentive structures facing physicians (and hospitals) in order to produce the peer regulation and cost consciousness that medicine has not heretofore provided.

Health Services: A Growth Enterprise

Anderson (1985) begins his book by writing that "any attempt to trace the development of the health services enterprise in the United States . . . borders on the arrogant." In a remarkably insightful fashion, he then proceeds to divide the history of the American health care delivery system into three periods. The first, running from 1875 to 1930, covers the emergence of the basic system of health services that still exists today. This period corresponds roughly to Starr's (1982) emergence of the sovereignty of medicine, although Anderson focuses more on the bricks-and-mortar aspects of the health care delivery system than on its cultural authority. As such, he details the coming of scientific and efficacious health care.

The second period, running from 1930 to 1965, concerns the era of the third-party payer for health care. Anderson (1985) notes that although health insurance had been discussed earlier, it was not until the 1930s that the idea began to catch on. One reason that health insurance began to emerge was simple economics; the cost of personal health services could be quite expensive,

especially when hospitals and the latest technology were needed. Health insurance provided a self-help resolution to this potential economic catastrophe, but only for those who could afford it. This aggravated what was already a basically inequitable system of access to medical care and thus laid the groundwork for the great debate over voluntary versus compulsory health insurance. In 1965, with the advent of Medicare for the elderly and Medicaid for the indigent, the debate ended in a compromise; compulsory health insurance emerged, but only for certain target populations.

The importance of the emergence of health insurance, especially in its dominant fee-for-service form, during this period cannot be underscored too much (Anderson, 1985). For patients it created what the economists call moral hazard. This is the situation that occurs when patients consume more health services than they really need, or at least more than they would have consumed in the absence of health insurance. For physicians it devalued the fiduciary agency relationships they were expected to maintain with their patients. Because the patient no longer directly paid for the health services provided, it became less salient for the physician to carefully avoid any hint of financially exploiting the patient's trust. Thus, services that might not have been provided if the patient had had to pay them out-of-pocket could now be provided and billed to the third-party payer. When taken together, these insurance-induced changes led to a remarkable increase in the demand for and supply of health services. As a result, the health care delivery system became one of the largest growth industries in the United States.

The third period, which Anderson (1985) describes as an era of management and control, began in 1965 and is expected to continue into the twenty-first century. In many ways, Anderson's description of this period is similar to Starr's (1982) discussion of the struggle for medical care after 1970. Anderson, however, focuses on newly emergent regulatory methods, such as the "discovery of competition" by the Nixon administration, federal support for health maintenance organizations as cost-containment stimulants, and the Prospective Payment System for reimbursing hospitals and physicians for treating Medicare patients. Thus, Anderson's evaluation of the federal government's current role in regulating the health care delivery is more consonant with our own. As indicated earlier, it is our view that the federal government now relies on manipulating the incentive structures that drive the reimbursement system rather than on regulating the supply and distribution of health services.

In the end, however, Anderson's view of the future is not that different than Starr's (1982). Anderson (1985) is fairly confident that by the year 2000 we will see

public demand for access to [health] services will continue, although it will stabilize at the current high level. . . . [H]ealth services will take on more corporate characteristics. Horizontal and vertical organizations will manage and deliver most health services. . . . There will be more competition among various types of financing and delivery systems. . . . Expenditures for health services will continue to increase because of sustained demand, new and horrendously expensive technology, the aging of the population, the low pain and anxiety threshold, and the general unwillingness to die. . . . There will never be universal compulsory national health insurance in the United States. . . . The greatly increased supply of physicians will result in their being more evenly distributed, but they will never be as equally distributed as planners would wish.

Regardless of whether Anderson, Starr, or anyone else's crystal ball speculations about the future come true, it is certain that the end of the twentieth and the beginning of the twenty-first centuries will witness remarkable changes in the American health care delivery system.

Summary

In this chapter we have provided a brief overview of the American health care delivery system, including its evolution, how it became a growth industry during the twentieth century, and where it is likely to go in the future. The first section focused on changes in the disease burden that we face. Four distinct periods were identified, containing: (1) epidemics of acute infectious diseases (1850 to 1900); (2) acute events, trauma, and infections affecting individuals (1900 to 1945); (3) chronic physiologically based conditions, such as heart disease, cancer, and stroke (1945 to 1985); and (4) chronic emotionally and behaviorally based conditions (now and in the future). We also learned that despite some gains over the past few years, the majority of adults have yet to consistently adopt healthy lifestyle behaviors.

In the second section we examined the remarkable growth of the health care delivery system during the twentieth century, beginning with a discussion of why what we do have really isn't a health care delivery "system." Indeed, of the four major (the middle-class, local government, military medical, and Veterans Administration) subsystems of health care delivery, only the military medical system has the crucial element of control. Because of the general lack of control over the health care industry, we now face an expensive excess of health services, including an estimated surplus of 55,800 physicians by 1990.

The third section focused on changes in the practice of medicine. Using the examples of tonsillectomy, hysterectomy, and cesarean section surgical rates, we saw how changes in the normative expectations of both physicians and patients have had marked effects on the way that medicine is practiced. Current patterns of health services use were reviewed in the fourth section, emphasizing the heterogeneity of health care provided out of doctors' offices and hospitals. In the fifth section we examined how the health care delivery system can be controlled, focusing on both planning and regulatory methods. Because money is the principal force that drives the health care delivery system, the federal government has adopted new regulatory techniques aimed at manipulating the reimbursement incentive structure in such a way as to constrain health care costs.

In the final section we considered two very important social histories of the American health care delivery system, Paul Starr's

(1982) *The Social Transformation of American Medicine* and Odin Anderson's (1985) *Health Services in the United States*. Although Starr focuses more on the rise and fall of the cultural authority of American medicine and Anderson focuses more on the growth of the health care industry, both agree on two crucial points. First, there have been three important growth periods in the history of American medicine: (1) from 1875 to 1920, when the rudiments of the health care delivery system that we know of today emerged and achieved sovereignty; (2) from 1920 to 1965, when the advent of health insurance made health care one of the largest growth industries of all times; and (3) from 1965 to the future, when the lack of self-regulation and control within health care led to the corporatization of American medicine. The second major point that Starr and Anderson agree on concerns what the future holds for medicine: increasing competition, the emergence of corporate medicine, vertical and horizontal integration of health care facilities, and the surrender of sovereignty.

II. Principles

4. Definitions and Assumptions in Health and Illness

A PHILOSOPHER ONCE remarked that "the problem of metaphysics is the problem of categories." A similar statement could be made about every scientific field indeed every intellectual discipline, because definition precedes sensible discussion, investigation, or action. All definitions demand consensus on the part of informed observers. This consensus is harder to achieve, however, in areas where "objective" yardsticks are few and human passions are at stake in the formulation [Wilson, 1970].

Wilson's statement is especially true with regard to the scientific study of health, including the sociology of health. Health and health care have become issues of great concern to the public, the government, and the academicians. In fact, since 1980 a national debate has developed within the United States over just how much we can afford for health care, and for whom we can afford it. It is not surprising, therefore, to find not only a lack of consensus over the definition of health and illness on the part of informed observers but also a failure of those observers to address systematically the entire issue of such definitions.

Sociologists of health have only recently recognized the ramifications of the definitional problem (for some interesting commentaries on the general issue of definitions see Caplan, 1981; Jago, 1975; Kelman, 1975; Liang, 1986; Susser, 1974a; Wolinsky and Zusman, 1980). Twaddle and Hessler (1977) may have said it best a decade ago: "We all know what health and illness are. Or do we?" Unfortunately, while sociologists of health have been addressing this problem with greater frequency during the 1980s, they have yet to be systematic about it.

This chapter will systematically examine the development of the definitions and assumptions of health and illness used in the sociology of health. To do this we have divided the chapter into four major sections. In the first we discuss the medical definition of health. Although this definition is primarily cast in physiological terms, it was accepted by most sociologists in the early days of the sociology of health. We document its continued popularity by analyzing the assumptions behind the numerous need-based measures of health status currently in use. In the second section we discuss the development of the sociological definitions of health and illness that began with the pioneering work of Talcott Parsons. The major refinements and critiques of his approach, as well as some of the more recent functional health status measures building upon these definitions, are also examined. In the third section we introduce the developing psychological or stress approach in defining health and illness. While this approach is still in its formative stages, it has become quite popular and has a considerable amount of promise for future study. The major stress-measuring devices are then presented and discussed. In the final section we take the three basic models for defining health and illness (medical, sociological, and psychological) and combine them to form the outline of a three-dimensional representation of health essential to recognizing the complexities involved in understanding health and illness behavior.

The Medical Model: Physiological Malfunctioning

Health as the Absence of Disease

The medical definition of health is straightforward and objective. According to Becker (1986), health is "a state of well-being of an organism or part of one, characterized by normal function and unattended by disease." This definition appears to be based on common sense. Health is simply defined as the absence of symptoms and signs. Symptoms and signs are used by health professionals, such as physicians, as evidence that the physiological entity, the human body, is in some state of biological disruption. This biological disruption reduces the capacity for normal physiological functioning and necessitates appropriate medical treatment in order to return the

body to its original state of health (see also Dorland, 1985; Stedman, 1982).

This medical definition is compatible with the germ theory and specific etiology discussed in chapter 1. It should be recalled that the germ theory assumes that germs cause disease and that medicine's job is to eliminate germs, thus eliminating disease and returning patients to their original healthy states. Physicians consider signs and symptoms as evidence that an invasion of the physiological body, by a particular variety of germs or a particular infirmity, has occurred. Relying on their training and clinical skill to determine what germs produce which particular signs and symptoms, physicians then proceed to combat those germs, cure the disease, and return the physiological body to its original state of health.

Within the medical model, then, health is defined in terms of the absence of disease, or the absence of physiological malfunctioning. At the same time, the medical definition of health is not really a definition of health, but rather a definition of what is not disease. This in itself is not necessarily bad. There are, however, four assumptions in the medical definition of health that need to be discussed.

Four (Questionable) Assumptions in the Medical Definition of Health

OBJECTIVITY. The first assumption in the medical definition concerns the objectivity of the presence of disease, its diagnosis, and its treatment. Before diagnosis and treatment, the physician examines the evidence at hand. This evidence takes the form of signs and symptoms. Signs consist of material evidence that may be directly observed by the physician in a nonverbal examination of the patient. Some of the more obvious signs of disease are temperature and pulse abnormalities, swelling, catatonia, and the like. Symptoms, however, are quite different. They are generally reported to the physician by the patient and would otherwise be unknown to the physician. Perhaps the most common symptoms are those that reflect changes in the general well-being of the patient. It is at this critical juncture that the assumption of the objective determination of the presence of disease, its diagnosis, and its treatment comes into question. While for the moment we may consider signs to be objective criteria by which physicians are able to diagnose and treat illnesses, we cannot consider symptoms to be objective. There is simply too extensive a body of evidence to the contrary.

Exemplary of such evidence is Zola's (1962, 1966) study of patients' presentation of symptoms to attending physicians. Zola demonstrated rather convincingly that patients' differing world views, or cultural heritages, had either a constraining or a stimulating effect on their presentation of symptoms. In his study, Zola interviewed Irish and Italian patients as they were waiting to see the doctor at an eye, ear, nose, and throat clinic. The symptoms presented by the patients were then compared with the examining physician's diagnosis and evaluation of the clinical urgency of the conditions. As indicated in the examples shown in Table 4-1, Zola found that in the general reporting of the same and equally severe conditions to the attending physician, Irish patients had a marked tendency to understate their symptoms, while Italian patients were more likely to generalize and overstate their symptoms. In analyzing the presentation of specific symptoms, Zola found that some symptoms were more typical of Irish than Italian patients, and vice versa. This supported his initial, radical assumption that most people possess symptoms that medical professionals are likely to interpret as disease.

Zola further argued that a selection process takes place in which patients identify those symptoms that require further action. In other words, there is a decision-making process involving which symptoms will need medical care and which symptoms will be reported to the attending physician. The selection and reporting of symptoms, according to Zola (1966), is closely related to the patient's particular sociocultural reference group. Thus, to the extent that the presentation of symptoms is a major part of the diagnostic process, the medical definition of

health becomes less and less objective. Subsequent research into symptom sensitivity and the lasting impact of mothers' health behavior on children's health behavior, even after they become adults, supports Zola's conclusions (see Hetherington and Hopkins, 1969; Mechanic, 1979b, 1980).

The underlying sociological principle in effect here is that the selection, salience, and presentation of symptoms are at least partially determined by sociocultural factors and conditioning. The presentation of symptoms is relative to the patient's sociocultural reference group. If the symptoms of disease are socioculturally relative, then disease itself must in part be defined relative to sociocultural phenomena. Accordingly, if disease must be considered as a culturally relative concept, so must the absence of disease, or health.

Now, let us turn to the question of the objectivity of signs. While we consider signs to be objective indicators, there is a related phenomenon that might dull that objectivity. In order for a physician to identify a sign and use it as evidence of the presence of disease, he or she must first observe that sign. To observe a given sign, the physician must have found that sign during the physical examination (a search for signs) of the patient. This leads us to an interesting question: Is there a uniform model for examining patients that all physicians follow in all cases? That is, if 10 of us were each to receive an examination by each of 10 physicians, would each of the 10 physicians give each of us the same examination, and would your 10 examinations be exactly like the other 9 peoples' 10 examinations. The answer to both of these questions is most likely no. While all physicians are rather comparably trained (including the rudiments of examination techniques; see Judge and Zuidema, 1974; Lodewick and Gunn, 1982; Raus and Raus, 1974), they are not likely to adopt a uniform procedure or mechanical algorithm for examining patients. Some physicians routinely check temperature, blood pressure, pulse, and respiration, while others do not.

Further, it is likely that two other patient-related factors will partially determine what signs are sought out: (1) which symptoms have been presented by the patient and (2) the sociocultural characteristics of the patient. With respect to the presentation of symptoms, we have already seen that these are socioculturally related and therefore not objective. The sociocultural characteristics of the patient often act as cues suggesting diseases linked to sociocultural traits (such as sickle-cell anemia or hypertension among blacks, or osteoporosis among elderly white women). In addition, some physicians may

Table 4-1. *A comparison of the responses to various questions by Irish and Italian patients having the same conditions and demographic characteristics.*

Diagnosis	Question of interviewer	Irish patient	Italian patient
1. Presbyopia and hyperopia	What seems to be the trouble?	I can't see to thread a needle or read a paper.	I have a constant headache and my eyes seem to get all red and burny.
	Anything else?	No, I can't recall any.	No, just that it lasts all day long and I even wake up with it sometimes.
2. Myopia	What seems to be the trouble?	I can't see across the street.	My eyes seem very burny, especially the right eye . . . Two or three months ago I woke up with my eyes swollen. I bathed it and it did go away but there was still the burny sensation.
	Anything else?	I had been experiencing headaches, but it may be that I'm in early menopause.	Yes, there always seems to be a red spot beneath this eye . . .
	Anything else?	No.	Well, my eyes feel very heavy . . . at night they bother me most.
3. Otitis externa A.D.	Is there any pain?	There's a congestion . . . but it's a pressure not really a pain.	Yes . . . if I rub it, it disappears . . . I had a pain from my shoulder up to my neck and thought it might be a cold.
4. Pharyngitis	Is there any pain?	No, maybe a slight headache but nothing that lasts.	Yes, I have had a headache a few days. Oh, yes, every time I swallow it's annoying.
5. Presbyopia and hyperopia	Do you think the symptoms affected how you got along with your family? your friends?	No, I have had loads of trouble. I can't imagine this bothering me.	Yes, when I have a headache, I'm very irritable, very tense, very short-tempered.
6. Deafness, hearing loss	Did you become more irritable?	No, not me . . . maybe everybody else but not me.	Oh, yes . . . the least little thing aggravates me . . . and I take it out on the children.

SOURCE: Irving Kenneth Zola. 1966. "Culture and Symptoms: An Analysis of Patients' Presenting Complaints." *American Sociological Review* 31:615–30. Reprinted by permission of the American Sociological Association and the author.

knowingly or unknowingly mete out different classes of medical care to different classes of patients. In effect, while signs are objective material evidence, it is not at all clear that the search for signs is an objective process.

THE MEDICAL PROFESSIONAL AS SOLE EVALUATOR. The second assumption in the medical definition of health is that the diagnosis—and hence the definition—of health is solely the domain of the medical professional (usually the physician, since most other health professionals cannot legally diagnose). It assumed that only physicians are capable of identifying and observing signs and interpreting symptoms. This capability presumably is derived from the training the physician receives prior to licensing. It follows, according to this assumption, that after the diagnosis has been completed, the physician will then be able to prescribe the appropriate treatment.

The problem with this assumption is twofold. First, in almost every case, there are more participants than just the physician. Obviously, there is always the patient. Because it is usually the patient (although sometimes a third party, as in the case of children) who decides to see the physician in the first place and then decides which symptoms to report or not to report, a considerable part of the diagnosis is determined, if only indirectly, by the patient. There may also be other people involved in the defining process, such as relatives, friends, and others (perhaps witnesses to accidents that have left the patient unconscious, governmental authorities in the case of entitlement patients, and so forth). To the extent that these nonphysician participants contribute to the diagnosis and treatment decision-making process by their presentation of symptoms, the authority and autonomy of the physician are reduced.

This leads us to the second problem. By vesting the sole authority to define health and illness in the physician, the medical definition takes away a remarkable amount of power from all the other participants. First, the patient surrenders control over his or her own physical body to the physician.

Second, the physician is given the power to constrain the liberty of the patient, through such techniques as diagnoses resulting in the quarantine of patients with contagious diseases or the confinement of the mentally ill. Additionally, because the physician is given the power to define health and illness within this system, the possibility of appealing a decision over the heads of physicians is ruled out; the profession of medicine is autonomously regulated and licensed, and thus there are no higher authorities to which decisions might be appealed.

PHYSIOLOGICAL CRITERIA ONLY. The third assumption in the medical definition of health is that health and illness are defined solely in terms of physiological malfunctioning. This assumes that nonphysiological functioning (excluding mental illness, which the medical profession asserts may be treated similarly to physiological malfunctioning) is not part of health. The difficulties encountered with this assumption are very important. People are not merely physiological beings having only physiological health. As you read this book you are functioning not only physiologically but socially and psychologically as well. Had you not been socialized, you would not be able to read. Had you not developed your own personality, you would not be able to interpret and evaluate. If you had been a feral child (completely unsocialized with no personality development), you would not have been able to read and evaluate this book—or anything else. In effect, you would have been unable to function socially or psychologically. According to the medical definition, however, you would still be considered healthy (assuming that you suffered from no physiological limitations). It is hard to imagine that such a feral child would have been evaluated as healthy, even by a physician.

THE RESIDUAL NATURE OF THE DEFINITION. The fourth assumption of the medical definition of health is that health is a quality that may be sufficiently defined as a residual value. In other words, the medical definition assumes that health is the absence of disease. As a result, it is not health that is discussed. Wilson (1970) has expressed this problem quite clearly: "By fixing the attention on familiar signs of malfunction, the definition of health as nondisease also tends to exclude analysis of the well-functioning individual. We learn much about what is wrong but little about what is right, and thus we are enfeebled in efforts to prevent illness or to foster superior functioning." The concern with nonhealth that the medical model stimulates has funneled most research efforts away from the pursuit of health and away from a definition of health.

The Historical Acceptance of the Medical Definition by Sociologists

Although the discussion of the four assumptions in the medical definition of health has shown it to be of limited heuristic or practical value, that definition was accepted in varying degrees by sociologists for quite some time. To be sure, the breadth and depth of that acceptance have been decreasing since Parsons (1951) first presented the sociocultural definitions of health and illness more than 35 years ago. The acceptance of the medical definition, however, persists. For example, sociologists rely upon morbidity and mortality rates in order to assess the health status of various populations. Carlson (1975), Fuchs (1974), and Illich (1976) have pointed to sociologists' mechanical use of these rates as health indicators in their critiques of the health care delivery system.

Perhaps anticipating such criticism, and partially in response to the availability of research funds from the federal government, a number of sociologists have been working on the development of better health indicators. Unfortunately, what has resulted from the efforts of these sociologists are health indicators that are more sophisticated in the technical sense but which continue to rely on the medical definition of health. The resulting indicators are called *need-based* measures of health or access to medical care (for an extensive review of these measures see Bergner, 1985).

One of the more sophisticated of these need-based measures is the "symptoms-response-ratio" developed by Aday and her associates (Aday and Andersen, 1974, 1975; Aday, Andersen, and Fleming, 1980; Aday, Fleming, and Andersen, 1980; 1984; Taylor, Aday, and Andersen, 1975). This measure begins by ascertaining the respondent's incidence of, and whether a doctor was consulted for, each of 22 symptoms experienced during the past year. These symptoms include coughs, feeling weak, headaches, diarrhea, vomiting, and pain in the gut. The respondent's actual number of visits to the doctor for these symptoms (represented by the symbol A) is then compared with the age-specific recommendation (represented by the symbol E) of the percentage of persons who *should* see a physician. The age-specific recommendation was based on guidelines established by 40 doctors at the University of Chicago School of Medicine. The symptoms-response-ratio was then computed using the following formula:

$$\text{symptoms-response-ratio} = ([A-E]/E) \times 100$$

The symptoms-response-ratio reflects (Taylor et al., 1975) "the extent to which the actual number of visits in response to a mix of symptoms is greater than, equal to, or less than the number a panel of medical professional experts would recommend." If the actual response is greater than the "should be" response, then the patient (or population) is overutilizing. If the actual response is less than the "should be" response, then the patient is underutilizing. If the actual and "should be" responses are the same, then access to health care is considered appropriate. The symptoms-response-ratio has been incorporated into several national health care surveys. The results indicate that some groups (e.g., children under the age of five) use more health services than they need, others (e.g., those without a regular source of medical care) use less than they need, and some (e.g., whites and those above the poverty level, in general) use exactly what they need.

As one can see from the definition of this need-based measure, health is determined by the "should be" estimate of the physician. Accordingly, the symptoms-response-ratio merely provides an opportunity to use the medical definition of health in situations where the patient does not actually come into contact with a physician, such as a large-scale survey. While this is beneficial in those cases where a strictly medical evaluation of the health of a person (or population) is desired, the symptoms-response-ratio by itself does not correct the deficiencies found in the original mortality and morbidity measures, as far as sociologists are concerned. Thus, measures such as this merely make the mechanical and physiological assessment of health sophisticated and extend its applicability to large-scale surveys.

The Sociocultural Approach: Capacity to Perform

In a pioneering effort to orient the sociology of health away from the medical definition of health, Parsons (1951; see especially chapter 10) presented the first fundamentally new analysis of health. Parsons's analysis considered health and illness in light of American values and social structure, rather than in isolation from them. His intent was to analyze the milieu of health and illness against the backdrop of the entire social system. As might be expected with any such fundamental shift in analysis, Parsons's original exposition became the center of much debate and commentary. More than twenty years after the first publication of his famous treatise, Parsons (1972, 1975) looked back upon his work and presented a restatement of the criteria for health and illness. The following section draws principally from this reevaluation of his work.

Health as the Capacity to Function Socially

HEALTH DEFINED. For Parsons (1951), the medical definition was just not appropriate for use in an advanced society such as the United States. In America, the level of structural differentiation was too high to rely on a definition of health based solely on physiological malfunctioning. Each person in so-

ciety had his or her own special jobs to perform. If those jobs were not carried out, the intricate network (the social system) of interlocking and interdependent jobs might well crumble. Assuming that the most sacred principle in American society is its continued existence, good health naturally becomes one of its most highly regarded values. Accordingly, Americans are obligated to pursue health and avoid illness wherever possible.

Parsons (1972) offered the following definition of health, based on the nature of the person's participation in the intricate social network: "Health may be defined as the state of optimum *capacity* of an individual for the performance of the roles and tasks for which he has been socialized." But the nature of a person's participation in the social system was not the only criterion on which to base a definition of health. In addition, Parsons argued that the status of the person is also important in defining health: "[Health] is also *relative* to his 'status' in the society, i.e., to differentiated type of role and corresponding task structure, e.g., by sex or age, and by level of education which he has attained and the like."

It is very important, according to Parsons (1972), that we do not confuse this sociocultural definition of health as the *capacity* to carry out roles and tasks with the individual's *commitment* to those particular tasks, roles, and their underlying values. It is not a health problem if the individual detests his particular tasks and roles. It only becomes a health problem if the individual does not have the capacity to carry out those roles and tasks. The performance of those tasks and roles, then, is the role of the healthy person.

ILLNESS DEFINED. According to Parsons (1972), illness, like health, is a socially defined and institutionalized role type. Parsons does not, however, present a true definition of illness. He prefers to define illness merely as the residual category of health, the opposite of the medical model's residual definition of health. For Parsons, illness is "most generally characterized by some imputed generalized disturbance of the capacity of the individual for normally expected task or role performance, which is not specific to his commitment to any particular task, role, collectivity, norm, or value." Illness, then, is an inferred reduction in the individual's capacity to perform the tasks or roles expected of him or her.

When illness occurs in an individual, it is necessary for the smooth and proper functioning of the social system that he or she be returned to his or her original state of health as soon as possible. An individual who is ill and can neither perform his or her expected tasks nor execute his or her expected roles is a liability to the social system. To deal with the ill individual, a sick role-set has been institutionalized in American society. Upon the recognition of the reduced capacity of the individual due to his or her illness, the individual is supposed to adopt the sick role (this concept is discussed at length in chapter 5). There are four features to this sick role, according to Parsons (1972). First, the individual is not placed at fault for his or her condition. The illness is recognized as being beyond his or her control and requiring some therapeutic process for recovery. Second, the illness is recognized as a legitimate basis for the exemption of the individual from certain normal role and task obligations. Third, although being ill is a partially legitimated state of being, it is an undesirable state of affairs. Accordingly, the sick person is given a new obligation, to both want to and try to get well. Finally, in order to get well the individual is obligated to seek out competent help, usually from physicians, and to cooperate with them.

Four Assumptions in
Parsons's Contribution

SOCIAL PERFORMANCE AS THE DEFINING CRITERIA. The most distinguishing feature in Parsons's (1972) sociocultural definition of health and illness is that the criterion for health is the optimum capacity for social functioning. This criterion is different from the medical model's criterion of biological functioning. Yet, the two are similar in that they are mutually exclusive and hence only partial definitions. Because the sociocultural definition of health ignores the entire issue of biological functioning, it cannot be considered a comprehensive definition of health.

RELATIVITY. The second assumption in Parsons's (1972) definition of health is that health must be defined relative to the individual's status and participation in the social system. By incorporating this notion of cultural relativity into his definition, Parsons lays the groundwork upon which he establishes universal criteria for defining health and illness, applying them to "all human beings in all societies." Of course, he admits that there is a major drawback to such a definition: it must be couched in terms so general that their operationalization appears to be impossible. Nonetheless, such terms do provide a heuristic framework on which the sociology of health may then be built.

The relativity assumption also provides the framework for a class-based definition of health; certain functional limitations may be considered as more or less important, depending upon the individual's position in the social structure. For example, a moderately severe head cold may not be seen as very important for a groundskeeper, while it would be viewed as a much more serious condition for an office-bound executive. More important, it is possible that the relativity assumption may be used to rationalize a medical care system in which the quantity and quality of care made available to an individual is based on his or her social status position. Such a system assumes that the tasks and roles of higher social status individuals are more important than those of lower social status individuals, so that individuals of higher social status receive more and better care than those of lower social status.

ILLNESS AS A SUBSET OF DEVIANT BEHAVIOR. The third assumption in Parsons's (1972) definition of health concerns the nature of illness behavior in light of American values. Parsons argues that in highly interdependent societies such as the United States, the nonperformance of social tasks and roles is intolerable and is considered to be deviant behavior. The sociocultural definition of health assumes that there are two basic types of such deviant behavior. In one type the individual is capable of carrying out his or her tasks and roles but chooses not to. According to Parsons's definition, that behavior is considered criminal by society, and the individual is culpable. In the second type of deviant behavior the individual is not capable of carrying out his or her social roles and tasks. Because the individual is unable to perform his or her obligations, he or she is considered to be sick rather than criminal. When an individual is sick, it is assumed that he or she will adopt the sick role and seek proper care in order to be returned to a fully functional state. By considering illness behavior as a subset of deviant behavior, the sociocultural definition of health allows for a more complete sociological analysis of health-related behavior.

THE SICK ROLE ASSUMPTION. The fourth assumption in the sociocultural definition of health and illness is that the sick person will adopt the sick role, which is assumed to be a normally institutionalized social role. From this assumption it follows that sick role behavior is a socially and culturally learned response that is universally accepted in American society. At this point, the logic of this assumption appears to be somewhat convoluted. The second assumption of the sociocultural definition assumed that health and illness were relative to an individual's particular status and participation in society, as well as his or her sociocultural heritage. After assuming such relativity in defining health and illness, it seems to be a change of orientation to assume that sick role behavior is universally conceived, accepted, and carried out by all sick persons in American society. As we shall see in detail in chapter 5, empirical studies of sick role behavior have not shown convincing support for this assumption.

Health Status Indicators Based on Social Functioning

In an initial attempt to operationalize Parsons's (1951) sociocultural definitions of health and illness, Fanshel and Bush (1970) presented the framework on which most subsequent health status measures have been developed. They began by hypothesizing the existence of 11 states along a continuum of social function and dysfunction. They reasoned that on any given day each individual could be said to exist in one or more of these states and that there would be a distribution of all persons in the various states. The eleven states were identified as follows:

1. *Well-being.* The individual is symptom-free, and his or her health state corresponds to the World Health Organization's (1958) definition of "physical, mental, and social well-being."

2. *Dissatisfaction.* The individual's health status is within the acceptable limits for his or her social status, although there is a slight deviation from total well-being, such as dental caries.

3. *Discomfort.* Daily activities are carried out with no significant reduction in efficiency, although some symptoms are present.

4. *Minor disability.* Daily activities are carried out but with a significant reduction in efficiency resulting from illness.

5. *Major disability.* Daily activities are restricted, and there is a severe reduction in functional efficiency.

6. *Disabled.* Individuals are unable to carry out their daily activities, but they are ambulatory and can move about the community.

7. *Confined.* Individuals are bedridden but not institutionalized.

8. *Confined and bedridden.* The individual's functional capacity is limited to his or her bed.

9. *Isolated.* The individual is separated from family and friends, and is institutionalized.

10. *Coma.* The individual is very near death, although there is a possibility that he or she may recover and move to a healthier state.

11. *Death.* The individual is completely unable to function and has no possibility of recovery.

In his subsequent works (Patrick, Bush, and Chen, 1973; Kaplan, Bush, and Berry, 1976),

Bush and his associates focused on three specific types of functional status: (1) body movement, (2) mobility (travel or confinement), and (3) major role activity. The last of these, major role activity, may be the most appropriate operationalization of the sociocultural definitions of health and illness because it is clearly based on social properties, while body movement and mobility are not.

Reynolds, Rushing, and Miles (1974) refined these three dimensions into a Function Status Index that is generally regarded as a reasonable measure of Parsons's (1951) sociocultural formulations of health and illness. The Function Status Index consists of three scales measuring role and other activity, mobility, and physical activity. Each scale has four or five steps, constructed from the respondent's answers to several questions, that summarize the health of the individual. For example, on the role and other activity scale the steps are (1) required assistance with self-care activities, (2) did not perform major activities but performed self-care activities, (3) performed major activities with limitations, (4) performed major activities but was limited on other activities, and (5) performed major and other activities. Following Parsons, major role activities were defined according to the individual's social status, with play being the major activity for preschool children, school being the major activity for school-age individuals, housework being the major activity for housepersons, and work activities being the major activities for those who are gainfully employed.

The Function Status Index has been found to be a reliable, valid indicator of the sociocultural definition of health in data from two large health surveys (see Reynolds et al., 1974; Stewart, Ware, and Brook, 1977b), but as with the sociocultural definitions they seek to operationalize, the functional status indicators are not without problems. Their major deficiency is that they do not take into consideration the cause of the functional limitation that is measured, nor the functional limitation itself. Nonetheless, the function status indicators have become quite popular in the

health services literature. (For a more extensive review of functional status indicators and other sociomedical indices, including how they have and have not changed over the last two decades, see Berg, 1973; Bergner, 1985; Bergner, Bobbitt, Carter, and Gilson, 1981; Brook, Davies-Avery, Greenfield, Harris, Lelah, Solomon, and Ware, 1979; Chen, 1976; Elinson, 1976; Gilson, Gilson, Bergner, Bobbitt, and Carter, 1975; Greenblatt, 1975; Haig, Scott, and Wickett, 1986; Renne, 1974; Siegmann and Elinson, 1977; Stewart, Ware, and Brook, 1977a, 1977b, 1981; Stewart, Ware, and Johnston, 1975; Sullivan, 1966; Ware, Brook, Davies, and Lohr, 1981; Wolinsky and Zusman, 1980.)

Other Sociological Approaches

Parsons's (1951) pioneering work on the sociocultural definition of health and illness, as well as the sick role concept, remains the major impetus for the sociology of health. Since then, however, several variations on the basic Parsonian theme have been offered. We shall briefly discuss three of these (returning to them in greater detail in chapter 6), before presenting the psychological or developing stress approach, and then conclude with our own framework.

MECHANIC'S COPING RESPONSE THEORY. Mechanic (1962, 1966a, 1968, 1978; Mechanic and Volkart, 1961) has suggested that illness behavior should be viewed as the individual's coping response to illness. As such, an individual's illness behavior will be determined primarily by the particular social network in which he or she is engaged, rather than by some all-encompassing, uniform role-set. In so doing, Mechanic has addressed the problems outlined in the fourth assumption under Parsons's (1951) sociocultural definition of health and illness. Mechanic's alternative model suggests that the assumption of illness behavior and the sick role is much more of a negotiated process between the individual and those with whom he or she interacts.

Ten factors are thought to be important in the negotiation and evaluation process. These include (1) the visibility, recognizability, or perceptual salience of the symptoms; (2) the perceived seriousness of the symptoms; (3) the extent to which the symptoms disrupt family, work, or other social activities; (4) the frequency of the symptoms' appearance, their persistence, or the frequency of their recurrence; (5) the tolerance threshold of those who are supposed to evaluate these deviant signs and symptoms; (6) the availability of information, the knowledge base, and the degree of cultural understanding of the evaluators (see number 5 above); (7) various perceptual needs that lead to subjective psychological processes; (8) other needs that compete with illness responses; (9) competing alternative interpretations that can be assigned to the symptoms once they are recognized; and (10) the availability of treatment resources, their physical proximity, and the psychological and monetary costs of taking appropriate action. As can be seen from the ten factors in Mechanic's (1968, 1978) theory of help-seeking behavior, it is too much to simply assume, as Parsons (1951) did, that once illness is perceived, the sick person automatically accepts the sick role. In fact, some persons never perceive that they are ill, and others will never assume the sick role.

SUCHMAN'S MODEL OF HELP-SEEKING BEHAVIOR. Building upon Mechanic's earliest works (Mechanic, 1962; Mechanic and Volkart, 1961), Suchman (1965a) presented a five-stage model of help-seeking behavior. His five stages were (1) the symptoms experience stage, (2) the assumption of the sick role stage, (3) the medical care contact stage, (4) the dependent patient stage, and (5) the recovery or rehabilitation stage. While studying only persons who had completed the entire cycle of illness behavior, Suchman concluded that all the stages "do not have to be present in every case of illness." In so stating, Suchman was taking the same position as Mechanic. Not every individual who is ill will recognize that fact, nor will he or she automatically assume the sick role and carry it out. Some people will progress only through the earlier stages of these models and will not ultimately receive

care. Others will never relinquish the sick role even though they recover. Thus, theories of help seeking need to explain why some people do not do what we expect of them.

PERFECT HEALTH, NORMAL HEALTH, AND SICKNESS. While Mechanic (1962, 1968, 1978, 1980) and Suchman (1965a) have primarily been concerned with the Parsonian model of the sick role (expanding it by addressing the issue of its uniform cultural acceptance and performance), Twaddle (1974) has addressed the more fundamental issue of defining health and illness. He builds upon the concept of sociocultural relativity. Because no one is perfectly healthy and everyone is not sick, Twaddle suggests we envision a continuum between perfect health and death (perfect sickness). Normal health and ill health lie somewhere between the two ends of this continuum. Building on the relativity notion, Twaddle argues that what may be healthy for one individual may be unhealthy for another. This results in "considerable overlap among behaviors, symptoms, or other clues considered as normal from those defining sickness. Depending upon the number of cultural traditions, groups, and definitions involved, this overlap will increase or decrease." Twaddle argues that two major points arise from this approach to defining health and illness. First, because we are forced to discuss normal health rather than perfect health, health must be recognized as a social norm. Second, the portion of the definition of health determined by social criteria is much larger than the portion determined by biological criteria. In addition, the saliency of the biological criteria is concentrated at the extreme ends of the continuum (i.e., perfect health and death). Accordingly, Twaddle argues that any definition of health should be primarily social and not biological.

Using these variations on the Parsonian (Parsons, 1951, 1972, 1975) model of health, Twaddle (1974) suggested a simple paradigm of the relationships between the health status designation that the individual assumes, and that which is assigned by the appropriate health status definers. Twaddle does this by cross-classifying the health status designation of the individual with the health status designation of the status definer. Both designations are dichotomized as well and ill. Individuals with consonant designations, well and well, or ill and ill, are classified as being in normal health and ill health, respectively. Individuals with noncongruent designations (well and ill, or ill and well) are considered to be deviant. The individual who believes he or she is ill in spite of the well designation of his or her status definers is labeled a crock, malingerer, or hypochondriac. The ill-evaluated individual who believes he or she is well is labeled as a denier. Using a similar paradigm, Maddox (1964) had earlier labeled the noncongruents as either pessimists (Twaddle's crocks) or optimists (Twaddle's deniers), and the congruents (Twaddle's normal and ill healths) as realists; Maddox's labels were perhaps more value-free than Twaddle's.

The value of such paradigms, and indeed the process models of Mechanic (1962, 1968, 1978, 1980) and Suchman (1965a), is that they allow the sociologist of health to consider both the status definer's and the individual's designation at the same time. The major difference is that some paradigms (Maddox, 1964) rely on the medical model, and some (Twaddle, 1974) rely on the sociocultural model to define health from the status definer's perspective. Both approaches rely on the individual's perspective as the contrast. This introduces the need to consider the third dimension in the process of defining health and illness, the individual patient. Although always a crucial source of information in the discussion of his or her health, the individual patient was considered only secondarily by both the medical and sociocultural models.

The Psychological or Stress Model: A Promising Development

A General Feeling of Well-Being

Since the early 1960s there has been a growing interest in the topic of psychological well-being among health services researchers from a variety of disciplines. As a result, a considerable amount of empirical data has been collected and analyzed. Conceptual development, however, has been rather slow (see Beiser, Feldman, and Egelhoff, 1972; Berkman, 1971; Bradburn, 1969; Bradburn and Caplovitz, 1965; Brenner, 1970; Fazio, 1977; Gaitz and Scott, 1972; Gurin, Veroff, and Field, 1960; Phillips, 1967; Veroff, Gurin, and Field, 1962, 1981; Ware, Johnston, and Avery, 1979). In general, the psychological model of health and illness presupposes that each individual is constantly and subjectively evaluating his or her own health status. The concept of self-evaluated psychological health was first thought to be a unidimensional, global phenomenon typically associated with an individual's general feeling of well-being. This subjective feeling of well-being has traditionally been operationalized by the "global happiness" question that asks (Gurin et al., 1960): "Taking all things together, how would you say things are these days—would you say you are very happy, pretty happy, or not too happy?" Frequently used during the 1960s and 1970s, the "global happiness" question was thought to be a straightforward indicator of psychological health.

In the 1980s researchers have relied on a more extensive approach to measure mental well-being, based on the self-reported number of *psycho-physiological symptoms*. Among the symptoms most frequently included are trouble sleeping, nervousness, headaches, upset stomach, dizziness, sweating or trembling hands, shortness of breath, and hearing one's heart beating hard. The focus here is primarily on the emotional problems that often result from situational stress (see Kessler and McRae, 1981; McClanahan and Glass, 1985). Other approaches focus more on *perceived stress*, such as that developed by Cohen, Kamarck, and Mermelstein (1983), shown in Table 4-2. Regardless of their particular focus, however, these measures tend to simply substitute a number of symptoms to tap the same phenomenon (psychological health) as the single-item global happiness measure.

A growing body of literature, however, suggests that psychological well-being (or

Table 4-2. *A global measure of perceived stress.*

In the last month, how often have you . . .

1. been upset because of something that happened unexpectedly?
2. felt you were unable to control the important things in your life?
3. felt nervous and stressed?
4. dealt successfully with intimidating life hassles? *
5. felt that you were effectively coping with important changes that were occurring in your life? *
6. felt confident about your ability to handle your personal problems? *
7. felt that things were going your way? *
8. found that you could not cope with all the things that you had to do?
9. been able to control irritations in your life? *
10. felt that you were on top of things? *
11. been angered because of things that happened that were outside of your control?
12. found yourself thinking about things that you have to accomplish?
13. been able to control the way you spend your time? *
14. felt difficulties were piling up so high that you could not overcome them?

SCORING SYSTEM: (0) never; (1) almost never; (2) sometimes;
(3) fairly often; and, (4) very often.

* These items are scored in the reverse direction. *
SOURCE: Adapted from Sheldon Cohen, Tom Kamarck, and Robin Mermelstein. 1983. "A Global Measure of Perceived Stress." *Journal of Health and Social Behavior* 24:385–96. Reprinted by permission of the American Sociological Association and the authors.

its stress sequelae) is not a unidimensional concept after all (see Fazio, 1977; Ware et al., 1979). Rather, psychological well-being probably results from a complex interaction among several different psychological processes. Based on data from the classic Sterling County studies in psychiatric epidemiology (see Leighton, 1959; Leighton, Leighton, and Danely, 1966), Beiser (1974) has identified (building on the works of Gurin et al., 1960; Bradburn and Caplovitz, 1965; Bradburn, 1969) at least three dimensions. The first is "negative affect," which includes such unpleasantness as boredom, unhappiness, loneliness, restlessness, and criticism from others. The second dimension is "pleasurable involvement," which includes transient good feelings derived from accomplishments, from things going one's way, from receiving compliments, and from being excited or interested in one's daily activities. "Long-term satisfaction" is the third dimension; it includes happiness of a more enduring nature associated with progress in personal, familial, and work situations, as well as a general sense of having achieved one's goals up to this point in life.

Beiser's (1974) analysis of the Sterling County data also confirms two important findings that had surfaced in previous studies. First, there was no simple inverse relationship between negative feelings (fears, worries, and so forth) and general happiness. Second, "negative affect" and "pleasurable involvement" were not correlated in any fashion with each other. As a result, Beiser was able to state that contrary to conventional wisdom, both popular and clinical, "the absence of factors promoting negative affect does not automatically ensure the emergence of positive feeling states and vice versa." Thus, Beiser was able to lay to rest two myths: (1) if there were no unhappy events or factors in an individual's life, then he or she would be happy; and (2) if an individual wasn't happy, he or she was unhappy. Psychological well-being just isn't that simple.

Psychological Stress as a Response to Social Interaction

Perhaps the most interesting outgrowth of the psychological model of well-being has been the examination of an individual's psychological response (i.e., distress) to stress-producing social events and the possible effect of stress on certain diseases (see especially the pioneering work of Selye, 1956). This process involves psychological responses of fear or anxiety in certain situations of social interaction in which the individual is unable to present a successful defensive coping mechanism. In effect, there are certain social events, usually changes in normal life events, that result in the production of the psychological responses of fear and anxiety or stress. The individual who is subject to such stressful conditions generally will not regard him- or herself as existing in a psychological state of well-being.

Holmes and Rahe (1967) based their approach on the assumption that any change in an individual's normal pattern of life would require some readjustment, and that any such readjustment would to some extent be of a stressful nature. They further hypothesized that although the degree of stressfulness would vary, stress is accumulative; if enough stressful events occurred, the accumulated stress might actually cause physical illness. Figure 4-1 graphically portrays this causal relationship.

The Social Readjustment Rating Scale

To measure the nature and degree of stressful life event changes in an individual's normal pattern of living, Holmes and Rahe (1967) developed the Social Readjustment Rating Scale. A sampling of 394 subjects were asked to numerically evaluate the amount of adjustment necessarily resulting from 42 commonly experienced life events. The rating was done by using a ratio-estimation technique in which one event (marriage) was arbitrarily assigned a necessary readjustment value of 50; the remaining 41 events were assigned readjustment scores in comparison to the amount of readjustment required by marriage. For ex-

ample, if an experienced life event was believed to require twice as much readjustment as marriage, it was assigned a readjustment score of 100. If an experienced life event required only half as much readjustment as marriage, it was assigned a readjustment score of 25. The average rankings of the 42 items in the Social Readjustment Rating Scale have been reproduced in Table 4-3. Building on the interaction of mind, body, and society that is evident in the whole-person approach to health and health care, Holmes and Rahe hypothesized that the accumulation of a certain amount of stress (the equivalent of 200 life change units) over a short period of time (one year) would drastically increase an individual's likelihood of having a serious disorder.

The introduction of the Social Readjustment Rating Scale has generated an enormous amount of research on the concept of stress and stress-induced behavior (for excellent resource collections on this topic, see Cohen and Syme, 1985; Dohrenwend and Dohrenwend, 1974b, 1981; Kaplan, 1983a; Lin, Dean, and Ensel, 1986a). Several studies have demonstrated a positive relationship between high scores on the Social Readjustment Rating Scale and health and illness behavior that Holmes and Rahe (1967) had hypothesized, including athletic injuries (Bramwell, Masuda, Wagner, and Holmes, 1975), coronary heart disease (Matthews and Glass, 1981; Rahe, Romo, Bennett, and Silaten, 1974; Theorell, Lind, and Flonderus, 1975), psychological distress symptoms (Dohrenwend, 1973), and various forms of psychiatric disorder (Brown, 1974; Paykel, 1978).

Gersten and her colleagues (Gersten, Langner, Eisenberg, and Simpcha-Fagan, 1977), however, have raised several questions following their examination of the etiological role of stressful life events in psychological disorders. They have demonstrated that if the stressful life processes that *produce* the stressful life events are taken into account, then the particular life events themselves make "no meaningful contribution to the prediction of any disturbed behavior." In effect, they suggest that it is the frequently hidden combination of

Figure 4-1. The Basic Causal Model in the Stressful Life Events Approach.

Life Events $\xrightarrow{+}$ Stress $\xrightarrow{+}$ Illness

Table 4-3. *Social Readjustment Rating Scale.*

Life events	Readjust-ment value	Life events	Readjust-ment value
Death of spouse	100	Son or daughter leaving home	29
Divorce	73	Trouble with in-laws	29
Marital separation	65	Outstanding personal achievement	28
Jail term	63		
Death of close family member	63	Wife beginning or stopping work	26
Personal injury or illness	53		
Marriage	50	Beginning or ending school	26
Being fired at work	47	Revision of habits	24
Marital reconciliation	45	Trouble with boss	23
Retirement	45	Change in work hours	20
Change in health of family	44	Change in residence	20
Pregnancy	40	Change in schools	20
Sex difficulties	39	Change in recreation	19
Gain of a new family member	39	Change in social activity	18
Change of financial state	38	Change in sleeping habits	16
Death of a close friend	37	Change in number of family get-togethers	15
Change of work	36		
Change in number of arguments with spouse	35	Change in eating habits	15
		Vacation	13
Foreclosure of mortgage	30	Minor violations of law	11
Change of responsibility at work	29		

SOURCE: Thomas H. Holmes and Richard H. Rahe. 1967. "The Social Readjustment Rating Scale." *Journal of Psychosomatic Research* 11:213–18. Reprinted by permission of the author and publisher.

life events, pathology, and sociocultural factors that result in behavioral disorders that *appear* to be the result of the stress of life events alone. Wheaton (1980) and Kaplan (1983a) have recently reached the same conclusion, although they provide more elaborate conceptualizations of the issues, arguing for the primacy of social factors in the genesis of psychosocial disorder.

Perhaps the greatest debate and lack of clarity in the stress literature involves the following question: What is the process by which stress is produced and results in illness? There is remarkable variation in the detail of the causal models presented to describe this process. At one extreme, Pearlin and Schooler (1978) suggest that role strains, such as life events, produce stress, which in turn produces illness or at least psychological distress. As shown in Figure 4-2, they argue that the effect of disruptive life events may be buffered by both coping responses (what people *do*, or their reactions), and coping resources (what people

Figure 4-2. *Pearlin and Schooler's View of How Coping Responses and Resources Buffer the Effects of Life Events.*

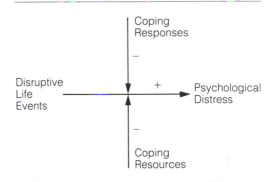

SOURCE: Leonard I. Pearlin and Carmi Schooler. 1978. "The Structure of Coping." *Journal of Health and Social Behavior* 19:2–21.

Figure 4-3. The Stress, Coping, and Health Process: Antonovsky's Complex View.

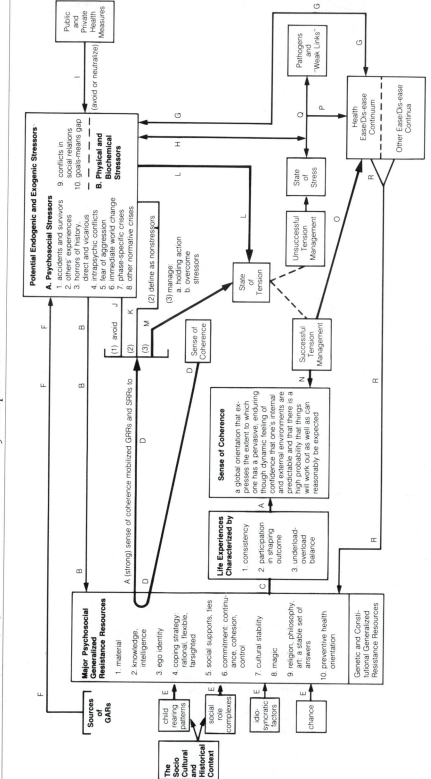

are, or their psychological composition). That explains why the same life events affect different people in different ways. After subsequent studies, Pearlin and his colleagues (Pearlin, Lieberman, Menaghan, and Mullan, 1981) expanded that basic model into a more complex version. In it, disruptive job (as an example of life) events produce (economic) strain, which reduces the individual's feeling of mastery over his or her life, as well as reducing his or her self-esteem. Both the disruptive job events and the economic strain serve to increase the level of depression, while the feelings of mastery and self-esteem (as examples of coping resources) serve to decrease (or buffer the individual from) worsening depression.

At the other extreme, Antonovsky (1979)

has presented a complex diagram (see Figure 4-3) of the stress, coping, and health process. This model has six major components, including stressors (life events), tension, stress, tension management, resources for resistance (coping resources), and the sense of coherence. Clearly the most important of these is the sense of coherence, which Antonovsky is unable to operationalize, other than saying it's sort of like Rotter's (1966) internal versus external locus of control, but not quite. This grave shortcoming notwithstanding, Antonovsky's scheme does represent the most detailed conceptual description of the process by which life events result in stress and how that may affect health status.

KEY TO FIGURE 4.3

Arrow A: Life experiences shape the sense of coherence.

Arrow B: Stressors affect the generalized resistance resources at one's disposal.

Line C: By definition, a GRR provides one with sets of meaningful, coherent life experiences.

Arrow D: A strong sense of coherence mobilizes the GRRs and SRRs at one's disposal.

Arrows E: Childrearing patterns, social role complexes, idiosyncratic factors, and chance build up GRRs.

Arrow F: The sources of GRRs also create stressors.

Arrow G: Traumatic physical and biochemical stressors affect health status directly; health status affects extent of exposure to psychosocial stressors.

Arrow H: Physical and biochemical stressors interact with endogenic pathogens and "weak links" and with stress to affect health status.

Arrow I: Public and private health measures avoid or neutralize stressors.

Line J: A strong sense of coherence, mobilizing GRRs and SRRs, avoids stressors.

Line K: A strong sense of coherence, mobilizing GRRs and SRRs, defines stimuli as nonstressors.

Arrow L: Ubiquitous stressors create a state of tension.

Arrow M: The mobilized GRRs (and SRRs) interact with the state of tension and manage a holding action and the overcoming of stressors.

Arrow N: Successful tension management strengthens the sense of coherence.

Arrow O: Successful tension management maintains one's place on the health ease/dis-ease continuum.

Arrow P: Interaction between the state of stress and pathogens and "weak links" negatively affects health status.

Arrow Q: Stress is a general precursor that interacts with the existing potential endogenic and exogenic pathogens and "weak links."

Arrow R: Good health status facilitates the acquisition of other GRRs.

SOURCE: Aaron Antonovsky. 1979. *Health, Stress, and Coping.* San Francisco: Jossey-Bass. Reprinted by permission of the publisher.

Some Problems in the Social Readjustment Rating Scale

While it represents a major contribution to the psychological model of health and illness, the Social Readjustment Rating Scale is not without its own problems. After using extensive analytic techniques, Ruch (1977) found that the concept of life event change is not unidimensional. In fact, she was able to identify three dimensions of life event change. The first dimension was identified as being very similar to Holmes and Rahe's (1967) initial scale; it refers to how much readjustment the life event causes in the individual's life. The second dimension reflects the qualitative nature of the life change event; in effect, this dimension refers to the desirability of the change (desirable, undesirable, or ambiguous). The third dimension is whether the life event change relates to the personal and interpersonal areas in the individual's life space, or to the financial and work life space areas.

Hough and his colleagues (Hough, Fairbank, and Garcia, 1976) have presented three major methodological criticisms. First, they suggested that there were some problems with the instrument construction and administration in the original Holmes and Rahe (1967) study in which the readjustment values were assigned to the life events. The range of items included was not sufficiently broad, and the rating format was biased; the life events were partially ordered before the raters even began. Second, they argue that there is clearly cultural variability; thus, life events should have different readjustment values for different sociocultural groups. Third, they posit that pertinent other variables were not reliably or adequately controlled in the analysis of the data, such as the stressful process itself, and other measures used in the study by Gersten and colleagues (1977).

Ross and Mirowsky (1979) have focused on the problem of how to score (count) the life events. Using data from the classic Myers, Lindenthal, and Pepper (1974) New Haven study, they compared 23 different methods of weighting the life events. After extensive analyses, it was determined that simply adding up the number of life events was the most efficient and accurate method of predicting psychiatric symptoms. Tausig (1986) has recently reached fundamentally the same conclusion. However, he is further concerned that the weighting schemes (readjustment values) do not make the important distinction between strain and emphasis (the degree of stressfulness to the individual). To measure emphasis, Tausig asked his respondents to indicate how desirable or undesirable each life event was to them, resulting in an indicator of relative importance. He argues that the simple addition of the number of life events measures strain, while the degree of desirability of those events measures their stressfulness, which may vary from person to person.

Funch and Marshall (1984) have explored threats to the reliability of life event inventories that result from respondents' inability to recall strains that occurred in the more distant past. Their analysis identified a rapid decline of about 5 percent a month in the ability to remember life events. (The decline levels off after about a year.) This drop-off in the accuracy of reporting varies by the nature of the life event, with the most salient events, like the death of a spouse, showing little decline, while less important events, such as family illnesses, have more marked and immediate drop-offs. These declines were also found to be related to various demographic characteristics, including age, 'sex, marital status, and education. Thus, the reliability of life event inventories is neither as good nor uniform as it was initially assumed.

Another methodological issue recently addressed is how to statistically model and interpret the buffering effects of social supports against life stress. This issue has prompted a most sophisticated technical debate beyond the limits of the present discussion (for comprehensive and detailed exegeses of these issues, see Cleary and Kessler, 1982; Finney, Mitchell, Cronkite, and Moos, 1984; Kessler, 1983; Lin, 1986; Lin, Woelfel, and Light, 1986; Thoits, 1982; Wheaton, 1985). Suffice it to say here that there is general agreement that social supports can moderate the stress of life events.

How this is conceptualized, statistically operationalized, and interpreted, however, is the subject of much debate.

General Assumptions in the Psychological and Stress Approaches

While the psychological model and the more recent stress model of health and illness have yet to be united into a clearly discernible position, there are several general assumptions rather consistently made. One of these assumptions should be quite familiar to us by now. As with the medical and sociocultural models of health and illness, the psychological model also has a narrow focus; it only considers psychological criteria in determining psychological well-being. This parallel, however, is somewhat misleading because, unlike the medical and sociocultural models, the psychological model generally makes no pretense at being an overall health status indicator. Its proponents seek only to develop an indicator of the general emotional well-being of the individual; in essence, they seek only to measure mental health.

A second important assumption in the psychological and stress models of health and illness is that both "good" and "bad" emotional feelings about life events affect an individual's psychological sense of well-being. For example, in the Social Readjustment Rating Scale (see Table 4-3) there are several "good" events that have been assigned necessary readjustment weights (including 28 points for an "outstanding personal achievement"). Explicit in the stressful life events approach, then, is the assumption that the greater the deviation from the patterns of normal life events, whether for the better or worse, the higher the level of stress in the individual.

This leads to the third general assumption in the psychological or stress model. It is generally assumed that as an individual's level of stress increases, so does the likelihood of his or her behavioral disorder or other serious impairment. In effect, the psychological or stress model incorporates the notion of interaction among the three dimensions of health—the medical, the social,

and the psychological—that we have discussed. A decrease in psychological well-being may result in a decrease in physiological and social health. At the same time, a decrease in the physiological or social dimension of health may result in an increase in the individual's level of stress, thus decreasing his or her psychological well-being. Coming full circle, this may make the individual more susceptible to further behavioral disorder or impairment.

Finally, the psychological or stress approach is highly dependent on the situational context in which the potentially stressful social interaction takes place. Many of the life events that have been used to measure potential stress accumulation may or may not result in stress, depending upon the individual's sociocultural heritage. If the individual's perception is that the situation (life event) is not a stressful one, then it will not produce stress. If the situation (life event) is perceived as stress producing, however, then it will produce stress. In the tradition of W. I. Thomas (see Thomas and Znaniecki, 1918), the proponents of the stress approach argue that if the life change event was one that could have been expected, based on the individual's prior socialization experience, then it is likely that the individual will be able to present a sufficient coping response and avoid stress. If the life change event was one for which the individual was not prepared, however, then sufficient coping responses could not be utilized, resulting in the psychological responses of fear and anxiety, or stress. In essence, whether or not the situation (life event) results in stress for the individual depends on whether or not the individual has learned an appropriate coping response for that, or a comparable, situation.

Toward a Three-Dimensional Conception of Health

Former Congressman Paul Rogers (1976) focused on the problem of defining health in his introduction to a government publication entitled *A Discursive Dictionary of Health Care:*

In order to inform and clarify the [health care] debate, I have asked our professional staff to prepare the dictionary which follows in order to define and explain as many as possible of the more important and common terms which will be used in the debate. This has been necessary because . . . a comparable dictionary . . . has not been prepared by the academic community, the executive branch, or any of the interested professional associations. Some limited or specialized glossaries and dictionaries are available and they have been consulted and listed in the bibliography for the interested reader, but so far as I am aware this is the first reasonably complete dictionary of terms relevant to the consideration of national health insurance and health care that we have available.

The implication of Rogers's statement is that the scientific study of health has been built upon a structure of faulty and unagreed upon definitions. If this is true, then much of the knowledge obtained through the scientific study of health may, at best, be tenuous and perhaps useless. Moreover, many of the policy discussions based on that knowledge would also be suspect.

One might be led, at first, to question the accuracy of Rogers's frank critique. The telling accuracy of his commentary, however, was given considerable professional credence in a review of the *Discursive Dictionary* in *Medical Care*, the official journal of the medical care section of the American Public Health Association, and a place where sociologists of health routinely publish their work. While pointing to several problems in the *Discursive Dictionary*, Viseltear (1977) was forced to conclude that "the *Discursive Dictionary* is . . . destined to be a best seller among all those who comprise the health care field, and not just legislators. . . . The achievements of the staff have been noteworthy. They have been inventive, resourceful, . . . they have also trod the path of scholarship." Some measure of the inventiveness and resourcefulness of this work becomes clear in the following entry for *health* taken from the *Discursive Dictionary*:

Defined by the World Health Organization as "a state of complete physical, mental, and social well-being and not merely the absence of disease

or infirmity." Experts recognize, however, that health has many dimensions (anatomical, physiological, and mental) and is largely culturally defined. The relative importance of various disabilities will differ depending upon the cultural milieu and the role of the affected individual in that culture. Most attempts at measurement have taken a negative approach in that the degree of ill health has been assessed in terms of morbidity and mortality. In general, the detection of changes in health status is easier than the definition and measurement of the absolute level of health.

This entry is accurate as far as it goes, but how far does it go? The answer, we think, is considerably further than the disciplinary definitions of health we have discussed up to now, but not far enough.

The mainstay of the *Discursive Dictionary*'s definition of health is the World Health Organization's (1958) terse statement, which defines health in terms of three areas: the physical, the psychological, and the social. Unfortunately, the WHO's statement does not define other levels of health, nor does it suggest a conceptual scheme in which to evaluate the full spectrum between health and illness. The remainder of the *Discursive Dictionary*'s entry for health accurately and succinctly suggests that the social and psychological areas need to be considered in any definition of health. Yet the definition falls short by failing to describe a comprehensive scheme. In the remainder of this chapter we shall present the rudiments of such a conceptual scheme. We shall rely heavily upon the works already mentioned, borrowing from them frequently and selectively.

Some Initial Assumptions

As we embark on the task of constructing a conceptual framework in which the three dimensions of health and illness will be included, we make several assumptions, which will serve to simplify the initial task. First, we assume that perfect health is an ideal and that normal health is what we will actually be discussing. Second, we assume that, although health and illness lie on a continuum with a wide range of values, such continuous variables are difficult to deal with, especially in the initial stages of a complex conceptual scheme. We will, therefore, limit the range of each of the three dimensions of health to two categories: well and ill. Third, we assume that all three dimensions are approximately equal in terms of their contribution to defining an individual's health status. This allows us to avoid using complicated weighting schemes in evaluating an individual's composite health status. Fourth, we assume that being healthy or sick is a dynamic process that results in a constantly changing, rather than a stationary, condition; we anticipate that individuals are in a constant process of moving from one health state to another. Finally, we assume that the resulting combinations (health states) are considered as ideal types. Ideal types may not exist in reality, but they can be useful when considered as abstractions formed by emphasizing certain aspects of typical behavior. These ideal types also serve as models for comparing behavior observed in similar situations within a variety of settings.

A Three-Dimensional Typology

In Figure 4-4 we have drawn a three-dimensional cube, with each dimension divided in half, producing eight subcubes. Each of these eight subcubes represents one of the possible health states of an individual. Only two of the eight health states have been labeled, because there is total congruence across the three dimensions of health in only two health states. The individual in health state 1 is normally well according to the World Health Organization's (1958) definition. The individual in health state 8 is most seriously ill, having ill evaluations within all three areas cited by the WHO's definition. But what about the six remaining health states? May we not affix labels similar to those developed for the two-

Figure 4-4. A Three-Dimensional Representation of Health.

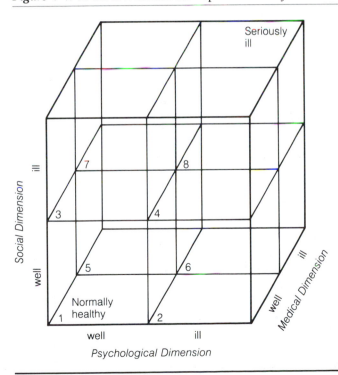

dimensional models described earlier to the health states represented by these subcubes?

We believe that it is feasible to assign labels to the health states in subcubes 2 through 7 as long as we remember our third assumption—that each dimension was to be considered approximately equal to the others in terms of its contribution to an individual's overall health. Accordingly, the only way in which the health of an individual in any one health state can be considered better than that of an individual in any other health state is to base that evaluation on the proportion of well evaluations that the individuals have received. This may be done by simply adding up the number of well evaluations. In a two-by-two-by-two scheme, this allows health states 2 through 7 to be divided into only two categories: two wells and one ill, and two ills and one well. Health states 2, 3, and 5 fall into the former (better health), while health states 4, 6, and 7 fall into the latter (poorer health). Within these categories our assumptions do not allow any further ranking of the individual's health state. We may, however, gain a better understanding of the various states of health possible. Table 4-4 shows the composition of the eight health states in the three-dimensional scheme, along with the tentative labels that we have affixed to individuals residing in each state.

HEALTH STATE 1: NORMALLY WELL. As we just mentioned, the normally well being is one who resides in one of the two health states that are the easiest to label. This is because

of the consistently healthy evaluations along all three of the dimensions of health. Individuals who are in this health state are normally healthy (although we are quick to remind you that they are not in perfect health, since perfect health is only an ideal).

HEALTH STATE 2: PESSIMISTIC. We affix the label of pessimist to that individual who believes him- or herself to be ill in the face of well evaluations along the medical and social dimensions. The pessimist will likely continue to search out ill evaluations from other groups of medical and social evaluators. In effect, the pessimist will seek "second opinions" that are more congruent with his or her own psychological health evaluation.

HEALTH STATE 3: SOCIALLY ILL. Socially ill is a label that we affix to an individual who has well evaluations on the medical and psychological dimensions, but an ill evaluation on the social dimension. An example of such an individual is the unwed pregnant female in American society. She considers herself to be well, and barring any complications, she is also considered to be well medically (pregnancy is generally not considered a medical illness). She is, however, often considered to be ill socially, and as a result is not allowed to carry out her social tasks and roles. A contemporary example of the unmarried female's plight is the enforcement of a leave of absence for unmarried pregnant schoolteachers, who are consid-

Table 4-4. *Composition of the eight health states in the three-dimensional model.*

Health state	Label	Psychological dimension	Physical dimension	Social dimension
1	Normally well	well	well	well
2	Pessimistic	ill	well	well
3	Socially ill	well	well	ill
4	Hypochondriacal	ill	well	ill
5	Physically ill	well	ill	well
6	Martyr	ill	ill	well
7	Optimistic	well	ill	ill
8	Seriously ill	ill	ill	ill

ered socially unfit to carry out their roles and tasks.

Perhaps a more publicized example during the last 10 years has been the homosexual schoolteacher. Since 1977 a national campaign of sorts has been waged by certain segments of the population to bar homosexuals from teaching in the public schools. Such teachers are considered to be socially ill even though they have well evaluations along the medical and psychological dimensions. The illness possessing these socially ill beings is social deviance.

HEALTH STATE 4: HYPOCHONDRIACAL. The hypochondriac is one who has a well evaluation on the medical dimension, but ill evaluations on the psychological and social dimensions. Unlike the pessimist, who continues to carry out his or her normal tasks and roles, the hypochondriac is considered as socially unable to perform such duties. This incapacity results from a successful (to a certain degree) presentation of an "ill self" by the hypochondriac to his or her social evaluators. The more often the individual opts for the hypochondriacal health state, the more permanent the label may become.

HEALTH STATE 5: MEDICALLY ILL. We affix the label of medically ill to one who, while medically ill, has well evaluations on the psychological and social dimensions. Such an individual denies the existence of medical illness and continues to adequately perform his or her social roles and tasks. An example of this type may be found in the traditional farmer's ideology concerning health. It has been shown that farmers will deny their physical limitations so long as they can work (Mechanic, 1978). Thus, although they may have a diagnosable medical problem, they consider themselves to be healthy. Because they are able to perform their social tasks and roles, they are also considered to be healthy socially. Another example of this type is the individual diagnosed as a victim of leukemia, but who is currently under the euphoric influence of a remission. Such an individual may feel well psychologically and may be evaluated as well along the social dimension, as long as the remission of the disease lasts.

HEALTH STATE 6: MARTYR. The label of martyr is applied to that individual who has been evaluated as being ill medically, who psychologically accepts the medical evaluation, yet who continues to perform his or her social roles and tasks and thus is considered to be socially healthy. Perhaps the most common example of the martyr is the terminally ill patient who accepts the medical evaluation but continues to perform his or her social roles and tasks. Another example of the martyr would be the public figure who accepts the deterioration of his or her physical health, yet continues to serve society by remaining in office.

HEALTH STATE 7: OPTIMISTIC. We affix the label of optimist to the individual who considers him- or herself to be healthy in the face of ill evaluations along the medical and social dimensions of health. The most common example of the optimist is the elderly person. Socially, the elderly are no longer considered capable of performing the social tasks and roles that they performed throughout their earlier careers. Medically, the elderly are in a state of physical deterioration closely related to the aging process. Psychologically, however, the elderly may feel that they are still useful to society and that they are in good health. Much of this propensity toward optimism on the part of the elderly can be explained through the concept of relative deprivation. Maddox (1964) has shown that people evaluate their health in relation to the health of their peers. Among the elderly, one's peers tend to have similar or worse medical problems. Therefore, inasmuch as psychological evaluation depends on the relative health of one's peers, many elderly people become optimists concerning their health; they are generally glad to be alive, all other things being considered.

HEALTH STATE 8: SERIOUSLY ILL. Seriously ill is the second category that is easy to label because of the consonant health status evaluation along all three dimensions. Individuals in this health state are very ill and need treatment, medically, socially, and psychologically.

Evaluating the Three-Dimensional Conceptualization

Using data on 500 North Carolinians, Wolinsky and his colleagues (Wolinsky and Zusman, 1980; Wolinsky and Wolinsky, 1981a) have conducted an initial assessment of the utility of the three-dimensional scheme. In these studies physical health was measured by the Health Status Proxy, which has been shown to be a reliable and valid substitute for physicians' examinations (see Carlton and Miller, 1971; Kisch, Kovner, Harris, and Kline, 1969). The social dimension of health was measured by taking the short forms of the activity and mobility scales from the Reynolds, Rushing, and Miles (1974) Function Status Index described earlier. Psychological health was measured by two variations on the global happiness question developed by Gurin and colleagues (Gurin et al., 1960). Individuals were assigned to one of the eight health states by dichotomizing each dimensional scale at its mean, yielding the distribution shown in Table 4-5. As these data indicate, nearly half of the respondents were classified as normally well, and 13.2 percent were

Table 4-5. *Frequency distribution of the eight discrete health states in a sample of North Carolinians.*

Health state	Label	Fre-quency	Per-centage
1	normally well	172	48.3
2	pessimistic	39	11.0
3	socially ill	8	2.2
4	hypochondriacal	14	3.9
5	physically ill	41	11.5
6	martyr	27	7.6
7	optimistic	8	2.2
8	seriously ill	47	13.2
Totals		356	100%

SOURCE: Fredric D. Wolinsky, and Marty E. Zusman. 1980. "Toward Comprehensive Health Status Measures." *The Sociological Quarterly* 21:607–21. Reprinted by permission of the publisher.

classified as seriously ill. Thus, three out of five persons had consistent evaluations on all three dimensions. Less than 4 percent were classified as being either hypochondriacal, optimistic, or socially ill. The remainder were about evenly distributed among pessimists, martyrs, and the physically ill. Overall, this was about the distribution that we had expected.

To assess the validity of the three-dimensional approach we used the eight health states to predict the respondents' use of health services. Andersen's (1968; see chapter 6 for a more detailed discussion of this and other models of health services utilization) behavioral model of health services utilization was employed. In the behavioral model, the use of health services is considered to be a function of the predisposing, enabling, and need characteristics of the individual. The predisposing characteristics are things like age and sex, which make some individuals more likely to use health services. The enabling characteristics include having a regular doctor, health insurance, and family income, which facilitate using health services once an individual is predisposed to do so. The need characteristics represent an individual's health status, which is considered to be the ultimate stimulus for using health services.

The results of our analysis were quite informative with regard to the percent of variation in the use of health services that could be explained at three different steps in the modeling process. In the first step only the predisposing and enabling characteristics were used to predict health services utilization, and the amount of variance that could be explained was small. The traditional measures of need were added into the model at the second step, and the explained variance increased considerably. This indicates that the need characteristics were more important than the predisposing and enabling characteristics in explaining why people used health services. In the third step we substituted measures of the eight health states for the traditional measures of need; the result was a remarkable increase in the amount of variance explained. Indeed, the amount of variance explained was about twice that explained when the conventional measures of health status were used. Thus, the three-dimensional approach appears to have considerable predictive value.

The last part of our analysis focused on the simple additivity and equality assumptions inherent in the model. Under these simplifying assumptions we expected that: the effects of any two health states with any one ill and any two well evaluations would be the same; the effects of any two health states with any two ill and any one well evaluations would be the same; the effects of any health states with any two ill evaluations would be equal to the effects of any two health states with any one ill evaluation each; and the effect of being seriously ill would be equal to the effects of any combination of health states having three ill evaluations.

To examine these assumptions we calculated partial unstandardized regression coefficients for each of the eight health states. The results told an interesting story. For example, they indicated that the socially ill averaged about 1.07 more physician visits per year than did the normally healthy, while the medically ill averaged 2.24 more physician visits. Similarly, the seriously ill averaged about 4.24 more days in the hospital per year than the normally healthy, while the medically ill averaged 4.64 more days in the hospital. Thus, these data indicate that the simple additivity and equality assumptions do not hold. Martyrs, optimists, and the seriously ill consistently used the most health services; the only common bond that they shared was having an ill evaluation on the physical dimension. Accordingly, physical health appears to be more important than social or psychological health, at least in terms of health services utilization.

What, then, can be said about the three-dimensional approach to defining health and illness? Empirically we know that it is a better predictor of the use of health services than traditional health status measures and that the simple additivity and equality assumptions do not hold. But perhaps the most important contribution of the three-dimensional model is its graphic portrayal

of the complexities involved in the health status picture. By so doing this model clearly shows the need to consider the physical, the social, and the psychological dimensions when defining health. A related contribution is that it allows us to distill six health states (those of the pessimist, the socially ill, the hypochondriac, the medically ill, the martyr, and the optimist) from what had been only two health states in former models. Thus, rather than lumping a wide range of health behaviors or states into two gross categories, such as Twaddle's (1974) crocks and deniers, or Maddox's (1964) optimists and pessimists, we are able now to identify six more discrete health states. This permits a more precise understanding of the combinations that are possible in an individual's composite health status.

The three-dimensional model, however, is not a panacea for the definitional problem; it is simplistic and does not provide *the* answer. Indeed, despite its intuitive appeal and our initial empirical assessment, a considerable amount of work remains to be done. This includes at least six major tasks: (1) evaluating each of the eight health states identified, (2) evaluating the relationships among these eight health states, (3) delineating the processes involved in arriving at one health state and in moving from one health state to another, (4) examining the effect of weighting the contribution of each dimension in the individual's composite health status, (5) describing the process by which the three dimensions of health interact with one another, and (6) delineating the relationship of the eight health states to the larger social system.

Despite its simplistic approach and the details yet to be ironed out, the three-dimensional model provides a framework upon which the fundamental issues in defining health and illness may be organized. At the very least, the three-dimensional model casts some light on the issues (medical, social, and psychological) to be considered in defining health and illness, and in developing health status indicators. Future recognition and systematic confrontation of the problems involved in defining health and illness will have a considerable impact on the direction and growth of the social scientific study of health, and on our understanding of this complex phenomenon (see Liang, 1986, for an extension of the three-dimensional model to the special case of the elderly).

Summary

In this chapter we have been concerned with the definition of health and the assumptions made in the three basic conceptual models—the medical, the sociocultural, and the psychological. In the medical model, health is defined as the absence of disease. Four faulty assumptions in the medical definition of health were discussed: (1) the nature of the disease, its diagnosis, and its treatment are assumed to be objective phenomena; (2) the medical professional is assumed to be the sole evaluator of the patient's health status; (3) health is assumed to be definable solely in terms of physiological malfunctioning; and (4) health is defined as a residual category of illness.

The sociocultural model of health and illness was then presented. In the sociocultural model, health is defined as the capacity to perform one's social roles and tasks. Four assumptions made in the sociocultural definition of health were discussed: (1) only social functioning is taken into consideration in defining health and illness; (2) health is defined relative to the individual's social status in society; (3) illness behavior is considered as a subset of deviant behavior; and (4) an institutionalized sick role is universally accepted.

In the psychological model, and the stressful life events approach emerging from it, health was defined as a general feeling of emotional well-being or global happiness. The stress approach assumes that changes for the better or for the worse in the normal pattern of an individual's life require some degree of readjustment in order to cope with the stress that these events produce. If too much stress accumulates from the individual's changing life events, then the individual becomes more susceptible to behavioral disorders or other impairments.

Finally, elaborating on the three previous approaches (the medical, the sociocultural, and the psychological) to defining health and illness, a three-dimensional conception of health status was presented. It was designed to aid our understanding of the complex phenomenon of health. In the three-dimensional conceptualization, eight specific health states were defined. The advantages of considering all three dimensions of health at the same time were discussed, as were the tasks yet to be done in order to further our understanding of health.

5. The Sick Role Concept

*I*N CHAPTER 4 we reviewed the three basic approaches used in defining health and illness. Of particular importance was the reorientation brought about by Parsons's innovative sociocultural approach to the sociology of health. In essence, he "rewrote the book" on the sociology of health. In his new orientation there were two major components: (1) the sick role concept and (2) the patient-practitioner relationship. This chapter will examine the concept of the sick role in detail (the patient-practitioner relationship will be examined in chapter 7). To accomplish this, we have divided this chapter into three sections. In the first section, we will review Parsons's sick role concept with respect to: (1) the sick role as the institutionalized social role by which we gauge our expectations about our behavior and the behavior of others, and (2) the four specific features that comprise the sick role. In the second section we will review the four basic types of criticism that the sick role concept has generated and how Parsons has responded to that criticism. In the final section we will examine Freidson's extension of the Parsonian sick role concept and review its utility by using the poliomyelitis victim as an example of an illness career.

Parsons's Sick Role Concept

When Parsons (1951) first presented his conceptualization of the sick role as an integral part of the sociocultural definition of health and illness, a new era was opened in the sociology of health. The basis for this new era is twofold. First, in order to understand illness-related behavior, Parsons suggested that we must identify the common theme behind the behavior of the majority of ill people. In other words, he suggested that from observing illness-related behavior we could distill a common response pattern or an institutionalized role set. Second,

Parsons suggested that there are four specific features of this institutionalized role set typical of Western industrialized societies.

Illness Behavior as an Institutionalized Role

As you may already know, most of the tenets of the functionalist perspective in American sociology may be traced back to Parsons. It should not be surprising, therefore, that when he began to write about the sociology of health, Parsons (1951) took a functionalist perspective. For the functionalist, the ultimate concern is the maintenance of the social system. In advanced industrialized Western societies like ours, the very high level of structural differentiation poses a potentially dangerous situation for the maintenance of the social system. Every individual has a specific social role to play, with its associated tasks to be carried out; therefore, the network of social roles (the social system) functions smoothly only to the extent that each individual adequately performs his or her roles and tasks. In other words, the stability of the social system is maintained only if all the interdependent social roles are carried out, because each specific role depends upon all other specific roles.

Several examples serve as good illustrations of this potentially dangerous situation. The first was the extended coal miners strike of 1977–1978. It exemplifies the problems that occur when, at the national level, all members of a particular class of workers (coal miners) refuse to do their jobs. When the coal miners first went out on strike, their impact was not initially felt by many segments of the population or related industries because substantial coal reserves had been built up for emergency use. Part of the rationale for such stockpiling involved the established tendency of the United Mine Workers union to go on strike (for a month or two) each time its contracts came up for renegotiation. After the first two months of the strike had passed, however, the effect of the strike began to be felt in all sectors of the population and the economy. By the end of the third month of the strike, the situation had become grave with many utility companies cutting back on their electricity output, many industries cutting back on their production schedules and laying off workers, reduced heating and lighting in private and public homes, schools being closed for lack of heat, and a serious decline in the rate of the nation's economic recovery. In essence, the historically anticipated "ripple effect" of the coal miner's strike of 1977–1978 gradually became a "wave effect"; eventually it threatened the stability and maintenance of the entire social system.

Another example of a nationwide strike, but by only one of several unions, is the 1986 TWA flight attendants' action. Although this labor dispute has been fairly devastating to TWA and its flight attendants, it has not had much impact on other airlines, other than increasing their load factors. At the subsystem level there have recently been four examples of local strikes by police (Chicago), doctors (San Francisco), garbagemen (New York), and nurses (Minneapolis). In these cases the entire class of workers in a specific community refused to do its job. As you might expect, some of these work actions were more crippling (effective) than others, given both the different values associated with each (safety, health, and sanitation) and the degree of interdependence involved with other occupations and industries (it's harder to run hospitals without nurses than it is without doctors).

The important point to be made here, and the one most evident in the coal miners' strike, is that in an advanced industrialized society with highly interdependent social roles we *expect* and *count on* individuals to adequately perform their social roles and related tasks. If an individual does not adequately perform his or her social roles and tasks, that individual deviates from our expectations. While the social system can usually survive deviation on the part of a few individuals at any given time, deviation by too many people in any one occupational class at any one point in time may well bring the social system crashing down around us. In order to avoid the collapse of the social system, society must devise some mechanism for the social control of deviants.

Parsons (1951) states that there are two main agents of social control in the United States, one for each of the two major types of deviant behavior. According to him, there are two reasons why an individual might deviate from the expected social role behavior. First, the individual may be capable of performing his or her roles and tasks but may choose not to do so. From the functionalist perspective, Parsons argues that this type of deviant behavior is considered a crime and the perpetrator a criminal, to be penalized by the appropriate legal authority. In the second situation, the individual is not capable of performing his or her social roles and tasks, through no fault of his or her own, and is considered to be sick rather than criminal. From the functionalist perspective, Parsons argues that sick people must be turned over to the appropriate medical agency in order to be returned to their original healthy state.

Both of the agents of social control—legal authorities for the criminal and medical agencies for the sick—have two common features (Parsons, 1972). First, regardless of why the individual is not performing his or her roles and tasks, that individual represents a potentially disturbing influence on others in the social system. As a result, it is important to have some way of *isolating* the nonperforming individual (either the criminal or the sick) from the others. If this isolation does not take place, we run the risk of having the infectious deviance (whether of the criminal or illness type) spread throughout the system. Second, and again regardless of why the individual is not performing his or her roles and tasks, we must develop a *therapeutic process* by which the individual may be restored to his or her adequate and acceptable performance level within the social system. Usually a time interval is involved between the isolation of the individual and his or her return to society, a time in which therapy is applied. In essence, regardless of the type of deviance exhibited

by the individual, he or she must be removed from the mainstream of society and returned only after therapy has "cured" him or her.

According to Parsons's (1951) functionalist perspective, society's need for the social control of deviant behavior has led to two institutionalized role-sets. The first involves the way in which we deal with criminal behavior. When an individual violates the rules and regulations established by the society, the social control arm of the legal authority pursues that individual in order to capture, isolate, and resocialize him or her. This pattern of behavioral reaction has become an accepted factor in our daily lives because it is necessary for the maintenance of the social system, and because our fundamental value or concern is the continued existence of the social system. In other words, the social control mechanism of the various legal authorities has become an institutionalized role-set internalized by Americans. We have been socialized to expect that if you violate the rules and regulations of society, you will be subject to the social control mechanism of capture, isolation, and resocialization. Just as the social control mechanism of the legal system has become an institutionalized role-set, so too has the pattern of behavior associated with being sick. We have come to expect that if an individual becomes sick, there are certain types of behavior that he or she should exhibit, or a certain social role that we expect that individual to play. That social role is the sick role, which defines a pattern of predictable behavior.

The Four Aspects of the Sick Role

Parsons's (1951) idea of the sick role is perhaps the single most important theoretical concept in the sociology of health (see Fox, 1979, 1985; Levine and Kozloff, 1978). Almost every subsequent theoretical concept or framework in the sociology of health has emerged as a result of attempts to refute or to extend the sick role concept. The sick role concept tells us what type of behavior we should be able to expect from and associate with the sick person. There are four basic aspects of the Parsonian sick role: (1) the nonresponsibility of the individual for his or her condition, (2) the exemption of the sick individual from normal task and role obligations, (3) the recognition that being sick is undesirable and one should want to get well, and (4) the obligation to seek out competent help.

NONRESPONSIBILITY OF THE INDIVIDUAL. The first aspect of the sick role is that the sick individual is not to be held responsible for his or her condition. The sick individual's incapacity to perform social roles and tasks is recognized as being beyond the individual's power to overcome by merely deciding to get well. Therefore, for the individual to become well, some therapeutic (curative) process is necessary. From a theoretical standpoint it does not matter whether the recovery process is a spontaneous one, such as a natural remission, or is aided by other factors, such as a physician or drugs. The point is that the sick individual is not capable of healing him- or herself merely by a personal desire or motivation to get well.

EXEMPTION FROM NORMAL OBLIGATIONS. Because of the individual's incapacity to perform social roles and tasks, he or she is defined as being sick. This incapacity to perform one's social roles and tasks becomes the basis for the legitimate social exemption from such performance, the extent of the exemption depending on the nature and severity of the illness. The more severe the illness, the greater the exemption; the less severe the illness, the less the exemption. The legitimate exemption, however is only partial and conditional; its continuation depends on the performance of the other aspects of the sick role.

BEING SICK IS UNDESIRABLE. The basic condition for the temporary exemption of the sick individual from his or her task and role obligations is rooted in the recognition that being sick is a socially undesirable state of affairs. Because it is so undesirable, the individual must want to get well (which also serves as a proscription against malinger-

ing), and is obligated to try to get well. To get well, the sick individual must cooperate with others because recovery is not possible through his or her efforts alone. Thus, while the sick person may enjoy the temporary but legitimate exemption from normal task and role obligations, he or she has the new obligation to want to get well and to try to get well as soon as possible.

SEEKING OUT COMPETENT HELP. It is the nature of most illnesses that spontaneous cures or recoveries cannot be expected to occur very often, to occur very fast, or to occur completely. The sick individual, however, is expected to recover completely and as soon as possible. Consequently, the sick individual (and other individuals such as family members who are responsible for their welfare) is saddled with a second obligation. The sick individual must seek out competent help and cooperate in a concerted effort to restore him- or herself to health from the incapacitating illness. Generally speaking, the competent helper who is sought out and whose instructions are complied with in American society is the physician.

To summarize, then, the sick individual is not held responsible for his or her condition and, in fact, is temporarily and conditionally exempted from some normal obligations. This exemption from normal obligations, however, is tied to the understanding that being sick is an undesirable state of affairs and, as a result, imposes on the sick individual two new obligations: (1) to want to and try to get well and (2) to seek out and comply with the treatment prescribed by competent helpers. Thus, associated with the sick role is one new benefit (the "secondary gain" of the temporary exemption of normal task and role obligations) and two new obligations (to want to and try to get well, and to seek out and cooperate with competent helpers). The sick role, if properly undertaken, becomes the social control mechanism necessary for the maintenance of the social system. Parsons (1951) succinctly described the essential need for the social control of illness by the use of the sick role-set when he wrote that the problem of health is intimately involved in the functional prerequisites of the social system. . . . Certainly by almost any definition health is included in the functional needs of the individual member of society . . . because illness incapacitates for the effective performance of social roles. . . . Insofar as [illness] is controllable, through rational action or otherwise [the sick role] it is clear that there is a functional interest of the society in its control, broadly in the minimization of illness.

Examining Parsons's Sick Role Concept

As we have already mentioned, Parsons's (1951) conceptualization of the sick role is the single most important contribution to the sociology of health. It offers the most systematic and consistent framework for analyzing the socially necessary behavior of sick individuals in American and other modern Western societies. The sick role concept, however, is not without its own problems. In fact, some sociologists have suggested that the concept should be abandoned entirely. Most sociologists, however, would agree that the sick role may be used as a viable concept as long as the user is aware of the four major areas of criticism (see Cockerham, 1986; Segall, 1987). These criticisms address the type of illness, variability in individual and group responses, patient-practitioner relationship, and middle-class value orientation.

Criticisms of the Parsonian Sick Role

TYPE OF ILLNESS. One of the major criticisms directed at the sick role concept is that it may only apply in the case of acute physiological illness. By their very nature, acute physiological conditions are usually readily observable by the individual, readily correctable by the appropriate medical professional, and pose no threat of stigmatization for the sick individual who seeks out competent professional help. On the other hand, chronic conditions such as coronary heart disease are not readily observable by the individual, nor are they readily correct-

able by the appropriate medical personnel. Thus, in cases of chronic illness (which as we saw in chapter 3 are becoming the major illness burden we face today), the initial definition of the individual as sick may be delayed for quite some time. Further, once the individual suffering from a chronic condition has been defined as sick, the nature of chronic illness makes it difficult, if not impossible, for the physician to effect a complete recovery and return the sick individual to health.

In their extensive research on the chronically ill and their perception of the sick role, Kassebaum and Baumann (1965) found four especially salient factors that differentiated the sick role of the chronically ill from the sick role of the acutely ill. First, for the chronically ill it is impossible to resume normal role performance at a pre-illness level. Second, the chronically ill are forced to adjust to a permanent condition, rather than merely overcome a temporary condition. Third, the chronically ill are forced to emphasize the retention of whatever level of role performance and autonomy that they now have, rather than to attempt to regain the higher levels of performance and autonomy they had prior to the onset of their illness. Finally, as we mentioned in chapter 1, the chronically ill are likely to find themselves on a downward slide with regard to socioeconomic status. As a result of this downward mobility, the chronically ill often fall to a lower socioeconomic status. Concomitant with this lower socioeconomic position is the closing of any opportunity to make use of the "secondary gains" of the sick role, because people of lower socioeconomic status must somehow continue to function (work) in order to stay alive.

Just as there was a problem in applying the Parsonian (1951) concept of the sick role to the chronically ill, there is a problem in applying it to the mentally ill (Segall, 1976a, 1987). At the root of this problem is the fact that while seeking help for *physiological* illness is expected, and the seeker is neither ridiculed nor stigmatized, seeking out competent help (the psychiatrist) for *psychiatric* illness often results in the stigmatization of the seeker, because in American society we have been socialized to believe that psychiatric disorders, unlike physiological disorders, are inherently bad or evil. In fact, it may be accurate to say that in American society we view the psychiatrically ill as partially responsible for their own condition. In any event, the act of seeking professional help for psychiatric illness often results in the painful stigmatization of the seeker by society. Because the nature of the human being is to avoid pain and to seek pleasure, an individual who begins to perceive signs, which are extraordinarily subtle in the first place, of his or her psychiatric illness will more often than not try to repress those signs and thus avoid the stigmatization of consulting a psychiatrist or other professional counselor. Accordingly, the institutionalized role-set of the sick role may not apply in cases of psychiatric illness. This apparent nonapplicability of the sick role concept to psychiatric disorders is rather ironic, because Parsons's (1951) original development of the sick role concept was based on its application to mental illness.

VARIABILITY. Another of the major criticisms directed against the Parsonian (1951) concept of the sick role is that there has been a lack of uniformity in sick role behavior for various individuals and social groups (Segall, 1976b). In other words, there are considerable variations in the ways that different people and social groups view illness, define the sick role for themselves and others, and adopt the sick role. For example, Gordon (1966) used a sample of New York City residents in order to empirically test Parsons's sick role formulation. At the more general level, Gordon found that the sick role, as Parsons had described it, was applicable only when the individual's prognosis was serious and uncertain. Under these circumstances, the sick role seemed to predict general illness behavior quite well. When the individual's prognosis was known and was not serious, however, a new "impaired role" seemed to be more appropriate. Under these conditions, there were no exemptions from normal task and role obligations. Even

though the individual was "impaired," he or she was held responsible for the performance of his or her task and role obligations.

As we mentioned in chapter 4, Zola (1962, 1964) demonstrated that some sociocultural groups perceive, select, and consider salient different illness symptoms than do other sociocultural groups. This means that there is a disparity among social groups as to who is ill and who will adopt the sick role. Zborowski (1952) examined these same phenomena on a more specific level. He found clearly different responses to pain among different sociocultural groups in his study of 103 male New Yorkers. "Old Americans" (second-generation white Protestant Americans) were less sensitive to what were assumed to be similar levels of pain associated with the same neurological ailments than were Italians or Jews. The similarity in response between Italians and Jews lasted only while they were hospitalized. When released from the hospital and returned home, the Italians resumed their "normal" authoritarian, masculine behavior patterns. The Jews, on the other hand, maintained their very emotional reaction to pain upon discharge from the hospital. Zborowski believed these findings represent the stoic nature of "Old Americans" who were taught to be aggressive and never show pain, and the overprotective and overemotional relationship between Italian and Jewish mothers and their sons. Along similar lines, Mechanic (1962; see also Verbrugge, 1985) and others have suggested that in general males take more stoical attitudes toward illness than females, as do older individuals compared to younger individuals.

In a slightly different vein, Monteiro (1973) has shown that while ill individuals may expect to take on the sick role, other lay individuals may not want to allow them that role. Specifically, Monteiro examined patients in Rhode Island who were recuperating from heart attacks. The heart attack patients expected to be exempted from normal task and role obligations under the umbrella of the sick role. Yet laypersons who had never been the victims of heart attacks were unwilling to grant such exemption. Instead, they felt that the recuperating heart attack patients should act out a role similar to Gordon's (1966) "impaired role"; they should resume their normal task and role obligations, but be careful not to do too much too soon. In essence, the heart attack patients and the laypersons were not in agreement about the nature and extent of the sick role.

THE PATIENT-PRACTITIONER RELATIONSHIP. Another of the major criticisms directed at Parsons's (1951) conception of the sick role involves the patient-practitioner relationship that is intertwined with it (the patient-practitioner relationship is discussed in detail in chapter 7). Parsons's discussion is based on the traditional one-on-one therapeutic relationship taking place in the office of the private physician (see Gallagher, 1976, for an excellent discussion of this general issue). There are four problems in applying this traditional one-on-one therapeutic relationship to illness behavior in contemporary American society. First, the prevalence of the solo practitioner providing medical care out of a private office has been gradually diminished in favor of collaborative or group practices. In the group practice setting, the patient may see one physician on one visit, and another physician on the next visit. The continuity of care often decreases with the increase of group practice, and this decrease results in a reduction of dependence by the patient on any one physician (see Wolinsky and Marder, 1985). Therefore, any control that the physician might have exerted in order to effect therapeutic results with the patient is somewhat deteriorated.

A second problem associated with the patient-practitioner relationship vis-a-vis the sick role is the shift in the site of their encounter. Since Parsons (1951) first presented the sick role concept, there has been a marked increase in the use of hospital emergency rooms, clinics, and mobile screening facilities for encounters between patient and practitioner. This had led their relationship away from the physician-controlled setting (the private office) to a more neutral setting. As a result, the dominance of the physician over the patient has been reduced (see Haug and Lavin, 1978).

A third problem associated with the patient-practitioner encounter and its relationship to the sick role is the changing nature of the interaction itself. The traditionally asymmetrical distribution of power between the physician (the active and powerful social actor) and the patient has become more symmetrical or balanced because of three major forces: the general consumer advocacy movement, which began in the late 1960s; the women's equal rights movement, which intensified about the same time; and the marked increase in the relative supply of physicians (as discussed in chapter 3). These movements have served to transform the traditionally passive patient into a much more active patient, who is not afraid to question the physician about his or her diagnosis, prognosis, or treatment regimen. The increasingly active participation on the part of the patient has also contributed to the deterioration of the control exercised by the physician (see Haug and Lavin, 1981, 1983).

The fourth problem associated with the patient-practitioner encounter and its relationship to the sick role is also concerned with the leverage needed by the physician to control the patient. This concern, however, runs along a somewhat different vein. In Parsons's (1951) formulation, the basis for control by the physician is vested in the necessity to provide therapeutic care to the sick patient. This is rather straightforward in the case of restorative medical care (especially when the patient wants to get out of the sick role), but not very clear in the case of preventive medical care. In receiving preventive medical care, the patient is not in the sick role. Therefore, the patient receiving preventive care from the physician is not in an undesirable state, and he or she is not directly obligated to comply with the physician's recommended regimen. Moreover, the target of preventive medical care is usually a social group (such as in an antismoking campaign) and not a specific individual.

Accordingly, in many instances of preventive medicine, there is little personal dependency by the patient on the preventive medical care provider (see Segall, 1987). As a result, in cases of preventive medical care, the physician must rely heavily on persuasive powers rather than authority and leverage as the social control agent.

MIDDLE-CLASS VALUES. The final major area of criticism usually directed at Parsons's (1951) sick role formulation is concerned with the sick role's middle-class value orientation. There are two basic points in this area of criticism. First, Parsons's sick role conceptualization emphasizes individual responsibility. Second, the sick role underscores the desirability of good health and the return to good health from ill health. Both of these points are clearly anchored in middle-class values, which emphasize a rational problem-solving orientation. A major assumption inherent in middle-class values is that when faced with an adverse situation, an individual can better the situation by hard work. Associated with this is the notion of "deferred gratification," in which it is assumed that by investing some resources (such as time and money) now, for which there is no immediate reward, there will come a time in the future when the investment will be paid back with interest (economists often refer to this as "investment in human capital").

While there is nothing inherently wrong with middle-class values, they are not shared by all segments of society (see Cole and Lejeune, 1972). For example, it may be very difficult for an individual living in an impoverished environment to accept the assumption that success can be achieved by hard work when there is very little evidence of such success in his or her environment. Further, under conditions of continued socioeconomic disadvantage, it also is unlikely that the logic of "deferred gratification" or investment in the future will carry much weight. Accordingly, a sick role formulation based on middle-class values may be valid only among people in the middle class.

Parsons's Response to His Critics

To be sure, a growing literature criticizing Parsons's (1951) concept of the sick role has developed (especially prior to 1975; for comprehensive reviews of this literature see Arluke, 1987; Arluke, Kennedy, and Kessler, 1979; Levine and Kozloff, 1978; Segall, 1976a, 1976b, 1987; Wolinsky, 1987; Wolinsky and Wolinsky, 1981b). In light of this controversy, a special session on the sick role was convened at the Toronto, Ontario, meeting of the International Sociological Association in 1974. At this special session, four review papers were presented criticizing Parsons's notion of the sick role. Parsons was on hand to respond to these papers (especially to the insightful paper by Gallagher, 1976), and he subsequently published his remarks (1975).

In particular, Parsons chose to respond to two major criticisms: (1) the apparent inability of his sick role conceptualization to apply to chronic or terminal illness, and (2) the suggestion by Gallagher (1976) and others that illness should no longer be sociologically viewed as deviance but as part of a more general adaptation framework. With regard to the apparent inability of the sick role to apply to chronic illness, Parsons (1975) suggests that we remember that health is conceived of as the capacity to perform. He grants that there are many conditions for which the art of medicine knows no cure, and for such conditions the notion of a complete recovery is impractical. The point for Parsons (1975), however, is that

recovery is the obverse of the process of deterioration of health, that is, a level of capacities, and in many of these chronic situations tendencies to such deterioration can be held in check by the proper medically prescribed measures based on sound diagnostic knowledge. An outstanding example is diabetes, where diabetics, by such measures as a modest regulation of diet, and stimulation in the milder cases by oral medication, in the more severe ones by the use of insulin, can maintain a relatively normal pattern of physiological functioning and the many activities of life which depend on normal physiological functioning. . . . The fact that diabetes is not, in the sense of pneumonia, "curable," does not put it in a totally different category from that of acute illness.

In other words, while the chronically ill or terminally ill patient may not be curable, such conditions may be *managed* so that the individual can lead a relatively normal life. To the extent that the chronically ill individual is able to manage his or her condition, holding deterioration in check, the chronically ill individual can recover, maintaining a relatively normal pattern of life activities.

In responding to the second criticism—that illness should no longer be viewed sociologically as deviance but rather as adaptation—Parsons (1975) took a different tack. First, he argued that deviance and social control are both phenomena concerned with the problems of integration in the social system. Second, he noted that illness is an impairment "of the sick person's integration in solidarity relationships with others" in a variety of contexts. Third, given this perspective, Parsons suggested that the therapeutic process is actually a reintegrative process. Citing the fact that integration and adaptation processes are the same phenomena viewed from different levels of analysis (the integration process is viewed from the societal or macro level, while the adaptation process is viewed from the individual or micro level), Parsons dismissed this second criticism by writing: "It therefore seems to me that the proposals to supplant the emphasis on deviance with one on adaptation is not very helpful unless it pays very careful attention to the relativities and complex interrelations between integration and adaptation." In essence, Parsons suggested that those clamoring for a shift in emphasis from deviance to adaptation are like those who are too close to the trees to see the forest. For Parsons, the integration and adaptation processes are the same phenomena seen from two different points.

The Relevance of the Sick Role for the 1980s and Beyond

Before leaving this section and the criticism of Parsons's (1951) conceptualization of the sick role, it is only fair to reiterate how important his work has been for the sociology of health, both then and now. The sick role concept is the most important and consistent approach to examining health and illness-related behavior. In fact, all efforts in the sociology of health may be linked to the sick role concept in one way or another. Therefore, if advancement in the sociology of health is to be made, it will only come about from a critical re-examination, reformulation, and expansion of the Parsonian sick role conceptualization. Perhaps Gallagher (1976) said it most eloquently when he wrote: "Whosoever sets out to acquire a sociologically-informed understanding of health and illness processes in contemporary society soon becomes aware of the profound contribution which Talcott Parsons has made. . . . When one considers how greatly sociological analysis has benefited from the original Parsonian formulations concerning the roles of physician and patient, my [and others'] criticism of that formulation here will seem perhaps petty and carping."

But two more convincing arguments for the contemporary relevance of the sick role may be made. The first involves clarifying the distinction between *expected* and *actual* behavior. Recall that Parsons's (1951) sick role concept describes the pattern of behavior that we expect of sick individuals, as well as those who interact with them. Many of his critics, however, focus on the fact that not everyone behaves the way we expect them to. Thus, these critics miss the boat by deriding the sick role concept for something that is not part of it.

Arluke, Kennedy, and Kessler (1979) have refocused that criticism by empirically assessing the degree of normative consensus Americans have for the sick role concept. Using questions developed by Segall (1976b) to tap the expectations associated with the four aspects of the sick role, they mailed questionnaires to a sample of adults who had recently been discharged from hospitals (for other than obstetrics and gynecology services). Results from 490 respondents indicated that the scale scores had extremely high means and small variances, indicating remarkably consistent acceptance of the sick role expectations. Moreover, as the data in Table 5-1 indicate, the scale scores were only weakly associated with various sociocultural characteristics. Indeed, age was the only factor consistently related to sick role expectations, with older persons accepting less the expectations about getting well but accepting more the expectations about not being considered responsible for their own illnesses. Arluke and his colleagues (1979) concluded that "a high degree of consensus exists. A balanced view, then, must acknowledge that there is a great deal of consistency in acceptance of these four behavioral expectations across the fairly comprehensive set of sociocultural contrast categories. . . . When the expectations are considered discreetly . . . Parsons's model is a fairly accurate description of the major patterns of sick role expectations."

The fact that only age was related to the four expectations associated with the sick role suggests a cohort effect. Older individu-

als who were socialized prior to the emergence of public responsibility for health care, and at times when most doctors were in solo practice and still made house calls, may have accepted and internalized the sick role more completely than their younger counterparts. Further support for this cohort effect has been reported by Haug and Lavin (1983). Similarly, in a study of who expects and receives sick role legitimation from their physicians, Wolinsky and Wolinsky (1981b) found older cohorts to be more likely to be in need of and receipt of prescription medicines.

The second more convincing argument for the contemporary relevance of the sick role concept involves examining the very way in which health services are configured. What exists in the United States today is a very centralized health care delivery system.

Table 5-1. *Adjusted means and standardized partial regression coefficients for the significant predictors of the sick role scales.* *

Predictor	1 Duty to get well	2 Duty to seek help	3 Right to be exempt from cause	4 Right to be exempt from roles
Income ($1,000s)				
Adjusted means				
0 to 5	—	—	4.93	—
5+ to 11	—	—	4.62	—
11 or more	—	—	4.51	—
Partial regression	—	—	.22	—
Family size				
Adjusted means				
1	5.52	—	—	4.66
2	5.26	—	—	4.78
3 or more	5.33	—	—	5.08
Partial regression	0.12	—	—	.16
Age				
Adjusted means				
0–39	5.52	4.16	4.47	—
40–59	5.41	4.54	4.50	—
60–69	5.38	4.73	4.76	—
70 or more	5.21	4.67	4.82	—
Partial regression	.41	.15	.23	—
R^2	.05	.02	.10	.03

*Education, sex, employment status, marital status, and religion produced no significant effects whatsoever. Scores range from low agreement (2) with sick role expectations, to high agreement (6).
SOURCE: Arnold Arluke, Louanne Kennedy, and Ronald C. Kessler. 1979. "Re-Examining the Sick Role Concept: An Empirical Assessment." *Journal of Health and Social Behavior* 20:30–36. Reprinted by permission of the American Sociological Association and the authors.

The bricks-and-mortar aspects are such that sick people are expected to come to identifiable and central locations for treatment. Underlying such a centralized method for delivering services, of course, is the implicit assumption that the sick role is accurate and that people will come to the delivery system rather than the delivery system going to those who need help. (Note that it has only been during the mid 1980s that effective efforts at decentralizing the health care delivery system have begun, such as home health care services.) Thus, the bulk of the health care delivery system presently in place remains highly centralized and dedicated toward the treatment of acute conditions (see Anderson, 1985; Starr, 1982). As such, it is quite consistent with the expectations associated with the sick role concept.

Freidson's Extension of the Parsonian Sick Role Concept

While many critics have attacked the Parsonian (1951) formulation of the sick role concept, few have offered viable alternatives in its place. The most widely acclaimed reformulation of the Parsonian framework was offered by Freidson (1970a) in his award-winning analysis of the medical profession. What Freidson did was to suggest that three dimensions be considered in expanding Parsons's sick role concept. These are (1) whether the individual is responsible for the deviance, (2) the imputed seriousness of the deviance, and (3) the imputed legitimacy of the deviance. He considered these three dimensions against the backdrop of the social construction of illness.

The Social Construction of Illness

Freidson (1970a) begins his discussion of the social construction of illness by establishing the social nature of illness. To do this, he relies heavily on the sociology of knowledge tradition expounded by Berger and Luckmann (1966), which states that the reality we perceive is often socially constructed rather than real in the biological or physical sense. In other words, the "reality" that we perceive is based on our interpretations of the social interactions and reactions rather than on the actual physical evidence. Because medicine may label one individual as ill and the next individual as well—regardless of the conditions of the individuals, which may actually be the same—Freidson argues that medicine is "engaged in *the creation of illness as a social state which a human may assume.*" For example, in some societies an individual may be labeled as sick, while in other societies an individual with the same physical condition is not labeled as sick. Unlike Parsons (1951), Freidson does not consider the physician the legitimator of one's acting sick but as the creator of the social possibility of acting sick. Thus, for Freidson medicine has the power to create illness as an "*official social role.*"

Freidson (1970a) sees two tasks for the analysis of such deviance or official social roles. The first task is to determine some stable quality of health, or deviation from that quality (i.e., illness), and to assess its causes. According to Freidson, this is what most of the sociological approaches to deviance are concerned with. The second task is to study how conceptions of deviance are developed and what the consequences are for the application of those concepts to human behavior. While he credits Parsons with "the most sophisticated and well developed theory of deviance," Freidson criticizes him for only being concerned with illness (as deviance) that motivates the individual to adopt the sick role (i.e., individual deviance).

According to Freidson (1970a), this ignores both the subsequent effects of the meanings the actors impute to their experience on their future behavior and the fact that the actors' behavior stems from their subjective understanding of the situation, rather than from the objective reality of the situation. Therefore, Freidson is concerned with the way individuals react to the one who has been labeled as ill. In other words, Freidson wants to investigate how the illness diagnosis affects both the individual's behavior and the behavior of others toward him or her. The analytic problem that

Freidson addresses, then, is "not the etiology of some state as much as the etiology of the *meaning* of a state. Thus it [Freidson's approach] asks questions like: How does a state come to be considered deviant? How does it come to be considered one kind of deviance rather than another? Is there any patterning in the way deviance tends to be imputed? What does the imputation of a particular kind of deviance do to the organization of the interaction between interested parties?" To answer these questions, Freidson states that we must focus on "the source and consequences of the meanings attached to behavior," which requires us to study those individuals who impute deviance to the behavior, as well as the deviants themselves.

Freidson (1970a) develops the framework for doing this by building on Lemert's societal reaction theory. Lemert (1951, 1964) had identified two types of deviance, primary and secondary. Primary deviance is merely symptomatic behavior, or an observable difference from the norm. Such differences in behavior are not significant until they are subjectively organized and transformed into new social roles, which may become the criteria for the assignment of a new social status. Once these new social roles have been created and the deviant and nondeviant individuals symbolically react to them as something different than the original socially acceptable role, then we have secondary deviance. In adopting such a secondary deviance role, the individual reorganizes his or her self-perception to match the new role and seeks out a deviant subculture that facilitates the new role. The difference between primary and secondary deviance, then, is that secondary deviance results from other individuals' responses to an individual or from one individual's response to him- or herself.

Freidson (1970a) describes this "interaction" process with the statement that "some primary deviations are singled out by others as undesirable, they penalize the deviant. This leads to more deviation and still stronger penalties, in the course of which the individual comes to resent those penalizing him. The deviant is stigmatized, social distance solidifies, and he turns to a deviant role . . . he becomes in essence a 'professional deviant.'" In the approach of societal reaction theory, then, it is the societal reaction that causes secondary deviance, not individual deviations in role performance. There are three important implications in this approach to deviance. First, social deviance does not exist in reality; it is only imputed. Thus, we should not study the attributes of the deviant, but those who label the individual as deviant. Second, the designation of behavior as deviant may be beyond the control of the individual. Therefore, the deviant individual's motivation is not essential to our understanding of the deviance. Third, because the deviance does not become secondary until it is socially organized, to understand deviance we must take into account the management of and responses to imputed deviance.

The Classification of Deviance

Freidson (1970a) relies on Parsons's (1951) notion of the nonresponsibility of the individual for his or her condition and the notion of variations in the sick role paralleling the seriousness of the condition. These specific notions are transformed into the general dimensions of imputed responsibility of the individual for his or her behavior and the imputed seriousness of the behavior's deviation from normality. The imputed seriousness of the deviation is dichotomized into minor and serious deviations. This dichotomization reflects the magnitude of the societal reaction. If the deviation is minor, then the societal reaction will be to leave the individual in his or her regular role, indicating only a primary deviation. If the deviation is serious, however, then the societal reaction will be to push the offending individual into a new, specifically deviant role indicating a secondary deviation.

The imputed responsibility of the individual is dichotomized into the individual's being held responsible, or not being held responsible. This distinction reflects the domain in which the deviant behavior occurs. If the individual is imputed to be respon-

Table 5-2. *Types of deviance, by the quality and quantity of the societal reaction.*

Imputation of seriousness	Imputation of responsibility	
	Individual held responsible	Individual not held responsible
Minor deviation	"Parking violation" Slight addition to normal obligations; minor suspension of a few ordinary privileges.	"A cold" Partial suspension of a few ordinary obligations; slight enhancement of ordinary privileges. Obligation to get well.
Serious deviation	"Murder" Replacement of ordinary obligations by new ones; loss of ordinary privileges.	"Heart attack" Release from most ordinary obligations; addition to ordinary privileges. Obligation to seek help and cooperate with treatment.

SOURCE: Eliot Freidson. 1970a. *The Profession of Medicine: A Study in the Sociology of Applied Knowledge.* New York: Harper & Row.

sible for his or her deviance, the deviant behavior falls into the domain of law and its social control mechanisms. If the individual is not responsible for the deviance, then the deviant behavior falls into the domain of medicine and its social control mechanisms.

The resulting cross-classification of these two dimensions results in the basic paradigm in Table 5-2. Just as in Parsons's (1951) framework (described in chapter 4), the right column in Table 5-2 represents the two types of illness behavior, while the middle column represents the two types of criminal behavior. Freidson (1970a) points out there are some cases of medical deviance that are treated as criminal deviance (such as venereal disease in the 1970s, or AIDS in the 1980s) because the individual could have avoided the illness. Thus, while the contraction of venereal disease is a medical condition in America, in some societies it may be treated as a criminal condition.

The examples in the cells of Table 5-2 are quite straightforward when viewed from the societal reaction perspective. Under the domain of law, a minor deviation such as a parking violation results in a slight addition to normal obligations (paying for the citation), along with the minor suspension of a few ordinary privileges (you might not be allowed to use that parking lot for 30 days). For a serious deviation such as murder, however, existing obligations are replaced by new ones and ordinary privileges are lost

(through incarceration, for example). The difference in societal reaction to a parking violation and to a murder is that for the former the individual maintains his or her previous social role, while for the latter a new social role is created. Parking violators may make us angry, but we do not consider them to be criminals in the same way that we consider murderers to be criminals.

Under the domain of medicine, the difference is similar. The individual with a cold receives a partial suspension from a few ordinary obligations and gains a few new ordinary privileges in exchange for accepting the new obligation of wanting to and trying to get well. The individual's normal social role is not changed; it is only slightly adapted. In contrast, the heart attack victim is released from most ordinary obligations and receives many new privileges in exchange for seeking out competent help and complying with its recommendations. The heart attack victim is given a new social role to perform, much as the murderer is given a new social role.

An Expanded Classification of Illness

The classification of deviance provides us with considerable insight into how law and medicine are alike with respect to social control and with an understanding of the importance of primary and secondary deviance. However, the classification of deviance is incomplete. What it lacks is the ability to take into consideration the third aspect of Parsons's (1951) sick role concept and one of its major criticisms. Parsons stated that the sick role was conditionally legitimate. In other words, the sick individual's exemption from task and role obligations was temporary, based on the individual's wanting to and trying to get well. But as his critics pointed out, the chronically ill don't get well. Therefore, any classification of illness (or deviance in general) must take into consideration the dimensions of the imputed legitimacy of the condition.

Freidson (1970a) identifies three major types along the dimension of imputed legitimacy. The first type is called conditional legitimacy, in which the deviant individual is temporarily exempt from normal task and role obligations. Some new privileges are gained, based on the condition that the individual try to rid him- or herself of the deviance. The second type is unconditional legitimacy. Unconditional legitimacy occurs when the individual is permanently exempt from normal task and role obligations, and obtains some new privileges in the face of the imputed hopeless nature of his or her deviance. Illegitimacy occurs when the de-

viant individual is exempt from some ordinary task and role obligations, but few if any new privileges are granted; some new handicapping obligations may even be taken on. The essence of these new handicaps is that the affected individuals are stigmatized (see Goffman, 1963), and other individuals react to the stigma rather than to the individual's true identity.

In combining these three dimensions into a conceptual model, the imagery becomes rather complex. Therefore, Freidson (1970a) cross-classifies the dimension of imputed seriousness with the dimension of imputed legitimacy, but only for those deviant behaviors falling under the domain of medicine, where the individual is not imputed to be responsible for his or her condition. The resulting paradigm is found in Table 5-3. In this table, the first distinction that needs to be made is between the top and bottom rows. In the top row, the deviance is considered to be symptomatic behavior associated with the performance of the individual's ordinary social role. In the bottom row, however, the deviant behavior is organized into new, special social roles that are distinct from and replace the individual's other roles. Thus, cells 4, 5, and 6

Table 5-3. *Types of deviance (illness) for which the individual is not held responsible, by imputed legitimacy and seriousness.*

Imputed seriousness	Illegitimate (stigmatized)	Conditionally legitimate	Unconditionally legitimate
Minor deviation	Cell 1 "Stammer" Partial suspension of some ordinary obligations; few or no new privileges; adoption of a few new obligations.	Cell 2 "A cold" Temporary suspension of few ordinary obligations; temporary enhancement of ordinary privileges. Obligation to get well.	Cell 3 "Pockmarks" No special change in obligations or privileges.
Serious deviation	Cell 4 "Epilepsy" Suspension of some ordinary obligations; adoption of new obligations; few or no new privileges.	Cell 5 "Pneumonia" Temporary release from ordinary obligations; addition to ordinary privileges. Obligation to cooperate and seek help in treatment.	Cell 6 "Cancer" Permanent suspension of many ordinary obligations; marked addition to privileges.

SOURCE: Eliot Freidson. 1970a. *The Profession of Medicine: A Study in the Sociology of Applied Knowledge.* New York: Harper & Row.

represent *new social roles*. Cell 4 represents the *stigmatized role*, cell 5 represents the *sick role* (as Parsons, 1951, originally conceived of it), and cell 6 represents the *chronically sick or dying role*.

In cell 1 the individual's normal identity is spoiled by the stigma associated with stammering, but it is not replaced with a new identity. In cell 2 the individual is recognized as being ill, but the role of being ill does not replace his or her regular roles; rather, it merely adds to them. Finally, in cell 3 the individual is recognized as having an impaired role, but again, this impaired role does not replace the individual's normal role. Thus, by cross-classifying the imputed seriousness of the deviance with its imputed legitimacy, Freidson has identified six analytically distinct types of deviance (illness) that would otherwise be lumped under Parsons's (1951) single, general notion of illness.

While the six distinct types of illness appear as static states in Table 5-3, Freidson (1970a) recognizes that health and illness are dynamic processes. These dynamic processes may be considered permanent or temporary careers demonstrating rather patterned behavior. To illustrate the process of going from one stage of an illness to another (i.e., from cell to cell), Freidson used the example of the possible processes associated with poliomyelitis. The sequential relationships of the analogs to cells 1 to 6 (as shown in Table 5-3) for the polio victim's career may be described as follows. To begin with, poliomyelitis usually appears as a cold (cell 2), gradually worsening to the point where the individual is labeled as a polio victim (cell 5). If the individual recovers with no ill effects, then he or she returns to his or her normal healthy state (and effectively escapes from Table 5-3).

There are, however, a number of other outcomes (from most of which the polio victim could possibly return to a healthy state). The polio victim may never recover, becoming an iron lung case (cell 6). Another outcome is for the polio victim to recover, although being left with some minor, concealable impairment, such as being weak (cell 3), preventing the performance of some task and role obligations but not resulting in stigmatization. Still another outcome is that the polio victim recovers but is left with severe paralysis resulting in the need of observable braces and crutches, stigmatizing him or her as a "cripple" (cell 4). Finally, the polio victim might recover and only be left with a slight, visible limp resulting in the mild stigmatization of part of his or her normal social roles (cell 1; this could occur directly from cell 5 to cell 1, or indirectly from cell 5 through cell 4 to cell 1).

Freidson (1970a) suggests that viewing illness as a career in this manner has a benefit in addition to the mere sequencing of illness types. Its paths provide a conceptual schema showing the linkage between individuals and their experiences throughout the range of illness between the top and bottom rows of Table 5-3, representing primary and secondary deviation, respectively. In cases of primary deviation, the contact is usually with the lay referral system, while in cases of secondary deviation contact is usually with the professional referral system. Presented in this manner, the illness career graphically demonstrates the sequence and type of agents and agencies with whom the individual comes into contact.

Unfortunately, Freidson's (1970a) extension of the Parsonian (Parsons, 1951) framework also contains flaws. First, it is only theoretical. Freidson's conceptualization has yet to be sufficiently tested, so that its utility in accounting for variations in illness behavior remains in question. Second, the conceptualization is based on the assumption of universal acceptance of middle-class values, as was the Parsonian framework. Third, just like Parsons's formulation, Freidson's classification of illness types does not explain why people define themselves as being ill or well, nor why they decide to seek or not to seek help. Nonetheless, Freidson advanced the Parsonian framework by identifying six different types of illness and by integrating societal reaction theory to show that illness is a socially created and labeled phenomenon. As such, Freidson's approach to the classification of different types of illness has considerable potential for future theory and research.

Summary

In this chapter, we have discussed Parsons's sick role concept, which serves as the cornerstone of the sociology of health. In the first section we began by setting the stage for the sick role concept. This was done by examining illness behavior as an institutionalized role in contemporary American society. As such, the sick role allows us to gauge our expectations of ourselves and others who either become sick or come into contact with the sick. Underlying this institutionalized role is the functionalist perspective, which states that all individuals must carry out their task and role obligations if the social system is to be maintained.

When people deviate from normal expectations, they become subject to the influence of one of two major social control agencies. If the individual is held responsible for his or her deviance, then the appropriate social control agency is the law. If the individual is not held responsible for his or her deviance, then the appropriate social control agency is medicine. These social control agencies are empowered to do three things: isolate (insulate) the individual from the rest of society, correct the deviation (illness) through therapeutic efforts, and return the well individual to society. We then found that there were four basic aspects to the institutionalized role: (1) the individual is not held responsible for his or her illness; (2) the individual is temporarily exempt from certain normal role and task obligations while he or she is ill; (3) the individual must realize that being sick is an undesirable state of affairs and that he or she is supposed to want to and try to get well; and (4) in order to get well, the sick individual must seek out competent professional help and cooperate in the therapeutic effort.

In the second section of this chapter, we turned to the four major criticisms of the Parsonian sick role concept: (1) the sick role appears to apply only to acute illness and not to chronic illness or psychiatric illness; (2) the sick role has not been uniformly adopted or perceived by individuals or social groupings; (3) the traditional one-on-one patient-practitioner relationship on which the sick role is based has changed; and (4) the sick role concept is deeply enmeshed in middle-class values, and therefore may be appropriate only among individuals of the middle class. We then reviewed Parsons's response to these criticisms, in which he dismisses his critics as being unable to "see the forest for the trees."

In the third section of this chapter we reviewed Freidson's extension of the Parsonian framework, based on societal reaction theory. Freidson constructed a detailed conceptualization of deviance by cross-classifying the imputed seriousness of the deviation with the imputed responsibility of the individual for the deviation. He then expanded his typology by adding the dimension of imputed legitimacy, resulting in six analytically distinct types of deviance (illness). Three of these six types resulted in new social roles for the individual, based on so-called secondary deviance: the stigmatized role, the sick role, and the chronically sick or dying role. The other three types of illness represent similar phenomena, but because the deviance was primary, no new social roles were created. There were three criticisms of Freidson's typology: it has never been sufficiently tested; it depends on the sick individual's acceptance of middle-class values, and it does not explain how and why people define themselves as being sick, or how and why they decide whether or not to seek professional care.

6. Seeking and Using Health Services

IN CHAPTER 5 we examined the sick role concept developed by Parsons (1951) and subsequently extended by Freidson (1970a). The sick role concept serves as the basic framework for understanding how and why people react to illness the way they do. In the present chapter we will go beyond the general conception of the sick role and explore in greater detail the seeking and using of health services. To do this, we have divided the chapter into three major sections. In the first we will examine two theories of illness behavior developed to explain the variations in sick role behavior that we observed in chapter 5. These two theories are Mechanic's (1968, 1978) general theory of help seeking and Suchman's (1965b) stages of illness and medical care model.

In the second section we will turn to the measurement and modeling of health services. This begins with a discussion of the basic issues involved in health services utilization, including an overview of the seven general approaches to health services utilization and a more detailed discussion of three of the most promising frameworks: the health belief model, the behavioral model, and the ethnomedical model. In the final section we will examine trends in the use of health services for the United States during the twentieth century. Here we will focus on hospital, physician, and dental utilization.

Two Theories of Illness Behavior

As we pointed out in chapter 5, Parsons's (1951) conception of the sick role serves as *the* major conceptual framework for understanding health and illness related behavior. Perhaps the most glaring defect in the sick role concept is the assumption that the sick role would be universally and uniformly adopted by all Americans. This is just not the case, as not everyone reacts to the same health conditions in the same manner. As a result of this and other criticisms of the sick role, several sociologists set out to expand and refine the sick role so that it would better explain health related behavior. Two of the most noteworthy of these efforts are Mechanic's (1968, 1978) general theory of help seeking and Suchman's (1965b) model of the stages in the illness and medical care process.

Mechanic's General Theory of Help Seeking

Mechanic (Mechanic and Volkart, 1961; Mechanic, 1962, 1968, 1976a, 1978, 1979a, 1979b, 1980, 1983, 1987) takes a social psychological approach to the study of illness behavior. As we mentioned in chapter 4, this approach is tied to the theoretical tradition of the looking glass self-concept (Cooley, 1964), the definition of the situation (Thomas and Znaniecki, 1918), the self process (Mead, 1934), the effect of group membership on health (Durkheim, 1956), and the effects of bureaucratization (Weber, 1968). At the base of Mechanic's (1978) general theory of help seeking is an emphasis on two factors: the perception or definition by the individual (or by the individual's significant others) of the situation at hand and, the ability of the individual (or of the individual's significant others) to cope with that situation. Mechanic uses these two factors to explain why "one person will hardly acknowledge a condition and refuse to allow it to alter his life, [while] another with a milder form of the same condition will display profound social and psychological disabilities." In essence, Mechanic is interested in explaining the variations in *illness behavior*, which he defines as behavior relevant to "any condition that causes or might usefully cause an individual to concern himself with his symptoms and to seek help." Thus, Mechanic's theory of help seeking focuses on understanding the behavioral process that takes place *before* an individual seeks out a health care provider. As a result, Mechanic sets out to expand Parsons's (1951) analysis of illness behavior by including all ill individuals, not just those who ultimately contact a physician.

TWO BASIC QUESTIONS. With this formidable task of explaining illness behavior in mind, Mechanic (1978) identifies two basic questions to be addressed. First, in order to explain an individual's illness behavior, we must seek to understand the particular factors of the individual's physical, social, and mental environments that resulted in the illness condition. In other words, one question in understanding how individuals respond to illness is how they acquired the illness in the first place. This is the etiology of disease question. The second question involved in studying illness behavior is to determine the factors that account for the variations in recognizing illness symptoms, associating these symptoms with their illness and then responding to the illness. This is the etiology of illness behavior question. Mechanic's general theory of help-seeking behavior concentrates on the second question, the etiology of illness behavior.

MECHANIC'S TEN DETERMINANTS OF ILLNESS BEHAVIOR. In concentrating on the etiology of illness behavior, Mechanic (1978) identifies a number of variables that affect an individual's response to illness. While recognizing that there is an overlap among some of these variables and that some factors that affect illness behavior may have gone unmeasured, he lists ten determinants of illness behavior:

1. Visibility, recognizability, or perceptual salience of deviant signs and symptoms.

2. The extent to which the symptoms are perceived as serious (that is, the person's estimate of the present and future possibilities of danger).

3. The extent to which symptoms disrupt family, work, and other social activities.

4. The frequency of the appearance of the deviant signs or symptoms, their persistence, or their frequency of recurrence.

5. The tolerance threshold of those who are exposed to and evaluate the deviant signs and symptoms.

6. Available information, knowledge, and cul-

tural assumptions and understandings of the evaluator.

7. Basic needs that can lead to denial.

8. Needs competing with illness responses.

9. Competing possible interpretations that can be assigned to the symptoms once they are recognized.

10. Availability of treatment resources, physical proximity, and psychological and monetary costs of taking action (included are not only physical distance and costs of time, money, and effort, but also such costs as stigma, social distance, and feelings of humiliation).

These ten determinants may be classified into four general categories. Determinants 1, 2, and 6 are concerned with the perception and salience of symptoms that will be largely determined by the medical orientation and sociocultural heritage of the individual. Individuals who have been socialized to perceive symptoms and who have been socialized to cope with those symptoms will respond to symptoms differently that those who have not. Determinants 3, 4, and 5 are concerned with the disruptive and persistent nature of the symptoms. In other words, this category of determinants focuses on the observable nature of the functional limitations imposed by the illness symptoms. Determinants 7, 8, and 9 are concerned with competing individual needs and alternative rationales for interpreting the observed disruptive symptoms. Finally, determinant 10 is a residual category that encompasses the effects of all nonsocial psychological factors in the response to illness. The fact that Mechanic relegates all nonsocial psychological factors to one of the ten determinants emphasizes his social psychological orientation.

SELF- AND OTHER-DEFINED ILLNESS SITUATIONS. In addition to identifying the ten determinants of illness behavior, Mechanic (1978) identifies two levels of analysis at which the determinants operate. The first level is called the other-defined level and refers to the process by which individuals other than the individual recognize the ill individual's symptoms and attempt to define

him or her as ill and in need of seeking professional care. This other-defined level of illness is most frequently used with psychotic conditions, although it also applies to the illness behavior of children and to somatic conditions denied by adults. At the self-defined level, the individual recognizes his or her symptoms and determines the need for help seeking independently. According to Mechanic, the major distinction between the self-defined and other-defined levels of analysis is that "in the latter the person tends to resist the definition that others are attempting to impose on him, and it may be necessary to bring him into treatment under great pressure and perhaps even involuntarily." In the main, the effects of the ten determinants of illness behavior are similar for both the self-defined and other-defined illness situations, as well as for psychotic and somatic illness situations.

THE CENTRAL THEME. There is a central theme that underlies all ten determinants of illness behavior at both levels of analysis. The theme is that *illness behavior is a culturally and socially learned response pattern*. Each time the individual (or the individual's evaluators) are confronted with illness symptoms, those symptoms will be perceived, evaluated, and acted or not acted upon on the basis of the individual's (or the individual's evaluators') definition of the situation. The individual's definition of the situation is determined by his or her sociocultural heritage and attendant socialization patterns. Therefore, individuals from the same sociocultural heritage should perceive, evaluate, and respond to illness conditions in a similar pattern, while individuals from different sociocultural heritages will respond to illness conditions in different ways.

The ten determinants in Mechanic's (1978) general theory of help seeking represent the criteria on which each illness symptom or condition is evaluated by the individual or by the individual's evaluators. In other words, the ten determinants of illness behavior represent the major decisions that are involved in the process of seeking or not seeking health care. Although it may appear that the ten determinants represent distinct and ordered stages in the decision making process, Mechanic states that they are not independent, and quite often interact with each other. The specific nature of their interdependence, however, has yet to be formally delineated.

THE EMPIRICAL EVIDENCE. Perhaps more than any other sociologist of health, Mechanic has consistently striven to use longitudinal data to gain a better understanding of illness behavior. His major research resource has been the continuing follow-up since 1961 of 350 children, their mothers, teachers, school records, and family health diaries (see Mechanic, 1983). At first, Mechanic (1964) found that the best predictors of the children's illness behavior was their age and sex. As time progressed, however, the role of developmental influences on their symptom reporting and illness behavior syndromes became increasingly clear (see Mechanic 1979a, 1979b, 1980). As the children reached young adulthood, psychological distress emerged as the most important correlate of the symptoms they reported and of the health services that they used. This has led Mechanic (1972) to focus on the role of psychological distress, for which he identified three aspects: (1) bodily sensations or symptoms that are different from those normally experienced by the individual, (2) social stress, and (3) cognitive orientations that suggest clues about the way the individual is feeling.

Based on the extensive analysis of the 16-year follow-up data at his disposal, Mechanic (1983) identified the existence of the "distress syndrome":

Changes in body sensations increase self-awareness, and stress contributes to body arousal and psychological disorientation that further motivate attention to inner feelings. The findings are consistent with the conclusion that factors that focus the child's attention on internal states and that teach a pattern of internal monitoring contribute to a distress syndrome. Respondents with such syndromes were more likely to come from families in which the mother was more upset and symptomatic, the child had more common physical symptoms such as colds and sore throats, and attention was directed to such symptoms by keeping the child away from school.

Mechanic goes on to make it clear that adulthood distress syndromes are *not* simply a continuation of childhood illness patterns. Although learned internal monitoring of bodily sensations is clearly an important aspect of psychological distress, it is not in and of itself a necessary and sufficient condition. Development of the distress syndrome in adulthood depends on many other factors, including the degree of psychological and bodily dysfunction, adverse life events, and experiences that intensify focusing on internal feeling states.

CRITICISMS OF THE GENERAL THEORY OF HELP SEEKING. While Mechanic's (1978) general theory of help-seeking behavior has expanded the scope of illness behavior to include individuals who are ill but do not seek care, identified ten major decision-making factors in the process of seeking care, and opened new vistas by isolating the psychological distress syndrome, the theory requires further clarification and testing. First, the nature of the interdependence among the ten determinants has not been specified. Knowing how these individual decisions affect one another is essential to our understanding of illness behavior. Second, the general theory of help-seeking behavior has not been submitted to testing in its entirety. As a result, it is impossible to assess its empirical validity even though it is intuitively reasonable. Third, while the general theory of help seeking has been expanded to include all illness behavior responses, it does not apply to health behavior, especially to preventive health behavior. It appears, however, that with some modification the general theory of help seeking could be applied to health as well as illness behavior. Fourth, the general theory of help seeking concentrates on the decision-making process leading up to seeking or not seeking care. It does not go beyond this process to the initial contact of the individual with the health professional. Finally, despite the exquisite longitudinal data available from the

16-year follow-up study, it is extraordinarily difficult to document a long-term developmental process such as the psychological distress syndrome or the increase in introspectiveness implied in Mechanic's (1987) recent work. The tandem problems here are first, to demonstrate the development (as opposed to the innate qualities) of the psychological distress syndrome or introspection and second, to identify those causative factors that bring it about.

Suchman's Stages of Illness and Medical Care

Like Mechanic and his colleagues, Suchman (1965b) was very concerned with illness behavior when defined as "the way in which symptoms are perceived, evaluated, and acted upon by a person who recognizes some pain, discomfort, or other signs of organic malfunction" (Mechanic and Volkart, 1961). Suchman's goal in analyzing illness behavior was to identify patterns in the "seeking, finding, and carrying out of medical care." From this he hoped to develop a model that followed the individual from the perception and recognition of illness all the way through his or her return to health at the hands of the health care professional.

FOUR PRINCIPAL ELEMENTS. In setting the stage for his model of illness behavior, Suchman (1965b) identified four elements that he thought were the principal components underlying the patterns of illness behavior: the content, the sequence, the spacing, and the variability of illness behavior. By combining various aspects of these principal components, Suchman was able to develop five useful concepts with which to analyze illness behavior: (1) "shopping," the process of seeking out several different sources of medical care, for one reason or another, although the purpose was usually to find a medical practitioner whose diagnosis and treatment were more in line with the ill individual's expectations; (2) "fragmentation," the process of being treated by several different medical practitioners, all at the same location; (3) "procrastination," the process

of putting off the seeking of care once the illness symptoms are recognized; (4) "self-medication," the process of home remedies and self-treatment; and (5) "discontinuity," the process of interrupting the treatment regimen.

To study the patterns involved in individual decision making in relation to the seeking, finding, and carrying out of medical care, Suchman (1965b) divided the sequence of events into five stages: (1) the symptom experience stage, (2) the assumption of the sick role stage, (3) the medical care contact stage, (4) the dependent-patient role stage, and (5) the recovery or rehabilitation stage. Each stage represents the place where a new and major decision is made in the help-seeking or illness behavior process. In constructing the five stages, Suchman relied heavily on Parsons's (1951) conception of the sick role, as well as Kadushin's (1958) description of the stages involved in the decision to seek psychotherapy (although Kadushin's description ends with the initial medical care contact, Suchman's approach continues throughout the treatment and recovery process).

STAGE I: SYMPTOM EXPERIENCE. At this stage the decision is made that something is wrong with the individual's organic functioning. In making this decision three separate aspects of the symptom experience may be identified. First, there is the physical experience of pain or discomfort that the individual actually feels. Second, there is the recognition that these things (pain and discomfort) are symptoms and that as symptoms they imply a state of illness. Third, there is the emotional response that accompanies the recognition of the presence of the state of illness as a potentially life-threatening condition. According to Suchman (1965b), the experience and definition of symptoms is usually recognized in terms of limitations on the individual's capacity for social functioning and not in terms of a specific medical diagnosis. In other words, we experience symptoms as limitations in our ability to function rather than as specific medical diagnoses.

STAGE II: ASSUMPTION OF THE SICK ROLE. At this stage the decision is made that the individual is ill and needs medical care. The ill individual begins to seek the alleviation of the symptoms through self-treatment and home remedies. At the same time, the ill individual seeks out information and advice about the symptoms from his or her family and friends. In addition, the ill individual requests "provisional validation" from these significant others, which, if granted, results in the temporary exemption from normal task and role obligations. In essence, at this stage of the illness and medical care process the individual turns to the lay referral system.

STAGE III: MEDICAL CARE CONTACT. At this point the decision has been made to seek professional medical care. Treatment seeking changes from the lay referral system to the professional referral system. Moving into this stage of the process is postponed whenever the individual aggressively pursues the lay referral system. The source of professional care sought will reflect the individual's knowledge, the availability, and the convenience of professional service sources. In addition, the initial diagnosis and treatment proposed by the professional will play an important role in the individual's future health behavior. This includes the issue of whether the individual shops around or complies with the proposed treatment.

STAGE IV: THE DEPENDENT-PATIENT ROLE. At this point the decision is made to transfer control to the health professional, and to accept and comply with the prescribed treatment regimen. According to Suchman (1965b), the ill individual is not a "patient" until this decision has been made. After the decision has been made, it may be reconsidered and perhaps terminated due to different conceptions of the illness and its treatment between the patient and the practitioner. In essence, communication and interaction between the patient and the doctor are essential if the dependent-patient role stage is to be successful. Of particular importance here are the barriers or obstacles that

the everyday activities of the ill individual place in the way of the treatment process.

STAGE V: RECOVERY OR REHABILITATION. At this point the decision is made to give up the patient role. The patient either is dismissed or withdrawn from the patient role (active medical care) in order to assume his or her old role as a healthy individual, or adopts a new role as a chronically ill invalid or long-term patient in cases where the illness is not curable, such as with chronic or terminal disease. During this stage the individual is frequently given a "grace period" during which the healthy role is gradually resumed. This grace period closely resembles the manner in which less than optimal functioning among adolescents is accepted. When the illness is chronic in nature, some resocialization of the ill individual may be necessary in preparation for his or her new role.

THE OVERALL PROCESS. For Suchman (1965b) these five stages represent the content and sequence of illness behavior. He explicitly recognized that all these stages do *not* have to be present in every case of illness, but that some part of the process, usually the earlier stages, will be involved. Thus, like Parsons (1951), Suchman has presented an ideal type model of illness and medical care-seeking behavior. Like Mechanic (1978) and Rosenstock (1960), however, Suchman emphasizes that individual perception is the key determinant of an individual's response to health and illness situations.

The overall process of Suchman's (1965a) model of the stages of illness and medical care is represented in Figure 6-1. In this figure the first row represents the stage of the illness and medical care process. The second row represents the specific decision made at this stage. The third row represents the behaviors typical for this particular stage. Finally, the fourth row represents the possible outcomes for the individual at each stage of the illness and medical care behavior process. The ideal movement through the illness experience is depicted by the flow of solid arrows from the symptom experience stage to the recovery and rehabilitation

Figure 6-1. Suchman's (1965a, 1965b) Sequences and Stages of Illness and Medical Care.

	I	II	III	IV	V
Stage	Symptom experience	Assumption of the sick role	Medical care contact	Dependent-patient role	Recovery and rehabilitation
Decision	Something is wrong	Relinquish normal roles	Seek professional advice	Accept professional treatment	Relinquish sick role
Behavior	Application of folk medicine, self-medication	Request provisional validation for sick role from members of lay referral system—continue lay remedies	Seek authoritative legitimation for sick role—negotiate treatment procedures	Undergo treatment procedures for illness—follow regimen	Resume normal roles
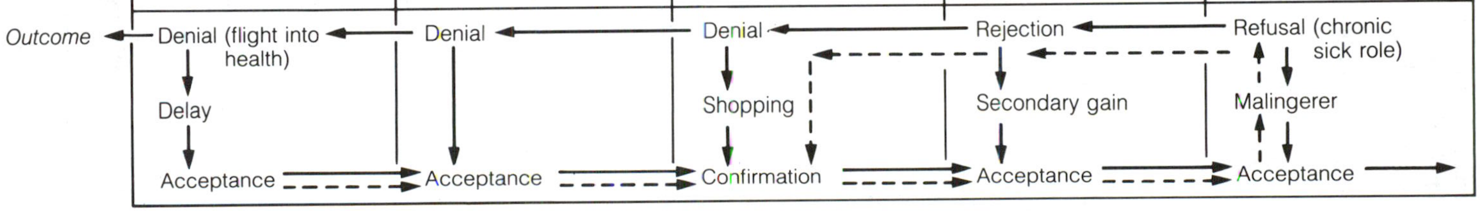 **Outcome**	Denial (flight into health) → Delay → Acceptance	Denial → Acceptance	Denial → Shopping → Confirmation	Rejection → Secondary gain → Acceptance	Refusal (chronic sick role) → Malingerer → Acceptance

SOURCE: Adapted from Rodney M. Coe. 1978. *Sociology of Medicine*, 2nd ed. New York: McGraw-Hill. Reprinted by permission of the publisher.

stage. In the ideal movement, the ill individual proceeds through all five stages without any significant delay in any one of them along the way.

The ideal movement, however, is not always the chosen path. Short of exiting from the process at any of the five stages, the individual may remain within a stage by exhibiting the behavior represented by the downward flow of solid arrows within a given stage. During the first stage the individual may try to deny the experienced symptoms and delay seeking care before eventually accepting the presence of the symptoms. In the medical contact stage the individual may not find the first physician's diagnosis and proposed treatment to be congruent with his or her own; as a result, shopping behavior may occur until a congruent physician's evaluation can be found. At the recovery and rehabilitation stage the individual may refuse to give up the patient role and delay the return to his or her normal role (malingering). Finally, there is the special case of the "hard-core malingerer" represented by the line of broken arrows. The malingerer retreats from stage V to stage III in search of continued congruent sick evaluations from a physician. This process may be repeated indefinitely, as long as the individual has sufficient resources for medical care costs and daily living expenses.

Suchman (1965a) next found that the variability and spacing of the five stage of illness and medical care-seeking behavior could be explained by the structure of the group to which the individual belonged and by the medical orientation of the individual. He identified two major types of group structure, parochial and cosmopolitan. Parochial social groups were characterized as being more traditional, sharing their experiences, having more affective relationships, and being closed to outsiders or anything "new." Cosmopolitan social groups were characterized as being more progressive and individualistic, having more instrumental relationships, and being more open to change. Suchman hypothesized that parochial groups would have a popular orientation to medicine with little knowledge of disease, more skepticism of medical care, and a greater dependency in illness. In contrast, cosmopolitan groups were expected to have a scientific orientation toward medicine with more knowledge of disease, little skepticism of medical care, and less dependency in illness.

Suchman (1965a) anticipated that individuals from parochial groups who held popular orientations toward medicine would be more likely to place their faith in the lay referral system. He also expected them to linger in the first two stages of illness behavior. In contrast, individuals from cosmopolitan social groups who held scientific orientations toward medicine were expected to move through the first two stages quite rapidly. The different emphases (rate of travel) of individuals from parochial and cosmopolitan groups through the five stages of illness behavior is represented in Figure 6-2. As can be seen from the figure, where the width of an illness stage represents the

Figure 6-2. *The Comparative Importance of the Five Stages for Parochial and Cosmopolitan Individuals.*

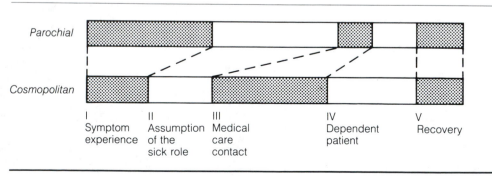

length of time spent in it, the postmedical care contact stages are the most important for cosmopolitan individuals, while the premedical care contact stages are the most important for the parochial individuals. In fact, many individuals from parochial social groups never enter the medical care contact stage.

CRITICISMS. While Suchman (1965a, 1965b) demonstrated considerable support for his model of illness and medical care behavior, his approach suffers from three methodological problems. First, he only studied persons who ultimately received medical care, so we don't know if his model really applies to illness behavior for which medical care is not ultimately sought. Second, he analyzed data only from persons who had serious symptoms, and he observed only those who recognized their own severe symptoms. This raises the question of whether or not the model applies to people who don't have or recognize their severe symptoms. Suchman suggests that such people are more likely to rely on the social or lay referral system than the professional referral system and that this may result in their not going beyond the second stage (assumption of the sick role). Third, the results of a replication of Suchman's research by Geersten, Klauber, Rindflesh, Kane, and Gray (1975) contradicted Suchman's hypotheses concerning parochial group behavior. Geersten and his colleagues found that Mormons, a very parochial group, have a scientific rather than a popular orientation toward medicine. Thus, they argue that modifications (or at least exceptions) to the parochial group expectations are in order. Nonetheless, Suchman's model of illness and medical care behavior represents a significant contribution to the sociology of health.

Measuring and Modeling Health Services Utilization

Before we begin to review both the major models of and the trends in the use of health services, you need to have a firm understanding of what we mean by and how we will measure these health services. To provide you with this understanding, we will first present the major conceptual framework of health services.

The Conceptual Framework of Health Services

As we have seen in the previous chapters, there are two levels or categories of health care: public or population-oriented, and private or individual-oriented. There are also two categories of health services. Health services falling in the public category consist of various sanitation services, mass immunization projects, water treatment, air quality protection, and the like. These *public health services* are directed toward the population at large rather than toward any specific individuals; *they generally require little if any initiative on the part of the individual. Private health services*, on the other hand, are directed toward the individual; *they require some initiative on the part of the individual* (or his or her significant others). Like most of medicine, most health services are directed toward the private use of the individual. In addition, most health services utilization studies are also concerned with the use of private health services. Therefore, we shall restrict our discussion of measuring health services to the private category.

In an informative and frequently cited article, Andersen and Newman (1973) presented a theoretical framework for the measurement of the use of private health services. The most important contribution of their work is the definition of the dimensions of health services utilization, which is now widely accepted although not always used by sociologists of health. The principal reason that Andersen and Newman's distinctions are not always used involves the difficulty of obtaining such detailed information in social surveys, which serve as the basic source of data for most studies of health services utilization (see Marcus and Crane, 1986; Mosely and Wolinsky, 1986). As a result, Andersen and Newman's approach serves more as an ideal type framework guiding the work of most health services researchers. Andersen and Newman identified three dimensions of primary importance in measuring and defining health services: the type, the purpose, and the unit of analysis.

TYPE. Type is the first dimension in Andersen and Newman's (1973) framework for measuring health services. It is used to separate the various health services from one another. Andersen and Newman demonstrated that there are different long- and short-term trends for the various types of services, such as hospitals, physicians, dentists, drugs, nursing homes, and so forth. They also showed that prior research found individual determinants of utilization varied considerably across the different types of health services. Because of these two factors (differing trends and determinants), it seems reasonable that one major component in the measurement of health services should be the type of health services used.

PURPOSE. Purpose is the second dimension in Andersen and Newman's (1973) conceptual framework for measuring health services. They suggest that the four distinctions of primary, secondary, tertiary, and custodial care made by the Commission on Chronic Illness in the United States be adopted. Primary care is preventive care, stopping illness before it begins. Secondary care is restorative care, returning the individual to his or her prior level of functioning. Tertiary care is care to stabilize the condition with respect to long-term illness. Custodial care is concerned with the purely personal needs of the individual patient and does not address the treatment of the disease; hospices offer custodial care. Andersen and Newman showed that differing determinants were in force when the purpose criterion was involved in the examination of utilization behavior, establishing purpose as a major component in measuring health services.

UNIT OF ANALYSIS. The unit of analysis is the third dimension in Andersen and Newman's (1973) framework for measuring health services. Three distinctions are proposed: contact, volume, and episodes. The major argument for this distinction is that, on the one hand, the individual's characteristics might be primarily responsible for the number of illness episodes incurred, as well as whether or not a doctor was seen for any of them. On the other hand, the characteristics of the delivery system (especially the physician) might be primarily responsible for the number of visits incurred as a result of each illness episode. Thus, because the issue of contact, the number of episodes, and the volume of health services used are determined by different factors, the measurement of health services utilization should clearly make a distinction among the different units of analysis.

Following Andersen and Newman's (1973) typology, for example, we might want to measure the number of hospital admissions per 100 persons in a given year, the number of physician visits per person in a given year, or the percent of persons having seen a dentist in a given year. In fact, in the final section of this chapter, we will examine the historical trends of health services utilization in the United States using these three indicators (and others). For the time being, however, we will concern ourselves with understanding the general nature of health services measurement, as reflected in the conceptual framework of Andersen and Newman.

The General Types of Health Services Utilization Models

During the past three decades a considerable amount of research has been done on the determinants of health services utilization (for an extensive list of references and findings see Andersen and Anderson, 1967; Andersen, 1968; McKinlay, 1972; Aday and Eichhorn, 1972; Flook and Sanazaro, 1973; Aday and Andersen, 1975; Andersen, Kravits, and Anderson, 1975, 1976; Andersen and Anderson, 1979; Aday, Andersen, and Fleming, 1980; Aday, Fleming, and Andersen, 1984; Hulka and Wheat, 1985; Wan, 1987). In most of this research, one or more models of existing health services utilization are developed and employed. These models are intended to be simplified versions of reality representing the causal process of health services utilization in the real world.

Andersen and Anderson (1979) suggest that these models of health services utilization may serve any one or more of the following purposes: (1) to illustrate the interrelationships among the determinants of health services utilization, (2) to facilitate the prediction of future health services needs, (3) to determine whether or not the distribution of the use of health services is equitable, (4) to suggest ways to manipulate policy relevant variables in order to bring about desired changes, and (5) to evaluate the impact of new health care delivery programs or projects. Because there has been so much research on health services utilization, it is nearly impossible to discuss every specific model that has been used. Instead, we shall briefly consider seven categories of models based on the types of variables used as determinants of health services utilization: demographic, social structural, social psychological, family resource, community resource, organizational, and health systems models.

DEMOGRAPHIC MODELS. In demographic models of health services utilization the variables typically used are age, sex, marital status, and family size. These variables are used as proxy measures or indicators of different physiological (age, sex) and life cycle (marital status, family size) states, assuming that different levels of health, illness, and health services utilization are associated with these different states. As we saw in chapter 1, these demographic characteristics may also reflect or be related to social characteristics, such as the social distinctions of gender that affect various types and modes of social interaction. Unfortunately, the nature of these relationships and their effects on health services utilization have yet to be fully explicated (see Nathanson, 1975; Verbrugge, 1985, 1986).

SOCIAL STRUCTURAL MODELS. In social structural models of health services utilization, the variables typically used are education, occupation, and ethnicity. These variables reflect the social position of the individual, or the family, in society. As such, they suggest the various lifestyles exhibited by individuals, and families, of certain social

positions. The use of health services is one aspect of those lifestyles that encompasses the social, physical, and psychological environments. The major problem of social structural models of health services utilization is that we don't know why these variables cause people to use health services. All we do know is that individuals of the same ethnicity, occupational, or educational level tend to have a common history of experience. This in turn influences how they perceive and react to their health. In other words, the social structural approach is based on the assumption that people of like social structural backgrounds will use health services in a similar manner.

SOCIAL PSYCHOLOGICAL MODELS. In social psychological models of health services utilization the variables typically used are measures of the individual's attitudes and beliefs. The social psychological variables generally fall into one of four categories: the perceived susceptibility to the disease or illness, the perceived seriousness of the disease or illness, the expected benefits of taking action (using health services) in the face of the disease or illness, or the cues that trigger the individual's actions. Models using these variables try to explain *why* people behave (use health services) the way they do, rather than just trying to show what characteristics are related to the use of services. The major problem with the social psychological models is that they assume a direct causal link between attitudes and beliefs, and behavior, which has yet to be demonstrated. One of the most well known of these models is the health belief model, which we will discuss in detail later in this chapter.

FAMILY RESOURCE MODELS. In family resource models of health services utilization the variables typically used are family income, health insurance coverage, and having a regular source of health care, such as a private family physician or dentist. These characteristics are used to measure the ability of the individual or family to obtain the health services it perceives as necessary. In essence, the family resource models emphasize the family's ability to procure health services for its members. These models assume that the more health services the family *can* procure, the more health services the family *will* procure. As such, the family resource models are basically microeconomic models.

COMMUNITY RESOURCE MODELS. In community resource models of health services utilization the variables typically used are the supply of health services and the resources available in the community, the rural versus suburban versus urban character of the community, and the accessibility of the available health services and resources in the community. Community resource models, then, are essentially macroeconomic supply models focusing on the aggregate of health resources available in a given geographic community. As such, community resource models move the analysis from the individual or family level to the community level. Thus, individual health services utilization is no longer explained; it is inferred from the explanation of community health services utilization.

ORGANIZATIONAL MODELS. In organizational models of health services utilization variables are used to represent the different forms of the health care delivery system. Some of the more commonly used variables are the style of medical practice (solo, partnership, group, or health maintenance organization), the nature of the delivery system (fee-for-service, salaried, or prepaid), the site of the service delivery (private offices, hospitals, or clinics), and the health workers who are first in the patient contact line (physicians, nurses, or physician extenders). Organizational models generally compare the use of health services of individuals in one health care delivery system with individuals of similar characteristics in another health care delivery system. Until recently, this consisted primarily of cross-national comparisons.

HEALTH SYSTEMS MODELS. As you may already have noticed, the preceding six categories of health services utilization models are not necessarily mutually exclusive,

although they are different in nature. It has become increasingly apparent that variables from all six of the categories of models need to be incorporated under one all-encompassing model of health services utilization. The general purpose of health systems models is to integrate the best of the other six models into a more cogent and complete model. For this task to be accomplished, the demographics, social structural characteristics, attitudes and beliefs of the individual and his or her family, the resources of the community, and the organization of the health care delivery system are all used in conjunction with contextual factors such as the health policy and economic structure of the larger society.

By using all these determinants, we can obtain a greater understanding of health services utilization. This occurs, however, at the cost of having to gather more data than in any of the six more limited models. Perhaps the major advantage of health systems models is that they illustrate how changes in one set of characteristics influence other characteristics throughout the entire health care system. This allows us to predict the outcome of health care planning and thus to avoid implementing potentially harmful programs and policies. The most widely used health system model is Aday and Andersen's (1974, 1975) framework for the access to medical care, which we will discuss in detail later in this chapter.

The Health Belief Model

The health belief model is one of the most well-known models of health services utilization (for a detailed history of the health belief model, see Becker, 1974; for a detailed review of variations on the health belief model see, Becker, Haefner, Kasl, Kirscht, Maiman, and Rosenstock, 1977; Becker and Maiman, 1983). It emerged from the efforts of several public health researchers who were independently confronting similar health problems during the 1950s and 1960s. Typical of these was the failure of the general public to accept disease preventatives or disease-screening tests, especially for tuberculosis, polio, and other asymptomatic diseases. It was the public's failure to accept and adopt such measures of prevention that spurred these researchers to develop a theory explaining preventive health behavior. They brought their social psychological training, especially their familiarity with Lewin's (1951) field theory, to bear on the problem. The result was the development of the health belief model.

THE THEORETICAL FRAMEWORK. As indicated, the health belief model is soundly based in Lewinian (Lewin, 1951) field theory. This approach implicitly accepts a conception of life in which each individual lives in his or her own social life space. Within this life space there are positively and negatively valued regions or valences. It is assumed that individuals are attracted or pulled to positive regions, while being repelled or pushed away from negative regions. When the Lewinian field theory was applied to health problems, it was assumed that disease and illness were negative valences, while health was a positive valence. Four key factors were thought to be involved in an individual's decision to take action against a disease: (1) the perceived susceptibility of the individual to the disease, (2) the perceived seriousness of the disease, (3) the perceived benefits and barriers of taking action against the disease, and (4) the cues that motivate the action process in the individual.

PERCEIVED SUSCEPTIBILITY. In order to take action against a disease, an individual must perceive that he or she is susceptible to it. For example, if AIDS strikes one out of every 10,000 people in the general population, the statistical probability of any one individual's contracting it is slim, certainly much slimmer than the probability of getting flu this winter (as indicated in chapter 2, the risk of AIDS is significantly higher among homosexual males and those who are intravenous users of illicit drugs). In other words, any avoidance or preventive action concerning disease "X" (AIDS, for example) will not be taken until and unless the individual perceives him- or herself to be susceptible to disease "X." This reflects the

health belief model's reliance on individual perception.

PERCEIVED SERIOUSNESS. Once the individual has perceived that he or she is susceptible to disease "X," then the individual must perceive the seriousness of contracting disease "X." The perceived seriousness of the disease may be measured by the anxiety aroused in the individual at the thought of contracting the disease and by the limitations that would be placed on the individual by contracting the disease. Most individuals would likely perceive AIDS as being far more serious than the flu but perceive their susceptibility to the two in the reverse order (unless they were in a high-risk category for AIDS). In any event, the individual is more likely to take preventive action when threatened by a disease perceived as serious than by a less seriously perceived disease.

PERCEIVED BENEFITS AND BARRIERS. If the individual perceives him- or herself as susceptible to a perceived serious disease, then he or she is more likely to take some type of action. The specific action taken, however, will depend upon the sum of the perceived benefits of and the perceived barriers to taking that specific action. In other words, the health belief model assumes that individuals choose their specific actions based on the perceived benefit of taking a specific action, less the perceived barriers to taking that specific action. Under this assumption, people will choose actions in which the perceived benefits outweigh the perceived barriers. As such, the health belief model assumes that human beings are rational.

CUES. In addition to having the right levels of perceived susceptibility, perceived seriousness, and perceived benefits less perceived barriers, the developers of the health belief model found that it was necessary for the individual's preventive action to be cued or triggered by some external factor. Some suggested common factors were mass media messages, friendly advice, or the illness of a family member, friend, or prominent citizen. In other words, the fully "perceiving" individual does not usually take action until and unless he or she is cued to take action. For example, recall the dramatic increase in mammographies (breast cancer-screening Xrays) after the much-publicized accounts of breast cancer and mastectomies of former First Lady Betty Ford and former Second Lady Happy Rockefeller. Or consider the more recent increase in colo-rectal cancer examinations following the much-publicized cancer surgery of President Reagan.

THE COMPLETE MODEL. Although it is not recognized as a major component in the health belief model, it is assumed that an individual's perceptions are modified and developed as a result of his or her sociocultural background. In other words, Lewinian (Lewin, 1951) field theory assumes that an individual's perceptions are by and large a product of his or her sociocultural heritage and concomitant socialization process. Therefore, when the various components of the health belief model are taken together, as in Figure 6-3, the modifying background factors are shown as antecedents of the perceptions of the individual. In this figure we can see that if the susceptibility, seriousness, and benefits less barriers are appropriately perceived in the presence of the right cues, the individual is likely to take the recommended preventive health action. In the absence of the appropriate perceptions or the appropriate cues, the individual is not likely to take the recommended preventive health action.

AN EMPIRICAL ASSESSMENT. While a number of studies have been conducted assessing the health belief model (see Becker, 1974; Becker, Haefner, Kasl, Kirscht, Maiman, and

Figure 6-3. *The Health Belief Model.*

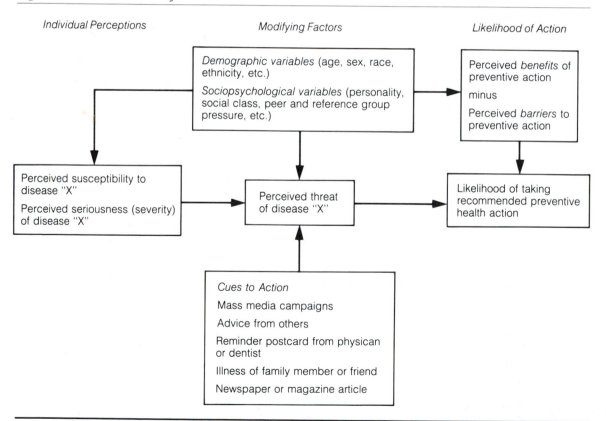

SOURCE: Irwin Rosenstock. 1974. "Historical origins of the Health Belief Model." *Health Education Monographs* 2:328–35.

Rosenstock, 1977; Becker and Maiman, 1983), a particular application of the model to the problem of child obesity and dietary compliance (Becker, Maiman, Kirscht, Haefner, and Drachman, 1977) is especially interesting. In this study, 182 eligible mothers and obese-diagnosed child pairs participated in an experimental assessment of the health belief model. The mother-child pairs had come to an ambulatory pediatric clinic, where the children were initially diagnosed by clinic physicians as obese. The children were then referred to the clinic dietitian for a weight reduction regimen, while the mothers were questioned about their health beliefs, concerns, and motives. Then the mother-child pairs were given the weight reduction regimen.

At this point the mother-child pairs were divided into three groups: high fear, low fear, and control. The mothers in the high-fear group were given a pamphlet that discussed in highly alarming terms the potential health hazards in later life for obese children. The mothers in the low-fear group were also given a pamphlet, although it was written with a much lower level of fear arousal. The mothers in the control group were not given any fear-arousing pamphlet. Each child was weighed at this initial visit and at each of the four subsequent follow-up visits, which were spaced two weeks apart.

At the end of the study the researchers calculated the average weight loss for each of the three groups over the course of the eight weeks. The amount of the weight loss was expressed as the cumulative percent of weight changes from the initial visit. When the experiment was over, the control group weighed just as much as when it began. The low-fear group lost weight, even though they put some of it back on between the second and third follow-up visits. Finally, the high-fear group lost the most weight. Moreover, they never put any of the weight they lost back on between visits. These dramatic results clearly demonstrate the importance of, in the presence of the appropriate cue (fear arousal), the perceived susceptibility, seriousness, and benefits of the dietary regimen (action) in avoiding future

illness (disease "X") among the obese children. Unfortunately, the general applicability of these results is somewhat limited because it was the mothers who chose to take action (dietary compliance) and not the children. It is difficult to say whether the same fear arousal techniques would have affected obese mothers' own compliance with dietary regimens.

WEAKNESSES IN THE HEALTH BELIEF MODEL. There are four major criticisms that can be directed toward the health belief model. First, as we have already mentioned, there is no evidence that attitudes and beliefs actually cause behaviors. Second, the health belief model appears to work well only if all other factors affecting the taking of preventive action are equal. In other words, while the health belief model appears to be intuitively acceptable, it has only been assessed in situations where the other factors causing action have been controlled or equalized. For example, in the mother-child obesity and dietary compliance study, access to the resources necessary for taking action was artificially equalized, for the follow-up visits were provided at no charge. Third, while the health belief model has been successful in predicting preventive health behavior (disease avoidance behavior), there is some question as to its ability to explain positive health action, such as the pursuit of good health unmotivated by the threat of specific disease. Finally, in a major field examination of the health belief model, Berkanovic and his colleagues (Berkanovic, Telesky, and Reeder, 1981; Berkanovic and Telesky, 1982, 1985) have shown that only health beliefs specific to disease "X" are predictive of disease "X" health behavior. No generalizable health beliefs that were predictive of a wide variety of health behaviors could be identified. Thus, the prediction of a specific health behavior required the knowledge of the health beliefs specifically related to that behavior. Therefore, the practical utility of the health belief model appears to be rather low, although its intuitive conceptual appeal remains rather high.

Andersen's Health Systems Model

The most widely adopted and empirically assessed model of health services utilization is Andersen's (1968) behavioral model. This model has been expanded, modified, and used extensively by health services researchers in the 1970s and 1980s; it is likely to continue to be the dominant model in the 1990s. The behavioral model originally focused on the individual determinants of the use of health services in a fashion similar to the health belief model. Aday and Andersen (1974, 1975), however, subsequently expanded the individual determinants model into a complete health systems model by incorporating a variety of contextual factors. In the original behavioral model there were three major categories of health services utilization determinants: predisposing characteristics, enabling characteristics, and need characteristics.

PREDISPOSING CHARACTERISTICS. The category of predisposing characteristics was used to reflect the fact that some individuals have a greater propensity to use services than other individuals. According to Andersen (1968), these propensities can be predicted by various individual characteristics occurring prior to the incidence of a specific illness episode. These individual characteristics were further classified into three groups: (1) demographic, such as age and sex; (2) social structural, such as education, occupation, and ethnicity; and (3) health benefits, such as the belief that medical care can be helpful in treating illness. In essence, Andersen believed that individuals with different demographic characteristics have different types and amounts of illness, resulting in different patterns of use of health services; individuals with different social structural characteristics have different lifestyles, resulting in differing patterns of health services use; and individuals believing in the efficacy of medical care are more likely to seek medical care than those who do not.

ENABLING CHARACTERISTICS. The category of enabling characteristics reflects the fact that while the individual may be predisposed to use health services, he or she does not use them unless able to do so. An individual's ability to use health services depends on both family (income and place of residence) and community (availability of health care facilities, including personnel) resources. If there are sufficient family and community resources to enable the individual to use health services, then the individual will be more likely to use them.

NEED CHARACTERISTICS. Finally, in the presence of the appropriate levels of predisposing and enabling characteristics, the individual (or those responsible for the individual) must perceive some need (such as illness or its perceived threat) for using health services. In other words, need is the basic and direct stimulus for the use of health services when the appropriate levels of predisposing and enabling characteristics exist. Need may be broken into two categories: perceived (or subjective assessments), or evaluated (clinical diagnoses).

THE RELATIONSHIP OF THE CHARACTERISTICS. The relationship among the predisposing, enabling, and need characteristics are shown in Figure 6-4. In this figure the sequence of the characteristics flows from left to right, and the categories within the predisposing, enabling, and need characteristics are listed in branch-form boxes beneath the more general characteristics. Thus, the first level of boxes represents the temporal sequence of events resulting in health services utilization, while the remaining levels of boxes represent the categories within the three major groups of characteristics.

EXPANDING THE ORIGINAL MODEL. The original model developed by Andersen (1968) has been empirically assessed in a number of regional and national studies with considerable success (see Andersen, 1968; Andersen and Newman, 1973; Wan and Soifer, 1974; Andersen et al., 1975, 1976; Berki and Kobashigawa, 1976; Wolinsky, 1976, 1978; Wolinsky and Coe, 1984; Wolinsky, Coe, Miller, Prendergast, Creel, and Chavez, 1983; Aday, Andersen, and Fleming, 1980;

Figure 6-4. *The Behavioral Model of Health Services Utilization.*

133

Measuring and
Modeling Health
Services
Utilization

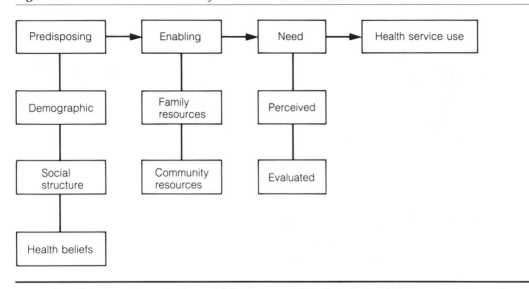

SOURCE: Ronald Andersen, Joana Kravits, and Odin Anderson. 1975. *Equity in Health Services.* Cambridge: Ballinger. Reprinted by permission of the author.

Aday, Fleming, and Andersen, 1984). Building on this success and on several suggestions emerging from the extensive application of the original model, Aday and Andersen (1974, 1975) have expanded the model into a full-fledged health systems model. They accomplished this by incorporating the contextual factors of "health policy" and the "characteristics of the delivery system," and by also adding "consumer satisfaction."

The resulting health systems model is reproduced in Figure 6-5, in which the predisposing, enabling, and need characteristics are now grouped under the general heading of "characteristics of the population at risk." The five major groups of variables are represented by the five blocks, with the nature of the groups of characteristics delineated within each block. The relationships of the groups of variables to one another are depicted by the arrows. Aday and Andersen believe that this health systems model accurately portrays the health care delivery system in the United States. Unfortunately, because the health systems model encompasses so many different variables at so many different levels of analysis, it is diffi-

cult to gather all the data necessary to test the complete model. Nonetheless, this health systems model is very useful because it provides both a conceptual and a methodological framework for the study of health services utilization. Indeed, it has become the standard framework used in health policy studies.

AN EMPIRICAL ASSESSMENT: ACCESS TO MEDICAL CARE IN 1982. Using data from a telephone survey of 4,800 families, Aday, Fleming, and Andersen (1984) applied the health systems framework to address four strategic health policy questions:

1) Have steady improvements in the access of traditionally disadvantaged groups such as minorities and the poor . . . continued into the 1980s? 2) Are there special access problems which traditional measures of access . . . fail to reveal? 3) Have the recession and high unemployment rates . . . accompanied by cutbacks in public health care programs and private health insurance coverage stymied or reversed the improving access trends of earlier periods? . . . 4) What are the implications for achieving or maintaining equity of access to medical care in the face of increasing constraints on the economy and the health care delivery system?

Central to these questions is the concept of equity. When applied to the use of health services, Aday and Andersen (1981) argue that an equitable situation is one in which only medical need determines health services utilization (in addition to some vestiges of a relationship with age and sex, as proxies of biological need). In contrast, inequity is said to exist when health services are distributed on the basis of race, income, or place of residence.

Aday and her colleagues (1984) found in their 1982 survey that 90 percent of the population have a regular source of medical care; this has not changed much since the early 1970s. Eighty-three percent of those surveyed reported spending 30 minutes or less in the doctor's waiting room before being seen; this actually represents a considerable reduction in average waiting times since the 1970s. About 10 percent of the sample was without any form of public or private health insurance; this figure is quite similar to that reported in the mid 1970s, suggesting that the poorer economic conditions of the late 1970s and early 1980s had not resulted in reducing this dimension of access to medical care. Thus, Aday and her

Figure 6-5. *The Health Systems Model.*

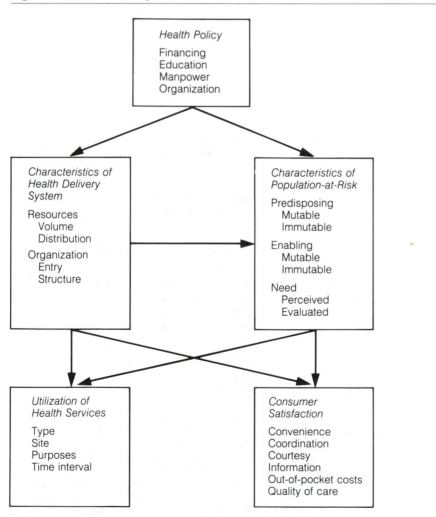

SOURCE: Lu Ann Aday and Ronald Andersen. 1975. *Access to Medical Care.* Ann Arbor: Health Administration Press. Reprinted by permission of the author.

colleagues (1984) were left to conclude that the answers to the four health care policy questions were favorable: "The country has come a long way toward achieving equity, measured in terms of services being primarily allocated on the basis of need. Further, the momentum toward equity did not appear to have been substantially diminished by 1982. Still, serious access problems remained for some groups, and these problems were exacerbated by the recession and constraints on federal and local spending for medical care."

Others, however, would disagree. Mechanic (1985) suggests that access to health care for the poor, the elderly, and other disadvantaged groups has been eroding during the mid 1980s. Moreover, he considers their access to be particularly vulnerable to further declines in the face of the current budgetary crisis. At the empirical level, Berki and his colleagues (Berki, Wyszewianski, Lichtenstein, Gimotty, Bowlyow, Papke, Smith, Crane, and Bromberg, 1985) have shown that the economic hardships of the early 1980s disenfranchised many of the un- and underemployed from traditional private and public health insurance programs. At the conceptual level, Wolinsky and his colleagues (Wolinsky, Coe, and Mosely, 1987) have argued that the case for equity is not established simply because medical need is the best determinant of the use of health services, even in the absence of any other significant predictors (such as race, income, or health insurance coverage). Noting that the health systems approach of Aday and her colleagues (1984) explains less than 25 percent of the variance in health services utilization, Wolinsky and his colleagues suggest that until more is known about why people use health services, it is premature to declare the health care delivery system to be equitable. Despite these concerns, the health systems approach remains the dominant model in the field.

An Ethnomedical Choice-Making Approach

Another very promising development in the construction of models of health services utilization may be found by looking to anthropology. Young (1981) presented and assessed the rudiments of a new way of looking at health services utilization. The choice-making model that he offered represents a refinement of the health belief model, extending its applicability to include the type of health services used. Young's approach is based on four considerations central to the individual's choice-making process, which he called gravity, knowledge of a home remedy, faith in the chosen remedy, and accessibility.

GRAVITY. The first component in Young's (1981) choice-making model is gravity, which is analogous to the perceived seriousness of the illness in the health belief model. Gravity, however, reflects more the perceived seriousness of the illness agreed on within the individual's particular reference group than the individual's personal perception. This evaluation represents the assumption that prior to the onset of any illness, there exists a classification of possible illnesses by their perceived gravity. When an individual is confronted with an illness, he or she symbolically turns to that classification, accepts the agreed-upon seriousness level, and uses that level of gravity in the choice-making process. This process is remarkably similar to Mead's (1934) notion of the "generalized other."

KNOWLEDGE OF A HOME REMEDY. The second component in Young's (1981) choice-making model is the ill individual's knowledge of an effective home remedy (lay referral system) for that particular illness. If an effective home remedy is available, the individual is more likely to choose that form of treatment than enter the professional referral system. If an effective home remedy is not known, however, the individual is more likely to turn to the professional referral system. In cases where known home remedies have not been particularly successful for this specific individual or his or her reference group in the past or when such a known home remedy is not successful in the present situation, the individual will then turn to the professional referral system.

FAITH. The third component in Young's (1981) choice-making model is faith, which is analogous to the perceived benefits of taking action in the health belief model. Faith reflects the individual's belief in the efficacy of folk remedies, as opposed to medical remedies, in treating a particular illness. In other words, faith refers to the individual's belief in the likelihood of cure associated with the different treatment choices. In most cases, medical treatment is perceived as being the most efficacious, while self-treatment is perceived as being the least efficacious (the middle ground is left to nonprofessional healers).

ACCESSIBILITY. The final component in Young's (1981) choice-making model is accessibility, which is analogous to the enabling characteristics in Andersen's (1968) behavioral model or to the perceived barriers to taking action in the health belief model. Accessibility reflects the costs and availability of the various types of health services. For example, in one community there may not be any professional health care providers, while in another community there may be several providers at various levels, such as doctors, nurses, and physicians' assistants. Thus, in making his or her treatment choices, the individual evaluates the costs associated with each treatment alternative.

THE CHOICE-MAKING MODEL. In developing and assessing the model, Young (1981) used data he collected in Pichataro, a small Mexican community. In Pichataro, there are several levels of both folk remedy and medical care providers. The choice-making model was constructed by predicting whether or not professional remedies are sought for a particular illness and, if so, what level of professional services are chosen. These possible choices are represented as the particular combinations of the four evaluated components in the model, which are presented in Table 6-1. In the upper panel of the table each column represents a possible combination of the four components for a given illness; in the lower panel each cell within the column represents a possible treatment choice for that illness. For example, column 1 indicates a nonserious (gravity level 1) illness for which a home remedy is known. There are four alternative treatment choices for this and every other column: (1) self-treatment, (2) a local, nonmedical curer, (3) a *practicante* (paraprofessional), or (4) a physician.

The numbers in the columns in the lower panel of the table represent the number of people in the Pichataro study choosing that specific treatment alternative; the boldface numbers represent the treatment selection

Table 6-1. *The ethnomedical treatment choice-making model.*

	Columns								
	1	2	3	4	5	6	7	8	9
Components									
Gravity*	1	1	1	2	2	2	3	3	3
Know home remedy	Yes	No	No	Yes	No				
Faith†		F	M	F	F	M	F	M	M
Accessibility								No	Yes
Choices									
Self-treatment	157			67		2			
Curer		4			8		8	2	
Practicante			5			20		4	2
Physician				1		7		2	11
Totals	157	4	5	68	8	29	8	8	13
Grand total = 300									

*Gravity was coded into three categories: (1) nonserious; (2) moderately serious; and, (3) grave.
†Faith was coded into two categories: (F) favors folk treatment; and (M) favors medical treatment.
SOURCE: Table 6.4, Decision Table for Initial Choice of Treatment. From James C. Young. 1981. *Medical Choice in a Mexican Village.* New Brunswick, NJ: Rutgers University Press. Copyright © 1981 by Rutgers, The State University of New Jersey.

predicted by Young's model. As we can easily see, of the 300 treatment choices analyzed, most fall in the predicted (boldface) patterns. In fact, 287 or 94.7 percent of the treatment choices were accurately predicted by the model. Thus, while it is still in the developmental stage and needs to be recast into Western medical terminology for more precise application to the United States, Young's treatment-choice model appears to be a promising development in our understanding of *why* people use *which* health services.

The Convergence of the Models

As you may already have noticed, there has been a considerable amount of convergence among the various models of health services utilization during the past decade. Advocates of the health belief model have placed increasing relevance on the role of the modifying (nonsocial psychological) factors. Health beliefs have become a more significant aspect of the behavioral model. Proponents of the general theory of help seeking have even begun to give greater credence to structural and organizational determinants of illness behavior. Until recently, however, the degree of overlap (or convergence) of the different models of health services utilization had not been empirically documented.

In 1979, Becker and his colleagues (see Cummings, Becker, and Maile, 1980; Becker and Maiman, 1983) contacted most of the living authors of the more popular models of health and illness behavior. These scholars were then asked to compare 109 variables that had been taken from their various models and to sort them into categories based on their similarities. Using smallest space analysis (a method of nonmetric multidimensional scaling), Becker and his colleagues found that nearly all of the 109 variables fell into six distinct categories: (1) perception of the illness, (2) threat of the disease, (3) knowledge of the disease, (4) social networks, (5) demographics, and (6) access to health care. This led Becker and Maiman (1983) to conclude that "the basic similarities identified among the variables contained in the different models examined are important to the advancement of research on understanding individual health-related behaviors. Clearly, the models are far from independent; despite differences in the labeling and defining of variables contained in the different frameworks, there is considerable overlap, *as judged by the model builders themselves.*" Despite the growing convergence of these models, it seems unlikely that a unified approach to the study of health services utilization will soon emerge. It seems reasonable to assume, however, that the traditional distinctions between the models will continue to blur, if not fade away entirely.

Trends in the Use of Health Services

Having reviewed the basic issues in the measurement and modeling of health services utilization, we now turn to an examination of the trends in the use of health services. To do this, we will examine the use of hospital, physician, and dentist services as they relate to the various social, family, and demographic characteristics of their users. We have chosen these particular health services because they represent not only the wide range of health services available, but the nondiscretionary, mixed, and discretionary use of health services by individuals. Discretionary services are those whose use is initiated by the individual; this is quite often the case with the use of dental services. The use of nondiscretionary services, such as the use of hospitals, is generally not initiated by the individual, but by the physician. Physician services are somewhat mixed, because the initial visit may be discretionary, but follow-up visits may be initiated or suggested by the physician (nondiscretionary). As we shall see, the determinants of the use of services vary by the discretionary or nondiscretionary nature of those services.

Hospital Utilization

The use of hospital services has changed drastically during the twentieth century, as the data in Table 6-2 demonstrate. Hospital admissions per 100 persons per year more than doubled between 1928 and 1982, going from 6 to 13 admissions per 100 persons per year. This appears to be directly related to two major factors: the growth in the number of hospital beds available, and the increasingly technological nature of medicine, which is best practiced by physicians in a well-equipped, modern hospital. The combined effect of these two factors has led to the postulation of Roemer's (1961) law, which states that as the supply of hospital beds increases, so does the demand for using that supply. While Roemer's law has been supported by sound research (see Harris, 1975), health services researchers have been unable to determine the causes of this phenomenon. The three most frequent explanations for the increase in hospital utilization are that (1) hospitals are motivated to provide and fill more beds by an organization version of the "keeping up with the Jones's" syndrome; (2) many health insurance plans only pay for expensive services

Table 6-2. *Number of hospital admissions per 100 persons per year by various characteristics, 1928–1982.*

Characteristic	Hospital admissions per 100 persons per year						
	1928–31	1952–53	1958–60	1963–64	1970	1974	1982
Sex							
Female	7	15	14	15	15	16	13
Male	4	9	9	10	11	12	12
Age							
0–5	3	8	7	8	9	10	9
6–16	4	8	7	6	6	6	5
17–24	5	15	15	17	17	14	11*
25–44	7	14	15	17	15	16	11*
45–64	7	12	12	15	15	18	18
65 and over	11	13	15	18	23	25	30
Family income							
Low	6	12	11	14	18	19	17
Middle	6	12	12	14	13	14	13
High	8	11	11	11	11	11	11
Race							
Nonwhite	—†	—	9	10	11	14	15
White	—	—	12	13	14	14	13
Education of head							
8 years or less	—	—	11	13	15	18	—
9–11 years	—	—		13	14	15	—
12 years	—	—	12		13	14	—
13 years or more	—	—		12	12	12	—
Residence							
SMSA	7	11	12	12	13	13	12
Non-SMSA, nonfarm	7	14	12	15	15	17	15
Non-SMSA, farm	5	12	10	11	12	14	15
Average	6	12	11	13	13	14	13

*These categories were collapsed in the 1982 data.
†Data unavailable.

SOURCE: Ronald Andersen and Odin Anderson. 1979. "Trends in the Use of Health Services." In Howard Freeman, Sol Levine, and Leo Reeder, eds., *Handbook of Medical Sociology,* 3rd ed. © 1979. Adapted by permission of Prentice-Hall, Inc. Englewood Cliffs, NJ: Prentice-Hall. Department of Health and Human Services. 1985. *Health, United States, 1984.* DHHS Publication No. 85–1232. Washington, DC: U.S. Government Printing Office.

when the individual has been hospitalized, motivating patients to seek hospitalization; and (3) physicians prefer to treat their patients in hospitals where they have access to the best technological equipment and support staff, and thus recommend hospitalization whenever hospital beds are available. Regardless of which explanation may be correct, the inescapable fact is that the use of hospital services has increased dramatically.

DEMOGRAPHIC CHARACTERISTICS. When the number of hospital admissions per 100 persons per year is examined within categories of various demographic characteristics, two interesting patterns emerge. First, although women had traditionally used many more hospital services than men, this no longer appears to be the case. Much of this difference was originally thought to be primarily biological in nature, reflecting women's use of obstetrical services. More recent evidence, however, suggests that most of this difference must have been of a more social nature, reflecting the differential socialization process. Men were supposed to be able to endure pain to a greater degree than women and, as a result, were less likely than women to be hospitalized for the same condition. The general narrowing of the gender gap in health services utilization during the 1970s and 1980s reflects the increasing social equality of the sexes, especially with regard to the increasing proportion of women in the labor force and in other fixed roles that had traditionally been dominated by men (see Marcus and Seeman, 1981a, 1981b; Marcus and Siegel, 1982; Marshall, Gregorio, and Walsh, 1982).

A second pattern that emerges from these data is that while age was once directly and positively related to hospital use—the older the individual, the greater the use of hospital services—age is now related to hospital use in a curvilinear manner, with high but stable use among the young, and high but ever-increasing use among the elderly. This curvilinear pattern reflects two factors: (1) the remarkable increase in access for the elderly to hospital services as a result of Medicaid and Medicare, and (2) the effect of

combatting the high infant mortality rate by increasing the use of hospital services among infants suffering from the birthing process and environmental conditions discussed in chapter 1.

SOCIAL STRUCTURAL CHARACTERISTICS. When hospital admission rates are examined by the social structural characteristics of education and race (as a proxy measure for ethnicity), an interesting pattern emerges. While higher levels of education and being white were associated with higher hospital admission rates earlier in this century, this is no longer the case. In fact, the relationship between education and hospital use had reversed itself by 1974, and racial differences in hospital admissions had reversed by 1982. Now, the lower the educational level, the higher the hospital admission rate. These changes are probably also the result of Medicaid and Medicare, which have greatly increased the access to health services of the poor and the elderly, a significant portion of whom are also nonwhite and poorly educated. Therefore, the change in the relationship between race, education, and hospital admissions may be a reflection of the parity seeking effects of Medicare and Medicaid.

FAMILY RESOURCE CHARACTERISTICS. When hospital admission rates are examined within categories of family income, a pattern similar to that of the social structural characteristics emerges. Family income used to be positively related to hospital admission rates; since the 1960s, however, it has become negatively related. Thus, it would appear that Medicare and Medicaid may also have eliminated family resource barriers to needed services. Indeed, it appears that Medicaid and Medicare are enabling families with low incomes to use those additional services necessary to overcome the greater illness levels that result from the vicious downward cycle associated with their disadvantaged socioeconomic status (as discussed in chapter 1).

The change in the relationship of place of residence to hospital admissions rates appears to reflect the increased access to hospital services among those living outside of major urban areas. The major factor behind this change was the Hill-Burton Hospital Construction Act of 1946. Its initial goal was to support the construction of hospitals in small towns and rural areas; its subsequent goal was to modernize hospital facilities serving inner-city urban areas. These data suggest that the Hill-Burton Program was quite successful in achieving its initial goal.

Physician Utilization

The use of physician services has increased during the twentieth century in a manner paralleling hospital use. In fact, the data in Table 6-3 show physician visits per person per year have nearly doubled, going from 2.6 in 1930 to 4.6 in 1982. This dramatic increase in the use of physician services may be linked to two major factors: the continued increase in the number of

Table 6-3. *Number of physician visits per person per year by various characteristics, 1928–1982.*

Characteristic	Mean number of physician visits per person per year						
	1928–31	1952–53	1958–59	1963–64	1970	1974	1982
Sex							
Female	3.1	5.1	5.3	5.1	5.1	5.6	5.1
Male	2.0	3.3	4.2	4.0	4.1	4.3	4.1
Age							
0–5	1.4	3.9	5.6	5.1	5.9	6.3	6.4
6–16	1.6	2.7	3.5	3.0	2.9	3.2	3.0
17–24	2.4	3.8	4.0	4.3	4.6	4.5	4.2*
25–44	3.2	4.3	4.7	4.5	4.6	5.0	4.2*
45–64	2.9	4.8	5.1	5.0	5.2	5.0	5.1
65 and over	4.9	5.7	6.7	6.7	6.3	6.7	6.3
Family income							
Low	2.2	3.7	4.4	4.3	5.2	5.3	5.3
Middle	2.5	3.8	4.6	4.5	4.4	4.8	4.5
High	4.3	6.5	5.5	5.1	4.9	4.9	4.4
Race							
Nonwhite	—†	—	3.2	3.3	3.8	4.4	4.7
White	—	—	4.9	4.7	4.8	5.0	4.6
Education of head							
8 years or less	—	—	4.2	4.2	4.4	4.8	—
9–11 years	—	—	4.6	4.4	4.4	4.6	—
12 years	—	—	6.1	5.4	4.6	4.8	—
13 years or more					5.1	5.4	—
Residence							
SMSA	3.5	4.4	5.0	4.6	4.8	5.2	4.7
Non-SMSA, nonfarm	2.7	4.3	4.6	4.4	4.5	4.5	4.4*
Non-SMSA, farm	1.9	3.7	3.6	3.6	3.3	4.1	4.4*
Average	2.6	4.2	4.7	4.5	4.6	4.9	4.6

*These categories were collapsed in the 1982 data.
†Data unavailable.
SOURCE: Ronald Andersen and Odin Anderson. 1979. "Trends in the Use of Health Services." In Howard Freeman, Sol Levine, and Leo Reeder, eds., *Handbook of Medical Sociology*, 3rd ed. © 1979. Adapted by permission of Prentice-Hall, Inc. Englewood Cliffs, NJ: Prentice-Hall. Department of Health and Human Services. 1985. *Health, United States, 1984.* DHHS Publication No. 85–1232. Washington, DC: U.S. Government Printing Office.

physicians available and the growing tendency of individuals to consult a physician for less serious conditions that in the past might not have warranted a visit to the doctor. In other words, as we are increasing the number of physicians per capita, we are also decreasing the severity level at which point we consult a physician. Thus, the number of physician visits per person per year has increased dramatically.

DEMOGRAPHIC CHARACTERISTICS. When the number of physician visits per person per year is examined within sex and age categories, the same patterns emerge that emerged for hospital admissions. Females have significantly higher levels of physician use than males, averaging one more visit per year. This difference, however, has been on the decline during the 1970s and 1980s. This is consistent with the general narrowing of gender gap socialization differences indicated earlier (see Marcus and Seeman, 1981a, 1981b; Marcus and Siegel, 1982). The relationship of age to physician utilization is much more pronounced than it was with hospital utilization. In 1928 age was positively associated with physician utilization, while by 1982 the relationship had become J-shaped, with high utilization by the young interrupting the remaining positive relationship. As with hospital utilization, the marked increase in physician utilization among the young probably represents the concerted effort to lower the high infant mortality rate by increasing neonatal, pediatric, and adolescent physician care. It may also reflect the general increase in the use of physicians for relatively minor illnesses for children.

SOCIAL STRUCTURAL CHARACTERISTICS. The patterns that emerged when hospital admissions were examined within categories of education and race appear to be reproduced for physician utilization. Although whites traditionally had used more health services than nonwhites, their utilization rates had become nearly identical by 1982. Indeed, nonwhites averaged one tenth of a physician visit more per year than whites. The better educated, however, continue to use more physician services than those with poorer educational levels. Yet this difference is also decreasing. Nonetheless, what may be inferred from these data (and from the hospital admission data) is that the more discretionary the health service is, the more important are the social structural characteristics as determinants of utilization. Use of the more discretionary health services appears to be a reflection of the general lifestyle of the individual in the social structure. People who are higher up in the social structure have a greater opportunity to exhibit a more discretionary lifestyle than those who are further down in the social structure.

FAMILY RESOURCE CHARACTERISTICS. When physician utilization is examined across a variety of family resource categories, a pattern similar to that of the social structural characteristics emerges. People living in major cities continue to have higher levels of physician utilization than those living outside such urbanized areas, although the gap is narrowing (see Rushing, 1975). This gap reflects the greater access by urban individuals to physicians. Family income, on the other hand, reveals a turnabout over time, just as it did with hospital admission rates. In 1930 income was positively related to physician utilization, but by 1982 family income was slightly negatively related to physician utilization. This reflects the access equalization effect of Medicaid and Medicare. As was the case when hospital admission rates were examined, the physician utilization data suggest that the greater access provided by Medicaid and Medicare has enabled the socioeconomically disadvantaged to use those additional physician services necessary to attempt overcoming their greater illness level (resulting from the cycle rooted in their disadvantaged socioeconomic status). If this is in fact the case, the utilization of physician services across family income levels should stabilize, once health status levels across family income levels have also stabilized.

Dentist Utilization

Like hospital and physician utilization, dentist utilization has also increased markedly during this century. In fact, the data in Table 6-4 show that the number of individuals seeing a dentist during a given year more than doubled from 21 per 100 in 1928 to 50 per 100 in 1982. This marked increase in dentist utilization probably reflects the impact of two factors: the increasing number of dentists per 1,000 persons, and the increasing emphasis in our society on physical appearance and resultant self-image, including such things as the Christie Brinkley smile. As a result of these factors, more of us are going to the dentist every year, resulting in a considerable increase in the use of discretionary health services.

DEMOGRAPHIC CHARACTERISTICS. When the numbers of those visiting a dentist in a given year are examined within age and sex categories, the results are quite interesting.

Table 6-4. *Percent seeing a dentist within one year by various characteristics, 1928–1982.*

Characteristic	Percent seeing a dentist within one year						
	1928–31	1952–53	1957–59	1963	1970	1974	1982
Sex							
Female	26	36	38	40	48	51	52
Male	17	31	35	36	46	48	48
Age							
0–5	12	10	14	12	17	21	25
6–16	23	44	48	47	61	63	65
17–24	27	44	49	46	56	57	54*
25–44	24	42	44	44	52	55	54*
45–64	20	32	32	38	44	47	50
65 and over		13	16	19	26	29	35
Family income							
Low	10	17	19	21	29	35	37
Middle	20	33	36	36	47	48	46
High	46	56	54	58	68	64	64
Race							
Nonwhite	—†	—	17	20	30	35	36
White	—	—	39	43	49	51	52
Education of head							
8 years or less	—	—	24	25	29	31	—
9–11 years	—	—	40	35	39	41	—
12 years	—	—		48	52	52	—
13 years or more	—	—	57	55	65	65	—
Residence							
SMSA	34	—	39	42	49	52	52
Non-SMSA, nonfarm	23	—	36	37	42	44	46*
Non-SMSA, farm	12	—	27	27	43	46	46*
Average	21	34	37	38	47	49	50

*These categories were collapsed in the 1982 data.
†Data unavailable.
SOURCE: Ronald Andersen and Odin Anderson. 1979. "Trends in the Use of Health Services." In Howard Freeman, Sol Levine, and Leo Reeder, eds., *Handbook of Medical Sociology,* 3rd ed. © 1979. Adapted by permission of Prentice-Hall, Inc. Englewood Cliffs, NJ: Prentice-Hall. Department of Health and Human Services. 1985. *Health, United States, 1984.* DHHS Publication No. 85–1232. Washington, DC: U.S. Government Printing Office.

At one time women used dental services more often than men. This gender gap has gradually narrowed to a point where the difference is barely perceptible. This equalization of the use of dentist's services reflects the increasing emphasis on the pleasing appearance of males as well as females in our society. Examining age categories indicates that dentist utilization has remained the highest among the 6-to-24-year-old group. Physical appearance for this age group may be most salient because of dating. It is important to note also that for this age group dental checkups may be a prerequisite to mandatory school enrollment. Furthermore, it is during this stage of life that an individual's permanent teeth emerge and most repairs to them are made.

SOCIAL STRUCTURAL CHARACTERISTICS. As might be anticipated, among the more discretionary health services, such as dental care, the social structural characteristics are strong determinants of utilization. In fact, the data in Table 6-4 show a consistently strong and positive relationship between the number seeing a dentist and both the level of education and the racial status of the individual. Thus, just as we suspected from examining physician utilization, the more discretionary the health service, the more important the social structural characteristics as determinants of utilization.

FAMILY RESOURCE CHARACTERISTICS. The data in Table 6-4 show that for both family income and place of residence, there is a positive relationship with dentist utilization, and that this relationship has continued over the years. Thus, for this discretionary health service, utilization is also positively related to the level of family resources. Coupled with data on social structural characteristics, this suggests that for the use of discretionary health services, equitable policies such as Medicaid and Medicare have not yet resulted in utilization parity. This failure to achieve parity appears to be linked to the affinity between discretionary health services use and social lifestyle, which seems to be unaffected by merely eliminating *economic* barriers to utilization. It may

also be linked to the fact that most parity-oriented programs either do not include any, or include only minimal, dental coverage. Thus, the economic barriers to dental utilization by and large remain in place.

Summary

In this chapter we have discussed the seeking and use of health services. The first section reviewed two of the major theories of illness behavior. While emphasizing that illness behavior was a coping response to the situation, Mechanic (1978) identified ten major factors involved in illness behavior: the recognition of signs and symptoms, the perceived seriousness of the symptoms, the extent of disruption caused by the symptoms, the frequency and persistence of the symptoms, the tolerance of the individual, the medical knowledge of the individual, basic needs that lead to the denial of the illness, competing needs, competing interpretations, and the availability of treatment resources. Suchman (1965a) identified five stages of the illness behavior process: (1) the symptom experience stage, (2) the assumption of the sick role stage, (3) the medical care contact stage, (4) the dependent-patient stage, and (5) the recovery or rehabilitative stage. Both Mechanic's and Suchman's models emphasize the importance of the individual's perception and definition of the situation; they also build upon Parsons's (1951) original conception of the sick role.

The second section of this chapter dealt with measuring and modeling health services. We learned that when measuring the use of personal health services, it is important that our indicators reflect the three dimensions of health services: the type of health service used, the purpose for which the health service was used, and the unit of analysis with which the health service was measured. Next, we reviewed the seven major health services utilization models: (1) demographic models; (2) social structural models; (3) social psychological models; (4) family resource models; (5) community resource models; (6) organizational models; and (7) health systems models. We then examined the health belief model (emphasizing perceived susceptibility, perceived seriousness, perceived benefits-less-barriers, and cues to action), the behavioral model (emphasizing the predisposing, enabling, and need characteristics of the individual), and an ethnomedical choice-making approach (emphasizing perceived seriousness, knowledge of a home remedy, perceived benefits, and accessibility) in greater detail.

In the final section of this chapter we examined trends in the use of health services for the United States during the twentieth century. Hospital admission rates, the num-ber of physician visits, and the number of persons seeing a dentist between 1928 and 1982 have doubled. Examining these utilization rates across categories of demographic, social structural, and family resource characteristics revealed two interesting patterns. First, the more discretionary the health service, the more important the social structural and family resource characteristics as determinants of utilization. Second, the less discretionary the health service, the more likely that equitable policy programs such as Medicaid and Medicare have accomplished their goals of creating parity in the access to health services.

7. The Patient-Practitioner Relationship

I N CHAPTER 4 we reviewed Parsons's (1951) innovative sociocultural approach to understanding health-related behavior and learned that it had two major components: the sick role concept and the patient-practitioner relationship. These components represent the beginning and end points in the health related behavior cycle. An individual first perceives the onset of an illness and adopts the sick role. Next, the ill individual decides whether or not to seek and to use health services. Finally, the ill individual enters into a social relationship with the health practitioner, which terminates upon the restoration of his or her health. The first link in this process, the sick role, was discussed in chapter 5. In chapter 6 we discussed the second link, the seeking and using of health services. In this chapter we will review the patient-practitioner relationship, the final link in the chain of health-related behavior.

The present chapter is divided into three sections. In the first we will review the Parsonian formulation of the patient-practitioner relationship. This includes (1) the asymmetrical nature of the relationship; (2) the four major components of the relationship; (3) the basic criticisms of the Parsonian formulation; and (4) Parsons's response to his critics. In the second section we will review two more conceptual extensions of the Parsonian model: the Szasz-Hollender (Szasz and Hollender, 1956) reformulation of the patient-practitioner relationship and the Hayes-Bautista (1976a, 1976b) model of the treatment modification process. In the third section we will focus on four more recent empirical studies of the patient-practitioner relationship: Stewart and Buck's (1977) analysis of physicians' knowledge of and response to their patients' problems; Haug and Lavin's (1983) study of challenges to physicians' authority; West's (1984) examination of patient-practitioner interaction patterns; and Coe's (1987; Coe and Prendergast, 1985; Coe, Prendergast, and Psathas, 1984) assessment of coalition formation when more than the doctor and patient are involved. We will conclude the chapter with a review of the current state of the art of research on the patient-practitioner relationship.

The Parsonian Formulation

According to Parsons (1951), the patient-practitioner relationship is a patterned component of our culture. In other words, just like the sick role concept, the patient-practitioner relationship is an institutionalized role-set in contemporary Western societies. As such, it provides both the primary parties (the patient and the practitioner) and the secondary parties (significant or concerned others) with a system of behavioral expectations. These behavioral expectations focus on the role of the practitioner and his or her interaction with the sick individual or patient.

The Role of the Practitioner

The role of the practitioner is a very straightforward one in the Parsonian (Parsons, 1951) framework. The practitioner is to function as the social control agent for society in situations where the deviant individual is not held responsible for his or her inability to perform normal task and role obligations. Thus, when the sick individual comes to the practitioner, the practitioner's obligation is to return the sick individual to a healthy and fully functioning state. The practitioner does this by calling on the tools of modern medicine. While applying these tools, the practitioner is supposed to maintain a professional attitude and demeanor, which includes four specific aspects: technical specificity, affective neutrality, universalism, and functional specificity.

TECHNICAL SPECIFICITY. The technical specificity aspect of the practitioner's role reflects the general professional credentials of achieved status and autonomy. These credentials (described in detail in chapter 9) are derived from the extensive technical training and established competence that qualify the practitioner as society's legitimate social control agent. Technical specificity, however, goes beyond this formal training. It also reflects the symbolic portrayal of the practitioner as the premier representative of the most important cultural value—health. As the symbolic representative of health, the practitioner's technical competency and prestige are immeasurably enhanced. This enhancement is typified by the awe and reverence in which most practitioners have traditionally been held by the public.

AFFECTIVE NEUTRALITY. The affective neutrality aspect of the practitioner's role implies social distancing. This enables the practitioner to prevent subjectivity from entering into the objective treatment process. Parsons (1951) argued that it was necessary for the practitioner to avoid becoming a copartner in the treatment of the patient. If the practitioner becomes emotionally too close to the patient, he or she might begin, knowingly or not, to allow that emotional closeness to influence or override the objective and technical considerations of medical treatment. As Wilson and Bloom (1972) suggest, the practitioner *should exhibit sympathy but not empathy* with the patient, understanding the patient's feelings but not feeling them. The importance of affective neutrality is most easily seen in dealing with psychiatric illness, especially when a female patient is under the care of a male practitioner. In such cases, the emotional involvement of the practitioner with the patient not only destroys the objective treatment of the patient, it may also aggravate existing—or create new—psychiatric disorders.

UNIVERSALISM. The universalism aspect reflects the fact that the professional practitioner is obligated to treat all patients alike, regardless of their social characteristics. In other words, the practitioner should consider all patients as equals, to be given the same quality of treatment and care that their particular illness requires. While the universalistic treatment of patients is a splendid philosophical goal, it is not easily accomplished. Like the rest of us, practitioners perceive and define the situations of individuals differently, based on the diffuse and extraneous characteristics of the individual. As a result, a patient's socioeconomic, ethnic, or marital status may affect the practitioner's demeanor, diagnosis, and treatment. For example, imagine that two women, one an unmarried black whose visit will be paid for by Medicaid and the other a married white who will pay cash for her visit, are treated by the same gynecologist for the same pregnancy-related problem. According to the universalism aspect of the practitioner's role, both women should receive the same (universal) treatment. It is more likely, however, that they will receive different treatment.

FUNCTIONAL SPECIFICITY. The functional specificity aspect is designed to limit the practitioner's behavioral arena to strictly medical matters. It places restrictions upon the social control agent and prohibits the practitioner from expanding his or her control over medical matters to include control over other matters. The functional specificity limitation is based on the fact that the technical expertise and competence of the practitioner is in medicine, not in social, religious, or psychological matters. Therefore, the power stemming from the medical professional's special status must be restricted so that it is used only in medical matters. If this restriction is not maintained, two complications may result. First, the patient might not receive the best possible nonmedical care. Second, the patient might be open to exploitation by the practitioner. The problem with the functional specificity aspect of the practitioner's role is knowing where the medical domain begins and where it ends. As we shall see in subsequent chapters, the medical domain is constantly growing; it is encroaching upon the social and psychological domains by redefining or medicalizing psychosocial behavior.

WHY ARE THESE EXPECTATIONS NECESSARY? In order for the practitioner to effectively and efficiently treat the patient, the patient must provide full and unlimited access to his or her body and soul. This includes not only the routine physical examination and presentation of symptoms but the innermost worries and fears of the patient as well. Such complete access is rarely voluntarily provided to anyone, including one's own significant others. For example, consider the fear of having contracted a sexually transmitted disease in an extramarital affair. Why, then, do patients provide such access to practitioners? This question is especially salient in situations where the patient has never met the practitioner before, as is the case when one moves to a new town and must select a new doctor (see Wolinsky and Steiber, 1982, for a detailed discussion of the doctor-selection issue).

The answer is trust. This trust is based on the four aspects of the practitioner's role described above. Put simply, patients expect that practitioners will adhere to the expectations associated with their role. Those institutionalized expectations provide stability, predictability, and guidance to to the interaction between doctor and patient. They are designed to prevent practitioners from exploiting the vulnerability of patients who have bared their bodies and souls to them. This potential for exploitation exists on a variety of levels, including the emotional, sexual, social, and economic. The expectations associated with the practitioner's role are perhaps most typified in the notion of doctor-patient confidentiality, which has obtained not only moral but legal status as well. In essence, patients trust doctors because of the expectations they have for the role doctors are supposed to play. This institutionalized trust is personally enhanced in those situations where an ongoing patient-practitioner relationship exists.

The Asymmetry of the Patient-Practitioner Relationship

When the patient and the practitioner meet, the resulting dyadic relationship, although mutually expected, is not an egalitarian one. The practitioner has a considerable advantage in the distribution of authority within the dyad. According to Parsons (1951), this asymmetrical relationship is necessary in any therapeutic relationship because the practitioner is charged with restoring the patient to a normal level of functioning. To accomplish this restoration, the practitioner must have control over the interaction with the patient, ensuring that the patient will comply with the prescribed regimen. If patient compliance is not ensured, then the ability of the practitioner to return the patient to a normal functioning state is undermined. In other words, although both parties know each other's role and task obligations and are mutually committed to the end result, they both expect the practitioner to wield more power and authority throughout the interaction. The practitioner's advantageous position rests on three interrelated leverage points intertwined in the patient-practitioner relationship: the professional prestige of the practitioner, the situational authority of the practitioner, and the situational dependency of the patient.

PROFESSIONAL PRESTIGE. The practitioner's professional prestige stems from two factors: the technical skills inherent in the trained practitioner, and the practitioner's certification by society as an official healer and minister of the ultimate value of health. As a result of this professional prestige, the practitioner enjoys a nonpareil social position in modern society. Therefore, in almost any social situation the practitioner commands more respect and prestige than does the patient. As a result, in everyday and *especially* in health-related interactions, the practitioner commands and receives deference from others. This facilitates the practitioner's domination of interpersonal encounters.

SITUATIONAL AUTHORITY. The situational authority of the practitioner reflects the seller's market nature of the patient-practitioner relationship. It is the practitioner who has the technical qualifications (or goods and services) to sell to the patient, who is the buyer-consumer. Therefore, the patient who wants or needs health care must come to the practitioner, who is the societally certified health care provider. In other words, the practitioner's power is rooted in his or her monopoly over what the patient wants or needs. To get what he or she needs, the patient must meet the terms of the practitioner. The reason for this is the fact that the demand for health care has traditionally exceeded its supply, making it a true seller's market.

SITUATIONAL DEPENDENCY. The situational dependency of the patient represents the obverse of the situational authority of the practitioner. The patient recognizes the need for health care and recognizes that this health care cannot be self-provided. As a result, the patient must seek health care from the certified health care provider (the practitioner). To receive the desired health care, the patient must meet the conditions for treatment established by the practitioner. In other words, the patient must establish a dependency relationship with the practitioner in order to receive health care.

Characteristics of the Patient-Practitioner Relationship

There is a more general pattern of behavior that reflects the internalization by patients and practitioners of their culturally prescribed roles and tasks. According to Parsons (1951), the patterned behavior of the patient-practitioner relationship is analogous to the child-parent relationship. In both cases there are three similar themes. First, both situations involve the social control of one individual (the child or patient) by another (the parent or practitioner) who is recognized by society as the legitimate social control agent. Second, both the child-parent and patient-practitioner relationships are heavily laden with emotion, although the parent or the practitioner must demonstrate a certain degree of affective neutrality in order to maintain the status distinctions. Third, both relationships focus attention on goals that include a time when the child or patient becomes a fully functioning member of society (i.e., a healthy adult). Drawing heavily on the psychoanalytic therapy model, Parsons and Fox (1952) identified four major features contained in both the patient-practitioner and child-parent relationships: support, permissiveness, manipulation of reward, and denial of reciprocity.

SUPPORT. By accepting the obligation to provide health care to the patient, the practitioner becomes a shoulder for the patient to lean on during the illness period. This includes making one's self available to the patient and trying to provide that dependent patient with the needed health care. The support offered by the practitioner, of course, is temporary and dependent on the patient's active efforts to get well and leave the sick role. If the patient does not live up to the necessary and expected sick role obligations, then the practitioner counters by withdrawing support and legitimization of the patient's sick role status; such actions redefine the patient as a socially undesirable malingerer.

PERMISSIVENESS. In the patient-practitioner relationship the patient is allowed to behave in a manner not normally permitted. Such aberrant behavior includes both the expression of feelings held and certain actions taken by the patient. This behavior is tolerated because the patient is not held responsible for his or her illness as long as he or she continues to fulfill and pursue the sick role and its obligation to want to and to try to get well. Thus, like the child who is given more leeway in his or her everyday behavior because he or she is not yet a completely socialized adult, the patient is permitted to exhibit aberrant behavior without suffering the normal societal response.

MANIPULATION OF REWARD. To provide additional leverage in obtaining compliance, the practitioner has the ability to set up and manipulate a reward structure. By controlling certain rewards that are highly valued by the patient (including approval of the sick role itself), the practitioner's authority and the patient's dependency are enhanced. For example, the practitioner can manipulate the duration of unpleasant aspects of the patient's life—such as the length of the hospital stay, the number of hypodermic injections, or other painful tests and treatments—in order to gain greater compliance to the prescribed regimen. Thus, if the patient tries very hard to get well, the practitioner can reward the patient by reducing the number of painful things, such as injections, or increasing the number of pleasant things, such as visits from family members. Parents have similarly been known to give children rewards when they earn good grades (a sign of growing up right) and to punish them when they earn bad grades (a sign of growing up wrong).

DENIAL OF RECIPROCITY. The fourth parallel between the child-parent and the patient-practitioner relationships is the denial of reciprocity. Despite extending support to the patient and being more permissive of normally aberrant behavior, the practitioner maintains the asymmetry of the relationship by keeping a discrete distance in interpersonal response. In other words, while accepting access to the patient's true feelings, the practitioner does not reciprocate by allowing the patient access to his or her own true feelings. Thus, even when confronted with a strong emotional expression by the patient, the practitioner remains sympathetic but not empathetic. As a result, the practitioner maintains the advantage necessary to effect the successful therapeutic treatment of the patient.

To summarize, the patient-practitioner relationship represents the interactions of two social actors, one playing the role of the patient and the other playing the role of the practitioner. Each actor may anticipate the behavior of the other based on internalized expectations and obligations associated with both social roles. As a result, the behavior they exhibit in the patient-practitioner encounter generally conforms to the patterned relationships described by Parsons (1951) and expanded by Parsons and Fox (1952). When taken together, the sick or patient role, the practitioner's role, and the patient-practitioner relationship constitute the general approach used by sociologists of health to explain health and illness behavior in Western societies.

Criticisms of Parsons's Patient-Practitioner Relationship

At this point you might ask what, if anything, is wrong with the Parsonian (Parsons, 1951) model of the patient-practitioner relationship? It seems to be intuitively convincing, and it provides a set of expectations that can be used to predict the pattern of social interaction between patient and practitioner. Nonetheless, there are three traditional sets of reservations about the Parsonian patient-practitioner relationship (see Levine and Kozloff, 1978): its applicability to all illnesses, the effect of the characteristics of the patient, and the effects of the characteristics of the practitioner. In addition to these traditional reservations, we will discuss three more that are beginning to emerge in the 1980s as a result of changes in the health care delivery system.

THE NATURE OF THE ILLNESS. The first set of reservations about the patient-practitioner relationship centers around the nature of the illness responsible for the patient-practitioner encounter. There seem to be two conflicts here. First, as discussed in chapter 5, there is the difference in the applicability of the patient-practitioner relationship for individuals with acute illness and those with chronic illness. In the acute illness situation the patient-practitioner relationship works very well. The patient expects to recover and depends on the practitioner for that recovery. In the chronic illness situation, however, the patient does not realistically hope to recover. This alters the relationship in that the patient no longer depends on the practitioner for recovery. The chronic patient depends on the practitioner only for assistance with the continuing management of the chronic illness. Second, there is the difference in the applicability of the patient-practitioner relationship for individuals seeking therapeutic care and those seeking preventive care. For individuals seeking therapeutic care the patient-practitioner relationship applies because the social control of the practitioner over the sick individual is maintained. When individuals seek pre-

ventive care, however, the practitioner's responsibility for social control vanishes because the individual is not sick. In the preventive care situation the practitioner must rely only on persuasion to effect patient compliance.

THE CHARACTERISTICS OF THE PATIENT. The second set of reservations about the patient-practitioner relationship focuses on the characteristics of the patient. There are two major concerns here: class barriers to communication, and cultural barriers to communication. The social class position of patients is reflected in their level of general knowledge and more critically in their level of specific knowledge of medicine, medical techniques, and medical vocabulary. When the patient and the practitioner come together, there is a certain amount of communication that takes place. The patient relays signs and symptoms to the practitioner; the practitioner relays probing questions, a diagnosis, and treatment to the patient. If the communication is to be effective, there must be a shared, basic level of knowledge, vocabulary, and techniques. Because the practitioner (regardless of social class origin) is trained by the upper social classes, he or she tends to adopt their communication skills. Accordingly, the lower the social class of the patient, the larger the communications gap and the less effective the patient-practitioner relationship.

Similarly, there may also be cultural barriers that limit the effectiveness of the patient-practitioner relationship. For example, in many of the newly developing countries to which physicians and other medical aid are sent, and from which new waves of immigrants are arriving, it is taboo for women to be examined by male physicians. As a result, when male physicians see women from these countries, the traditional patient-practitioner relationship does not work very well. Another example would be the "hot and cold" theory of illness dominant in many Hispanic-speaking cultures. In these cultures the people believe that illness is the result of an imbalance between the hot and cold forces in the body. Therefore, when an individual suffers from a too hot condition, the treatment includes cold things, and vice versa (see Young, 1981). Such contradictions to the scientific model of medicine, which also occur to a lesser degree in the United States, limit the applicability of the patient-practitioner relationship.

THE CHARACTERISTICS OF THE PRACTITIONER. The third set of reservations about the patient-practitioner relationship reflects the variety of practitioners available and active in health care. As we have already seen, there has been a marked departure from the traditional one-on-one patient-practitioner encounter for which the Parsonian (Parsons, 1951) scheme was originally constructed. In addition, there are more and more practitioners available, perhaps including a surplus of physicians. Taken together, these factors decrease the dependency of patients on any one practitioner and increase the incidence of provider-shopping among patients. Moreover, there is a growing number of nonphysician practitioners, such as nurse practitioners, physicians' assistants, and so forth, from whom the patient may receive health care. Because of the changes in the social setting, the increase in the physician supply, and the greater availability of alternative providers, the asymmetry of the traditional patient-practitioner relationship has decreased, placing in question the continued applicability of the relationship.

EMERGING CRITICISMS. In addition to the three traditional criticisms discussed above, three more have begun to emerge during the 1980s. The first of these focuses on the expansion of the practitioner's side of the dyad. As we move into the 1990s, the provision of health care is becoming more and more of a team effort. Although the physician is still the captain of the team, he or she is becoming more removed from initial patient contact and frequently assumes the role of a collaborative consultant to the growing number of paraprofessionals. Instead of having only one practitioner to deal with in the encounter, the patient often meets several, many of whom are not physi-

cians. As a result, the continuity of care and the asymmetrical power distribution are decreasing, because the paraprofessional does not hold the same special social position as the physician.

Just as the practitioner side of the dyad is increasing, so too is the patient's side. We are seeing an increase in the involvement of the patient's family in the treatment process and an increase of familial efforts concerning the patient's life space and health care. Thus, the health care practitioner must deal with the family unit, which carries collectively more influence and authority than the individual patient. As a result, the asymmetry of the power distribution in the patient-practitioner relationship continues to diminish, although it will not disappear completely.

The third emerging area of criticism concerns the expansion of our conception of health and illness beyond strictly physiological criteria. In chapter 4 we learned that the World Health Organization (1958) suggests that we consider three dimensions of health—the physiological, the social, and the psychological. Only when an individual is healthy along all three dimensions is he or she a truly healthy being. Because of our expanding definitions of health and illness, nonmedical practitioners are being brought into the patient-practitioner encounter in order to effect and maintain complete health. Thus, the power of the physician as the sole social control agent is being diminished as more and more other social control agents are brought into the relationship.

These three emerging criticisms suggest changes that need to be made in the traditional patient-practitioner interaction model. In the 1980s the situation is far more complex than the simple interaction of patient and practitioner described by Parsons in the 1950s. At the very least, the patient-practitioner relationship must now consider three additional dimensions: the involvement of the entire array of health care professionals, the involvement of the patient's family, and the expansion of health and illness to include the larger sociocultural matrix (consisting of the physiological, psychological, and social dimensions of health). Both the patient and the practitioner interact with all three of these dimensions. Indeed, they are subsets of these larger social systems, and their interactions must be viewed in that context.

Parsons's Response to His Critics

In responding to his critics, Parsons (1975) focused on the issue of the asymmetrical power relationship. His detractors had said that the advantaged position held by the practitioner permitted the degradation and exploitation of the patient. This conflicted with the nature of relationships in the competitive market and in voluntary associations. In responding to this charge, Parsons first reviewed the types of social structures warranting symmetrical equality. He then based his case on the therapeutic nature of the patient-practitioner relationship and how that therapeutic nature necessitated the advantaged position of the practitioner.

RELATIONSHIPS NECESSITATING SYMMETRICAL EQUALITY. According to Parsons (1975), there are three general types of social relationships in which a symmetrical distribution of power is necessary. The first is the competitive economic market. Market transactions are based on the assumption that rational social actors participate as long as their interaction remains economically interesting. In the absence of a symmetrical power distribution, it is difficult for individuals to consider market transactions economically interesting. The communications network is the second situation that necessitates the presumption of symmetry. Parsons defines the communications network as the transmission of information, which assumes equal access to the symbolic meanings attached to that information because communication cannot be made in its absence. Voluntary associations are the third type of situation that Parsons identifies as requiring symmetry among the participants. All members of voluntary associations are formally declared to be equals, and all are eligible for the rotating leadership roles, if any, within the association. The basic principle here—one person, one vote—is the essence of a symmetrical power distribution. According to Parsons, these are the only types of social structures that necessitate the assumption of a symmetrical power relationship.

THE NECESSITY OF ASYMMETRY IN THERAPEUTIC RELATIONSHIPS. Therapeutic relationships, in contrast, necessitate an asymmetrical relationship between patient and practitioner. The practitioner's task is to return the patient (or deviant individual) to his or her normal functioning state. To do this, the practitioner must have the leverage necessary to control and alter the patient's behavior. Because illness represents a major threat to the maintenance of society, the elimination of illness has been assigned a high priority. Therefore, society has institutionalized the necessity of the asymmetrical relationship by granting the practitioner the fiduciary responsibility of being *the* health care (social control) agent. Parsons (1975) argued that this fiduciary responsibility has been institutionalized as the central theme of the patient-practitioner relationship.

THE PRINCIPLES OF THE FIDUCIARY RELATIONSHIP. The fiduciary relationship is based on three principles: the presumption of the competence of the practitioner, the full-time nature of the practitioner's role, and the expectation that the patient will cooperate. Two of these principles, the presumption of the physician's competence (based on his or her moral and intellectual probity, technical skill, and trusteelike status) and the patient's expected cooperation, have already been discussed. The full-time nature of the practitioner's health-related occupation introduces a new dimension to the patient-practitioner relationship. Parsons (1975) points out that the health care practitioner is involved in caring for the sick (even if indirectly through teaching, research, or administration) day in and day out; this is his or her full-time job. In contrast, unless the patient is a "professional," being sick is a part-time, temporary job and usually does not replace all of that individual's normal roles. The patient is usually not absorbed in or excited by the sick role; he or she is merely content to play a passive and complacent rather than an active role. As a result, the fiduciary role has traditionally been granted virtually in default to the practitioner by the patient.

AN ANALOGOUS ASYMMETRICAL RELATIONSHIP. According to Parsons (1975), the necessity for the asymmetry of the patient-practitioner relationship can be clarified by presenting the analogous situation of the professor-student relationship. The student is considered to be ignorant (or at least inferior) in terms of knowledge. Because ignorance compared to knowledge is as undesirable as illness compared to health, society desires the elimination of ignorance. To accomplish this a social control agent is selected and empowered to rid individuals of their ignorance. At the higher education level this social control agent is the professor, whose role is, in effect, the trustee of the cultural tradition. As such, the professor has the fiduciary responsibility of "healing" the ignorant. Of course, Parsons recognized that in some of the less advanced sciences, the additional expertise of professors compared to the knowledge of the laity is questionable. Nonetheless, he submits that the professor-student relationship is analogous to the patient-practitioner relationship; it is basically therapeutic and requires an asymmetrical distribution of power and authority in order for the intended therapy to be effected.

In sum, Parsons (1975) argued that any therapeutic relationship must be asymmetrical, favoring the practitioner if the therapy is to be successful. This asymmetry was to be anchored in the responsibility, competence, and occupational concern of the professional. Parsons, however, conceded that the exact formula for the distribution is not known and that it changes as new knowledge and social conditions emerge. In so conceding, Parsons accepted the minor criticisms of the patient-practitioner relationship as suggestions that resulted from the ongoing process of social change. At the same time he maintained that his conceptualization remained the most valid and may be generically applied to all patient-practitioner encounters.

Extending the Parsonian Formulation

While the Parsonian (Parsons, 1951) model of the patient-practitioner relationship has maintained its position as *the* framework for analyzing the social interaction between patients and practitioners, several proposals for extending it have emerged. Two of these proposals complement the Parsonian framework quite well, and we shall review them here. The first, the Szasz-Hollender model, is primarily a clarification of Parsons's original model, while the second, the Hayes-Bautista model, represents a more detailed description of the negotiations potentially involved in the patient-practitioner relationship.

The Szasz-Hollender Patient-Practitioner Models

Parsons's (1951) formulation of the patient-practitioner relationship emphasizes the social nature of illness and human interaction. It relegates the contribution of physiological symptoms to a minor role as the cue that stimulates the adoption of the sick role. Szasz and Hollender (1956), however, believe that the physiological symptoms are much too important to be relegated to such a minor role. In fact, they argue that the nature of the patient-practitioner relationship is directly related to the physiological symptoms that the patient brings to the encounter. In cases of serious symptoms an asymmetrical model like Parsons's might apply, but in cases of more minor symptoms a different type of model is necessary. Szasz and Hollender, both physicians themselves, specified three types of patient-practitioner relationships based on the severity of the symptoms: the activity-passivity model, the guidance-cooperation model, and the mutual participation model.

THE ACTIVITY-PASSIVITY MODEL. In the activity-passivity model the patient plays a passive role to the physician's active one. This model emerged from physicians' responses to the desperately ill. It is especially applicable to emergency cases where the patient is virtually helpless, such as those critical trauma cases where the patient has suffered severe injuries, excessive blood loss, or is comatose. In these situations the physician proceeds by giving the necessary treatment regardless of the patient's contribution or lack of contribution. Szasz and Hollender (1956) equate this situation with that occurring between the parent and the helpless infant. In essence, the activity-passivity model represents the unilateral action, power, and decision making of physicians working in desperate situations. Whether or not the patient contributes to the process is irrelevant.

THE GUIDANCE-COOPERATION MODEL. Most of the time that patients encounter physicians the situation is not as desperate as that depicted by the activity-passivity model. Usually the purpose for physician contact is the alleviation of some acute condition, perhaps an infectious condition such as influenza or measles. Although the patients in these situations are ill, they know what is going on and are capable of making judgments about their treatment process, especially when those judgments pertain to treatment compliance. Under these conditions patients seek out physicians because they can provide the needed care. Physicians guide the relationships by way of diagnosis, prognosis, and treatment, while patients cooperate by providing the information necessary (symptoms and medical history) for the physicians' guidance and complying with that guidance. In essence, the guidance-cooperation model represents the classic Parsonian (parent-child) model of the patient-practitioner relationship, although its scope is somewhat more limited by the presentation of the other two models.

THE MUTUAL PARTICIPATION MODEL. The third patient-practitioner model that Szasz and Hollender (1956) present is designed for use in the management of chronic illness. Here the patient plays an active role

with the periodic consultation of the physician. Thus, the physician "helps the patient to help himself." An excellent example of the mutual participation model is the case of the patient with diabetes mellitus. The treatment regimen prescribed by the physician, such as oral medication or insulin injections, is carried out by the patient on a day-to-day basis. This mode of the patient-practitioner relationship, however, places a considerable demand on the skill of the patient, limiting its applicability to mature, informed individuals. As such, the mutual participation model is analogous to the relationship of one adult to another, with one of them having the specialized knowledge needed by the other. Although Szasz and Hollender do not specifically mention it, the mutual participation model appears to apply also to situations in which preventive medicine is the reason behind the patient-practitioner encounter. In preventive care physicians help patients to help themselves, thereby investing in their own future. The management of a preventive health care regimen can be carried out by the patient in periodic consultation with the physician, as can the management of a chronic health care regimen.

THE UNDERLYING THEME. The common theme that underlies the three patient-practitioner models proposed by Szasz and Hollender (1956) is the adaptation or recalibration of the original Parsonian (1951) framework. That theme is based on the severity and manageability of the illness. In choosing to adapt the Parsonian framework to better fit a variety of situations, Szasz and Hollender have implicitly accepted his assumptions. As a result, their models are subject to the same criticisms, except that in their models the asymmetrical child-parent nature of the patient-practitioner relationship was subdivided into infant-parent, adolescent-parent, and adult-adult relationships. The purpose behind this reformulation was not to outdo Parsons's model but to make it more readily adaptable to different situations. As they put it, "it would be inaccurate and misleading to maintain that one model is better than another. It is rather a question of which model is more appropriate for (or works better in) a given situation." In essence, the Szasz-Hollender models represent a clarification and extension of the original Parsonian concept by taking into account the severity and manageability of the illness symptoms.

The Hayes-Bautista Model of Treatment Modification

In a somewhat similar vein, Hayes-Bautista (1976a, 1976b) has sought to clarify and extend our knowledge of the process by which the treatment regimen is followed or modified. His approach is grounded in the "negotiated order" tradition of Glaser and Strauss (1965, 1968) and is based on their theoretical sampling approach to "grounded theory" (Glaser and Strauss, 1967). Hayes-Bautista hoped to develop a theoretical model of the social process of modifying the treatment in the patient-practitioner relationship by culling commonalities from the recounted illness episodes of 200 Chicanos in the San Francisco Bay area.

Much like Freidson's (1970a) expansion of the sick role concept, Hayes-Bautista's (1976a, 1976b) elaboration of the patient-practitioner relationship is based on the perceptions of the patient and not on the objective reality of the situation. As such, the modification process is initiated only after the patient perceives that the treatment is inadequate, regardless of the perception of the practitioner. The perception of the treatment's inadequacy serves as the patient's cue for the need to modify the situation. According to Hayes-Bautista, there are two basic strategies open to the patient for doing this: convincing tactics, and countering tactics.

CONVINCING TACTICS. The purpose of convincing tactics is to bring to the practitioner's attention the fact that the patient perceives the treatment regimen to be inappropriate and desires some *other* treatment. The patient hopes that after doing this, the practitioner will modify the treatment regimen to more closely coincide with what he or she considers to be appropriate. Hayes-

Bautista (1976a) identified four convincing tactics along the continuum of the directness of the tactic. The most direct convincing tactic is the *demand*, in which the patient straightforwardly insists that a change be made in the treatment regimen. Usually the patient threatens to withdraw patronage from the practitioner if the changes are not made. A slightly less direct convincing tactic is the patient's *disclosure* that the prescribed treatment regimen has not been as successful as it should have been. The *suggestion* is a more tactful and even less direct tactic; here the patient attempts to modify the treatment regimen by suggesting additional treatments. Finally, the least direct convincing tactic available to the patient is the *leading question*. This is used to guide the practitioner's thoughts on the treatment regimen in the direction of the patient's perception of the treatment's inadequacy.

The initial selection of which of the four convincing tactics will be used depends on the patient's perception of the severity of the treatment's inappropriateness. The more direct tactics are chosen when the perceived inappropriateness is high, and the less direct tactics are chosen when the perceived inappropriateness is low. Once the initial selection has been made, the level of convincing tactics may be escalated if the patient perceives that the treatment has not been properly modified. Although not a steadfast rule, this escalation usually progresses through the sequence of convincing tactics. In sum, patients use the four convincing tactics to get practitioners to reorient their treatments to an acceptable regimen.

COUNTERING TACTICS. Countering tactics are employed by the patient who feels that the treatment regimen is inappropriate in that either *more* or *less* "things" should be done. Before employing countering tactics, the patient usually has perceived that the physician is unable or unwilling to change the treatment regimen. Although convincing tactics need not have been already employed, they are usually used as a prelude to countering tactics. The complete realm of convincing tactics, however, need not have been exhausted. As with the convincing tactics, there are four types of countering tactics. These are based on whether or not the patient perceives the treatment regimen is not strong enough or too strong. *Simple augmentation* is the countering tactic used when the patient perceives that the treatment is not strong enough and that this situation may be resolved by merely increasing the quantity of treatment prescribed by the physician (such as doubling the dosage of medication). *Additive augmentation* is the countering tactic used when the patient perceives the prescribed treatment as too weak and can be rectified by adding treatments in order to "fill in the gaps."

When the patient perceives that the prescribed treatment regimen is more than adequate, then he or she employs one of the diminishing countering tactics. If the overadequacy of the treatment may be corrected by merely reducing the intensity of the prescribed treatment (such as halving the dosage of medication), then the patient exhibits the tactic of *simple diminishment*. In contrast, if the overadequacy of the treatment results in undesirable side effects, the patient may exhibit *subtractive diminishment*. In this case the faulty aspect of the treatment is discontinued entirely or a milder alternative is substituted. The selection of the simple or complex forms of augmentation and diminishment depends on the perceived level of the inadequacy or overadequacy of the original treatment regimen. In essence, the patient turns to countering tactics on perceiving that convincing tactics do not work or that an acceptable modification of the treatment regimen can be obtained unilaterally.

PRACTITIONER TACTICS. Once the patient has embarked on a plan for modifying the treatment regimen, there are several tactics available to the practitioner. On the one hand, if the practitioner does not perceive that the patient has modified the treatment regimen, then he or she takes no action. In this situation the patient has unilaterally arranged a satisfactory modification. On the other hand, if the practitioner recognizes that the patient has attempted to modify the treatment regimen, he or she may rely on four

tactics. These tactics are somewhat similar to those employed by the patient, but they are used from the advantaged position of the practitioner.

The most devastating of these is the *overwhelming knowledge* tactic. In this case the practitioner cites his or her societally certified expertise as diagnostician and treatment prescriber. Somewhat similar in nature is the *medical threat*; here the practitioner warns the patient of the dire consequences for the patient's health of noncompliance with the treatment regimen. At a much less drastic level are the disclosure and personal tactics, which are usually preludes to treatment bargaining. The *disclosure* involves the practitioner's reassertion that the prescribed treatment is the right one, but that in this particular patient's case it may take a little longer than anticipated. The *personal tactic* constitutes an appeal for patient compliance based on personal acquaintance. If the practitioner perceives that the patient is still attempting to modify the treatment regimen, a bargaining or negotiated-order process takes place in which both parties modify their tactics in an attempt to produce a satisfactory outcome.

BARGAINING OUTCOMES. As you can well imagine, there are a number of possible outcomes from the bargaining process involved in modifying the treatment regimen. Hayes-Bautista (1976b) identifies four such outcomes by first dichotomizing and then cross-classifying patient and practitioner satisfaction with the modification process. One possibility is when both the patient and the practitioner are satisfied, resulting in their mutual desire to continue the patient-practitioner relationship. Another is when the patient is not satisfied but the practitioner is. This results in a considerable strain on the interaction and may cue the unilateral termination of the patient-practitioner relationship by the patient. A third possibility is when the patient is satisfied but the practitioner is not. This also results in a considerable strain on the interaction and may cue the unilateral termination of the patient-practitioner relationship by the physician. The final possibility is when neither the patient nor the practitioner is satisfied. These circumstances usually lead to a mutual desire to terminate the patient-practitioner relationship.

THE OVERALL BARGAINING PROCESS. While the above discussion clarifies the outcomes of the bargaining process, it does not delineate the bargaining process itself. Hayes-Bautista (1976a) suggests that the bargaining process is represented in Figure 7-1, which he claims provided "the unifying theoretical threads which would tie together the experiences of those who decide to modify the treatment in some aspect." The figure begins with the patient's perception that the prescribed treatment is inadequate. The patient may respond with uneasy compliance (convincing tactics) or noncompliance (countering tactics). The practitioner may (calling on countermanagement tactics) or may not perceive the patient's actions (resulting in unilateral modification). If the practitioner is perceptive, a bilateral redefinition of the situation may be negotiated. The outcomes of the definition of the situation involve the four possibilities discussed earlier: a mutual decision to continue the relationship, the patient's desire to terminate the relationship, the practitioner's desire to terminate the relationship, or a mutual desire to terminate the relationship.

LIMITATIONS OF THE HAYES-BAUTISTA MODEL. While the Hayes-Bautista (1976a, 1976b) model represents a considerable explication of the negotiated process of modifying treatment regimens, the model has some problems of its own. First, it is theoretical and has never been submitted to empirical testing beyond the limited sample of 200 urban Chicanos from which it was developed. As a result, the generalizability of the model has not been established. A second problem is that while the model focuses on the perceptions of the patient, it does not consider the perceptions of the practitioner, nor how the perceptions of the two may be reconciled. Finally, while the general process is presented in considerable detail, no indicators (either proposed or those used in the urban Chicano study) are presented for measuring the tactics or the perceptions of either the patient or the practitioner. This leaves other researchers at a loss to replicate the initial experiment. Nonetheless, the Hayes-Bautista model adds considerably to our understanding of patient noncompliance and physician control in the treatment process. This is especially important given the increasing tendency toward symmetry that the patient-practitioner relationship is experiencing in the 1980s. In this vein, the model allows for the modernization of the original Parsonian (Parsons, 1951) formulation of the patient-practitioner relationship by developing and clarifying the possibility for negotiation in the treatment process.

Four Recent Empirical Studies

Although there have been a number of recent studies conducted on the patient-practitioner relationship, four seem especially salient for discussion here. The first investigated the extent to which practitioners are aware of their patients' non-medical problems and, if aware, what they do about them. In the second study patients and physicians were surveyed about the rising tide of consumerism in medicine: does it exist and, if so, for whom? The other two studies focused on the analysis of verbal communication between doctors and patients in the ambulatory care setting. We conclude this section with a brief overview of the burgeoning empirical literature.

The Stewart and Buck Study of Practitioner Knowledge and Response

An area of growing concern regarding the patient-practitioner relationship is the extent of practitioners' knowledge of patients' problems and their responses to them. As the definition of health continues to expand, encompassing more of the non-physiological aspects, we expect practitioners to have better comprehension or perception of their patients' total health problems, including the psychosocial aspects. Two questions that arise are what practitioners really do know about their patients' prob-

Figure 7-1. The Treatment Modification Process.

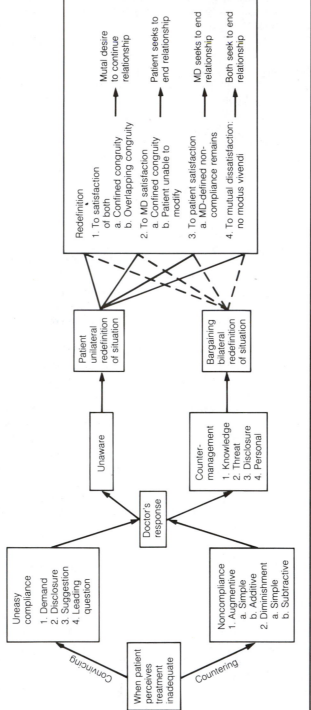

SOURCE: David Hayes-Bautista. 1976. "Modifying the treatment: Patient compliance, patient control, and medical care." *Social Science and Medicine* 10:233–8. Reprinted by permission.

lems and what response do they make to them? Building on previous studies of practitioner awareness and response (see Hulka, Kupper, Cassel, and Mayo, 1971; Hull, 1972; Korsch, Gozzi, and Francis, 1968; Querido, 1963), Stewart and Buck (1977) gathered data by interviewing 299 rural Canadians who had at least one chronic condition and the five clinic physicians they frequented over a three-month period. Stewart and Buck addressed three principal areas: the extent and association of practitioners' knowledge of their patients' problems, the extent and association of practitioners' responses to their patients' problems, and the association between the practitioners' knowledge and response to their patients' problems.

PRACTITIONERS' KNOWLEDGE OF PATIENTS' PROBLEMS. Stewart and Buck (1977) focused their analysis of the practitioners' knowledge of the patients' problems on five specific areas: complaints, discomforts, worries, daily living disturbances, and social problems. To assess the practitioners' knowledge of their patients' problems, Stewart and Buck compared the patients' self-reports in these five problem areas with practitioners' self-reports of their awareness of the patients' problems. They found that while the practitioners had a high level of knowledge concerning patients' complaints, discomforts, worries, and daily living disturbances (in 46 percent to 62 percent of the cases the practitioner was aware of all these problems), they had a low level of knowledge concerning the patients' social problems (practitioners were aware of the patients' social problems in only 23 percent of the cases). Further, while the practitioners' knowledge of the patients' nonsocial problems were all highly correlated with one another, their knowledge of the patients' social problems was not. In essence, Stewart and Buck found that the practitioners' knowledge of patients' problems is generally high and correlated, with the exception of social problems. Practitioners' knowledge of their patients' social problems was low and unrelated to their knowledge of their patients' other problems.

PRACTITIONERS' RESPONSES TO PATIENTS' PROBLEMS. After examining the practitioners' knowledge of the patients' problems, Stewart and Buck (1977) turned to an analysis of the practitioners' response to four of those problems: discomforts, worries, daily living disturbances, and social problems. By making comparisons between practitioner and patient self-reports, Stewart and Buck found that practitioners responded very well to patients' complaints of discomfort but not very well to patients' worries, daily living disturbances, or social problems. Further, practitioners' responses to the various areas of patients' problems were unrelated to one another. In essence, except for the area of patient discomfort, practitioners did not respond well to patients' problems. Contrary to what might be expected, the practitioners' poorest responses were not to the patients' social problems but to their daily living disturbances. Thus, although the patients' social problems were usually not well perceived, once they were perceived, the practitioners responded to them just as they would respond to the patients' worries and daily living disturbances.

THE RELATIONSHIP BETWEEN KNOWLEDGE AND RESPONSE. Finally, Stewart and Buck (1977) focused their analysis on the relationship between the practitioners' knowledge of and response to their patients' complaints. By correlating the knowledge of a problem with the response to that problem, they found significant but modest relationships of comparable size for the discomfort, worry, daily living disturbance, and social problems. These findings support their earlier assumption that when a patient's problem is perceived by the practitioner, he or she responds regardless of the specific nature (social or psychological) of the problem. The consistently low correlation between knowledge and response, however, indicates that practitioners are not very responsive to patients' problems, even when those problems have been perceived by the practitioner.

IMPLICATIONS FOR THE PATIENT-PRACTITIONER RELATIONSHIP. Stewart and Buck's (1977) findings have serious implications for the patient-practitioner relationship in general, and especially for Hayes-Bautista's (1976a, 1976b) elaboration of the treatment modification process. Overall, this research indicates that practitioners are not very aware of their patients' social problems. Even when they are aware of their patients' social or other problems, the practitioners do not respond very well. Thus, as the inclusion of social and psychological factors in our definition of health increases, it appears that practitioners will become more and more remote from the patients' nonmedical problems. This will undoubtedly decrease practitioner effectiveness and may justify an increased emphasis on teaching the skills of social interviewing and social perception in graduate medical education.

These results are especially salient for the Hayes-Bautista (1976a, 1976b) model of the treatment modification process. The low correlation between knowledge and response indicates that practitioners are not very likely to redefine the treatment situation in order to placate an unhappy patient. Thus, the negotiability of the treatment process becomes severely restricted. This increases the likelihood that patients who feel their treatment is inadequate will resort to terminating their current patient-practitioner relationships and searching for new ones.

LIMITATIONS OF THE STUDY. Although the Stewart and Buck (1977) study provides some much-needed insight for our understanding of the patient-practitioner relationship, there are some methodological problems with the study. First, the data are based on a small and highly selective sample (five physicians and 299 rural Canadian patients). This limits the study's generalizability to the population at large. Second, all of the patients were suffering from one or more chronic conditions during the period of the study. This calls into question the study's generalizability to those using medical care for different purposes (chronic, acute, or preventive). Finally, the data on the individuals were gathered only for the first three months following the initial visit. This may not have allowed sufficient time for patient-

practitioner rapport to develop, possibly resulting in lower levels of practitioner perceptions and responses. Nonetheless, these data are sufficient to demonstrate that a considerable gap exists between the practitioner's technical competence and his or her ability to perceive and respond to the psychosocial problems of the patient.

The Haug and Lavin Study of Consumerism in Medicine

In a remarkably detailed book Haug and Lavin (1983) have examined the power relationship between patients and their physicians. Using data from two 1976 surveys of 640 Ohio residents and their 88 doctors, as well as a 1978 national survey of 1,509 adults, Haug and Lavin sought to determine whether the time had come that people no longer unquestioningly accepted their doctors' diagnoses and treatment regimens. Most specifically, they examined attitudes toward and behaviors representative of consumerism in medicine.

FINDINGS ABOUT PATIENTS AND PRACTITIONERS. The consumer attitudes and behaviors that Haug and Lavin (1983) discovered were most interesting. They found a fairly consistent consumerist attitude among younger, more knowledgeable individuals. These individuals were also more skeptical of medicine's efficacy and of the dedication of physicians to their patients. This profile is not surprising; indeed, it is entirely consistent with the consumerist profiles generated by research on other types of transactions. What is surprising is the fact that these attitudes did not uniformly result in actual behavior. In fact, although health knowledge was predictive of health behavior, age and educational attainment were not. The most important predictor of consumerist health behavior turned out to be whether or not the individual had experienced a medical error. In sum, although the modernistic theme depicted by the youthful questioning of authority seemed to explain the public's attitudes, it was their health status and prior experience of physicians' mistakes that explained their behavior.

Similarly interesting were the results obtained from the 88 physicians. Haug and Lavin (1983) found that the physicians who were more willing to tolerate the consumerist patient were more likely to be younger themselves, to exhibit a general antiauthority stance, to be willing to delegate tasks to allied health care workers, to work in a prepaid versus a fee-for-service setting, and to live in a more urban community. These findings suggest the existence of a cohort phenomenon in which the idealism of younger physicians is coupled with the increased competition induced by the growing physician surplus. Together these factors may have created a set of circumstances more conducive to tolerating consumerist patients.

IMPLICATIONS FOR THE PATIENT-PRACTITIONER RELATIONSHIP. Haug and Lavin's (1983) work has important implications for studying patient-practitioner interactions. It suggests the cross-classification of patient and practitioner orientations, as shown in Table 7-1; this identifies the four most likely outcomes. When a consumerist patient goes to see a physician who likes to take charge of the situation, the outcome is likely to be conflict and the patient is likely to wind up with a different doctor. When a consumerist patient goes to see an accommodating physician, a bargaining process is likely to occur (not unlike that described by Hayes-Bautista, 1976a, 1976b); this will likely result in the development of an ongoing relationship of mutual trust. When a dependent (nonconsumerist) patient goes to see a doctor who likes to control the situation, a happy congruence of controller and controlled is likely to emerge. Finally, when a dependent patient goes to see an accommodating physician, the situation will likely be somewhat uncomfortable; the patient may shop around to find a more "take charge" doctor, or the accommodating doctor may take on a more "take charge" orientation.

LIMITATIONS OF THE STUDY. Despite the important identification of the medical consumer and modern physician profiles, Haug and Lavin's (1983) study cannot be considered definitive for several reasons. First, comparable data on patients and physicians from earlier periods is not available. Therefore, it is not possible to demonstrate whether the attitudes and behaviors of the patients and their doctors is any different from that of their forebearers. Second, these data were gathered more than 10 years ago. Thus, there is no way to know whether the alleged tandem trend toward consumerism and accommodation has continued, accelerated, or even reversed. Third, the practitioner data is based on the responses of only 88 Ohio physicians. They may not be representative of all physicians in the United States, or even of all the doctors in Ohio. Finally, the majority of the variance in both patient and physician attitudes and behaviors is unexplained despite the use of rather complex predictive models. Thus, the profiles of the medical consumer and the accommodating

Table 7-1. *The dynamics of who's in charge.*

Patient orientation	Physician orientation	
	Take charge	Persuade or accommodate
Consumerist	Conflict; the patient will get, or be told to get, a new doctor.	Bargaining to agreement; it may lead to the development of mutual trust.
Dependent	A happy congruence of controller and controlled.	An uncomfortable disjuncture; it may decay into the doctor taking charge, or the patient may try to find a more "take-charge" doctor.

SOURCE: Adapted from Marie Haug and Bebe Lavin. 1983. *Consumerism in Medicine: Challenging Physician Authority.* Beverly Hills, CA: Sage. Reprinted by permission of Sage Publications, Inc. and Marie Haug.

physician are somewhat tentative. Nonetheless, Haug and Lavin's carefully executed analysis provides us with considerable insight into the patient-as-consumer issue, and suggests the emergence of an ever-increasing cohort of more accommodating physicians.

West's Study of Doctor-Patient Communications

West (1984) has also examined the patient-practitioner relationship, albeit from a very different approach. The focus of her research is at the micro level; it involves the actual verbal exchange between patient and doctor rather than their attitudes toward such encounters. The data are taken from 532 pages of transcribed dyadic interactions between 18 physicians and 20 patients who had routinely given their consent to have their encounters audio- and videotaped. The physicians were all residents in the same university-based family practice training program to which the patients had come for an office visit. The questions that West set out to answer were these: what actually happens when doctor and patient meet, who says what to whom, why, and how? Her approach involved the use of conversational analysis to address the social organization of medical dialogues.

THE ISSUE. The sociological issue underlying West's (1984) study is the existence of the asymmetrical power distribution. As such she cuts to the heart of the Parsonian (1951, 1975) model of the patient-practitioner relationship. Focusing on an apparent paradox, she notes that "if, as Parsons argues, communication is predicated on *symmetrical* relations, and if, as he also contends, the practitioner-patient relationship is *essentially* asymmetrical, then communication between physicians and patients is theoretically impossible." Thus, she questions whether the Parsonian scheme, which is primarily theoretical, can be shown to exist in actual patient-practitioner encounters. She underscores the salience of the issue by noting that the analysis of actual medical dialogues has heretofore fundamentally escaped the interests of medical sociologists.

THE METHOD. One reason that medical dialogues have not been used to examine the patient-practitioner relationship is the difficulty involved in analyzing them (see Inui and Carter, 1985). In other words, how do you tell if the power distribution is asymmetrical or not? West (1984) argues that asymmetry can be measured by several methods. These include counting the number of times each party interrupts the other, who asks the questions and who answers them, who misunderstands whom, and who invokes laughter. She then proceeds to painstakingly apply these techniques to the 532 pages of transcribed medical dialogues.

THE RESULTS. What West (1984) found is most interesting. The male physicians interrupted their patients twice as often as their patients interrupted them. Black patients were more likely to be interrupted than white patients. Both of these findings lend support to the asymmetrical relationship described by Parsons (1951, 1975). For exchanges involving women physicians, however, the situation was reversed; patients interrupted women physicians more often than women physicians interrupted their patients. Thus, while the traditional physician-dominant relationship occurs when the doctor is a man, it does not occur when women doctors are involved.

Further support for the asymmetrical nature of the relationship was found in the analysis of who asked the more direct questions and who answered them. West (1984) found that the doctors were much more likely to initiate questions and that the patients were much more likely to answer them. Indeed, of the 773 direct questions recorded, only 68 were asked by patients. Moreover, when patients did ask questions of their doctors, the patients tended to stutter, indicating deference to the more powerful social actor.

In contrast to the findings about direct questioning are the results obtained for what West (1984) calls "conditionally relevant" questions. These fall into three types, each of which is in response to the other actor's previous utterance, including requests for clarification, requests for repair, and markers of surprise. West found that the patients initiated about half of each of these three types of more indirect queries. Moreover, although patient-initiated direct questions were not very welcome by the physicians, the conditionally relevant queries were viewed as acceptable modes of interaction. Thus, they seemed to offer a mutually acceptable method of doctor-patient communication.

IMPLICATIONS FOR THE PATIENT-PRACTITIONER RELATIONSHIP. The conclusions that may be drawn from West's (1984) work are mixed. On the one hand, she finds considerable support for the asymmetrical nature of the patient-practitioner relationship: "In general, physicians were the ones who asked the questions, interrupted their co-parties to talk, and initiated the familiarities in these encounters. Conversely, patients generally were the question answerers, the recipients of interruption, and the ones to use formal terms of address in naming their co-participants." On the other hand, the evidence for asymmetry disappeared for women doctors, and it receded in less direct situations: "For example, patients interrupted women doctors more than the reverse; the organization of conditionally relevant queries exhibited a symmetrical distribution between parties to talk; and for doctors and patients alike, terms of address were the exception rather than the rule."

Thus, West's conclusion is that the patient-practitioner relationship contains considerable amounts of both asymmetry and symmetry. In other words, Parsons's (1951, 1975) theoretical description of the interaction between doctor and patient is oversimplified. The physician does not always dominate the patient, although the physician does seem to have the upper hand in several aspects of the encounter (especially in asking questions, interrupting, and initiating familiarities). Thus, the perennial stereotypes of omnipotent physicians and helpless patients seem to be gross simplifications of empirical reality. What West's research suggests is more of an unfolding drama that is negotiated between two actors, one of whom has a bigger reputation, but both of whom are likely to improvise the final scene.

THE LIMITATIONS OF WEST'S WORK. To be sure, West's (1984) work represents a considerable breakthrough in the analysis of the patient-practitioner relationship. It has focused the issue at the micro level by examining what actually happens when doctors and patients talk to each other. There are, however, a number of limitations to the study. First, conversational analysis is a difficult method to use and a line of inquiry that is relatively new. The application of these techniques is not without controversy (see Inui and Carter, 1985). Second, all the data come from the interactions of 18 physicians and 20 patients associated with one family practice residency program. This raises a multifaceted issue of generalizability. It is difficult to know if the physicians, patients, and residency program are representative of all physicians (not just family practice residents), all patients (not just those who come to medical school clinics for their care), and all practice settings (not just graduate medical education facilities). Third, because the doctors in the medical residency program were only there for a maximum of three years, these medical dialogues do not involve any long-standing patient-practitioner relationships. Thus, it is possible that the observed degree of asymmetry would be different if there had been more "history" between the doctors and the patients. Finally, because all of the medical dialogues were gathered during a brief period, they are analogous to one cross-sectional survey. Therefore, it is not possible to determine whether the asymmetry in the patient-practitioner relationship has been changing (becoming more symmetrical) or not. Nonetheless, West's analysis has provided considerable insight into the complexities involved in doctors and patients talking to each other.

Coe's Analysis of Coalition Formation

Coe (1987; Coe and Prendergast, 1985; Coe et al., 1984) has also turned to the micro-level approach for analyzing patient-practitioner relationships. Unlike West (1984), Coe is motivated by more practical concerns. Particularly salient to him is understanding the structure and process of communication between doctor and patient that results in defective behavior by one or the other. Thus, he focuses on the outcomes of patient-practitioner interactions, including cognitive gain, satisfaction, compliance, and clinical improvement. Coe's ultimate goal is to improve training programs for health care providers.

DIFFERENCES BETWEEN COE'S AND WEST'S RESEARCH. There are two other significant differences between Coe's (1987) research and West's (1984). First, all of the medical encounters that Coe has studied involve elderly patients. This requires consideration of three special factors: cohort effects, aging effects, and unmet expectations. Elderly patients are of a generation far more likely to accept the doctor's answers and regimens without question (see Haug and Lavin, 1981, 1983; Wolinsky and Wolinsky, 1981b). They are also less likely to seek detailed information about their conditions (see Haug, 1979; Nuttbrock and Kosberg, 1980). There may also be significant age declines in the elderly's ability to hear, see, and remember, as well as in their ability to coordinate psychomotor responses (see Botwinick, 1985). Therefore, physicians may need to take special care to be sure that communication with their elderly patients is successful. Finally, there is the issue of unmet expectations that stems from the fact that most of the elderly's ailments are of a chronic nature, for which medical treatments are not very successful. As a result, dissatisfaction with health outcomes may be more frequent among elderly patients.

The second way in which Coe's (1987) work differs from West's (1984) is that all of his medical encounters involved the doctor, the patient, and the patient's significant other (usually the oldest surviving daughter). Thus, Coe's work represents an impor-

tant shift from studying patient-practitioner relationships in dyadic situations to studying these interactions in triads. This allows Coe to focus on coalition formation and maintenance, which represents a considerable contribution given the rapidly expanding nature of the patient-practitioner relationship beyond the traditional one-on-one encounter.

THE RESULTS: SPECIAL STRATEGIES AND COALITION FORMATION. One of the most important findings that Coe (Coe et al., 1984) has reported is the documentation of a special strategy used by physicians to enhance communication with and compliance by elderly patients. Coe and his colleagues found that the physician engaged the elderly patient's relative (the third party, usually the daughter) as a "manager" or "supervisor." In effect, the relative becomes a "partner in the therapeutic enterprise," primarily responsible for managing the patient's medical regimen at home. Although one interpretation of this strategy would be that the physicians were genuinely concerned about enhancing compliance with the drug regimen, these same data may indicate that the physicians were willing (if not eager) to write off any further attempts at more successful direct communication with the elderly patients. In essence, the physicians may have begun to treat these elderly patients as nonadults, in much the same manner in which doctors communicate more directly to the parents of children than to the children themselves.

The second principal finding to emerge from Coe's (Coe and Prendergast, 1985) work concerns the effect of the third party (the relative) on the patient-practitioner relationship. To focus on this issue, Coe and his colleagues taped two encounters of each doctor with each elderly patient. The relative was absent from the first encounter but present during the second. Analysis of the transcriptions indicated that the relative played the roles of an interpreter, negotiator, and caretaker. What the relative did most often as an interpreter was elaborate and update the patient's presentation of symptoms and medical history, sometimes even correcting the elderly patient's initial report. In the negotiator role the relative mediated the frequency of appointments and the substitution of less expensive treatments, especially generic or otherwise cheaper drugs. As a caretaker the relative monitored the elderly patient's health, supervised medication taking, and provided psychological support.

In the process of playing out these roles, a number of coalitions formed in which two members of the triad adopted a common strategy for influencing the third. In most of the encounters two or more coalitions were formed, with the old coalitions dissolving as new alignments emerged. There was no consistency in how long the coalitions lasted, which actors were paired up, or the successes of the coalitions. According to Coe and Prendergast (1985), the important point to be made from studying the formation and subsequent dissolution of coalitions is that in doctor-patient-relative triads there is no preordained script that the actors consistently follow. This is quite consistent with West's (1984) analysis of dyadic patient-practitioner encounters and suggests that the stereotyped conceptions of the omnipotent doctor and totally deferent patient do not coincide with the reality of triadic interactions either.

THE LIMITATIONS OF COE'S WORK. As was the case with West's (1984) analyses, Coe's (Coe, 1987; Coe and Prendergast, 1985; Coe et al., 1984) work is limited in a variety of ways. First, there is the multifaceted question of generalizability. All of the medical encounters transcribed by Coe and his colleagues involved a small number of elderly patients and their relatives who came to see only two physicians who practiced at one medical school's ambulatory clinic. Thus, it is not clear how atypical their findings are. Second, the use of conversational analysis is a relatively new and complex technique (see Inui and Carter, 1985). Moreover, it has rarely been applied to the study of coalition formation. Thus, the validity of the methods for assessing coalition formation has yet to be substantiated by replication. Third, there was very little "history" between these doctors, the patients, and their relatives. It is unclear what effect the establishment of more ongoing and trusting relationships

would have on the results. Finally, there are the special considerations of using elderly patients, including the cohort, aging, and unmet expectations factors. Nonetheless, Coe's work has significantly advanced our understanding of the patient-practitioner relationship by examining what happens when a third party is introduced.

The State of the Art of Patient-Practitioner Studies

The patient-practitioner relationship has been the subject of study by social and medical scientists for quite some time. Traditionally, most of that research has taken a macro-level perspective, focusing on the characteristics of physicians and patients in relation to various medical outcomes. More recently, the focus has shifted to the micro level, as exemplified in conversational analysis. In addition to the level of analysis, research on the patient-practitioner relationship may be classified in terms of its theoretical orientation and its disciplinary orientation or motivation.

THREE THEORETICAL ORIENTATIONS. Coe (1987) suggests that descriptions of what happens when doctor and patient meet may be categorized into three groups based on their theoretical perspective: functionalism, exchange, and conflict. The *functionalist* perspective is typified by Parsons (1951, 1975) and by Szasz and Hollender (1956). As indicated before, they focus on social role expectations, emphasizing the necessity of the asymmetrical relationship. The *exchange* perspective (see Bloom, 1963a) sees things somewhat differently. Building on Homans's (1959) classic work in social psychology, proponents of the exchange perspective emphasize the notion of transactions, implying rational social actors who essentially calculate cost-benefit ratios to determine how to proceed in the interaction. Finally, there is the *conflict* perspective (see Freidson, 1970a). The emphasis here is on the dissimilar interests and resources of doctor and patient, and how their encounter necessitates a negotiated outcome. West (1984) argues that the work of those who take the functionalist perspective is more likely to be theoretically based and supportive of the traditional stereotypes of the omnipotent physician and the helpless patient. In contrast, the work of those who take the conflict perspective is more likely to be empirically based and critical of the medical profession (see Mishler, 1984).

DISCIPLINARY ORIENTATIONS. Inui and Carter (1985) suggest that a more pertinent distinction among the numerous studies of the patient-practitioner relationship is not their theoretical orientation but rather their disciplinary bias. They distinguish between research conducted by sociobehavioral scientists and that conducted by clinicians. The sociobehavioral scientists focus on the process of doctor-patient communications.

Their concern is more likely to involve the dynamics of the interaction, including power, the elements and dynamics of decision making, nonverbal behavior, and the language of the encounter. In contrast, the clinicians focus more on the outcome of that process. Their concern is more likely to involve explicating history taking, increasing diagnostic accuracy, and enhancing patient compliance. In essence, Inui and Carter suggest that sociobehavioral scientists are primarily interested in understanding the process of medical encounters while clinicians are primarily concerned with maximizing the outcomes of those encounters.

A GENERAL CONCEPTUAL MODEL. Despite differences in theoretical perspectives and

Figure 7-2. A General Model of Doctor-Patient Communication.

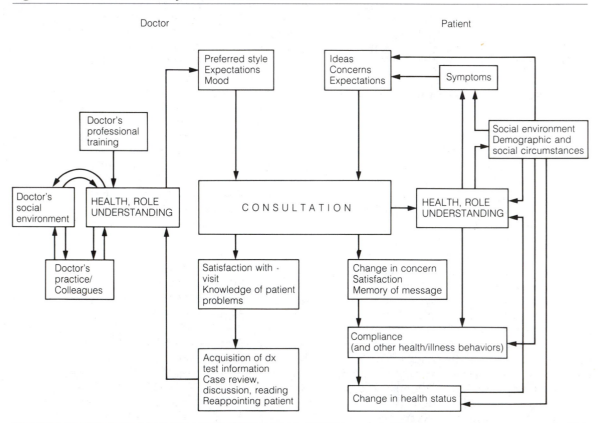

SOURCE: Thomas S. Inui and William B. Carter. 1985. "Problems and prospects for health services research on provider-patient communication." *Medical Care* 23:521–38.
Reprinted by permission of the author and publisher.

disciplinary interests, there seems to be a considerable amount of consistency in the issues addressed in studying patient-practitioner communications. Inui and Carter (1985) believe that most studies involve some or all of the issues shown in Figure 7-2. Although the model is fairly detailed, they note that it is an oversimplification of what actually happens. In particular, except in instances of one-time episodic care, the process shown is an iterative one involving several layers, or repetitive encounters, of the model.

After reviewing the extensive literature, Inui and Carter (1985) concluded that considerable evidence exists to support the model:

Inputs . . . that have been shown to affect the process . . . include prior experience with medical care, patient objectives for the visit, patient age, type of medical problem, the number of patient concerns, prior physician knowledge of the patient's concerns, and characteristics of the physicians' practice setting. Outcomes . . . have included patient knowledge, provider-patient congruence on problems or recommendations, patient satisfaction (in many dimensions), patient compliance with provider recommendations, and resolution of patient concerns or symptoms.

Thus, a great deal is now known about what actually occurs when doctor and patient meet.

FUTURE RESEARCH QUESTIONS. There are, however, two serious gaps that have yet to be bridged in the literature. First, no single study has looked at all of the aspects of the patient-practitioner relationship simultaneously. As a result, the relative importance of each of the doctor and patient inputs on each of the outcomes is unknown. In particular, it is not clear how the modification of some inputs affects the effect of other inputs. Second, there have been virtually no long-term studies of ongoing patient-practitioner relationships; most studies have been analogous to one cross-sectional survey. As a result, it is not clear whether the observed relationships between inputs and outcomes are truly causative or merely relational. Moreover, without longitudinal studies it is impossible to determine if the

effects of manipulating inputs are permanent or if their half-life may be measured in episodes. Thus, future research on the patient-practitioner relationship needs to take a more systematic and longitudinal approach.

Summary

In this chapter we have reviewed the patient-practitioner relationship originally proposed by Parsons (1951), the comments and criticisms raised and made about it, and some recent extensions of that formulation. We began the first section by presenting Parsons's original conceptualization of the role of the practitioner, reviewing the four specific aspects of that role: technical specificity, affective neutrality, universalism, and functional specificity. These aspects of the practitioner's role are closely related to the asymmetry in the patient-practitioner relationship, which is necessary if the therapeutic action of returning the patient to his or her healthy state is to be successful. Practitioners rely on three leverage devices to maintain this asymmetry, which results in a patient-practitioner relationship analogous to the child-parent relationship. Three major reservations concerning Parsons's formulation were then discussed: (1) its applicability only to acute illness, not to chronic illness or instances of preventive care; (2) class and cultural communication barriers between the patient and the practitioner; and (3) the number and types of practitioners available have drastically changed since 1951. Parsons's (1975) response to these criticisms focused on the necessity of asymmetry in therapeutic relationships. He illustrated his argument with the example of the student-professor relationship.

In the second section we turned to two conceptual modifications of the Parsonian patient-practitioner relationship. First, we examined the Szasz-Hollender (Szasz and Hollender, 1956) models. Based on the severity and manageability of the illness condition, they proposed three more specific forms of the patient-practitioner relationship: the activity-passivity model, the guidance-cooperation model, and the mutual participation model. We then examined the Hayes-Bautista (1976a, 1976b) model. It elaborated on the process of treatment modification within the patient-practitioner relationship. This model showed that by using convincing tactics or countering tactics patients who perceived their treatment to be inappropriate attempted to negotiate a new one. In response, the practitioner used his or her own tactics in the negotiating process, resulting in four general classes of outcomes: a mutual decision to continue the relationship, the patient decided to terminate the relationship, the practitioner decided to terminate the relationship, or a mutual decision to discontinue the relationship.

In the final section we reviewed four more recent empirical studies of the patient-practitioner relationship. Stewart and Buck (1977) studied practitioners' knowledge of and responses to their patients' problems. They found that (1) while most patients' problems are perceived by their practitioners, social problems are not; (2) once a patient's problem is perceived by the practitioner, it is responded to, regardless of its psychosocial or physiological nature; and (3) although the practitioner responds to the perceived problems of the patient, regardless of the nature of the problem, the response rate is uniformly low reflecting the unresponsive nature of the practitioner. Haug and Lavin (1983) studied patient and practitioner attitudes toward and actual behavior about consumerism in medical care. They identified profiles of the medical consumer (younger, better-educated individuals who take a dim view of authority) and the accommodating physician (younger physicians more likely to practice in a prepaid setting and to live in a more urban community). When it came to actual consumerist behavior, however, Haug and Lavin found that the best predictor was whether or not the individual had previously been involved in a physician's mistake. West (1984) used conversational analysis to assess the extent of asymmetry between patients and their doctors. Her results were mixed. On the one hand, male physicians were more likely to ask the more direct questions and to interrupt their patients. On the other hand, patients asked about as many clarifying questions as did their doctors, and these were rather well tolerated. Using the same techniques, Coe (1987; Coe and Prendergast, 1985; Coe et al., 1984) focused on the special strategies that physicians use when seeing elderly patients and their relatives. The distribution of power in these triadic relationships was similar to that observed in dyads by West. The third party, usually the patient's oldest daughter, filled several roles, including that of interpreter, negotiator, and caretaker. The coalitions that formed were neither consistent nor lasting, underscoring the need to reconsider the role of asymmetry in patient-practitioner relationships. Finally, we reviewed the state of the art of research on the patient-practitioner relationship, noting in particular the need for more comprehensive studies of a longitudinal nature.

8. Applying the Principles to Aging, Death and Dying, and Mental Illness

*I*N CHAPTERS 4 through 7 we have reviewed the four basic principles in the sociology of health: the definitions and assumptions of health and illness, the sick role concept, the seeking and use of health services, and the patient-practitioner relationship. This chapter will use these principles to gain a better understanding of the social problems of aging, death and dying, and mental illness. These three social problems have been selected for two reasons. First, all three are health-related, and all three are on the increase. As such they underscore the relevance of the sociology of health for sociology in general, as well as for public policy in particular.

The second reason is that all three social problems involve what Preston (1979) has called "ambiguous" people. These are incomplete individuals who either are, or are perceived to be, unwhole, deformed, or incapacitated. Building on Becker's (1973, 1975) writings about human frailty and mortality, Preston characterizes the ideal type of the ambiguous person by recounting Kafka's discussion of Gregor Samsa in *The Metamorphosis*. Gregor, you will recall, wakes up one morning to find that in appearance he now has the body of a six-foot-long cockroach, although he has retained his human intelligence and personality. According to Preston, the reaction of others to Gregor is conceptually similar to that of others to any "incomplete" individual, including the aged, the dying, and the mentally ill. Although interested primarily in how normative witnesses (ordinary people) are affected by coming into contact with such human abnormality (like Gregor), Preston's concept of the ambiguous person identifies the common thread among the aged, the dying, and the mentally ill. All three are special cases for the application of the principles of the sociology of health.

The present chapter is divided into three sections. In the first we consider aging, be-

170

*Applying The
Principles to
Aging, Death and
Dying, and Mental
Illness*

ginning with a review of the life cycle and the social roles associated with each of its stages. This is followed by an analysis of where the increase in the number of elderly people has come from. We then review the five major theoretical approaches to social gerontology, emphasizing their dependence on the sick role concept. The section on aging concludes with a view of the aged role from both sides: the perceptions of the aged and the perceptions of others.

In the second section we address death and dying. We begin with a discussion of the changing societal attitudes toward death, including some of the more controversial plans for defining brain death. We then take up the issue of how people deal with the death and dying process. This includes reviewing both the stages and contexts of dying, which are variations of the traditional patient and practitioner roles. Concluding the section on death and dying is a discussion of what it is like to be clinically dead, yet return to life.

In the final section we examine mental illness. We begin with a review of the definitional problems. The societal reaction and social learning approaches to mental illness that have been offered as alternatives to the traditional psychiatric and psychoanalytic models are considered next. We then discuss the career or modified sick role of the patient in the "total institution" of the mental hospital. We conclude this section with a brief review of the leading indicators of mental illness and their social correlates.

Aging

When we speak of aging we must remember that, as with health, aging contains three major dimensions: the physiological, the social, and the psychological. Individuals age along all three of these dimensions, but not necessarily at the same rate or at the same time. Accordingly, if we are to understand the aging problem, we must begin by gaining an understanding of the three dimensions of the life cycle and the roles associated with each of its stages.

The Life Cycle and Its Associated Roles

Although there are several specific models of the life cycle, Figure 8-1 represents its basic stages and the approximate chronological age associated with each. Although nine distinct stages are represented in the figure, most of us would consider only the last three (middle age, later maturity, and old age) as relevant to a discussion of aging. That is, when we think of aging and the aging process, we usually think of the elderly. In reality, everyone is part of the aging process from their very beginning (birth), if not before. We are simply accustomed to referring to and studying the aging processes that occcur prior to middle age by other names, such as child development, adolescent psychology, or marriage and the family. Nonetheless, the aging process by any other name is still the aging process; life cycle stage-specific courses merely reflect how the

Figure 8-1. The Nine Stages of the Life Course and Their Chronological Boundaries.

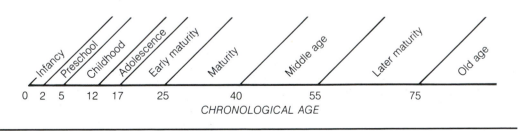

CHRONOLOGICAL AGE

aging process affects individuals and their social roles at that particular point in life. When viewing aging as a social problem, however, it simplifies matters somewhat to restrict our discussion of aging to the latter stages of the life cycle, especially those most clearly associated with "the elderly." Accordingly, our first task should be to review the physiological, psychological, and sociological aspects of the aging process among the elderly.

PHYSIOLOGICAL ASPECTS OF AGING. In studying the physiological aspects of aging one discovers several theories—including the programmed theory, the mutation theory, and the autoimmune theory—that have been separately advanced in order to explain the underlying biological processes (for a detailed elaboration of these theories and processes, see Finch and Schneider, 1985). In the past three decades these theories have been combined under the more general senescence theory, which seeks to explain why the human body becomes less viable and more susceptible with age (Cape, Coe, and Rossman, 1983). While total agreement has not been reached as to the underlying processes making up senescence, it has been distinguished from other biological processes in at least four ways (Atchley, 1985): it has universal characteristics, its changes occur entirely within the individual, it is a gradual process, and its effects are negative for the individual.

Kart (1985) has identified eight consistent biological aspects of senescence: (1) the skin becomes wrinkled and rough; (2) the joints stiffen and height is reduced by a stooping posture; (3) the sensory perceptions and reflex actions are reduced; (4) the brain mass deteriorates while its arteries harden and occlude; (5) the circulatory system's output and elasticity decrease; (6) the respiratory capacity is significantly reduced; (7) the digestive system deteriorates; and (8) the effectiveness of the reproductive, kidney, and temperature-regulation systems declines. Kart also points out two important facts concerning these eight aspects of the senescence process. First, this physiological

aging does not occur for all individuals at the same chronological age nor at the same rate. Indeed, the elderly are considerably heterogeneous with respect to the ways that the aging process affects them. Second, this aging is also affected by social and psychological considerations. In essence, the physiological aspect of aging represents the biological deterioration of the human body that, although it begins with the individual's birth, is accelerated once the individual nears and reaches old age.

PSYCHOLOGICAL ASPECTS OF AGING. According to Birren (1968; see also Birren and Schaie, 1985), an individual's psychological age may be defined as "the level of his adaptive capacities." This definition is based on the individual's declining ability to adapt to the total environment and includes declines in the accuracy and speed of perception, reasoning, memory, and learning capability. Thus, the central issue is whether or not the mental functioning of the aged *typically* deteriorates over time. For many years the conventional wisdom was that mental abilities do indeed decline with age. The basis for this belief was the strong negative relationships typically revealed in cross-sectional data. Further examination of two conceptual and methodological issues, however, has shown this not to be the case.

The first issue was the identification and resolution of the APC or age, period, and cohort problem (see Nesselroade and Labouvie, 1985; Schaie and Hertzog, 1985). When using data from just one cross-sectional survey, it is not possible to separate the effects of aging from the effects of historical factors (or periods) or from the effects of a birth cohort's experiencing the same historical events at the same point in his or her life cycle. As a result, the negative correlation between age and mental ability, most frequently measured by intelligence test scores, was mistakenly interpreted as evidence of age-related declines. In fact, these differences represent a cohort effect associated with different educational attainment patterns. Older cohorts typically received less education than younger cohorts; as a result,

172

*Applying The
Principles to
Aging, Death and
Dying, and Mental
Illness*

they typically scored lower on standardized intelligence tests. When longitudinal (or synthetic panel) data were brought to bear on the issue, no age-related declines in mental ability were detected.

The second issue was quite similar. It involved the failure to control for physical health status when examining declines in mental abilities. Birren (1968) addressed this issue by conducting his own longitudinal research and examining the data on declining mental abilities first without, and then with, the appropriate controls. When the data were examined without controlling for physical health, the group of aged subjects were found to have typically suffered mental decline while the group of younger subjects had not. Then the data were reexamined after dividing the aged subjects into two groups, those who were physically healthy and those who were not. Birren found that the physically unhealthy group typically showed a decline in mental functioning over the five-year study period, although the physically healthy group did not. This lead him to conclude that

the average person's growing older in our society need not expect to show a typical deterioration of mental functioning in the last years. Rather, limitation of mental functioning occurs precipitously in individuals over the age of 65 or 70 and is closely related to health status. For this reason the expectations of mental performance must be based upon the elderly individual's characteristics rather than on the assumption about the average in the population at large. The expectation is, therefore, given good health and freedom from cerebral vascular disease and senile dementia, [that] individuals can expect high-level mental competence beyond the age of 80.

In essence, Birren concluded that higher rates of mental decline among the aged are the results of associated physiological disorders and are not the results of some universal deterioration process.

SOCIAL ASPECTS OF AGING. The social aspects of the aging process can best be illustrated by the changing social roles that the individual is assigned and plays as he or she grows older (for a detailed compendium of these changes, see Binstock and Shanas,

1985). From infancy through early maturity, the individual proceeds through a long and careful apprenticeship for that "real" adult role to be assumed at maturity. Shortly after achieving this "real" adult role, however, the individual enters the middle-age stage where the self-realization of aging occurs, coupled with the recognition that death is a "real" phenomenon from which no one is exempt (Atchley, 1985). As a result of this recognition, middle-aged individuals begin to reorient their time perspectives from the future to the past, attempting to avoid the inevitability of death's approach. In addition, activities begin to be reoriented by middle-aged individuals from the physical to the intellectual as a result of the perceived reductions of their energy levels. As the individual enters later maturity, these reorientations in activity and time perspective continue; they are accelerated by retirement, which usually brings about a reduction in income. This in turn curtails the individual's general activity and social relationships. The death of one's spouse, coupled with one's own continued physiological deterioration, income reduction (fixed retirement incomes seldom keep pace with inflation), and the death of one's other significant others increases the likelihood that the elderly individual will become bored, lonely, and despondent. All of this is concomitant with the ever-increasing recognition of one's impending death. In sum, the prospect of entering old age is not a very pleasant one (see Fischer, 1978, and Butler, 1975, for detailed accounts of what it is like to grow old in the United States).

Negative Aspects of Aging Process as Social Problem

The negative effect of the physiological, psychological, and social aging processes on the aged may be viewed as a social problem for two reasons. First, as with most other contemporary social problems, we have been unable to deal with the aging problem in a totally satisfactory manner. While we recognize the negative aspects that occur along all three dimensions of the aging process, we haven't found cures for them. Thus,

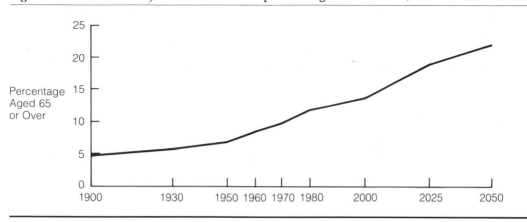

SOURCE: United States Bureau of the Census. 1982. *Projections of the Population of the United States: 1982 to 2050.* Current Population Reports, Series P-25, No. 922. Washington, D.C.: Government Printing Office.

the aged continue to suffer through the aging process. Second, like most other contemporary social problems, the negative aspects of the aging process are affecting more and more people. The extent of the growth of the aged population is represented in Figure 8-2, which shows that the percentage of individuals aged 65 or over in the United States has increased from 4.0 percent in 1900 to 11.3 percent in 1980, with a prediction of 19.5 percent by 2025, when most of you will still be approaching the age of 60. This fivefold increase in the number of elderly persons raises two interesting questions: where did all these old people come from, and what effect does their increasing number have on the health care system.

REASONS FOR INCREASE IN NUMBERS AND PROPORTION OF ELDERLY. In 1900 the average life expectancy for an American was only 47 years. By the mid 1980s the average life expectancy had risen to 74 years, and it continues to climb (see Rice and Feldman, 1983). As we saw in chapter 1, this increase in life expectancy (or decrease in mortality rates) may be traced to two principal factors. First, the increasing industrialization and urbanization of American society during the past two centuries has brought about an increase in public health measures, especially sanitation. Along with improvements in sanitation came advances in housing

and working conditions, nutritional intake levels, and expanded leisure-time facilities. These public health improvements and healthier lifestyles have been the major factor in lowering mortality rates. A second factor has been the increase in the quantity, quality, and availability of health services. We now have more physicians and other health personnel per person who are better trained and more readily accessible than at any other time in American history; this has also contributed to our increased life expectancy, but not nearly so much as better sanitation and healthier lifestyles.

The combination of the factors described above has clearly reduced mortality levels, which has resulted in the larger absolute number of elderly persons. The increase in the relative number of the elderly (or their proportion of the total population) is, however, also a function of declining fertility levels (see Myers, 1985). Population aging can best be explained by the theory of the demographic transition. The demographic transition argument states that most societies will eventually move through the four stages shown in Figure 8-3, based on their fertility and mortality rates. In developing societies (i.e., those at stage I) both fertility and mortality rates are high; the result is a population pyramid that clearly resembles a pyramid. As a society develops the mortality rate drops first, followed somewhat

174

*Applying The
Principles to
Aging, Death and
Dying, and Mental
Illness*

later by a concomitant drop in the fertility rate. As a result, both the mortality and fertility rates are low in developed societies (i.e., those at stage IV), and their population pyramid looks more like a flashlight battery. By the year 2020 the population pyramid for the United States will be much more batterylike than pyramidlike. As the batterylike population pyramid stretches upward (i.e., as the angles at its base more closely approximate 90 degrees), the reliance of the elderly on those in the peak labor force years increases. This is indicated by the dependency ratio, or the ratio of the population aged 65 and over to that aged 20 to 64. If current population projections are accurate and the traditional retirement age remains at or about age 65, the generational burdens (both financial and social) on working individuals in the United States will grow to phenomenal levels. Indeed, although the dependency ratio was less than 0.2 in 1960, it is expected to reach nearly 0.4 by 2040. That is what makes aging such a pressing social problem.

THE IMPACT OF THE ELDERLY ON HEALTH CARE. The second interesting question that we face is what impact the expanding group of the elderly has on the health care delivery system. Fuchs (1974), Coe (1983), and others have addressed this question intensively and generally agree on three likely effects. First, there will be a considerable

shortage of geriatricians who specialize in the treatment of the elderly. Although currently there is one pediatrician for every 4,300 persons under the age of 20, there is only one geriatrician for every 67,000 persons aged 65 and over. By the year 2000 the ratio of geriatricians to the elderly will have decreased; there will be more elderly, although the number of geriatric specialists will remain about the same.

Second, the diseases and illnesses that especially affect the elderly, such as arteriosclerosis, heart disease, and arthritis, are those against which medicine is least effective. Thus, there will be more old people who have conditions for which medicine currently is not very effective. This in turn will result in an increased level of maintenance-oriented rather than curative-oriented medical care. Third, the medical expenses of the elderly are much higher than those for any other age group. This disparity may be illustrated by the fact that in 1985 the per capita medical bill for the aged was nearly triple that of the nonelderly. As the number of elderly persons increases, so will medical care expenditures (see Berki, Lepkowski, and Wyszewianski, 1986). It has been estimated that the health care costs of the elderly will rise to $2 trillion by the year 2000, representing more than a 20-fold increase over the next 15 years, even if there is *no inflation* in the cost of health services. Such an astronomical increase in health

Figure 8-3. *The Theory of the Demographic Transition.*

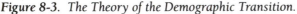
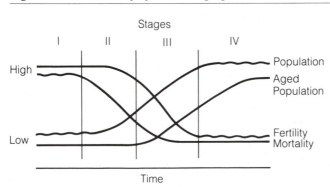

care spending for the aged (which would itself be about equal to the current national debt) makes the aging process a serious social issue.

Five Theoretical Approaches to the Aging Process

There are a variety of theoretical approaches addressing the topic of social gerontology, or the social aspects of the study of aging. Most of these theoretical approaches have been borrowed from the older social sciences, especially sociology and psychology, and then adapted to explain the aging process. None of these is sufficiently well developed to warrant a detailed discussion of its strengths and weaknesses. Therefore, we shall only briefly review the five most notable of these: the role theory approach, the disengagement theory approach, the subcultural theory approach, the activity theory approach, and the age-stratification theory approach.

THE ROLE THEORY APPROACH. The role theory approach to aging suggests that when people age, they must adjust to a variety of conditions that were not part of their previous social roles (Phillips, 1957). These adjustments generally fall into two major categories: relinquishing social roles and relationships typifying adulthood, and accepting social roles and relationships typifying old age (Cavan, Burgess, Havighurst, and Goldhamer, 1949). Cottrell (1942) has suggested that the most efficient way of understanding the aging process is to analyze the changing social relationships of the aged by using a role theory perspective. In essence, just as Parsons (1951) identified the sick role, Cottrell identified the aged role. While the aged role is not nearly as well delineated as the sick role (see Rosow, 1985, for a detailed discussion of the limitations of the aged role), it is generally agreed that it includes the aged person's adjustment to nine changes from the adult role: (1) retirement from or relinquishment of employment or household management, (2) withdrawal from leadership roles in the community and other organizations, (3) dissolution of marriage through the death of a spouse, (4) elimination of an independent place of residence, (5) reduced interest in planning for distant goals, (6) increased dependency on others for a variety of support, (7) subordination to one's own children and to agency personnel, (8) joining of voluntary associations for the aged, and (9) adoption of a day-to-day orientation for planning purposes. As with the four aspects of the sick role, these changes represent the behavior society has come to expect of the aged.

Research on the social aspects of aging using the role theory perspective focuses on how the aging individual adjusts to these changes from the adult social role. In essence, the role theory approach to social gerontology assumes that as an individual ages he or she takes on new social roles corresponding to the new life cycle stage that is being entered. When the individual enters old age, the social role of the adult (later maturity) is relinquished and the social role of the aged (old age) is assumed. Approached in this manner, social gerontology is mainly the study of how individuals adjust to or cope with the last (or second to the last, if dying is considered as a separate stage) social role change in the life cycle.

THE DISENGAGEMENT THEORY APPROACH. The disengagement theory approach to social gerontology was originally proposed by Cumming, Dean, and Newell (1960), elaborated by Cumming and Henry (1961), and subsequently revised by Cumming (1963). While similar to the role theory approach, the approach of the disengagement theory suggests that in "normal aging" the aging individual and others in the social system mutually withdraw or disengage from social relationships with each other. Either the individual or others may initiate the disengagement process that, when complete, results in significantly greater distance between the aging individual and all others, and a radically different basis for solidarity relationships that are based not on interdependent role performance (i.e., organic solidarity) but on similarity and common sentiment bonds (i.e., mechanical solidarity). In essence, the changes in solidarity

176

*Applying The
Principles to
Aging, Death and
Dying, and Mental
Illness*

represent a shift from the organic solidarity enjoyed by the adult to the mechanical solidarity extended to the aged individual. This shift is considered to be a functional necessity by disengagement theorists because the aging individual is likely to die soon, and the loss of an interdependent worker is too disruptive to the social system. While the loss of a noninterdependent nonworker is sad, it is not societally disruptive. Therefore, to avoid disrupting the social system, the aged must be disengaged from their roles in the interdependent social structure before the likelihood of their imminent and disruptive death becomes too great. If their disengagement is properly timed, their impending death poses no threat to the maintenance of the social system.

As such, the disengagement theory is decidedly functionalist. Old age (death) is viewed as a potential problem for the social system, to be avoided by disengaging the aged from important social roles. In addition to "saving" the social system, the disengagement process also benefits the aging individual. The more social roles that are taken from or given up by the aging individual, the more freedom he or she has from society because there are fewer obligations and expectations placed on him or her. Thus, as the aging individual is allowed to relinquish all social roles, except that of the retired individual, he or she has more time to devote to that single role, becoming more self-oriented and self-occupied in the process. In sum, disengagement theory holds that the process of mutual withdrawal of the aged individual and society from each other is typical, inevitable, and necessary for mutually successful aging.

THE SUBCULTURAL THEORY APPROACH. The subcultural theory approach to social gerontology originally suggested by Rose (1965) parallels the role theory and disengagement approaches. According to Rose, a subculture emerges when a group of people interact with each other more than they do with others for either of two reasons: as a result of a positive affinity with each other, or because all members of one group are ex-

cluded from interacting with members of other social groups. Although it is hard to say which of these conditions occurred first, it is clear that both conditions apply to the aged in America, as evidenced by the growing proportion of the aged to the general population, their self-segregation into retirement communities, the increase of compulsory and voluntary retirement, and the extensive development of social welfare services specifically for the aged. The subculture of aging, however, contains several characteristics that differentiate it from the larger culture or any other subculture. These include a dual status system based on the status afforded to the elderly individual by the general society and the status afforded to the individual by the subculture, a reduced and declining interest in sex, reduced and declining differences in economic roles based on social and sexual criteria, a distinct attitude concerning the imminent nature of death, and the domination of everyday life by leisure activities. Subcultural theory suggests that the behavior of the aged be viewed and analyzed from the perspective of their participation in the aged subculture. In essence, this approach suggests that the social problems of aging should be viewed as subcultural problems, just as other social problems like juvenile delinquency.

THE ACTIVITY THEORY APPROACH. The activity theory approach to social gerontology focuses on the relationships between social activity and life satisfaction originally presented by Havighurst and Albrecht (1953), and subsequently expanded by many others. This approach is built on Mead's (1934) assumption that the social self emerges from interaction with other social actors. Any structural barriers placed in the way of continued social interaction (such as disengagement by retirement) demoralize and alienate the individual (the aged), resulting in lower levels of life satisfaction. In this approach, social activity is tied to social roles, so that if one is disengaged from those roles, one's social activity decreases. This results in decreased life satisfaction.

Lennon, Bengston, and Peterson (1972) formalized this approach by axiomatically identifying the four basic postulates (P's) of activity theory:

P1 The greater the role loss, the less activity one is likely to engage in.

P2 The greater the activity, the more role support one is likely to receive.

P3 The more role support one receives, the more positive one's self-concept is likely to be.

P4 The more positive one's self-concept, the greater one's life satisfaction is likely to be.

By merging these four basic postulates and then combining them with the resulting theorems, Lennon and his colleagues were able to generate a number of hypotheses concerning the social behavior of the aged. These were neither conclusively accepted nor rejected when submitted to empirical testing. In essence, activity theory suggests that the aging individual's behavior may be analyzed as a result of the reduction of the social activity brought about by the loss of adult social roles. As such, activity theory concentrates on the changes in the individual's self-concept as he or she passes into old age, the last stage in the life cycle.

THE AGE-STRATIFICATION THEORY APPROACH. The age-stratification theory approach to social gerontology was proposed by Riley (1971, 1986) and suggests that the aging and death and dying processes be analyzed by a class theory based not on socioeconomic status but on age status. In other words, Riley suggests that the aging phenomenon, like most social class phenomena, may best be understood by examining the stratification of the age classes. Specifically, Riley identifies four sets of questions concerning the age process that an age-stratification theory would be used to explain: (1) how does an individual's age channel his or her attitudes and behaviors; (2) how do individuals communicate to other individuals between and across age classes; (3) what difficulties does an individual's aging place upon those in the new age stratum he or she is entering, as well as those in the age stratum left behind; and (4) how do

these differences in the attitudes and behaviors of individuals in different age strata generate pressures for social change? In other words, Riley argues that "*people* at varying ages differ in their capacity and willingness to perform social roles . . . the age strata differ in the social *roles* members are expected to play . . . old people must live as members of such a society, finding their place in relation to the other members . . . (all the while) people of different ages are *all* growing older." In essence, the age-stratification approach to social gerontology may be equated to an aggregate-level version of the role theory approach. Each stratum represents a different social role to be learned by those who enter it, played by those who remain in it, and given up by those who leave it. Accordingly, the proponents of the age-stratification approach suggest that we concentrate our analyses on the social relationships between, emphasizing social cleavages, and within, emphasizing social bonds, age strata.

A COMMON THEME. As you may already have noticed, while the five major approaches to social gerontology emphasize different aspects of the aging process, they all focus around one factor, the changing social role of the aging individual. This focus is explicit in the role theory, while the disengagement theory focuses on the withdrawal from one role and the assumption of another. In the subcultural theory the importance of the aging role emerges from the common perception of typical behavior. Activity theory presumes that the loss of an individual's adult social role results in reduced social activity, which in turn results in reduced self-concept and lowered life satisfaction. The age-stratification theory assumes that each age-stratum has its own social roles, to be acted out by the individuals who pass through that stratum. In sum, all five theoretical approaches to social gerontology may be viewed as variations from a general role theory perspective similar to Parsons's (1951) role theory and systems conceptualization of the sick role. This should not be too surprising, because social gerontology is a somewhat recent outgrowth of medical sociology. As we have mentioned throughout these chapters, the sociology of health is built soundly upon the Parsonian structural functional framework.

Aging Viewed from Both Sides

Regardless of which theoretical approach one takes to social gerontology, there are two major issues to be considered: how society views the aged, and how the aged view themselves. In the best of all situations, we might expect these two views to be similar if not identical, just as the expectations concerning the sick role might be for the patient, the practitioner, and society. This, however, is not the case.

SOCIETY'S IMAGE. While there is currently no official policy toward the aged, there is a very consistent and negative societal reaction to both the aged and the aging process. This reaction, however, has not always been the case. Indeed, in a fascinating book Fischer (1978) has identified five major ways in which aging has historically been viewed in the United States: a period of gerontocracy (from 1607 to 1820), in which age was honored, obeyed, venerated, and served as the basis for a hierarchically stratified society; a period of deep change (1780 to 1820), during which a revolution in age relations occurred and equality masked over youthful ascendancy; a period of gerontophobia (1780 to 1970), in which the cult of youth emerged and society began to loathe aging in others and fear it in itself; another period of deep change (1910 to 1970), during which aging began to be viewed as a social problem and which marked the emergence of social gerontology and geriatrics as scholarly disciplines; and a potential period of gerontophratria (the present), in which a fraternity of youth and age are possible if the economic dependence of one on the other is eliminated, if the aged are recognized as a heterogeneous group, and if there is a change from the traditional work ethic to a more modern creativity ethic. Other gerontologists, such as Butler (1975), how-

ever, are less optimistic about this last stage; they argue that the United States is still firmly entrenched in a gerontophobic period.

The pervasive negative attitude associated with gerontophobia is readily apparent. Thumbing through several of the more popular American magazines, such as *Time, Newsweek, Better Homes and Gardens, Good Housekeeping*, or the *Ladies' Home Journal* reveals numerous advertisements and articles focusing on how to stay young-looking, young-feeling, young-acting, and so forth. The same attitude can be found in television or radio commercials broadcast daily, or in the books on the best-sellers' list. To be sure, America has become a youth-oriented society in which the aging process and becoming aged are viewed with anxiety and fear. Indeed, an extensive negative stereotype of what it means to be old has developed; it is typified by the 10 myths shown in Table 8-1. Despite the fact that careful research has proved these 10 statements to be false,

Table 8-1. The 10 myths of aging.

Read each statement carefully and indicate whether you believe it to be true or false.

1. Senility inevitably accompanies old age.
2. The majority of old people are miserable.
3. Most old people are lonely and isolated from their families.
4. The majority of old people are in poor health.
5. Old people are more likely than younger people to be victimized by crime.
6. The majority of old people live in poverty.
7. Older workers are less productive than younger ones.
8. Old people who retire usually suffer a decline in health and early death.
9. Most old people have no interest in, or capacity for, sexual relations.
10. Most old people end up in nursing homes and other long-term care institutions.

SOURCE: Cary S. Kart. 1985. *The Realities of Aging: An Introduction to Gerontology,* 2nd ed. Copyright © 1985 by Allyn and Bacon, Inc. Reprinted with permission.

they remain securely entrenched in contemporary American society (Kart, 1985).

According to most social gerontologists, it is this negative stereotype that begins to threaten individuals as they enter the middle stage of the life cycle. This fear and anxiety appear to increase the closer one gets to old age (Atchenbaum, 1985). Once old age is reached, the aged are faced with both inevitable physiological decline and assignment to a lower social status (such as in disengagement theory). As a result, it has been argued that the closer an individual gets to old age, the more fully he or she accepts the negative stereotype of the aged, and the more fearful and anxious he or she becomes about being identified as an old person (see Thomas and Yamamoto, 1975). Once the individual has been so identified, society reacts to that label rather than to the individual's true identity. This redefines the individual as something different, and of less value and status. In sum, contemporary American society views the aged as less than useful, and it is not quite sure what to do with them.

AGED'S SELF-IMAGE. While it is quite obvious how much of society views the aged, it is not at all clear how the aged view themselves. The research literature comparing the aged's self-concept with society's stereotypes is contradictory, to say the least. Some research studies portray the aged as accepting of the stereotype; others portray the aged as stable contributors with high levels of self-worth. Neugarten (1971; see also Binstock, 1985) has attempted to reconcile these apparently contradictory findings by noting that the aged, like other social groups, are not homogeneous. Rather, they are heterogeneous. In fact, from a study of 2,000 aged individuals Neugarten was able to identify four major personality types: the integrated personality, characterized by openness, satisfaction, mental alertness, and a positive self-concept; the defended personality, characterized by ambitious, achievement-oriented individuals striving to reject the aged stereotype by maintaining their adult roles and their health; the passive-

dependent personality, characterized by a strong need to be responded to by others and to depend on them; and the disintegrated personality type, characterized by an extensive psychological disorganization requiring elaborate familial assistance if the individual is to be maintained ouside of an institution. Thus, she concludes that there is more variation among the aged than is typically assumed. As studies of the aged become more representative of the total population, rather than concentrated among the poorer and lower-educated aged who in the past have been the most convenient to study, this heterogeneity will become more evident.

Personality differences, however, are not the only factors affecting how the aged view themselves and adjust to the aging process. Three other important factors are health, sex, and socioeconomic status. Aged individuals who are in better health, whether this is only their perception or that of the health professional as well, typically adapt better to the aging process, and they do so with less anxiety (Maddox, 1962). Similarly, aged and nonaged individuals' attitudes toward the elderly are also affected by the health of the evaluating individual; healthy individuals consider the aged in a better light than do ill individuals. Males have more difficulty adapting to old age and are more anxious about it because they were more attached to the social structure through their jobs and other social roles than were aged females. Thus, when disengagement occurs at the end of the adult role, males suffer greater structural and status changes, face the prospects of old age more anxiously, and adapt to it less readily (Cumming and Henry, 1961).

Finally, although everyone who reaches old ages faces a significant reduction in socioeconomic status, the economic well-being among the aged is not equal (see Schulz, 1985). Those aged individuals who have more resources than others may remain in closer contact with people and exhibit more activity. This results in a higher self-concept, better adjustment, and less anxiety than others. In essence, the aged's view of themselves depends on factors of personality, health, sex, and socioeconomic status. As social gerontology matures and socially based subgroups among the aged are studied in greater detail, a clearer understanding of what motivates the aged to view themselves the way they do is likely to emerge. For the time being, all that can be said is that the aged generally do not conform to their societal stereotype, nor do they all respond to the aging process or old age in the same way. In short, the aged are a heterogeneous group, not a homogeneous one.

To summarize, although aging per se is the study of the entire life cycle, we usually associate it with the study of the elderly. Most important to our understanding of the aging process is the fact that we all age along three dimensions—the physiological, the psychological, and the social—although not necessarily at the same time or in the same way. There are, however, sufficient similarities in the processes that we all go through to warrant the discussion of an "aged role" patterned after the sick role. We expect the elderly to withdraw or be disengaged from their normal adult roles and to take on a new, societally detached role. By and large, this new role evokes a negative reaction from society. Therefore, adopting this role is something that is feared by most of those approaching old age. Because the number and proportion of elderly people in our society are rapidly increasing, we may soon find ourselves being forced to redesign a more appropriate role for the aged, to reconsider how they might be better treated, and to reevaluate whether or not they should be so totally disengaged from society.

Death and Dying

Closely related to the aging issue is the social problem of death and dying. Their relationship stems from the fact that as an individual ages, his or her likelihood of dying increases. Thus, the death and dying process is much more common among the aged than among any other social group. More subtly, death and dying may be viewed as

placing individuals in a special version of the sick role, a version from which there is no hope of recovery (see Freidson, 1970a, and the discussion of the more specific sick roles in chapter 5).

The death and dying process may be viewed as a social problem for at least two reasons. First, we understand very little about the dying process. Social research in this area only began to appear after 1965, and our lack of knowledge about this social process poses several problems. Second, and perhaps more timely, is the fact that technological developments, both inside and outside of medicine, have enabled us to prolong biological functioning almost indefinitely (at least as long as the bill can be paid). This capability raises the issue of when a human being, as opposed to merely a biological one, is dead or alive. It becomes especially significant when one considers the expanding use of organ transplants, whether they be human, xenografts, or mechanical. We shall begin our discussion of death and dying at the logical starting point by tracing historical attitudes toward death and their subsequent modification.

Redefining Death

When we think of death, we generally think of it in common terms such as the loss of life, the cessation of vital functions, or the act of dying. We generally take for granted the notion that death has always been viewed as it is now. Moreover, we assume that it is relatively easy to determine when a person has died. Many of these assumptions, however, are not accurate. The nature of death and its definition have been changing for some time.

CHANGING IMAGES OF DEATH. Although every modern society has had its own image of death (usually viewed as the absence of life), there seems to be some consistency in how those images have changed over time (see Feifel, 1977; Gonda and Ruark, 1984; Rachels, 1986). In fact, Illich (1976) has identified six distinct stages in the historical development of the image of death. The first appeared around the fifteenth century and may be labeled as the "dance of the dead." During this period death was used as an occasion for reveling in life, with dancing on the tombs occuring as a typical affirmation of the joy of life. In the Renaissance this image gave way to a conception of death as marking the end of life and the beginning of eternity. One indication of the switch to this "danse macabre" was the proliferation of clocks, symbolizing the new time-bound perspective. The third image of death appears with the emergence of the bourgeois class and is appropriately labeled "bourgeois death." As they could afford it, the bourgeois started to pay physicians to keep death away, marking the first use of doctors as death-delayers or preventers. This image matured until the nineteenth century; at that point physicians promulgated the "clinical" image of death. It held that death was the result of specific diseases identifiable by the physician.

By the 1900s this image had transformed into a "natural death" image in which doctors were supposed to step in and keep all patients from dying. The image of natural death has recently evolved into "death under intensive care." "Unnecessary deaths" are to be prevented at all costs by using every medical technique available. In essence, Illich (1976) argues that our image of death has been transformed from death as a natural event (not to be fought), to death as a force of nature (to be avoided), to death as an untimely event, to death as something caused by specific diseases, to society's obligation to fight the unnatural death of all of its members, to an all-out war against death. Thus, although death was once recognized as a natural part of the living process, it has come to be viewed as an evil to be avoided and fought at every step. This includes the use of highly sophisticated life-support systems capable of keeping "alive" in intensive care units individuals who would surely die without such life-support devices.

TOWARD A DEFINITION OF DEATH. We have seen that the image of death has changed drastically over the centuries from a natural and expected event to an unnatural event to be avoided at all costs. Perhaps the most perplexing issue concerning dying that faces us today is how we define death. As was the case with health, we generally all assume that we know exactly what death is, at least until we are asked to define it. Only then does it become clear that the matter is quite complex and the definitions are rather controversial. Consider, for example, the following extended definition of death taken from a leading medical dictionary (Becker, 1986):

Cessation of life, generally considered to ensue in the absence of spontaneous breathing or heartbeat. In a society of high technology, however, absence of discernable brain function has sometimes been substituted for the above criteria. In the United States, a presidential commission voted in 1981 that a Uniform Determination of Death Act be adopted by all states, an action endorsed by the American Medical Association and [the] American Bar Association. The Act reads: 'An individual who has sustained either (1) irreversible cessation of circulatory or respiratory function, or (2) irreversible cessation of all functions of the entire brain, including the brain stem, is dead. A determination of death must be made in accordance with accepted medical standards.'

Despite its length, this definition fails to provide any clarification of what would be consistent with "accepted medical standards" for determining death under either option. This is not an uncommon shortcoming, even among the more elite or "standard" medical dictionaries. Indeed, the entry in another (Thomson, 1984) states that

the only certain sign of death . . . is the *stoppage of the heart*, and to ensure this is permanent it is necessary to listen over the heart, that is, over the chest at the inner side of the nipple, for five minutes. This can be done by means of a stethoscope or by listening directly with the ear on the chest. *Stoppage of breathing* should also be noted, and this can be confirmed by observing that a mirror held before the mouth shows no haze, that a feather placed on the upper lip does not flutter, or that a reflection on the ceiling from a cup of water placed on the chest of the dead person shows no movement. . . . In the vast majority of cases there is no difficulty in ensuring that death has occurred. The introduction of organ transplantation, however, and of more effective mechanical respiration, whereby an individual's

182

*Applying The
Principles to
Aging, Death and
Dying, and Mental
Illness*

heart can be kept beating almost indefinitely, has raised difficulty in a minority of cases. To solve the problem in these cases the concept of '*brain death*' has been introduced. In this context it has to be borne in mind that there is no legal definition of death.

Thus, although this entry provides straightforward, if not simplistic, methods for assessing death in most cases, it only identifies a general principle for defining death in unusual circumstances. It is precisely this disagreement surrounding the determination of death in extraordinary cases that poses the crucial problem. Moreover, it has focused the controversy on defining brain death, as evidenced by the cases of the late Karen Ann Quinlan (see Bush, 1978) or Baby Jane Doe (see Rachels, 1986).

REFINING THE CRITERIA OF DEATH. In an initial attempt to resolve the sensitive issue of extending our conventional definition of death to these extraordinary situations, a Task Force on Death and Dying was established by the Institute of Society, Ethics, and the Life Sciences (1972). They recognized countless biological, ethical, psychological, and social factors to be considered in defining death. While scrupulously avoiding the task of defining death, the Task Force identified eight "good" criteria for a definition of death: (1) the criteria should be clear and distinct, with unambiguous tests; (2) the tests should be simple and be able to be performed by any physician or nurse; (3) the tests should indicate the permanence and irreversibility of the condition; (4) the determination of death should not be based on one criterion alone, so as to avoid error; (5) the criteria should parallel existing techniques of determining death; (6) the criteria should be adhered to as closely as existing criteria; (7) the criteria should be readily communicable to the laity; and (8) the soundness and accuracy of the criteria should be pretested on the basis of autopsy findings.

THE HARVARD PLAN AND THE KANSAS STATUTE. Although no definition of death has been proposed that satisfies all the criteria established by the Task Force on Death and Dying, at least two subsequent proposals

have come fairly close. We shall review them both briefly. The first was advanced in 1968 by the Ad Hoc Committee of the Harvard Medical School to Examine the Definition of Brain Death. The Harvard plan, reproduced in its entirety in Figure 8-4, contains four criteria for defining brain death: (1) the existence of an irreversible coma, defined as the unreceptivity and unawareness of external stimuli and internal needs; (2) the absence of any spontaneous muscular movements, respiration, or responses to any external stimuli; (3) the absence of all elicitable reflexes; and (4) the existence of flat brain waves. In addition to these four stringent criteria, the Harvard plan mandates that these four sets of tests must be repeated at least 24 hours after the initial testing and must reveal absolutely no change.

In 1973 the state of Kansas enacted a statute reflecting the Harvard plan in principle. The Kansas statute (Kansas, The State of, 1970) established two definitions of death: the permanent absence of spontaneous cardiac and respiratory functioning, and the permanent absence of spontaneous activity. Both of these definitions are clearly drawn from the Harvard plan and, like it and similar proposals, are based on three questionable assumptions (Task Force on Death and Dying, 1972):

(1) that the existence of human life, no less than its essence, is defined in terms of activities normally associated with higher brain function; (2) that such activities are exclusively centered in the anatomical locus known as the neocortex; and (3) that the EEG provides a full and complete measure of neocortical function. From these assumptions the following conclusion is drawn: In the absence of a functioning neocortex, as determined by an isoelectric [flat] EEG, human life has ceased.

All three of these assumptions have come under fire. Brierly, Adams, and Graham (1971) have questioned the third assumption, because their research revealed that patients with flat brain waves continued to respirate for up to six months. Oakley (1971) has questioned the second assumption, based on his research involving instrumental learning among neocordicate rabbits. Silverman, Masland, and Saunders (1969)

Figure 8-4. Criteria of the Harvard Plan for Defining Brain Death.

1. Unreceptivity and Unresponsivity. There is a total awareness to externally applied stimuli and inner need and complete unresponsiveness—our definition of irreversible coma. Even the most intensely painful stimuli evoke no vocal or other response, not even a groan, withdrawal of a limb, or quickening of respiration.

2. No Movements or Breathing. Observations covering a period of at least one hour by physicians is adequate to satisfy the criteria of no spontaneous muscular movements or spontaneous respiration or response to stimuli such as pain, touch, sound, or light.

After the patient is on mechanical respirator, the total absence of spontaneous breathing may be established by turning off the respirator and observing whether there is any effort on the part of the subject to breathe spontaneously. (The respirator may be turned off for this time provided that at the start of the trial period the patient's carbon dioxide tension is within the normal range, and provided also that the patient had been breathing room air for at least 10 minutes prior to the trial.)

3. No Reflexes. Irreversible coma with abolition of central nervous system activity is evidenced in part by the absence of elicitable reflexes. The pupil will be fixed and dilated and will not respond to a direct source of bright light. Since the establishment of a fixed, dilated pupil is clear-cut in medical practice, there should be no uncertainty as to its presence. Ocular movement (to head turning and to irrigation of the ears with ice water) and blinking are absent. There is no evidence of postural activity (decerebrate or other). Swallowing, yawning, vocalization are in abeyance. Corneal and pharyngeal reflexes are absent.

As a rule the stretch of tendon reflexes cannot be elicited; i.e., tapping the tendons of the biceps, triceps and pronator muscles, quadriceps and gastrocnemius muscles with the reflex hammer elicits no contraction of the respective muscles. Plantar or noxious stimulation gives no response.

4. Flat Electroencephalogram. Of great confirmatory value is the flat or isoletric EEG. We must assume that the electrodes have been properly applied, that the apparatus is functioning normally, and that the personnel in charge is competent. We consider it prudent to have one channel of the apparatus used for an electrocardiogram. This channel will monitor the EEG so that, if it appears in the electroencephalographic leads because of high resistance, it can be readily identified. It also establishes the presence of the active heart in the absence of EEG. We recommend that another channel be used for a noncephalic lead. This will pick up space-borne or vibration-borne artifacts and identify them. The simplest form of such a monitoring noncephalic electrode has two leads over the dorsum of the hand, preferably the right hand, so the EEG will be minimal or absent. Since one of the requirements of this state is that there be no muscle activity, these two dorsal and hand electrodes will not be bothered by muscle artifact. The apparatus should be run at standard gains $10\mu v/5mm$. $50\mu v/mm$. Also it should be isoletric at double this standard gain which is $5\mu v/mm$ or $25\mu v/5mm$. At least ten full minutes of recording are desirable, but twice that would be better.

It is also suggested that the gains at some point be opened to their full amplitude for a brief period (5 to 100 seconds) to see what is going on. Usually in an intensive care unit artifacts will dominate the picture, but these are readily identifiable. There shall be no electroencephalographic response to noise or to pinch.

All of the above tests shall be repeated at least 24 hours later with no change.

The validity of such data as indications of irreversible cerebral damage depends on the exclusion of two conditions: hypothermia (temperature below 90 F [32.2 C]) or central nervous system depressants, such as barbiturates.

SOURCE: Harvard Medical School, Ad Hoc Committee. 1968. "A Definition of Irreversible Coma: Report of the Ad Hoc Committee of the Harvard Medical School to Examine the Definition of Brain Death." *Journal of the American Medical Association* 205:337–40. © 1968, American Medical Association. Reprinted by permission.

have questioned the reliability and validity of using the flat EEGs as the sole determinant of brain death. Finally, the first assumption is a philosophical one, which Freidson (1970a) suggests should not be made by the physician, but left up to the patient and his or her family. Based on the controversy surrounding these three assumptions, the Task Force has recommended that the first three criteria of the Harvard plan (the clinical criteria of unreceptivity and unresponsivity, no movements or breathing, and no reflexes) be used as the principal

criteria, using the criterion of flat EEGs only as a confirmatory technique.

In 1981 the Presidential Commission for the Study of Ethical Problems in Medicine and Biomedical and Behavioral Research published its own guidelines for determining death under the *Uniform Determination of Death Act*. That Act simply states "[that] an individual who has sustained either (a) irreversible cessation of circulatory and respiratory functions, or (b) cessation of functions of the entire brain, including the brain-stem, is dead. A determination of death must be made in accordance with acceptable medical standards." Not so simple, however, is operationalizing brain death. Indeed, although the Presidential Commission is somewhat more rigorous than the Harvard plan by including the brain stem in its definition of brain death, the issue remains unresolved. Gonda and Ruark (1984) suggest that the rapidly rising cost of maintaining life in irrevocably vegatative patients (especially those without neocortical function, which provides consciousness, personality, and all other behavioral attributes, but who still have intact brain-stem functions) will force revisions in the definition of brain death. That is, they expect economic pressures will necessitate a resolution of the definitional problems in the near future.

THE ESSENTIAL QUESTION. Regardless of which particular definition of death you prefer or which definition we discuss, there is a growing recognition of one essential fact. Like health and illness, life and death are not two polar opposites. Rather, as with health and illness (see chapter 4), there is a continuum with absolute life at one end and absolute death at the other. There are an infinite number of gray shades in between. This continuum is portrayed in Figure 8-5, where the letters A, B, and C represent three of the places along the continuum where death may be defined. You may choose to define death as occuring at point A, while I choose point C, and another individual chooses point B. The essential queston in defining death is locating the point where a given individual may be appropriately labeled as dead. According to the Task Force (1972), this involves decision making at five levels: "(1) establishing a concept of death; (2) selecting general criteria and procedures for determining that a patient has died; (3) determining in the particular case that the

patient meets the criteria; (4) pronouncing him dead; and (5) certifying the death on a certificate of record." As we have seen, there was once a consensus as to the meaning of death (although the meaning has changed throughout history), but this is no longer the case. Having shared agreement on the first decision, we used to leave the last four decisions up to the physician. Now, however, there is a growing concern as to who shall decide what criteria and which tests are to be used to determine death (see Gonda and Ruark, 1984; Saunders and Baines, 1983; Turnbull, 1986). For the moment, there are neither absolutely right nor absolutely wrong answers to these questions. There is only a great deal of controversy that may not be resolved for several years.

Stages in the Dying Process

What is it like to be dying? Are there certain things or phases that we all go through when it is our time? How is the onset of death viewed by the dying patient? These are but three of the many questions that emerge when we begin to speak of death and dying. Until as recently as the mid 1960s these questions were confined to the philosophical literature; they were considered to be unpleasant issues inappropriate for public discussion. More than any other person, Elisabeth Kubler-Ross threw open the doors hiding these issues in 1968 with the publication of her widely acclaimed book *On Death and Dying*. (For an alternative but fundamentally quite similar model of the stages in the dying process see Weisman, 1980, who identifies four comparable stages: existential plight; mitigation and accommodation; decline and deterioration; and, preterminality and terminality.) Almost overnight a new movement began to form,

Figure 8-5. The Continuum of Life and Death.

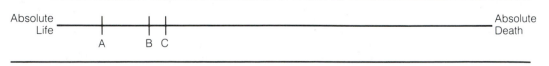

Absolute Life ———————————————————————————— Absolute Death

A   B C

and a growing audience awaited new theories and the results of new research. Perhaps still the dominant figure in the death and dying movement, Kubler-Ross opened a fountainhead of knowledge on the subject with her analysis of in-depth interviews with more than 400 terminally ill patients. Kubler-Ross was able to identify five distinct stages that patients passed through during their dying process: denial, anger, bargaining, preparatory grief, and acceptance. When taken together, these stages tentatively constitute a variation of the traditional sick role that may be referred to as the dying role or process. The latter term—*process*—is preferred, because the concept is not nearly so well articulated as the concepts of the sick or aged roles.

DENIAL. When most patients are confronted with a diagnosis of terminal illness, their initial response is one of shock and denial. Kubler-Ross (1968) found that a typical reaction was "no, it can't be me; it's not possible." In a general sense, we never expect *this* time to be *our* time. Such things may be happening to other people every day, but not to us, at least not today. This deep-seated denial stems from the contemporary conception of death as something to be fought at all costs. Being told that we have a terminal illness is like being told that we have failed at the ultimate task of living. We are shocked by such information; we attempt to deny its reliability and validity. The denial stage begins to erode when the dying individual is confronted by the task of getting everything in order. This erosion is aided by the patient's perception that facing the reality of impending death will help make it easier on his or her significant others.

ANGER. After the denial stage comes anger. The typical reaction that Kubler-Ross (1968) found at this stage is epitomized in the "no, not me," and "why me?" responses. Angry patients are difficult patients because of their rage at being "singled out" for death while others have escaped. Patients in this stage of the dying process may attempt to conceal their anger by venting it on those who care for them, claiming that they have

been awakened, disturbed, and so on. Nurses and other hospital personnel often react to such dying patients by delayed responses to their calls and other requests. In essence, during the anger stage of the dying process the patient is enraged, sensing his or her own impotence and helplessness. The only recourse for an angry patient is to complain about everything to everyone, because there is no one to whom he or she can appeal the final judgment.

BARGAINING. The bargaining stage of the dying process occurs when anger is given up for a different approach: making a deal for the extension of whatever time remains. In this stage the patient recognizes that anger will have no effect on the terminal illness. Therefore, a better strategy is to bargain for as much time as possible. The majority of such bargaining takes place between the patient and his or her conception of God; it is typified with statements—often internalized—such as "if you give me one more year to live, I will be a good Christian," or "for one more year of life I will donate my organs." This bargaining with the gods represents a promise of some behavioral change in order to prolong life. Bargaining, however, may also occur with the practitioner. Under these circumstances it takes the form of an exchange of patient compliance for a weekend at home with the family, or for permission to walk around the hospital grounds at will.

PREPARATORY GRIEF. In the preparatory grief stage of the dying process the "no, not me" reaction changes to a "yes, me" reaction. The dying patient begins to acknowledge the fact that the time has come and that the bargaining process is over. Depression sets in and the dying patient may withdraw contact from all visitors, save for that one special beloved friend. At this point the dying patient begins to prepare for the loss of not just one good friend, which we all face in the death of someone else, but for the loss of all good friends. Accordingly, the dying patient prepares to separate him- or herself from all others. All that is left is to prepare for the end.

186

*Applying The
Principles to
Aging, Death and
Dying, and Mental
Illness*

ACCEPTANCE. In the final stage of the dying process, the dying individual accepts the inevitable not as a feeling of resignation but as a good feeling. Kubler-Ross (1968) portrays the typical reaction in the acceptance stage with "I have now finished all of my unfinished business. I have said all of the words that have to be said. I am ready to go." The assumption of the acceptance stage in the dying process represents the declaration of accomplishment by those who are dying. They have reviewed their lives and found that while they may not have been perfect or famous, they have lived their lives fully and are now ready to accept the final act of life, which is death. She equates the patient in this stage of the dying process with those at the beginning stages of life; both have similar physical needs that must be met by others (such as feeding and bathing), and both have other needs that only one beloved individual can provide.

EVALUATING KUBLER-ROSS'S MODEL. In delineating five distinct stages in the dying process, Kubler-Ross (1968) has significantly advanced our understanding of what it is like to die and what we may expect to feel when it is our turn. There are, however, three kinks yet to be ironed out of her theory. First, the five stages in the dying process may only apply to the terminally ill who have sufficient time and ability to confront and evaluate the fact of their own dying process. In other words, to pass through the five stages in the dying process requires the dying individual to be aware of his or her impending death, to be dying somewhat slowly (as opposed to death from a traumatic accident), and to have retained enough mental capacity to grasp the implications of the dying situation. Thus, the stages of the dying process may not apply to all situations. Second, like the Parsonian (1951) sick role concept, Kubler-Ross's stages in the dying process are anchored to middle-class American values, especially at the bargaining and acceptance stages. The attitudes and emotional responses portrayed in the five stages of dying represent typical middle-class reactions to trying situations. To the extent that middle-class values are not shared by others, neither are the five stages in the dying process. Third, while the five stages in the dying process specify certain behavior, not all individuals complete all five stages, nor do they necessarily complete them in the same order. There is considerable variation in the behavior of dying individuals, just as there is considerable variation in the behavior of sick individuals (consider Suchman's, 1965a, 1965b, argument that all individuals need not proceed through all the stages of illness behavior, nor spend the same amount of time in each). To be sure, Kubler-Ross makes this point herself. She argues that the various stages may reoccur a number of times in different sequences for the same individual. Nonetheless, it has become commonplace for both professionals and lay individuals to interpret her model as a staged set of ordered passages (see Gonda and Ruark, 1984). Despite these limitations and misinterpretations, Kubler-Ross's theory provides us with a set of expectations on how dying people are likely to behave and how they are likely to feel.

USING THE THEORY TO HELP THE DYING. When viewed as an ideal-type model, Kubler-Ross's (1968) fives stages of dying suggest a number of ways in which others can help the terminally ill patient pass through the stages to arrive at the least distressful death possible. Specifically, Pattison (1969, 1977) has identified six ways in which assistance can be provided to ease the passage of the dying patient: share the responsibility for the individual's dying crisis, reducing his or her anxiety and bewilderment; clarify the specific realities of the patient's life, so that they may be focused and clearly put in order; maintain rewarding human contact throughout the dying process; assist in the separation of the dying individual from the living role, while maintaining meaningful relationships with those being lost; assume the physical and psychological needs of the dying individual without depreciating his or her self-respect; and encourage the dying individual to accept the final life situation with dignity and integrity. According to Pattison, if we could accomplish these six tasks in sequence to match the stages of dying, then we would have helped the dying patient deal with the dying process.

In addition to helping the dying patient deal with the dying process, the work of Kubler-Ross (1968), Pattison (1969, 1977), and others suggests how we may help the bereaved deal with the grieving process. For example, Lindemann (1944) has presented the classic description of the acute grief syndrome. This syndrome, which usually begins to dissipate after six weeks, is characterized by tightness in the throat, choking, shortness of breath, sighing, a feeling of emptiness in the gut, a loss of muscular strength, and psychic pain. By accepting this syndrome as a natural reaction to grief, others can help the bereaved through this transitional period. More recently, Turnbull (1986) has argued that there are four distinct phases in the grief process: numbness, initially in the form of disbelief and subsequently in the form of an intense forward-looking orientation; pining, or an overwhelming desire for the deceased; apathy and depression, during which the bereaved may feel inadequate, tense, and irritable; and reorganization, or when the bereaved begins to make "a new start." By extending support to the bereaved, much like the temporary and conditional exemption from normal task and role obligations associated with the sick role, we facilitate their return to their prebereavement state.

Awareness of Dying

In order for us to help and to understand the dying patient, we must first be aware of the dying situation. While this may seem to be an obvious point, Kubler-Ross (1968) was astonished at the unwillingess of hospital personnel to identify dying patients. It seems that when she first started her research no one in the hospital was dying, although some were "too sick" to be interviewed. Because more than half of all Americans die in hospitals and most of the remainder die in hospital-like nursing homes, the various contexts of the awareness of death and dying in hospitals are of considerable importance in understanding the overall issue.

Hospital personnel view death and dying as highly disruptive to their ordered social setting. Accordingly, they tend to manipulate the social situation, which may be viewed as a variation of the patient-practitioner relationship, in order to minimize this disruption. In *Awareness of Dying*, Glaser and Strauss (1965) identified four types of hospital awareness settings that may be seen as contextual analogs of Kubler-Ross's stages of dying: closed awareness, suspected awareness, mutual pretense awareness, and open awareness. According to Glaser and Strauss, the interplay between patients and hospital personnel (the patient-personnel relationship) depends on the awareness context in the dying situation and how earlier awareness evolves into later awareness.

CLOSED AWARENESS. The closed awareness situation exists when hospital personnel and others are aware that the patient is dying, but the patient is not. Glaser and Strauss (1965) identify five factors that contribute to closed awareness: most patients have had insufficient experience in recognizing the signs of impending death; physicians generally do not inform their patients outright that death is coming, avoiding emotional scenes and the admission of failure by telling the family instead; families tend to keep this information from the dying patient, so as not to upset him or her; the structure of hospitals is such that medical information, in the form of both documents and staff knowledge, is inaccessible to the patient; and the dying patient has no allies in the pursuit of such information. There are several benefits in the closed awareness situation as long as the dying process is not prolonged. First, the physician does not have to discuss the dying process with the patient. Second, the emotional trauma of a "graceless" dying patient may be avoided. Finally, the patient may be spared the agonizing stages of the dying process.

SUSPECTED AWARENESS. The suspected awareness context of the dying process occurs

188

*Applying The
Principles to
Aging, Death and
Dying, and Mental
Illness*

when the patient suspects but is not sure that he or she is terminally ill, although the hospital personnel and others are sure. In this context the dying individual tries to draw information out of whatever sources are available. The hospital personnel and the patient's significant others attempt to evade the patient's requests for information in order to maintain the advantages of the closed awareness situation. As a result, the dying patient begins to play a version of the bargaining game, except that the purpose is latent rather than manifest, and the reward is information rather than privileges.

MUTUAL PRETENSE AWARENESS. In the mutual pretense situation both the hospital staff and the patient are aware of the fact that the patient is dying. The patient generally refuses to talk about his or her impending death; the hospital staff assumes the position that they are not obligated to discuss the matter with the patient, although they may if asked to do so. Thus, if neither the hospital staff nor the patient chooses to initiate a discussion on the topic, all parties remain informed but incommunicative. Because both parties are aware of the patient's impending death, the mutual pretense context allows them to avoid the potential embarrassment or distress of either party. Knowledge of the impending death coupled with discussion-avoidance, however, eliminates the possibility for cathartic relief.

OPEN AWARENESS. The final situation that Glaser and Strauss (1965) identify is the open awareness context. In this situation the dying patient and the hospital staff know of the patient's impending death and openly acknowledge it. The hospital staff is expected to make the dying patient's last days as comfortable and painless as possible (see Saunders and Baines, 1983), while the dying patient is expected to face his or her death with responsibility and dignity (see Gonda and Ruark, 1984). In this context, dying patients and hospital personnel are allowed to support each other. The hospital personnel support the dying patients in various ways as they face their death; the dying patients absolve the hospital person-

nel for failure (their impending death) because they tried their best.

THE UNDERLYING THEME. The theme that underlies the awareness contexts identified by Glaser and Strauss (1965) is based on the social setting, which includes talking, activity, and other aspects of social interaction, and the control of information concerning the dying patient in the hospital. At one extreme—in the closed awareness context—the social setting is closed and relevant information about the dying patient is not shared with him or her. At the other extreme—in the open awareness context—the social setting is open and relevant information is shared with the patient. The different awareness contexts represent different ways of managing the dying experience. Once the experience has begun and the dying patient and the hospital personnel begin to interact, the awareness context may be modified from more closed to more open situations.

Unlike Kubler-Ross's (1968) stages of dying, however, Glaser and Strauss's (1966) four awareness contexts are not considered to be a series of stages, ordered or not, that all who are dying are expected to pass through. Quite to the contrary, in some cases it may be much easier for everyone involved if the context of dying remains closed. What makes the contexts of the awareness of dying increasingly important is the fact that more and more Americans are dying from chronic conditions that require them to be hospitalized for a prolonged period prior to their death. As a result, the dying process frequently takes place in a hospital setting. By manipulating the social setting and controlling the flow of information, hospital personnel may bring about the awareness context with which they are most comfortable and which they believe will best suit the dying patient. This manipulation may be rapid or gradual, and the dying situation may pass through only one or all four contexts.

EVALUATING THE AWARENESS CONTEXTS APPROACH. Glaser and Strauss's (1965) awareness contexts approach suffers from three limitations similar to those of Kubler-Ross's

(1968) stages of the dying process. First, the four awareness contexts are only appropriate when the patient is conscious and in the hospital for a reasonable period of time prior to his or her death. This rules out comatose patients, infants, and emergency situations. Second, the awareness contexts approach applies only when there is an attempt by the hospital staff to manage the knowledge of the patient's dying. Finally, all of the dying patients that Glaser and Strauss studied were paying for their own care and were of above-average socioeconomic status. This placed these dying patients in a more advantaged position to negotiate with the hospital staff for information; as a result, they may be atypical. Nonetheless, Glaser and Strauss were clearly able to show that death and dying are viewed as disruptive processes by hospital personnel who alter the social setting and control the flow of information in order to minimize such disruptions.

Coming Back from Death: Life After Life

When the time comes for the dying patient to die, one of the most puzzling questions known to humankind arises. This occurs regardless of the stage of the dying process the individual has entered or the nature of the awareness context. The puzzling question is this: "Now that the dying process is over, *what is death really like?* Does everything go dark and cease to exist, or is there really some form of life after death?" For centuries this question has given rise to great speculation. There are no authoritative answers because the dead do not come back to testify about the ultimate experience of death—not even Houdini.

About 10 years ago, however, a physician named Raymond Moody, Jr., published two very popular and controversial books based on his analysis of the recounted stories of individuals who have been clinically dead and then come back to life. While the scientific community has yet to accept the data or the conclusions reached by Moody in *Life After Life* (1975) or in *Reflections on Life After Life* (1976), there is a strikingly common theme that runs through the ex-

periences recalled by those who had "returned." This theme is encapsulated in the following vignette concerning a dying young mother:

I had a heart attack, and I found myself in a black void, and I knew that I had left my physical body behind. I knew that I was dying and I thought 'God, I did the best I knew how at the time I did it. Please help me.' Immediately, I was moved out of that blackness, through a pale grey, and I just went gliding and moving swiftly, and in front of me, in the distance, I could see a grey mist, and I was rushing toward it. It seemed that I would just not get to it fast enough to satisfy me, and as I got closer to it I could see through it. Beyond the mist, I could see people, and their forms were just like they are on earth, and I could also see something which one could take to be buildings. The whole thing was permeated with the most gorgeous light, a living, gold yellow glow, a pale color, not like the harsh glow we know on earth. As I approached more closely, I felt certain that I was going through that mist. It was such a wonderful, joyous feeling: there are not words in the human language to describe it. Yet it wasn't my time to go through the mist, because instantly from the other side appeared my Uncle Carl, who had died many years earlier. He blocked my path, saying, 'Go back. Your work on earth has not yet been completed. Go back now.' I did not want to go back, but I had no choice, and immediately I was back in my body. I felt that horrible pain in my chest, and I heard my little boy crying, 'God, bring my mommy back to me.' (Moody, 1975) (Reprinted by permission.)

In this vignette, as well as in nearly all the other recounted incidents in *Life After Life*, there are eight elements in the dying experience that appear with astounding regularity. First, there is the feeling of leaving the physical body and moving off into space. Second, there is the awareness and acceptance of dying. Third, there is the memory of moving (floating) through a tunnel-like conduit that was filled with a gray mist. Fourth, the dying individual perceives that he or she is not moving through the tunnel fast enough; this is the first indicator that something may be awry. Fifth, as the dying individual comes to the end of the tunnel, he or she encounters other people and physical settings comparable to those experienced in the first life, except that these objects are

190

*Applying The
Principles to
Aging, Death and
Dying, and Mental
Illness*

seen as if on an unusually clear and bright day. Sixth, the dying individual is overcome with the splendor and joy of everything that appears so perfect. Seventh, just as the dying individual is ready to enter this enchanted existence, the path is blocked by a significant other who has died before. This significant other states that the dying individual's final time has not yet come and that he or she is to return to life. Finally, almost immediately after encountering the significant other, the dying individual is returned to his or her physical body in this life.

Whether these strikingly common elements in the experience of those returning from clinical death are an accurate representation of the final act of dying or whether they are merely the subconscious reflection of a dominant Judeo-Christian traditional belief in life after death cannot be ascertained. In fact, this question may never be answered, unless individuals can convince us that they have indeed come back from death, and not just from the dying process, to tell us about it. Nonetheless, the accounts that Moody has collected suggest that a very interesting scenario takes place at the ultimate dying point, where we shift from one life to another. We suggest you read his books and draw your own conclusions.

Euthanasia: Letting People Die

During the past 10 years the issue of euthanasia—or when to let (or help) people die—has received increasing attention. This is indicated by the proliferation of "living wills," the publication of two popular books on self-deliverance (the British Voluntary Euthanasia Society's, 1935, *How to Die with Dignity*, and Humphrey's, 1984, *Let Me Die Before I Wake*), and the emergence of several organizations devoted to helping their members achieve successful self-destruction (such as the Hemlock Society founded in the United States in 1980). In part this trend is due to several situations that have received considerable media exposure. Among the most notable of these were the cases of Karen Ann Quinlan, who succumbed to death only years after her parents won a court order permitting them to take her off a respirator; Hans Florian, who felt compelled to kill his Alzheimer's disease-stricken wife rather than have her suffer through a prolonged, unthinking existence; Baby Jane Doe, who suffered from numerous birth defects, including the absence altogether of a significant portion of her cerebral cortex, and whose parents refused to authorize surgical procedures that might have allowed her to survive as a severely retarded, paralyzed, epileptic unlikely to reach the age of 20; and Barney Clark, the first human to receive a permanent artificial heart, who had been given a key to turn off the air compressor that kept him alive if he should wish not to continue living a life tied to machines.

Another reason for the increased discussion of euthanasia has been the pressures of numbers and technology. As we have already seen, there is a growing number of individuals in circumstances where euthanasia is likely to be considered. This results in part from the increase in the number of persons who live long enough to reach old age and are then faced with prolonged deaths from chronic conditions. Such technological developments as respirators and artificial hearts also add to the problem by providing the means for maintaining bodily functions of otherwise nonfunctioning patients.

According to Rachels (1986), the euthanasia issue ultimately comes down to a question of morality. In a discussion of the concept of the individual's welfare, he argues that we should cease speaking about maximizing happiness, the traditional moralist's approach, and shift instead to speaking about maximizing interests. This leads to a more utilitarian conception that results in the following justification of euthanasia (Rachels, 1986): "(1) If an action promotes the best interests of everyone concerned, then that action is morally acceptable. (2) In at least some cases, euthanasia promotes the best interests of everyone concerned. (3) Therefore, in at least some cases euthanasia is morally acceptable." Determining what circumstances constitute an acceptable case for euthanasia, however, is most difficult. It raises several issues beyond the scope of the present discussion. These include the distinction between active (i.e., doing something to bring the patient's death about in a more timely fashion) and passive euthanasia (i.e., letting the patient die); reaching consensus on what constitutes life; the "slippery slope" argument (i.e., if euthanasia is allowed under any circumstances, what will prevent its progressive expansion to ultimately justifying genocide); and arriving at a rational and generalizable protocol for policy implementation. We recommend that you read Rachels's book and reach your own conclusion on the merits and demerits of euthanasia.

To summarize, death and dying is the newest subfield of interest within the sociology of health, emerging no more than 25 years ago, when death and dying started to become less of an individual event occurring at home and more of a social event occurring in a hospital or nursing home setting. Although theory and research in death and dying are rapidly increasing, they are by and large too speculative for use in establishing hard facts or defining dying roles analogous to the sick or aged roles. In essence, the major accomplishment of the death and dying movement has been to focus individual and public attention on the physical, social, and psychological issues associated with death and dying. This has forced American society to reconsider questions concerning the nature of death, how people die, under what circumstances they may be allowed to die, and how interaction with dying individuals should take place. Only time will tell what the answer to these questions will be.

Mental Illness

Mental illness may be viewed as a social problem for at least three reasons. First, there is no general agreement as to what constitutes a mental disorder, although as we have already seen there is a general recognition that mental illness is bad and that the mentally ill are stigmatized (see Goffman, 1963). Second, there are several competing and contradictory models used to explain and treat mental illness, none of

which provides a truly satisfactory explanation or treatment. Finally, whatever mental illness may be, it appears to be rather widespread in the general population; at least 20 million Americans suffer from one or another of its forms. Accordingly, the topic of mental illness has become both an important social issue and an important social problem in the United States (see Eaton, 1980; Ricks and Dohrenwend, 1983; Grusky and Pollner, 1981).

Defining Mental Illness

At the root of the controversy surrounding mental illness is a lack of agreement about what constitutes it. As we learned in chapter 4, it is impossible for informed, rational discussion to take place prior to the definition of the problem at hand. In that chapter we defined an individual's general health to include his or her well-being along the three dimensions suggested by the World Health Organization (1958): the physiological, the social, and the psychological. It would seem, therefore, that mental illness must be the absence of well-being along the psychological dimension. That much is rather straightforward. What is not at all clear is how the absence of, or deviation from, psychological well-being is defined and treated.

THE PSYCHIATRIC APPROACH. As the societally authorized social control agent in charge of mental illness, most of the responsibility for caring for the mentally ill falls on psychiatry. It seems reasonable, then, to begin there with our search for a definition. Unfortunately, there is little agreement among psychiatrists as to what constitutes mental illness (see Leifer, 1969). Spitzer and Wilson (1975), however, have identified three questions that psychiatrists routinely use to diagnose a condition as a mental illness: (1) Is the condition undesirable? (2) If so, how undesirable is it? and (3) Does the diagnosis or treatment of the condition fall within the domain of psychiatry, or elsewhere? These questions reflect the inherently subjective process by which psychia-

192

*Applying The
Principles to
Aging, Death and
Dying, and Mental
Illness*

trists determine whether an individual's condition indicates mental illness.

Regardless of the inherent subjectivity in defining mental illness, however, psychiatrists have strived to establish "objective" diagnostic criteria comparable to that of the medical model. This is reflected in the American Psychiatric Association's publication of its procedural code, known as the *Diagnostic and Statistical Manual of Mental Disorders*, third edition (1980), or *DSM-III*. It lists seventeen major categories of mental disorders:

1. Disorders usually first evident in infancy, childhood, or adolescence.

2. Organic mental disorders.

3. Substance use disorders.

4. Schizophrenic disorders.

5. Paranoid disorders.

6. Other psychotic disorders.

7. Affective disorders.

8. Anxiety disorders.

9. Somatoform disorders.

10. Dissociative disorders.

11. Psychosexual disorders.

12. Factitious disorders.

13. Other impulse control disorders.

14. Adjustment disorders.

15. Psychological factors affecting physical conditions.

16. Personality disorders.

17. Conditions not attributable to a mental disorder that are a focus of attention or treatment.

Although the *DSM-III* goes on to provide detailed decision trees for reaching differential diagnoses within each category and for every specific condition, it fails to provide a general definition of mental disorders. Indeed, it clearly states that "there is no satisfactory definition that specifies precise boundaries for the concept 'mental disorder' (also true for such concepts as physical disorder and mental and physical health)." Nonetheless, the *DSM-III* provides the following statement as a framework for why certain conditions are included while others are not:

Each of the mental disorders [included in the *DSM-III*] is conceptualized as a clinically significant behavioral or psychological syndrome or pattern that occurs in an individual and that is typically associated with either a painful symptom (distress) or impairment in one or more important areas of functioning (disability). In addition, there is an inference that there is a behavioral, psychological, or biological dysfunction, and that the disturbance is not only in the relationship between the individual and society. (When the disturbance is *limited* to a conflict between an individual and society, this may represent social deviance, which may or may not be commendable, but is not by itself a mental disorder.)

Thus, the *DSM-III* goes to great lengths to make the differential diagnosis of mental disorders appear to be an objective process (as in the medical model), even though it recognizes that mental disorders cannot generally be defined. In essence, the psychiatric approach provides an objectified scheme to use in subjectively determining whether or not an individual is mentally ill.

AN ALTERNATIVE APPROACH. After reviewing the poor state of the psychiatric art of defining mental illness, Spitzer and Wilson (1975) proposed an alternative definition. It represents a considerable advancement over the existing psychiatric approach, which fails to define mental illness. For Spitzer and Wilson, a given condition is a mental disorder if and only if it meets three criteria. First, the condition must be principally a psychological one, although this psychological condition may produce changes in physiological functioning as a result of psychologically altered behavior. Second, in its most advanced state the condition is highly correlated with psychosocial stress (as we discussed such stress in chapter 4), reduced general functional capability, and irregular voluntary behavior patterns, all of which the ill individual would like to end because they are physically harmful. Third, the condition under scrutiny must be analytically distinct from any other condition, and it must be responsive to the proper treatment regimen.

These criteria serve three important, separate purposes. The first separates psychological from nonpsychological conditions, limiting the realm of mental illness to the psychological dimension. This guards against the psychiatric medicalization of nonmedical behavior, which we will discuss in detail in chapter 14. The second criterion specifies three things: that the mental disorder is usually not recognizable at its onset (as are acute conditions), but only after it is rather well developed, like many other asymptomatic chronic conditions; that the mental disorder arises from a condition impairing the individual's functioning in general, rather than from a social reaction to the individual's impaired functioning in any specific context; and that, congruent with the framework of the dominant medical model, mental disorders must be distinct and treatable. The third criteria requires mental disorders to be distinct from other factors, as opposed to being a manifestation of them.

Models of Mental Illness

The medical model, as represented by psychiatry, is the dominant approach to mental illness. Other models have been advanced that offer radically different explanations. Three of these—the psychoanalytic approach, the societal reaction approach, and the social learning theory approach—have received more attention than others. After looking at the medical model, we shall briefly discuss these alternative approaches in the order in which they are recognized as being reasonable alternatives to the psychiatric or medical model.

THE MEDICAL MODEL. The dominance of the medical model is based on the simple fact that psychiatry is one of many specializations within medicine. As such, psychiatrists are physicians who have elected to take their residency in psychiatry rather than in one of the other specialties. Thus, prior to their concentration in studying psychiatric conditions, psychiatrists have been subjected to and accepted the basic medical model. The medical model considers mental illness to be a disease or diseaselike phenomenon treatable by purely medical means, because all mental illness is the result of physiological causes, which includes biochemical and genetic disturbances. Of the utmost importance in understanding psychiatry's approach to mental illness is the reliance on the germ theory of the medical model. Germ theory, as discussed in chapters 1 and 4, holds that each illness is caused by its own special set of germs and that the goal of medicine is to find the right "magic bullets" to kill those germs and consequently restore the individual's health. When applied to mental illness, germ theory forms the basis for the massive reliance on the physiological—and established pharmaceutical—treatment of the mentally ill. This reliance is typified in the search for and widespread use of new wonder drugs in combating mental illness, almost to the exclusion of nonmedical treatments such as social and psychological casework. In sum, the medical or psychiatric approach represents the extension of the objectively based physiological model and its treatments to subjectively based psychological phenomena. As such, the traditional approach defines mental illness as a condition to be eliminated by properly trained physicians who have completed specialized training in psychiatry, which provides them with the best ammunition (physical and chemical bullets) for use in combating the germs of mental illness.

PSYCHOANALYTIC APPROACH. Psychoanalytic theory is based on the extensive work of Sigmund Freud (1953–1966). Freud believed that mental illness results from an improperly balanced personality, which develops as a result of stressful events occurring during the individual's infancy and childhood adolescence. These stressful events occur specifically during the oral, anal, phallic, latency, and genital stages of the individual's psychosexual development. If the child is subjected to stressful events during one of these stages of psychosexual development, the result will manifest itself as a particular personality disorder in adulthood.

According to Freud (1953–1966), personality is a dynamic system in which the ego balances the tensions between the id and the superego. The id represents the reality of the individual's pleasure seeking, in the general sense. This includes the instinct to satisfy fundamental needs. The superego represents the moral aspect of the individ-

194

*Applying The
Principles to
Aging, Death and
Dying, and Mental
Illness*

ual's personality, recognizing the moral standards of society. A balanced personality contains an ego capable of balancing the instinctual pleasure seeking of the individual world (the id) with the striving for moral perfection in the ideal world (the superego). In essence, Freud's concept of personality may be likened to an individual's ability to balance his or her own basic needs and wants against society's codification of ideal expectations. If the ego fails to balance the id and the superego, one of four general emotional problems appears: *personality disorders*, which direct the conflict resulting from the failure to balance the id and superego outward from the individual; *neuroses*, which cause excessive ego defense mechanisms to develop within the individual; *psychophysiological disorders* (such as stress), which result in organic tissue change; or, *psychoses*, in which the individual loses the ability to cope with the real world.

The major form of treating emotional disorders in the psychoanalytic perspective is psychoanalysis. Psychoanalytic treatment involves a one-to-one relationship between the patient and the therapist. This usually lasts for at least two years. The reason that psychoanalysis takes so long is that it involves the use of free association. In free association the patient is encouraged to say whatever comes into the mind. At the same time, the psychoanalyst attempts to keep the patient focused on the same sequence of events, encouraging the patient to hold nothing back. The assumption of psychoanalysis is that eventually the patient can bring to the surface the event or events that prove to be the cause of the emotional disorder. Following this the psychoanalyst can give the proper counsel to the patient so that he or she can effectively deal with the problem.

Because of the time and cost involved, psychoanalysis is neither appropriate for nor accessible to everyone. Therefore, the treatment that is most commonly used is psychoanalytic therapy, a modified version of pscyhoanalysis. In psychoanalytic therapy, extensive interviewing and counseling by the analyst takes place after sufficient information has been obtained about the patient's history. The major distinction between the two treatments is that psychoanalysis depends on the technique of free association to allow the patient to bring the root of the problem to the surface, while psychoanalytic therapy depends on the practitioner's guiding and directing the patient to gain insights into his or her own problems through an extensive interviewing process. Although less time-consuming and expensive than psychoanalysis, psychoanalytic therapy still consumes more time and money than most of us can afford, limiting its utility for application on a wide scale.

Cockerham (1981) has identified five major criticisms of the psychoanalytic model in general. First, psychoanalysis assumes that Freud's conception of the id, ego, and superego is correct, even though there has never been any evidence to support this assumption. Second, human beings are portrayed as instinctual animals with no ability to will their own behavior. Third, psychoanalysis assumes that stressful events occurring in childhood dictate adult behavior. Fourth, psychoanalysis underemphasizes the cognitive abilities of human beings while overemphasizing their emotional development. Finally, psychoanalytic theory is at best vague, if not impossible, to test or to use in predicting future behavior. Nonetheless, psychoanalytic theory remains as the major alternative to the traditional medical model; it has even partially been incorporated into psychiatric training.

THE SOCIETAL REACTION APPROACH. In 1960 the psychiatrist Thomas Szasz (see also 1961, 1970, 1974) came out with a new and revolutionary view of mental illness. Put quite briefly, he argued that mental illness is not an *illness*; therefore, it should not be regarded or treated as such in the medical sense. Szasz's argument is based on four propositions. First, a disease can be evidenced only by the presence of demonstrable physical lesions. Second, physical lesions are objective signs, independent of societal norms. The symptoms of mental illness are subjective and societally dependent. Third, mental problems arise from problems in social living. Fourth, mental problems are not diseases; rather, they are indicators of a conflict in social values that have been labeled as mental illness by the medical profession for the purpose of social control. In essence, Szasz argued that the concept of mental *illness* is a myth. What really exists are deviations from socially normative behavior. When a psychiatrist identifies a particular aspect of an individual's deviant social behavior as a symptom of mental illness, he or she is clearly making the social judgement that this deviant behavior is so different from the norm that it is unacceptable. Such unacceptable behavior is socially controlled by labeling the "offender" as mentally ill. Then, as is done with the physiologically ill, that individual is labeled and isolated from the rest of society so that proper treatment can be given. The individual is returned to the mainstream of the social system upon completion of a successful therapeutic regimen.

At the root of Szasz's (1960, 1961, 1970, 1974) argument is the fact that what constitutes mental illness is determined by the kind and degree of deviance from normal behavior that the ruling social audience will tolerate. Once an individual's behavior exceeds those limits, he or she is labeled mentally ill and submitted to treatment. The problem here is that different social groups have different social norms. Therefore, what may be acceptable behavior to one social group may be unacceptable (deviant) to another. This raises the question of which social group's norms are chosen as the standard for comparing all individuals' behavior. According to Szasz, the social norms chosen are likely to be those of the most powerful group, which is usually the upper middle class. As a result, individuals who are not members of the upper middle class are more likely to be labeled mentally ill simply because they have been socialized to respond differently to various situations than have members of the upper middle class. In this context Szasz raises two major questions: Is this a good and reasonable way to define and approach mental illness? and Can so subjectively determined deviance really be considered as illness in the germ theory tradition? Of course, Szasz's answer to both is

no. His approach, however, has gained little support from psychiatry, aside from the tacit recognition in the *DSM-III* conceptualization presented above that conditions of *purely* social deviance do *not* constitute mental disorders, although they may be treated as such. The primary reason that Szasz's approach has not been readily accepted is its failure to provide a better way of treating mental illness than does the medical model.

While the societal reaction theory has not gone very far in psychiatry, it has been picked up with considerable fervor by sociologists of health and by other behavioral scientists. Scheff (1964, 1966, 1974, 1975, 1984) is the foremost proponent of the societal reaction theory of mental illness. He has taken Szasz's (1960, 1961, 1970, 1974) basic approach and added the notion that in American society our stereotypes of mental illness and the mentally ill profoundly affect the labeling process. According to Scheff, the stereotypes of mental illness and the mentally ill are social roles that are internalized in early childhood. Indeed, he argues that by eighth grade we have learned what mental illness is and, more importantly, how to react to the mentally ill and how to expect them to act. Moreover, our childhood socialization is such that once an individual has been *labeled* mentally ill, we respond to that person as if he or she *is* mentally ill, and we expect him or her to *behave* as we expect a mentally ill person *should* behave.

This raises the interesting question of how one is labeled mentally ill in the first place. Scheff (1975, 1984) argues that this usually occurs by the individual's violation of "residual norms." These are defined as ordinary social conventions, such as looking at your conversational partners and responding to your name when it is called. The violation of these residual norms is viewed as so unnatural (badly deviant) that it can only be explained by the fact that the violator is mentally ill. Once the violator has been so labeled, others react to the label rather than to the violator's true identity. This perpetuates the stereotype of the violator as being mentally ill. As a result, society expects the violator to adopt and play the social role of being mentally ill, which, unlike the sick or other social roles, the violator is never allowed to relinquish. (You may recall, for example, reading about the 1972 presidential election. Senator Thomas Eagleton was forced to withdraw as the Democratic vice-presidential nominee because, although he had been "cured," he had once received psychiatric treatment.) In essence, the societal reaction approach to mental illness holds that an individual is labeled mentally ill because of his or her violation of the residual norms. From that point on, all interaction with the individual is based on a stereotype of how to react to the mentally ill, and how to expect the mentally ill to act.

While Scheff (1964, 1966, 1974, 1975, 1984) has added a great deal to Szasz's (1960, 1961, 1970, 1974) original formulation, the societal reaction approach still has several weak points (Cockerham, 1981). First, the existing behavioral studies of mental illness do not support the societal reaction explanation. Second, recent advances in drug therapy have shown that some mental disorders, especially schizophrenia, may be physiologically based. Third, an individual's occasional violation of residual norms does not always result in his or her being permanently labeled as mentally ill. Fourth, societal reaction theory fails to explain why individuals violate the residual norms in the first place. Finally, and perhaps most importantly, societal reaction theory fails to suggest a treatment procedure for the mentally ill. As a result, the societal reaction approach to mental illness remains popular only within the behavioral sciences where the examination of mental illness is more concerned with social interaction processes than with treatment regimens.

THE SOCIAL LEARNING THEORY APPROACH. The third alternative to the medical model of mental illness has developed out of social learning theory (Bandura, 1969). The assumption underlying this approach is that all social behavior is learned. Therefore, if an individual has learned the "wrong" social behavior—behavior which would be identified as mental illness—it is possible to have

that individual *unlearn* the behavior and replace it with the learning of new and more appropriate behavior. Behavioral modification is the therapeutic regimen used to get the individual to learn the new and more appropriate behavior. It contains five major techniques: desensitizing fearful social situations, reinforcing appropriate behaviors, punishing inappropriate social behaviors, conditioning new responses, and increasing group orientations.

While behavioral modification therapy has been quite an effective alternative to the traditional medical model, there are four major criticisms directed against it (Cockerham, 1981). First, there is a question as to whether individuals can actually be conditioned like programmable computers, or whether free will and creativity enter the situation at some point. Second, there is some doubt as to whether successful results achieved in the clinical laboratory can be sustained once the patient is back in the "real" world. Third, there are a number of mental disorders for which the learning of new behavior is not a sufficient treatment by itself. Fourth, there is an assumption that the patient wants and is able to learn the new, more appropriate behaviors; this is not always the case. Nonetheless, social learning theory represents a significant alternative to the medical model because it does provide a treatment process, behavior modification. It is also more readily applicable on a massive scale than psychoanalysis or psychotherapy.

Mental Institutions and the Career of the Mental Patient

Perhaps the most interesting aspect in the study of mental illness is the *social* process that brings an individual to a mental institution, what happens to that individual as an inmate, and, if lucky enough, what happens to that individual as a former inmate. A popular novel, later a movie that won the 1975 best picture Academy Award, was *One Flew Over the Cuckoo's Nest* (Kesey, 1962). In this story, one nonmentally ill patient (McMurphy) attempted to create a viable social system within the mental hospital comparable to the real social situation on the outside.

As a reward for his successful efforts to humanize life within the institution McMurphy was given a frontal lobotomy, the ultimate act of the dehumanization process of mental institutions. Although *One Flew Over the Cuckoo's Nest* is a fictional account, it does provide considerable insight into the four major aspects of the social process of being a mental patient: the nature of total institutions, the pre-inmate experience, the inmate experience, and the ex-inmate experience.

TOTAL INSTITUTIONS. The concept of the total institution was developed by Goffman (1961) to set the stage for the explanation of the social situation of mental patients and other inmates. Goffman defines a total institution as "a place of residence and work where a large number of like-situated individuals, cut off from the wider society for an appreciable period of time, together lead an enclosed, formally administered round of life. Prisons serve as a clear example, providing we appreciate that what is prison-like about prisons is found in institutions whose members have broken no laws." Total institutions fall into five general categories: homes for the blind and the indigent; sanitaria for those who pose a threat to community health and cannot care for themselves, such as lepers, those with tuberculosis, or the mentally ill; prisons and penitentiaries for intentional wrongdoers; instrumentally oriented institutions, such as the armed forces, boarding schools, and work camps; and religious training stations, such as monasteries, convents, and cloisters.

Common to each of these institutions is the component breakdown of the sleep, work, and play spheres of our everyday lives. In essence, in the total institution all three of these spheres are regulated by the same authority (the supervisory staff). Individuals (or inmates) in such institutions are collectively forced to perform their activites in these three spheres. Each incoming individual is stripped of his or her personal identity and given the new identity of the inmate. *All* privileges and rights are taken from the inmate and doled out at the sole discretion of the staff. This leaves the

inmate dependent and helpless, as portrayed in the following vignette (Johnson and Dodds, 1957):

Probably anybody who has never been in a similarly helpless position cannot realize the humiliation to anyone able bodied yet lacking authority to do the simplest offices for herself or having to beg repeatedly for even such small necessities as clean linen or a light for her cigarette from nurses who constantly brush her aside with, 'I'll give it to you in a minute, dear,' and go off and leave her unsupplied. Even the canteen staff seemed to share the opinion that civility was wasted upon lunatics, and would keep a patient waiting indefinitely, while they gossiped with their friends.

Such depersonalization and dehumanization are the nature of total institutions like mental hospitals.

THE PRE-INMATE EXPERIENCE. Because the total institution is such a bad place to be sent, the question that naturally emerges is how people arrive there in the first place. Usually the identification or labeling of an individual as mentally ill begins with his or her family and significant others. These are the people who best know the potential inmate and who interact with him or her most often. That makes them the most likely to observe the onset of mental illness. Goffman (1961) suggests that this recognition by family or friends launches the future inmate's career as a mental patient. The transformation to the patient role is affected by the interaction of three parties: the next of kin, the complainant who actually initiates the patient's career as a patient, and the mediators or agents and agencies who review and examine the patient to determine the need for institutionalization. Institutionalization may occur by either of two processes, voluntary or involuntary commitment. Under voluntary commitment the patient presents him- or herself to the mental hospital for hospitalization. This is a very easy process; almost anyone can be committed who wants to be. More important than the act of voluntary commitment, however, is the initial diagnosis. Once the patient is hospitalized, the admitting diagnosis is viewed as accurate and shapes the staff's perception and subsequent evaluation of the patient.

In involuntary commitment power and authority are used to force the institutionalization of the patient. Although the rules for involuntary commitment vary from state to state, they usually require several complainants, a psychiatric exam on initial hospitalization, subsequent reexamination by at least two court-appointed psychiatrists, a court-appointed lawyer to represent the patient, and a judicial hearing. Regardless of the voluntary or involuntary nature of the commitment, Goffman (1961) has identified a number of other factors that affect the decision to institutionalize the patient. These include the patient's socioeconomic status, the visibility of the deviant behavior, the availability and convenience of treatment, and the whims of those involved in the judicial proceeding. In sum, the pre-inmate experience represents the identification, labeling, isolation, and institutionalization of the mental patient.

THE INMATE EXPERIENCE. Once the patient has become an inmate and is subjected to the confines of the total institution, depersonalization is the first order of the day. Rosenhan (1973) has attributed this emphasis on depersonalization within mental institutions to two major factors. First, the societal attitude toward the mentally ill is a bleak one; the mentally ill are stereotyped as evil, nonuseful nonpersons. Because they are not viewed as real people, the mentally ill are not afforded the treatment due to "real" people. Second, the hierarchical structure in the mental hospital is such that the lower-echelon staff, who have the most contact with inmates, try to emulate the upper-echelon staff. Because the upper-echelon staff spends very little actual time with the inmates, preferring instead to sedate or physically restrain them, their apparent attitudes of depersonalization are picked up and reflected in the actions of the attending staff. As a result, a general atmosphere of depersonalization prevails throughout the mental hospital.

From their disadvantaged position, inmates have little choice but to conform and adapt to their new social situation in one of

four ways (Goffman, 1961): situational withdrawal; intransigence or rebellion; colonization, the process of using pre-inmate experiences to make the inmate life look desirable; or conversion, the process of adapting to the ideal role proposed for the inmate by the staff. According to Denzin (1968), the ideal role proposed by the staff holds the expectation that the patient will: believe that recovery is possible, recognize his or her illness and the need for treatment, believe and trust the therapists, present an orderly confirmation to institutionalized life, and accept and comply with the treatment regimen. Until such role acceptance or conversion by the inmate occurs, the hospital staff is not likely to view the patient as a cooperative one who might eventually be returned to society. Because uncoverted inmates are never recognized as being returnable, many inmates convert solely for the purpose of getting out. To make their stay in the institution as humane as possible, inmates generally form a society of their own. This provides them with moral and social support, and maintains some semblance of the normal social relationships that they experienced prior to being institutionalized.

THE EX-INMATE EXPERIENCE. If the inmate is fortunate enough to gain release from the mental hospital, he or she is not granted the same healthy status accorded to those released from the standard hospital. The released mental inmate is stigmatized as an ex-inmate. In general, that stigma is more indelible than that of the ex-convict. This indelibility is based on the social attitude that being a mental patient is more than just being sick; it is a sign of something evil that, although it has been brought under control, may still be lurking in the inmate's mental configuration. As a result, once an inmate is released, society reacts to his or her new role as an ex-inmate rather than to his or her own true identity. Most social interaction results in the rejection of the ex-inmate; that often results in the ex-inmate's subsequent return to the mental hospital and the inmate role. According to Miller (1971), the likelihood of recidivism can be reduced if four supports are extended to the ex-inmate: material support, the personal support of a significant other, the experience of several positive social relationships, and the placement of the ex-inmate in a situation where he or she can experience some control. In the absence of any of these supports, the ex-inmate is likely to become an inmate all over again. Each successive institutionalization reduces the possibility of permanent release and emotional recovery.

The Social Epidemiology of Mental Illness

Having reviewed the process by which individuals are defined as being mentally ill, the theories explaining mental illness, and the career of the mental patient, we will now examine briefly how extensive a social problem mental illness is and who, if anyone, is most likely to become mentally ill. The social epidemiology of psychiatric disorders is an area to which the sociology of health has made a number of classic contributions (such as the works of Faris and Dunham, 1939; Hollingshead and Redlich, 1958; Leighton, 1959; and Srole, Langner, Michael, Opler, and Rennie, 1962; see also Srole, 1975), resulting in its receiving considerable respect as an academic specialty. Much of that respect has been based on two accomplishments: differentiating between "official" and "true" categories of mental illness; and discovering how mental illness is distributed by sex, socioeconomic status, and rural-urban differences within the general population.

"OFFICIAL" AND "TRUE" LEVELS OF MENTAL ILLNESS. Official data on mental illness are based upon the number of treated cases. As part of the ongoing national Health Interview Survey, the National Center for Health Statistics (1986) reported that there were 7.2 hospital admissions per 1,000 persons in the United States during 1984 for which a mental disorder was listed as the primary diagnosis. When secondary and tertiary diagnoses were included, the rate rose to 19.8 admissions per 1,000 persons. Table 8-2 shows the number of hospital discharges in 1984 (for primary diagnoses only) within each of 20 major categories of mental disorders. These data indicate that the bulk of hospital admissions occurred within only

Table 8-2. *Number of discharges from short-stay hospitals in the United States during 1984 by primary diagnostic category for mental disorders.*

Primary diagnostic category	Number of discharges (1,000s)
Senile and presenile organic psychotic conditions	34
Alcohol psychoses	53
Drug psychoses	9
Transient organic psychotic conditions	8
Chronic organic psychotic conditions	8
Schizophrenic disorders	173
Paranoid states	10
Other nonorganic psychoses	50
Neurotic disorders	197
Personality disorders	30
Sexual deviations and disorders	10
Alcohol dependence syndrome	392
Drug dependence	55
Nondependent abuse of drugs	81
Physiological malfunction arising from mental factors	15
Acute reaction to stress	9
Adjustment reaction	76
Specific nonpsychotic mental disorders due to organic brain damage	62
Disturbance of emotions specific to childhood and adolescence	3
Hyperkinetic impulse disorder	3

SOURCE: National Center for Health Statistics. 1986. *Detailed Diagnoses and Procedures for Patients Discharged from Short-Stay Hospitals, United States, 1984.* DHHS Publication No. 86–1747. Washington, DC: U.S. Government Printing Office.

four categories: alcohol dependence syndrome, nondependent drug use, neurotic disorders, and schizophrenic disorders. Although these numbers may seem rather large, they do not tell the whole story. Much of the mental illness that exists in the United States goes untreated or is treated on an ambulatory basis. A major problem is determining how much mental illness, treated and untreated, truly exists in the general population.

To accomplish this, a number of psychiatric screening devices have been developed that take the form of a series of questions

Table 8-3. *Langner's 22-item psychiatric screening score.*

Item	Response
1. I feel weak all over much of the time.	1. Yes* 2. No
2. I have had periods of days, weeks, or months when I couldn't take care of things because I couldn't "get going."	1. Yes* 2. No
3. In general, would you say that most of the time you are in high (very good) spirits, good spirits, low spirits, or very low spirits?	1. High 2. Good 3. Low* 4. Very Low*
4. Every so often I suddenly feel hot all over.	1. Yes* 2. No
5. Have you ever been bothered by your heart beating hard? Would you say: often, sometimes, or never?	1. Often* 2. Sometimes 3. Never
6. Would you say your appetite is poor, fair, good, or too good?	1. Poor* 2. Fair 3. Good 4. Too Good
7. I have periods of such great restlessness that I cannot sit long in a chair (cannot sit still very long).	1. Yes* 2. No
8. Are you the worrying type (a worrier)?	1. Yes* 2. No
9. Have you ever been bothered by shortness of breath when you were not exercising or working hard? Would you say: often, sometimes, or never?	1. Often* 2. Sometimes 3. Never
10. Are you ever bothered by nervousness (irritable, fidgety, tense)? Would you say: often, sometimes, or never?	1. Often* 2. Sometimes 3. Never
11. Have you ever had any fainting spells (lost consciousness)? Would you say: never, a few times, or more than a few times?	1. Never 2. A few times 3. More than a few times*
12. Do you ever have any trouble in getting to sleep or staying asleep? Would you say: often, sometimes, or never?	1. Often* 2. Sometimes 3. Never
13. I am bothered by acid (sour) stomach several times a week.	1. Yes* 2. No
14. My memory seems to be all right (good).	1. Yes 2. No*
15. Have you ever been bothered by "cold sweats"? Would you say: often, sometimes, or never?	1. Often* 2. Sometimes 3. Never
16. Do your hands ever tremble enough to bother you? Would you say: often, sometimes, or never?	1. Often* 2. Sometimes 3. Never
17. There seems to be a fullness (clogging) in my head or nose much of the time.	1. Yes* 2. No

Table 8-3. (*continued*) 201

Mental Illness

Item	Response
18. I have personal worries that get me down physically (make me physically ill).	1. Yes* 2. No
19. Do you feel somewhat apart even among friends (apart, isolated, alone)?	1. Yes* 2. No
20. Nothing ever turns out for me the way I want it to (turns out, happens, comes about, i.e., my wishes aren't fulfilled).	1. Yes* 2. No
21. Are you ever troubled with headaches or pains in the head? Would you say: often, sometimes, or never?	1. Often* 2. Sometimes 3. Never
22. You sometimes can't help wondering if anything is worthwhile anymore.	1. Yes* 2. No

*Asterisked responses indicate psychiatric impairment; the sum of such responses is the Screening Score.
SOURCE: Thomas Langner. 1962. "A 22-item Screening Score of Psychiatric Symptoms Indicating Impairment." *Journal of Health and Human Behavior,* 3:269–76. Reprinted by permission of the American Sociological Association.

that may be asked of the general public in a large-scale survey. Once the data have been collected, the response patterns are analyzed and the number of mentally ill individuals may then be determined. The most widely used, modified, and discussed of these psychiatric screening devices are Langner's (1962) 22-item psychiatric screening score, which has been reproduced in Table 8-3, and the Center for Epidemiological Studies Depression Scale (Radloff, 1977), which has been reproduced in Table 8-4. We shall consider each in turn.

The asterisked responses to the 22 questions in the Langner scale (see Table 8-3) indicate psychiatric illness, and the screening score is the simple sum of the asterisked responses given by the respondent. Based on an extensive methodological evaluation, Langner determined that a score of four or more indicated the psychiatric impairment of the respondent. In the Midtown Manhattan Study of 1,438 respondents representing the general population of New York City (see Srole et al., 1962), 28 percent had scores of four or more (indicating their psychiatric impairment). As is evident, this 28 percent is a much larger estimate of the true extent of mental illness than that indicated by the 7.2 hospital admissions per 1,000 persons for which a mental disorder was the primary diagnosis.

The Langner (1962) index, however, is not without controversy (see Wheaton, 1983). The principal issue is the index's validity. Critics point out that its questions tap both psychological and psychophysical symptoms, such as feeling hot, having fainting spells, or experiencing gastric distress. Each of these could be caused by either psychological or somatic factors. Thus, the index does not tap psychiatric symptoms alone. After an extensive review of these criticisms, however, Wheaton has recently reached the conclusion that the Langner index is a useful tool in screening and identifying individuals with depressive symptomatology in large-scale surveys. It remains widely used today.

Nonetheless, the Center for Epidemiological Studies Depression (CES-D) scale was developed in the early 1970s as an alternative to the Langner index (see Comstock and Helsing, 1976; Radloff, 1977; Weissman, Sholomskas, Pottenger, Prusoff, and Locke, 1977). The CES-D scale contains 20 straightforward questions (see Table 8-4) that tap depressive symptoms. The response to each question is given a score from zero to three depending on the frequency with which the symptom occurred during the past week. Extensive analyses indicate that the CES-D scale is both reliable (its coefficient alpha averages

0.85), and that a combined scale score greater than 15 is a valid indication that the individual is clinically depressed (see Eaton and Kessler, 1981). Indeed, after fielding the CES-D and several other psychiatric assessment techniques in five populations, Weissman and her colleagues (1977) concluded that "the [CES-D] scale is a sensitive tool for detecting depressive symptoms and change in symptoms over time in psychi-

atric populations, and that it agrees quite well with more lengthy self-report scales used in clinical studies and with clinician interview ratings."

Eaton and Kessler (1981) have used the CES-D scale in a national survey of 3,059 adults aged 25 to 74 who were interviewed as part of the 1975 National Health and Nutrition Examination Survey. Their results are shown in Table 8-5 within categories of several sociodemographic characteristics. The numbers in the first column indicate the actual percentage of persons in that group having CES-D scores greater than 15, which indicates clinical depression; the numbers in the second column have been statistically adjusted for the effects of the other sociodemographic factors shown in the table. These data indicate that depressive symptomatology is greater among women, young adults, those who are divorced or separated, the less educated, the unemployed, the poor, whites, those who live in large households, and those who do not live in rural areas. For the most part, these findings are consistent with previous studies and common expectations about the epidemiology of mental illness. It is important to emphasize, however, that these data reflect global psychiatric impairment or depressive symptomatology. They do not indicate specific mental disorders.

In 1979 the National Institute of Mental Health began a most ambitious effort called the Epidemiological Catchment Area (ECA) program to obtain prevalence rates for specific mental disorders at the national level (see Eaton and Kessler, 1985). The principal objective of the ECA program is to gain a better understanding of the etiology, clinical course, and response to the treatment of each particular psychiatric illness. A secondary goal is the identification of the sociodemographic and other correlates of these mental disorders. To accomplish these goals, five geographic catchment areas have been defined: New Haven, Connecticut; Baltimore, Maryland; Saint Louis, Missouri; Durham, North Carolina; and Los Angeles, California.

Within each catchment area detailed, face-to-face interviews are being conducted

Table 8-4. *The Center for Epidemiological Studies Depression (CES-D) scale.*

Below is a list of the ways you might have felt or behaved. Please tell me how often you have felt this way during the past week.

Responses
(0) rarely or none of the time (less than 1 day)
(1) some or a little of the time (1–2 days)
(2) occasionally or a moderate amount of time (3–4 days)
(3) most of the time (5–7 days)

Questions
 1. I was bothered by things that usually don't bother me.
 2. I did not feel like eating; my appetite was poor.
 3. I felt that I could not shake off the blues even with help from my family and friends.
 4. I felt that I am just as good as other people.*
 5. I had trouble keeping my mind on what I was doing.
 6. I felt depressed.
 7. I felt that everything I did was an effort.
 8. I felt hopeful about the future.*
 9. I thought my life had been a failure.
10. I felt fearful.
11. My sleep was restless.
12. I was happy.*
13. I talked less than usual.
14. I felt lonely.
15. People were unfriendly.
16. I enjoyed life.*
17. I had crying spells.
18. I felt sad.
19. I felt like people dislike me.
20. I could not get "going."

*Asterisked items are reverse-coded.
SOURCE: L. S. Radloff. 1977. "The CES-D Scale: A Self-Report Depression Scale for Research in the General Population." *Journal of Applied Psychological Measures* 1: 385–401. Copyright 1977. Reprinted with permission of Applied Psychological Measurement Incorporated.

Table 8-5. *Unadjusted and adjusted percentages of persons in a national sample with CES-D scale scores over 15 (indicating impairment).*

Sociodemographic characteristic	Unadjusted percentage	Adjusted percentage*
Sex		
Males	10.8	10.8
Females	20.8	20.8
Age		
25–44 years old	16.9	18.6
45–64 years old	16.4	16.2
65–74 years old	14.8	8.2
Marital status		
Single	17.1	15.1
Married	14.5	16.1
Widowed	23.4	16.6
Other	28.8	20.4
Education		
0–7 years	25.3	22.1
8–11 years	24.6	23.1
12 years	15.6	15.5
13 or more years	8.8	10.8
Employment status		
Working	13.1	15.6
Houseperson	20.6	15.6
Retired or student	14.8	20.7
Other	28.1	25.6
Income		
$000–3,999	31.1	28.2
$4,000–5,999	25.4	23.6
$6,000–14,999	14.3	14.1
$15,000 or more	9.7	11.7
Race		
Blacks	15.3	16.0
Whites	28.5	21.3
Household size		
1 person	21.8	16.7
2 persons	12.6	12.8
3 persons	18.6	19.0
4 or more persons	16.9	17.8
Place of residence		
Cities	19.2	18.8
Suburbs	13.9	16.4
Towns	19.7	18.8
Rural areas	16.0	12.9

*Adjusted for the effects of the other sociodemographic factors shown in the table.

SOURCE: Adapted from William W. Eaton and Larry G. Kessler. 1981. "Rates of Symptoms of Depression in a National Sample." *American Journal of Epidemiology* 114:528–32. Reprinted by permission of the author and publisher.

on representative samples of at least 3,500 noninstitutionalized and 500 institutionalized persons using the Diagnostic Interview Schedule (DIS). Each interview takes about 90 minutes to complete and yields data that will subsequently be used to determine which, if any, specific conditions the respondent has, including 36 of the diagnoses listed in the *DSM-III*. By 1985 more than 20,000 persons had been interviewed; each of them was reinterviewed one year later.

Because the second wave of data collection was finished very recently, the investigators on the ECA program have only just begun to report their findings. As this volume went to press, those reports were limited to either descriptions of the general methodology used in the ECA study itself or prevalence rates based on whether the respondent had one or more of the numerous mental disorders for which differential diagnoses algorithms are available in the DIS. No data have yet been released on the prevalence of specific mental disorders. Therefore, the following review of the relationships between sex, socioeconomic status, and rural-urban differences is limited to previously published reports.

SEX AND MENTAL ILLNESS. In reviewing more than 80 previous studies on sex differences in the rate of mental illness, Dohrenwend and Dohrenwend (1976) made a major contribution by identifying the reason that these studies vacillated between saying males had a higher rate of mental illness than females, and vice versa. According to the Dohrenwends, the results of these studies appeared to be in conflict because of a false assumption that mental illness is unidimensional, with a high correlation between all subtypes. Indeed, this was not the case; manic-depressive psychoses and neuroses are more frequent among women, personality disorders are more frequent among men. Thus, depending on which subtype of mental illness one uses for comparing male and female rates, one arrives at different answers to the same question.

The sex difference in psychoses, neuroses, and personality disorders may be attributed to both biological and sociocultural factors. Biologically, depressive and other neuroses are linked to the hormonal changes occuring in women during regular menstrual cycles and at menopause. Socioculturally, men and women are subjected to different socialization processes and face markedly different opportunity structures as adults. This is evidenced dramatically in the socially restrictive, low-prestige, common occupation of women as housewives. As a result, women more often than men are "locked into" depressing social situations that tend to foster neurotic reactions. Men more often than women are found in high-pressure situations that tend to foster personality disorders. Accordingly, in comparing the rates of mental illness between males and females it is necessary to specify which particular psychiatric condition is being discussed so that the effects of biological and sociocultural factors may be isolated.

SOCIOECONOMIC STATUS AND MENTAL ILLNESS. A most striking relationship emerges when mental illness rates are examined across categories of socioeconomic status. For the general gamut of mental disorders, and especially for schizophrenia and other personality disorders, the lower social classes consistently have higher rates. (An exception involves the rates of neuroses and manic-depressive psychoses, which are higher for the higher social classes.) This negative relationship of socioeconomic status to mental illness rates has remained stable throughout this century. Three popular but incomplete explanations are generally offered to account for these differences (Cockerham, 1981). First, there is a genetic explanation that holds that the lower social classes are more predisposed to mental illness as a result of poorer genetic inheritance. Prospective studies of the incidence of schizophrenia between separately adopted identical twins, however, have cast considerable doubt on genetic differences as the only factor. It has been shown that the rate of schizophrenia varies more by social than by genetic factors. Second, there is the social stress explanation that suggests that lower-class individuals are subjected to higher social stress that results in a higher rate of mental ill-

ness. While perhaps more intuitively pleasing than the genetic explanation, the social stress explanation is based on data that are inconclusive. Third, there is a version of the drift hypothesis (discussed in chapter 1), which states that the mentally ill drift downward in socioeconomic status, causing their number to be overly represented in the lower social classes. (There is also a "residue" version of this explanation that asserts that the mentally stable in the lower class move up the socioeconomic ladder, leaving behind a residue of the mentally ill.) As with the social stress explanation, the data do not show a sufficient level of socioeconomic mobility to support the drift (or residue) hypothesis. Finally, Kohn (1974) has offered a promising alternative explanation that holds that the conditions of life for those in the lower socioeconomic classes often can promote a fatalistic psychological orientation. This involves feeling that it is the unknown forces beyond one's control that determine one's life. Individuals with such a fatalistic orientation are likely to withdraw from the social reality that they do not understand. Recalling that schizophrenia is characterized by a withdrawal from reality, Kohn's alternative explanation seems to be rather promising; however, it has yet to be empirically validated.

RURAL-URBAN DIFFERENCES IN MENTAL ILLNESS. Another common stereotype is that the stress of urban living is responsible for the higher rate of mental illness in urban as compared to rural areas. Just as in the case of sex differences in the rate of mental illness, Dohrenwend and Dohrenwend (1974a) argue that it is inappropriate to compare rural and urban rates unless specific subtypes of mental illness are examined. According to their extensive review of the literature, some disorders—general and manic-depressive psychoses—are more prevalent in rural areas. Others—neuroses, personality disorders, and schizophrenia—however, are more prevalent in urban areas. Unfortunately, while the mass of data consistently supports these differences, it is not known why they exist. The more popular explanations suggest that manic-depressive psychoses are the result of the sense of physical isolation in rural areas, while schizophrenia, neuroses, and other personality disorders result from the increased stress of urban living. A factor presently confounding the distillation of rural-urban differences in mental illness rates is the migration of stress-weary urban residents to areas of country living, and the reciprocal migration of isolation-weary rural residents to urban areas. Because both types of migrants take their mental disorders along with them, the determination of which place of residence contributes to what mental disorders becomes even more difficult.

Summary

In this chapter we have looked at three of the more popular health-related issues as social problems through the principles of the sociology of health. In the first section we approached the issue of aging. We began with a discussion of the life cycle process and the roles associated with each of its stages, emphasizing the physiological, psychological, and social aspects. Next we discussed where the increasing number of elderly people are coming from and how they affect the health care delivery system. The five basic theoretical approaches to aging were then reviewed, including role theory, disengagement theory, subcultural theory, activity theory, and age-stratification theory. The first section concluded with a look at the aging process from both sides, the societal view, and the aged's own view.

In the second section we examined the health-related social problem of death and dying. We began with an evaluation of the changing social attitudes toward and the definitions of death. Since the fifteenth century the image of death has changed at least six times, going from the view of death as a celebration of life, to a view of death as the ultimate failure to be avoided at all costs. Concomitant with this have been changes in formal definitions of death, such as the Harvard plan and the Kansas statute. These approaches focus on defining brain death. We then turned to how people deal with death, discussing five stages of the dying process (denial, anger, bargaining, preparatory grief, and acceptance). These may occur in any of four awareness contexts (closed awareness, suspected awareness, mutual pretense, or open awareness), based on the control of the social setting and the flow of information concerning the dying patient. Our examination of death and dying concluded with an excerpt from and discussion of the provocative research on individuals who have experienced clinical death and returned to life. Regardless of the circumstances surrounding the individual's clinical death, strikingly similar ultimate experiences were reported.

In the third section we addressed the issue of mental illness. As was the case with the definition of health, the definition of mental health is rather clouded, although the traditional psychiatric version of the medical model remains the dominant perspective. Alternatives to the medical model's approach include the psychoanalytic approach (based on Freud's conception of the id, the ego, and the superego), the societal reaction approach (urging moderation in social labeling as a determinant), and social learning theory (involving the use of behavioral modification). We then looked at mental institutions from the perspective of the mental patient's career, including the concept of the total institution and the pre-inmate, inmate, and ex-inmate experiences. Finally, we reviewed the social epidemiology of mental illness, focusing on how mental illness is measured in social surveys, and how these measures correlate with sex, socioeconomic status, and place of residence.

III. Practitioners

9. Physicians

As we learned in chapter 2, the physician has been one of the major topics of interest throughout the development of the sociology of health. In fact, McIntire's (1894) first formal definition of medical sociology addressed the study of physicians as a unique and separate social group. The reason for the continued interest in the physician is quite simple. When we think of health and medicine, we usually think of the physician. The doctor has traditionally been society's premier representative of the ultimate value of health. In this chapter we will examine how the modern physician achieved and maintains that position.

To do this the present chapter is divided into three sections. In the first we examine the historical development of the modern physician. This includes three major periods in modern medicine's evolution: the Hippocratic oath and the emergence of medical ethics and morality, the great advances in medical history, and the rise of medicine in the United States. In the second section we will take up the profession of medicine. We focus on the "great trade," which resulted in the professionalization of physicians and has also produced the complex and powerful social organization known as the American Medical Association. In the third section we will examine the medical education process through which an individual becomes a physician. Our focus will be on the medical student subculture, the socialization process in medical schools, and the process of selecting a medical specialty.

Historical Development of the Modern Physician

As we learned in chapter 1, modern scientific medicine is just that, *modern*. It has emerged after a long and arduous journey that began at least as far back as the ancient Greece of Hygeia in the fifteenth century B.C. Sigerist (1951) notes that archeologists have turned up evidence of the therapeutic practice of cauterization and amputation in fossil relics of Cro-Magnon man, which date between 5,000 and 18,000 B.C. Thus, the modern scientific medicine that we know of today did not come about overnight; rather, it passed through the eight periods discussed in chapter 1: (1) the philosophy of Hygeia; (2) the cult of Asclepius; (3) the age of Hippocrates; (4) the constraints of the Church; (5) Descartes and seventeenth-century rationalism; (6) the age of advances in public health; (7) Pasteur, Koch, specific etiology and germ theory; and (8) whole-person health. The most important of these periods, however, was the age of Hippocrates. It brought about the beginning of scientific medicine and established the basics of medical ethics and morality.

The Hippocratic Contributions

As we have already learned, historical accounts generally show the Greek physician Hippocrates appearing late in the fifth century B.C. This was a time when the dominant world view held that illness was caused by evil spirits and when physicians were primarily magicians and soothsayers. More than any other individual, Hippocrates sought to change this conception into one in which deviations from normal physiological functioning were viewed as the major causes of illness. He felt that physicians were to be competently trained practitioners who treated those deviations systematically, morally, and ethically in their attempt to restore the patient's health.

THE SCIENTIFIC APPROACH. What appears to have motivated Hippocrates most in his quest for scientific medicine was the paradox he found in Greek culture. Although there was an increasing emphasis on rational and systematic problem-solving approaches in most aspects of Greek life, medicine remained a mythological phenomenon. With the emergence of his new school of medicine, Hippocrates led his colleagues to-

ward the teaching and practice of a scientific medicine. His efforts were greatly aided with the publication of his medical treatises, including *The Aphorisms*, *Medical Geography*, and especially *The Book of Prognostics*. *Prognostics* combined theory with observation in order to determine what treatments were most successful for the various conditions a Greek physician was likely to encounter. At the base of Hippocrates' approach were two principles: theory and observation. Recorded observations allowed the detection of patterns of specific treatments that were successful for particular conditions. (Note that this is a forerunner of the classic experimental design in science.) Generalizations based on those observations and on the intuition of the physician were used to explain the underlying medical processes.

For Hippocrates the basic theory of medicine was an equilibrium or balance model. Good health was portrayed as the balance of the four body humors: blood, phlegm, black bile, and yellow bile. When one of these body humors was out of balance, the individual was sick. To restore the patient's health, the physician had to restore the natural balance. This was done by relying on dietary regulation and the cautious use of drugs and other potions. As such, Hippocrates' approach represented a considerable deviation from the reliance on the supernatural and the practice of divination to make the evil spirits flee from the patient's body. In so doing, Hippocrates set the stage for the development of modern scientific medicine, even though we may now look back on his humor-balance theory and consider it to be "unscientific." In his time, Hippocrates epitomized science and scientific medicine.

MEDICAL ETHICS AND MORALITY. While Hippocrates' major contribution to the development of scientific medicine is not generally recognized by the nonphysician, we are all somewhat familiar with the Hippocratic oath. The oath was an invocation sworn to by all those aspiring to become physicians under Hippocrates' training. It was intended to bind their commitment to medicine and humanity. Not only did it serve that purpose back then, it subsequently became the foundation for modern medical ethics and morality. Because the Hippocratic oath has played such a central role in the development of modern medical ethics and because it is still relevant today, it bears repeating in full (as found in Clendening, 1960). As you read it, note its five basic principles and try to see how they apply to the pressing ethical and moral issues facing contemporary physicians.

I swear by Apollo Physician, by Asclepius, by Health, by Panacea and by all the gods and goddesses, making them my witnesses, that I will carry out, according to my ability and judgment, this oath and this indenture. To hold my teacher in this art equal to my own parents; to make him partner in my livelihood; to consider his family as my own brothers, and to teach them this art, if they want to learn it, without fee or indenture; to impart precept, oral instruction, and all other instruction to my own sons, the sons of my teacher and to indentured pupils who have taken the physician's oath, but to nobody else. I will use treatment to help the sick according to my ability and judgment, but never with the view to injury or wrongdoing. Neither will I administer a potion [poison] to anybody when asked to do so, nor will I suggest such a course. Similarly, I will not give a woman a pessary to cause abortion. But I will keep pure and holy both my life and my art. I will not use my knife, not even, verily, on sufferers from stone, but I will place to such craftsmen therein. Into whatsoever houses I enter, I will enter to help the sick, and I will abstain from all intentional wrongdoing and harm, especially from abusing the bodies of men or women, bond or free. And whatsoever I shall see or hear in the course of my profession, as well as outside of my profession in my intercourse with men, if it be what should not be published abroad, I will never divulge, holding such things to be holy secrets. Now if I carry out this oath and break it not, may I gain forever reputation among all men for my life and for my art, but if I transgress it and foreswear myself, may the opposite befall me.

The first principle in the oath addresses the close-knit, secretive nature of the brotherhood of physicians. The knowledge of medicine is to be kept within the brotherhood by imparting it only to one's sons or the sons of fellow physicians. The second principle prescribes that proper medical treatment will be rendered to those who need it (a form of universalism). The use of medical knowledge for terminating or harming human life (the antithesis of preserving life) is prohibited under *any* circumstances, including poisoning and abortion. The third principle, a proscription against surgery, was originally intended to separate the science of medicine from the nonscientific, nonmedical, barber-oriented surgical craft of the times. The fourth principle stipulates that physicians will avoid any wrongdoing to, or exploitation of, their patients. Finally, the fifth principle constitutes the basis for claiming the patient-practitioner relationship is sacred. Any information obtained by the doctor during an encounter with a patient is to remain confidential. As you can see, although the Hippocratic oath and its fundamental ethical and moral principles emerged more than 2,300 years ago, it is as relevant and timely today as it was then. Indeed, four of the six fundamental concepts in contemporary medical ethics are explicitly contained in the oath (i.e., nonmaleficence, beneficence, universality, and rationality), and the other two are implicit (i.e., autonomy and justice).

From Hippocrates to Harvey and Beyond

From the moment that Hippocrates first began to practice and train other physicians, medicine began a metamorphosis from mostly magic and some science to mostly science and some magic. While this metamorphosis was immediately evident, it was not until the nineteenth century that this process changed from a gradual to a rapid one. Only then did major medical discoveries begin to occur with astonishing rapidity. According to Coe (1978), the development of modern medicine since Hippocrates may be traced through five periods: Greco-Roman advances, medieval progress, Renaissance advances, post—sixteenth-century medicine, and American medicine.

GRECO-ROMAN ADVANCES. After Hippocrates, the movement toward scientific medicine continued at a slow but steady pace. This was primarily a result of the continued recording of observed experiments. The first major theoretical advance came from Aristotle. He proposed a soul theory, as an alternative to humoral theory, in order to explain why the body reacts to treatment the way it does. Soul theory held that in each individual there are three souls: a vegetation soul (explaining nourishment processes), an animal soul (explaining environmental adaptation), and a rational soul (explaining the power of conceptualization). Following Aristotle's death, the soul theory was advanced by his disciples. They grounded the theory in some speculative physiology, holding that the vegetation soul is lodged in the heart, the animal soul in the lungs, and the rational soul throughout the nervous system. Like Hippocrates' theory of humors, the new soul theory was an equilibrium theory. That is, an imbalance among the three souls results in illness, and the proper treatment is to adjust that soul. This can be accomplished by means of bloodletting, when the animal soul is excessive, and by similar procedures for other soul imbalances.

When Greek civilization gave way to the Roman Empire, the advance of scientific medicine took a different turn. Around the time of Christ's appearance, Roman medical encyclopedists compiled and organized all available medical knowledge and observations. Unfortunately, these encyclopedists were rather selective in their work. This resulted in different compilations of scientific medicine for the different medical factions in Rome at the time. Nonetheless, this central codification of knowledge brought together all that was known about medicine and made it available to all medical practitioners. It represents the first major attempt at standardizing medical diagnoses and treatment. Another major contribution of the Roman Empire was the development of hospitals and the notion of public health. This included not only the construction of sewers and public bathing facilities but also basic sanitary regulation, mandatory street cleaning, voluntary health education programs, and the provision of some health care to the indigent.

MEDIEVAL MEDICINE. As we learned in chapter 1, the rise of the Catholic church followed the fall of Rome. With it came an increase in scholasticism reflecting the dogmas of the Church. This approach, emphasizing the otherworldly pursuit of rewards in the next life, produced a conflict between scientific medicine based on theory and observation, and philosophical medicine based on religious truth and dogma. Because the Church was more powerful than the emerging medical profession, it won the conflict. This resulted in the near stagnation of scientific medicine and the production of a dependent, illiterate population. In fact, because the Church viewed illness and disease as a punishment for sins, rather than as natural phenomena, the general populace turned to the healing powers of folk medicine, the clergy, and the royalty. Thus, the market for physicians' services dropped; those who remained were retained primarily by the nobility, who managed to maintain some semblance of literacy and knowledge.

Aside from the negative effects of the Church's dogmatic approach to scientific medicine, three significant structural changes occurred. First, the training of physicians evolved from the master-apprentice relationship established by Hippocrates to the university setting. This began in Italy during the tenth century. In the university setting whatever information existed (and was nonoffensive to the Church) was made available to the medical student. Second, specialization occurred; although clerics were allowed to study medicine, they were not allowed to draw blood. As a result, surgery was formally relegated to the barber-surgeon who enjoyed much less prestige than the physician and relied on barbering as his major craft—surgery was merely a sideline. In addition, an even less prestigious occupational group of apothecaries emerged. They were primarily responsible for extending folk medicine to the masses. The third structural change was that the hospital system was transformed from municipal control to church control. This increased the Church's authority over the everyday life of the people, as well as its control over medicine. During the medieval period, there were also several horrendous epidemics that ravaged the world's population. While these were tragic events, they did lead some physicians and scientists to postulate the notion of contagious disease and to suggest that it might be contained by isolating those already infected. Unfortunately, the medieval practitioners had no real notion of how contagious diseases were transferred; they simply relied on the observation that isolation seemed to help stem epidemics.

RENAISSANCE ADVANCES. During the Renaissance (approximately the fifteenth and sixteenth centuries) a very important change took place that gave considerable impetus to the scientific medicine movement. That impetus was the change in values from dogmatic scholasticism to an inquisitive scholarship seeking to make things better in this life. The Church's control over values and the production of knowledge eroded, and there was a return to the quest for knowledge and the alleviation of suffering. Thus, the focal point of the times moved from the Church to the arts and sciences. Among the sciences some of the most significant advances came about as a result of the return to the use of cadavers for dissection, a practice that was forbidden by the Church. The advances made in the study of anatomy challenged the Church's position. In addition, new surgical techniques emerged in the field hospitals of military surgeons. These developments lowered surgical death rates and increased the status of surgery from the low level of the barber-surgeon to something closer to the high level of the physician. Coupled with these anatomical and surgical advances was the return to the basic scientific (experimental) procedure of recording observations in order to cull out patterns of successful and unsuccessful treatment for various conditions. This resurgence was enhanced when previously unavailable scientific literature surfaced through actual rediscovery and the Church's willingness to make available what it had previously sequestered.

POST—SIXTEENTH-CENTURY MEDICINE. While scientific medicine was revived during the Renaissance, it was still a far cry from modern medicine. In fact, many Renaissance physicians continued to believe in Hippocrates' humoral theory as the underlying explanation of health and illness. It was not until the seventeenth century that the growth of scientific medicine began to accelerate and important discoveries began to be made with regularity. Perhaps the most significant milestone was William Harvey's description of the circulation of blood in 1628. Unfortunately, while Harvey's discovery was of immense theoretical value, little application was made of it until the nineteenth century. Nonetheless, beginning with his description of the circulation of blood, the basic principles underlying modern medicine began to emerge in the 1600s.

Although the history of modern medicine is fascinating in its own right, a review of the chronological order of the major medical discoveries is most informative (see Bender, 1965; Bordley and Harvey, 1976). It suggests two important points. First, the discovery and application of the more powerful tools of medicine has occurred only rather recently. For example, the all-purpose penicillin compounds were not discovered and used until 1928, anticoagulants were first used in 1941, the defibrillator was first used in 1956, and the first immunizations against measles occurred in 1965. Second, the closer one gets to the present time, the more temporally compacted have been the discoveries. This reflects the explosive growth of scientific knowledge in medicine, especially during the past two decades. Thus, we can gain a better sense of the statement that "modern medicine is really *modern* medicine."

THE DEVELOPMENT OF AMERICAN MEDICINE. Modern scientific medicine developed in the United States just as it did in Europe, with one major distinction. In Europe the development of modern medicine went through several stages and nearly 2,400 years as it progressed from Hippocrates to the present. In the United States, however, similar stages were gone through in something less than three centuries. As a result, American medicine represents the most rapid development of any major social institution in our society. Coe (1978) argues that this occurred because of the New World values that emphasized three ethics above all others. The first was an exploratory ethic promulgated by the opportunity for continued growth and expansion. It was especially evident in the rapid charting, settlement, and development of what was formerly wilderness in the push from east to west. The second was a belief in doing things as well as they could be done. This was reflected in the deep-seated sense of craftsmanship that dominated America's history. The third was a predisposition toward doing things as quickly as possible, of not wasting time or materials, and of inventing new ways to help increase productivity.

Coupled with the almost instantaneous economic success and immeasurable resources of the United States, these three dominant ethics—exploration, craftsmanship, and productivity—created an optimal medium for the phenomenal development of modern medicine. As a result, medicine evolved rapidly in America, making it the worldwide center of modern medicine by the mid 1900s. This tremendous advance, however, has brought about one very serious side effect. By providing and encouraging such extensive medical development a unique situation has been created in which medicine has gradually usurped the responsibility for a considerable number of the aspects of our daily lives. We will discuss the full implications of this "medicalization of society" in chapter 14. For the time being, it is sufficient to say that the social institution of medicine in America is unlike that of any other country. It is more powerful and has accumulated control over a wider range of activities that are normally associated with other social institutions.

The Profession of Medicine

As we know it today, the profession of medicine is *one* of the strongest, if not *the* strongest profession in the United States. It is autonomous and self-regulating. Moreover, through its own professional union,

the American Medical Association (AMA), the profession of medicine has the power to regulate and certify the training process of would-be physicians. In essence, the profession of medicine and the AMA enjoy an advantaged position unknown to any other occupational group in the United States. This enhanced position came about almost overnight, resulting in what we shall call the "great trade" made between society, government, and the AMA in 1910. To understand the current profession of medicine, therefore, we must begin with a discussion of the "great trade." (For alternative interpretations of these events, see Anderson, 1985; Starr, 1982; and Stevens, 1971.)

The Flexner Report of 1910

We have already learned that the development of modern medicine in America was a very rapid process, taking less than 300 years compared to the 2,400 years it took in Europe. The development of the medical profession that we know of today, however, is an even more recent phenomenon. It occurred as the result of a historical accident. This accident may be traced back to the turn of the twentieth century when a considerable gap existed between the level of medical knowledge and its practical application.

THE GAP BETWEEN KNOWLEDGE AND APPLICATION. While the level of medical knowledge was advancing rapidly throughout American history, that knowledge was not finding its way into practical application at the hands of physicians. This perplexing situation occurred as a result of the structure of medicine. Until the twentieth century there were no central licensing organizations for individual physicians, nor were there any national accrediting institutions for medical colleges. Many physicians received their only training as apprentices to other doctors. Physicians in rural and pioneering areas resembled the barber-surgeons of medieval Europe. Indeed, as late as the nineteenth century it was still possible to buy a medical diploma without ever having studied medicine.

There were two dire consequences of this

situation. First, although scientific medicine had made and continued to make marked advances, these were not transformed into everyday practice. The reason for this was that most "physicians" were not trained in the academic settings where this scholarship took place. Second, because most physicians were not scientifically trained, they were not very successful in treating their patients. As a result, doctors were not generally held in high regard, nor did the public seek them out when they became ill. Instead, home remedies and folk medicine were usually the first choice for cures.

DOCUMENTING THE EXTENT OF THE GAP. Although it had become clear that such a gap existed, the extent of the gap had not been formally documented by the turn of the twentieth century. Recognizing the seriousness of the situation, the Carnegie Foundation supported Abraham Flexner's 1906 review of the then extant 155 medical schools. It was not long before his careful and extensive review of medical colleges revealed the extent of the gap between medical knowledge and its application. In fact, 20 medical colleges permanently closed their doors to avoid revealing the poor quality of their programs.

When Flexner's final report was published in 1910, it revealed the stark medical travesty. Most medical schools were inadequate and most physicians were improperly and insufficiently trained. Thirty-nine percent of the 155 original medical schools were closed by 1915, and 45 percent were closed by 1920. Private foundations began to withhold their funds pending the upgrading of the medical school facilities and faculties. Because such funds were the principal sources of support for most medical schools, this particular action was devastating. Moreover, individual states began to institute procedures for the licensing of adequately trained physicians. In general, there was a distinct and extensive push for an instantaneous remedy of this medical travesty. Someone had to be chosen to determine who was properly trained and who wasn't. Someone had to accept the responsibility for regulating the medical profession.

The "Great Trade"

It just so happened that the only national standards available for accrediting medical schools were those of the AMA's Council on Medical Education. Accordingly, the individual states and the federal government turned to the Council on Medical Education for the purpose of setting the standards for accreditation. As a result, by 1925 the AMA had obtained a monopoly over the production and licensing of physicians. This included the power to determine what the curriculum should be, how many students should be admitted, which students should be admitted, and how many faculty there should be for each student. Thus, 1910 marked a trade of immeasurable importance between society (as represented by state and federal governments) and the AMA. The trade gave the AMA the exclusive right and the sole power to regulate the medical profession. In return, the AMA was to give society the best and most efficient medical care system possible. Society has clearly lived up to its part of the bargain by providing the profession of medicine an advantaged monopolistic position known to no other occupation or industry. What is not at all clear is whether the AMA has provided society with the best possible medical care system.

THE IMMEDIATE EFFECTS. The great trade produced three rather immediate, positive effects on the health care delivery system. First, the number of medical schools plummeted from 175 in 1906 to 107 by 1920. More than 80 percent of those that survived began requiring a college education prior to admission. Second, the licensing requirements instituted in most states by 1925 resulted in a substantial decrease in the number coupled with a substantial increase in the quality of physicians. Third, medical education was significantly upgraded. Emphasis was placed on combining theory and research findings, and incorporating both into an application-oriented, university- and hospital-based curriculum. The end result of all this was that physicians became more scarce and more prestigious at the same time. The AMA has worked hard to maintain this situation ever since.

There were also, however, some negative effects of the great trade. Perhaps the most important of these was the fact that the smaller, shoestring budget medical schools went out of existence. They were financially unable to come up with the resources necessary to meet the stiff new accreditation requirements (i.e., they were caught in a "catch-22" situation). Unfortunately, most black physicians had received their training at such schools, and because of their closing, the number of black physicians declined markedly. This situation continues to exist today, even in the face of affirmative action programs that have generated considerable controversy (as evidenced by the controversial United States Supreme Court action in the 1978 Allan Bakke decision). In fact, while blacks constitute about 11 percent of the general population, they account for only 2.2 percent of the physician work force.

Similarly, just as the black medical schools closed, so too did the part-time and night schools. This occurred because of the shift in medical education to a demanding, expensive, full-time, and lengthy process. Those who could not afford the luxury of a full-time education were kept away from medical schools. Thus, lower socioeconomic status groups rapidly became underrepresented in medical schools and, subsequently, in the medical profession. Accordingly, although the great trade brought about a rapid increase in the quality of physicians and medical education, it also resulted in the establishment of the profession of medicine as an occupation for white, middle- or upper-class men. What is most important here, however, is that the great trade established the AMA as *the* force behind and in charge of American medicine.

The American Medical Association

Although the AMA was organized in 1847, its meteoric rise to power did not begin until 1910 when the Flexner report was released. It has since grown into the most powerful and effective health care lobbying group in the United States. To understand

Table 9-1. *Number of physicians in various medical specialties, December 31, 1983.*

Specialty	Number
Total physicians	482,635
Aerospace medicine	695
Allergy	1,551
Anesthesiology	20,003
Cardiovascular diseases	12,298
Child psychiatry	3,606
Colon/rectal surgery	793
Dermatology	6,315
Diagnostic radiology	11,345
Family practice	35,952
Forensic pathology	291
Gastroenterology	5,398
General practice	28,202
General preventive medicine	871
General surgery	36,323
Internal medicine	82,462
Neurology	7,140
Neurological surgery	3,873
Obstetrics/gynecology	29,306
Occupational medicine	2,648
Ophthalmology	14,294
Orthopedic surgery	16,193
Otorhinolaryngology	7,051
Pathology	14,940
Pediatrics	32,831
Pediatric allergy	399
Pediatric cardiology	759
Physical and rehabilitative medicine	2,902
Plastic surgery	3,701
Psychiatry	30,763
Public health	2,112
Pulmonary diseases	4,696
Radiology	10,403
Therapeutic radiology	2,054
Thoracic surgery	2,169
Urology	8,529
Other specialty	16,158
Unspecified	7,771
Not classified	12,643

SOURCE: Gene Roback, Lillian Randolph, Diane Mead, and Thomas Pasko. *Physician Characteristics and Distribution in the U.S., 1984 Edition.* Chicago: American Medical Association. Reprinted by permission.

the AMA's extensive power, its effective use of that power, and its implications for the health care delivery system, we must examine its size and structure in greater detail.

SIZE. The size of the AMA clearly reflects the specialized occupation that it represents. On December 31, 1983, there were 482,635 physicians actively practicing medicine in the United States. Of these, 48 percent were members of the AMA. Members and nonmembers are divided into dozens of specialty areas, as shown in Table 9-1. Although physicians' incomes vary from specialty to specialty, as shown in Table 9-2, they are quite high. Indeed, the average physician's net income before taxes in 1985 was $113,188. Thus, these data demonstrate that physicians are both highly specialized and highly paid. To provide a sense of perspective, the median family income in 1985 was only about $25,000.

FORMAL STRUCTURE. The AMA consists of seven major bodies: (1) city and county societies, (2) state associations and specialty groups, (3) the House of Delegates, (4) the Scientific Assembly, (5) the Secretary-Treasurer, (6) the headquarters staff, and (7) the Board of Trustees. The interrelationship of these bodies is shown in the organizational chart in Figure 9-1. The primary function of the county or city societies is to screen and award membership to petitioning physicians so that they may apply for admission to the state societies. Similarly, the primary function of the state societies is to screen and award membership to petitioning physicians so that they may apply for membership in the AMA. Until 1981 membership in state and local medical societies was a prerequisite for membership in the national association. Since then, the AMA has been

Table 9-2. *Annual net income of physicians by major medical specialty categories, 1985.*

Medical specialty	Net income
All physicians	$113,188
General or family practice	77,912
Medical specialties	93,229
Surgical specialties	146,841
Other specialties	117,829

SOURCE: American Medical Association. 1986. *Socioeconomic Monitoring System Core Surveys.* Chicago: Author. Reprinted by permission of the American Medical Association.

Figure 9-1. *An Organizational Chart of the American Medical Association.*

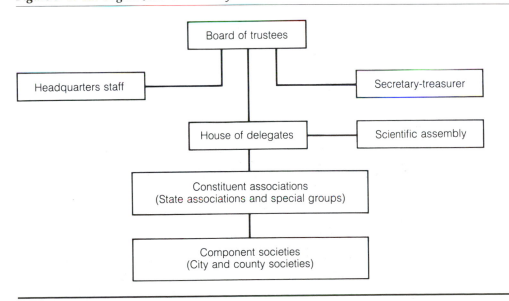

SOURCE: Rodney M. Coe. 1978. *Sociology of Medicine,* 2nd ed. New York: McGraw-Hill. Reprinted by permission of the publisher.

able to directly recruit members, but only during a brief, specified time during the year. Therefore, for all practical purposes it remains the case that members of the AMA are usually also members of their state and county medical societies.

The House of Delegates is charged with the responsibility for constitutional amendments and regulations in a manner similar to the United States Congress. The Scientific Assembly considers new developments in medicine and their implications for the AMA. The assembly's function is similar to that of the congressional staff made available to Congress for investigating scientific problems, but not for setting political policies. The Secretary-Treasurer is responsible for the maintenance of the appropriate financial and procedural affairs of the AMA. The headquarters staff is in charge of the day-to-day business and research affairs. Finally, the Board of Trustees functions in the same way as any other corporation's board of directors; they have legal charge over the property and financial affairs of the AMA.

In most organizational charts the higher up one goes, the more power one finds. In the AMA, however, this is not quite the case. As we have seen, membership has traditionally been granted only on the recommendation of, and with membership in, the state medical society. Membership in the state medical society has traditionally been granted only on the recommendation of, and with membership in, the county medical society. Membership in the county medical society is obtained by the petition of the physician to the Board of Censors or some similarly named, elected group within the county society (Garceau, 1961). In theory, all "reputable and ethical licensed physicians" (M.D.s) are eligible for membership. In practice, county medical societies have been known to reject qualified physicians for a variety of reasons including race, the setting in which the physician practices (such as the nontraditional health maintenance organizations or free clinics), and the perceived economic threat that the petitioning physician poses to established physicians in the community. As a result, some have charged county medical societies with

having arbitrary and capricious admissions policies.

Regardless of the validity of the above concerns, the county medical societies remain quite powerful because of their traditional hold on admission to the AMA. Admission to the AMA is important for two reasons (Freidson, 1970a). First, there is no comparable alternative association for general membership of any significance to the physician. Therefore, the AMA is "the only game in town." Second, membership in the AMA is frequently used as a criterion for professional competence by employers and certifying agencies. It is also used by prospective patients as a form of quality assurance in selecting a new doctor (see Wolinsky and Steiber, 1982). This makes membership an important item for the successful career of the physician. As a result, the AMA is a rather monolithic institution with an inverted power structure.

INFORMAL STRUCTURE. The concentration of formal and informal power at the local level is the principal force for homogeneity within the AMA. As Denton (1978) points out, the incoming physician is forced to adapt to the existing power structure if he or she desires admission, rather than having it adapt to him or her. Further, the dominant, conservative attitudes of the founding fathers of the AMA have been preserved through both the formal and informal "old boy" networks for the selection of future officers, trustees, and delegates. Freidson (1970a) describes this process as follows:

On the county level, the president appoints the nominating committee, which puts up a slate to be voted on. The state president does the same. Since state and national associations forbid electioneering, organized opposition to the official slate has rarely succeeded and the official slate is almost always elected. The reelection of incumbent delegates is common and "new blood" is uncommon. These electoral practices are of course not very unusual for occupational associations in general, being by no means peculiar to the AMA.

Thus, within the formal structure of the AMA most of the actual power and control are allocated along informal, nondemocratic lines. This is exemplified in the detailed organizational chart of a typical state medical society shown in Figure 9-2. In the figure the broken arrows represent appointed positions and committees; the solid arrows represent elected ones. As is evident, the more important committees and positions (such as editor of the state journal and executive secretary) are not directly elected; rather, they are appointed by elected officials. The election of the officials who make these appointments are structurally controlled at the local level; the county officials select the committees who then nominate candidates for election at the higher levels. These county officials obtain and maintain their power by virtue of the admissions and expulsion process. Thus, the informal or "true" power base is at the county level; it regulates what goes on higher up in the AMA.

WANING POWER. Although the AMA has managed to maintain its position as the most powerful and effective health care lobbying group in the United States, this position has been on the decline since the mid 1960s. There are three principal reasons for this. First, the American Association of Medical Colleges (AAMC) and the individual medical colleges themselves are taking a much more active and independent role in directing and reorienting medical education. Indeed, the Federal Trade Commission has been investigating the AMA's traditional control over medical education; it may choose to divest the AMA of that control in the future. The second reason for the general decline in the status and prestige of the AMA is the current crisis in the health care delivery system. Most health care critics point to the AMA as a major source of the current crisis. This has eroded the public's trust and confidence in the AMA.

Third, while the AMA is still "the only game in town," the percentage of physicians who are members has declined. Twenty-five years ago three out of four doctors were members. Today, membership in the AMA has fallen to slightly less than 50 percent of all active, licensed physicians. This has occurred for two reasons. One is the free-rider problem. Because the AMA lobbies on behalf of all physicians, nonmembers are able to reap its benefits just as members do. They, however, do not have to pay any of the associated costs. Thus, as long as enough other physicians support the AMA, nonsupporting physicians will enjoy most of the benefits anyway. The other reason for the decline in AMA membership is the proliferation of medical specialization and specialty societies. Many specialists feel that the AMA has nothing to offer them beyond what they accrue from being members of specialty societies. Thus, membership in the AMA is more typical among office-based primary care physicians. Despite these problems, the AMA remains the single most important health care group on the national scene.

The Professionalization of Physicians: The Freidsonian Perspective

As we have seen, the great trade between society, government, and the AMA left physicians in charge of the health care delivery system. In the process the occupation of being a physician has come to be regarded as a profession; those who occupy it are regarded as professionals. The public image of physicians has traditionally been one of prestige, trustworthiness, and responsibility. To understand the relevance of the professional status of medicine, we must understand the difference between a profession and an occupation, distinguish between professions and professionals, determine how an occupation becomes a profession, examine how the profession regulates itself, and consider the implications of medicine's professional status. Our discussion of these issues relies heavily on Eliot Freidson's (1970a) award-winning book, *The Profession of Medicine*. We will conclude this section with a brief review of the two major schools of criticism of Freidson's perspective and his response to them.

THE DEFINITION OF A PROFESSION. What exactly is a profession? It is an occupation that is set apart from other occupations. How is that occupation set apart from other occupations? Society conceives of that occupation as being different than the other

Figure 9-2. A Detailed Organizational Chart of a State Medical Society.

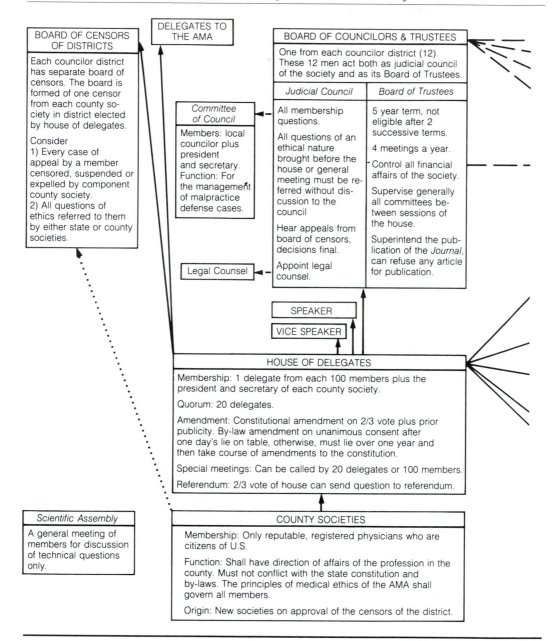

BOARD OF CENSORS OF DISTRICTS

Each councilor district has separate board of censors. The board is formed of one censor from each county society in district elected by house of delegates.

Consider
1) Every case of appeal by a member censored, suspended or expelled by component county society.
2) All questions of ethics referred to them by either state or county societies.

DELEGATES TO THE AMA

BOARD OF COUNCILORS & TRUSTEES

One from each councilor district (12). These 12 men act both as judicial council of the society and as its Board of Trustees.

Judicial Council	*Board of Trustees*
All membership questions.	5 year term, not eligible after 2 successive terms.
All questions of an ethical nature brought before the house or general meeting must be referred without discussion to the council	4 meetings a year.
	Control all financial affairs of the society.
	Supervise generally all committees between sessions of the house.
Hear appeals from board of censors, decisions final.	Superintend the publication of the *Journal*, can refuse any article for publication.
Appoint legal counsel.	

Committee of Council

Members: local councilor plus president and secretary. Function: For the management of malpractice defense cases.

Legal Counsel

SPEAKER

VICE SPEAKER

HOUSE OF DELEGATES

Membership: 1 delegate from each 100 members plus the president and secretary of each county society.

Quorum: 20 delegates.

Amendment: Constitutional amendment on 2/3 vote plus prior publicity. By-law amendment on unanimous consent after one day's lie on table, otherwise, must lie over one year and then take course of amendments to the constitution.

Special meetings: Can be called by 20 delegates or 100 members.

Referendum: 2/3 vote of house can send question to referendum.

Scientific Assembly

A general meeting of members for discussion of technical questions only.

COUNTY SOCIETIES

Membership: Only reputable, registered physicians who are citizens of U.S.

Function: Shall have direction of affairs of the profession in the county. Must not conflict with the state constitution and by-laws. The principles of medical ethics of the AMA shall govern all members.

Origin: New societies on approval of the censors of the district.

SOURCE: Oliver Garceau. 1941. *The Political Life of the American Medical Association.* Cambridge: Harvard University Press. Reprinted by permission of the publisher.

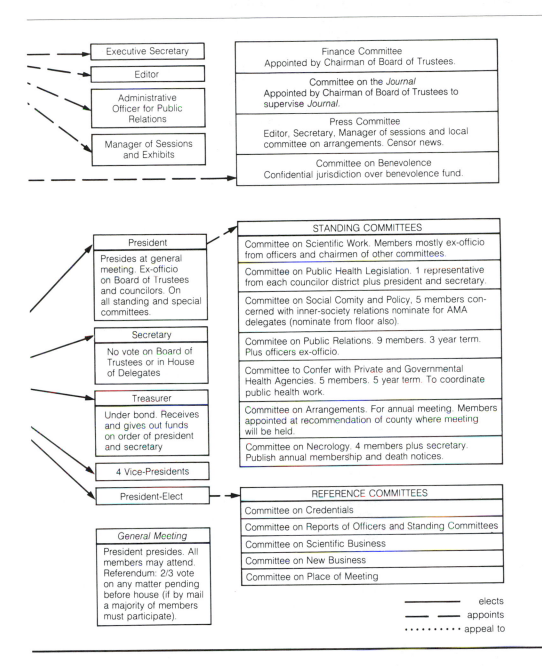

Executive Secretary	**Finance Committee** Appointed by Chairman of Board of Trustees.
Editor	**Committee on the *Journal*** Appointed by Chairman of Board of Trustees to supervise *Journal*.
Administrative Officer for Public Relations	**Press Committee** Editor, Secretary, Manager of sessions and local committee on arrangements. Censor news.
Manager of Sessions and Exhibits	**Committee on Benevolence** Confidential jurisdiction over benevolence fund.

President
Presides at general meeting. Ex-officio on Board of Trustees and councilors. On all standing and special committees.

Secretary
No vote on Board of Trustees or in House of Delegates

Treasurer
Under bond. Receives and gives out funds on order of president and secretary

4 Vice-Presidents

President-Elect

General Meeting
President presides. All members may attend. Referendum: 2/3 vote on any matter pending before house (if by mail a majority of members must participate).

STANDING COMMITTEES

Committee on Scientific Work. Members mostly ex-officio from officers and chairmen of other committees.

Committee on Public Health Legislation. 1 representative from each councilor district plus president and secretary.

Committee on Social Comity and Policy, 5 members concerned with inner-society relations nominate for AMA delegates (nominate from floor also).

Commitee on Public Relations. 9 members. 3 year term. Plus officers ex-officio.

Committee to Confer with Private and Governmental Health Agencies. 5 members. 5 year term. To coordinate public health work.

Committee on Arrangements. For annual meeting. Members appointed at recommendation of county where meeting will be held.

Committee on Necrology. 4 members plus secretary. Publish annual membership and death notices.

REFERENCE COMMITTEES

Committee on Credentials

Committee on Reports of Officers and Standing Committees

Committee on Scientific Business

Committee on New Business

Committee on Place of Meeting

——————— elects
— — — appoints
· · · · · · · · · appeal to

occupations. What makes society consider this occupation as being different? A variety of things, depending on the particular society or social scientist trying to define a "profession." For example, Carr-Saunders and Wilson (1933) state that a profession "exhibits two principal features, the spontaneous coming together of the practitioners in associations, and the regulative intervention of the State. . . . It is the purpose of the professional association to achieve, and of the State, when it intervenes, to grant some degree of monopoly of function to the practitioners." Thus, Carr-Saunders and Wilson recognize two key elements, a strong association, representing the occupation desiring to be a profession, that works together with the political authorities to establish a legal monopoly over the pursuit and practice of that occupation.

Taking a more historical approach, Wilensky (1964) argues that occupations become professions by passing through five typical stages: (1) making the occupation a full-time pursuit, (2) linking the training of workers to a special training institute, (3) establishing an association like that Carr-Saunders and Wilson described, (4) obtaining a legal monopoly over their sphere of work, and (5) developing a code of ethics that regulates their professional behavior. While Wilensky's approach seems rather straightforward, it runs into problems when we consider the fact that many of our present trades (plumbing, electrical work, and bricklaying) have completed these five stages but are not regarded as professions. The definition (or criterion) of a profession, then, must contain something more.

Recognizing this need, Goode (1960) identified two core characteristics of a profession: "a prolonged specialized training in a body of abstract knowledge, and a collectivity of service orientation." From these two core characteristics, Goode went on to derive ten additional characteristics of professions, five of which form a cluster around *autonomy*: "(1) the profession determines its own standards of education and training; . . . (3) professional practice is often legally recognized by some form of licensure; (4) licensing and admission boards are manned

by members of the profession; (5) most legislation concerned with the profession is shaped by that profession; . . . and (7) the practitioner is relatively free of lay evaluation and control." Although there are many other specific ways to approach the definition of a profession, they generally contain some semblance of Goode's two core characteristics (for an extensive review of the various definitions, see Cogan, 1953; for an excellent review of the issues under discussion in the literature on professions, see Freidson, 1983, 1986).

As indicated earlier, Freidson is generally regarded as *the* major analyst of the profession of medicine (see his 1970a, 1970b, 1980, 1983, 1984, 1985, and 1986 works). He has built on Goode's core characteristics by arguing that the word *profession* has two meanings. On the one hand, it represents a special kind of occupation. On the other hand, it represents an avowal or promise. These meanings correspond to Goode's reference to specialized training and a service orientation. For Freidson (1970a), the study of a profession such as medicine should place emphasis on both. He writes that

it is useful to think of a profession as an occupation which has assumed a dominant position in a division of labor, so that it gains control over the determination of the substance of its own work. Unlike most occupations, it is autonomous or self-directing. The occupation sustains this special status by its persuasive profession of the extraordinary trustworthiness of its members. The trustworthiness it professes naturally includes ethicality and also knowledgeable skill. In fact, the profession claims to be the most reliable authority on the nature of the reality it deals with. When its characteristic work lies in the attempt to deal with the problems people bring to it, the profession develops its own independent conception of these problems and tries to manage both clients and problems in its own way.

Thus, Freidson defines a profession as an occupation that has achieved autonomy or self-direction. He defines a professio*nal* as an individual who carries out the duties of his or her occupation in a manner befitting the avowed promise of that profession.

HOW DOES A PROFESSION GET AUTONOMY? If autonomy is truly the test of any occupation's professional status, then the next interesting question is how a profession achieves that prized autonomy and the service orientation. Freidson argues that autonomy is granted by society in recognition of the occupation's accomplishments and advances. As such, autonomy is always a granted, legal process. It is not something that the occupation may obtain on its own. In the case of medicine, autonomy was granted to physicians and the AMA in exchange for their promise to provide quality medical care and eliminate the sad state of affairs described in the Flexner (1910) report. This promise included a vow to assure the specialized knowledge of physicians through educational requirements, licensing procedures, the adoption of a professional code of ethics, the control over fellow physicians to ensure professional work, and the development of a professional association to organize the profession and continually upgrade its quality. According to Freidson, these conditions represent the first stage in the professionalization process that eventually distinguishes it from an occupation. Once these qualities have been demonstrated, then society *may* recognize the value and reliability of that occupation as a special one and extend autonomy to it.

While many occupations meet the first-stage requirements, Freidson (1970a) argues that only medicine, law, and the ministry have been extended autonomy. He notes that "the only truly important and uniform criterion for distinguishing professions from other occupations is the fact of autonomy— a position of legitimate control over work. . . . Autonomy is the critical outcome of the interaction between political and economic power and occupational representation, interaction sometimes facilitated by educational institutions and other devices which successfully persuade the state that the occupation's work is reliable and valuable." Accordingly, while nursing has progressed to the first stage of the process, it has not become a true profession. The nature and extent of the work that nurses can do is regulated and controlled not by nurses but by physicians. Thus, nurses do not have autonomy. Similarly, physicians' assistants have

achieved the first stage in the professionalization process, but their work is also controlled by physicians. This bars physicians' assistants from professional status as well.

Once autonomy has been granted to an occupation, the public recognizes that occupation *as if* it had an extensive collectivity and service orientation. Whether the profession actually does or not is irrelevant (Freidson, 1970a):

Other occupations may actually have as great a proportion of members with such an orientation—that is not the issue. They may have codes of ethics, oaths, and other institutional attributes reflecting such an orientation—that, too, is not the issue. *The profession's service orientation is a public imputation it has successfully won in a process by which its leaders have persuaded society to grant and support its autonomy.* Such imputation does not mean that its members more commonly or more intensely subscribe to a service orientation than members of other occupations.

In essence, the societal reaction to a profession is to label it as service-oriented and subsequently react to that label rather than to the true nature of the profession.

The overall process of achieving professional status is summarized in Figure 9-3. In this figure an occupation (in this case occupation C) is elevated to stage 1 when it achieves educational requirements, licensing procedures, a code of ethics, a professional association, and peer control. If the occupation remains at stage 1, it may be considered a paraprofession, such as nursing. If the occupation is to become a profession, however, it must demonstrate its worthiness and be officially rewarded with autonomy (especially the control over its own work). That causes society to impute a collective service orientation to the profession, as with physicians.

SELF-REGULATION. Autonomy, then, is the single most important criterion for determining whether an occupation has achieved the status of a profession. When society grants an occupation autonomy, it gives up its oversight or dominion over that occupation. According to Freidson (1970a), self-regulation (that is, self-imposed peer review) then becomes the test of professional

Figure 9-3. *The Stages of the Professionalization Process.*

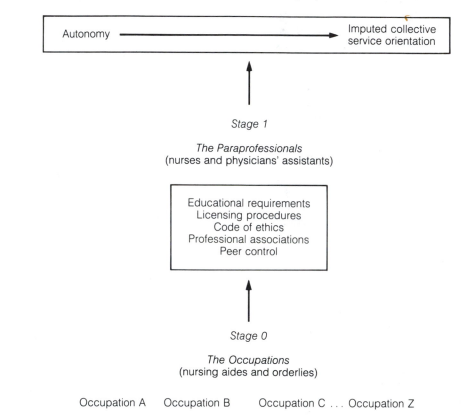

Stage 2

The Professions
(medicine, law, and religion)

| Autonomy ⟶ | Imputed collective service orientation |

Stage 1

The Paraprofessionals
(nurses and physicians' assistants)

Educational requirements
Licensing procedures
Code of ethics
Professional associations
Peer control

Stage 0

The Occupations
(nursing aides and orderlies)

Occupation A   Occupation B   Occupation C . . . Occupation Z

autonomy. What this means is that if society grants the profession its autonomy, then the profession must be self-regulating, providing its own quality control. No one else has the power to regulate that profession anymore. Although this seems rather simple and straightforward, the possible implications of granting professional autonomy are staggering. If the autonomous profession so chooses, it may go lax on the issue of self-regulation, leaving its members to practice as they please. Because there is no other social control agency over the profession but the profession itself, the possibility arises for the profession to misuse its autonomy and abuse its clientele. Therefore, the pro-

fession must have both formal and informal ways of regulating the performance of its members.

At the formal level the self-regulation of physicians has traditionally not been very common in most medical settings. In fact, it is the marked absence of formal review processes that has spurred the consumer movement, in collaboration with governmental cost containment strategies, to push for the establishment of professional review standards and quality care assessment programs. These would force the periodic recertification and evaluation of a physician's knowledge and its clinical application (see Brook, Davies-Avery, Greenfield, Harris, Lelah, Solomon, and Ware, Jr., 1977; LoGerfo and Brook, 1984). At the national level no such systematic review procedures currently exist. What does exist are review committees that are supposed to evaluate the credentials of physicians initially seeking hospital privileges, review the laboratory analysis of surgically removed tissue, and review medical records on a random basis. These formal reviews are concentrated in hospitals, especially in the larger teaching hospitals. They are seldom found in office practices. Even among hospitals, however, the formal review process is not as stringent as it should be. Therefore, although it may be assumed that where such formal self-regulation takes place it functions to increase the quality of physicians' performances, there is virtually no information on how much performance is monitored, nor the standards against which that performance is measured. (The basic methods of quality assurance, including their strengths and weaknesses, will be discussed in detail in chapter 14.)

As in most large, formal organizations, the majority of the self-regulation and review processes that occurs for physicians is informal. Physicians begin to regulate themselves only when they have informally received information that a fellow physician is not performing at an acceptable level. Once this information has been obtained, the self-regulation that follows is almost always also informal and takes on one of four basic forms. The first two forms of negative sanctions are the "talking-to," which may occur as a single physician-to-physician interaction or as an interaction between a group of physicians and a single physician. In either case, the physician or physicians who have come to be aware of the less-than-acceptable performance of their colleague informally raise the issue with him or her. The intent is to bring the performance question out into the open among the physicians but not among anyone else. This exerts pressure for the offending physician to get back in line. The talking-to, of course, carries no formal weight and does not show up on the offending physician's records. Unfortunately, the talking-to is often the only informal sanction available to one's colleagues.

Usually, the initial talking-to is between a single physician and the offending colleague. If this is unsuccessful, another physician may try talking to the offending physician. If this also fails, other physicians may try this one-on-one or dyadic talking-to. If these interactions do not succeed, then the concerned physicians may elevate the process. Here, several colleagues talk to the offending physician at the same time. It is important to note that physicians prefer to limit the talking-to process to one-to-one situations whenever possible for two basic reasons. First, in so doing their colleagues are neither criticized nor corrected in a public way, even among their colleagues. Thus, the offending physician does not become widely recognized as a poor performer. This is especially important if it is the first talking-to that the offending physician has received. Second, physicians highly value their own independence as practicing professionals. They do not want to be told what to do by a review committee. Thus, they would much rather be advised in private by a single colleague.

If these interactions fail to correct the performance of the offending physician, then they are usually elevated to the next and only other level—the boycott. The boycott, like the talking-to, may be either a personal or group phenomenon. At the personal level, an individual physician may decide that the talking-to has not had the desired effect on the poorly performing colleague. Short of any formal action to delicense the offending physician or to remove his or her hospital staff privileges—neither of which is likely to occur unless a strong public case has been made against the physician—the physician may be independently or collectively boycotted by his or her colleagues. Such a boycott constitutes the personal and economic sanctions of colleagues in their refusal to refer patients to the poorly performing physician. If enough physicians boycott another physician, the offending physician will have to come into line or be left without patients.

THE POWER OF INFORMAL SANCTIONS. At this point you may be ready to say that while there are very few formal self-regulation processes among physicians, the two methods of informal negative sanctioning (at the individual and collective levels) should be more than sufficient. While this seems to be a reasonable point, there is a serious drawback to these informal sanctions. Freidson (1970a) notes that "all these methods of exclusion are practiced by *individuals*: they are not actions of the collegium. Therefore, they do not prevent an offender from working and maintaining his work relations with colleagues whom he has not offended. *They punish him only insofar as he is sensitive to the good opinion of those particular individuals whom he has offended.*"

There are, unfortunately, a variety of situations in which poor performance can be noted and informal sanctions taken without any success. For example, the poor performer can flourish in areas where there is an insufficient supply of physicians because, regardless of the personal boycott of other physicians, the demand for physician services keeps the poor performer well supplied. The offending physician's clientele may, however, suffer from a high degree of turnover; patients may seek other sources of care after they perceive their doctor's poor performance. This is especially true in inner-city, rural, and other aesthetically unpleasing areas where the demand for physician services usually exceeds the available supply. This compounds the traditional problem of poor access to health care in these areas with poor-quality health care.

In addition to these limitations, one must realize that whatever informal sanctions are applied come only after the information concerning poor performance has been received. This raises the question of how that information is compiled and becomes available to the offending physician's colleagues. Unless the information describing the poor performance of the offending physician is brought to the attention of his or her colleagues, not even informal actions will take place. Because offending physicians do not advertise their poor performance and there are no real formal review processes, the collection of such information takes a considerable amount of time. Moreover, it is largely informal except for the use of patients' medical charts. The use of medical charts in itself raises two serious problems. First, medical charts are the working tools of the physician. They are usually not detailed enough to accurately reconstruct the treatment episode of any given patient. In addition, most of the physician-related data in the medical chart is entered by the physician. It is unlikely that an offending physician will systematically enter potentially incriminating evidence.

The second major problem in reviewing patients' medical charts is that it constitutes a formal process that is rather visible to much of the hospital staff. This violates the private, individual nature of the talking-to and boycott sanctions. As a result, short of the rare formal review brought about by malpractice suits or other litigation, most information is obtained informally through physician encounters and discussions with nursing and other ancillary staff. Such informal information retrieval takes considerable time. The negative effect of this time factor is augmented by medicine's fragmentation. Different physicians, nurses, and other ancillary workers know a little about one aspect of the offending physician's performance. Others know a little bit about another aspect. Thus, the assembly of the information necessary to instigate informal sanctions is hard to come by and comes in little bits and pieces. These must be carefully pieced together to form the total picture of a poorly performing physician.

And these problems with the formal review process are compounded by a myriad of control deficiencies at the system level. For example, there is no mechanism for sharing information about disciplinary actions initiated, or taken, against physicians in one state with counterpart control agencies in other states. Indeed, it was only in the mid 1980s that the armed services agreed to forward information related to the dishonorable discharges, for reasons of malpractice, of its former physicians to the states. Moreover, there are even bureaucratic barriers that constrain (if not prevent) the flow of such information from agency to agency within the same state.

Thus, the disciplinary system is so loose and uncoordinated that if they desire to do so, incompetent physicians can find a variety of ways to remain in practice.

THE FLAW OF PROFESSIONAL AUTONOMY. Obviously, then, there is a flaw in the notion of professional autonomy. It produces a host of negative results that may ultimately outweigh the benefit of better scientific medical knowledge. To fully comprehend this flaw we must be sure of what we mean by professional autonomy. The notion of professional autonomy is epitomized by four characteristics: *organized autonomy*, *occupational dominance*, *self-education*, and, *client regulation*. When taken together these traits produce a profession that is remarkably insulated and isolated from related occupations, its own clients, and society in general. The flaw of professional autonomy, then, is that it allows and encourages (Freidson, 1970a) "the development of self-sufficient institutions, it develops and maintains a self-deceiving vision of the objectivity and reliability of its knowledge and the virtues of its members. . . . [Medicine's] very autonomy has led to insularity and a mistaken arrogance about its mission in the world." In essence, the granting of professional autonomy has allowed physicians to pull the wool not only over the eyes of their clientele but over themselves as well. Over the years, medicine has deceived itself to the point where it believes that it really is self-regulating, deserving of professional autonomy, and acting in the public interest.

THE EFFECTS OF PHYSICIANS' AUTONOMY. Having learned what autonomy really means and how it sets the profession of physicians off from other occupations and paraprofessions, especially those in medicine-related fields, we will now assess the four major effects of that autonomy. The first two are best understood when a distinction is made within the realm of medicine. Freidson (1970a) has argued that in medicine and all other consulting professions "*the practice, exercise, or application of expertise is analytically distinct from the expertise of knowledge itself*." Thus, a distinction must be made between the level of medical knowledge and the nature of its application. In making this distinction, Freidson suggests that granting autonomy has had a Dr. Jekyll and Mr. Hyde effect: "*While the profession's autonomy seems to have facilitated the improvement of scientific knowledge about disease and its treatments, it seems to have impeded the improvement of the social modes of applying that knowledge.*" Thus, on the one hand professional autonomy has spurred the development of the best system of codified, scientific knowledge about medicine. On the other hand, however, professional autonomy has stifled the development of the best system for applying that knowledge to the human condition. This stifling effect may be traced to two factors: the lack of self-regulation among physicians, which we have already discussed, and the resistance of the AMA to social change. The AMA views any external regulation of the application of medical knowledge as an affront to the profession of medicine and a threat to the quality of medical care in the United States.

The third major effect of professional autonomy has been the ever-increasing redefinition of reality by physicians and the growing medicalization of America. Medicine has become one, if not the prime, avenue for societal reactions to deviant behavior. This clearly encroaches on the social control functions of the fellow professions of law and the ministry (Freidson, 1970a): "Disapproved behavior is more and more coming to be given the meaning of illness requiring treatment rather than of crime requiring punishment, victimization requiring compensations, or sin requiring patience and grace." While this encroachment began gradually, it has been increasing at an alarming rate. Szasz (1975) has documented its growth with specific examples:

At first slowly, such things as hysteria, hypochondriasis, obsessive-compulsive neurosis, and depression were added to the category of illness. Then, with increasing zeal, physicians and especially psychiatrists began to call "illness" . . . anything and everything in which they could detect any sign of malfunctioning, based on no matter what norm. Hence, agoraphobia is illness because one should not be afraid of open spaces.

Homosexuality is an illness because heterosexuality is the norm. Divorce is illness because it signals failure of marriage.

In essence, the granting of professional autonomy to medicine has allowed it to redefine and relabel reality. In redefining and relabeling reality, medicine has gotten into the habit of affixing the label of *illness* to almost every type of *social* deviance. As American life becomes increasingly pluralistic, social deviance increases by definition—there are more and more deviations from "typical" social behavior. This results in the further medicalization of American life (see Conrad and Schneider, 1980).

Finally, there is the economic effect of professional autonomy. Whenever any occupation becomes a profession, it is granted a legal monopoly over its services, which are usually scarce and in high demand. This includes the responsibility to set prices. Of course, in the ideal sense professional ethics and self-regulation dictate that physicians will set prices in the public interest and will not abuse their privileged position. Freidson (1970a), however, argues that the ideal and real situations are markedly different: "By and large, I think it is fair to say that the profession [of medicine] in the United States has made virtually no effort to insure that its members do not abuse their privileged economic position by seeking more than a 'just price.'" At issue here is the basic question of who should set medical care prices in the first place. Rayack (1967) simply and eloquently argues that "wherever there is a need to set standards in the medical market and the possibility of a conflict of interest exists, physicians should not be in policymaking positions." Unfortunately, it is precisely in such conflict of interest situations that physicians *are* in policymaking situations. For example, Blue Cross, Blue Shield, and other third-party reimbursors have national and regional advisory boards. These boards determine how much a physician or hospital should be paid for certain procedures and what procedures are or are not warranted. Almost all the members of these boards are physicians; most of the remainder are hospital administrators. Therefore,

when issues of rate increases or extended coverage come up, "what the doctor wants is what the doctor gets." As a result, medical care expenditures have grown from $12 billion in 1950 to nearly $400 billion in 1986 (Department of Health and Human Services, 1987).

LIMITING PROFESSIONAL AUTONOMY. Self-deception and the concomitant failure to fulfill the public trust are not characteristics unique to the profession of medicine. Rather, it is the nature of professional autonomy itself that is the villain. They need to be limited if the public interest is to be served. To protect the public interest, Freidson (1970a) suggests two cardinal principles for limiting professional autonomy. The first is that when a question of the public, the family, or an individual's interest in a health problem arises, it should be the public, the family, or the individual's decision as to what is in its true best interest. It should not be the decision of the physician(s) or of the AMA. The second principle calls for a drastic increase in the general external regulation of the profession.

From these cardinal principles, Freidson (1970a) makes four concrete proposals for limiting the professional autonomy of medicine. First, there should be a special effort to recruit medical students from a wider range of social backgrounds. At the same time there should be a systematic effort to limit the number of children of physicians who are admitted to medical school. These two policies would increase the heterogeneity of the profession. Second, the virtual isolation of medical schools from the rest of the university should be modified. Medical education should not be wholly dominated by its own perspective. Third, once in professional practice the physician must not be so isolated from colleagues. Increased interaction with colleagues makes physicians more informed about their knowledge and performance. This facilitates the exchange of new therapeutic techniques and increases the likelihood of effective self-regulation. Finally, there should be some form of professional standards review to regularly consider the technical, economic, and social practices of all physicians. These review groups should focus on professional *and* lay concerns, be composed of both physicians *and* laypersons, and be empowered to prevent poorly performing physicians from continuing their practices.

TWO CRITICAL VIEWS OF THE FREIDSONIAN PERSPECTIVE. In the two decades since the publication of the *Profession of Medicine*, much has changed in the United States, both in general and in medicine. Indeed, a number of scholars now argue that the traditional autonomy of the professions is eroding. With respect to the autonomy of physicians, two schools of thought have emerged. One focuses on the notion of deprofessionalization; the other focuses on the notion of proletarianization.

Haug (1973, 1975, 1977; see also Haug and Lavin, 1978, 1981, 1983) has been the primary force behind the deprofessionalization argument. Her view is that the profession of medicine has been losing its prestigious societal position and the trust that goes with it. She cites five principal reasons for this loss. First, medicine's monopoly over access to its defined body of knowledge has been eroded by the increased use of automated retrieval systems, such as computerized algorithms for symptom assessment. Second, marked increases in educational attainment have made the public less likely to view medical knowledge as mysterious. As a result, people are more likely to challenge physicians' authority. Third, the increasing specialization within medicine has made doctors more dependent on each other and also on nonphysician experts, especially engineers. Dependence on the former diffuses the power of any single physician inasmuch as he or she must rely on the advice and expertise of colleagues. Dependence on the latter diffuses the power of all physicians inasmuch as they must rely on advice and expertise from outside the profession. Fourth, the growth of consumer self-help groups coupled with the emergence of a variety of allied health care workers has increased the reliance on the lay, or at least the nonprofessional, referral system. For many people the experiential information exchanged in these lay encounters poses a rather attractive alternative to the physicians' academic knowledge. Finally, the physicians' altruistic image has not weathered well the recent storms over the rising cost of health care. Indeed, Haug notes that physicians are now being held far more accountable for their role in cost containment.

The proletarianization thesis has been advanced most eloquently by McKinlay (1973, 1982, 1986). He builds on Marx's theory of history, emphasizing the inevitability of all workers in capitalistic societies like the United States to eventually be stripped of their control over their work. This occurs when individuals are reduced to selling their services rather than producing finished goods. McKinlay argues that the growing corporatization, or bureaucratization, of medicine has resulted in eliminating the self-employment and autonomy of physicians. As the number and extent of intermediaries between patients and their doctors increases, physicians become more like other laborers. Moreover, as the medical workplace becomes more bureaucratized, physicians are increasingly subject to rules and other hierarchical structures that are not of their own making. As a result, the ability of doctors to govern themselves, especially by using their preferred informal methods of self-regulation, declines.

FREIDSON'S RESPONSE. As you might expect, Freidson does not find much support for either of the critical appraisals of his analysis of medicine's privileged professional status. His dismissal of the deprofessionalization thesis asserts that although some specifics may have changed over the last two decades in the absolute, the overall situation remains relatively the same (Freidson, 1984):

The professions . . . continue to possess a monopoly over at least some important segment of formal knowledge that does not shrink over time, even though both competitors and rising levels of lay knowledge may nibble away at its edges. New knowledge is constantly acquired that takes the place of what has been lost and thereby maintains the knowledge gap. Similarly, while the power of computer technology in storing codified knowledge cannot be ignored, it is the members of each profession who determine what is to be stored and how it is to be done, and who are equipped to interpret and employ what is retrieved effectively. With a continual knowledge gap, potentially universal access to stored data is meaningless. In sum, while the events highlighted by proponents of the deprofessionalization thesis are important, the argument that members of the professions are losing their relative prestige and respect, their expertise, or their monopoly over the exercise of that expertise over time is not persuasive.

In dismissing the proletarianization thesis, Freidson (1984) emphasizes that although the autonomy of individual physicians may have been reduced, the autonomy of the profession of medicine remains intact:

While rank and file professional workers may have to take orders just as blue collar or clerical workers have to, these orders are given by a superordinate colleague, not by someone trained in management or some other field. Where the work of the professional employee is formally delineated in some detail . . . it is not done by outsiders who have expropriated the professional's skills, but rather by members of the same profession who have specialized in the accomplishment of such tasks. While this formatting does reduce the use of discretion and judgement by *individual* rank and file professional workers, it does not represent a reduction in the control of professional work by the *profession* itself, for other professional workers create it and supervise and manage the rank and file. It is therefore entirely inaccurate to say that the professions as corporate bodies have lost their capacity to exercise control over their members' work, even though individual professionals may have.

In Freidson's view, the fundamental changes are not occurring on the *outside* of medicine, but rather on the *inside*. He (1985) emphasizes that these changes

might be interpreted as bureaucratization in Weber's ideal-typical sense, for they are accompanied by an increase in hierarchical positions as health care organizations grow in size, records become more elaborate, specific standards govern the formal evaluation of more and more work, supervision in the form of evaluation of work becomes more and more widespread, and hierarchical positions of responsibility increase in number and variety. . . . [They] do not affect the position of the profession as a corporate body

in the social as well as institutional division of labor so much as they affect the *internal* organization of the profession, in the relations among physicians. In essence . . . they are creating more distinct and formal patterns of stratification within the profession than have existed in the past, with the position of the rank and file practitioner changing most markedly.

Thus, Freidson believes that the stage is not set for the profession of medicine to have its advantaged position wrestled away from the outside. Rather, he believes it will be modified from within. Principal among the alterations currently taking place is the formalization of professional controls. The informal practice of using face-saving normative methods of self-regulation is on the wane. It is being replaced by formalized, bureaucratic methods. Nonetheless, dominion over these new formalized methods of control remains within the profession itself. Therefore, the deprofessionalization and proletarianization theses seem to be without supporting evidence.

A FEW WORDS IN DEFENSE OF THE PROFESSION OF MEDICINE. While the profession of medicine is seriously flawed, it is neither inherently evil nor the worst profession practicing in the United States. All professions are subject to forgetting that their members are mere humans. Caught up in demanding practices, all professionals have the tendency to let slide their standards of self-regulation and client satisfaction. In this respect, medicine is one of the most regulated, client-oriented, and honest of the professions. For example, consider the self-regulation, client concern, and honesty of university teaching. By comparison, the profession of medicine is clearly superior. Nonetheless, the superior levels of self-regulation, client-concern, and honesty among physicians are not nearly high enough. Moreover, they won't be unless structural changes are made to correct the flaw of professional autonomy. Because we grant professional autonomy to medicine and the other professions, we too are responsible for their flaws and the effects of those flaws.

The Social Organization of Medical Practice and Self-Regulation

Not all physicians have the same type of medical practice. Indeed, there is considerable variation in the nature of the social organization of physicians' practices. Generally speaking, however, there are five major forms of medical practice: solo practice, associations, partnerships, group practices, and corporate entities, such as health maintenance organizations (HMOs). According to Freidson (1970a; see also Wolinsky and Marder, 1985), each of these forms of medical practice affects the self-regulation process in different ways. These include both the assembly of information concerning an offending physician and the invocation of sanctions against him or her.

SOLO PRACTICE. The solo practitioner's patients have chosen him or her on their own as their personal physician. This has traditionally been the typical model of medical practice in the United States. However, the number of physicians entering group prac-

tices and HMOs is increasing at a phenomenal rate. Although it is the national stereotype, the solo practitioner's practice is inherently unstable (Freidson, 1970a). In the ideal setting the solo practitioner becomes either client- or colleague-dependent. In reality it is the general or family solo practitioner who becomes client-dependent, because without clients his or her practice will fall apart. In addition, the general or family practitioner is not usually the recipient of clients from the referral system; rather, he or she refers clients to specialists when their services are needed. It is the specialist solo practitioner who becomes colleague-dependent, because he or she relies on referrals from other specialists or from general practitioners.

The ideal referral system among general practitioners (GPs) and specialists (SPs) who are in solo practice is portrayed in Figure 9-4, where the different dependencies of the general (patient-dependent) and specialist (colleague-dependent) practitioners are evident. The solo general practitioner operates in an independent and unobserved

Figure 9-4. The Ideal Referral System and Dependencies Among General Practitioners (GPs) and Specialists (SPs) in Solo Practice.

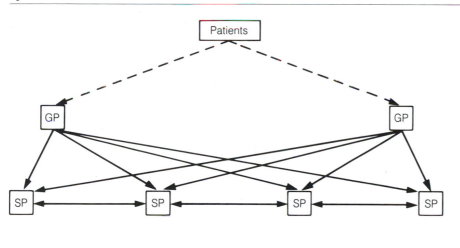

- - - → Private patient flow, reflecting client dependency

——— → Referred patient flow, reflecting colleague dependency

fashion in regard to his or her colleagues. Therefore, the assembly of information indicating poor performance is increasingly difficult. Moreover, the power of informal negative sanctions are drastically reduced because of the limited interaction and referrals made with the offending physician. The solo practice specialist is in a much different situation. He or she is constantly interacting with colleagues. Being dependent on them allows information on his or her performance to be more readily available. In addition, informal negative sanctions are likely to be more effective.

THE ASSOCIATION. The association is a formal cooperative agreement in which physicians share the expense of maintaining office facilities, equipment, and auxiliary personnel. At the same time, however, they maintain their own private patients. Thus, the effect of this type of medical practice on self-regulation is similar to that of the general practitioner in solo practice, with one exception. The exception is that by sharing the same auxiliary personnel, the collection of information from the informal subordinate grapevine is enhanced. Because economic factors are not brought into play since the participating physicians are not sharing profits, however, this enhanced access to informal information is seldom acted upon.

THE PARTNERSHIP. Quite similar in structure but not in effect is the small legal partnership. Usually partnerships consist of two physicians. They share not only the expenses of office and auxiliary staff maintenance but the profits of their practices as well. The particular method of dividing profits is always a bone of contention. This is especially true when different specialties are involved, some of which may handle more or fewer patients and generate larger or smaller fees. The most important factor here, however, is that each physician has a clear and definite monetary interest in the other. Thus, the increased flow of information and partnership dependency makes informal negative sanctions far more effective.

GROUP PRACTICE. Group practice is becoming more and more popular. In fact, about one out of every four (or 143,392) physicians actively practicing in 1985 was involved in group practice. This represents more than a 10-fold increase in both the number and proportion of physicians in group practice since the 1930s (Havlicek, 1985). Group practice is the formal organization of three or more physicians who provide medical care by the joint use of equipment, auxiliary staff, and office facilities. The resulting income is distributed on a prearranged basis. Because there are so many different types of group practices based on size and specialty, our understanding of the effects of group practice on self-regulation will be facilitated by examining Table 9-3. This table shows the number of physicians in group practice by the size and type of their group. Two trends stand out. First, more than one third of all the physicians in group practice are in groups of seven physicians or less. Second, about 60 percent of all the physicians in general practice and single-specialty groups are in groups that have seven physicians or less. Among the multispecialty groups the re-

Table 9-3. *Number of physicians in group practice by size and type of group, 1984.*

Type of group	Size of group						
	All sizes	3–4	5–7	8–15	16–25	26–49	50+
All physicians	139,127	27,117	20,270	18,955	10,208	11,972	50,605
Single-specialty	59,917	20,775	15,053	11,351	4,099	2,812	5,827
Multispecialty	69,371	2,384	3,181	6,615	5,306	8,370	43,515
Family or general practice	9,839	3,958	2,036	989	803	790	1,263

SOURCE: Adapted from Penny L. Havlicek. 1985. *Medical Groups in the U.S., 1984.* Chicago: American Medical Association. Reprinted by permission of the American Medical Association.

verse is true; 60 percent of all the physicians in multispecialty groups are in groups that have 50 or more physicians. This reflects a general distinction within group practice. The smaller groups (seven or fewer physicians) tend to be enlarged versions of the private partnership where physicians own the group; the larger groups tend to be owned and operated by a third party who salaries the physicians they employ.

Even among the smaller groups self-regulation is easier because the size of the practice's organization requires a greater bureaucratic structure than solo or partnership practices. This provides easier access to information regarding poor performance (Mechanic, 1976b). The self-regulation process remains primarily in the hands of the physicians as a result of their vested financial interest (poor performance loses patients and lowers fee schedules). In the larger groups there are two significant differences. On the one hand, there is not as much of an economic incentive to prompt self-regulation among colleagues. On the other hand there is the added regulatory effect of administrative review of poor performance by the third party, either administrators or owners. As a result, self-regulation among the larger groups is often motivated more by professional rather than economic concerns. Self-regulation will be higher in any group practice when there are more physicians practicing the same specialty as the offending physician, because this increases the overlap in the patients that they see. There is also generally more interaction among same-specialty colleagues that increases the flow and collection of information.

HEALTH MAINTENANCE ORGANIZATIONS. Health maintenance organizations (HMOs) are one of the newest forms of medical practice in the United States. They have five essential characteristics (Luft, 1981): contractual responsibility, an enrolled defined population, voluntary enrollment, fixed periodic payment, and financial risk. Contractual responsibility means that HMO members have legal rights to medical care provided by the HMO. In conventional health care systems, physicians have the

right to decide whether to take on a new patient. In the HMO, physicians must provide the care that any HMO member needs. Having an enrolled, defined population means that the HMO knows to whom it is obligated to provide care and can therefore estimate how much care it will need to provide. This allows HMOs to engage in more accurate planning than conventional delivery systems. Voluntary enrollment means that enrollees can choose either a conventional plan like Blue Cross or Blue Shield, or the HMO. The choice, however, is theirs to make. Fixed periodic payment means that regardless of the number of services used, a given enrollee pays the same predetermined monthly fee. This means that the HMO does not make more money by providing more services, as is the case in the conventional, fee-for-service health care delivery system. Finally, financial risk means that the HMO will either financially suffer or benefit from the care that it delivers.

There are three basic types of HMOs, although within each type there is considerable variation: group models, staff models, and individual practice associations (IPAs). In a group model HMO all physicians are members of the same group practice. Their medical group contracts with the HMO to provide its services but remains legally and fiscally separate from the HMO. The group usually services the HMO exclusively and either owns or contracts with the hospital to which its patients are admitted. Members of the group are reimbursed on a salary or salary-plus-profit-sharing basis. The key element, then, in group model HMOs is that the physicians have a clear proprietary interest in the success or failure of the group and of the HMO. In essence, they are partners in its financial success or failure. The classic example of group model HMOs is the Kaiser Foundation Health Plan.

Unlike physicians in group models, physicians in staff model HMOs are employed directly by the HMO itself. As a result they are employees rather than partners. Therefore, they do not have as clear a proprietary interest in the HMO. They are usually reimbursed on a salary basis, although adjustments may be made based on average patient loads. The classic example of a staff model HMO is the Group Health Plan of Puget Sound.

The IPA is a loose federation of independent, individual physicians who agree to treat patients enrolled in a third-party HMO on a fee-for-service basis in their own offices. Frequently the IPA is jointly sponsored by local medical societies and insurance companies. When an IPA physician provides service to an HMO enrollee, the physician is reimbursed by the IPA for services rendered, less a modest allowance for the administration of the plan. Unlike staff and group model physicians who usually have the majority of their patients coming from the HMO, IPA physicians usually have no more than 10 percent of their patients coming from the HMO. As a result, although the HMO practice is usually the major, if not the entire, practice for staff and group model physicians, it is a small sideline for physicians in IPAs. The classic example of an IPA is the Forbes Health Maintenance Plan in Pittsburgh.

THE UNDERLYING THEME. Figure 9-5 facilitates summarizing the relationship between the social organization of medical practice and self-regulation. This figure graphically portrays the approximate relative differences in self-regulation expected as one proceeds from solo practice to group model HMOs. Underlying the continuum are three dimensions: organizational constraints, peer review, and fiscal incentives. The organizational constraints represent the increasing bureaucratic nature of medical practice as one moves from right to left. As medical practices get larger, the opportunity and need for more formalized review processes increases. Peer review also increases as medical practices get larger, because of the increased access to and coordination of information concerning colleagues' performance. This is especially true in single-speciality group practices or in large group practices that have a number of physicians in each specialty. The effect of fiscal incentives is as follows. In smaller practice settings (i.e., solo practices, associations, and partnerships), physicians are usually reimbursed on a fee-for-service basis; this creates an incentive structure that emphasizes doing more. In the larger practice settings, however, physicians are usually reimbursed on a salaried basis; this creates an incentive structure more supportive of doing what's right. When taken together, then, the likelihood of self-regulation increases as one moves from right to left on the continuum shown in the figure.

The Making of a Physician

We have seen how the profession of medicine has come into being, and we have learned what the results of the "great trade" for professional autonomy have been. We now turn our attention to the making of a physician. For quite some time the process of becoming a physician and practicing medicine has been the subject for a wide variety of entertainment media, including television series ("Dr. Kildare," "Ben Casey," "Marcus Welby, M.D.," and "St. Elsewhere"), movies (*The Interns* and *Doctors' Wives*),

Figure 9-5. Approximate Relative Differences in Self-Regulation Expected in Different Medical Practice Settings.

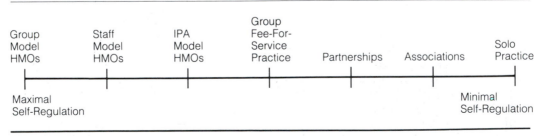

and books (*The Making of a Surgeon*). These descriptions of the process of becoming a physician are generally overglorified and underemphasize the hard work and grueling discipline required in medical school. More importantly, their portrayal of the social selection elements in the making of a physician are inaccurate. (If you are interested in a more detailed discussion and analysis of the making of a physician, we recommend that you read *Boys in White* by Becker, Geer, Hughes, and Strauss, 1961, and *The Student Physician* by Merton, Reader, and Kendall, 1957, which are the two classic sociological studies of medical education. The more recent works of Atkinson, 1981; Bloom, 1963a, 1963b, 1973, 1979; Bosk, 1979; Coser, 1979; Light, 1980; Millman, 1977; and Mumford, 1970, continue this fine tradition.) From the social science perspective there are two major stages in the process of becoming a physician: the medical student years, and the selection of a medical specialty and practice location.

Being a Medical Student: An Overview

Becoming a physician requires a long, strenuous career as a medical student (see Bloom, 1963a, 1973, 1979). This is usually preceded by the pursuit of at least a baccalaureate degree. That normally requires four years of college in a premed program or in one of the associated basic sciences, such as biology, chemistry, physiology, or pharmacology. After this undergraduate college precareer has been completed, the would-be physician faces five distinct phases—acceptance into medical school, the basic science years, the clinical years, the internship, and the residency—and an evolving medical student subculture.

GETTING INTO A MEDICAL SCHOOL. Of the many aspects of medical education, we know the least about the recruitment of medical students. In 1985 there were 127 accredited medical schools. They claimed a total enrollment of 66,604 medical students and graduated 16,191 physicians. As Table 9-4 indicates, this is a considerable increase from the 76 accredited medical schools in 1930, which enrolled 21,982 medical students and graduated 4,735 physicians. Indeed, the yearly production of physicians has increased nearly fourfold, a much faster increase than that of the general population. As a result, the physician per capita ratio is now the highest it has ever been in American history.

At this point an interesting question can be raised: Who gets into medical school? Or, put another way: What are the common traits of medical students? Medical students have traditionally had four common characteristics. First, they tend to have fathers or other close relatives who have already been physicians or other professionals. This at-

Table 9-4. *Students and graduates of United States medical schools, 1930–1985.*

Academic year	Number of schools	Total enrollment	First year	Graduates
1930–31	76	21,982	6,456	4,735
1940–41	77	21,379	5,837	5,275
1950–51	79	26,186	7,177	6,135
1960–61	86	30,288	8,298	6,994
1970–71	103	40,487	11,348	8,974
1980–81	126	65,497	17,204	15,667
1981–82	126	66,485	17,320	15,985
1982–83	127	66,886	17,230	15,824
1983–84	127	67,443	17,175	16,327
1984–85	127	67,093	16,992	16,347
1985–86	127	66,604	16,929	16,191

SOURCE: "Medical Education in the United States, 1985–86." 1986. *Journal of the American Medical Association* 25(12): 1561. © 1986, American Medical Association. Reprinted by permission.

tracts their children into medicine. Hall's (1948) telling explanation of this common trait is classic:

> One can see why doctors tend to be recruited from the families of professional workers. The latter possess the mechanisms for generating and nurturing the medical ambition. Only the members of a profession can translate the public protestations of the profession into the vernacular of useful advice. . . . In most cases family or friends played a significant role by envisaging the career line and reinforcing the efforts of the recruit. They accomplished the latter by giving encouragement, helping establish appropriate routines, arranging the necessary privacy, discouraging anomalous behavior, and defining the day to day rewards.

Thus, Hall notes that a professional orientation emerges from the socialization process in professional families. Such an orientation is almost a necessity in training for and assuming the professional career of a physician.

The second common characteristic of medical students is quite related to the first. Because of their increased likelihood of coming from a professional family, medical students are also likely to have significantly higher family incomes than the national average. Indeed, a number of studies have shown that medical students are about 10 times more likely to come from families with high incomes than their same-age peers not enrolled in medical schools (see Department of Health, Education, and Welfare, 1974). Although this income discrepancy has started to decline in recent years, parity has yet to be achieved.

The third common characteristic of medical students is that they are more likely to be men than women. Table 9-5 shows the number and percent of women in various stages of medical school from 1939 to 1985. While the percentage of women in the entering classes of medical school has in-

Table 9-5. Enrollment of women in medical schools, 1939–1985.

Academic year	Women applicants		Women in entering class		Total women enrolled		Women graduates	
	Number	Percent of total	Number	Percent of total	Number	Percent of total	Number	Percent of total
1939–40	632	5.4%	296	5.0%	1,145	5.4%	253	5.0%
1949–50	1,390	5.7	387	5.5	1,806	7.2	595	10.7
1959–60	1,026	6.9	494	6.0	1,710	5.7	405	5.7
1964–65	1,731	9.0	786	8.9	2,503	7.7	503	6.8
1969–70	2,289	9.4	952	9.2	3,390	9.0	700	8.4
1970–71	2,734	10.9	1,256	11.1	3,894	9.6	827	9.2
1971–72	3,737	12.8	1,693	13.7	4,755	10.9	860	9.0
1972–73	5,480	15.2	2,315	16.9	6,099	12.8	924	8.9
1973–74	7,202	17.8	2,743	19.6	7,731	15.4	1,264	11.1
1974–75	8,712	20.4	3,260	22.3	9,786	18.1	1,706	13.4
1975–76	9,575	22.6	3,656	23.8	11,527	20.5	2,200	16.2
1976–77	10,244	24.3	3,876	24.7	13,059	22.4	2,611	19.2
1977–78	10,195	25.1	4,149	25.7	14,373	23.8	3,086	21.4
1978–79	9,561	26.1	4,184	25.2	15,293	24.4	3,445	23.0
1979–80	10,222	28.3	4,748	27.9	16,315	25.4	3,497	23.1
1980–81	10,644	29.5	4,970	28.9	17,373	26.5	3,892	24.8
1981–82	11,673	31.8	5,343	30.8	18,555	27.9	3,991	25.0
1982–83	11,685	32.7	5,445	31.1	19,627	29.3	4,229	26.7
1983–84	11,961	33.9	5,659	32.9	20,685	30.7	4,706	28.8
1984–85	12,476	34.7	5,705	33.6	21,287	31.7	4,903	30.0
1985–86	11,562	35.1	5,788	34.2	21,624	32.5	4,968	30.7

SOURCE: "Medical Education in the United States, 1985–86." 1986. *Journal of the American Medical Association* 256(12):1562. © 1986, American Medical Association. Reprinted by permission.

creased from 5 percent in 1939 to 34 percent in 1985, women are still considerably underrepresented. After all, they compose 54 percent of the total population. These data also point out two rather important trends. First, until the mid 1970s female applicants were more likely to be admitted to medical school than were male applicants (the percent of women entering was greater than the percent of women applying). Since then, however, female applicants have been slightly less likely to be admitted. Second, until the mid 1970s exit with the medical degree was also easier for women than for men (the percent of women graduates was larger than the percent of women entering four years earlier). Since then, however, female medical students also have been slightly less likely to graduate. These trends suggest that reverse sex discrimination policies may have increased both women's access to and exit from medical schools during the 1960s and 1970s; however, that situation reversed itself by the late 1970s and early 1980s. This is entirely consistent with the general shift in both public attitudes toward and federal enforcement of sex discrimination policies. In any event, women have a long way to go before they are equally represented in medical schools.

Finally, just as women are underrepresented in medical schools, so are nonwhites. Although blacks constituted 11 percent of the total population in 1985, they made up only 5.3 percent (or 3,556) of the total medical school enrollment. In a relative sense, blacks appear to be the most underrepresented racial minority in medical schools. Moreover, they have also made very little progress in achieving equity, inasmuch as they constituted 4.7 percent of the total medical school enrollment back in 1971. By comparison, the proportion of American Indian, Mexican American, American Oriental, and Puerto Rican American medical students increased substantially during this same period.

When taken together, the four common characteristics of medical students—coming from a professional family, having higher family incomes, being white, and being male—have served to maintain the homogeneity of the profession of medicine brought about by the "great trade." While recent efforts have sought to make the medical student population more representative, they have not been entirely successful. Moreover, the whole notion of reverse discrimination and the use of quotas in order to ensure adequate representation has come into question (see *Bakke v. The Regents of the University of California, Davis,* United States Supreme Court, 1978). It seems that although we have recognized the underrepresentation of certain social groups in the profession of medicine, we haven't yet agreed on how to go about correcting it and making the medical student population more heterogeneous.

THE BASIC SCIENCE YEARS. Once a student has been fortunate enough to be admitted to medical school, the first grueling part of the four years of undergraduate medical education begins. This involves the basic science years. Traditionally, most of the first two years of medical education (or most of the first 12 months in the compacted three-year-round programs) is devoted to the study of anatomy, biochemistry, biophysics, cellular biology, genetics, microbiology, pathology, pharmacology, and physiology. Perhaps the two most striking characteristics of the basic science years are the extensive range of knowledge to be absorbed and the expectation by the faculty that each medical student will study his or her basic science field and master it as if they had chosen to take a Ph.D. in it. In fact, many scientists teach medical students as if they were conducting a seminar for Ph.D. candidates whose primary interests were in theory and research rather than in clinical application. As a result, medical students typically find themselves spending 80 hours a week either in the classroom or studying for the classroom.

A considerable factor behind these long student hours is the nature of medical school instruction. Teaching in medical schools is far more individual and aggressive than anything the students have experienced in their baccalaureate training. Instead of semester-long courses, the curriculum in medical schools is divided into one to four blocks of intensive lecture, laboratory, and discussion units. Faculty members intersperse their lectures and laboratory presentations with questions. They demand specific and meticulous answers, and they single out specific medical students to give those answers. As you can well imagine, the embarrassment of being unable to completely and immediately answer such questions is devastating.

In sum, the basic science years are far more academic than clinical. There are two major deviations from the baccalaureate experience. First, the curriculum is highly compacted and structured into short, intense units rather than semester-length courses. Second, the basic science faculty teach as if they were conducting Ph.D. seminars in their research interests specialties, rather than courses for first-year medical students.

THE CLINICAL YEARS. In the clinical years things change (see Atkinson, 1981). Medical students are no longer solely engaged in formal academic pursuits. They are introduced to the hospital, the patient, and the role of student physician. At this point much of the academic knowledge learned in the basic science years begins to be applied to real, live patients. This becomes an increasingly trying situation for students because the nature of the examination process changes markedly. First of all, the faculty are now more concerned with clinical or applied issues than with the research and theoretical concerns of the basic sciences faculty. Second, the faculty now have the opportunity to orally examine the medical student in every aspect of the clinical setting, including making the rounds at the bedsides of patients. Here a clinical faculty member may pose any question relevant to the case. This represents far greater latitude in questioning than that of the basic science faculty, whose grueling questions were at least tied to the formal topic of their lectures. As a result, to avoid the embarrassment of giving wrong answers or being unable to answer at all, the medical student in the clinical years must be

on top of everything rather than just that day's lecture.

A third difference that makes the clinical years more trying is the social organization of the learning setting. The clinical years are based in the hospital (see Coser, 1979; Millman, 1977). Here the medical student is no longer the center of attention, as was the case in the classroom. In fact, the medical student is at the bottom of the hierarchy in the hospital. The prize "students" are the residents and interns; they occupy most of the clinical faculty's time. Moreover, the medical student lacks the legal authority to practice medicine. All of those with whom he or she associates, however, have that authority.

Perhaps the major shift in the clinical years is that accumulated facts and textbook authority are outweighed by the practical experience of the clinical faculty. This causes medical students to wonder why they studied all those textbooks and learned so many facts in the first place. In essence, the clinical years are the times when the medical student becomes the student-physician. He or she takes on an apprenticelike status and position to the clinical faculty. It is here that the medical student is shown and learns how to translate the codified knowledge of medicine into practical applications.

THE MEDICAL STUDENT SUBCULTURE. In addition to the structural and organizational characteristics that we have described concerning the medical student's basic science and clinical years, a more interesting cultural phenomenon occurs throughout the medical education process. This phenomenon is the development and periodic reorientation of the medical student subculture. This includes the dominant perspective or outlook that medical students adopt throughout the various stages of their careers. The flow of these perspectives throughout the medical education process is portrayed in Figure 9-6 (based on the work of Becker, Geer, Hughes, and Strauss, 1961). When students first enter medical school, the perspective or outlook they hold is the obsession to learn all the facts of medicine. This

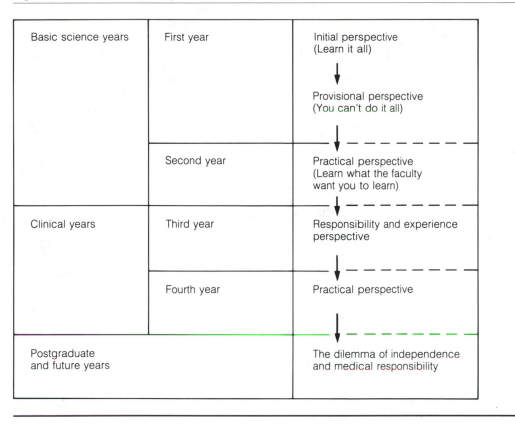

perspective changes into a provisional one, just prior to their first examination, when they realize that they can't possibly learn all there is to know. Following their first exam a new practical perspective emerges. At this point medical students seek to learn what they perceive the faculty want them to learn. They try and pick up on the cues that the faculty give off about what is really important and what is not. Then, only the really important things are learned. This practical perspective is maintained throughout the remainder of the basic science years.

Just as this practical perspective is developing, a related phenomenon takes place. An informal agreement emerges within the subculture that imposes limits on the amount of studying the medical students will do. The reason for this is to avoid having "rate busters" who will make the ma-

jority of medical students look bad. This represents a collective effort to exert some control over the amount of work that the medical students can reasonably be expected to do. More than anything else, this allows them to deal with the tension and fear of having to work too much and having to face public, oral examinations.

In the clinical years the guiding perspective changes from a practical orientation to one in which the medical students' responsibility and experience become the primary concerns. As the clinical years progress, however, the medical students are faced with the problem of deciding what to learn about these two concerns. As a result of this insecurity or lack of confidence in making the right decision, they adopt another version of the practical perspective. Once again they try to concentrate on learning what they perceive the faculty want them to learn. As the medical students leave medical school for their postgraduate training, they adopt a new perspective. They become very concerned about balancing their desire for independence and a solo practice against their goal of medical responsibility, which they have learned is best served by group and hospital-like staff practice. Thus, the newly graduated physicians begin their careers with a strong desire for independence as well as a felt need to be in close enough association with their colleagues for consultation and support.

THE INTERNSHIP. When the medical student begins his or her internship (which used to be a one-year process, but since 1975 has technically been merged with the first year of the residency), a new stage is entered in the medical career. At this point the medical student is legally permitted to practice medicine under the supervision of established physicians. There are two significant ramifications of this change in the medical student's status. First, the intern may legally be given the responsibility for the care of patients and is held accountable for that care. As such, the intern is able to assume a role in the health care hierarchy more like a colleague, although still in a subservient position. In fact, as the medical student crosses over to the status of intern, he or she is catapulted into an authoritative position above most of the ancillary staff, especially the nurses. What had been more casual interaction patterns between medical student and ancillary staff quickly become more distant and formal. In essence, it is during the internship that the medical student is formally recognized as a physician, even though the informal recognition had been building throughout the basic science and clinical years.

This formal change in status activates and accelerates changes in interaction patterns. These changes continue throughout the residency that follows. Another ramification of this changing status (from student to intern) is that the intern is assigned a wide variety and extensive amount of the more basic, routine, and boring "physician work" in the hospital. In essence, the intern is the major source of cheap general physician labor. He or she is assigned long hours so that established physicians can maintain their private practices and social life. For example, interns are usually the major physician component in the emergency room and outpatient situations where they work with very little supervision unless an unusual (either medically or politically) case is brought in. At such times, the resident or hospital staff physician is brought in to supervise and make teaching use of that case.

In essence, the intern is thrown into the physician's role. This occurs in the hectic, combatlike situation of the emergency room as well as in the other unpleasant or undesirable physician roles in the hospital. It prompts the intern to question and compare the impersonal and detached treatment given under such circumstances with the ideal, patient-oriented treatment that was so recently a part of his or her training. For these reasons, being an intern appears to be one of the most disheartening experiences in the medical student's career. Perhaps this explains why more dissatisfaction is expressed at this stage than at any other (see Mumford, 1970).

THE RESIDENCY. The internship is designed to expose the physician in training to a variety of tasks that doctors face in the hospital setting. It also provides supervision for the first flexing of their medical wings. The residency, however, is quite different. It exposes the resident to a concentrated apprenticeship and supervised practice in his or her specialty area. The purpose of the residency is to transform the "general utility intern" into a "specialist." At the present time almost every physician elects to take a residency in one of the many specializations acknowledged by the AMA. This has become especially true since the family practice specialty was introduced as a modernized version of the older general practice, which did not require a residency. In becoming a resident the physician reaches a new stage in the medical career. Residents are given partial responsibility for the training of interns and for their supervision. As a result, the role of the resident represents the final stage before the independent physician emerges from the medical training process.

The emergence of the independent physician is reflected in the process by which residents, unlike interns and medical students, evaluate their own competence. Bucher and Stelling (1977; see also Bosk, 1979; Light, 1980) have provided a classic analysis of the socialization of residents. Their study revealed that most residents have gained the self-confidence to evaluate their own work by the end of their training. Moreover, they begin to do so in part by ignoring the comments of patients and paying little attention to those of nurses and supervising physicians. This process of emerging self-evaluation is revealed in the following remarks of a senior resident. Bucher and Stelling had asked him: "How do you tell how you're doing?"

The pat answer to that is you have—if you see a patient that walks out the wards . . . and say, "Damn, that's the *third* case of poulypopituitorism I've seen," then you've been around too long. . . . I think as I read . . . if I go back and review things and say, you know, I've already read this somewhere else, that means that I have at least accumulated a certain amount of basic knowledge. . . . I still haven't accumulated as much as I want to accumulate. . . . I have grown but I'm obviously not satisfied with how much I've gotten done. . . . Being able to effectively manage patients, seeing them get along well, recognizing problems, testing myself against attending personnel who I consider to be good people—I mean in their particular fields—and coming away with the same understanding of problems as they have, means to me that I have advanced somewhat . . . to be able to effectively manage more and more of a patient's problems in a quicker period of time tells me that I have advanced from where I was when I first started. And lastly, of course, maybe not least—certainly not least—is peer considerations and being asked to see patients on other residents' services and being asked for my interpretations of problems.

Thus, the resident evolves to the point where self-assessments can comfortably be made about what knowledge has been learned, what diagnostic skills have been developed, whether diagnoses and treatments can be matched with supervisory physicians, and finally, whether or not fellow residents refer their patients for consultation. In essence, the resident has become capable of matching the desire for independent practice with the goal of medical responsibility. There is the recognition that although everything may not be known, the resident can match the performance of established physicians and has earned the respect of colleagues. The latter is the earliest indication of one's future referral patterns as a specialist. Thus, as the residency is completed, an independent physician is turned out, having successfully passed through the resident's marginal status of being a physician but not quite an established colleague.

Specialty and Location Selection: Effects of the Socialization Process

Two of the most interesting aspects of the socialization process that medical students go through are the selection of a medical specialty and a location in which to practice. In the ideal situation medical students would be opting for those specialties that the public needs and those locations where they are needed. In reality, however, this is not the case. In fact, there is a considerable difference between the supply and the demand for medical specialties (recall the physician surplus data discussed in chapter 3). As a result, we often hear people say that they can't find a doctor when they need one, despite the fact that there are more doctors available today than ever before in American history. In order to understand this apparent doctor "shortage," we must examine three parts of the problem in some detail: the maldistribution of physicians, the "specialty surplus," and the specialty-location selection process.

THE MALDISTRIBUTION OF PHYSICIANS. We are all aware of the fact that most physicians, like other professionals, prefer to live in metropolitan areas. These areas provide greater access to cultural, educational, and recreational activities. Most of us, however, would be shocked at the extent of the inequity of their geographic distribution. Fuchs (1974) has shown that the number of physicians per person in metropolitan counties is *three* times as high as it is in nonmetropolitan counties. Rushing (1975, 1985) has shown that there is more than just a metropolitan versus nonmetropolitan effect; the number of physicians per 100,000 persons is directly related to the percentage of urban residents. His data reveal a constant, linear relationship between physician supply and the degree of urbanization. The higher the degree of urbanization, the higher the per person supply of physicians. This clearly demonstrates the reluctance of physicians to live and work in the more remote, nonurban areas. It would seem that this situation could be rectified if we simply produced more physicians so that extra or excess physicians would move into rural areas. Unfortunately, although this would have some effect, it wouldn't solve the problem. Indeed, producing more physicians does not necessarily guarantee that they would be distributed in a more equitable fashion geographically.

THE "SPECIALTY SURPLUS." While geographic inequality is one part of the doctor shortage, another part is the "specialty surplus." It seems that there are more physicians specializing in some fields, especially in surgery and in subspecialties within internal medicine, than there is a demand for such specialists. At the same time, the reverse occurs in other specialties; there the demand far exceeds the supply. Although the spe-

cialty surplus has been recognized for quite some time, efforts to correct the trend have not been successful. For example, since the early 1970s there has been an increasing push for more residencies in family practice. Table 9-6, however, shows that as of 1985 internal medicine was still the specialty having the highest number of residency positions, of which 99 percent were filled. In family practice there were 7,513 residency positions available, and 97 percent were filled. Thus, despite the recognition of the specialty surplus, more subspecialists in internal medicine and surgery continue to be produced than necessary, and fewer general (family) practitioners are produced than needed. When new residency positions are made available in the needed areas, they somehow tend to go unfilled. As a result, that part of the doctor shortage caused by the specialist surplus continues to exist.

PICKING A SPECIALTY AND A LOCATION. This begs the fundamental question: How does the medical student come to select a specialty and a practice location? If it is the result of the socialization process that occurs in medical school, then we could change the results by changing that process. If entering medical students already know what specialty and location they desire, then we need only admit those whose preferences match current or projected needs. Unfortunately, it is not certain what causes medical

Table 9-6. *Number of approved residency programs, total positions filled and vacant during 1985.*

Specialty	Number of approved programs	Total positions offered	Total positions filled	Total positions vacant	Percent of positions filled
Family practice	385	7,513	7,276	237	97%
Surgery	306	8,183	8,070	113	99
Internal medicine	442	18,031	17,832	199	99
Obstetrics-gynecology	292	4,591	4,630	−39	101
Pediatrics	236	6,312	6,088	224	96
Psychiatry	211	5,077	4,809	268	95
Radiology, diagnostic	211	3,151	3,132	19	99
Anesthesiology	165	4,050	4,025	25	99
Other	2,551	19,416	18,657	759	96
Total	4,799	76,324	74,519	1,805	98

SOURCE: Adapted from "Medical Education in the United States." 1986. *Journal of the American Medical Association* 256(12):1586. © 1986, American Medical Association. Reprinted by permission.

students to select the specialties and practice locations that they do. During the past 35 years, however, a growing number of research studies have been conducted that attempt to identify the factors related to specialty and location selection. The general nature of these studies, from the classics (see Merton, Reader, and Kendall, 1957; Becker, Geer, Hughes, and Strauss, 1961) on down (see Ernst and Yett, 1985) has been epidemiological. They have only sought to compile all those common factors in the backgrounds of students choosing one specialty or practice location. They have not sought to unearth the process by which these decisions were made in the first place. Comprehensive reviews of these studies have shown that factors of background, experience, personality, and ability are related to specialty and location selection, although the level of empirical support has been only moderate and at times inconsistent (see Otis, 1975; Ernst and Yett, 1985).

In commenting on this situation, Mitchell (1975) has presented a conceptual scheme that represents the overall decision-making process. It consists of four major components: (1) the personal characteristics domain (past experience, present life circumstances, personality, and attitudes, beliefs, values, and predispositions); (2) the cognitive lens (how the individual conceives and deals with his or her environment); (3) the educational environment (reflected self-images and refracted faculty images); and (4) the choice domain (specialty selection, work settings, community type, and practice type). Underlying the process by which these components determine the selection of a medical specialty and practice location are two basic assumptions: "(1) The student will seek to select that niche which he sees as optimally satisfying his preferences and priorities, and which is compatible with the limitations imposed by his abilities and life circumstances. (2) From his medical training experiences the student acquires information about (a) himself, and (b) the career niches which he will use in attempting to make an optimal match between the two." Mitchell's (1975) conceptualization of the decision-making process clearly emphasizes the negotiated order and perceived process

that occurs within the medical school environment. It underemphasizes, however, the importance of the socialization and other processes that determine which student gets into which medical school environment in the first place.

Drawing on the works of Levinson (1967), Olmstead and Paget (1969), Bucher and Stelling (1977), and others, we suggest that the overall process of specialty and practice location selection may be portrayed as in Figure 9-7. Here the arrows flow from the earlier phenomena (causes) to the later phenomena (effects). As you can see, we have added two phenomena to this figure: the type of medical school that the student gets into (representing the general orientation or reputation of that medical school, such as producing the best specialists or generalists) and the type of faculty contacts that the student is able to make (such as close faculty supervision, or the protege type versus distant associations or role models). Thus, this figure suggests that to understand the decision-making process, the processes and factors that brought a particular student to a particular medical school must be considered. The nature of the medical school and the faculty contacts made within it are also important factors.

Accordingly, the causal process portrayed in Figure 9-7 begins with the medical student's background. It affects his or her personality, which affects his or her abilities, which affect the type and nature of the medical school that he or she gets into, which affect the type of faculty contacts that the student will have, which finally affect the specialty and practice location selection that the medical student ultimately makes. For example, a very bright and able female student from the East Coast may enroll in the Rochester (N.Y.) School of Medicine. Because she is bright and able, she is likely to do very well in her two years of basic science courses. Thus, she will be identified by the faculty as a first-rate student. As a result, the more prestigious clinical faculty at Rochester will consider taking her under their tutelage. Because Rochester's School of Medicine is famous for training pediatricians, the most prestigious of the clinical faculty are likely to be pediatricians. There-

Figure 9-7. An Expanded Model of the Medical Speciality and Practice Location Selection Process.

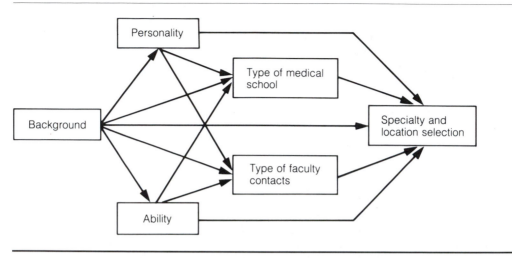

fore, the prize student most likely will be drawn into pediatrics. Because of this, she will be more likely to select an urban practice location that will support her pediatrics specialty. Moreover, because of the nature of pediatric practice (the need for large waiting rooms and the frequency of emergency calls at all hours), she is likely to prefer a group practice. There the initial cost of setting up a practice is lower, and it is possible to rotate with her partners the evenings and weekends for which she must be "on call."

Summary

In this chapter we examined the physician in contemporary American society. We did this by reviewing the historical development of modern medicine, the emergence of medicine as a profession, and the making of a physician. In the first section we saw that there were several distinct stages in the development of modern medicine. Each stage brought about its own particular contribution. There were six of these: (1) the Hippocratic contributions of the scientific approach, medical ethics, and medical morality; (2) the Greco-Roman stage, which contributed the first major theoretical paradigms attempting to explain how the body reacted

to various treatments; (3) the medieval period, which saw the beginnings of the development of university-trained physicians; (4) the Renaissance, in which scientific medicine was allowed to flourish as the dogmatic scholasticism of the Church receded; (5) post–sixteenth-century advances in clinical and biological medicine, including Harvey's theoretical discovery of the circulation of blood; and (6) the development of American medicine and its exploratory ethic, which facilitated medical research and development.

In the second section we saw that the profession of medicine emerged in the early 1900s as a result of the "great trade" induced by the 1910 Flexner report. That report revealed the generally low quality and remarkable variation in the training of physicians. The great trade gave physicians professional status and vested their autonomy in the AMA. The immediate effects of the great trade were most beneficial; only competent physicians having the requisite skills were licensed. The long-term effects, however, have not been entirely pleasing. Although it has accelerated the development of scientific medical knowledge, granting autonomy to physicians has impeded the social application of that knowledge. As a result, the public has been left with a health care delivery system that is fundamentally unresponsive to its needs and desires. We brought closure to our discussion of professional autonomy by reviewing two theories, deprofessionalization and proletarianization, that suggest that medicine's advantaged position is on the decline.

In the final section we examined the way in which one becomes a physician. We began by considering what it is like to be in medical school and what the medical school student typically experiences during the conversion from baccalaureate student to in-dependent practitioner. This included five relatively distinct stages: (1) getting into medical school; (2) the basic science years; (3) the clinical years; (4) the internship; and (5) the residency. It also includes the changing medical student subculture. We then examined how medical students are socialized into selecting a medical specialty and a practice location. We concluded by considering how this process has resulted in both a geographic maldistribution of physicians and a "specialty surplus."

10. Alternatives to Physicians

IN CHAPTER 9 we noted that physicians have long been the centerpiece of the health care delivery system in the United States. Although many things have changed in the past few decades, physicians have retained their dominant role (Freidson, 1980, 1983, 1984, 1985, 1986). Nonetheless, it is not always a physician that people seek when they have health problems. Saunders and Hewes (1969) may have said it best when they wrote:

A person may consult somebody (a druggist, an electrotherapist, a naturopath), may visit an institution (a shrine, a hot spring, a gymnasium, a Turkish bath), may change his residence, may purchase and use an appliance (a sun lamp, an electric stocking, a hot-water bottle, an exercising machine), may seek relief in drugs (Hadacol, Lydia Pinkham's Vegetable Compound, Carter's Liver Pills), may change his diet (fewer vegetables, nuts, gravies, starches, fruits), may choose a household remedy (bicarbonate of soda, salt, vinegar, oil of cloves), may follow a procedure (sun-bathing, cold baths, eye exercises, prayer), or may turn to the written word (a home medical book, a newspaper, a copy of *Reader's Digest*) for information and advice. *All of these and innumerable other choices may fall outside the field of scientific medicine and can be made without any contact with a licensed physician* [emphasis added].

In essence, when health care is sought, it is not always found at the door of the physician, or the hospital, or the clinic. Rather, what is often sought is some alternative to the physician.

There are numerous alternative healers from which to choose. Table 10-1 provides comparative data on the frequency of use and associated costs for a selected subset of these. As a whole, the alternative providers shown accounted for nearly 375 million visits and over $9 billion in total charges during 1980. This compares to 714 million visits to physicians and nearly $24 billion in total charges for those services during the same period.

There are two points to be made from these data. First, although there are fewer visits to, and at a lower cost than those made to physicians, the use of alternative sources of health care represents a sizable market. Moreover, accurate data on the use of alternative health services is incomplete and hard to come by. These statistics represent the best and most recent information available (Department of Health and Human Services, 1986b). Indeed, no comparable data exist prior to 1980, nor do similar data exist on alternative providers not shown here (such as osteopathic physicians, homeopaths, midwives, or faith healers). Therefore, the true extent to which Americans use alternative practitioners is seriously underestimated.

The second point to be made involves the considerable variation in both the per capita utilization rates and average charges for going to see these alternative providers. This underscores the significant differences between them. It suggests that an informed discussion must focus on but a few exemplary cases.

Accordingly, the present chapter is divided into four sections. In the first we compare three alternative healing occupations that began from similar roots at about the same point in time. Since then they have clearly gone very different ways. These include osteopaths (who have gradually been co-opted into the mainstream of traditional medicine), chiropractors (who have remained limited if not marginal practitioners by retaining their distinctive theory base), and homeopaths (who have become an endangered species). In the second section we consider the case of midwives and their struggle for licensing and acceptance by medicine. Special consideration will be given to the implications of licensure and regulation on the very nature of midwifery. In the third section we will review the role of faith healers and how their use underscores the duality between magic and science in modern medicine. Finally, we will discuss quacks and their devices. This will include guidelines on how to spot quackery in the medical marketplace.

Osteopaths, Chiropractors, and Homeopaths

Osteopathy, chiropractic, and homeopathy have a lot in common and yet they are very different. They all represent alternatives to traditional medicine, which for want of a better name is often referred to as allopathic medicine. All three trace their roots to the late 1800s. Each identifies a charismatic individual as its founding father. All three were initially viewed as healing cults. Today, however, things are quite different. Osteopathy has nearly achieved fusion with traditional medicine. Chiropractors are now viewed as somewhere between being marginal and limited practitioners. And homeopathy, at least in the United States, borders on extinction. To understand why these providers have the status that they have today, we must first consider the alternative theory with which each began and then trace its historical development. We begin with osteopathy.

Osteopathy

THE ORIGINAL THEORY. Osteopathic theory came into existence by divine revelation to Andrew Still, a licensed frontier physician. At precisely 10:00 A.M. on June 22, 1874 he (Still, 1908) "saw a small light in the horizon of truth. It was put into my hand, as I understand, by the God of Nature. That light bore on its face the inscription: 'This is my medical library, my surgery and my obstetrics. This is my book with all the directions, instructions, doses, sizes and quantities used in every case of illness, and birth, the beginning of man, in childhood, youth, and declining days.'" The fundamental precept in Still's system of medicine was that osteopathic lesions were the causes of all diseases and symptoms. The diseases and symptoms themselves were mere manifestations or effects.

Osteopathic lesions were defined as dislocations of bones, muscles, ligaments, or viscera. Thus, restoration of a sick individual to his or her originally healthy state re-

Table 10-1. *Number of visits to selected health care practitioners, total charges, and average charges in the United States, 1980.*

Item	M.D.'s	All others	Optometrists	Chiropractors	Podiatrists	Psychologists
Total number of visits (1,000s)	714,416	374,586	28,499	74,662	13,456	27,793
Number of visits per person with visits	4.5	4.8	1.4	8.3	3.1	9.7
Total charges ($1,000,000s)	$23,704	$9,197	$1,331	$1,186	$350	$843
Median charge	$20	$14	$33	$12	$15	$25
Average annual charge per person with visits	$150	$118	$65	$132	$80	$294

SOURCE: Department of Health and Human Services. 1986. *Visits to Selected Health Care Practitioners, United States, 1980.* DHHS Publication No. 86–20208. Washington, DC: U.S. Government Printing Office.

quired the proper realignment of the dislocated structure. The principal method of realignment involved manipulation of the small bones in the spinal column. Indeed, Still (1908) wrote that "I could twist a man one way and cure flux, fever, colds, and the diseases of the climate; shake a child and stop scarlet fever, croup, diphtheria; and cure whooping cough in three days by a wringing of the child's neck." Thus, the alternative that osteopathy posed to traditional medicine's germ theory of disease was also a unified one. It focused on structural dislocations and their realignment by spinal manipulation.

EARLY HISTORICAL DEVELOPMENTS. Because of Still's considerable success in practicing manipulative therapy, the demand for his services rapidly began to exceed his capacity to provide them. At first his sons and a few others began to work with him as apprentices. By 1892 the demand was such that the first "college" of osteopathic medicine was established in Kirksville, Missouri. A year later it graduated its first class of 17 men and 5 women. In 1896 Vermont became the first state to license osteopaths. The American Osteopathic Association (AOA) was founded in 1897. By 1902 standards were established for the approval of osteopathic medical colleges, and graduation from them became a prerequisite for

membership in the AOA. When Still died in 1917, there were more than 5,000 osteopaths in practice.

OSTEOPATHY AND THE FLEXNER REPORT. As discussed in chapter 9, the Flexner (1910) report on the status of medicine and medical training had important implications for traditional or allopathic medicine. Albrecht and Levy (1982) point out that the effect on osteopathy was crucial. Of the 37 osteopathic colleges of medicine that existed prior to 1910, only 6 survived to 1960. However, because Still and his followers had modeled osteopathic training as a close analog of traditional medical training (requiring four years of training by 1915), osteopathy was significantly better positioned to survive the "great trade" than were other alternative healing occupations. Indeed, while other competitors faded away, osteopathy continued moving toward professional recognition.

THE FIGHT FOR PROFESSIONAL STATUS. Between 1910 and 1962 both osteopathy and traditional medicine continued the professionalization process and the consolidation of resources. However, they did so at remarkably different rates (Albrecht and Levy, 1982). As we have already seen, by 1960 there were about 100 traditional medical schools and nearly 300,000 M.D.'s. In con-

Nurses	Paramedics	Physical therapists	Social workers	Lab technicians	Radiology technicians	Other technicians	Other practitioners
109,359	5,833	31,220	12,319	$25,104	8,707	5,166	32,288
3.8	2.1	11.4	7.8	1.7	1.5	3.2	NA
$1,502	$145	$830	$314	$948	$568	$284	$887
$6	$13	$18	$19	$21	$50	$25	$15
$52	$53	$302	$198	$65	$95	$175	$86

trast, there were only 6 osteopathic medical colleges (today there are 14 with full accreditation and 1 with provisional status) and about 14,000 D.O.'s (today there are over 25,000; see Table 10-2). Moreover, during this period traditional medicine focused on the creation of specialties and subspecialties. This involved a shift to graduate medical education (involving internships and residencies) supported by a considerable investment in research training facilities. By the 1920s quite a few specialty boards were recognized by the AMA. In contrast, osteopaths did not approve a mandatory internship program until 1936 or an optional residency program until 1949. Indeed, osteopathy was quite reticent to shed its wholistic orientation to health care for the emerging fascination with specialization that was sweeping the health care delivery system.

Something else was occurring during this period. Traditional medicine was rapidly flexing its muscles in order to gain control over the provision of health care. It effectively succeeded in eliminating its competition, with one exception—osteopathy. According to Albrecht and Levy (1982), osteopathy was spared because it had originally developed as a discordant cult within medicine. Moreover, its leaders had the foresight to monitor the political activity of the AMA and take a proactive stance to meet that threat.

Table 10-2. *Growth of the osteopathic profession, 1932 to 1986.*

Year	Total D.O.'s	Percent AOA members	New graduates
1932	8,410	50	325
1940	9,950	53	447
1950	11,250	69	373
1960	13,708	76	427
1970	13,454	79	432
1980	18,820	77	1,032
1981	19,686	78	1,128
1982	20,559	78	1,040
1983	21,618	74	1,317
1984	22,746	75	1,300
1985	24,014	75	1,474
1986	25,479	73	1,667

SOURCE: Adapted from American Osteopathic Association. 1986. *Yearbook and Directory of Osteopathic Physicians, 1985–1986* Chicago: Author. Reprinted by permission of the publisher.

Although others would disagree with Albrecht and Levy's (1982) interpretation (see Wardwell, 1979, 1980, 1982), there is a clear consensus on what ultimately occurred. After trying to eliminate osteopathy as a competitor failed, traditional medicine changed course and began a program to bring osteopaths into the fold by co-optation and merger. As they put it (Albrecht and Levy, 1982):

Traditional medicine and osteopathy moved towards each other ideologically and in practice. . . . Influenced by modern science, traditional medicine began to give up some of the practices of heroic medicine such as bleeding and purges and some iatrogenic drugs like arsenic. In fact, some allopaths quietly began to use manipulation much like physical therapists and osteopaths. On the other hand . . . osteopaths became increasingly convinced through research and clinical practice of the efficaciousness of some drugs and surgery. . . . These influences were reflected in a changing definition of osteopathy.

The merger, however, was not (and is not today) complete. Traditional medicine has remained the dominant force, and osteopathy has retained some of its special orientation.

During 1961 a significant milestone in the resolution of the "osteopathic problem" occurred. At the urging of the AMA, the osteopathic and allopathic physician organizations in California merged under four provisions (Albrecht and Levy, 1982): (1) the sole college of osteopathic medicine would become a traditional medical school; (2) all licensed osteopaths would be given M.D. degrees; (3) these new M.D.'s would be accepted into the county medical societies; and (4) there would be a combined effort to support a ban on future licensing of D.O.'s and to eliminate the Board of Osteopathic Examiners. The last point was accomplished with a public referendum in 1962.

Although the ban on licensing new osteopaths in California was eventually overturned by that state's supreme court in 1974, the die had been effectively cast. Osteopathy had been committed, somewhat involuntarily, to a process of assimilation with traditional medicine. Although the two have not completely merged, the differences between them are now a matter of degree rather than kind. In 1970 the first college of osteopathic medicine affiliated with a university was established at Michigan State. There students are admitted to study medicine, and the colleges of osteopathic and allopathic medicine jointly share basic science departments. It is only after the first year of coursework that Michigan State medical students choose between osteopathic and al-

lopathic training. By 1973 osteopaths had gained full practice rights in all 50 states and the District of Columbia.

OSTEOPATHY TODAY. Osteopathy is very different today than it was when Still founded it in the late 1800s. Osteopaths now specialize in a variety of fields and subfields just as M.D.'s do. These are shown in Table 10-3. What is different about specialization in osteopathy is its extent. Less than one in four D.O.'s specialize, compared to the majority of M.D.'s. Similarly, although M.D.'s are concentrated in more urban locations, osteopaths are much more likely to practice in rural areas and small towns. Indeed, nearly half of all osteopaths practice in communities with fewer than 50,000 persons. Thus, osteopaths are much more likely than traditional physicians to be engaged in primary care and to practice in small communities. In this regard, the tradition established by Still and his followers continues.

THE ULTIMATE QUESTION: IS OSTEOPATHY STILL UNIQUE? Perhaps the most hotly debated question surrounding osteopathy today is whether it has shed its unique orientation and become completely assimilated into traditional medicine. Albrecht and Levy (1982) note that "many people see no distinction between osteopaths and allopaths." Moreover, they argue that the changing nature of the health care delivery system is forcing osteopaths to align themselves more closely with allopathic medicine in order to survive. They expect this trend to accelerate in light of the increasing relative supply of physicians.

The view of the osteopathic profession, itself, is somewhat less clear. For the past several years there has been much debate in its journal (the *Journal of the American Osteopathic Association*), at the annual meetings of the AOA, and at the meetings of its accrediting body (the American Association of Colleges of Osteopathic Medicine [AACOM]) about what constitutes "osteopathic" as opposed to traditional medical training. Some osteopaths argue that they are modern-day physicians and that their

Table 10-3. *Degree and diversity of specialization in osteopathy, 1986.*

Area of board certification	Number of D.O.'s certified	Area of board certification	Number of D.O.'s certified
Anesthesiology	227	Otolaryngology	17
Dermatology	58	Otorhinolaryngology	132
Emergency medicine	108	Oro-facial plastic surgery	67
Fellows of AAO	85	Orthopedic surgery	193
General practice	2,582	Pathology	
Internal medicine	695	Anatomic pathology	119
Allergy and immunology	8	Cytopathology	1
Cardiology	110	Forensic pathology	1
Endocrinology	13	Laboratory medicine	105
Gastroenterology	43	Pediatrics	161
Hematology	4	Proctology	72
Hematology and oncology	13	Public health and preventive medicine	12
Infectious diseases	8	Radiology	313
Medical diseases of the chest	58	Diagnostic radiology	68
Nephrology	25	Diagnostic roentgenology	40
Oncology	25	Radiation therapy	3
Rheumatology	18	Roentgenology	28
Neurology and psychiatry	4	Rehabilitation medicine	82
Neurology	34	Surgery	
Pediatric neurology	1	General surgery	398
Psychiatry	96	Neurological surgery	17
Pediatric psychiatry	4	Plastic and reconstructive surgery	3
Nuclear medicine	80	Thoracic surgery	28
Obstetrics and gynecology	41	Urological surgery	59
Obstetrical-gynecological surgery	139		
Ophthalmology	114	*Total*	6,566

SOURCE: Adapted from American Osteopathic Association. 1986. *Yearbook and Directory of Osteopathic Physicians 1985–1986.* Chicago: Author. Reprinted by permission of the publisher.

training is no different than that of allopathic physicians. Others argue that osteopathy is quite different. They, however, often have difficulty identifying what is really different.

In the early 1980s the AOA began an extensive public relations campaign aimed at meeting two goals: to underscore the fact that osteopaths are "real" physicians, and to explain the added skills that osteopaths bring to their patients. This campaign was carried out on two fronts. The first was directed at the mass media. Its intent was to educate and inform those who control most of what the public sees and hears. An example of this aspect of the public relations campaign is shown in Figure 10-1. Note that it provides a variety of facts and figures in bullet form. This approach serves two

purposes. First, the bullets convey their information in terse fashion that facilitates comprehension and retention. Second, they may easily be cut and pasted and used as filler items or add-ons to other pieces about the health care delivery system.

The second front of the AOA's public relations campaign was targeted directly at the general population. In a 1982 leaflet it prepared for mass distribution the AOA set out to make its first point. It did so by posing and answering these questions: What is a D.O.? What is an M.D.?

In the first place, let's define what we mean by a "complete" physician. In general use of the term, a complete, fully trained physician has taken the prescribed amount of pre-medical training, graduated from an undergraduate college, and received four years of training in a medical school.

Half the media believe that M.D.s are the only comprehensive health-care professionals in America.

Yet 25 million Americans visit another type of fully-trained and licensed physician or surgeon for medical care. Their doctor is a D.O. or osteopathic physician.

The D.O. has essentially the same qualifications, medical education, internship, licensure and specialties as an M.D. They are equal with M.D.s under the laws of all 50 states, they serve as commissioned officers in the medical corps of all armed forces plus the Veterans Administration and Public Health Service. And they're recognized by the A.M.A. as physicians.

Yet there is great misunderstanding about the existence and role of osteopathic physicians in our society. That's why the American Osteopathic Association is calling attention to D.O.s in this message and striving to communicate their philosophies, distinctions and service to the American people.

Some facts:
- Osteopathic medicine was founded by a physician, Andrew Taylor Still, seeking options to the rudimentary drugs and surgery of the late 1800s.
- Central to osteopathic medicine is the body's musculoskeletal system and its importance to a patient's well-being. This system includes the bones, muscles, tendons, tissues, nerves, and spinal column–about 60% of the body mass.
- Osteopathic medicine views the human body as a single, individual organism–a basic tenet of Hippocrates.
- There is a fundamental concern with the whole body, preventive medicine, holistic medicine, proper diet and keeping a patient fit.
- Today's osteopathic physician typically offers primary care (86% are in family practice, general practice, internal medicine and gynecology).

- Today's osteopathic physician typically practices in smaller towns and rural areas (55% do).
- Fourteen percent of the profession is board certified in a full range of 18 medical specialties, including surgery, anesthesiology, emergency medicine, psychiatry, obstetrics, pediatrics, radiology and other fields.
- Today's D.O. provides comprehensive medical care, including preventive medicine, diagnosis and appropriate use of drugs, surgery, manipulation and hospital referral.
- Osteopathic manipulation of the musculoskeletal system is a viable and

- 50 million patient-visits are made to D.O.s annually.
- D.O.s are fully licensed to practice in every state. Strong concentrations of D.O.s are found in Michigan, Pennsylvania, Ohio, New Jersey, Florida, Texas and Missouri.
- 15 colleges of osteopathic medicine (about half state supported) now enroll nearly 6,500 medical students.
- 25% of osteopathic medical school students are women; women

You Probably Think All Doctors Are M.D.s. If So, You're Wrong!

proven technique for many "hands-on" diagnoses and treatments. It can provide an alternative to many drug therapies.
- Sports medicine is a natural outgrowth of osteopathic medicine, with concern for the musculoskeletal system, manipulation, diet, exercise and fitness. Many professional sports team physicians, Olympic physicians and personal sports medicine physicians are D.O.s.
- Osteopathic medicine is the fastest-growing health care field today.
- The D.O. is entitled to practice medicine and surgery in all its branches along with the M.D. and should be included in any discussion of "physician" when the reference is to providers of unlimited, comprehensive medical care. Comparison to physicians with limited practice rights is inappropriate.

Some Statistics:
- 21,000 D.O.s practice in America today, with 30,000 expected by 1990.
- 5% of all U.S. physicians and 10% of all U.S. military physicians are D.O.s.
- 25 million Americans visit D.O.s annually.

have been enrolled in osteopathic medical schools since their inception in 1892.
- 215 osteopathic hospitals offering 28,000 beds serve people in 30 states.

Osteopathic Medicine—proud to be a major force in America's health care delivery system.

The American Osteopathic Association is ready to fulfill your editorial queries about the profession and its contribution to U.S. health care. Information packets are available by mail and questions will be answered by phone. Please contact any osteopathic medicine state society or:

Public Relations Department
The American Osteopathic Association
212 East Ohio Street
Chicago, IL 60611
(312) 280-5882

The young physician then takes a year's internship in a hospital program with an approved intern-training program. If he or she elects to enter any one of a number of medical specialties, the doctor engages in a further two- to six-year residency program. Whether one becomes a D.O. or an M.D., the route of complete medical training is basically the same.

To make its second point the AOA published another leaflet in 1983. It focused on the added skills that D.O.'s bring to their patients (American Osteopathic Association, 1983):

Osteopathic medicine focuses special attention on the biological mechanisms by which the musculoskeletal system, through the nervous and circulatory systems, interacts with all body organs and systems in both health and disease. The emphasis is appropriate since osteopathic research and practice have demonstrated that disorders of the musculoskeletal system, in some degree, almost invariably are present when illness occurs. Sometimes these disorders are simply outward manifestations of internal distress. At other times they may set off a neurological chain reaction that perpetuates disease and interferes with the body's natural recuperative powers. At still other times the disorder may trigger the disease process itself.

According to the AOA, it is osteopathy's ability to diagnose and treat these disorders through palpation and manipulation that gives it an "added dimension of health care." Whether osteopathy is ever fully assimilated into traditional medicine or whether it retains its heritage as a unique alternative depends on the effectiveness of this public relations effort on both the public and the osteopathic profession itself.

Chiropractic

THE ORIGINAL THEORY. Chiropractic began in September 1895 when Daniel Palmer restored Harvey Lillard's lost hearing by adjusting (manipulating) the bones in his spinal column. Palmer had been a practitioner of magnetic healing for some time and had learned about vertebral manipulation from another doctor. He was soon confronted with a case of heart trouble that did not respond to any of his normal treatments. Examining that patient's spinal col-

umn, he found a displaced bone pressing on the nerves that go to the heart. After adjusting the spinal column the patient experienced immediate relief. This lead Palmer (1910) to speculate about his discoveries:

If two diseases, so dissimilar as deafness and heart trouble, came from impingement, a pressure on nerves, were not other diseases due to a similar cause? Thus, the science [knowledge] and art [adjusting] of Chiropractic were formed at that time. I then began a systematic investigation for the cause of all diseases and have been amply rewarded. I founded Chiropractic on Osteology, Neurology and Functions—bones, nerves, and the manifestation of impulses. . . . The amount of tension determines health or disease. In health there is normal tension, known as tone, the normal activity, strength and excitability of the various organs and functions as observed in a state of health. The kind of disease depends upon what nerves are too tense or too slack.

As you can see, in the beginning the theoretical bases for chiropractic and osteopathy were quite similar. What has subsequently happened is that osteopathy has been assimilated into, if not become synonymous with, traditional medicine. Chiropractic, however, did not stray from its original precepts and remains a marginal health occupation. To understand why this occurred, we must trace its historical development.

THE EARLY DAYS OF CHIROPRACTIC. Because of his success, Palmer, like Still, soon had more work than he could handle. Therefore, he established the Palmer Infirmary and Chiropractic Institute in Davenport, Iowa, in 1897. A year later he began to instruct a limited number of students in a six-month course in chiropractic. One of these students was his son, B. J. Palmer. By 1910 the diploma issued by the institute was changed to a Doctor of Chiropractic (D.C.) degree. Shortly thereafter B. J. Palmer became the driving, charismatic force behind the chiropractic movement. By 1921 the institute was graduating 1,000 chiropractors a year. It was recognized as the focal point for "straight" practice. "Straight" chiropractors eschewed their independence from traditional medicine and refused to use their skills in combination with any other medical therapies (see Wardwell, 1982).

A competing tradition in chiropractic began to develop at much the same time. These chiropractors mixed adjustment therapy with other therapeutic techniques, including those used by traditional medicine. Hence, they came to be called "mixers." The leader of this group was John Howard, who had been an unhappy member of the faculty at the Palmer Institute. In 1906 he established the National School of Chiropractic, also in Davenport. By 1908 the school had moved to Chicago and been renamed the National College of Chiropractic. It rapidly became, and remains today, the center of the "mixer" movement in chiropractic. In 1934 it offered the first standard, four-year course of training (see Wardwell, 1982).

With the exception of their ideological differences, both the "straight" and the "mixer" branches of chiropractic developed in much the same way. Indeed, by 1930 both had their own national organizations. The International Chiropractors Association (ICA) was established for the "mixers," and the American Chiropractic Association (ACA) was developed for the "straights." Neither branch of chiropractic had its colleges associated with universities. As a result, they fared poorly during two significant environmental confrontations. The first occurred in 1910 with the publication of the Flexner report. In the absence of strong university affiliations and consistent, medical school–like standards, chiropractic was seen as a marginal occupation. Indeed, for several decades thereafter chiropractors were attacked and prosecuted by traditional doctors as incompetent individuals attempting to practice medicine without a license (see Wardwell, 1979, 1982). The second environmental confrontation was with the Great Depression. Although colleges and universities in general were hit hard, chiropractic colleges suffered more. They simply had smaller financial bases with which to absorb the decline in enrollments and philanthropy.

During the four decades following the Great Depression chiropractic began to re-build. At first this recovery process was a gradual development. It was significantly aided by an infusion of students enrolling under the benefits of the GI Bill. By 1950 a four-year course of study became the educational standard. About 20,000 D.C.'s were actively engaged in chiropractic practice by 1960. These developments led Gibbons (1980) to write that the "proprietary period" in chiropractic history, as he called the early days of Palmer and Howard, had come to an end. The "professional period" of chiropractic's history, during which licensure and limited professional recognition would emerge, was about to begin.

THE TURNING POINT. According to Wardwell (1979), 1974 actually marked the major turning point in chiropractic's struggle for acceptance. Four things happened during that year. First, Louisiana became the last of the 50 states to license chiropractors. Second, the U.S. Office of Education gave the Chiropractic Commission on Education the power to accredit chiropractic colleges. Third, chiropractors' fees were declared reimbursable under Medicare. Fourth, the Congress set aside $2 million of the National Institutes of Health annual budget to ascertain the scientific merits of and basis for chiropractic. Within a year the AMA disbanded two of its committees that had been dedicated to the elimination or containment of chiropractic.

Chiropractic and medicine, however, have remained distant from and uneasy with each other. The educational standards of chiropractic fall considerably short of those of medicine. They have, however, been considerably improved in the last decade. The 16 chiropractic schools, which graduate 1,700 students annually, now all require two years of general college credits prior to admission. The chiropractic curriculum itself lasts another four years, making a minimum training period of six years. Coupled with the availability of third-party reimbursements, these educational changes have considerably enhanced chiropractic's image and the public's reliance on and use of it (see Caplan, 1984).

WHAT THE FUTURE HOLDS. Chiropractic's future remains uncertain. On the one hand, Caplan (1984) believes that it depends on how chiropractic and traditional medicine work together:

Either inside or outside of a hospital setting, chiropractors must demonstrate a willingness and desire to cooperate with the medical community. . . . As long as the chiropractic profession itself is seriously divided on this [i.e., the "straights" versus the "mixers"], or any other major issue, the likelihood of reconciliation with the medical establishment is greatly reduced. Such internal divisions and disagreements weaken the profession from within, give ammunition to its opponents, and represent significant obstacles to progress.

He believes that chiropractic would be best strengthened by a merger of the two competing associations (the ICA and the ACA), an increased research effort to better establish the profession's scientific credentials, and an emphasis on chiropractic as a legitimate paradigm distinct from but compatible with traditional medicine.

On the other hand, Wardwell (1979) believes that the future of chiropractic depends on how the relationship between osteopathy and traditional medicine develops:

Medical absorption of osteopathy could impede the acceptance of chiropractors by bringing more experts in manipulative therapy within orthodox medicine. [But at the same time] . . . osteopathy's disappearance could further upgrade the more progressive chiropractors (perhaps joined by dissident osteopaths), in which case the more marginal chiropractors might form a new association of drugless practitioners hostile toward physicians and chiropractic "mixers" alike. The cycle might then repeat itself.

Ultimately, however, both Caplan (1984) and Wardwell (see also Wardwell, 1980) agree that for the immediate future chiropractors are likely to remain as marginal or be elevated to limited practitioner status. The reason for this is their explicit decision to maintain, to varying degrees, their unique orientation to health care. Unlike osteopaths, chiropractors have neither been, nor intend to be, assimilated into traditional medical practice.

Homeopaths

THE ORIGINAL THEORY. The principles of homeopathy were identified by the German physician Samuel Hahnemann in the early to mid 1800s; they came to the United States around 1825. Building on the balance-based theories of Hippocrates and Aristotle, Hahnemann focused on the concept of "similars," but with a new twist. Coulter (1984) writes that at the turn of the nineteenth century, Hahnemann discovered "a new interpretation of 'similarity.' Knowing that quinine was curative in malaria, he decided to ascertain its effects on a healthy person. He took a strong dose himself and soon started to exhibit the typical symptoms of malaria. He concluded that quinine acts curatively in this disease because of its capacity to elicit malarial symptoms in a healthy person." Hahnemann continued exploring this phenomenon by experimenting with the administration of other substances and noting the symptoms they produced. This process of correlating inducing agents and resultant symptoms came to be known as proving. It represents the methodological basis on which homeopathic knowledge has been built.

Homeopathic practice, then, is based on the "law of similars" and the "science of therapeutics." The fundamental notion in homeopathy is that "like cures like." That is, by administering to the patient that medicinal substance that causes the patient's symptoms to be mimicked in healthy individuals, the patient's underlying vital forces are stimulated to function efficiently (see Law, 1975). Coulter (1984) describes the process of homeopathic treatment as follows: "When treating a patient the homeopathic physician first notes down his symptom-pattern and then compares it to patterns from the provings. The medicine whose symptomatology in the provings is closest to that of the patient will be the 'most similar' medicine (the 'simillimum') and thus the one indicated. Mere superficial similarity between the two symptom-patterns is not sufficient. Only the medicine which is 'most similar' will have a truly curative effect." In the process of administering the "most similar" medicinal compound, there is considerable emphasis on using the smallest dosage possible. Two concerns are involved here. The first is to avoid overmedicating the patient. The second is centered around Hahnemann's belief that the body reacted more favorably to less potent and smaller doses.

THE EARLY DAYS OF HOMEOPATHY IN THE UNITED STATES. Although homeopathy began in Europe at the turn of the nineteenth century, it did not spread to the United States until 1825. According to Coulter (1984), it was accepted by a number of prominent physicians on the East Coast within two decades. Indeed, in 1844 the American Institute of Homeopathy was established as this country's *first* national medical association. That predates the founding of the AMA by two years. Moreover, there is some evidence to suggest that the AMA was established by the allopathic medical community as a reaction against and in order to control the homeopaths (see Coulter, 1982, 1984). To be sure, during the next half century the relationship between homeopathy and traditional medicine was less than cordial. Nonetheless, homeopathy flourished in the United States during the nineteenth century. By 1900 there were 14 homeopathic medical schools, about 15,000 homeopathic practitioners, and a number of scholarly homeopathic journals and medical societies.

HOMEOPATHY IN THE TWENTIETH CENTURY. It is important to note that most homeopathic practitioners had first been trained in allopathic medicine. Only then had they gone on to study homeopathy. This proved to be quite significant for two reasons. First, in the aftermath of the Flexner (1910) report, medical education was transformed into a prolonged, full-time, and rigorous enterprise. Therefore, it became very difficult for would-be homeopaths to afford the luxury of first spending six to eight years training in traditional medicine and then enroll in an additional course of homeopathic training. Second, because most homeopaths were also allopathic physicians and traditional

medicine sought to gain complete control over the health care delivery system as a result of the "great trade," the stage was set for the extraordinarily rapid disappearance of homeopathy as a separate identity. That is, homeopathic physicians' loyalties were primarily to medicine and only secondarily to homeopathy. As a result, by 1960 the number of homeopathic practitioners in the United States declined to about a hundred. Although a resurgence of interest in homeopathy began in the 1960s, in part stimulated by a general dissatisfaction with traditional medicine, there are still only a few hundred practicing homeopaths in the United States today. And all of them are allopathically trained physicians.

THE FUTURE OF HOMEOPATHY. One thing is certain about the future of homeopathy. There are nearly polar-opposite predictions for it. On the one hand, Wardwell (1979) simply argues that homeopathy has disappeared as a distinct group. He believes that it has essentially been relegated to the level of a very small splinter group within traditional medicine. Coulter (1984), on the other hand, believes that the future of homeopathy is bright. He cites as a milestone the enactment in 1980 of a homeopathic licensing law in Arizona and a similar statute enacted in Nevada in 1983. To him this marks the beginning of the reestablishment of a dual licensing system for allopathic and homeopathic physicians. In light of the increasing relative supply of physicians, however, it would seem that Wardwell is more on target. It will be difficult for homeopathy to reestablish itself as a viable, separate entity in the increasingly competitive environment of today's health care delivery system.

Midwives

In this section we turn our attention to midwives. We begin with a historical review of midwifery. We then shift to the development of midwifery in the United States. After that we consider the implications of the growing chasm between lay and certified midwives brought about by licensing and regulation. We conclude this section with a discussion of the future of midwifery in the United States, especially in light of the increasingly competitive health care delivery system.

A Brief History of Midwifery

In most dictionaries a midwife is simply defined as a woman who assists other women in childbirth. In some dictionaries the definition is somewhat more extended; it specifies that the assistance to be provided is not merely limited to the mechanics of childbirth. Rather, the midwife is responsible for ministering to the emotional and social needs of the delivering woman as well as her physiological needs. Thus, the role of the midwife is defined as wholistic assistance for women in childbirth.

Throughout history midwives have been and continue to be the major health care attendants at the birthing process. Indeed, Bayes (1968) estimates that about two thirds of all live births involve midwives. Others (see Sousa, 1976) put that estimate closer to four fifths. (The fact that midwifery plays an insignificant role in the United States will be discussed in detail below.) According to DeVries (1982), midwifery has been documented as a distinct healing occupation since the time of the Jewish captivity in Egypt. To be sure, much has been made of the general refusal of midwives to carry out the Pharaoh's order to kill all male children born to the Hebrews (see Gregory, 1974; Litoff, 1978).

According to DeVries (1982), midwifery's dominance over the birthing process began to decline in the 1500s. There were two primary reasons for this. First, it was during the sixteenth century that the Church extended its power to include a variety of essentially nonreligious institutions, including health (see chapter 9). Accordingly, the Church began a system of registration of and regulation over midwives. Although the concerns of the Church primarily involved the social and religious aspects of childbirth, it did come to impose barriers on midwifery. These basically involved the Church's fundamental opposition to witch-

craft. Because a variety of herbs, potions, and spells were used by midwives to assist in the birthing process, a number of midwives were mistakenly accused of being witches. Moreover, most were at least considered somewhat suspect. Although the Church's control over health care began to wane in the eighteenth century, the damage had already been done.

The second reason for the erosion of midwifery's dominance in the birthing process involved the increasing encroachment of male practitioners into the "lying-in chambers" (DeVries, 1982). Previously it had been considered inappropriate, if not taboo, for the barber-surgeons of Europe (who were, of course, men) to attend disrobed and bed-bound women. Although this encroachment began gradually, it was rapidly accelerated when male doctors introduced the use of forceps. With forceps, which could only be legitimately used by (male) physicians, came the promise of shorter labor. And with shorter labor came the promise of lower maternal and infant mortality rates. As a result, midwifery's control over the birthing process rapidly dissolved. Indeed, most medical historians consider the development of the forceps as the single most important event in the downfall of midwifery (see Donnison, 1977; Litoff, 1978; Rousch, 1979).

Midwifery in the United States

The situation of midwifery in the United States has been similar to that in Europe, with two exceptions (DeVries, 1982). First, until the twentieth century American midwifery has been relatively free of regulation. Second, when traditional medicine "turned" on midwifery as part of its post-Flexnerian attempt to obtain dominance over the health care delivery system, it did so with a vengeance. Moreover, unlike the other "alternative practitioners" discussed above, midwives were poorly positioned to fend off medicine's charges. The result was devastating. Although national statistics on midwifery are hard to come by, evidence from New York City indicates that the number of midwives there declined from 1,700 in 1919 to

170 in 1939. By 1957 there were only two midwives practicing in New York City.

It is important to note why midwifery nearly became extinct in the United States but not in Europe. Physicians on both continents agreed that the traditional midwife was grossly inadequate to assist in even uncomplicated birthings during the twentieth century. They disagreed, however, on the solution (DeVries, 1982). European physicians suggested and implemented a program for upgrading the skills of midwives by more rigorous and standardized training. American physicians preferred to simply eliminate midwifery. Their justification was that enhanced training for midwives would result in a "double standard" of obstetrics; those who could afford it would have access to physicians, and those who could not would have access to midwives. American physicians' outward claims focused on the immorality of such a solution.

DeVries (1982), however, suggests it was more a matter of the fear of competition. His explanation is entirely consistent with the experiences of the other "alternative practitioners" discussed above. It is also well supported by Starr's (1982) thesis on medicine's creation of a vast industry under its sovereignty. Moreover, DeVries cites explicit recognition of the competition theme in statements made by influential physicians as late as 1968. For example, in comments made at the Macy Conference on midwifery in the United States, Johnson (1968) stated "Let us be above board about it. We [physicians and organized medicine] have a financial interest in delivering babies. If you [midwives] don't include us in deliveries, we have no choice but to be obstructive to whatever thing you start." Thus, it seems rather clear that regardless of any initial shortcomings in the training of midwives, medicine's current opposition to them stems from their competitive threat.

The Implications of Certification and Licensure

Almost driven out of existence, except in economically depressed urban and rural areas where physicians have little desire to

practice, midwifery seems to be on a comeback in the United States. DeVries (1982) notes that this is actually occurring on two levels:

On the one hand, the certified nurse-midwife is slowly gaining medical recognition and acceptance, and on the other, the lay midwife—who is often beyond the realm of legal or medical control—is gaining popular appeal. The status of the American midwife is somewhat confounded by the fact that each of the fifty states must establish its own regulations relating to the practice of midwifery. This allows for a range of situations, including everything from the active prohibition of all midwives, to the allowance of only certified nurse-midwifery, to what one writer calls "legality by default."

The legal issues surrounding the licensing and regulation of midwives are, indeed, fascinating. We, however, are more concerned here with their effect on the nature of midwifery.

DeVries (1982) argues that the licensing and regulation of midwives has led to the development of two distinct practitioners: the lay midwife and the certified nurse midwife (CNM). The role-set of the lay midwife has traditionally focused primarily on the patient, with little involvement with the formal health care delivery system. The role-set of the CNM, however, is clearly more oriented toward hospital personnel in particular and the health care delivery system in general.

The CNM's role-set is unavoidable given her recruitment and training under current regulations (DeVries, 1982): "To become a CNM, an individual must first be a registered nurse and then complete a nationally approved education program in midwifery at one of 16 schools which offer such training." Thus, by the time a CNM begins to practice, she has had at least six years of specialized training, all of which have been under the general direction of traditional medicine. As a result, the CNM is not really a midwife. Rather, as Arms (1977) notes: "She is a registered nurse with a post-graduate degree in a specialty called midwifery. And she looks and acts much like the physician authority whom she is licensed to assist. . . . Further [she] is trained . . . to defer to the authority of rank. She believes that the physician, not the birthing mother, knows best and holds the power to heal. By training, she sees life as a physician does, full of problems, abnormalities, and complications." Thus, despite the fact that the role-set of the lay midwife has been becoming less patient-oriented, there is a marked difference between what she does and how she does it, and what a CNM does and how she does it.

The Future of Midwifery in the United States

The future of midwifery seems uncertain. A principal reason for this is that, as indicated above, each state is responsible for licensing and regulating midwives. There is considerable variability in the way that they go about it. Thus, it is difficult to know whether the recent and much discussed experience of midwives in California (see De-Vries, 1982) will actually be repeated in other states. Moreover, it seems unlikely that the federal government will intervene in the near future. Rather, it is more likely to pass the issue back to the states by referring only to "practitioners of midwifery with current state licenses" in subsequent reimbursement legislation.

Increasing competition at several levels within the health care delivery system is likely to change the nature of midwifery even more. Competition among physicians induced by their increasing relative supply will stimulate them to take a more restrictive stand toward alternative providers in general. Given the considerable amount of funds expended around the birthing process, midwives (both lay and CNMs) are likely to be especially attractive targets for such restrictive campaigns.

Competition among hospitals, however, may work on behalf of midwives, at least for CNMs. Hospitals are under considerable pressure to reduce their costs of providing care. This has traditionally been done by attempts to shorten the amount of time that patients spend in the hospital (i.e., reducing the average length of stay). More recently, however, hospitals have begun to employ

cost-saving techniques utilized in the business world. Among these are the substitution of cheaper goods and labor for more expensive goods and labor. When it comes to delivering babies, especially in the absence of complications, CNMs represent a considerably less expensive labor force than physicians. Therefore, in the pursuit of cost containment hospitals may find the employment of CNMs a very attractive alternative to maintaining extensive obstetrics-gynecology services at their current levels.

In either case, however, the nature of midwifery will continue to shift from its client-oriented role-set to a more hospital personnel–oriented role-set. As a result, the traditional midwife appears destined for extinction. The contemporary midwife (whether in the form of the CNM or some subsequent version) will become more of a limited practitioner of medicine, rather than a wholistic minister to delivering women. In the process another "real" alternative practitioner will have been lost.

Faith Healers

Faith (or psychic) healing is quite different than the other alternatives we have discussed. First, faith healing makes no claims about being based in scientific theory. Second, faith healing includes an extraordinarily diverse group of practitioners and methods. Benor (1984) has underscored these points:

Psychic healing . . . refers to the beneficial influence of a person on another living thing (either animal or plant) by mechanisms which are beyond those recognized and accepted by conventional medicine. These mechanisms may include focused wishes, meditation, prayers, ritual practices, and the laying-on-of-hands. Some healers believe that in healing they are merely activating innate recuperative forces from within the healee. Other healers believe they are transferring their own energies to the healee. Others state they are merely acting as channels for healing energies from universally available cosmic sources. Many believe they must involve the intervention of spirits or of God.

There does, however, appear to be some consensus that faith healing works best if the recipient is receptive and in a quiet or meditative state of mind. Because of the remarkable diversity in faith healing, we shall only briefly review its history, the evidence of its efficacy, its current status in the United States, and its future prospects.

The History of Faith Healing

Accounts of faith healing can be found in the earliest of documents. Since then they have appeared in all manner of recorded materials. Consider, for example, the numerous instances of faith healing attributed to Christ in the New Testament, such as the healing of lepers, the restoration of sight to the blind, and the reambulation of the crippled. To be sure, faith healing is widespread and knows neither ideological nor religious bounds.

What is intriguing about the history of faith healing is its pendular relationship to conventional medicine. From the beginning of recorded history there has been a strong duality in medicine involving both science and magic (or the supernatural). As we saw in chapters 1 and 9, the magical side of this duality started from a position of strength. That strength was maintained by the separation of body and soul in Cartesian philosophy. It was not until the decline of the Church and the beginning of the scientific revolution in medicine that the role of magic in health care started to wane. Only after the Flexner (1910) report was published did the science side of the duality began to rapidly gain the upper hand. The last two decades, however, have seen a resurgence of the supernatural in health care. This may in part be due to the growing dissatisfaction with scientific medicine's inability to cope with the current chronic disease illness burden, as well as the trend toward more wholistic health care.

Coupled with the return to a wholistic orientation toward health has been an increased interest in the power of positive thinking. Indeed, Schaller and Carroll (1976) note that

over the past fifty years, many individuals have adopted a more "holistic concept" of humanity

and health as well as disease. The intimate, inseparable interactions between mind (psyche) and body (soma) have led to the recognition of psychosomatic illness: demonstrable physical illness caused by underlying mental conflict. Indeed, the relationships between mind and body are so powerful that some researchers have proposed the idea of psychosomatic health. For if one contends that the mind can create physical illness, then it may be assumed that the mind can relieve physical illness too.

Although there is considerable controversy surrounding the efficacy of psychosomatic health, there is general agreement that the 1980s have witnessed a renewed interest in faith healing.

Does Faith Healing Work?

Parallel with the renewed interest in faith healing in the latter half of the twentieth century has been a burgeoning research effort to assess its efficacy (see Benor, 1984; LeShan, 1974). Prior to the mid 1960s most of the evidence supporting faith healing was anecdotal. Since 1965, however, a number of controlled studies have been conducted. According to Benor (1984), these studies

have repeatedly demonstrated significant effects of healing in plants (Grad 1967; Loehr 1969), yeast (Grad 1965; Barry 1968), bacterial (Nash 1982) and cancer cell (Snell 1980) cultures, and mice (Onetto and Elguin 1966; Watkins, Watkins, and Wells 1973; Grad 1967; Solfvin 1982). Controlled studies in humans demonstrated systolic blood pressure in hypertensives was reduced with distant healing (Miller 1980), and that anxiety in cardiac patients was reduced with on-the-body (Heidt 1979) and near-the-body (Quinn 1982) healing.

Not everyone, however, is as swayed by these studies as Benor. Indeed, most would argue that although the more recent "evidence" looks promising, the jury is still out.

Faith Healing in the United States

Much like midwives, faith healers in the United States face a much different situation from their counterparts in Europe and elsewhere. There is little willingness by the American public or other health practitioners to accept faith healers' claim for efficacy. Indeed, the AMA and other health associations have lobbied against faith healers, citing their nonscientific nature as the principal justification. Although forced in 1980 to change its code of ethics that had previously barred physicians from associating with faith healers (or other alternative providers), the AMA has retained its negative stand toward them. This has led some physicians to form the American Holistic Medical Association (AHMA) as an independent entity to promote alternative healers and their approaches. Even in this fledgling association, however, faith healers are viewed with considerable suspicion.

There appear to be two reasons why faith healing has not become as respected an alternative to traditional medicine in the United States as it has abroad. First, there is the unique situation of the social transformation of American medicine (see Anderson, 1985; Starr, 1982). As a result of the "great trade," it obtained dominance over the health care industry and set out to control, if not eliminate, its competition. This has been a limiting factor for all alternative practitioners. Second, there is the unique situation of faith healers in the United States. It is typified in what Benor (1984) calls "an aversion to exclusivity": "[Faith] healers hesitate to sit in judgment of each other, at least publicly or openly. In part it may also represent an honest approach to the subject of healing. It has been suggested . . . that most people possess some healing abilities. Combined with the great difficulty in defining and demonstrating what healing is and/ or is not, this poses problems in establishing clearer criteria for testing healing ability and licensing healers." In the absence of any criteria or method for training, testing, and licensing faith healers, poorly performing practitioners and quacks are allowed to practice. As a result, the "good name" of faith healing, in general, is not so good.

The Future of Faith Healing

The future of faith healing in the United States is not unlike that of the other alternative practitioners we have discussed. That is, it is somewhat unknown. On the one hand, there would appear to be considerable potential for faith healing given the chronic disease burden that we face. In this regard, faith healing may have an edge on some of the other alternatives to traditional medicine (Benor, 1984): "At present there is more evidence from controlled studies to advance [faith] healing as a therapeutic modality than there is to support the efficacy of chiropractic or osteopathic manipulations." In particular, this evidence has been linked, albeit tentatively, to the major chronic conditions of our times (i.e., cancer and heart disease). Therefore, the promise of what faith healing could do is considerable.

Faith healing's potential, however, must not be allowed to overwhelm reasoned judgment in the establishment of licensing and regulatory processes. As Benor (1984), who is perhaps the staunchest scholarly advocate of faith healing, warns:

Hopefully the zeal of proponents of alternative therapies will not override the call for deliberate and cautious steps in certifying healers before they are sanctioned by social and legal agencies. Though rapidly legitimizing alternative therapists such as [faith] healers would have a short-term benefit of increasing their availability, it could too easily be a long-term detriment in leading to abuses of this license. Ultimately a backlash of rejection of the wheat with the chaff could ensue.

Thus, it is ironic that one of faith healing's fundamental precepts, the "aversion to exclusivity," stands as the major obstacle to its recognition and development.

On the other hand, the future of faith healing is not so bright. Traditional medicine holds a rather negative opinion of faith healing. Because of traditional medicine's dominance, if not control, over the health care delivery system, it is not likely that faith healing will be permitted to develop either very much or very rapidly. Moreover, as the competitive environment among physicians intensifies, organized medicine will probably seek to reduce that tension by lobbying for even greater restrictions on what alternative providers may do. Therefore, the future for faith healing in the United States is likely to remain considerably more bleak than it is in Europe or elsewhere.

Quacks and Their Devices

Of all the alternative healers the quack is the furthest removed from traditional medicine. This is perhaps most ironic, because it is precisely scientific medicine that quacks try to imitate and exploit. The basic ploy of medical quacks is to profess medical skills or qualifications, especially through the use of sophisticated-looking equipment that they frequently do not even possess. Most of the time the quack knows that he or she is only pretending to cure the patient. Some quacks, however, believe their healing claims. The most common technique of quacks is to introduce machines, "little black boxes," special foods, or drugs guaranteed to cure the disease at hand.

According to Schaller and Carroll (1976), there are three important aspects of quackery. First, it is *very big* business. Even in the scientific era of the 1980s, tens of billions of dollars are spent annually on quacks and their nostrums. Second, quackery has a progressive nature to it. It becomes increasingly sophisticated over time. For example, in the nineteenth century "snake oils" were used as cure-alls; today it is "moon dust." Third, the prime targets of quackery are those individuals who have illnesses that traditional medicine cannot cure. Such individuals often feel that they have no place else to go. They turn to quacks out of desperation.

The elderly are especially likely to be targeted as "marks" by quacks. There are several reasons for this. Two take precedence over the rest. First, the elderly are more likely to have chronic conditions, such as cancer and heart disease, for which traditional medicine can do very little. Second, although the average educational level of the United States in general is now slightly more than 12 years of public schooling, for those over 65 the average educational attainment level is barely beyond the completion of grade school. It has been shown that the less educated are more susceptible to quackery. Additional factors that make the elderly prime targets for quacks include heightened levels of loneliness and grief, an acute fear and distaste of aging, increased levels of human credulity, the reality of death, inactivity during retirement, and sensory impairments related to the aging process (Schaller and Carroll, 1976).

The elderly, however, are clearly not the only ones who fall prey to quacks and their gadgetry. Indeed, most of us do not have as good an understanding of health quackery as we should. For example, despite the fact that it is not true, many Americans believe that copper bracelets are an effective treatment for rheumatism, hormonal creams can prevent the wrinkles of aging, malnutrition in this country is widespread because our food is grown on depleted soil, and recent federal laws prevent false and misleading health information and products from appearing on the market (see Lanese, 1973). As long as these and other falsehoods are believed, the market for quackery remains.

To help avoid being taken in by a quack, Bauer and Schaller (1965) suggest that if in any medical proposition you detect a faint, or not so faint, aroma of one of the following, be suspicious:

(1) A claim to cure or alleviate a disease that puzzles doctors. . . . (2) "Satisfaction or your money back" guarantees. . . . (3) Any medicine, appliance, diagnosis, or other remedial service offered by mail. . . . (4) The use of testimonials by "cured" or "satisfied" users. . . . (5) Claims to the possession of secret formulas, secret ingredients, and secret methods. . . . (6) Demands for payment in advance. . . . (7) Endorsed by "high government officials". . . . (8) Trial package free, or in plain wrapper. . . . (9) Limited supply reserved for special customers. . . . (10) "Doctors recommend," "nurses prefer it for their own personal use," or "leading hospitals insist on it". . . . (11) "Proved by leading research laboratories". . . . (12) Use of high-sounding degrees. . . . (13) Attacks, oblique or direct, on legitimate doctors, hospitals, nurses, or other genuine professional personnel. . . . (14) Use of current scientific interests as basic appeals to victims.

Applying these guidelines to contemporary advertisements for healing aides and devices indicates the extent of quackery in the United States today.

Perhaps the two most notorious of the documented quacks have been Drs. James Graham and Albert Abrams. Dr. Graham was an English physician who practiced during the late eighteenth century. His scheme was both relatively simple and seemingly scientific, exactly the sort that seems to work best. Moreover, Dr. Graham treated only patients with "the most desperate diseases" (Jameson, 1961). He either placed his patients on a "magnetic throne" or in a bath and administered mild electric shocks. Dr. Abrams was an American physician who in the 1920s claimed that his diagnostic devices could determine *by mail* the disease, sex, race, and religious status of the sick individual from a single drop of blood, or from an autograph. Dr. Abrams's operation was so extensive that the AMA wrote on the occasion of his death that he was "easily ranked as the dean of all twentieth century charlatans" (Holbrook, 1959). Unfortunately, American quackery did not die out with Dr. Abrams's demise.

There are two principal reasons why quackery persists in the United States and elsewhere. First, on occasion quackery appears to be effective. It is important to note, however, that it is not really quackery that is effective, but the patient's belief in it that makes it work. In this regard, the limited success that quackery sometimes has stems more from faith healing (i.e., psychosomatic *health*) than from quackery. Second, individual's are not immortal. When traditional medicine cannot fend off death, many individuals turn to quackery out of sheer desperation. Thus, as long as all individuals must ultimately face death, a market for quackery will always exist.

Summary

In this chapter we have examined alternatives to the physician. We began by considering three alternatives that emerged at the same time, had similar theoretical bases, and enjoyed relatively equally charismatic leaders. Within a hundred years, however, osteopathy had been accepted as part of traditional medicine, chiropractic remained an occupation of limited if not marginal practitioners, and homeopathy virtually disappeared. The reasons for the different routes that these alternatives have taken appear to focus on the co-optation of osteopathy by traditional medicine, the maintenance of ideological purity by chiropractic, and the effect of the "great trade" on homeopathy.

In the second section we focused on midwifery. After tracing the historical dominance of midwives at the birthing process, we noted the sharp decline in their position following the encroachment of physicians into the "lying-in chambers." In the United States midwifery appears to have lost its original identity as a result of the licensing and regulatory processes. Indeed, the traditional lay midwife is rapidly becoming extinct, while the newer certified nurse midwife is rapidly becoming much more like a physician.

The focus in the third and fourth sections was on faith healers, and quacks and their devices. Because of the marked diversity among both groups, our emphasis was on what makes them so popular and whom do they especially attract. The answer was much the same in both cases. Those with incurable and chronic conditions and those with lower levels of education are most likely to seek out both faith healers and quacks. They do so often out of desperation and as a last resort after having exhausted all avenues of traditional medicine.

11. Nurses and the Paraprofessions

THROUGHOUT THE first nine chapters we have focused our attention primarily around the traditional social interaction between the patient and the physician. As medicine has developed, the traditional doctor-patient relationship has changed. It now includes a considerable variety of non-physician health care practitioners. Having talked about *alternative* providers in chapter 10, we now turn our attention to *assistant* health care practitioners. To do this, we have divided the present chapter into four major sections. In the first we will examine the common traits that assistant health care practitioners share. We will emphasize their dependent relationship to physicians, their resulting positions in medicine and society, and their continued use of the physician's characteristics as benchmarks against which self-comparisons are made.

In the second section we will examine nursing, which is the largest and most important of the assistant health care occupations. We will trace its development from the days when nursing was synonymous with being a nun, through the professionalizing efforts of Florence Nightingale, to the decentralization and divergence of contemporary American nursing education. Then we will examine the making of a nurse and the internal struggle the nursing profession currently faces. In the third section we will examine nursing's bid for professional status. Special attention will be given to those factors that both enhance and limit that bid. In the final section we will look at the two new paraprofessionals—nurse practitioners and physicians' assistants—who stand a good chance of gaining some measure of professional autonomy. We will pay special attention to the differences between the two and how these may affect their success at becoming full-fledged health care practitioners.

Nonphysicians as Paraprofessionals

There are clearly more people involved in the delivery of health care than simply the patient and the physician. On the patient's side of the interaction there is a wide variety of laypersons including the spouse, other family members, close friends, and various social, legal, and religious authorities. On the physician's side of the interaction there is a wide variety of health care workers, such as nurses, physicians' assistants, pharmacists, nursing aides, orderlies, and the like. The patient's lay helpers influence and assist in the decision to seek or not to seek health care. The health care workers assist the physician in his or her treatment of the sick. A closer examination of the latter reveals the reason that nonphysician health care workers are considered paraprofessionals and the implications of this distinction.

Physician Dominance: The Absence of Professional Autonomy Among Assistant Healers

Within the health care delivery system almost all occupations are organized around the work of the physician, and they usually come under his or her direct control. As a result, nonphysician health care occupations lack the professional autonomy discussed in detail in chapter 9. As you recall, Freidson (1970a) reduced to a nutshell the notion of a profession as distinct from an occupation by stating that

the only truly important and uniform criterion for distinguishing professions from other occupations is the fact of autonomy—a position of legitimate control over work. That autonomy is not absolute, depending for its existence upon the toleration and even protection by the state and not necessarily including all zones of occupational activity . . . the single zone of activity in which autonomy must exist in order for professional status to exist is in the content of the work itself.

Thus, according to Freidson, all nonphysician health care workers are employed in occupations, not in professions. This is true regardless of the fact that many of them espouse professionalism and desire to be professionals. The context of their work is simply dominated by physicians. This lack of professional autonomy has both positive and negative aspects.

The negative aspect is that nonphysician health care workers cannot be considered professionals in the true sense of the word. Although nurses and other paraprofessionals may emulate the role of the professional and may indeed have advanced to the status of a paraprofession, professional status cannot be obtained unless professional autonomy is granted by society. Our society has recognized and appointed physicians as the principal ministers of health care and the official representatives (and interpreters) of the ultimate value of health. Therefore, the conferral of professional autonomy on any emerging health occupation or paraprofession must be done by physicians. They are not likely to voluntarily divest themselves of any portion of their monopoly on professional autonomy. Thus, nonphysician health care workers are likely to be kept at the paraprofessional level as long as physicians continue to dominate and control the field.

The positive aspect about not having professional autonomy is not having its flaw either. Because they are not professionals, paraprofessionals must face both external and internal regulatory groups. In fact, paraprofessionals find themselves answerable to four distinct authorities: physicians, hospital or clinic administrators, patients, and fellow paraprofessionals. As a result, their work is under almost constant scrutiny from several different perspectives. This serves to make paraprofessionals more sensitive to these groups and their perspectives. Unfortunately, these different perspectives are sometimes in conflict with one another, and this places the paraprofessional in the middle of a tug-of-war. Such conflict produces a great deal of strain on those who occupy paraprofessional roles. This strain accounts for their high job-turnover rate, which is especially evident in the hospital setting. (We will examine the effects of such strain on paraprofessionals in the next chapter.)

Regardless of the effects of such strain, nonphysician health care workers are much more responsive than physicians to patients and their families. This responsiveness is heavily influenced by two related factors. First, in comparison to physicians the relative demand for paraprofessionals is much smaller; this enhances the patient's ability to pick and choose among them. Second, most of what paraprofessionals may do is severely restricted to being done "out of the office of" or "in conjunction with" a physician. Thus, paraprofessionals are highly dependent on the good graces of the physician in order to keep working. As a result, they have traditionally been thrust into the front line of patient-practitioner interactions. They bear the brunt of the burden for caring for the patient as a person, while the physician holds him- or herself in reserve for the "scientific diagnosis and treatment of diseases." Having been thrust into such a role and being dependent on the physician's protective umbrella for their livelihood, paraprofessionals are faced with the choice of becoming patient-oriented and responsive or getting wet.

Resultant Social Positions and Hierarchies

The restriction of nonphysician health care workers to paraprofessional status produces a distinctive set of social positions and hierarchies in both the health care field and the larger social community. Because paraprofessional health care workers are subordinate to and dominated by physicians, their social position is clearly less than that of physicians. But how much less, and how does that compare to the rest of the occupations within society? One way to answer these questions is to examine the occupational prestige assigned to various health care occupations by the public. Another way is to examine the hierarchy of so-

cial positions within the health care delivery system itself.

THE EXTERNAL PRESTIGE HIERARCHY AND HEALTH CARE OCCUPATIONS. The most widely accepted and used measure of socioeconomic position is Duncan's Socioeconomic Index (see Reiss, Duncan, Hatt, and North, 1961). It assigns occupational prestige scores to each of the 446 positions in the detailed occupational classification of the United States Census. These prestige scores were determined from the subjective ratings of representative samples of Americans as follows. The income and education levels normally associated with each occupation were taken into consideration, and each occupation was assigned a prestige score between 0 (the lowest) and 99 (the highest). The results are quite interesting. Physicians (with a score of 92) enjoy a considerable amount of occupational prestige, although dentists and osteopaths receive slightly higher scores (96). The only other health care occupations to be ranked close to physicians are pharmacists, optometrists, and veterinarians. The remainder fare rather poorly. Indeed, registered nurses (46) were assigned occupational prestige scores similar to those assigned to postal clerks (44), and licensed practical nurses (22) were ranked lower than bus drivers (24), machinists (33), and plumbers (34). What these occupational rankings indicate is that although physicians, surgeons, osteopaths, dentists, and veterinarians, all of whom carry the title "doctor," command a great deal of prestige from the general public, the remaining health care occupations, which do not carry the title of "doctor," do not. It appears, therefore, that the enormous respect and admiration that the public generally had for medicine during the 1960s and 1970s (when these surveys were conducted) was concentrated around the role of the medical professional, or the *doctor*. Whether this remains the case in the 1980s and 1990s remains to be seen.

THE INTERNAL PRESTIGE HIERARCHY IN HEALTH CARE OCCUPATIONS. Within the health care

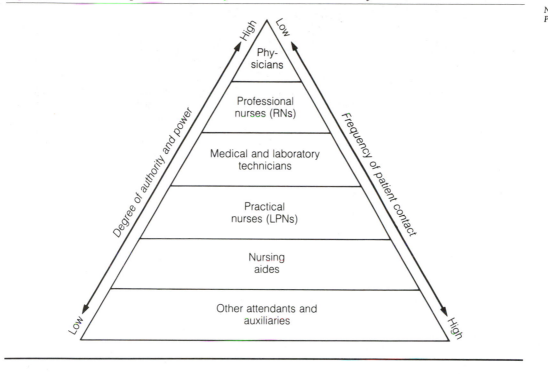

Figure 11-1. The Occupational Hierarchy in Health Care As Seen By Health Care Workers.

field itself, the hierarchy of health care occupations is somewhat different from the way the public views it. The view from within looks like the pyramidic structure in Figure 11-1. The physician is clearly seen as the captain of the team, to whom all other health care workers are directly responsible. It is the professional nurse, however, who usually serves as the "acting manager" in the physician's absence. This is especially true in the hospital setting where the physician is really an outside, part-time worker. The physician merely uses the facilities and support staff of the hospital when his or her patients require more sophisticated equipment or round-the-clock medical care than his or her private office can provide. As a result, the professional nurse bears the responsibility for managing, coordinating, and supervising the delivery of health care by the remainder of the paraprofessionals. Thus, physicians and nurses are often viewed

as the major health care workers, while those in health care occupations with less prestige are viewed as allied health care workers. For comparative purposes, the active supply of major health care workers is shown in the upper panel of Table 11-1. The active supply of allied health care workers is shown in the lower panel, according to the level of educational preparation needed for such positions.

Immediately below the professional nurse in prestige is the growing number of medical and laboratory technicians. These technicians maintain and operate the sophisticated medical and laboratory equipment that physicians use in the war against disease. Practical nurses receive less prestige than the medical technicians because they are viewed as less scientifically skilled. That is, practical nurses (and those who have even less prestige) do not require the breadth or depth of formal training required of profes-

Table 11-1. *Supply of active major and allied health care workers, 1960 to 1990.*

Major health care workers

Year	All health professions	Physicians (M.D. and D.O.)	Dentists	Registered nurses	Optome-trists	Pharmacists	Podia-trists	Veterinarians
				Number active				
1960	1,029,620	251,900	90,120	527,000	16,100	117,800	7,000	19,700
1970	1,329,120	323,200	102,220	723,000	18,400	129,300	7,100	25,900
1980	1,885,370	446,800	126,170	1,099,600	21,800	146,100	8,500	36,400
1990	2,484,410	593,800	154,910	1,466,700	28,000	179,900	13,000	48,100
				Percent distribution				
1960	100.0	24.5	8.8	51.2	1.6	11.4	0.7	1.9
1970	100.0	24.3	7.7	54.4	1.4	9.7	0.5	1.9
1980	100.0	23.7	6.7	58.3	1.2	7.9	0.4	1.9
1990	100.0	23.9	6.2	59.0	1.1	7.2	0.5	1.9
				Rate per 100,000 population				
1960	572.1	140.0	50.1	292.8	8.9	65.5	3.9	10.9
1970	652.1	158.6	50.2	354.7	9.0	63.4	3.5	12.7
1980	830.8	196.9	55.6	484.5	9.6	64.4	3.8	16.0
1990	991.3	236.9	61.8	585.2	11.2	71.8	5.2	19.2

Allied health care workers

Occupation	1970	1975	1980	1985	1990
	Basic educational preparation at least baccalaureate in level				
Dietitians	15,300	16,140	18,170	20,470	22,340
Medical record administrators	4,200	4,500	5,140	5,850	6,430
Medical technologists	45,000	60,160	80,620	103,010	123,520
Occupational therapists	7,300	9,270	11,760	14,500	16,880
Physical therapists	11,550	16,640	23,030	30,080	36,570
Speech pathologists and audiologists	13,300	23,560	37,070	53,720	70,930
	Basic educational preparation less than baccalaureate in level				
Certified laboratory assistants	6,700	13,590	22,260	31,950	41,160
Cytotechnologists	2,400	3,400	4,670	6,090	7,400
Dental assistants	9,200	23,490	39,100	55,880	71,530
Dental hygienists	15,100	23,310	34,190	46,320	57,650
Dental laboratory technicians	1,600	3,970	7,070	10,670	14,290
Respiratory therapists	3,850	6,800	10,510	14,720	18,810
Licensed practical nurses	400,000	464,680	565,890	693,410	819,790
Medical record technicians	3,800	4,160	4,900	5,720	6,460
Occupational therapy assistants	600	2,320	4,360	6,620	8,820
Radiologic technologists	41,000	63,570	93,560	127,770	161,280

SOURCE: Department of Health, Education, and Welfare. 1975. *The Supply of Health Manpower: 1970 Profiles and Projections to 1990.* Washington, DC: U.S. Government Printing Office.

sional nurses and technicians. Similarly, nursing aides receive less training and learn fewer skills than practical nurses. Other attendants and auxiliaries require even less. Thus, they are rated as unskilled workers. In essence, the internal hierarchy of medical care workers is based on how closely each meets the criteria for becoming a profession described in chapter 9.

Two interesting features of this occupational hierarchy warrant further discussion. First, authority and power are greatest at the apex of the pyramid (the physician), steadily diminishing as one progresses to its base (auxiliary attendants). In contrast, patient contact is at its maximum at the base of the pyramid and decreases as one progresses to its apex. This indicates that the more authority a health care worker has, the more removed he or she is from patient contact. This inverse relationship between the levels of authority and patient contact is rather ironic. The conferred authority is based on one's ability to treat and cure patients; yet, the better one is trained, the more removed one becomes from patient contact.

The Physician as a Benchmark

As we have learned, there are at least three professions in the United States: medicine, law, and the ministry. Of these, medicine is recognized as the archetype because it most clearly possesses professional autonomy. As a result, whenever any occupation is examined to see if it meets the criteria of being a profession, the profession of medicine is used as the benchmark. This is especially true when the occupation being examined is from the health care field. In these cases, it is not only the examiners who use the physician as *the* benchmark, but the examinees as well (Wilson, 1970): "Each variety of health worker gauges his status and professional self-hood in terms of how closely he approaches the doctor on a scale of privileges and responsibility." Such comparisons have both positive and negative effects.

By making comparisons between themselves and physicians, health paraprofessionals are encouraged to imitate and emulate physicians. This may translate into physicianlike attitudes and ethics, or into the establishment and pursuit of high work standards among fellow paraprofessionals. Such imitation and emulation is encouraging. Moreover, it should be encouraged. The more professionalism demonstrated on the part of the health paraprofessionals, the better the quality of care that they will deliver.

The pursuit of having one's paraprofes-

sion emerge as its own profession, however, is simply unrealistic. This is due to the historical development of American medicine, and to the exalted position and autonomy that has been granted to physicians. Without massive and fundamental changes in the fabric of American social structure, there will be no health profession other than that of the physician. Furthermore, because of the American Medical Association's (AMA) continued efforts, the premier position held by physicians is sufficiently secure to weather any political storm directed toward establishing a competing health profession. As a result, the pursuit of professional status and comparisons to the physician by the non-physician almost always produce a frustrating situation for the would-be professional. It may well be precisely this frustration that causes trained health care paraprofessionals to take extended leaves of absence or to seek out other occupations.

The Development of the Nursing Profession

Among all the paraprofessions, the one that we know the most about, the one about which there is the greatest controversy and debate, and the one within which there is the most evident bid for increased status is nursing. By nursing we are referring only to those who are registered nurses (RNs). As can be seen from Table 11-1, registered nurses comprise nearly 60 percent of the total supply of all active health professionals. The current nurse per capita rate is about two and a half times the current physician per capita rate. Although they are the largest health care occupation, nurses are generally not happy with their situation. As Dachelet (1978) has written, "Sociologists can document the hierarchical status system in the medical establishment and the public can discern it, but it is the health care team members who must deal with it and its implications daily. Perhaps most acutely aware of the status hierarchy is the health practitioner working closest with the physician—the nurse. The general status disparity and concomitant income differential between the two has not gone unnoticed by the nursing profession."

In essence, just as medicine is the archetypical profession, nursing is the archetypical paraprofession. Accordingly, our understanding of the paraprofessions will be enhanced by a detailed examination of nursing. We begin with nursing's major historical turning points and then we look at its appearance in the United States, how one comes to be a nurse, and the internal struggles that threaten to tear nursing apart.

Historical Turning Points in Nursing

Like medicine, nursing has its own set of special historical turning points and key personalities (see Bullough and Bullough, 1969; Mauksch, 1972). Unlike medicine, however, the historical development of nursing may be reduced to two fundamental periods: before and after Florence Nightingale. To be sure, these two periods are not internally homogeneous. Nonetheless, they do reflect the dramatic change that has swept through nursing.

NURSES AND NUNS: "MOTHER SURROGATES" AND SISTERS. While men have traditionally filled the medical role and have been referred to as father-surrogates, women have traditionally filled the nursing role and have been referred to as mother-surrogates (see Davis, 1966, 1972; Mauksch, 1972; Olesen and Whittaker, 1968; Schulman, 1972). Accordingly, the traditional relationship between physician and nurse has been that of father figure to mother figure. The father figure has been aggressive and dominant, while the mother figure has been passive, subservient, and supportive (Mauksch, 1972). Mauksch has succinctly summarized the nature of this early era of nursing's history:

In Western culture those who care for the sick are identified with labels which are profoundly female. The term "sister" is applied not only to the religious functionary, but in many European languages generally identifies the nurse. In the English language, "nursing" implies the essence of the mother's relationship to her offspring. . . .

The history of nursing is inextricably interwoven with the history of women. The selection of nurses, their relationships, and the image they evoke can be fruitfully examined by linking them to the past. The quasi-innate qualities which were perceived to be the attributes of the mother represent images which influence the fate of nursing education to this day. *The natural tendency of a mother to care for her family without having formal boundaries to her area of competence as well as her tendency to manage her home, underlie the expectation still held today about the appropriate role of the nurse* [emphasis added].

In short, pre-Nightingalean nursing was simply the application of the mother surrogate perspective to sick people in the public hospital. These early-day nurses were completely without specialized training in medical care. Indeed, early nurses practiced neither medical nor health care. They only served the personal needs of the patients, especially their religious and spiritual needs. More often than not, early period nurses were either nuns or "women off the streets and of bad character." As a result, the early occupational prestige of nursing was quite low.

FLORENCE NIGHTINGALE AND THE NIGHTINGALE SYSTEM: EMERGING PROFESSIONALISM. In the middle of the nineteenth century, the role of nursing was dramatically changed. Most of this change has been attributed to Florence Nightingale, an English Protestant woman from a respectable middle-class family who had a religious vision in 1837. After her mystical experience, Nightingale was not sure what she was supposed to do. As a woman she knew that the only way to serve God was as a Catholic nun. Catholicism, however, was a faith that she could not profess. After much consideration Nightingale set out to answer her "call" by becoming a nurse. Instead of going out untrained she went to Germany and secured better training from a Protestant minister. On her return to England in 1853 she founded a hospital for "women from good families." She fought to make nursing an honorable occupation and put her nurse-recruits (all "honorable" women) through a rigorous training program. Unfortunately, her hospital was not successful and was forced to close. To a considerable extent, the hospital's closing resulted from the conflict with "acceptable behavior for ladies" that her nurses posed (see Freidson, 1970a).

In 1854 Nightingale got another opportunity concomitant with the outbreak of the Crimean War. She took her nurses to the battlegrounds to help care for the wounded. At first the army refused to hire them. After seeing the results they produced while working as volunteers, however, Nightingale and her nurses were widely acclaimed at the end of the war. They had reduced the death rate at the Surtari hospital from 42 per thousand to 22 per thousand. On her return to England in 1859 Nightingale published the first textbook on nursing, *Notes on Nursing*. Capitalizing on her fame from the Crimean War, she raised sufficient funds to set up a true nursing school at Saint Thomas' Hospital in London. There the "Nightingale System" of nursing was the order of the day and soon spread to other hospitals and nursing schools. The fight to change nursing from "mother surrogate" to "professional nurse" was on, and Nightingale (1914) called for an all-out war: "A woman who takes a sentimental view of nursing (which she calls 'ministering' as if she were an angel), is, of course, worse than useless. A woman possessed with the idea that she is making a sacrifice will never do; and a woman who thinks that any kind of nursing work is 'beneath a nurse' will simply be in the way. . . . For us who nurse, our nursing is a thing, which, unless in it we are making progress every year, every month, every week, take my word for it, we are going back." Florence Nightingale had clearly charted the future course for nursing and charged her followers never to quit traveling down the chosen path. She feared that if they did, they would be swept back to the mother surrogate role.

Nursing Education in the United States: Decentralization and Divergence

The Nightingale System of nursing soon spread to the United States and resulted in the firm entrenchment of specialized training. At the same time, however, a number of factors have kept nursing education from becoming centralized and uniform. As a result, although we generally think of a nurse as a nurse, there is a considerable divergence in the formal training and expectations among them. To understand the overall nature of nursing education in the United States, we must examine the early schools of nursing, the diploma schools, the baccalaureate schools, the associate degree schools, and the current controversy surrounding technical versus professional nursing.

THE EARLY SCHOOLS. The first three accredited schools of nursing in the United States—the Bellevue Hospital School, the Connecticut Training School, and the Boston Training School—were founded in 1873 and were based on the Nightingale System. All three were financially dependent on the hospitals with which they were affiliated. The hospitals provided the money and materials needed to train nursing students in exchange for the use of those nursing students to staff the hospital and provide the requisite nursing services. (Although this might appear to have been an amicable relationship, we shall soon see how it has tempered the perspective and outlook of hospital-trained nurses.) This "hospital connection" provided the initial opportunity to firmly implant the Nightingale System of nursing in the United States. Because of the prestige of Nightingale System nurses and concomitant with the increasing migration from rural to urban areas, nursing came to be viewed as a rather respectable occupation for American women. Moreover, it was, and is, one at which they could earn a comfortable living. As a result, there was a significant rise in the number of hospital nursing schools during the late 1800s and early 1900s. Three distinct types of nursing education have emerged from these early nursing schools. Unlike the uniformity found among medical schools, however, nursing education is quite varied and produces rather different types of nurses.

DIPLOMA SCHOOLS. The earliest schools of nursing in the United States were closely associated with hospitals. This type of nursing

Table 11-2. *Graduates of initial registered nurse programs in the United States, 1963–64 to 1982–83.*

Academic year	Diploma			Associate degree		Baccalaureate	
	Total number	Number	Percent of total	Number	Percent of total	Number	Percent of total
1982–83	78,474	11,704	14.9	42,372	54.0	24,398	31.1
1981–82	74,975	11,682	15.6	38,770	51.7	24,523	32.7
1980–81	74,890	12,903	17.2	37,183	49.7	24,804	33.1
1979–80	76,415	14,495	19.0	36,509	47.8	25,411	33.3
1978–79	77,932	15,820	20.3	36,763	47.2	25,349	32.5
1977–78	78,697	17,131	21.8	37,069	47.1	24,497	31.1
1976–77	78,461	18,014	23.0	36,158	46.9	23,632	30.1
1975–76	77,633	19,861	25.6	35,094	45.2	22,678	29.2
1974–75	74,536	21,673	29.1	32,622	43.8	20,241	27.1
1973–74	67,628	21,280	31.5	29,299	43.3	17,049	25.2
1972–73	59,427	21,445	36.1	24,850	41.8	13,132	22.1
1971–72	51,784	21,592	41.7	19,165	37.0	11,027	21.3
1970–71	47,001	22,334	47.5	14,754	31.4	9,913	21.1
1969–70	43,639	22,856	52.4	11,678	26.8	9,105	20.8
1968–69	42,196	25,114	59.5	8,701	20.6	8,381	19.9
1967–68	41,555	28,197	67.8	6,213	15.0	7,145	17.2
1966–67	38,237	27,452	71.8	4,654	12.2	6,131	16.0
1965–66	35,125	26,278	74.8	3,349	9.5	5,498	15.7
1964–65	34,686	26,795	77.3	2,510	7.2	5,381	15.5
1963–64	35,259	28,238	80.1	1,962	5.6	5,059	14.3

SOURCES: American Nurses' Association. 1975. *Facts About Nursing, 1974–75.* Kansas City: Author. American Nurses' Association. 1985. *Facts About Nursing, 1984–85.* Kansas City: Author. Reprinted by permission of the publisher.

school is called the diploma program. It usually requires two and a half to three years of study. As the data in Table 11-2 indicate, diploma programs have traditionally been the most popular. They produced 50 percent or more of all the registered nurses graduated annually until 1970–71. As a result, the majority of all living and active registered nurses have been trained and socialized in diploma schools. Habenstein and Christ (1955) have described the graduates of diploma programs as *utilizers*, whose principal concern is with the technical and organizational details of nursing work. Mauksch (1972) describes their training program as follows:

Typically, the three-year hospital school combined education with a considerable admixture of apprenticeship. . . . The diploma school taught the nurse subordination to institutional goals and needs; it ritualized status subordination to the physician, stressing it beyond the necessary functional dependence of nursing tasks upon medical initiative. . . . Hospital control [of the nursing

school] meant that the nursing student, and therefore the nurse, could be used any place, any time, to do whatever needed to be done.

In sum, the hospital diploma programs focused on the practical production of a nurse who, as a surrogate-generalist, could be expected to serve the hospital in any way it deemed fit.

BACCALAUREATE PROGRAMS. In contrast to the diploma programs, baccalaureate nursing education has a more professional orientation. This reflects its close association with academic institutions. From the very first baccalaureate nursing program offered by Columbia University in 1899, baccalaureate nursing education has produced the majority of nursing faculty, nursing leaders, and nursing administrators. All of these have gone through a carefully mixed program of occupational training *and* liberal arts education. This has resulted in their adoption of what Habenstein and Christ (1955) label as the *professionalizer* role, which holds that nursing is a distinct profession based on formal, rational knowledge. These programs also emphasize the nurse's role as the patient's advocate. Baccalaureate training has become quite similar to graduate medical education in that the emphasis is not on practical application but on the theory and knowledge of how and why a particular disease receives a certain treatment. As indicated from the data in Table 11-2, the production of baccalaureate nurses has historically been rather small. Nonetheless, it has increased to the point where it is now producing about a third of all the registered nurses graduated annually.

ASSOCIATE DEGREE PROGRAMS. During the early 1950s a middle-ground nursing program emerged. In it nursing students attend a junior or community college for two years and receive both the registered nurse's license and an associate of arts degree (Hiatt, 1961; Meyer and Hoffman, 1964). The associate degree nursing schools, however, have not really resolved the *professionalizer* versus *utilizer* conflict; they have merely "straddled the fence." On the one hand, they moved the locus of control over nursing education from the hospital to the academic setting. Although this was intended to upgrade the nursing education that diploma nurses had received, it only served to alienate them. On the other hand, the move to the community college was not far enough for the baccalaureate advocates; they viewed the community college setting as a *vocational* rather than a *professional* one. As a result, the associate degree nurse has become the focus of the controversy in nursing; she generally adheres to the role of the *traditionalizer*, believing that bedside care and knowledge is the distinctive domain of nursing. The data in Table 11-2 show that the associate degree programs currently have the upper hand in nurse production. Their share of the market has increased from less than 6 percent in 1963–64 to a little over 50 percent today.

THE AMERICAN NURSES' ASSOCIATION POSITION: TECHNICAL VERSUS PROFESSIONAL NURSING. The three basically distinct forms of nursing education prepare their nurses in different ways and for seemingly different positions. Nonetheless, they all take the same national nursing board examinations and receive the same RN licenses. It is not surprising, therefore, that the majority of the American public adheres to the notion that a nurse is a nurse is a nurse. As a result, there has been a great deal of confusion over what nursing is and is likely to become. In its attempt to resolve this issue, the American Nurses' Association (ANA) took the "official position" that there were two types of nursing: technical and professional (American Nurses' Association, Committee on Education, 1965). Graduates of diploma or associate degree programs were declared *technical* nurses. To be a *professional* nurse, one had to graduate from a baccalaureate program. Thus, the ANA decreed that only baccalaureate degree nurses would be considered professionals.

This official position was met with immediate disgust and resistance by rank and file nurses, 70 percent of whom were trained in diploma or associate degree programs. Moreover, even among members of the ANA, to which only about 13 percent of the 1.4 million registered nurses in the United States belong (see American Nurses' Association, 1985), the decision was not well received; the majority of them are not baccalaureate nurses either. To nonbaccalaureate nurses, the official position was both an insult and a foolish mistake. They did not feel that an extra liberal arts education made their baccalaureate colleagues any better at nursing. As a result, the ANA's official position, which was adopted by its baccalaureate degree–dominated council, failed to resolve the controversy surrounding the diverse and decentralized state of nursing education. Moreover, it served to rub salt into the open wound resulting from the debate over who was and who was not a professional nurse.

In the two decades since the ANA took its official position, there has been little resolution of the professional versus technical nursing question. A mid 1970s survey of associate and baccalaureate degree graduates (see Hogstel, 1977) found that although there was a slight salary differential, there was no difference in the functions performed or positions filled by them. A subsequent study (see Soules, 1978) found absolutely no difference between baccalaureate, diploma, or associate degree nurses on either salary or professional advancement issues. Results such as this have lead Hogstel (1977) and others to suggest that "perhaps it is time to review the ANA position paper on education for nursing. If associate and baccalaureate nurses are not being utilized differently, different kinds of educational preparation for nursing practice must be questioned." A more recent survey (see Mattera, 1985), however, has once again documented a modest salary differential. It indicates that baccalaureate nurses averaged about $1,500 more a year than their diploma or associate degree colleagues. According to this survey, the average nurse's salary in 1985 was $24,200; hospital-based nurses averaged about $1,000 more per year.

Another recent survey focused on the attitudes that nurses have toward colleagues trained in the three different types of schools (see Gulack, 1983). In this study a representative sample of 2,000 nurses were asked to rank the "professional status" of baccalaureate, diploma, and associate degree nurses on a scale of 1 to 10. The results were quite interesting. Baccalaureate degree nurses received the highest scores, averaging 8.6. Nurses trained in diploma programs were a close second, averaging 8.2. Associate degree nurses, however, fared more poorly; they had an average score of 7.4. This suggests that nurses' perceptions of professional status may be tied to the length of the training experience.

Although the professional versus technical nursing issue remains unresolved, two things seem clear. First, the question of whether there ever will be two levels of entry into nursing depends more on sociopolitical factors than differences between baccalaureate and nonbaccalaureate trained nurses. The reason for this is that although there are no documented differences in their performance levels, there are clear differences in their relative positions of power and authority within nursing. Second, there has been and will continue to be a move to-ward baccalaureate training. Moreover, this trend is occurring at two levels. One of these involves the training received by new recruits. As indicated in Table 11-2, baccalaureate degree programs now account for about a third of all new nursing graduates. The other mechanism involves registered nurses returning to school to receive the baccalaureate degree. By 1985 there were 170 "RN to BSN" programs in the United States (see Zusy, 1986). Enrolling in one of these can be a nerve-wracking experience for two reasons. First, the registered nurse is treated as if she were a *student* who doesn't know much about nursing, although she is already a registered nurse. Second, there is usually a prolonged debate about how many of the registered nurse's previous credits will be counted toward the baccalaureate degree (see Tomajan, 1986).

The Making of a Nurse

As was the case with the making of a physician, there is a definite pattern of events involved in the making of a nurse. Unlike the sequence involved with medical students, however, the pattern of events in the making of a nurse is not nearly so regular. Most of this variation is caused by the type of schooling the nurse receives. Nonetheless, five distinct aspects of the nurse-making process warrant special attention: who chooses nursing; why they choose nursing; the socialization stages in nursing; the career quandary; and learning to play the "doctor-nurse game."

WHO CHOOSES NURSING? Physician recruits tend to be from the upper social classes, from families already containing physicians, and these recruits tend to be males from urban areas. In nursing, however, a quite different pattern emerges. Hughes, Hughes, and Deutscher (1958) found that nursing students were predominantly women, from small towns or rural areas, and of lower middle-class or working-class backgrounds. These students generally perceived of nursing as the most appealing avenue of social mobility available to them. In more recent studies Davis (1972) and Mauksch (1972) have found similar patterns, although it appears as if a growing number of nursing students are now coming from middle- to upper-middle-class urban families. This change reflects the stabilization of urban migration during the late 1960s and early 1970s. As a result, the typical nursing student has become a woman from the middle class.

WHY DO THEY CHOOSE NURSING? After knowing who selects nursing, perhaps the most interesting and telling question emerges: Why do they choose nursing? Nursing has historically been associated with the mother surrogate role, although modern nursing reformers such as Florence Nightingale have fought hard to change that image. Existing studies indicate that the reformers' efforts have not yet been successful. In fact, Mauksch (1972) summarized the results of two decades of his own research studies on nurses and nursing students as follows:

Significantly more than a comparison group of female college students, the entire group of nurses seemed to desire nurturant and affiliative relationships, and they also sought a succorant environment. These strongly evident needs to help, and for close relationships, were accompanied by the consistent finding that they also sought to avoid individual risks and blame-producing situations, and that they preferred the safety of the institutionally established social order of specific task demands.

In other words, the typical nursing student desires a role in which she may help others and develop close interpersonal relationships. At the same time she desires the safety and protection of an institutionalized social setting where her tasks and roles are clearly defined by someone else. Such an image of the nursing student does not seem to be very "professional." Indeed, it appears to be an adaptation of the mother surrogate role. Mauksch suggests that it is this very image of the nurse as a symbolic mother that makes nursing such an appealing occupational choice for middle-class women.

SOCIALIZATION STAGES IN NURSING: Given the mother surrogate orientation of entering students and the professional product that

emerges from nursing school upon graduation, there must be a strong socialization process in nursing education that accounts for the change. By studying a baccalaureate school of nursing, Davis (1972) has identified six stages in the nursing socialization process that are quite reminiscent of those found in medical schools (see Becker et al., 1961). The first stage is *initial innocence*. Students enter nursing intending to be mother surrogates and provide kindness and care in the Judeo-Christian tradition. Very soon they begin to feel disillusioned and frustrated because their instructors do not support this image of the mother surrogate role. Instead, the faculty emphasize the technical aspects of bed making and other chores that have little direct bearing on succor. This disillusionment and frustration begins to peak during the first academic term. It gives rise to the second socialization stage that Davis calls *labeled recognition of incongruity*. In this stage students openly vent their frustration by questioning their career choice and despairing over the incongruence between their expectations for and the realities of nursing. As a result, there is an exodus of resolute mother surrogates from the nursing school.

Those who remain enter a new stage in which they try *psyching out* the faculty. This is analogous to the "learning what the faculty want" perspective discovered in medical students. In essence, the students collectively participate in determining what the faculty does and does not think is important for the graduate nurse. Once the faculty have been psyched out, the students concentrate only on those things that they perceive the faculty consider important. As the faculty are psyched out, it becomes apparent that they want the students to adopt a professional orientation toward nursing. Although they do not like the idea, the students begin to act like professionals and enter the *role simulation* stage. By the end of the first year they begin to feel more confident as future nurses, and their discomfort with the acting role declines. As they begin the last half of their program, their confidence increases and they enter the *provisional internalization* stage. When graduation is about a year away, the students enter the final stage of the socialization process. Here the professional role achieves *stable internalization,* and the nursing student is ready to be turned out.

Davis's (1972) identification of the six stages in the nursing socialization process is based on the study of a baccalaureate program. Psathas (1968), however, reported similar results from his examination of a hospital's diploma school of nursing. Moreover, our own observations of an associate degree program point to similar stages. Thus, it appears as if nursing students are heavily influenced by the faculty with whom they study. These faculty usually have a professional rather than a mother surrogate orientation toward nursing. The intensity of this orientation among faculty members appears to be strongest in baccalaureate and weakest in diploma programs. This results in the more professional orientation of the baccalaureate student.

THE RN AS INSURANCE: A CAREER QUANDARY. Although all three types of nursing schools instill some sense of professionalism among their students, nursing presents a unique career quandary. Although most nursing faculty view nursing as a career, most nurses do not. In fact, a special version of "marital sweepstakes" takes over most nursing schools during the last few months of the program. Announcing one's engagement to be married becomes the center of attraction and *the* most important event. Of particular interest in this marital sweepstakes is the fact that most researchers (see Davis, 1972; Davis and Olesen, 1967; Psathas, 1968) have found that nursing students' first intent was to marry physicians-to-be. They soon learn that medical students are not from the same social background and relegate themselves to having affairs with physicians. Eventually they seek marital partners from a more compatible social class background.

Thus, although nursing students have studied and trained for a career in nursing, it appears that they view this career as an insurance policy. It may be used while waiting to get married or as something to do or fall back on after being married and raising

a family. Indeed, only about two thirds of all female nurses are ever actively employed at the same time. Because of this career quandary two distinct groups have developed in the nursing profession. One consists of professionally oriented nurses, who typically have baccalaureate training. The other consists of occupationally oriented nurses, who move in and out of nursing practice according to their marital status and life cycle position. This split within nursing poses a considerable barrier for its future recognition as an independent profession.

WORKING WITH DOCTORS: LEARNING TO PLAY THE "DOCTOR-NURSE GAME." Perhaps the most important aspect in the making of a nurse is learning how to play the "doctor-nurse game." According to Stein (1967), it is through the practice of the doctor-nurse game that nurses seek more equitable positions in the medical care hierarchy within the hospital, where three fourths of all active nurses are employed. Stein considers this interaction pattern to be a game because it contains the three features common to all games: an objective, rules, and scoring. The objective is for the nurse to show initiative and to take situations into her own hands while appearing to remain totally supportive of the physician and a passive reactor to his orders. The primary rule is to avoid open disagreement between the physician and the nurse.

To accomplish this, the nurse must act and communicate in such a way that she does not appear to be making recommendations. In addition, the physician who is seeking recommendations from the nurse must not appear to be doing so. If he does, his superior status position is jeopardized. Thus, for an effective game to take place both doctor and nurse must be well aware of each other's modes of communication. This implies that the best players at the doctor-nurse game are those who have worked with each other before and are able to "sense" the full meaning of each other's actions. The scoring aspect of the game involves the outcome. Is the nurse able to make a recommendation without actually appearing to do so? Is the physician able to ask for a nurse's recommendation without actually appearing to do so?

In essence, the doctor-nurse game is a facade designed to maintain the image that the doctor is the *practitioner* and the nurse is the *assistant*. The maintenance of these status distinctions is especially important in the hospital setting. In the hospital, doctors are outsiders who entrust their patients to the staff. The principal paraprofessional in the hospital is the nurse. It is the nurse who knows the most about the hospitalized patient and his or her progress, even though the nurse is not allowed to make important decisions relevant to that progress. Therefore, it is especially important that the doctor-nurse game be played well in the hospital. If it is not played well by the nurse, she tends to be fired. If it is not played well by the physician, there tends to be a problem in having work orders carried out in an efficient and timely manner. To be a good nurse in the eyes of the doctor or a good doctor in the eyes of a nurse, one must be good at the doctor-nurse game.

A good example of a well-played doctor-nurse game in the hospital setting is as follows. The doctor and nurse are treating a patient. The nurse notices that the patient should have an intravenous feeding, although the doctor has forgotten about it. The nurse asks, "Should I get the intravenous feeding ready?" The doctor responds to her suggestion by saying, "Yes, do that." This way the doctor gets to tell the nurse what to do, even though it was her idea in the first place.

Nursing's Bid for Professional Status: Internal Struggles

As we have seen, nursing is currently facing an internal struggle over its future status. This struggle may be linked to several factors, including the "structured-in" conflict between physicians and nurses, the significant disparity between the average physician's salary ($113,118 in 1985; see American Medical Association, 1986) and the average nurse's salary ($24,200 in 1985; see Mattera, 1985), the fact that nurses are

the single largest group involved in patient care, and the fact that the doctor-nurse relationship may well be the most important one in the hospital, where the bulk of American health care takes place (see Duff and Hollingshead, 1968; Pellegrino, 1964). In addition, because physicians are usually men and nurses are usually women, their status relationships are inexplicably drawn into focus around the women's equal rights movement (Roberts and Group, 1973; Cleland, 1971; Lamb, 1973).

It would seem, then, that regardless of whether one speaks of the need for new "collegial" relationships (see Bates, 1972), "collaborative co-professionals" (see Cohen, 1973), "congruent roles" (see Lysaught, 1973), "interdependent" practitioners, or for "equality" (see Smoyak, 1974), the time has come, as Schlotfeldt (1974) has written,

for nurses to assert their professional prerogatives and with confidence communicate and demonstrate the nature and value of their contribution. . . . The time is long overdue for nurses, without embarrassment, to declare the scope of their responsibilities, demonstrate their competencies and expect appropriate rewards—not only those that are intrinsic to their work, but also those that include recognition and compensation commensurate with their contribution to the health care system.

Thus, the stage seems to be set for nursing's bid to enhance its professional status.

According to Smoyak (1974), nursing has a proper claim to its own true professional status. She argues that nursing uses its separate and distinct skills and expertise in "caring, comforting, counseling, and helping patients and families cope with their health problems." This contrasts with the physician's expertise, which lies in diagnosing and curing diseases. Smoyak's distinction, then, is based on the difference between medical care (as provided by physicians) and health care (as provided by nurses). Unfortunately, this is a distinction that the public has yet to accept. Furthermore, if it is not presented carefully, this distinction could relink nursing to the mother surrogate role, which is not where nursing would like to go. To fully understand nursing's bid for enhanced social position in the health care delivery system, we must look at those factors that hamper and favor such a change (Dachelet, 1978).

Factors Hampering Nursing's Bid for Increased Status

There are a number of factors both within and outside of nursing that hamper its drive for independent professional status. From within there are problems in how nurses are socialized and trained. There is also the debate over professional versus technical nursing. The factors external to nursing include the fact that most nurses are women while most doctors are men, the public's perception that nursing is a relatively unskilled occupation, and the effects of the economic recession (Dachelet, 1978).

NURSING SOCIALIZATION. When the socialization process that nurses go through is compared to that of doctors, a striking difference emerges. A student doctor, as we see in the following description by Knowles (1968), is socialized to be an independent, individualistic practitioner: "At the end of four years, he is a highly individualistic person cloaked with the charismatic values of the profession, trained to take immediate action with the individual patient and to expect immediate rewards with his knowledge firmly grounded in science." Nursing education, however, is quite different. De Tourngay (1971) writes that

we have socialized nursing students to the submissive role. We have helped students to be tactful and diplomatic to the point of obscuring their collaborative role. We have also filled nursing students with the fear of making a mistake [to the extent] that they are low risk takers. Along with fostering this fear of making mistakes, we socialize our students to depend on physicians and to be reluctant to accept responsibility and accountability for their own actions.

In short, medical students are socialized into being aggressive, individualistic practitioners. Nurses are socialized (by other nurses) into being handmaidens to the physician. Indeed, a considerable amount of nursing socialization focuses on making the student nurse good at playing the doctor-nurse game. To the extent that such so-cialization mechanisms are successful, nursing's bid to be an independent profession is likely to fail. Its socialization processes are self-defeating.

FORMAL EDUCATION AND TRAINING. As with socialization for physicians and nurses, there is a significant difference in their educational processes. First, academic screening for admission to medical school far exceeds the best processes involved in baccalaureate nursing. This implies that the intellectual and studious qualities of medical students exceed those of nursing students. Second, the formal education processes themselves are quite different. Medical students are taught in an academic environment typified by the logic of scientific inquiry; nursing students are trained in technique. Thus, medical students learn *why* something happens and *why* a certain treatment is preferred. Nursing students learn *what* treatment is to be used in *which* situations. In the end, nurses are trained as technicians while physicians are trained as scholar-scientists.

THE PROFESSIONAL-TECHNICAL SCHISM. There is a considerable split within nursing between baccalaureate, diploma, and associate degree nurses over the issue of professional versus technical nursing. Although they comprise only about 30 percent of all RNs, baccalaureate (and higher degree) nurses tend to be career-oriented and have taken over control of the ANA. As a result, in 1965 the ANA decreed that to be a *professional* nurse one needed a baccalaureate degree; anything less made one a *technical* nurse. Because "professional" connotes something better than "technical," this position caused a tremendous rift between baccalaureate and nonbaccalaureate nurses. The continued existence of this split impedes nursing's chance to become an independent profession. Nursing's leadership (baccalaureate nurses) appears unable to pull the rank and file (diploma and associate degree nurses) into line behind them. To win the struggle and emerge as a profession, nursing must first resolve its internal strife over the professional versus technical nursing distinction.

THE PUBLIC IMAGE OF NURSING. One of the three most serious external impediments to nursing's bid for enhanced status is the public's image of it. The general image held by the public is that "anyone, or at least any female, can provide basic nursing service" (Dachelet, 1978). Thus, nursing suffers from a professional identity crisis in which the public fails to associate any special skills with it that make it worthy of being a profession. This is exemplified in the relationship between nurse and patient, which is far more symmetrical than the patient-practitioner relationship. Moreover, there is a vicious cycle at work here. Nurses are assigned low occupational prestige scores by the public. This limits their advantageous position in nurse-patient situations, which in turn reinforces the low prestige of nursing. The only way out of this cycle appears to be the provision of the best, most sophisticated nursing care. As Dachelet points out, however, this actually works against the emergence of nursing as a profession because "part of the skill in providing this sophisticated nursing care is that the care and facilitating be provided unobtrusively. It is ironic but quite possible that to the extent the nurse is effective as a nurse the profession will be accorded less prestige." Thus, the very nature of the nursing role is such that doing it well diminishes its professional prestige-producing qualities.

NURSING AND WOMEN. The second major external impediment to nursing's bid for professional status is the fact that 95 percent of all active and practicing nurses are women. Thus, the claim has been repeatedly made that the disadvantaged position of the nurse relative to the doctor is due to the relationship of women to men. Dachelet (1978) argues that it is hard for nursing to reach first-class status when society views most of its members as second-class citizens. Indeed, Twaddle and Hessler (1977) suggest that in contemporary American society the plight of female nurses may be compared to the plight of black professionals in the early 1960s. At that time skin color was viewed as a more important credential than achieved formal qualifications. In a society where women are not considered to be on a par with men, being a distinctly female occupation presents a considerable disadvantage for nursing's bid to become an independent profession.

THE RECESSION AND NURSING. The third major external impediment to nursing's bid for enhanced professional status is the economic recession experienced during most of the 1980s. Because many of their husbands became un- or underemployed, a significant number of nurses elected either to return to the labor force, or if they were already in it, to change from part-time to full-time positions. At the same time the economic downturn and major modifications in the health insurance industry forced hospitals to trim costs wherever possible (see Lee, 1984). As a result, the traditional nursing shortage rapidly disappeared, although unemployment levels among nurses remained quite low— about 1.6 percent in 1983 according to the American Nurses' Association (1985)—and job security has remained quite high (see Mattera, 1986). Nonetheless, the decline in the relative scarcity of nurses brought about by the economic downturn has put nursing in a less advantageous position to vie for enhanced status.

Factors Enhancing the Bid for Nursing as a Profession

Just as there are factors that hinder nursing's bid for enhanced professional status, there are also factors that enhance it. Some of these come from within nursing. They include changes in the education process, a trend toward research and inquiry in nursing, and the admission of more men into nursing schools. Other factors that enhance nursing's bid for increased status are external to it. These include increased public appreciation of nursing, favorable new legislation, and the feminist movement (Dachelet, 1978).

CHANGES IN NURSING EDUCATION. One of the most significant developments in nursing has been the shift from hospital diploma programs to associate and baccalaureate degree schools. As a result, nursing education has become much more clearly associated with the university. It has also become more formalized and consistent from school to school. In addition, as the baccalaureate programs become more popular, nursing education becomes a longer process. The effect of these changes is that the *utilizer* role model is giving out to the *traditionalizer* role model. Moreover, it will eventually give out to the *professionalizer* role model. Because of this, society will begin to confer higher social status on nursing. These education-based changes, however, will not take place overnight. It will take at least two more decades for the number of traditionalizers in nursing to be surpassed by the number of professionalizers. Although nursing education is clearly moving toward professional education, there is a considerable history of nonprofessional nursing to overcome. This will only be accomplished by the systematic replacement of retiring cohorts of utilizers and traditionalizers by emerging cohorts of professionalizers.

RESEARCH IN NURSING: A NEW OUTLOOK. Closely related to the changes in nursing education is the emerging perspective of research in nursing. Not only are baccalaureate schools of nursing becoming more popular, so are graduate schools of nursing. Indeed, about 6 percent of all nurses now hold graduate degrees (American Nurses' Association, 1985). Because graduate schools of nursing are housed within academic university structures, they emphasize research as an integral part of their program, as do most graduate professional programs. When graduate nurses go out into practice, their training in nursing research goes with them. Moreover, it is dispersed to their coworkers. As a result, nursing education has changed from the technique-only perspective to a scientific-inquiry perspective with nurses seeking to scientifically expand their knowledge. As Schlotfeldt (1974) has written, this new perspective has transformed nursing to the point where it now sees its obligation to "advance, verify and continuously restructure the expanding body of knowledge known as nursing science."

MEN AND NURSING. A third change internal to nursing is the increasing number of men choosing to enter it. Although the number of men in nursing is still quite small—less than 2 percent of all nurses are males—admission rates for them have increased from less than 4 percent of all nursing students in 1969 to about 10 percent in 1985 (American Nurses' Association, 1985). This represents a considerable trend toward breaking down nursing's image as a female-only occupation. As that image fades and more men become nurses, the societal conception of nursing as something less than professional (because of its women-only status) will decrease. Indeed, the fact that more and more men are being attracted to careers in nursing serves to legitimize and emphasize its importance, at least in the public image. When men in a male-dominated society increasingly choose a traditionally female-dominated occupation, it indicates that the occupation in question must have become worthwhile.

NURSING APPRECIATION. Three factors external to nursing also enhance its bid for increased status. The first is a general trend toward better public appreciation of nurses and their skills. This is partially a function of the movement away from hospitals and toward neighborhood health care facilities and centers for primary and secondary care. In these new facilities nurses play a much more important role than they do in the hospital. This is primarily because these centers are not where physicians bring their sickest patients. Rather, this is where sick individuals come when they do not have access to a physician (Dachelet, 1978). As a result, the people using these facilities receive most of their care from nurses and other paraprofessionals. Therefore, they have a much better view of how well qualified nurses are for providing health education and counseling, well-baby care, and other aspects of nursing care. In fact, after seeing how well received they were while working in neighborhood clinics, some nurses have begun to set up their *own* offices to practice nursing independently.

LEGISLATION AND NURSING. Perhaps the most important of all external factors enhancing nursing's bid for increased status has been the emergence of legislation favoring nurses as practitioners. Dachelet (1978) notes that in the past few years more than 30 states have adopted or revised their statutes that define and/or restrict the practice of nursing. The typical phraseology of these new nursing acts defines nursing as (Kelley, 1974) "diagnosing and treating human responses to actual and potential health problems through such services as case finding, health teaching, health counseling and provision of care supportive to or restorative of life and well being." Because this definition of nursing includes diagnosis and treatment, it has received considerable opposition from physicians and the AMA. Nonetheless, nursing acts such as this have become law in a number of states. They provide nursing with a considerable air of legitimacy in its quest for increased status.

THE FEMINIST MOVEMENT. The third factor outside of nursing that enhances its bid for increased status is the women's rights movement. Because it is a female-dominated occupation, nursing stands to gain a great deal from the success of the feminist movement. At the very least, the feminist movement has brought a greater sense of positive self-assessment and worth to nurses. It emphasizes women's abilities to be decisive and independent. This general change of perspective in women has made nurses much less subordinate, dependent, and deferential than ever before. Moreover, the feminist movement instructs us all to no longer *expect* women to play the mother surrogate role. As a result, the role of women in our society is significantly changing. Because most women in health care are nurses, the social prestige of nursing is in for quite a change.

In sum, there are forces from within and outside of nursing that serve both to enhance and impede its bid for increased professional status. Perhaps the most difficult factors to overcome are internal ones, especially the historical dominance of the mother surrogate image. If nursing is to become an independent profession, the majority of nurses must begin to view themselves as professional practitioners and not as patient and physician handmaidens. Whether or not nursing can overcome its tradition is unclear. Dachelet (1978) writes: "It is too early to predict success or failure. The health care system as a whole is in a period of transition. Changes are occurring not only in interprofessional relationships but also in modes of delivering services and in the attitudes of consumers. It is left for the observer of perhaps twenty years hence to reflect upon the events of this decade and assess the impact and effect of nursing's bid for increased professional status."

We can, however, turn our attention toward a weather vane of nursing's bid for higher status: the nurse practitioner. We can also examine the most potentially threatening obstacle in the way of nursing's becoming a profession: the physicians' assistant. Both of these new roles may be evaluated against a common background, the desire to create a new set of paraprofessionals generally known as *physician extenders*.

The New Paraprofessionals: Nurse Practitioner and Physicians' Assistant

One of the most universally encountered yet least understood scenarios in the American health care delivery system is that you cannot find a doctor when you need one. This phenomenon is primarily due to the maldistribution of physicians and the surplus of specialists, as discussed in chapter 9. It would appear that the optimal answer to this problem might be to produce more primary care physicians and direct them to practice in rural and ghetto areas. Unfortunately, this is not feasible. The principal reason is that the AMA is quite opposed to it because it violates the individual doctor's freedom to choose a medical specialty and a practice location. Therefore, a new breed of paraprofessional practitioners known as physician extenders began to emerge in the mid 1960s as a more practical resolution. Of these, the nurse practitioner and the physicians' assistant represent the most researched and important examples.

Nurse Practitioners

The term *nurse practitioner* appears to have come into being in 1965 when the first pediatric nurse practitioner program was established at the University of Colorado (Levine, 1977). This program, and those that followed it, emerged from a series of nurse training acts that provided federal support for physician extender programs (see Public Laws 88–581, 90–490, 92–158, and 94–63). These programs are especially interesting because of their bearing on the delivery of primary health care, health maintenance, disease prevention, and cost containment. All four have become increasingly important issues in the debate over America's health care.

THE NATURE OF THE NURSE PRACTITIONER. Although nurse practitioners have been around for two decades, it is not yet clear what role they have been trained to play in the health care delivery system. In reviewing the state of nurse practitioner programs Levine (1977) concluded that they "provide preparation in extended nursing roles, that is, such primary care skills as history taking, physical examination, ordering laboratory tests, and assuming responsibility for management of selected cases with emphasis on primary care; and required that students be registered nurses." He found that by the mid 1970s there were 130 nurse practitioner programs with about 1,100 students enrolled. Nearly one third of these students were pursuing a master's degree in nursing, underscoring the more "professional" orientation of the nurse practitioner's role. More than 80 percent of the students were specializing in either pediatric, adult, or family practice, indicating that most nurse practitioners would, indeed, go into primary care areas. Moreover, on graduation nearly two thirds of all nurse practitioners went into ambulatory care settings, representing a considerable break from the tradition of registered nurses, 75 percent of whom go into hospital-based inpatient care.

Waters and Arbeiter (1985) have more recently examined the status of nurse practitioners themselves. They were able to iden-

tify about 24,000 nurse practitioners in 1985, and they estimate that there will be about 30,000 by 1990. Perhaps more important than this rapid growth in numbers is the fact that the identity crisis that had originally beset the field seems to be going away. Thirty-five states have changed their nursing practice acts to accommodate the expanded role of the nurse practitioner. Moreover, 18 states now allow nurse practitioners to write prescriptions on a limited basis. Their salaries, however, are anything but special. The nurse practitioners earn no more than hospital staff nurses, and in some cases (especially in family planning clinics) even less.

PATIENT ACCEPTANCE. Regardless of how well trained nurse practitioners may be, their future will be determined by two related factors: patient acceptance and physician receptivity. Although the public has yet to fully comprehend the nature and scope of the nurse practitioner, several researchers have investigated the public's acceptance of them (see Merenstein, Wolfe, and Barker, 1974; Public Health Service, 1976). In general, these studies have shown a high degree of acceptance of nurse practitioners among those who have used their services. They have also shown a general level of "alleged" acceptance among those who have yet to use their services. Thus, it appears that as far as the public is concerned, nurse practitioners *are* acceptable. There is, however, some hesitancy the first time that a nurse practitioner is used in lieu of a physician.

PHYSICIAN RECEPTIVITY. The other side of the acceptance issue is whether or not physicians are receptive to the idea and use nurse practitioners. Lawrence, DeFriese, Putnam, Pickard, Cyr, and Whiteside (1977) have studied this issue in detail using data from an extensive study of North Carolina physicians. To determine physician receptivity, Lawrence and his colleagues asked 1,665 physicians whether or not they were willing to delegate 35 tasks, which ranged from routinely recording laboratory results to delivering babies and setting fractures. They found that the majority of physicians were willing to delegate many of these tasks to nurse practitioners, but only so long as the task in question was not important. This hesitancy to delegate important tasks was lower among physicians who had previously worked with a nurse practitioner. Physicians with nurse practitioner work experience were about 25 percent more receptive than their colleagues without such experience. These data, however, do not indicate that nurse practitioners "have it made" in terms of physician receptivity. In fact, when Lawrence and his colleagues asked physicians to whom they would rather delegate these tasks, the physicians preferred physicians' assistants 18.5 percent more often than nurse practitioners (although 69.3 percent said they would delegate tasks equally). Moreover, there have been a number of boundary disputes between doctors and nurse practitioners in which the former have sued the latter for practicing without a license.

IS THE NURSE PRACTITIONER REALLY A NURSE? After reviewing the current status of the nurse practitioner, the following question seems warranted: Are they really nurses? To be sure, the nurse practitioner bears the title of *nurse* practitioner and to enroll in such a program one needs to be a registered nurse. Nonetheless, it seems as if in the course of their training nurse practitioners have taken the same route for equal status that osteopaths took earlier in this century. That is, if you cannot be accepted by the physician as a coprofessional on your own merits, then become more like a physician. The osteopaths carried this to its logical conclusion; they have become accepted as physicians and are now more or less viewed as an identifiable specialty within traditional medicine. Nurse practitioners, however, have not gone that far. Their view is that although they are not physicians, they are surely better trained and more professional than registered nurses (see Waters and Arbeiter, 1985). In essence, because it is impossible for a nurse to be accepted as a coprofessional, a new and expanded nursing role has been developed. It, however, results in a health care practitioner rather than a nurse.

The Physicians' Assistant

Like the nurse practitioner, the physicians' assistant concept began in 1965 when Duke University established the first program. Since then more than 50 quite diverse programs training physicians' assistants have emerged. Although these are too varied to be succinctly described, their general purpose is to train physicians' assistants to be quasi-independent, junior-level practitioners under the general supervision of physicians. Concomitant with the growth of this new paraprofession, the literature examining the physicians' assistant has dramatically increased. Several extensive reviews are available (see Gairola, 1982; Lewis, 1975; Perry, 1976, 1977; Perry and Breitner, 1982; Perry and Redmond, 1980; Sadler, Sadler, and Blessa, 1972; Schneller, 1974, 1975, 1978; Weston, 1980, 1984). They point to three distinct and interesting phenomena: who becomes a physicians' assistant; into what work setting does the physicians' assistant go; and the acceptance of the physicians' assistant.

WHO BECOMES A PHYSICIANS' ASSISTANT? In an informative overview, Perry (1977; see also Perry and Redmond, 1980) provides a detailed description of who becomes a physicians' assistant. The most significant characteristic is that most physicians' assistants are men. This represents a considerable reversal from the predominance of women in nursing and the other paraprofessions. A second significant characteristic is that about half of all physicians' assistants have previously served as medical corpmen. An additional 20 percent or so had been medical technicians. Less than 5 percent were registered nurses before becoming physicians' assistants. On average physicians' assistants have worked for five years in a related medical field and had taken about two and a half years of postsecondary school training before entering their program.

The background characteristics of the physicians' assistant, then, are remarkably different from those of the nurse practitioner or the registered nurse. Although the training program for the physicians' assistant is quite varied, it is also rather different from that of the nurse practitioner. Nurse practitioner programs maintain stiffer entrance requirements, are of longer duration (especially since being a registered nurse is a prerequisite to admission), and have more uniform and demanding exit requirements. Nonetheless, the salaries for physicians' assistants are higher than those of nurse practitioners.

WORK SETTINGS. The second interesting phenomenon about physicians' assistants involves the work setting that they enter following training. Like nurse practitioners, physicians' assistants were expected to go into primary care and nonmetropolitan areas in order to ease the doctor shortage. These expectations have been met. Although less than half of all physicians enter primary care, more than three fourths of all physicians' assistants do. Moreover, nearly half of all physicians' assistants are involved in general practices. Similarly, although only about a tenth of all physicians practice in small communities, more than a fourth of all physicians' assistants do. Thus, just like their nurse practitioner counterparts, physicians' assistants seem to be extending primary care to those who do not have access to primary care physicians. There is, however, a major difference between them. The physicians' assistant is much more likely to enter private practice (nearly 50 percent) than the nurse practitioner (less than 15 percent). Thus, although nurse practitioners are trained as independent practitioners and physicians' assistants are trained as quasi-independent practitioners (under clear supervisory linkages to a physician), it is the physicians' assistant who actually practices most independently.

ACCEPTANCE OF THE PHYSICIANS' ASSISTANT. The third interesting phenomenon about physicians' assistants is their acceptance by patients, fellow paraprofessionals, and physicians. Patients' acceptance of physicians' assistants is similar to that of their acceptance of nurse practitioners, although the former receive slightly higher evaluations (see Schneller, 1978; Nelson, Jacobs, and Johnson, 1974). There are two reasons for this preferential treatment. First, to the patient the nurse practitioner is still a *nurse*; the physicians' assistant, however, is a *physicians'* assistant. Second, because nurses are usually women and physicians' assistants are usually men, the latter have more ascribed prestige in our male-oriented stratification system.

As indicated above, physicians are more willing to delegate tasks to physicians' assistants than to nurse practitioners. There are four chief reasons for this. First, physicians' assistants are *physicians'* assistants; they are dependent on the physician for their livelihood. Nurse practitioners are independent and alternative *practitioners*; they are viewed as competitors to the physician. As one might suspect, physicians are more receptive to paraprofessionals who accept a subordinate role (i.e., physicians' assistants) than to those who demand a coequal role (i.e., nurse practitioners). Second, physicians' assistants are usually men, like the majority of physicians. Nurse practitioners are usually women, like the majority of nurses. The status privileges generally extended to men in our society carry over into the physician-paraprofessional relationship. This results in physicians being more likely to accept male physicians' assistants than female nurse practitioners. Third, the physicians' assistant concept was largely initiated and backed by physicians as a counteroffensive to the nurse practitioner concept. Therefore, physicians are predisposed to favor their own "creation" over that of nurses. Finally, physicians' assistants are trained by physicians, while nurse practitioners are trained by nurses. This means that physicians' assistants receive *medical* training as opposed to *nursing* training. It also allows the physicians' assistant to be socialized by physicians into a physicianlike role. In contrast, the nurse practitioner is socialized by nurses into an extended nursing role.

The acceptance of physicians' assistants by other health care workers (excluding physicians and hospital administrators), however, is not so favored. Coe and Fichtenbaum (1972) point out that "the general attitude . . . was, at best, ambivalent. Much of it was negative. The ambivalence stemmed from envy of the physician's assistant's close relationship with the physician, his freedom to make decisions (which most felt were the sole responsibility of the physician) and greater financial rewards with less formal training than most of the personnel with whom he worked." Indeed, Coe and Fichtenbaum described the root of the problem in physicians' assistants' acceptance by their coworkers as an "entry" problem. Unlike any other emerging health paraprofession, physicians' assistants did not enter at the bottom of the status hierarchy and work their way up (either by the "bootstrap" or "subsequently emerging" paraprofession method). Rather, with less formal training than their coworkers, physicians' assistants were immediately given, by physicians, a status position above nursing and directly below doctors (as quasi-independent, "junior level" practitioners). Because this is what other paraprofessionals have always wanted, they felt slighted and envious. Particularly slighted were nurses, who had been the "top" candidates for such a position before being preempted by physicians' assistants. As a result, one out of four physicians' assistants reports having problems getting nurses to follow orders. In addition, physicians' assistants encounter 50 percent more problems of acceptance by nurses than acceptance by physicians (see Perry, 1977). Clearly, nurses and other paraprofessionals appear to be far more resistant to and offended by the concept of the physicians' assistant than are physicians.

The Future of Nurse Practitioners and Physicians' Assistants

The future for nurse practitioners and physicians' assistants is not entirely clear. They were originally expected to work out of ambulatory care settings as physician extenders in areas without access to doctors. Brooks and Johnson (1986), however, have recently shown that this is no longer the case. In 1975 they began to track a national cohort of 44 rural satellite health centers that were initially staffed only by nurse practitioners and physicians' assistants.

Twelve of the centers had gone out of existence by 1984. Eight of these had been replaced by physicians' practices. Of the 32 remaining health centers only 18 were still staffed solely by nurse practitioners and physicians' assistants. This led Brooks and Johnson to write that "the growth in the number of physicians and the decrease in the number of NPs and PAs practicing in the study communities suggests that the period when NP/PA satellite centers were important forms of organization for the delivery of primary care to previously underserved, isolated rural areas may be ending." This interpretation is consistent with the results of several recent reports on the effects of the increasing relative supply of physicians on the geographic maldistribution problem (see Newhouse, Williams, and Bennett, 1982; Williams, Schwartz, and Newhouse, 1983). Those studies indicate that the growth in competition brought about by the increased relative supply of physicians has begun to force doctors into previously "unacceptable" locales. As a result, the market for physicians' assistants and nurse practitioners in those settings is eroding.

The situation for nurse practitioners and physicians' assistants, however, is not entirely bleak. Perry and Breitner (1982) have shown that physicians' assistants have begun to move toward institutional settings in order to provide their care. Similarly, Cruikshank, Clow, and Seals (1986) have reported that nurse practitioners are becoming more likely to enter institutional and tertiary care settings than ever before. Moreover, there is some evidence to suggest that hospitals are starting to turn to physicians' assistants and nurse practitioners to serve as "junior house staff" in order to further reduce operational costs. Thus, the future for these physician extenders may be quite good, although it appears that it will be in institutional as opposed to ambulatory care settings.

In the end, the future of nurse practitioners and physicians' assistants depends on how they respond to the marked changes presently occurring in the health care delivery system. Weston (1984) may have said it best when he wrote:

The future . . . may rest on how well they and their educational programs adapt to the changes in the number of physician providers and the needs of the population. There is little evidence that "hard core" rural areas will be able to attract and support primary care physicians, yet this possibility has already led to controversy with local medical societies. The federal government alone has invested some $200 million in the training of nurse practitioners and physician assistants. That investment was made to meet a demand. While the need as originally conceived may change during the next decade, their potential contributions will not change if the constraints on their practice can be mitigated by more than experimental projects and their important contributions to health care can be fully utilized.

Whether this will be allowed to occur or not is unknown. It depends a great deal on how organized medicine in general and the AMA in particular respond to the perceived competitive threat.

Summary

In this chapter we have examined assistant health personnel. The first section focused on the principal reason why assistant healers are unlikely to achieve true professional status; they are dominated by physicians who deprive them of autonomy. Because autonomy is *the* prerequisite to professional status, physicians remain atop the pyramid of power and prestige, controlling the work setting of all those further down in the health care hierarchy. Within this hierarchy the gulf between the occupational prestige of the doctor and the next highest health care worker, the nurse, is considerable. Nonetheless, all paraprofessionals use the physician as a benchmark for comparative assessments of their own status. This produces frustration and bad feelings, because no matter how hard paraprofessionals try, they can never achieve the status and prestige of physicians.

In the next section we turned to an examination of the history and social organization of nursing, which has a larger contingent of workers than all of the other health occupations combined. Two turning points in nursing's historical development were identified. In the beginning the English word *nurse* was synonymous with "sister" or "nun." The result has been a general perception of the nurse as a "mother surrogate" who provides unspecialized, "motherly" care to the sick and needy. This view was drastically altered with the introduction of the Nightingale System of nursing, which emphasized scientific and technical nursing training along with a professional perspective. Although the Nightingale System was universally adopted, nursing education remains diverse and decentralized. This has resulted in the painful struggle between the *technical* (diploma and associate degree trained) and *professional* (baccalaureate trained) factions.

As with the making of a physician, several identifiable characteristics are involved in the making of a nurse. These include the fact that nurses are predominantly middle class women from smaller-sized communities; choose nursing because of unusually strong needs to help others and work in a clearly defined social structure; pass through six stages en route to being resocialized out of a "mother surrogate" orientation and into a professional one; choose nursing not only as a full-time career but also as an insurance policy if they remain single or for when their children are grown; and have to learn how to play the "doctor-nurse game." In the third section we analyzed nursing's bid for increased status in the health care hierarchy. We found a number of external and internal factors that hamper their bid. These included patterns of nursing socialization, formal education, the professional-technical schism, the public image of nursing, and the fact that most nurses are women. Factors enhancing their bid included changes in nursing education, a new nursing research outlook, the increased interest of men in nursing, a growth in the public's appreciation of nursing, favorable legislation, and the feminist movement.

In the final section we turned our attention to the newest paraprofessionals that have the most promise for professional status: nurse practitioners and physicians' assistants. We found that both are viewed as physician extenders, intended to increase access to primary care among the poor and the geographically disadvantaged. While these extender roles are succeeding, there are both differences and conflicts between the two. Nurse practitioners are better trained and view themselves as alternative practitioners. Physicians' assistants are given higher status within the health care hierarchy and view themselves as assistant practitioners. As a result, nurse practitioners tend to be envious of the advantageous entry and quick acceptance of physicians' assistants in the health care hierarchy.

12. Hospitals

IN THE last three chapters we have examined the profession of medicine, alternatives to physicians, and nursing. We saw that the principal place where these health care workers interact is the hospital. Accordingly, we now turn our attention to the hospital and its role as the center stage of the American health care delivery system. To examine the hospital we have divided the present chapter into two sections. In the first we will examine the emergence of the modern hospital. To do this we will delineate the changing social posture of the hospital from its early religious orientation, through the poorhouse and deathhouse perspectives, and finally into the modern orientation. Special attention will be given to the hospital as the center for medical technology. We next look at various aspects of the modern hospital, including differences in ownership, size, type, organization, utilization, and costs. We conclude this section by discussing the emergence of multihospital systems.

In the second section we will examine the social organization of the hospital from two perspectives. First we will look at the two lines of authority within hospitals. To do this we will focus on traditional bureaucracies, the special case of the professions, the concept of an advisory bureaucracy, changes in hospital domination, and the plight of nurses caught between the doctor and the administrator. Then we will look at the social organization of hospitals from the patient's perspective. This includes an accentuated sick role, identity stripping, resource control, mobility control, and the "good" (i.e., subordinate) patient.

The Emergence of the Modern Hospital

As was the case with all the other components of contemporary medicine, the modern hospital is quite a recent development. In fact, it is completely a product of the twentieth century. Contemporary hospitals were brought about by the same social and cultural phenomena that gave birth to modern medicine, physicians, and nurses. Therefore, if we are to fully understand the modern hospital, we must first be aware of its historical development. Only then may we explore its contemporary mode.

Historical Orientations of the Hospital

Modern medicine has evolved from its earlier religious-mythical orientation to its present technological and scientific orientation. Physicians and nurses have followed the same evolutionary line, shedding the religious and magical for the scientific, technical, and professional. The place where modern physicians and nurses practice is the hospital. It too has evolved from a religious orientation, through poorhouse and deathhouse perspectives, and into a modern technological medical orientation. (For the classic work on the social history of hospitals, see Rosen, 1963. For more recent reviews in the same tradition, see Anderson and Gevitz, 1983; Croog and VerSteeg, 1972; Rushing, 1984; and VerSteeg and Croog, 1979.)

THE RELIGIOUS ORIENTATION. While the first hospitals appeared at the time of the Roman Empire, the development and growth of the hospital is usually associated with the ebb and flow of Christianity. Whereas the Judaic religion, from which Christianity emerged, emphasized the family's duty to provide assistance to its sick and needy, the Christian religion expanded the obligatory concept to the entire community. Moreover, Calvinistic logic held that one way of ensuring salvation and the grace of God was to provide such care for those who could not afford it. Accordingly, the development of a network of community-based hospitals began to flourish as the Church flourished. They were located on or near the Church's campus and were controlled by the clergy. This served to further integrate and extend the Church into everyday life.

Religious hospitals grew and spread so rapidly that by the 1400s hospitals were common entities throughout western Europe (Rosen, 1963). These religious hospitals, however, were nothing like modern hospitals. Most of the care given to patients in these early hospitals was provided by nuns and priests. This care was much more spiritual than medical in nature. In fact, nursing care was not the major feature of these hospitals. Moreover, these hospitals did not have anything resembling "staff physicians." In essence, the early hospitals served as social service centers for the sick, the poor, and especially for the religious traveler or pilgrim. They provided the rudiments of nursing along with a variety of other social services. Nonetheless, even these early hospitals were guided by three principles common to the modern hospital: a service orientation, a universalistic approach, and a custodial orientation (see Coe, 1978).

THE POORHOUSE ORIENTATION. During the Renaissance and Reformation the control of many hospitals passed from religious to secular hands. This brought about a period of decline for the hospital movement. On the one hand, this divestiture allowed each hospital to pursue its own course of action. On the other hand, it severed hospitals' steady source of revenue, and many were forced to close for budgetary reasons. During this period the cost of hospitalization was not borne by the patient; instead, it was financed by the hospital's endowments. As a result, much of the English hospital system collapsed after being liberated from monastic control.

By the late 1500s, however, this situation began to change. The primary forces behind the change were the increasingly dismal life of the poor and their growing number. The hospital movement was given new life by private philanthropists and community funding; the purpose was to take the "undesirables" off the streets and keep them out of sight and out of mind (see Rosen, 1963). This upsurge was not oriented toward health care. Rather, hospitals served as poorhouses where the orphans, the aged, the crippled, and the mentally incompetent were stored.

If these new inmates were able to work, they were forced to pay for their room and board by going out and working during the day and returning to the hospital at night. This poorhouse perspective is vividly portrayed in the classic tale of *Oliver Twist*.

THE DEATHHOUSE ORIENTATION. Throughout the 1600s very little changed in the poorhouse perspective of the hospital, especially from the public's viewpoint. Physicians, however, were gradually making a startling discovery. There were large numbers of people in hospitals who were sick or injured, especially from the rising number of industrial accidents. These individuals could be studied and used as experimental fodder for newly developing treatments. Moreover, because the sick and injured who were forced into the hospital had no alternatives, they were perfect subjects for experimentation. There were two reasons for this. First, society wanted them off the streets because their presence was offensive. This meant that there was little or no social concern over their well-being. Second, the sick and injured were of such disadvantaged social position that they could not defend themselves against such exploitation. Accordingly, physicians began to view the hospital as an asset. There they could learn a great deal among live patients about how the body functioned and reacted to treatment. Having already cornered the market on what little medical knowledge there was, physicians began to move toward taking control of the care of hospital patients. By the early 1700s physicians had changed the primary function of hospitals from providing social services to providing extremely primitive medical services. By the 1800s hospitals had become institutions of medical care where research and education flourished (see Rosen, 1963).

THE TECHNICAL MEDICAL ORIENTATION. By the early 1900s the image of the hospital began to change again. It became *the* place where anyone of whatever social class went to receive the highest-quality medical care. The deathhouse orientation had faded as medicine became modern, scientific, and

successful. Much of this success could be attributed to two factors. One was the increased quality of hospital personnel. This included better-trained physicians as a result of the "great trade" and better-trained nurses as a result of the Nightingale System. The other was the discovery of antiseptic procedures that drastically reduced infectious diseases as well as the likelihood of dying following simple surgery. In fact, at the turn of this century the probability of coming out of the hospital alive climbed to over 50 percent for the very first time. As a result, the deathhouse perspective gave way to the emerging image of the modern hospital (see Rosen, 1963).

The major stimulus for the emergence of the modern hospital has been the increasing technological nature of contemporary medicine. Put quite simply, the technology of modern medicine requires very extensive and expensive facilities. Consider, for example, the requirements for the surgical, laboratory, and radiation therapy equipment involved in treating cancer patients. Few physicians, whether in solo practice or in groups, are likely to be able to afford or provide such facilities out of their own office or clinic. Therefore, a central location had to be chosen where all physicians could bring those patients whom they could not adequately treat in their offices. The latest technological equipment and the technicians to operate it would be at this location. This location, of course, is the modern hospital. It is the most inexpensive place to provide sophisticated technical medical facilities. Here their expense is borne by a constant collection of patients much larger than any physician or group of physicians could assemble at any given time. Thus, the hospital has become the focal point of the American health care delivery system. (For a truly superb and timeless collection of essays on all aspects of the hospital, see Freidson, 1963.)

Contemporary American Hospitals: An Overview

The first American hospital was established by William Penn in Philadelphia in 1713. Like its sister hospitals in Europe,

Penn's hospital was principally a poorhouse providing social rather than medical services. Things soon changed, however, as the deathhouse orientation emerged and ultimately gave way to the hospital as the center of medical technology. The latter orientation received considerable support with the establishment of the Public Health Service. It marked the entrance of federal, state, and local governments into the hospital industry.

By the mid 1980s there were about 6,900 hospitals in the United States. All of these, however, were not alike. Indeed, a decade ago Fuchs (1974) provided a classic description of American hospitals that still holds today:

The American hospital is large, impersonal, and dominated by elaborate technology. The American hospital is small, inefficient, underequipped, and understaffed. The American hospital exists primarily to further the professional and economic interests of physicians. The American hospital exists to serve the community. The American hospital is crowded to the point of inefficiency and even danger, and serious delays are encountered in obtaining admission. The American hospital is half-empty, and many of its patients should be at home or in extended-care facilities. The American hospital is the noblest expression of philanthropic impulse. The American hospital is a business run to show a profit for its owners. Will the "real" American hospital please stand up? Which of these many contradictory characterizations of United States hospitals is correct? To some extent all of them are. No other country has such a heterogeneous collection of institutions comprising its hospital "system."

Thus, in order to understand the modern American hospital we must consider further six of its aspects: (1) ownership, (2) type, (3) size, (4) organization, (5) utilization, and (6) costs.

HOSPITAL OWNERSHIP. The 6,900 hospitals in America during the mid 1980s may be placed into three categories based on their ownership (American Hospital Association, 1986). The largest category are the voluntary or nonprofit short-term hospitals, of which there are about 3,400. About 25 percent of these are church-related; the re-

mainder are community hospitals. Voluntary or not-for-profit hospitals provide high-quality medical care and typically direct their services toward the middle and upper social classes. These individuals either pay directly or indirectly (through third-party insurance mechanisms) for the services they use. Access to voluntary hospitals for the poor comes about more through outpatient clinics and teaching programs than through inpatient services. This emphasizes the self-supporting nature of voluntary hospitals, where the bulk of the hospital's expense must be offset by patient revenues. This dictates a preference for patients who can afford to pay for the services that they use.

The next largest category of hospitals is those that are *government*-owned. Federal, state, and local governments owned and operated about 2,000 hospitals during the mid 1980s. More than 90 percent of the nearly 1,600 hospitals owned and operated by local governments are general service hospitals. In contrast, hospitals owned by the federal government are usually veterans' or psychiatric hospitals; those owned by the states are usually psychiatric hospitals or tuberculosis sanitariums. In all of these government-owned hospitals the major source of revenue is the government. Very little money comes from the patient, either directly or indirectly. Indeed, lower-class patients are more likely to use government hospitals because they do not have to pay for their services if they cannot afford to. Thus, the government hospital has become the major source of medical care for most poor people. Unlike voluntary hospitals where the staff is made up primarily of private physicians who bring their own patients to the hospital, government hospitals are typically staffed with interns, residents, and graduates of foreign medical schools. This difference is being reduced, however, with the increasing affiliation between government-owned hospitals and U.S. medical schools. That trend has considerably upgraded the quality of care and facilities available at government hospitals.

The smallest category is called *proprietary* hospitals. These are owned and operated by private corporations or groups of

Table 12-1. *Utilization, personnel, and finances in short-term hospitals during 1985.*

Classification	Hospitals	Beds	Admissions	Occupancy, percent	Average daily census	Adjusted average daily census	Avg. stay, days
TOTAL	6,339	1,111,584	35,767,238	65.7	730,784		
GENERAL	5,938	1,069,960	35,039,278	65.5	701,123		
Nongovernment not-for profit	3,262	696,963	23,876,278	67.2	468,204	560,650	7.2
6–24 beds	79	1,548	41,574	35.7	553	753	4.8
25–49	391	14,778	429,033	41.2	6,086	7,870	5.1
50–99	631	46,531	1,377,344	53.6	24,942	31,292	6.6
100–199	823	118,298	3,981,056	61.9	73,225	90,965	6.7
200–299	529	129,782	4,612,048	67.1	87,135	105,800	6.9
300–399	357	123,545	4,420,607	68.6	84,699	100,540	7.0
400–499	199	89,076	3,124,399	70.8	63,066	74,077	7.3
500 or more	253	173,405	5,890,217	74.1	128,498	149,353	8.0
Investor-owned (for-profit)	774	101,217	3,171,697	52.4	53,040	61,774	6.1
6–24 beds	24	470	13,378	37.2	175	211	4.7
25–49	104	3,990	110,959	38.5	1,535	1,891	5.0
50–99	223	16,662	525,241	46.6	7,771	9,212	5.3
100–199	276	38,440	1,200,384	51.0	19,603	23,140	5.9
200–299	104	24,647	801,620	56.7	13,968	15,966	6.4
300–399	26	9,007	271,152	59.0	5,313	6,039	7.2
400–499	13	5,520	165,115	57.0	3,144	3,572	7.0
500 or more	4	2,481	83,848	61.7	1,531	1,743	6.7
Local government	1,486	160,785	5,155,155	61.1	98,163	120,055	6.9
6–24 beds	105	2,035	45,724	32.0	652	903	5.2
25–49	451	16,766	439,778	38.3	6,425	8,138	5.3
50–99	487	34,298	963,297	51.2	17,552	21,717	6.6
100–199	257	35,884	1,086,268	62.0	22,238	27,031	7.5
200–299	88	21,427	806,634	66.2	14,179	17,109	6.4
300–399	40	13,881	535,735	69.4	9,627	12,112	6.6
400–499	20	8,955	318,307	69.0	6,182	7,523	7.1
500 or more	38	27,539	959,412	77.4	21,308	25,522	8.1
State government	111	27,353	874,669	71.5	19,556	23,885	8.2
6–24 beds	11	179	3,540	30.2	54	174	5.7
25–49	23	785	15,760	41.1	323	524	7.6
50–99	15	1,091	29,131	51.2	559	838	7.0
100–199	16	2,245	77,204	64.3	1,444	1,873	6.9
200–299	8	2,056	72,050	69.0	1,418	1,891	7.2
300–399	11	3,874	127,753	75.8	2,936	3,559	8.4
400–499	7	3,102	115,630	75.7	2,349	2,783	7.4
500 or more	20	14,021	433,601	74.7	10,473	12,243	8.8
Federal government	305	83,642	1,961,479	74.3	62,160		
6–24 beds	28	509	27,435	51.3	261		
25–49	60	2,082	102,774	53.9	1,123		
50–99	37	2,367	120,270	59.0	1,397		
100–199	45	6,705	257,533	68.6	4,600		
200–299	33	7,591	196,863	72.4	5,496		
300–399	23	8,367	213,821	71.9	6,020		
400–499	26	11,249	251,614	77.9	8,762		
500 or more	53	44,772	791,169	77.1	34,501		

| | | Newborns | | | Expenses (In thousands of dollars) | | | |
| | | | | | Labor | | | |
Surgical operations	Outpatient visits	Bassinets	Births	FTE personnel	Payroll	Employee benefits	Total	Total
21,134,071	274,605,612	77,168	3,629,696	3,301,063	$67,812,016	$12,479,591	$80,291,607	$142,953,926
20,813,025	269,495,259	76,142	3,563,616	3,200,593	65,755,232	12,055,581	77,810,813	138,683,101
14,952,559	157,641,349	50,776	2,459,932	2,179,473	44,409,794	8,410,499	52,820,293	94,425,207
14,580	774,292	250	3,290	3,381	67,942	12,687	80,629	132,278
167,223	3,408,030	1,891	36,317	30,779	514,116	88,620	602,736	1,112,932
753,531	10,003,695	4,330	126,790	105,807	1,875,487	337,804	2,213,291	4,036,776
2,501,852	28,290,278	9,197	365,356	320,805	6,158,309	1,120,488	7,278,797	13,354,038
2,964,494	31,438,137	9,464	446,234	391,699	8,011,427	1,498,339	9,509,766	17,067,971
2,890,387	26,819,056	9,065	482,002	393,724	8,110,537	1,506,325	9,616,862	17,178,709
1,964,280	19,320,973	6,297	354,266	299,103	6,208,415	1,175,910	7,384,325	13,063,175
3,696,212	37,586,888	10,282	645,677	634,175	13,463,561	2,670,326	16,133,887	28,479,329
1,938,387	12,123,709	5,745	248,276	215,295	4,237,633	831,319	5,068,952	11,217,188
5,640	56,737	60	782	929	12,661	2,576	15,237	31,580
48,581	559,777	294	6,794	7,585	122,710	22,667	145,377	303,961
292,327	2,224,754	1,168	39,355	35,171	630,390	127,318	757,707	1,702,663
743,664	4,750,201	2,176	91,183	78,940	1,520,735	296,806	1,817,541	4,111,886
511,707	2,840,957	1,235	64,110	54,158	1,115,272	216,107	1,331,379	2,893,307
184,142	857,304	384	19,061	20,164	451,869	90,662	542,531	1,184,883
95,860	477,438	303	16,957	11,739	223,708	44,546	268,255	596,533
56,466	356,541	125	10,034	6,609	160,288	30,637	190,925	392,375
2,457,544	37,617,819	15,677	633,277	441,588	8,448,283	1,686,670	10,134,954	17,697,588
11,820	366,474	387	4,660	4,066	56,788	9,762	66,550	119,711
129,983	2,598,454	2,393	39,274	30,630	478,247	81,927	560,174	1,005,839
401,904	5,804,490	3,771	98,668	69,150	1,121,544	198,895	1,320,439	2,383,526
545,435	6,390,605	3,378	124,481	82,383	1,416,033	261,194	1,677,228	3,024,532
486,934	4,679,703	1,974	95,463	62,838	1,212,935	246,545	1,459,481	2,599,583
306,338	4,989,492	1,087	79,594	52,460	1,122,925	238,035	1,360,960	2,367,067
186,357	2,875,406	613	42,484	33,533	689,590	128,064	817,654	1,408,151
388,773	9,913,195	2,074	148,653	106,528	2,350,220	522,248	2,872,468	4,789,179
536,790	12,190,355	1,675	113,731	110,134	2,239,781	499,315	2,739,096	4,867,174
3,208	424,402	7	206	627	8,882	1,474	10,356	13,562
11,191	771,964	24	258	1,642	30,524	5,227	35,751	50,764
26,075	844,143	83	3,678	2,376	46,056	10,350	56,406	94,415
59,863	1,003,516	203	11,211	5,430	97,932	20,568	118,501	205,428
47,741	1,565,639	121	10,646	8,114	163,417	33,138	196,555	366,279
67,921	1,388,243	239	18,763	18,441	417,276	96,015	513,291	869,514
51,389	1,275,701	228	17,571	13,925	288,206	65,857	354,063	630,742
269,402	4,916,747	770	51,398	59,579	1,187,489	266,685	1,454,174	2,636,470
927,745	49,922,027	2,269	108,400	254,103	6,419,740	627,777	7,047,518	10,475,943
11,498	1,612,039	107	3,136	3,737	37,160	4,773	41,933	69,591
37,559	5,618,599	429	14,858	13,226	263,533	18,727	282,260	372,464
64,625	5,863,687	489	19,748	15,359	356,480	32,474	388,954	549,277
139,765	10,497,153	587	27,779	30,115	773,865	52,782	826,648	1,158,243
107,494	4,476,475	206	12,150	22,480	538,386	49,113	587,500	904,428
107,676	5,105,596	176	9,463	25,817	745,377	71,918	817,295	1,272,041
108,636	5,169,831	47	3,955	33,036	810,000	97,053	907,054	1,431,993
350,492	11,578,647	228	17,311	110,333	2,894,939	300,937	3,195,876	4,717,906

Table 12-1. (*continued*)

Classification	Hospitals	Beds	Admissions	Occupancy, percent	Average daily census	Adjusted average daily census	Avg. stay, days
PSYCHIATRIC	246	23,559	286,803	75.4	17,754		
Nongovernment not-for-profit	60	4,887	61,296	73.5	3,592		
6–24 beds	4	83	1,878	84.3	70		
25–49	14	529	8,928	73.7	390		
50–99	29	2,143	23,915	69.1	1,480		
100–199	11	1,554	20,732	79.0	1,228		
200–299	1	196	2,500	96.9	190		
300–399	1	382	3,343	61.3	234		
Investor-owned (for-profit)	152	11,934	138,768	68.8	8,207		
6–24 beds	4	71	791	63.4	45		
25–49	29	1,036	14,866	67.4	698		
50–99	83	6,017	71,116	68.4	4,116		
100–199	33	4,160	45,094	70.7	2,940		
200–299	3	650	6,901	62.8	408		
Local government	9	2,249	27,181	90.1	2,027		
25–49 beds	1	34	927	64.7	22		
50–99	4	330	16,264	87.9	290		
200–299	2	558	2,107	88.2	492		
400–499	1	439	1,715	96.4	423		
500 or more	1	888	6,168	90.1	800		
State government	25	4,489	59,558	87.5	3,928		
25–49 beds	3	112	1,446	91.1	102		
50–99	5	358	4,727	85.2	305		
100–199	6	823	9,882	89.8	739		
200–299	8	2,006	29,096	90.9	1,823		
300–399	2	731	8,407	68.4	500		
500 or more	1	459	6,000	100.0	459		
TB AND OTHER RESPIRATORY DISEASES	2	275	2,761	63.6	175		
State government	2	275	2,761	63.6	175		
100–199 beds	2	275	2,761	63.6	175		
ALL OTHER	153	17,790	438,396	65.9	11,732		
Nongovernment not-for-profit	102	10,843	312,059	69.0	7,479		
6–24 beds	4	63	2,040	47.6	30		
25–49	24	850	17,772	55.3	470		
50–99	35	2,440	44,798	59.9	1,462		
100–199	26	3,498	117,902	63.6	2,223		
200–299	7	1,558	60,168	78.9	1,230		
300–399	4	1,306	50,741	81.1	1,059		
500 or more	2	1,128	18,638	89.1	1,005		
Investor-owned (for profit)	31	2,704	69,823	41.6	1,126		
6–24 beds	5	63	3,121	20.6	13		
25–49	5	192	7,978	39.1	75		
50–99	10	779	17,164	48.9	381		
100–199	9	1,248	30,429	40.5	506		
200–299	2	422	11,131	35.8	151		

| | | Newborns | | | Expenses (In thousands of dollars) | | | |
| | | | | | | Labor | | |
Surgical operations	Outpatient visits	Bassinets	Births	FTE personnel	Payroll	Employee benefits	Total	Total
1,261	1,755,312	0	0	40,740	823,639	173,156	996,795	1,612,877
374	632,380	0	0	10,166	200,657	41,584	242,241	384,152
0	96,191	0	0	438	6,654	1,380	8,033	12,933
8	212,689	0	0	1,504	25,780	4,596	30,376	46,055
345	109,498	0	0	3,576	69,399	14,216	83,615	137,574
21	83,273	0	0	2,880	61,452	11,475	72,927	114,817
0	130,268	0	0	1,362	29,174	8,445	37,619	55,307
0	461	0	0	406	8,198	1,472	9,670	17,466
883	480,888	0	0	18,194	390,073	83,289	473,363	842,058
1	9,507	0	0	118	2,451	537	2,988	5,507
18	45,592	0	0	1,636	35,243	7,452	42,695	78,235
92	301,070	0	0	9,247	195,236	39,682	234,918	414,528
772	121,815	0	0	6,310	137,128	30,102	167,230	301,653
0	2,904	0	0	883	20,016	5,517	25,533	42,134
0	328,240	0	0	3,230	66,380	18,437	84,817	122,276
0	9,012	0	0	77	1,092	160	1,252	2,144
0	115,823	0	0	757	16,865	3,755	20,620	31,986
0	13,258	0	0	567	10,471	2,848	13,319	16,653
0	37,950	0	0	450	8,937	2,405	11,342	15,342
0	152,197	0	0	1,379	29,015	9,268	38,283	56,150
4	313,804	0	0	9,150	166,528	29,847	196,375	264,391
0	115,955	0	0	713	15,955	2,606	18,561	24,622
4	46,752	0	0	837	15,539	1,916	17,456	25,035
0	51,901	0	0	1,666	32,353	4,333	36,685	48,215
0	76,085	0	0	3,730	67,210	11,888	79,098	107,651
0	23,111	0	0	1,458	21,181	5,671	26,852	33,631
0	0	0	0	746	14,291	3,432	17,723	25,237
1,487	17,533	0	0	554	11,654	3,315	14,969	22,657
1,487	17,533	0	0	554	11,654	3,315	14,969	22,657
1,487	17,533	0	0	554	11,654	3,315	14,969	22,657
318,298	3,337,508	1,026	66,080	59,176	1,221,490	247,539	1,469,029	2,635,291
231,434	2,360,493	654	47,517	37,658	832,071	167,144	999,215	1,813,341
946	21,904	44	361	197	4,123	681	4,803	8,072
13,877	243,751	24	1,343	3,647	64,649	11,587	76,236	136,011
29,925	476,322	42	1,464	7,725	149,665	25,601	175,266	311,957
116,092	905,046	90	8,202	12,015	262,540	53,299	315,839	577,692
35,406	287,947	249	21,612	6,040	144,796	30,013	174,809	297,051
24,013	277,182	205	14,535	4,908	91,566	18,016	109,582	211,858
11,175	148,341	0	0	3,126	114,732	27,947	142,679	270,700
64,316	253,838	372	18,563	5,524	100,751	20,219	120,970	269,041
7,324	44,396	0	0	234	3,246	672	3,918	7,976
9,846	76,093	40	1,719	511	10,024	1,717	11,741	21,882
12,349	37,581	69	3,275	1,426	25,467	4,917	30,384	66,794
26,968	82,239	205	7,734	2,391	45,926	9,762	55,688	130,580
7,829	13,529	58	5,835	962	16,088	3,152	19,240	41,809

Table 12-1. (continued)

Classification	Hospitals	Beds	Admissions	Occu-pancy, percent	Average daily census	Adjusted average daily census	Avg. stay, days
Local government	7	1,730	9,205	80.2	1,388		
50–99 beds	1	54	955	48.1	26		
100–199	3	398	4,797	65.8	262		
300–399	2	652	2,467	79.1	516		
500 or more	1	626	986	93.3	584		
State government	11	1,543	32,195	68.4	1,055		
25–49 beds	4	134	1,378	47.0	63		
50–99	3	229	2,857	51.1	117		
100–199	1	159	1,048	81.1	129		
200–299	2	514	12,546	63.8	328		
500 or more	1	507	14,366	82.4	418		
Federal government	2	970	15,114	70.5	684		
400–499 beds	2	970	15,114	70.5	684		

SOURCE: American Hospital Association. © 1986. *Hospital Statistics, 1986 Edition.* Chicago: American Hospital Association. Reprinted by permission.

individuals. They are run in order to make a profit. These hospitals tend to be smaller than voluntary or government hospitals. They avoid unprofitable services in favor of profitable ones. Moreover, all of the revenue for the operation of these proprietary hospitals is patient-generated. This makes the flow of incoming patients based on the referral system the *major* concern of such hospitals. In the mid 1980s there were about 1,000 proprietary hospitals in the United States.

HOSPITAL TYPES. In addition to the three major categories of hospital ownership, there are two major types of hospitals: general and specialty. *General* hospitals (or medical or surgical hospitals, as they are sometimes called) provide a full range of general and specialty services to their patients. *Specialty* hospitals are organized around and limited to the treatment of one particular set of problems, such as obstetrics and gynecology, psychiatry, or tuberculosis. Approximately 95 percent of all voluntary and 85 percent of all proprietary hospitals are general ones. This contrasts with less than half of all government hospitals.

The differences in hospitals may be seen in Table 12-1. It breaks down utilization, personnel, and financial considerations according to the different types and ownership modes of the nation's 6,339 short-term hospitals in 1985. In these hospitals the average length of stay is less than 30 days, or half of the patients stay 30 days or less. Short-term hospitals are what we usually think of when we talk about hospitals (see Anderson and Gevitz, 1983). As indicated, these hospitals have more than 1.1 million beds, about two thirds of which are filled at any given time. Moreover, they provide about 275 million outpatient visits each year. Thus, the short-term hospital has clearly become the center of the health care delivery system. To provide this care these hospitals employ about 3.3 million persons and require nearly $143 billion to cover their expenses. Voluntary, general hospitals bear the brunt of this utilization. They provide two thirds of the beds, admissions, surgical operations, and newborn facilities. They also provide more than half of all outpatient facilities. In essence, the voluntary, general, short-term hospital has become the backbone of the American health care delivery system.

Surgical operations	Outpatient visits	Newborns		FTE personnel	Expenses (In thousands of dollars)			
					Labor			
		Bassinets	Births		Payroll	Employee benefits	Total	Total
1,374	66,913	0	0	2,524	47,015	11,150	58,165	93,856
718	10,836	0	0	257	4,899	827	5,727	9,943
0	34,343	0	0	799	16,155	3,847	20,003	30,931
368	9,271	0	0	905	13,721	2,632	16,353	25,317
288	12,463	0	0	563	12,239	3,843	16,082	27,665
17,361	518,933	0	0	10,507	171,409	36,868	208,277	316,385
583	29,740	0	0	480	8,580	1,176	9,756	15,473
833	51,643	0	0	1,021	16,903	3,445	20,348	32,843
871	24,703	0	0	531	10,100	1,160	11,260	13,467
8,316	84,963	0	0	2,507	44,197	7,137	51,334	85,064
6,758	327,884	0	0	5,968	91,629	23,950	115,579	169,539
3,813	137,331	0	0	2,963	70,244	12,158	82,402	142,668
3,813	137,331	0	0	2,963	70,244	12,158	82,402	142,668

HOSPITAL SIZE. As Table 12-1 indicates, hospitals also come in different sizes. Indeed, they range from 6 beds (the minimum number of beds necessary to meet the standards for a hospital established by the American Hospital Association) to more than 500 beds. Several teaching hospitals even have more than 1,000 beds. There are two reasons why size is an important distinction to be made in any discussion of hospitals. First, the larger the size of a community hospital, the more services it is likely to be able to provide. Table 12-2 shows the relationship between bed size and the percent of community hospitals offering selected services. For the most essential services (i.e., emergency rooms) there is very little difference between hospital size and the likelihood of providing the service. For more specialized and costly services (such as cardiac catheterization), however, the likelihood of having such services is directly related to hospital size. The larger the hospital, the more likely such services will be available.

The second reason why size is important in discussing hospitals is its relationship to cost. Cost is usually measured in terms of adjusted expenses per patient day. Table 12-3 shows such costs by bed size for community hospitals during 1984 and 1985. As indicated, although larger hospitals may provide a greater mix of services to their patients, they are able to do this only at considerably higher costs. In fact, the average adjusted expense per patient day in the largest hospitals is more than a third again as high as it is in the smallest hospitals. This raises the question of what size hospital is optimal. According to some health economists (including Fuchs, 1974), the most efficient size is in the 200 to 500 bed range. Other health economists (including Feldstein, 1983), however, argue that economies of scale disappear after hospitals pass the 200 bed size.

HOSPITAL ORGANIZATION. Just as hospitals come in different sizes, types, and modes of ownership, each has its own unique organizational structure. There is, however, one theme common to the organization of hospitals. They are designed for efficiency and ease of operation, not for patient comfort or patient amenities. Because the major goal of the hospital is to provide medical treatment,

Table 12-2. *Percent of hospitals having selected services during 1984, by hospital size.*

Type of service	Size of hospital (beds)							
	6–24	25–49	50–99	100–199	200–299	300–399	400–499	500 or more
Ambulatory surgery	60.8	73.0	77.9	86.3	91.0	88.8	86.0	73.0
Ultrasound	28.6	51.9	68.4	83.4	89.9	91.3	88.5	76.1
Cardiac catheterization	0.5	0.2	0.7	6.1	23.0	45.2	57.3	64.4
Physical therapy	43.8	70.9	84.8	91.1	94.9	98.8	97.8	97.3
Social work	28.6	50.1	79.1	92.4	97.6	99.0	99.7	100.0
Premature nursery	1.8	3.5	10.8	22.5	40.3	56.8	59.6	55.1
Hemodialysis	0.5	1.0	4.5	17.1	41.2	58.2	70.7	65.1
CT scanners	0.9	5.4	18.4	45.6	74.0	84.6	84.1	69.0
Emergency department	85.7	87.3	84.3	86.2	90.0	89.5	86.0	74.2
Open-heart surgery	0.0	0.0	0.2	2.9	11.7	28.2	38.9	53.8
Chemical dependency program	9.2	8.5	9.8	15.7	21.6	28.0	37.9	42.6
Health promotion	27.6	25.5	33.5	49.1	61.7	69.8	70.7	66.1

SOURCE: Adapted from American Hospital Association. © 1985. *Hospital Statistics, 1985 Edition.* Chicago: Author. Reprinted by permission.

Table 12-3. *Adjusted expenses per inpatient day in community hospitals during 1984 and 1985.*

Hospital size	Adjusted expense per patient day		Percent change
	1984	1985	
All community hospitals	$411	$460	12.0
Bed-size categories			
6–24 beds	347	380	9.6
25–49	339	379	11.7
50–99	323	363	12.4
100–199	362	402	11.1
200–299	398	449	12.8
300–399	433	484	11.8
400–499	434	489	12.6
500 or more	468	527	12.5

SOURCE: Adapted from American Hospital Association. © 1986. *Hospital Statistics, 1986 Edition.* Chicago: Author. Used by permission.

hospitals are organized to facilitate the provision of that medical care. Although varied in particulars, hospital organization *is* rather uniform (see Croog and VerSteeg, 1972; Georgopoulos and Mann, 1962; Coe, 1978; Wilson, 1970). As a result, the typical large (200 to 500 bed) general, short-term, voluntary hospital, which is what we usually think of when we think of a hospital (see Anderson and Gevitz, 1983), is usually organized in a fashion similar to that portrayed by the chart in Figure 12-1. The chart shows five major divisions within the hospital. They represent the very specialized and interdependent division of labor,

and the direct (solid) and indirect (broken) lines of authority associated with them. As indicated, there are quite formal patterns of authority. Within each division there is a vertical stratification system. The higher up one is within it, the more power one has. Each of these divisions is fairly autonomous, although each is ultimately responsible to someone.

You may have noticed, however, that there are really two large entities in the hospital structure. One is the medical division (primarily the physicians), and the other is the administrative or support divisions (everyone else). Given the special nature of

Figure 12-1. *An Organizational Chart of a Typical, Large General Hospital.*

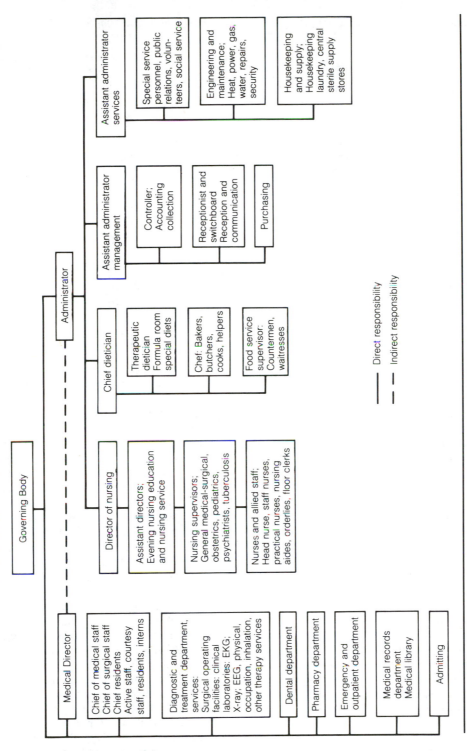

SOURCE: Department of Labor. 1967. *Technology and Manpower in the Health Service Industry.* Washington, D.C.: Government Printing Office.

Table 12-4. *Trends in the utilization of short-term, general hospitals, 1946 to 1985.*

Year	Hospitals	Beds (in thousands)	Admissions (in thousands)	Average daily census (in thousands)
1946	4,444	473	13,655	341
1950	5,031	505	16,663	372
1955	5,237	568	19,100	407
1960	5,407	639	22,970	477
1965	5,736	741	26,463	563
1970	5,859	848	29,252	662
1971	5,865	867	30,142	665
1972	5,843	884	30,777	664
1973	5,891	903	31,761	681
1974	5,977	931	32,943	701
1975	5,979	947	33,519	708
1976	5,956	961	34,068	715
1977	5,973	974	34,353	717
1978	5,935	980	34,575	720
1979	5,923	988	35,160	729
1980	5,904	992	36,198	748
1981	5,879	1,007	36,494	764
1982	5,863	1,015	36,429	763
1983	5,843	1,021	36,201	750
1984	5,814	1,020	35,202	703
1985	5,784	1,003	33,501	650

SOURCE: Adapted from American Hospital Association. © 1986. *Hospital Statistics, 1986 Edition.* Chicago: Author.

the profession of medicine, the organizational structure of hospitals takes on nontraditional bureaucratic qualities that we shall discuss later on in this chapter. For the moment we shall limit our discussion of hospital organization to the typical pattern of the five divisions. Each has its own departments. They are all operationalized (or interrelated) through a codified system of rules, regulations, and administrative procedures. The purpose behind all of this bureaucratic formalization is the efficient provision of medical treatment to patients.

HOSPITAL UTILIZATION. Like the characteristics of American hospitals, their utilization also varies. In chapter 6 we saw that the number of hospital admissions per 100 persons has more than doubled since the 1920s and 1930s. Table 12-4 details how hospital utilization has changed for nonfederal, short-term hospitals between 1946 and 1985. As indicated, the number of general admissions has risen from about 14 million to more than 33 million. Moreover, the number of outpatient visits has increased from less

than 92 million to more than 222 million. The bulk of this increase in outpatient hospital utilization has been due to the increased use of the emergency room. Clearly, the use of the hospital has been increasing and changing throughout this century.

Turning back to Table 12-1 we can see that the type of hospital service provided and used varies by the other characteristics of the hospital. For example, of the 275 million outpatient visits that took place in short-term hospitals during 1985, more than 98 percent occurred in general hospitals. Occupancy figures indicate that although the overall average rate for short-term hospitals was 65.5 percent, this varied remarkably by the size of the hospital. The rates range from 35.7 percent among the smallest voluntary hospitals to 74.1 percent among the largest voluntary hospitals. Length of stay also varies by hospital size. In the smallest voluntary hospitals the average stay was 4.8 days; this compares to 8.0 days in the largest voluntary hospitals. Although it is not easy to straightforwardly interpret these differences without knowing

Adjusted average daily census (in thousands)	Occupancy (percent)	Average length of stay (days)	Outpatient visits (in thousands)	Births
	72.1	9.1		2,087,503
	73.7	8.1		2,660,982
	71.5	7.8		3,304,451
	74.7	7.6		3,678,051
620	76.0	7.8	92,631	3,413,370
727	78.0	8.2	133,545	3,403,064
736	76.7	8.0	148,423	3,337,605
739	75.2	7.9	166,983	3,119,446
768	75.4	7.8	178,939	2,987,089
793	75.3	7.8	194,838	2,947,342
806	74.8	7.7	196,311	2,998,590
816	74.4	7.7	207,725	2,962,305
820	73.6	7.6	204,238	3,111,756
825	73.5	7.6	204,461	3,156,570
841	73.8	7.6	203,873	3,287,157
861	75.4	7.6	206,752	3,408,699
876	75.9	7.6	206,729	3,465,683
882	75.2	7.6	250,888	3,514,761
869	73.4	7.6	213,995	3,490,629
824	68.9	7.3	216,474	3,456,467
780	64.8	7.1	222,773	3,521,296

more about each hospital, the point to be made is that hospital utilization varies by the type, size, nature, and ownership of the hospital.

HOSPITAL COSTS. Almost every American can agree on one thing when discussing hospitals—using them is expensive. Indeed, hospital costs account for over 60 percent of all health insurance claims. On average, the daily charge per patient day in community hospitals during 1985 was $460 (American Hospital Association, 1986). This is an extraordinary increase from the $40 average daily charge in 1965, and the $135 average daily charge in 1975. Indeed, over the last two decades hospital costs have grown more than 10-fold. What is it that makes hospitals cost so much and those costs increase so fast? To understand that question we must first look at the simple equation for hospital costs. Most health economists agree that:

Total Hospital Costs = Admissions × Length of Stay × Cost per Patient Day

Accordingly, to alter total hospital costs one needs to alter one or more of the three components that define them. Let us first consider admissions. We have already seen that admissions have more than doubled during this century. This would only have accounted for a doubling in hospital costs if the other two components had remained unchanged. Therefore, the rising total cost of hospitalization is not likely due to the doubling of admissions. A second possibility is changes in length of stay. But length of stay in hospitals has not changed dramatically during this century. In fact, where length of stay has changed, it has generally decreased as a result of experimental "shorter stay" programs such as the Prospective Payment System now used in Medicare, which will be discussed at length in chapter 13. Therefore, length of stay is probably not the cause of increasing hospital costs either. This leaves the cost per patient day as the major culprit. We have already seen that it has increased more than 10-fold between 1965 and 1985.

Why has the cost per patient day increased so much? Government studies (see Department of Health, Education, and Welfare, 1975) suggest that four factors are involved. These include additional staff, higher prices, wage increases, and other changes. Fifteen percent of the increased cost is due to hiring additional staff members to meet the increased demand for hospital services. Sixteen percent of the increase is attributed to higher prices for goods and services (non–wage-related) that the hospital consumes in providing medical care. Thirty-six percent of the growth in costs is due to increases in salaries and wages paid to hospital employees. The remainder, fully one third of the increase in costs, is charged to new equipment and more extensive patient care. That is, one third of the increase is due to the fact that patients are getting more care—especially more sophisticated, technological care—than ever before. This reflects the tendency of physicians to use and order more tests and laboratory equipment for diagnosis and treatment. These procedures have become very expensive, ballooning the daily per patient hospital cost. An additional factor can be identified at the societal level. There is a general sentiment that greater health care expenditures mean better health care. This has encouraged an escalating cycle of hospital cost increases.

To illustrate the costs involved, Table 12-5 contains the summary billing statement for an episode that occurred in a 175-bed hospital in the Southwest during 1986. The patient was a 34-year-old white female with endometriosis, a common cause of infertility among professional women. Surgery was performed (a laparotomy using laser techniques), and the patient stayed in the hospital five days. The total hospital charges came to $3,576. This included $182 a day for a private room (semiprivate rooms at this hospital are $15 a day less), and $750 for the use of the operating room. The remainder of the charges are for "ancillary services" such as supplies, laboratory tests, and medications. Thus, more than half of this hospital bill was for ancillaries over and above the regular room rate. Moreover, the $3,576 hospital bill does not include the primary surgeon's fee ($2,015), the assisting

Table 12-5. *Summary billing statement for a 1986 hospital episode involving endometriosis.*

Item category	Charge
Private room (5 days)	$910
Operating room use (2.5 hours)	750
Recovery room use (1.0 hours)	96
Lab fees	281
Radiology	58
Anesthesiology supplies	310
Pharmaceutical supplies	382
Respiration therapy	61
Surgical pathology	160
Admission kit	19
Hematology workup	45
Central supplies	175
Surgical supplies	47
Medical supplies	49
Orthopedic supplies	19
Intravenous solutions	193
Dressings	9
Telephone and television	12
Total	$3,576

surgeon's fee ($441), the anesthesiologist's fee ($561), or the pathologist's fee ($105). The total cost of this five-day hospital episode, then, comes to $6,698. And this amount falls within most insurance companies' "usual, customary, and reasonable" charge guidelines.

The Emergence of Multihospital Systems

Having described and considered the distribution of hospitals, we may now turn to the emergence of hospital systems. According to Ermann and Gabel (1984), hospital systems may be defined as "three or more hospitals owned, or managed by a single organization." The rapid growth of hospital systems during the 1970s and 1980s has led to much debate over the coming of the "medical industrial complex" (see Relman, 1980), the "corporatization of health care" (see Starr, 1982), and the future of the freestanding (i.e., unaffiliated) single hospital (see Schulz and Johnson, 1983). Although more than 500 articles have been published on these topics in the last decade, there remains little agreement on what the trend toward multihospital systems actually means for the health care delivery system (see Ermann and Gabel, 1985). Therefore, to understand more about multihospital systems we must consider their anticipated benefits, stages of development, distribution and growth, and performance.

ANTICIPATED BENEFITS. Underlying the growth of multihospital systems is the belief in their anticipated benefits. Schulz and Johnson (1983) identify six reasons why multihospital systems seem so attractive: (1) economies of scale, especially through group purchasing; (2) the reallocation of marginal services, which reduces losses at one or more institutions at the same time that such consolidation increases the volume of services provided at other institutions; (3) reduced capital needs; (4) enhanced ability to recruit qualified personnel and negotiate more effectively, including collusive behavior in employee compensa-

tion; (5) opportunities for the survival of small rural hospitals; and (6) a means for improving the quality of health care. For the most part, Schulz and Johnson's reasons focus on the benefits that accrue to the hospital. Zuckerman (1979) provides a more detailed summary of the benefits that accrue from multihospital systems at three levels—economic, manpower, and organizational—for both the hospital and the community. His cross-classification of the type and level of benefits is shown in Table 12-6. According to Zuckerman, the principal benefits to the community include lower prices, reduced duplication and excess facilities, better resource allocation, better management expertise, and improved access to and more comprehensive health services.

STAGES OF DEVELOPMENT. Multihospital systems seldom develop overnight. Rather, there is usually some evolutionary process

Table 12-6. *A summary of anticipated benefits of multihospital systems to both the institution and the community.*

Type of benefit	Level of benefit	
	Institution	Community
Economic	Cost savings via economies of scale. Operating advantages: increased productivity, improved utilization of resource capacity, lower staffing requirements, reduced unit costs from joint activities. Financial advantages: access to capital markets, improved credit standing, reduced borrowing costs.	Lower prices. Reduced duplication and excess capacity of facilities. Improved resource allocation.
Manpower	Improved recruitment of clinical and management manpower. Improved retention of clinical and management manpower. Strong clinical and management capability.	Greater access to and availability of breadth and depth of clinical and management manpower. Improved distribution of health manpower.
Organizational	Organizational growth: extend referral networks, penetrate new markets, expand existing markets. Organizational survival: financial improvements, accreditation standards. Greater political power.	Improved access to care. Increased availability of services. Broader, more comprehensive scope of services.

SOURCE: Adapted from Howard Zuckerman. 1979. "Multi-Institutional Hospital Systems." *Inquiry* 16:289–302. Reprinted by permission of the publisher. All rights reserved.

that results in a gradual shift from free-standing hospitals to an integrated system. Barrett (1979) has proposed a developmental theory of multihospital systems that involves three stages. The first is the building or establishment stage. In it the "prime mover" behind the push for the multihospital system initiates the process. This typically involves a more external or environmental (in the organizational sense) focus of activities. The prime mover is usually one hospital, although it may be an outside force such as the state legislature. The solidifying stage is characterized by internal or organizational work. In it the chief executive officer (CEO) of the hospital prepares the way for the merger and finalizes the arrangements. The selling or legitimizing stage occurs when the multihospital system becomes comfortable with its internal configuration and turns toward marketing itself to potential buyers of its services.

Not all analysts of multihospital systems, however, agree with Barrett's (1979) model. Starkweather (1971), for example, considers the development of multihospital systems to be far more complex. He identifies seven dimensions on which health care facilities can be combined and a continuum from pluralism to fusion along which each of them may be located. The resulting cross-classification shows how multihospital systems can be formed by the vertical, horizontal, or regional integration of facilities. It also indicates that the degree of integration may vary from shared services or joint undertakings to formal mergers and consolidation. Unfortunately, at the same time that Starkweather's model more accurately portrays the manifold possibilities for the development of multihospital systems, it underscores how different they may be and how those differences may account for their varied performance.

DISTRIBUTION AND GROWTH. Although multihospital systems have existed for quite some time (note that the Veterans Administration represents one of the largest multihospital systems with its 174 medical centers), it is only in the last decade or so that they have become an important issue in the delivery of health care (see Arrington, 1985; Ermann

and Gabel, 1984, 1985). In 1975 there were 202 multihospital systems involving 1,405 hospitals and 293,000 hospital beds. This amounted to about 25 percent of all community hospitals and beds in the United States. By 1985 there were over 250 multihospital systems involving almost 2,000 hospitals and over 360,000 beds (Ermann and Gabel, 1985). Included in these figures are one third of all community hospitals. The hospitals in multihospital systems fall roughly into three major categories. About 40 percent of them are involved in investor-owned or for-profit systems. Another 35 percent of the hospitals are involved in systems owned and operated by religious groups, such as the Sisters of Mercy. The remainder, about one fourth of the total, involve voluntary and city hospitals.

Although there is a wide range in terms of the size of these multihospital systems, a substantial number of hospitals are now owned or operated by the three largest, national, for-profit chains: the Hospital Corporation of America (HCA), Humana Hospital Corporation (Humana), and American Medical International (AMI). Indeed, HCA alone owns or manages about 350 community hospitals, 25 international hospitals, and 25 psychiatric hospitals. Moreover, it owns about one fifth of Beverly Enterprises, which is the largest chain of nursing home facilities. In 1985 HCA grossed over $4 billion. It is the potential impact of the large, for-profit systems like HCA, Humana, and AMI that concerns the critics of the multihospital system movement (see especially Relman, 1980; Starr, 1982). They fear that this corporatization of hospitals marks a major philosophical shift from the collectivity notion traditionally underlying health care to a more business and profit orientation. For them this shift portends a decline in both the integrity and quality of American health care. In essence, they fear that the for-profit hospital chains replace the "caring" component of health care with a "business" component, and that this is bad for the patient, the doctor, and society as a whole.

PERFORMANCE. At present there are no definitive studies on the performance of multi-

hospital systems. Although more than 40 empirical assessments have been published, each is limited by different factors (see Arrington, 1985). Even when taken together, they fail to provide a clear answer. Nonetheless, Zuckerman (1979) argues that three observations can be made. First, although the economic benefits at the institutional level appear uncertain depending on which study is considered, there is *no* evidence that multihospital systems provide economic benefits (lower prices, better access, and so on) to the community. Second, there is some evidence to suggest that multihospital systems do improve the recruitment and retention of personnel. Third, there is evidence that demonstrates the organizational benefits of multihospital systems to the institution.

Beyond these statements, however, it remains unclear exactly what effect multihospital systems will have on the institutions involved and their communities. Much more research is needed, especially in terms of how different organizational configurations affect performance (for several interesting yet preliminary studies in this vein, see Alexander and Fennell, 1986; Alexander, Anderson, and Lewis, 1985; Alexander, Morrisey, and Shortell, 1986; and Morlock, Alexander, and Hunter, 1985). For the time being, further discussion of the performance of multihospital systems is premature. All that can safely be said is that the trend toward multihospital systems will continue, there will be more vertical integration within them, and the debate on whether they constitute a violation of the anti-trust laws will intensify (see Zuckerman, 1981).

The Social Organization of the Modern Hospital

As indicated above, the modern American hospital system, if indeed there is such a system, is quite heterogeneous. Nonetheless, there is a common perception of the modern hospital that usually comes to mind. It is the not-for-profit, private, short-stay, general hospital. There are more of these (about 3,400) than any other kind of hospital. More interesting than these physical details of the typical hospital, however, are its social details. Although the modern American hospital varies considerably in its physical characteristics, there is very little variation in its social organization. In fact, there are two characteristics that consistently emerge from analyses of the hospital: the existence of two lines of authority, and the new task and role expectations placed on the hospitalized patient.

Two Lines of Authority

Just like any other complex organizational entity, the hospital must have a formal authority structure and concomitant bureaucracy if it is to fulfill its charge with maximum efficiency. There is, however, something especially interesting and uniform about hospital bureaucracies and authority structures. Instead of having just one traditional line of authority, they have two. To understand how these came to be and how they affect efficient operations, we must examine several related aspects of the social organization of hospitals. These include traditional bureaucracies, the special case of the professions, the notion of an advisory bureaucracy, the plight of those caught between the two lines of authority, and historical changes in hospital domination.

TRADITIONAL BUREAUCRACIES. Every organization has a goal that it wants to achieve and a power structure designed to facilitate meeting that goal. The overall goal of the hospital is to provide medical care to its patients. In the process of achieving this goal, the hospital must perform a variety of other functions, because it, as Wilson (1970) notes, "is at once a business, a hotel, a university, a social services agency, and so on through the long list of functions [the hospital] is called on to perform. Hospitals resemble a business or factory in rapid flow of work, heavily practical emphasis on speedy results, and perhaps in the tangibility of desired outcome levels of wellness." In order to provide these functions as efficiently as possible, the hospital generally takes on the formal bureaucratic structure portrayed in Figure 12-1. Such formal bureaucratic structures represent the mechanism through

which the goals of the organization are achieved. This mechanism is a hierarchical arrangement of offices and positions designed for the rational coordination of tasks and roles. When completed, these tasks and roles fulfill the goals of the organization (see Weber, 1968).

The bureaucracy of the hospital is designed in a rational manner. The authority and responsibility of each office and position is clearly defined, and the interrelated or interdependent nature of all of the offices and positions is clearly spelled out. As a result, each of the five major divisions in Figure 12-1 is responsible for its particular aspect of the hospital's operation. Within each division tasks and roles are subdivided into departments. They are then specifically assigned to individuals. This allows each individual, who is a specialist at his or her assigned tasks and roles, to function as efficiently as possible. The authority linkage within and between departments and divisions allows for the most efficient overall operation of the hospital. In sum, the hospital's bureaucracy is rationally designed; each aspect of the hospital's operation is placed in the hands of those most qualified to handle it. As such, the bureaucratic structure of the hospital is reminiscent of the bureaucratic and hierarchical arrangement within traditional bureaucracies, such as the armed forces or any other large corporation.

Coe (1978; see also Christman and Counte, 1982), however, points to two major differences between the hospital's bureaucracy and that of the armed forces or big business. First, the hospital bureaucracy is much more horizontally differentiated (note the five divisions). It resembles more of a "comb" than the bureaucracies of other formal organizations. Those organizations more closely resemble "trees." Second, in the armed forces the lines of authority come from the top ranks directly *and* indirectly through all the lower ranks. In the hospital these lines of authority come down to the lower ranks only indirectly. This is especially true where non–patient contact roles are involved. For example, in Figure 12-1 there are no direct lines of authority from the governing body to the lower-level positions in any division except the medical di-

vision (where there is a great deal of patient contact). Thus, in the nonmedical divisions the line of authority from the hospital administrator reaches only to the division and department heads. The authority lines do not extend directly to subordinates within the departments. This is a very significant difference from the military bureaucracy. In it all personnel are directly responsible to the commander in chief.

THE SPECIAL CASE OF THE PROFESSIONS. As indicated above, the bureaucratic structure in Figure 12-1 does not tell the whole story of the social organization of the hospital. As Smith (1955) and many others have pointed out, there are two lines of authority within the hospital. The reason for their existence and the problems that they create is rooted in the nature of the professional autonomy conferred on physicians by society as a result of the "great trade" (see chapter 9). Wilson (1970) has eloquently summarized the problem of dual lines of authority and their continued existence:

Given the doctor's scientific and curative prestige and his legal responsibility for the patient's fate, it is perhaps understandable that he should also come to assume command over the organizational aspects of medical care. Yet, his administrative dominance . . . is clearly unrelated to his therapeutic knowledge. Indeed, one might argue persuasively that the physician's very absorption in clinical detail, his concentration on the individual as a closed system of biological events, tends to make him unfit for that interpersonal and structural purview that is the essence of the administration role. Nevertheless, the doctor has traditionally served as executive in medical institutions or at least as the power behind the layman or nurse who bore the formal executive title. . . . The basic problem of split authority remains. No lay administrator can effectively dictate the course of bedside action or intrude into general clinical management. And neither can the physician, increasingly often, seriously pretend to master hospital personnel policy or the coordination of diverse interdependent departments. Administrative and medical lines of authority coexist in varying degrees of harmony or unease.

In essence, the true social organization of the hospital may be more accurately portrayed by Figure 12-2. In it the medical staff

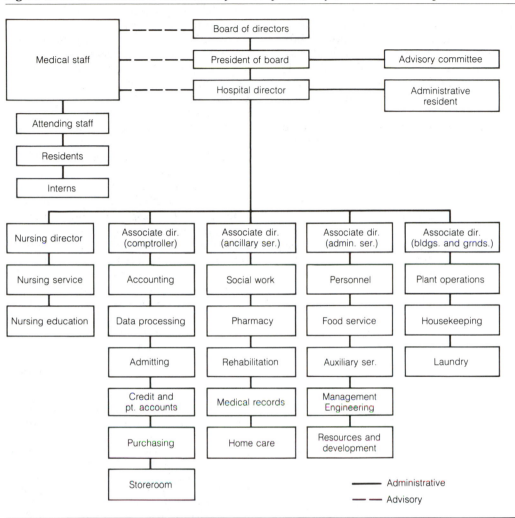

SOURCE: Rodney M. Coe. 1978. *Sociology of Medicine,* 2nd ed. New York: McGraw-Hill. Reprinted by permission of the publisher.

(i.e., physicians, who are primarily associated with the hospital only on a part-time basis when one of *their* patients is admitted) enjoys an exalted position of authority. This results from their prestige and ultimate responsibility for patients. The broken lines linking the medical staff with the board of directors, the board president, and the hospital director reflect the medical staff's indirect responsibility and authority. In the formal bureaucratic sense these physicians are subordinates to the board, the president, and the director. In the informal or practical sense, however, these physicians direct the board, the president, and the director (and all those below them) when it comes to medical matters. This informal line of authority is based on the physician's being *the* premier minister of health, as well as society's designated health care team captain.

What usually happens in the hospital is that the formal, bureaucratic authority structure serves as a framework for day-to-day operations. These day-to-day formal lines of responsibility are nullified or superseded when the physician must exercise informal authority for medical reasons. This occurs when the appropriate treatment of a patient necessitates exemption from the day-to-day rules in order to ensure the fulfillment of the hospital's ultimate goal, restoring health to the patient through the delivery of medical care. The effect of having the second line of authority is that whenever the physician deems it necessary (i.e., declares a "medical emergency"), the day-to-day formal bureaucratic structure of the hospital may be upset and temporarily replaced by the physician-dominated authority structure.

Having two lines of authority is justifiable. On the one hand, the hospital, like any other large organization, must have a bureaucratic structure in order to function efficiently and effectively. On the other hand, when a true "medical emergency" arises, everything else becomes secondary to meeting that emergency. Nonetheless, having two lines of authority raises basic conflicts and generates friction among hospital personnel. This is especially true when physicians perceive too many situations to be "medical emergencies." Such repeated requests for a suspension of the everyday rules suggest that physicians are abusing their privileged position (i.e., "throwing their weight around").

THE "ADVISORY BUREAUCRACY." The special case of the bureaucracy within the hospital has been labeled as a "collegial" bureaucracy combined with the traditional "administrative" bureaucracy common to most organizations (see Anderson and Gevitz, 1983; Coe, 1978; Freidson and Rhea, 1963, 1965; Wilson, 1970). Goss (1961, 1963), however, has suggested the term *advisory bureaucracy* as being more appropriate. She focuses on the fact that in traditional administrative bureaucracies, such as the armed forces, the consulting staff act as technical specialists. They advise management of the pros and cons of each situation and the possible outcome of various decisions. Management then makes the decision. In advisory bureaucracies, however, it is the consulting or medical staff who possess and wield the authority. They make all the decisions that are

directly related to issues of patient care and "medical emergencies." As a result, in an advisory bureaucracy the role of formal management is reduced to providing the ways and means for the successful execution of physicians' orders. Therefore, the medical staff tends to direct the activity of the hospital personnel, while the administrative staff's functions are restricted to devising the most efficient and economical ways of meeting the physicians' demands.

In addition to the advisory nature of the formal bureaucracy to physicians, there is also an advisory atmosphere among physicians. The extensively detailed division of labor within the hospital extends not only across the five major divisions but within each one as well. Within the medical division physicians are loosely organized into separate departments that are practically autonomous and over which there is little central authority (see Freidson and Rhea, 1963, 1965). Wilson (1970) succinctly describes this decentralization among physicians and its effect on overall hospital functioning:

Each department of the medical institution cultivates its domains of activity, in treatment, research, teaching, or whatever, as a relatively autonomous fief. So the large general hospital, despite bearing one name and one spatial location actually consists of the duchy of surgery, the principality of obstetrics, the free state of psychiatry, and so on. This system works reasonably (some might say astonishingly) well most of the time. Its twin defects are that interdepartmental collaboration in the patient's interest is problematic and that the hospital administration finds it difficult to execute general organizational policy.

Thus, in the hospital the formal bureaucracy is in an advise-only situation with respect to physicians. Within each medical department each physician is in an advise-only situation with each other physician and medical department. As a result, there is more strained interaction within advisory bureaucracies than in more straightforward administrative bureaucracies.

CAUGHT BETWEEN THE LINES: SPECIAL CONSEQUENCES FOR NURSES. More often than not the "strain" produced within the advisory bureaucracy of the modern hospital is borne by the nurse. The reason for this is that the nurse is in a situation of "multiple subordination" (see Henry, 1954, for an elaboration of this concept). First, the nurse is an extension of the physician and second-in-line in the medical hierarchy. As such, her task is to aid the physician whenever and wherever possible. This may be translated as "doing what the physician tells you to do when he or she tells you to do it." Thus, in the medical hierarchy the nurse is subordinate to the physician. The nurse is, however, also subordinate to the hospital administrator. Moreover, it is the hospital administrator who is technically the "boss" of the hospital. As such, he or she makes the important decisions about hiring, firing, and merit increases. Consequently, the nurse is subject to all of the house rules set down by management in order to promote an efficient operation. As a result, the nurse is subordinate to two different bosses: the physician and the hospital administrator.

There is nothing inherently wrong with multiple subordination. In fact, many people are directly subordinate to more than one person or office at the same time. Nonetheless, problems arise when the multiple superiors disagree over *what* the subordinates should be doing at any given time and *how* it should be done. Given the right of physicians to declare a "medical emergency" and thereby supersede normal hospital bureaucratic protocol, they may make demands on nurses that violate established administrative procedure. But because nurses are subordinate to physicians and do not have the right to question the existence of a "medical emergency," they are obligated to comply. At the same time, however, the nurses must also work within the rules and regulations laid down by the hospital's administrators, who truly *are* the nurses' employers. Thus, nurses find themselves in a predicament where they can follow the orders of one superordinate only by disobeying those of another.

The extent and intensity of this conflict has increased for two reasons. One is that physicians have been declaring "medical emergencies" more and more often in response to a variety of pressures. These pressures include physicians' own habitual behavior and their tendency toward the practice of "defensive" medicine. Under the latter each patient's condition is examined as carefully as possible, and all possibly useful diagnostic procedures are followed in an attempt to avoid mistakes that might result in malpractice litigation. The other reason for increased conflict lies with hospital administrators' growing concern over cost containment and financial responsibility.

The conflict that results from multiple subordination is a major factor in the rapid turnover of nursing staffs from hospital to hospital, and from department to department within the same hospital. It produces a considerable amount of strain by continually forcing the nurse to choose between the administrator's line of authority and the physician's. If the physician's line is chosen, then the consequence may be the loss of a job. If the administrator's line is chosen, then the consequence may be the patient's death. The choice between these two lines of authority and their consequences is not an easy one. More often than not, however, the situations that nurses face are neither this clear-cut nor conflicting.

CHANGES IN HOSPITAL DOMINATION. Fortunately, the negative aspects of having two lines of authority within the hospital may be reduced as the domination of the hospital moves into a new era. According to Perrow (1963; see also Schulz and Johnson, 1983), four distinct periods in hospital domination may be described: trustee domination, medical domination, administrative challenge, and multiple leadership. The first period covered the emergence of the voluntary general hospital, up through about the early 1900s. During this period the hospital was dominated by its board of trustees. Recall that at this time hospitals were supported primarily by philanthropic means. It was the board of trustees who were responsible to see that sufficient funds were available for operation. Therefore, these early hospital trustees used the authority that came with their responsibility and "ran" *their* hospitals.

By the 1930s the period of trustee domination gave way to one in which the medical staff was given and used more authority. Perrow (1963) cites three important factors leading to this "medical domination" period: a fee-for-service orientation replaced the philanthropic nature of the hospital; the quality of medical care improved as a general function of the post–Flexnerian era; and, hospitals began to seek more prestige than their competitors by having the "best" physicians on their staffs. As a result, the physician's position in the hospital hierarchy improved considerably and physicians rather than trustees became the more responsible force. Indeed, the changing nature of the hospital and American medicine brought physicians to the center of the limelight in the most showcased theater—hospitals.

Physicians soon began to abuse their new power, however, and the hospital became the kingdom of the physician rather than the place where patients were to be treated. To counter this development, the formal training and legal status of the hospital administrator began to appear during the 1940s and 1950s. Perrow (1963) labels this period the "administrative challenge." Although formally trained management staff were brought into hospitals, physicians retained their dominant position. By the 1960s and 1970s, however, the businesslike nature of hospitals had become so complex that physicians' relative advantage began to erode. This resulted in a period of "mutual leadership" or two lines of authority. During this period the advisory bureaucracy became entrenched. In it the central authority within the hospital was uneasily shared between hospital administrators and physicians (with some rumblings still coming from the trustees).

During the 1980s the health care industry has faced increasing pressures for cost containment and fiscal responsibility. As a result, "mutual leadership" is giving way to a new period of "hospital administrator leadership." The reason for this is that the hospital administrator (just like the trustee of the first period) must be sure that there is sufficient operating revenue available. Moreover, he or she must be sure that the daily charges per patient are reasonable. Ac-

cordingly, as the 1980s slip by there should be less and less conflict between the two lines of authority within the hospital. This should relieve some of the strain on nurses by more clearly identifying *the* authority within the hospital.

Nonetheless, physicians remain a strong second authority within the hospital and continue their dominance in *true* "medical emergencies." There are three reasons for this. First, physicians are not employees of the hospital. Indeed, they are actually its truest customers. The hospital is simply where they frequently come to practice medicine. Second, physicians continue to have high social standing. This allows them considerable advantage in any interactional context. Finally, because they are *the* medical professionals, physicians remain the *ultimate* authority in strictly medical matters (see Georgopoulos and Mann, 1972).

The Hospitalized Patient: More Roles and Less Freedom

So far our discussion of the hospital has avoided what many consider to be the most important component: the patient. In any service organization there are always at least two perspectives and two roles: those of the staff and those of the consumers. To fully understand the hospitalized patient, we must examine a series of related issues. These include models of patient care, how the sick role is accentuated, identity stripping, control over the patient's resources, control over the patient's mobility and other activities, different modes of patient response, and what being a good patient means to the hospital staff.

MODELS OF PATIENT CARE. As different orientations of hospitals have emerged (spheres of religious activity, poorhouses, deathhouses, and centers of modern medical technology), so too have different models of patient care. Coe (1978) suggests that three distinct models have come into being. They may be compared and contrasted with each other in terms of their goals, assumptions, patient motivations, and resulting institutional models. Table 12-7 presents the distinctions that

Table 12-7. *Models of patient care.*

Dimension	Custodial	Classical	Rehabilitative
1. Stated goals	Comfort	Cure	Restoration
2. Assumptions about the disease process	Incurable	Reversible	Mutable
a. Therapy	Sporadic	Central	Supplementary
b. Sick role	Permanent	Temporary	Intermittent
3. Patient motivation	Obedience to institutional rules	Obedience to "doctor's orders"	Achieve mastery
4. Resulting institutional model	Total institution	Acute general hospital	Rehabilitation center

SOURCE: Rodney M. Coe. 1978. *Sociology of Medicine,* 2nd ed. New York: McGraw-Hill. Reprinted by permission of the publisher.

Coe makes between the custodial, classical, and rehabilitative models of patient care.

The *custodial* model of patient care is most closely associated with the earlier orientation of the hospital. That was a time when hospitals functioned primarily as social service, poorhouse, or custodial homes for the less fortunate or more undesirable elements of society. In the custodial model the hospital served as a "total institution" in the same manner that Goffman (1961) has described the mental institution (see chapter 8). That orientation served to keep the "offensive" people off the streets in keeping with America's "out of sight, out of mind" approach to social problems.

The *classical* model of patient care is one that is most closely associated with the general voluntary hospital. As indicated above, the modern hospital emerged as a result of the significant advances in medicine. It has become the center of modern technology. Moreover, it is usually *the* place where physicians bring their patients in hopes of curing them. Thus, the character of the modern general voluntary hospital is one in which medical therapy is the central concern. It is oriented toward curing the patient and helping him or her move out of the temporary sick role as soon as possible. Accordingly, the ultimate authority (or motivating factor) in the classical model of patient care is the "doctor's orders." This contrasts with the emphasis on "institutional rules" in the custodial model.

The *rehabilitation* model of patient care is most often associated with the long-term hospital. Its principal task is to restore patients to a higher level of functioning by helping them learn to manage (or master) their generally chronic ailments (such as paraplegia, diabetes, or leukemia). In the rehabilitative model the emphasis is on rehabilitation. This requires patient care of much longer duration, and it generally involves chronic rather than acute or emergency situations. In fact, many trauma patients (especially amputees or paraplegics) may at first be taken to a short-term, general hospital to stabilize their condition and help them past its initial traumatic medical aspects. They are subsequently transferred to the rehabilitative hospital. There the concern shifts from relatively fast trauma care to a more gradual rehabilitative process.

THE SICK ROLE ACCENTUATED. When the patient is hospitalized, the sick role becomes accentuated and strongly reinforced. As noted in chapter 5, the sick role carries with it the obligation of the patient to want to and try to get well. In order to do this, the patient must seek out the physician and comply with the proscribed regimen. In the case of the hospitalized patient (especially those in the acute, short-term, voluntary hospital), this obligation is even greater. Hospitalized patients are more dependent on physicians by virtue of the severity of their illnesses (see chapter 7 and the discussion of the Szasz-Hollender model [Szasz and Hollender, 1956] of patient-practitioner interaction).

Because physicians delegate some of their authority to the hospital personnel who look after their patients, the sick role for the hospitalized patient is expanded to include cooperation and compliance with the general hospital routine. This includes its rules, regulations, and attendant personnel (see Tagliacozzo and Mauksch, 1972). At the same time that this general acceptance of the hospital routine accentuates the patient's subordination within the sick role, it also fundamentally modifies it. The one-on-one intimacy and permissiveness of the traditional patient-practitioner relationship that is present for the outpatient is absent for the inpatient (see Lorber, 1975a). Thus, although most of the aspects of the sick role are accentuated for the hospitalized patient (especially those which relate to subordination and compliance), other aspects of the sick role (especially permissiveness) are reduced.

In general, however, the sick role for the hospitalized patient may be considered an acute case of the traditional sick role. It is reflected in the following account of what a physician went through when he was forced to accept the hospitalized sick role within his own hospital (Geiger, 1975):

I had to be hospitalized, suddenly and urgently. . . . In the space of only an hour or two, I went from . . . staff to inmate in a total institution. At one moment I was a physician: elite, technically skilled, vested with authority, wielding power over others, affectively neutral. The next moment I was a patient: dependent, anxious, sanctioned in illness only if I was cooperative. A protected dependency and the promise of effective technical help were mine—if I accepted a considerable degree of psychological and social servitude.

Coming from a physician, such a description of the accentuated sick role for the hospitalized patient is quite revealing. It suggests three distinct techniques used by hospitals to control patients (see Coe, 1978): identity stripping, resource control, and mobility control.

IDENTITY STRIPPING. The first thing that happens to the hospitalized patient is that his or her identity is stripped away (Coe, 1978). Each patient comes to the hospital as an individual with his or her own unique personality and background. On admission, however, the individual's unique identity is stripped away. First, normal clothing ("street clothes") is taken away, and he or she is forced to wear either a hospital gown or some type of sleepwear. Next, other personal belongings (including valuables like rings, watches, or money) are taken away. They are either stored in the hospital safe for return when the patient is released or sent home with relatives. Finally, the individual is placed in a room that looks and is equipped like every other room in the hospital. In essence, every aspect of an individual's personal identity and individuality that can be taken away is taken away. This results in a remarkable reduction of the individual's self-image. It serves as an initiation into the social world of the hospital.

RESOURCE CONTROL. The second distinct aspect of being hospitalized is called resource control (Coe, 1978). After the individual's identity has been stripped away, the next thing that the staff does is establish control over the resources in the hospital. This includes both physical resources, such as soap, toilet paper, and mouthwash, and information or knowledge resources, such as patient charts, test results, and other medical information concerning the patient. As a result, if the patient wants to use a resource, he or she must apply to the hospital staff for it. This further reduces the self-image of the patient because it makes him or her more dependent than before. In addition to having to ask for such resources, the patient must be prepared to have that request denied. This occurs because the hospital staff is the superordinate in the interaction; therefore, they have the power to refuse or delay the request. When this occurs, the patient's self-image drops even lower than it had been.

MOBILITY CONTROL. The third technique that hospitals and their staffs use to control patients and prepare them to adapt to the accentuated inpatient version of the sick role is mobility control (Coe, 1978). If you have ever been hospitalized or have visited someone in the hospital, you know that the activities a patient may engage in, as well as where these may take place, are determined by hospital staff. In other words, once hospitalized, any patient activity or mobility is left to the discretion of the staff. The restrictions placed on mobility range from whether or not you can have visitors in your room, to whether or not you can go to the hospital chapel to worship, to whether or not you may have access to roam the halls or visit other people in the hospital. The purpose of such restrictions is to increase the hospital staff's control in the staff-patient interaction.

MODES OF PATIENT RESPONSE. When confronted with the hospitalized version of the sick role and the three control-inducing techniques, not every patient responds in the same way. Based on Merton's (1957) classic study of adaptation, Coe (1978) has identified four modes of patient response to the hospitalization experience. The first response mode is *withdrawal*. In it the patient tries to escape the hospital just as one would try to escape from a burning building. Because of the controlled patient mobility within the hospital (you cannot leave until the doctor discharges you, except in the unusual case where you are allowed to leave against medical advice), however, withdrawal is more likely to be psychological than physical. Usually the patient constructs a "psuedocommunity" within the hospital as an illusionary tactic to avoid the pain of the hospital. This is a very typical response in long-term facilities, especially in mental hospitals (see Goffman, 1961).

The second response mode is called *aggression*. It occurs when the patient responds to the hospitalization experience by "overt resistance to the rules and regulations." This includes disobeying physicians, showing physical aggression against hospital staff members, or destroying hospital equipment and facilities. Aggressive reaction in total institutions usually results in the utter confinement and isolation of that patient from all other patients. In the voluntary hospital setting the aggressive patient runs the risk of having the hospital staff give up and discharge him or her before treatment has been effective.

The third response is called *integration*. It represents the patient's coming to terms with being hospitalized by abiding by most of the hospital's rules and regulations. In so doing, the patient becomes an active member of the hospital patient subculture. As a result, the integrated patient satisfies the compliance requirement and is also able to reestablish some identity as a member of the patient subculture. While this might be the optimum response in terms of benefits to staff and patient alike, it requires the establishment of extensive social interaction patterns with other patients. This is not likely to occur in the short-term, general hospital setting where the average length of stay is about seven days. It may also result in the problem of weaning away a patient who has become *too* well integrated into the hospital and does not want to leave when it is time to be discharged.

The fourth response mode of patients experiencing the hospitalization process is called *acquiescence*. The patient who acquiesces to the hospital's routine "plays it cool" at first while reevaluating his or her own situation. Essentially, the acquiescent patient is so shocked by the hospital regimen that at first he or she merely sits back and numbly complies with the demands and restrictions imposed by the hospital staff. Such a response is very typical of patients, especially those with an acute illness, who experience hospitalization in a short-term, general hospital. Here, the initial shock does not really have time to wear off before the patients are "cured" and discharged.

BEING A "GOOD" PATIENT. Although there are four distinct modes of patient responses to the hospitalization experience, there is one that is preferred above all others by the staff. The preferred or "good" patient response is the acquiescent response. Acquiescent patients create the least problems for the hospital staff. Therefore, caring for them takes the least amount of effort. For example, the acquiescent patient does not consume a lot of the hospital staff's time by violating rules and regulations for which he or she must then be reprimanded. The acquiescent patient also does not ask lots of questions about his or her prognosis, treatment, or physician. In essence, the acquiescent or conforming patient makes the hospital staff's job that much easier and more pleasant.

In an insightful study of individuals identified by physicians as "good" patients, Lorber (1975a) found that older and more poorly educated individuals were more likely to be so labeled. This finding reflects the fact that younger and better-educated people generally tend to be more inquisitive and less awed by physicians. Lorber also found that the physician's description of a "good" patient generally focuses on the fact that the patient is stoic, uncomplaining, cooperative, and requires very little care. Apparently, as far as physicians are concerned, "good" patients are *easy* patients.

Summary

In this chapter we examined the hospital from two perspectives: the emergence of the modern hospital and the social organization within it. We began by tracing the development of the modern hospital through four distinct periods during which its orientation was that of (1) the religious center, (2) the poorhouse, (3) the deathhouse, and (4) the modern, technical medical center. We then surveyed modern hospitals and found that they vary considerably along six dimensions: ownership (government, proprietary, and not-for-profit); type (general or specific); size (6 beds to more than 1,000); organization (at the general level, a five-division organizational chart is typical); utilization (short-term versus long-term, and inpatient versus outpatient); and cost (from $323 to $468 per day). Nonetheless, we found that what we usually mean when we talk about a "typical" hospital is a short-term, general, not-for-profit hospital of from 150 to 500 beds. It is usually oriented toward the care of patients with acute illnesses and conditions. We concluded this section by discussing the emergence of multihospital systems.

In the second section we turned to the social organization of the typical modern hospital. There we found two lines of authority. One was the traditional administrative line similar to the chain of command in the armed forces. The other was the special authority of physicians who can declare a "medical emergency" and breach (or supersede) all of the hospital's rules and regulations necessary for the treatment of a patient. The physician's authority in the hospital is derived from the cultural belief that no one else knows what is best for the patient. Therefore, the hospital bureaucracy becomes an advisory one. In a true "medical emergency" the physician's ultimate decision-making authority is justified because he or she has the responsibility for the patient's health. The most serious side effect of this dual authority is that nurses are caught in the middle. They are simultaneously subordinate and responsible to both physicians and administrators. As a result, whenever the two lines of authority clash, nurses are "crunched" in the middle.

Finally, we turned our attention to how the social organization affects the patient's role in the hospital. We found that in the hospital the dependency and compliance aspects of the sick role are accentuated, although the one-to-one and permissive aspects of the patient-practitioner relationship are diminished. In order to increase control over patients, the hospital staff strips away their personal identity, restricts their mobility, and maintains control over the resources within the hospital. Patients respond to these techniques and to the general hospitalization experience in one of four ways: withdrawal, aggression, integration, or acquiescence. Physicians and other members of the hospital staff prefer the acquiescent patient response. They generally label such patients as "good" patients.

IV. Issues

13. Health Care Economics

As THE preceding chapters have indicated, the delivery of health care in the United States is big business. In 1984 health care expenditures totaled $387 billion, or 10.6 percent of the gross national product (GNP; see Levit, Waldo, and Davidoff, 1985). By 1990 those expenditures are expected to rise to $690 billion, or 12 percent of the GNP. For the year 2000 those expenditures are forecast to be $1.9 trillion, or 14 percent of the GNP (see Tyson and Merrill, 1984). It is most important to note that these sharp increases in health care costs are not the result of ordinary inflation. Indeed, after adjusting for rises in the consumer price index (CPI), the real growth in health care expenditures during the 1970s and 1980s has averaged 4.6 percent annually (see Merrill and Wasserman, 1985). If this trend continues, it will jeopardize the progress that has been made throughout the twentieth century toward improving access to quality health care. Therefore, a number of innovative programs have been or are being developed to curb these rapidly rising costs (Robert Wood Johnson Foundation, 1986). To better understand these programs, why they were needed in the first place, and how they may or may not work, we must draw on the related field of health care economics.

To familiarize you with the basic concepts of health care economics, the present chapter is divided into three sections. The first will focus on the applicability of traditional economic theory to the health care industry. Of special interest here is why traditional economic assumptions are not valid in the medical marketplace. In the second section we will consider how health care is financed. This will include a brief review of the theory behind and distribution of insurance, and an overview of patient, physician, and hospital reimbursement methods. The final section will focus on the most hotly debated innovation in the health care industry—Diagnostic Related Groups (DRGs).

After explaining what DRGs are and how they came to be, we will examine the experience with them to date. We will conclude this section with a discussion of whether or not the cost-containment movement has gone too far.

Is Traditional Economics Applicable to the Health Care Industry?

Perhaps the most interesting issue in health care economics is its validity. That is, does it make sense to apply standard economic theory to the health care industry? For most health care delivery analysts, the answer is no. For most health economists, however, the answer is yes, albeit in modified form. The difference in opinion rests on how economic theory is defined. If it requires the presence of an economist's ideal market, then the answer is no. If it requires only the ability to apply economic principles through public policy initiatives in order to modify the health care industry, then the answer is yes. To better understand these issues we will consider first the analyst's perspective, and then the economist's.

The Analyst's Perspective

The analyst's perspective is well demonstrated in the report of the National Commission on the Cost of Medical Care of the American Medical Association (1978). That commission was established in 1976 to independently explore the problem of rapidly escalating health care costs. Twenty-seven commissioners were recruited from business, labor, health care industries, academia, consumers' groups, and government. Their charge was to provide a comprehensive overview of health care costs and identify possible approaches for resolving those problems. They were asked to complete these tasks within two years.

The commission established four task forces to facilitate their analysis. These focused on the system for delivering health care, those factors that affect the demand for health care, the supply and distribution of health care providers, and those technological innovations that impact health care delivery. After each task force completed its initial report, the commissioners met as a whole to consider the overall problem. They soon discovered a most recurrent theme (American Medical Association, National Commission . . . , 1978):

Certain characteristics inherent in the health care delivery system affected all areas under consideration. The following discussion of this system, necessary to any analysis of costs, centers on the system's divergence from an economist's notion of an ideal market. Among the most important differences are the structure of health insurance and the associated subsidy effect; the lack of consumer and provider knowledge regarding the cost, efficacy, or necessity of specific medical procedures; and the potential ability of the provider to affect demand.

In essence, the commissioners concluded that the medical marketplace had become rather unique, at least in an economic sense.

As the commissioners indicated, there are three reasons why the health care industry is economically unique. The first involves the effect of health insurance on consumer and provider behavior. In traditional economic markets the consumer is also the payer. For example, when you buy a car, you are expected to pay for that car. You know what your available resources are, and you take your financial situation into account when deciding which car to buy. Indeed, one of the more salient factors in deciding which car to buy is whether you can afford it. This represents price consciousness on your part.

When purchasing health services, however, things are different because of the associated subsidy of health insurance. If you have a traditional policy, such as Blue Cross or Blue Shield, your insurance company will typically pay 80 percent or more of the costs involved in purchasing necessary health services. As a result, your price consciousness is significantly reduced, if not eliminated. The reason for this is that the effective price of the health services you desire is quite low given the insurance subsidy. Therefore, you do not consider the entire cost of the health services, but only that portion you must bear when you decide whether or not to purchase. Under such circumstances, you may buy more, or more expensive, services than you really need.

Just as the insurance subsidy affects consumer behavior, it also affects provider behavior. Because the effective price of health services is so low, physicians may order or recommend that more (or more expensive) health services, such as laboratory tests, be consumed by (or for) their patients. If they or their patients had to bear the full cost of each ordered health service, however, it is likely that fewer health services would be consumed. Thus, the perverse incentive of health insurance is that it significantly reduces, or eliminates, price consciousness from the repertoires of both patients and physicians.

A second reason why the health care industry is economically unique concerns both consumer and provider knowledge. At issue here is knowledge about the cost of health care, its efficacy, and its necessity. Lack of knowledge (or ignorance) from the patient's perspective is the greater of the two. Consider patients' knowledge about the cost of health care that they receive, both in the hospital and in the ambulatory setting. Patients seldom are aware of what costs are associated with an overall hospital episode, let alone with a particular procedure or test. Recall the summary hospital bill associated with the endometriosis episode discussed in chapter 12. At least half of that bill was for various and sundry ancillary charges over and above the daily room rate.

The situation in the ambulatory setting is not much better. Few patients know what they will be charged by their doctors for any given office visit. Moreover, in selecting a new doctor (such as when you move to a new community; see Wolinsky and Steiber, 1982), it is infrequently the case that "price lists" are readily available. Indeed, many physicians are loathe to discuss their fee structures with established patients, let alone with prospective ones.

Patients' knowledge of how effective health services may be is generally even lower than that about their cost. This stems from the considerable gap between the pa-

tient's and the practitioner's medical knowledge (see chapter 7). After all, patients come to the physician for help because they do not know what to do (or how and why to do it) for themselves. Thus, the patient is unlikely to be able to make qualified judgments about the efficacy, comparative or otherwise, of medical treatments. Accordingly, the patient depends on the fiduciary agency relationship with the physician for sound advice and guidance about what will and will not work.

The patient is also dependent on the physician for advice and guidance concerning the necessity of various medical procedures. Although he or she may know that something is wrong (either a general or specific sense of feeling badly), it is unlikely that the patient has sufficient knowledge to determine whether or not action must be taken. Therefore, the patient most often relies on the recommendation of the physician in his or her role as the fiduciary agent acting in the patient's best interest.

The physician or other provider, however, is not infallible. To a large part, this is because medicine is not an exact science. Therefore, it is simply not clear what medical procedures are more efficacious or necessary in a particular set of circumstances involving any given patient. Moreover, studies have shown that physicians are relatively unfamiliar with the costs associated with common diagnostic and therapeutic procedures (see Feldstein, 1983). They frequently do not know what the procedures they are recommending will cost. And this includes their most frequent, if not routine, regimens.

A third reason why the medical marketplace is economically unique involves the potential ability of providers to affect the demand for their services (Ramsey, 1980). Part of the nature of the fiduciary agency relationship between patient and practitioner involves the former placing considerable trust in the latter to recommend only those procedures that are necessary. An unscrupulous practitioner, however, may recommend procedures (or return visits to the office) that are not in the patient's best interest but are financially rewarding.

Although such economic exploitation of

patients (and their insurance companies) violates both the letter and the spirit of the Hippocratic oath and contemporary medical ethics, it is not uncommon. Moreover, it is not at all unexpected. After all, the traditional patient-practitioner relationship places physicians in a most tempting position in which it is very easy to induce more (or more expensive) demand for their services. This inducement may range from relatively mild forms such as suggestions for "rule-out" tests in marginal situations (including throat cultures every time you have a cold), to more moderate forms such as an extra follow-up visit or two, to more extreme forms such as unnecessary surgery.

The potential for supplier-induced demand also applies to such institutional providers as hospitals. Indeed, there is a phenomenon known as "Roemer's law" that suggests that each new hospital bed added to a community's supply will add to its demand (see Pauly and Satterthwaite, 1980). In other words, if additional hospital beds are introduced, somehow they will manage to be filled. Harris (1975) has empirically demonstrated this to be the case using data from several counties in New York. He found that the occupancy rate remained constant despite the introduction of many new hospital beds. The reason for this is that hospitals need to maintain a certain occupancy level for minimal operating efficiency. Therefore, when occupancy rates fall, either through improved health status in the community or increased competition, hospitals focus on a variety of methods to increase the demand for their services. This is quite evident in the current push by hospitals to develop home health care and other outreach programs that serve as "feeders" or sources of future inpatients.

In order to overcome the problems of the associated subsidy effect of health insurance, the lack of price consciousness on the part of consumers and providers, and the potential for supplier-induced demand, the National Commission on the Cost of Medical Care of the AMA (1978) issued 48 recommendations. For the most part, these recommendations focused on two areas: strengthening price consciousness and ex-

panding regulatory controls over providers. To accomplish the former the commissioners advocated: (1) creating economic incentives on the part of employers and employees in the purchasing and selection of health insurance plans, (2) increasing the cost sharing of the patient at the point where health care is consumed, (3) fair market competition that did not favor any particular form of medical practice, (4) conducting experiments to test the effectiveness of different ways of financing health care, (5) preparing regional directories of physicians that would include pricing information, (6) establishing "truth in insurance," or simplified and easier-to-understand descriptions of health policy benefits, (7) setting minimum standards for insurance carriers, and (8) implementing quality assessment methods and making the results available to consumers.

The commissioners' recommendations on how to better regulate providers included calls for (1) considering the application of public utility regulation techniques to the health care industry, (2) a thorough review of current regulatory mechanisms, (3) supporting the notion of health planning, (4) establishing Certificate of Need (CON) legislation, (4) implementing programs to decertify or convert excess acute care beds into long-term beds or congregate housing for the elderly, (5) developing regional as opposed to national health manpower supply guidelines, (6) shifting to consensus criteria for the location of expensive facilities and capital equipment, (7) supporting the regionalization of high-cost special technology centers, and (8) imposing limits on capital expenditures made by hospitals. As you may notice, although these recommendations were made a decade ago, they identify the current state of thinking about cost containment. Unfortunately, they have yet to resolve the problem.

The Economist's View

Economists view the applicability of their discipline to the health care industry in a different manner. As Feldstein (1983) notes, there tend to be two levels at which the applicability questions arise. The first involves the accuracy of the assumptions that underlie the economic behavior of providers and consumers. The second addresses the implicit values associated with health care. Feldstein concisely summarizes the bulk of these arguments:

Critics have claimed that it is inaccurate to assume that the consumer of health services is rational, and that he or she has sufficient information when deciding on use of services. Such critics also claim that the purchaser of medical services is not the consumer, as in non-medical markets, but the physician, who also has a financial interest in the services to be purchased. . . . critics claim that these providers are organized as nonprofit organizations and therefore do not have the same motivations as for-profit firms in other industries. Further, since consumers may be irreparably harmed by incompetent providers, more stringent controls must be exercised over the provision of medical services than over non-medical goods and services. Lastly, such critics claim that access to medical services is considered a right by society and its distribution cannot be left solely to the marketplace.

Thus, Feldstein expands the issue by shifting the focus from the fundamental principles of economics in isolation, to their role within the social and political context of the American health care delivery system.

According to Feldstein (1983), it is also important to separate the criticism directed at the validity of economic assumptions (e.g., rationality, informed consumers, for-profit firms) from criticisms of using economic criteria to evaluate the performance of the health care delivery system. Indeed, he argues that economic principles are only tools to be used; they are not ends in and of themselves. Although it is true that these tools assume the health care industry to be a "free market," deviations from that assumption do not negate their utility. Rather, deviations from classic market structures require that public policy measures be initiated to change the health care industry's performance. Economic incentives must be introduced to effectively alter consumer and provider behavior. In this regard, the economist's view of the situation is consistent with the view of the health care analyst.

Where health care economists and policy-makers differ most is on where the root of the problem lies. Policymakers are more prone to adjust the current health care delivery system on a piecemeal basis in order to bring about desired changes. Health economists, however, suggest that greater attention be paid to the underlying social and moral questions that subsequently dictate the form of the health care delivery system. In particular, Feldstein (1983) identifies three basic choices that must be made:

The first choice is determination of both the amount to be spent on health and medical services and the composition of those services. The second choice is a selection of the best method for producing medical services; two such methods are prepaid group practice and fee-for-service. Even within a given delivery system, choices must be made regarding the amounts of capital and equipment to use relative to the amounts and types of labor providing a service. The third choice is a selection of the method for distributing health services among the population.

According to Feldstein, the first two choices involve economic efficiency, while the last choice concerns the equitable distribution of the resources to be provided.

Although he takes a slightly different perspective, Fuchs (1974; see also 1986a, 1986b) fundamentally agrees. He notes that a permanent resolution of the current crisis in health care costs is only possible if we first address the basic social and moral issues. How much can society, which now pays for the bulk of health care, afford to spend on one individual? Should this amount depend on the social position of the individual, or should the amount be the same for all individuals? These are questions that cannot be answered by economists; they must be answered by society. But the questions do not stop there. Fuchs notes that even if agreement can be reached on the maximum amount of medical care that society can afford for any individual, another issue arises. How much can we allow the individual (or the individual's family or friends) to spend on his or her medical care? In an economic system of limited resources society must not only choose what it owes to each individual but also how much of the total resources available may be spent on any one individual regardless of who that individual may be. This question represents the classic debate over the proper balance between individual and collective responsibility in industrialized societies (see Durkheim, 1957). Thus, although the economists recognize the divergence of the health care industry from an ideal marketplace, they argue that their principles are readily applicable. Before those principles are applied, however, fundamentally moral and social decisions about the nature of the health care delivery system must be made.

Financing Health Care

Three important points emerge from the above discussion. First, the medical marketplace's deviation from economic ideals requires public policy manipulations of existing incentive structures in order to achieve the desired goals. Second, the incentive structure most likely to be effectively manipulated is the method of payment for health care. And third, almost all payments involve health insurance. Thus, it would seem most fruitful to focus any policy changes on health care financing methods. To understand health care financing we must first review the theory and distribution of health insurance, and then discuss patient, physician, and hospital reimbursement methods.

The Theory and Distribution
of Health Insurance

The economic literature on the demand for health insurance is both extensive and mathematically sophisticated (see Feldstein, 1983, for a thorough review of these issues). It is based on the assumption that individuals wish to maximize their utility functions, as in all economic demand theory. The underlying problem is not knowing, or being able to accurately forecast, whether you will need health insurance, and how much of it you will need. In most cases individuals simply do not know if they will be ill or how seriously ill they will be. Therefore, one must guess at the expected need (demand) for health care.

There are two basic scenarios or alternative paths that an individual may envision. Feldstein (1983) describes them this way: "1. He or she can purchase insurance and thereby incur a small loss in the form of the insurance premium, or, 2. He or she can self-insure, which means facing the small possibility of a large loss in the event that the illness occurs, or the large possibility that the medical loss will not occur." This suggests that risk-takers will be un- or underinsured, and that more conservative types will insure, if not overinsure, themselves.

The situation, however, is not that simple. Some individuals will have more knowledge about their health status; they may have chronic conditions for which future needs are more readily anticipated. Others may have fewer options from which to select; they may have limited disposable incomes, or they may not be able to obtain group insurance rates. Moreover, the rapidly rising cost of health care has made the risk of voluntarily being un- or underinsured catastrophic for everyone. Therefore, Feldstein (1983) underscores the following factors as a more complete set of determinants of the demand for health insurance: "1. How risk averse the individual is. . . . 2. The probability of the event's [illness] occurring. . . . 3. The magnitude of the loss. . . . 4. The price of insurance. . . . [and] 5. The income of the individual." Thus, the demand for health insurance is seen as a complex function of both economic (such as price and income) and social (or welfare) factors (such as the preference for risk aversion). The relative importance of these factors depends on the individual's personal and financial situation.

Just as the demand for health insurance is a complex phenomenon, so too is its differential distribution in the population. The problem here is twofold. First, there is the question of who are the uninsured. Second, there is the question of the adequacy of the coverage of those who are insured. Unfortunately, detailed data that bear on these questions are hard to come by. Indeed, the most recent comprehensive study of health insurance coverage in the United States was conducted in 1977 as part of the National Medical Care Expenditure Survey (NMCES). The

NMCES involved six interviews with each of over 40,000 individuals over an 18-month period during 1977 and 1978 (see Kasper, Walden, and Wilensky, 1978). Before summarizing the findings from the NMCES, it is important to note the changes in health insurance brought about by the economic downturn of the late 1970s and early 1980s. These have made the situation considerably more bleak (see Berki, Wyszewianski, Lichtenstein, Gimotty, Bowlyow, Papke, Smith, Crane, and Bromberg, 1985).

With regard to the first question, the NMCES data indicate that at any given time over 25 million Americans have *no* health insurance coverage from either private plans or public programs (Kasper et al., 1978). In the absence of such coverage, the uninsured are often turned away from hospitals even in emergency situations, although some states (like Texas) have recently (1986) adopted statutes forbidding such practices. Those who are not turned away face a variety of dismal scenarios (Davis and Rowland, 1983): "Some neglect obtaining preventive or early care, often postponing care until conditions have become life-threatening. Others struggle with burdensome medical bills. Many come to rely upon crowded, understaffed public hospitals as the only source of reliable, available health care." The reliance on such "residual institutions" by the uninsured underscores the multitiered nature of the American health care delivery system (see chapter 3).

Salloway (1982) has cogently described such "residual institutions" and the situation of patients who must use them as follows:

They serve the needs of a patient population that has been lost to the traditional health care delivery system by default. The private system of health care delivery [i.e., involving insurance] cannot meet the needs of these people, because they have no means whatever of entering into the payment system . . . or because they are not the kinds of people that the private health care delivery system is comfortable taking care of. Often they are dull and uninteresting [from the health professional's perspective] cases; they are very difficult to communicate with; they are intransigent; and they scare off more desirable patients. These are the patients who will be described not by diagnoses, but by epithets: gomer, chronic, crock. . . . It is the vocabulary used for those

who are different, who are helpless, who don't understand the language and norms of a middle-class, highly technical bureaucracy, and who have, for these reasons, lost control of their own lives.

To be sure, the more than 10 percent of Americans without health insurance of one form or another face a dismal situation when they are sick.

And who are the uninsured? The NMCES data indicate significant relationships between health insurance coverage, age, race, and income. More than 98 percent of those over age 65 were always insured (over the 18-month study period), primarily as a result of the Medicare program. For those younger than 65, however, the situation was somewhat different. About 84 percent of the white nonelderly, and about 74 percent of the nonwhite nonelderly were always insured. Thus, although Medicare has brought about nearly universal access to health insurance among the elderly, one out of six nonelderly whites and one out of four nonelderly nonwhites remain disenfranchised from any health insurance program.

As one would expect, income is positively related to health insurance coverage. Among families whose incomes are below 125 percent of the federal government's officially declared poverty level, 27 percent are uninsured. Those who are significantly better off, with family incomes between 125 and 200 percent of the poverty level, fare only slightly better; about 21 percent of them are uninsured (Wilensky and Walden, 1981).

Although the situation of the insured is definitely better than that of the uninsured, it is not always rosy. The reason for this is that health insurance coverage is not uniformly comprehensive. Indeed, the extent of coverage among the insured is quite heterogeneous, as Davis and Rowland (1983) suggest:

Many individuals in the insured category may have actually had very limited health insurance coverage, leaving them basically uninsured for most services. For example, many individuals classified as insured have coverage for inpatient hospital care, but are not covered and are, therefore, essentially uninsured for primary care in a physician's office. In contrast, insured individuals also include those enrolled in a health maintenance organization offering comprehensive coverage for both inpatient and ambulatory care.

As a result, answering the question of who is insured and who is not begs the second question: How insured are the insured?

To address this question, Wilensky, Farley, and Taylor (1984) used the NMCES data to profile the characteristics of the benefits held by the nonelderly who had any employment-related health insurance. Their findings are shown in Table 13-1. These data indicate that almost 138 million Americans have employment-related health insurance. Of these, nearly 70 percent have both basic and major medical coverage. The breadth of that coverage, however, varies remarkably. Although nearly 88 percent have some coverage for outpatient prescription drugs, less than 7 percent have any coverage for routine physical examinations by a physician. Similarly, although nearly 90 percent have some form of hospital coverage, only 42 percent have something that approximates complete coverage. Moreover, nearly two thirds of the individuals surveyed are subject to out-of-pocket costs that can exceed $750 per person per year.

This raises the question of the adequacy of health insurance coverage. Using these same NMCES data, Farley (1985) conducted a series of analyses using different definitions of inadequate coverage. These definitions were based on the actuarial probabilities of out-of-pocket expenses adjusted for an individual's age, sex, race, income, perceived health status, and degree of limited activity due to health problems. The results indicated that 8 percent of those with health insurance in 1984 had out-of-pocket costs equal to at least 10 percent of their family's income (the definition of inadequate insurance coverage). This led Farley to conclude that the traditional focus on only the uninsured leads to too optimistic of a picture:

While roughly 10 percent of the population is uninsured throughout the year according to these estimates, a similar proportion are underinsured. The proportion with lapses in coverage during the year is also about equal to the proportion who are always uninsured. In total, the number of people under age 65 with inadequate

coverage is three times the number who are always uninsured. At least a quarter of the nonelderly population—about 50 million people in 1977 and a projected 56 million in 1984—are inadequately protected against the possibility of large medical bills.

The absence of universal, comprehensive (i.e., adequate) health insurance creates significant strains within the social fabric of our society. As Davis and Rowland (1983) note, it tarnishes our image as "a just and humane society when significant portions of the population endure avoidable pain, suffering, and even death because of an inability to pay for health care."

Patient Reimbursement Arrangements

There are basically three types of health insurance policies from the patient's perspective. The first is the indemnification plan. Under such an arrangement the insured person receives a cash benefit in the event of a loss. This type of policy operates quite similarly to traditional life insurance. When a loss occurs (such as a day in the hospital) in the health insurance situation, a flat benefit is paid to the insured individual (or his or her creditors). Indemnity policies typically contain a schedule of benefits, such as $150 a day for a hospital room, $500 for a surgeon's fee for the repair of a hernia, and the like. More often than not the individual may choose between several different schedules upon signing up (enrolling) for the indemnity policy. The more generous the benefit schedule is, the higher the monthly premiums to be paid. Such policies are more typical in farming and small rural communities, where they are the basic policy, and among the elderly, where they are a supplement to Medicare coverage.

It is important to note that under the indemnity system the insurance company has no incentive to work toward cost containment. The reason for this is that the insurance company's liabilities are fixed. It is only obligated to pay up to the fixed schedule benefit in the event of a claim. Therefore, the indemnity insurance company is only sensitive to the number of claims submitted. This allows its actuaries to focus

Table 13-1. *Characteristics of health insurance benefits held by those under age 65 with employment-related group insurance.*

Characteristics of benefits	Number with benefit (in thousands)	Percent with benefit
Any employment-related group coverage	137,700	100.0
Type of coverage		
Any HMO	5,900	4.3
Basic only	13,200	9.6
Major medical only	21,700	15.8
Basic and major medical	95,600	69.4
Other/unknown	1,200	0.9
Breadth of coverage		
Coverage for dental care	39,000	28.3
Coverage for vision or hearing care	16,100	11.7
Coverage for outpatient prescription drugs	120,500	87.5
Coverage for routine physical	8,700	6.3
Coverage for outpatient psychiatric care	106,400	77.3
Identical to other outpatient physician benefits	10,600	7.7
Different from other outpatient benefits	95,800	69.6
Hospital benefits[a]		
No deductible, semiprivate, generous limit	57,700	42.0
No deductible, semiprivate, less generous limit	41,000	29.9
No deductible, less than semiprivate	20,900	15.3
Deductible, semiprivate, generous limit	4,100	3.0
Deductible, semiprivate, less generous limit	3,600	2.6
Deductible, less than semiprivate	7,900	5.8
No hospital coverage	2,000	1.5
Physician office benefits		
No deductible, less than 20% coinsurance	10,700	7.8
No deductible, 20% or more coinsurance	9,500	6.9
Deductible, less than 20% coinsurance	18,200	13.2
Deductible, 20% or more coinsurance	82,800	60.1
No physician office coverage	16,500	12.0
Maximum major medical benefit[b]		
Less than $250,000	51,000	37.1
$250,000 or more	55,000	39.9
Unlimited	13,800	10.1
No major medical coverage	17,800	12.9
Out-of-pocket maximum under major medical[c]		
$750 or less	30,800	22.3
$751 or more	32,000	23.3
Unlimited	57,100	41.5
No major medical coverage	17,800	12.9

[a]A "generous" limit is defined as 365 days or more of basic benefits, or $250,000 of major medical coverage for those with no basic hospital benefits.
[b]Maximum benefit for hospital room and board charges, miscellaneous hospital expenses, surgery, inpatient physician visits, outpatient physician visits, outpatient diagnostic and laboratory tests, and any other expenses included under the maximum benefit for those services.
[c]Out-of-pocket maximum applicable to most of the services covered under the policy.
SOURCE: Gail R. Wilensky, Pamela J. Farley, and Amy K. Taylor. 1984. "Variations in Health Insurance Coverage: "Benefits vs. Premiums." *Milbank Memorial Fund Quarterly* 62:53−81. Reprinted by permission of the publisher.

on the projection of the number of future claims and adjust its premiums accordingly.

The patient with an indemnity policy, however, is faced with some incentives for cost containment. Assuming that something close to an economist's ideal marketplace exists, it is in the patient's best interest to shop around for those providers who will deliver the desired services at or closest to the level of reimbursement established in his or her benefits schedule. Under such a scenario the cost of health care would reach an equilibrium point at the intersection of the supply and demand curves. Unfortunately, the health care industry is not an ideal market, and the benefit schedules of indemnity policies are seldom at the "usual, customary, and reasonable" (UCR) level. Therefore, individuals so insured are likely to be inadequately insured.

The second type of health insurance is the service benefit policy. Under it the insurance company guarantees its policyholders of the services that they need and that are included in the agreement, rather than a cash amount for them. One of the most typical services guaranteed is the full charge for a semiprivate room in a hospital, as long as it does not exceed the UCR rate in the community. The most well-known service benefit policies include Blue Cross and Blue Shield, as well as the more popular commercial insurers, such as Equitable, Lincoln National, and Prudential. Under the service benefit approach the insurance company has some incentive to fight for cost containment because it is liable for the actual charges. Therefore, if those charges inflate faster than projected, the insurance company's profits are jeopardized.

For the patient, however, the incentives for cost containment are somewhat reduced. As long as the service provider's charges do not exceed the UCR level, they will be paid for by the insurance company. This creates a low effective price for the patient, which in turn introduces the problem of moral hazard. Economists (see Feldstein, 1983) define moral hazard as occurring when the demand for health care is inelastic to its associated out-of-pocket costs. That is, because health insurance significantly reduces the out-of-pocket costs associated with the consumption of medical care, the more fully insured individuals are, the more likely they will use health services. The reason for this is that the marginal cost of consuming additional health services is virtually nonexistent.

To counter the incentive that moral hazard induces in patients to use more health services than they might otherwise consume, service benefit policies have introduced two modifications to their basic designs. These are deductibles and copayments. Deductibles are an amount to be paid by the patient before the insurance coverage begins. A typical deductible associated with major medical policies is about $200 per person per year. Deductibles, however, only serve as a constraint at the onset of the coverage period. Once they have been met, their cost-containment effect is neutralized.

In contrast, the effect of copayments lasts throughout the policy period. The principle here is that the patient is required to pay a portion of the cost of the health services being consumed at the time of consumption. This serves to associate some out-of-pocket cost with each service consumption. As such, it is generally regarded as a more effective, long-term curb on patients' moral hazard. Copayments frequently take the form of $5 to $10 per office visit, or 20 percent of the cost of ambulatory services. Many service benefit insurance policies employ some combination of deductibles and copayments.

The third type of health insurance involves enrolling in a prepaid medical practice like a health maintenance organization (HMO; see chapter 9). In an HMO the individual pays a fixed monthly premium. This entitles him or her to receive all the care needed without any additional charge. As a result, moral hazard is at its maximum in prepaid settings because the effective (or marginal) price of consuming health care is zero. To offset this, most HMOs have adopted a modest copayment system associated with their ambulatory services. In addition, they frequently impose two- or three-week delays in scheduling nonemergency visits to the doctor.

Physician Reimbursement Methods

Just as there were three types of insurance plans to which patients may subscribe, there are three ways in which physicians are typically paid. The first is fee-for-service. Under this arrangement the physician is reimbursed for each service or procedure that he or she provides. This has been the traditional method of payment for physicians in the United States. The patient, or more often the patient's third-party insurer, pays the physician for the services rendered. Given the increasing use of copayments (both in fixed dollar and percentage form), both the patient and the insurance company are involved in paying the doctor.

The problem with the fee-for-service system is its perverse incentive. It encourages physicians to violate their fiduciary agency relationship with patients and their insurers, thus providing and charging for more (or more expensive) services. In this way, the fee-for-service system leads to the overutilization of health services. When coupled with the moral hazard facing the adequately insured patient, the perverse incentive of the fee-for-service system accounts for a considerable part of the problem of rapidly rising health care costs.

A second method of paying physicians involves capitation techniques. Under such a system the physician receives a fixed amount per patient per year regardless of the amount or nature of services provided. On the one hand, this eliminates the incentive to provide more (or more expensive) services than their patients actually need. This represents an improvement over the fee-for-service system. On the other hand, the capitation system creates a new but equally perverse incentive. It motivates physicians to provide fewer services or to substitute less expensive ones than their patients actually need. This incentive leads to underutilization or skimping, because the fewer (or less costly) services provided results in greater profit-taking for the physician.

The third method for the payment of physicians involves straight salaries. Under this arrangement the physician is paid for a fixed-length workweek. Therefore, the perverse incentives of the fee-for-service and capitation systems are avoided. Placing physicians on salaries, however, has its own problem. It promotes what Mechanic (1975) identifies as a "target-time" orientation wherein salaried physicians respond to increased work loads (more patients) by spending less time with each patient. This occurs because the physicians are neither paid for each service provided (as in fee-for-service), nor for each patient (as in capitation), nor for each time-unit spent (as in wage labor). In the absence of any supplemental rewards, salaried physicians apparently expand or shrink the demand for their services to fill or fit their time allocation.

Hospital Reimbursement Methods

Describing the ways in which hospitals have (prior to the Prospective Payment System introduced as part of Medicare in 1983) traditionally been reimbursed is at the same time both an easy and a difficult task. It is easy in that there is a perverse incentive that has been involved in nearly all forms of hospital reimbursement. It is the reliance on cost-plus techniques. Under such arrangements the hospital had no incentive to contain costs. Indeed, the more costly a hospital episode was, the more profit the hospital traditionally made. This is because hospitals had traditionally been reimbursed for the actual costs of the services they provided plus an operating margin (the moral equivalent of a profit margin in not-for-profit settings) of about 3 to 5 percent. Therefore, bigger (more costly) always meant better (more profitable) for the hospital. This served as a major inducement for ever-increasing hospital costs.

Describing traditional methods of cost-plus (or subsequently cost or cost-minus; see Wolinsky and Marder, 1985) reimbursement techniques becomes more difficult when one turns to particular methods. Generally speaking, there were five basic types (see Glaser, 1986; Richardson, 1984). The first involved reimbursement for specific services rendered. As such, it is the organizational analog of the fee-for-service system of paying physicians. The hospital merely billed the patient's third-party insurer for the charges incurred for services provided. Similar to this was the per case method in which the hospital was paid for all the care provided to the insured patient. A third reimbursement method involved capitation payments. This, too, represents an organizational version of the same technique used to pay physicians.

Two slightly more complicated methods were proportional budgeting and per diem reimbursement. Proportional budgeting operated as follows. The hospital was paid for the amount of services consumed by the enrollees of a specific insurance plan based on the proportion that that plan's patients constituted of the hospitals overall patient load. For example, if subscribers to Blue Cross accounted for 40 percent of the hospital's patient load, then Blue Cross reimbursed that hospital for 40 percent of its total costs. Per diem reimbursement was slightly more straightforward. Under it the hospital was paid based on the number of days the patient was hospitalized. The daily rate was determined by adding up the total annual costs of running the hospital and dividing by the total number of patient days. Thus, the per diem approach arrives at an average cost per patient day.

It is important to note two features about these traditional methods of hospital reimbursement. First, with the exception of the specific services technique, all the reimbursement methods necessitate an ongoing agreement between the hospital and the third-party insurer. The reason for this is that it is most difficult to determine precisely the real cost of services provided to any given patient in the hospital. This leads to the second point. With the possible additional exception of the capitation technique, all these reimbursement methods are based on retrospective audits and year-end adjustments. That is, although the hospital and the third-party insurer agree to a tentative per diem (for example) payment rate for 1988 based on the known costs for 1987, it is not until the hospital's total costs for 1988 are known (in early 1989) that the financial books are closed. (Note that pro-

spective budgeting takes a per diem approach but estimates the target year's cost and then reimburses at that level with no year-end adjustment. Thus, under that scenario hospitals that come in under their projected budget make a profit, and those that do not incur a loss.)

It is the compounded effect of the perverse incentives of patient, physician, and hospital reimbursement that is fundamentally responsible for the crisis in health care costs. Insured patients face only limited barriers to the consumption of health services. Physicians, and other providers approved by third-party insurers, are more often than not faced with the incentive to provide more (and more costly) services in order to maximize their incomes. And the same has been true for hospitals. In order to overcome these traditionally perverse incentives, new methods of paying for health care have been developed. Because the bulk of health care costs occur in the hospital, it has become the primary target for such initiatives as Diagnostic Related Groups.

Diagnostic Related Groups: The Biggest Name in Cost Containment

On September 3, 1983, the Congress of the United States passed the Tax Equity and Fiscal Responsibility Act (TEFRA). No single piece of legislation has ever had the impact on the health care delivery system like TEFRA. It mandated a fundamentally new method by which the federal government pays for the hospital care received by its Medicare program beneficiaries. This new method significantly altered the way that hospitals and the doctors associated with them do their business. To fully understand the implications of this momentous change in the health care delivery system, we must first review the history and definitions behind it, and then consider the experience of its effects to date. Only then can we turn to the issue of whether cost containment has gone too far.

History and Definitions

Perhaps the most reasonable question associated with TEFRA is why Congress waited until 1983 to implement it. Two answers to that question come to mind—one immediately and one only after some reflection. The first is that the development and refinement of a new method for hospital reimbursement is a Herculean task. It requires the initial theoretical identification of an appropriate set of incentives designed to facilitate cost containment. These incentives must then be translated into practical techniques for the accurate and timely transfer of billions of dollars in insurance funds. Finally, the new plan must be successfully demonstrated at least on a statewide basis for several years. And that was the easy part.

The second part of the answer to the question of why it was only in 1983 that TEFRA was adopted is somewhat less obvious. To effectively introduce a radically new method of reimbursing hospitals requires the introducer to have some control over the health care delivery system. Otherwise, who will pay any attention? As indicated in chapter 3, there is no health care delivery system in the United States in a true sense. Unlike the situation in Britain or Canada, the federal government does not own or operate the health care industry. Similarly, no other commercial insurer has a large enough share of the market to dictate terms to the providers from which it buys services for its enrollees.

At least not until very recently. By the early 1980s the federal government was picking up the tab for close to half of all health care expenditures. As such, it gained near monopsonist power. That is, the federal government clearly emerged as the principal buyer of health services. Therefore, it obtained the power to effectively dictate the price (and the method of establishing that price) that it would pay for the services its beneficiaries needed. Coupled with the rapidly rising cost of medical care, the achievement of this near monopsonist power set the stage for the passage of TEFRA.

The fundamental component within TEFRA is the use of Diagnostic Related Groups (DRGs) as the method of paying hospitals for services received by Medicare beneficiaries. The concept of DRGs was developed by Thompson and Fetter (see Fetter, Youngsoo, Freeman, and Thompson, 1980) at Yale University's School of Organization and Management. The fundamental logic was to construct a method that would define specific hospital case types (470 of them based on initial diagnosis, surgical versus medical treatment, complications or comorbidities, and the patient's age) for which there would be considerable internal homogeneity with regard to outputs and services consumed. Then, average costs could be calculated for that particular DRG, and hospitals could be reimbursed based on their actual DRG case load rather than on a per diem or service basis. (For extensive critiques of and alternatives to the DRG system see Horn, 1983; Horn and Sharkey, 1983; Horn, Sharkey, and Bertram, 1983.)

At the same time that the concept of and logic behind DRGs is straightforward if not intuitively pleasing, its alteration of the incentive structure for hospital reimbursement represents a monumental achievement. The reason for this is as follows. Under DRGs the hospital receives a predetermined and fixed payment for each DRG-type patient regardless of the actual costs associated with that particular patient. For example, consider a hypothetical case involving a Medicare beneficiary having coronary bypass surgery with cardiac catheterization, or DRG-106. Assume that the current DRG schedule, which is adjusted on an annual basis, for DRG-106 is $15,000. This means that the hospital in which our hypothetical patient is operated on will receive a flat payment of $15,000 for all of the care associated with this particular coronary bypass episode.

In 1984 DRG-106 episodes averaged about a 14-day stay in the hospital. If for some reason this particular patient needs to stay in the hospital longer or if for some reason the associated costs of treating this particular patient exceed $15,000, the hospital absorbs the loss. The reason for this is that the hospital is paid by the episode and not by the particular services provided. If, however, the hospital can provide care for this particular patient for less than the set $15,000 payment, then it will show a profit. In this regard, DRGs are comparable to the capitation reimbursement techniques described above, albeit based on episodes rather than person-years of care.

Because they are quite similar to capitation payment methods, DRGs create comparable perverse incentives for hospitals. The two most important of these are skimping on the services associated with each episode and selectively focusing on only those DRGs for which it can make a profit. Skimping at the hospital level includes substituting cheaper labor and material inputs for more expensive ones (e.g., using licensed practical instead of registered nurses or generic instead of name-brand drugs), providing fewer services per episode (e.g., reducing the number of laboratory tests ordered and the frequency of their repetition), and discharging the patient sooner than would be the case under traditional insurance mechanisms. Selectively focusing on only profitable DRGs involves a shift to a "product line" management orientation. As a result, "orphan" product lines, at which the hospital is inefficient due to their low frequency, are discontinued, as are high-risk products.

Because they are based on episodes of care rather than person-years, however, DRGs have an additional perverse incentive. It is quite reminiscent of that associated with the fee-for-service system. Under DRGs the hospital is paid for each episode of care that it provides. This creates an incentive for the hospital to generate additional (but separate) episodes. This is especially likely to occur after the hospital identifies its more profitable DRGs (i.e., product lines). At that time the hospital may take action to generate the demand for DRG episodes that it is profitable at providing. Although utilization review techniques have been implemented to prevent hospitals from generating needless episodes, it is generally believed that there is a considerable amount of unmet need in the population. This is especially true among the elderly (who are the major

targets of DRG-based reimbursement systems), and includes lens procedures (DRG-39), atherosclerosis (DRG-132), chronic obstructive pulmonary disease (DRG-88), simple pneumonia (DRG-89), cardiac arrythmia (DRG-138), and angina pectoris (DRG-140). Therefore, many hospitals have begun "outreach" programs that specialize in bringing in elderly patients with these conditions.

The Experience with DRGs to Date

As Light (1986b) indicates, DRGs have clearly become the major strategy for containing hospital costs. Through them the federal government can more easily tighten the health care delivery system by either freezing or reducing the amount it pays for each DRG. As the number of individual states that have also adopted a DRG-like reimbursement system increases, the monopsonistic power of the federal government is enhanced, as its competitive buyers mimic its behavior. Therefore, there can be little doubt that DRGs have brought about a change in the health care industry.

What is not quite clear is exactly what effect DRGs have had on cost containment. There are two reasons for this. First, there is the problem of agreement over what are appropriate indicators of costs, so that changes in them can be tracked over time. Second, there is the problem of time itself. TEFRA was adopted in 1983. Depending on the anniversary date of their fiscal year, however, hospitals did not have to shift to the DRG system for Medicare patients until October 1, 1984. Therefore, it is not clear that either the manifest (better cost containment per episode) or latent (more episodes) effects of DRGs will yet be noticeable. Neither of these problems can be resolved here.

What can be done, however, is to look at the facts as they exist today based on data taken from the National Hospital Discharge Survey (see Department of Health and Human Services, 1986). These data reveal three important points about the average length of stay. First, length of stay varies by region. It is higher in the Northeast and lowest in the West, regardless of age. Second, regardless of age or region, the average length of stay has decreased over the past 15 years. Third, the decline in average length of stay is considerably larger among the elderly than among the nonelderly, regardless of region. This is to be expected, because the cost containment effects of DRGs are fundamentally directed at the elderly. Therefore, if DRGs are effective, then the reduction in the average length of stay among the elderly should exceed that of the nonelderly. And indeed it does, as the average annual percent of change between 1980 and 1984 (shown in Table 13-2) demonstrates.

Another indicator with which to assess the effect of DRGs is the number of hospital episodes. Table 13-3 contains such information (as well as average length of stay) at the general level for all hospital discharges among those 65 and over, and more specifi-

Table 13-2. Annual percent of change in average length of stay for persons in short-stay, nonfederal hospitals, 1980 to 1984.

Age and region	Year				
	1980	1981	1982	1983	1984
Under 65 years					
Northeast	+0.27	−1.74	−1.58	−3.09	−2.64
North Central	+1.64	−2.22	+1.20	−2.71	−2.13
South	−0.59	−0.03	−2.18	−0.53	−6.22
West	+1.92	−0.36	−2.76	−1.74	−0.22
65 years and over					
Northeast	−0.59	−0.46	−6.15	−1.32	−6.57
North Central	−0.71	−2.57	−1.55	−6.42	−9.68
South	−0.99	−0.39	−4.38	−3.41	−8.05
West	−4.37	−3.50	−0.52	−2.86	−7.81

SOURCE: Department of Health and Human Services. 1986. *Utilization of Short-Stay Hospitals by Diagnostic-Related Groups, United States, 1980−84.* DHHS Publication No. 86−1748. Washington, DC: U.S. Government Printing Office.

Table 13-3. Number and average length of stay for patients 65 years and older discharged from short-stay hospitals by selected DRGs, 1980 to 1984.

DRG number and group	Number of cases (1,000s)					Average length of stay (days)				
	1980	1981	1982	1983	1984	1980	1981	1982	1983	1984
All DRGs (1–470)	9,864	10,408	10,697	11,302	11,226	10.7	10.5	10.1	9.7	8.9
DRG-14 Strokes	281	294	295	305	339	15.1	15.8	15.4	14.4	12.0
DRG-39 Lens procedures	313	387	429	473	394	3.7	3.2	2.9	2.6	2.3
DRG-88 Chronic obstructive pulmonary disease	270	304	300	320	272	9.8	9.9	9.8	9.6	9.0
DRG-89 Simple pneumonia or pleurisy (age 70 and over)	282	281	276	303	350	11.0	11.2	10.7	10.7	9.3
DRG-127 Heart failure and shock	349	363	387	402	456	10.0	9.9	9.7	9.5	8.4
DRG-132 Atherosclerosis (age 70 or over)	442	422	427	406	282	9.8	9.4	8.8	8.7	7.1
DRG-138 Cardiac arrythmia (age 70 or over)	140	168	181	193	218	7.8	7.3	7.1	7.0	6.1
DRG-148 Angina pectoris	147	161	195	217	272	7.1	7.0	6.6	6.2	5.6

SOURCE: Department of Health and Human Services. 1986. *Utilization of Short-Stay Hospitals by Diagnostic-Related Groups, United States, 1980−84.* DHHS Publication No. 86−1748. Washington, DC: U.S. Government Printing Office.

cally for selected conditions most salient to the elderly. If DRGs have had their anticipated effect, then some changes should occur between the 1980 to 1983 (pre-DRG) levels, and the 1984 (post-DRG) data. It is important to note, however, that there are two alternative explanations for any observed changes, either of which is as viable as the effect of DRGs. These alternative explanations involve real changes in inpatient morbidity and the artifactual change in hospital record keeping associated with DRGs. Nonetheless, several relatively large changes are evident between 1980 to 1983 and 1984.

With regard to all discharges there is a minuscule (less than 1 percent) drop between 1983 and 1984 of about 76,000 episodes. This is accompanied by a very large (more than 8 percent) average decline in the length of stay of about 0.8 days. Because the former decline (slight as it is) comes after three years of more sizable increases, and because the latter decline is at least twice as large as any previous one-year drop, these data suggest that DRGs have had a significant effect on the health care delivery system.

The data for the specific DRG categories shown, however, yield an apparently more complicated picture. On the one hand, the number of episodes for strokes are up by more than 11 percent, simple pneumonia among those 70 years or older is up by 16 percent, heart failure is up by about 13 percent, cardiac arrythmia is up by about 13 percent, and angina pectoris is up by 25 percent. On the other hand, the number of episodes for lens procedures is down by nearly 17 percent, chronic obstructive pulmonary disease is down by 15 percent, and atherosclerosis is down by nearly 31 percent. When other factors are taken into consideration (such as the shift from the performance of lens procedures as inpatient to outpatient surgeries), however, it appears that these selected DRGs most directly associated with the elderly have experienced a considerable increase in frequency between 1983 and 1984. This suggests that the perverse incentive of DRGs (to generate more episodes) is also occurring.

The changes in length of stay associated with the increase in the volume of episodes

similarly suggest that the perverse incentives of DRGs (in terms of too-early discharges) are operating. All of the DRGs shown in Table 13-3 experienced a considerable decline in their associated average length of stay. When considered together, then, the volume of episodes and average length of stay data suggest that hospitals have begun to discharge Medicare patients earlier as well as to reach out and generate more DRG episodes. Unfortunately, it is not possible to reach a definitive conclusion with these data.

Has Cost Containment Gone Too Far?

There can be no doubt that cost containment has become the principal issue facing the health care delivery system today or that DRGs have become the principal weapon in the armamentarium. The reasons why cost containment efforts were necessary are also well established (see Anderson, 1985; Fuchs, 1986a; Starr, 1982). In fact, the only thing that remains in doubt is how far cost containment efforts will be allowed to go. Although a philosophical discussion of what the most desirable health care delivery system should include and whom it should serve is beyond the scope of this chapter, it seems appropriate to beg the issue of whether cost containment has already gone too far.

In an insightful essay addressing this issue, Fuchs (1986b) notes that there are only three basic ways in which cost containment can be achieved. The first is to force health care providers to increase their production efficiency, thereby delivering the same amount and kind of health services using fewer inputs, thus reducing costs. Although there are always inefficiencies to be eliminated, doing so will not have much of an effect. After all, as Fuchs points out, the issue was never how health care was produced, but rather what health care was delivered.

The second way in which costs may be contained is by reducing the amount of money paid for the goods and services input to produce health care (Fuchs, 1986b). As was the case with production efficiency, it is also possible to trim some "fat" from the input matrix (such as reducing physicians' fees or nurses' salaries). But this is also not likely to have a major effect, unless the suppliers of these inputs are perpetually elastic (always willing to have their prices reduced). And it is likely that at some point these suppliers will leave the marketplace rather than accept further reductions in the prices of their goods and services.

This brings us to the third and easiest way to contain health care costs (Fuchs, 1986b). It simply involves the delivery of fewer health services. This may take the form of fewer hospital admissions, more truncated lengths of stay, or less laboratory testing and imaging (e.g., X rays, CT scans). Indeed, the simplicity of this approach is self-evident. Unfortunately, continued reliance on this method of achieving cost containment raises an entirely new question. What effect do such reductions in the amount of health services provided have on health and social welfare?

According to Fuchs (1986b), the answer depends on how the reductions are made. He identifies three likely scenarios that involve equal absolute reductions (such as two days less hospitalization per patient), equal percentage reductions (the same relative amount per patient), and unequal percentage reductions (wherein the heaviest users of health services would receive the largest reductions). Fuchs notes that the outcome will also be influenced by how sensitively the reductions are made (i.e., how effectively they will be concentrated on those patients who receive too much care). Unfortunately, there is insufficient data to definitively determine either which scenario is taking place or what its outcome will be.

Fuchs's (1986b) discussion, however, does bring us full circle in this chapter. We began by noting that regardless of whether traditional economic principles may be straightforwardly applied to the health care industry, three noneconomic decisions must be made before we attempt to apply them. These decisions include the amount to be spent on health services and their composition, the best method for producing those health services, and the method for dis-

tributing them. Health care economics can only resolve the cost containment problem after these fundamentally moral and social decisions have been made.

Summary

This chapter was divided into three sections. The first focused on the applicability of traditional economic theory to the health care industry. Three factors make the medical marketplace economically unique: the subsidy effect associated with health insurance; insufficient knowledge on the part of patients and their doctors about the cost of health care, its efficacy, and its necessity; and the potential for supplier-induced demand for health services. Accordingly, public policy initiatives are needed to achieve the goals desired for the health care delivery system. Before those goals can be reached, however, economists note that they must first be defined. This requires that three decisions be made: the amount to be spent on health services and their composition; the best method for producing those health services; and the appropriate method for distributing them.

The second section focused on financing health care. It began with an overview of the theory of insurance and its distribution in society. Although only about 10 percent of all Americans are consistently without any form of private or public health insurance, nearly 25 percent of those under age 65 are inadequately insured. From the patient's perspective, health insurance policies come in three basic forms: indemnity, service, and prepaid plans. Although the former creates some price consciousness on the patient's part, the latter creates moral hazard. There were also three ways of paying physicians: fee-for-service, capitation, and straight salaries. Each has its own perverse incentive, respectively resulting in overutilization, skimping, and a target-time mentality.

Reimbursing hospitals involves more numerous and complex methods. Nonetheless, the traditional approaches have generally been referred to as cost-plus techniques, which generate perverse incentives similar to those facing physicians under fee-for-service arrangements. Only with the advent of the DRG system of reimbursement for Medicare patients in 1983 was this tradition modified. DRGs were discussed at length in the last section of this chapter. After reviewing both the concept and its implementation, it was suggested that the perverse incentive associated with DRGs may be to both skimp on the care provided per episode of illness (as in too-early discharges) and to generate additional episodes that would not otherwise have occurred. Although the limited evidence presently available appears to bear this out, it is too early to reach a definitive answer.

14. Quality Assurance, the Medicalization of Life, and the Coming of the Physician Surplus

IN THIS final chapter we shall shift our attention to three of the most interesting and pressing issues facing the health care delivery system today. The first issue is quality assurance. As more attention is focused on the rapidly rising cost of health care, less seems to be paid to the quality of that care. We will begin by presenting a brief overview of the issues involved in quality assessment. Then we will review the three major approaches for assessing health care quality (process, outcome, and structural methods). This section will conclude with a consideration of the effects of current cost-containment policies on the quality of health care delivered in the United States.

The second issue to be addressed is the medicalization of life. Medicalization involves the redefinition of behavior previously considered to be socially deviant as a medical problem. It is especially concerned with the labeling of certain behaviors as constituting an illness syndrome. To gain a better understanding of this issue, we will first review the basic postulates of the medicalization perspective, including the notions of social and cultural iatrogenesis. Then we will illustrate the medicalization process by examining how the hyperkinetic impulse disorder came to be identified.

The third section of this chapter will focus on the coming of the physician surplus. It will begin by considering the conceptual and methodological issues associated with determining how many physicians are too many. Then it will focus on the implications of the coming surplus. This will include the potential effects on individuals, on the cost of health care, and on other health care practitioners.

336

*Quality Assurance,
the Medicalization
of Life, and the
Coming of the
Physician Surplus*

Quality Assurance

Overview

There are two important components to any discussion of the quality of health care (see Brook, Davies-Avery, Greenfield, Harris, Lelah, Solomon, and Ware, Jr., 1977; Donabedian, 1980, 1981). The first involves measuring the quality of the health care provided at any given point in time, usually referred to as quality assessment. Quality assurance is the second component. It involves the ongoing monitoring of health care quality against some minimally defined standard. Implicit (if not explicit) in the notion of quality assurance is the assumption that failure to meet the established minimum standards initiates some corrective mechanism. Although neither quality assessment nor assurance is any easy task, the latter is more difficult. It requires some degree of social and moral consensus about how good health care must be in order to be acceptable.

Health care quality may be defined as the degree of excellence or conformity to standards. That definition, however, requires the completion of five important tasks (LoGerfo and Brook, 1984). These include (1) setting the standards (whether they be goals to be met or averages to be obtained); (2) establishing reliable and valid methods of measuring those standards; (3) comparing actual performances of health care providers to the standards; (4) determining how much of any observed deviation is the result of who's performance (i.e., patient, physician, or environment); and (5) implementing appropriate and effective mechanisms to eliminate the deficiencies. These tasks are exacerbated by the fact that much of medical practice is based on the personal, independent, clinician's experiences rather than on a straightforward, codified system of knowledge. As a result, discussions of quality assessment are frequently, sometimes permanently, mired in a debate over the proper definition of standards.

To a considerable extent the issues behind evaluating health care quality are analogous to the reporter's traditional guidelines for good storywriting. These guidelines focus on the "who," "what," "where," "when," "why," and "how" questions. With respect to health care quality, the "who" refers to the population from which the assessment will be made. An example would be all those individuals operated on by the hypothetical Doctor Smith. "What" refers to the particular services (or topic) to be evaluated. In the case of Dr. Smith it might involve the appendectomies that he has performed. "Where" refers to the site at which the care was delivered. Because Dr. Smith, like most physicians, has admitting and surgical privileges at more than one hospital, it is necessary to specify which of those will be considered. "When" refers to the point in the process of delivering health care at which the quality assessment takes place. The three typical modes include prospective, concurrent, and retrospective assessments. "Why" refers to the reasons or motivation for the evaluation process. It may be that Dr. Smith is being reviewed because of malpractice accusations, in consideration of admitting and surgical privileges at yet another hospital, or for promotion to chief of surgery. Depending upon the motivation behind the review, different issues will be raised and different answers may be found. Finally, the "how" refers to the actual method to be used in assessing quality. This represents the most important of the six questions. The three basic methods of quality assessment, which focus on structure, process, and outcome, are discussed below.

The Three Basic Methods of Quality Assessment

Each of the three basic methods of quality assessment focuses on a different dimension of the delivery of health care. Structural measures reflect primarily the setting in which that care is delivered. This includes the facility itself, the personnel in it, and its organizational structure (see Donabedian, 1980, 1981; LoGerfo and Brook, 1984). In its simplest form, the underlying assumption in structural assessments of

health care quality is this: If the structural characteristics of the setting are good, then it necessarily follows that the process of medical care that occurs within it and the resulting outcomes will also be good. Among the structural characteristics most often examined are compliance with existing codes and regulations (such as fire and safety standards), the number and training level of personnel (such as the ratio of physicians and nurses per patient, whether the doctors are board-certified or whether the nurses are registered or licensed), the clarity of rules, regulations, and other aspects of bureaucratic structure, and the existence of peer review mechanisms.

Structural assessments of health care quality are attractive to administrators and health services researchers for the same reason. They are relatively easy and inexpensive to conduct. Most of the information needed is either readily available from existing documents or from a quick inspection of the facility. That is the greatest strength of structural assessments. Their greatest weakness, however, is that good structure is a *necessary* but not a *sufficient* criteria for quality assurance.

An excellent example of using structural methods to assess health care quality is Shortell and LoGerfo's (1981) examination of myocardial infarction and appendectomy cases drawn from a representative sample of hospitals. They performed regression analyses on a considerable amount of data obtained on the hospital facilities, their personnel, and their organizational structure. The results show that after the volume of patients per physician (an indicator of the degree of regionalization and specialization), the most important predictor of standardized mortality ratios for acute myocardial infarctions was whether the president of the medical staff was on the hospital's governing board. In those hospitals where this was the case, the standardized mortality rates were considerably lower. Similarly, the most important predictor of whether the appendectomies were necessary (i.e., the pathology reports were not normal) was the frequency of medical staff committee meet-

ings (an indicator of the intensity of peer review). The more frequent the staff meetings, the less likely normal appendices were to be removed.

These results led Shortell and LoGerfo (1981) to emphasize the importance of organizational structure on achieving and maintaining quality health care. Indeed, they conclude that

the actual organization of the medical staff itself, as reflected partly by participation in hospital-wide decision-making bodies and communication through committee meetings, appears to be most strongly associated with the quality of care provided. Thus, activities aimed at changing medical staff organization and articulating its relationship and involvement with the overall hospital organization and decision-making process may be a key factor in improving the quality of hospital care.

At the same time that Shortell and LoGerfo's work demonstrates the utility of structural methods of quality assessment, however, it underscores one of their major weaknesses. Because most such structural assessments rely on cross-sectional data, it is not possible to establish the direction of the causal relationship. On the one hand, it is possible that the organizational structure (in which the president of the medical staff serves on the hospital's governing board) caused the quality of health care. On the other hand, it is also possible that the consistently high quality of health care provided in these hospitals led to their development of organizational structures in which the hospital's governing board recognized the medical staff's contributions by inviting their president to serve on the board. Therefore, it is not certain that changes in medical staff organization would necessarily result in better-quality health care, although Flood and Scott (1978) have reached similar conclusions from their work.

Process measures of health care quality focus on what is done to patients (see Donabedian, 1980, 1981; LoGerfo and Brook, 1984). Perhaps the most typical approach to process measures involves the use of checklists or treatment protocols of what should be done for a particular condition. The

338

Quality Assurance,
the Medicalization
of Life, and the
Coming of the
Physician Surplus

actual care delivered is compared to the checklists, and any discrepancies are noted as deviations from acceptable standards. At the heart of this approach is the following assumption. If the right things (i.e., those on the checklist) have been done in the right sequence, then quality health care has been provided. The most common form of quality assessments using the process method are medical audits.

Process methods are popular for two reasons. First, they are relatively easy to operationalize. Usually a panel of physicians specializing in the condition under consideration, such as upper respiratory infections (URIs), is selected. They are then asked to collectively indicate what should be done in the process of treating URIs. After consensus has been reached about the minimally required regimen, a checklist is drawn up to indicate this process. The checklist is then given to medical records technicians who review (audit) the files of the providers under scrutiny. That suggests the second reason why process measures have become so popular. They are seldom patient- or time-dependent. Therefore, they can be conducted without intruding upon the patient during the sick role, and without relying upon either the patient's or the provider's recollection of what was actually done.

Although process measures focus more directly on what was done to patients than their structural counterparts, they are not without their own problems. The most practical problem is their reliance on the medical record for information about whether the procedures contained on the checklist were performed. Simply put, it is not always the case (especially in noninstitutional settings) that medical records contain all of the information necessary. When such information is absent, process measures assume that the procedure in question was not performed. Although this provides some incentive for better record keeping, it limits the utility of medical audits to more bureaucratized practice settings.

A more damning weakness of process methods is the absence of a clear relationship between the process of delivering health care and the outcome of that care (see Brook

et al., 1977). There simply is no compelling evidence that adequate diagnostic workups and treatments result in favorable health outcomes. Accordingly, the validity of the fundamental assumption underlying process methods is questionable. It is also possible that the use of process (especially checklist) measures of health care quality simply results in the increased use of "appropriate" tests with no demonstrable gain in outcome quality. Adherents to this criticism suggest that the growing reliance on such checklist approaches merely stimulates the practice of "defensive medicine." They argue that physicians come to order all the laboratory tests contained in the approved algorithm only to cover themselves from malpractice litigation, seldom making use of all the information obtained.

An additional criticism of the checklist approach is often mentioned by physicians (see LoGerfo and Brook, 1984). They argue that medicine is not practiced in a "laundry-list" fashion; rather it involves an iterative decision-making process that is not well reflected by checklist methods. In response to this criticism, the criteria-mapping approach has been introduced to measure the process of delivery health care (see Greenfield, Lewis, and Kaplan, 1975). In it good care is defined more loosely and in an iterative fashion based on the provider's response to signs, symptoms, laboratory test results, and severity of the illness. Greenfield et al. have effectively demonstrated the utility of this technique with medical record data for cases involving diabetes mellitus. As was the case with checklists, however, criteria mapping requires reasonably detailed medical records for review.

The third method of quality assessment focuses on the effects or results of the health care delivered. In so doing, outcome measures avoid the tenuous linkages that the structural and process methods must assume exist (see Brook et al., 1977; Donabedian, 1980, 1981; LoGerfo and Brook, 1984). Therefore, the face validity of outcome measures is somewhat more intuitively pleasing. As we shall soon see, however, they, too, are not without their own problems.

Outcome measures generally come in

two forms. The first involves the use of general health status measures, such as the Sickness Impact Profile (SIP; see Bergner, Bobbitt, and Krenel, 1976). As indicated in chapter 4, the SIP involves an individual's response to an extensive series of questions tapping a number of dimensions of health status. These include a general feeling of well-being, functional abilities, and social interaction. As such, the SIP or other general measures of health status are appropriate for use with a variety of different disease entities. For example, the SIP could be used to measure the effect of treatment regimens on diabetes, hypertension, cardiovascular disease, or cancer patients. All of these conditions would likely have some effect on the SIP, indicating its suitability for monitoring the illness course. This utility of general health status measures, however, also suggests their limitations. Principal among these is their lack of disease-specific precision in detecting changes in outcomes.

The second form of outcome measures involves disease-specific measures. These trade off the general applicability of global health status measures for their enhanced sensitivity to the particular condition under scrutiny. Among the most well known of the disease-specific measures is the use of mortality (or survival) rates for particular illnesses. For example, five-year survival rates are typically calculated for each of the various types of cancer. These are especially useful in determining the relative value of different treatment regimens for the same condition. For example, it was the comparison of five-year survival rates calculated separately for breast cancer victims who received surgical, chemotherapy, radiation, and mixed (a combination of surgery and either chemotherapy or radiation) regimens that led to the identification of mixed therapy as the treatment of choice (see LoGerfo and Brook, 1984).

Although outcome measures eliminate the validity problems associated with either the structural or process methods of quality assessment, they introduce three equally formidable limitations. First, the outcome of a particular illness episode is affected by other factors in addition to the treatment regimen.

One of the most important of these is patient noncompliance. Despite the best-laid plans of health professionals, patients and their families may unintentionally, or even intentionally, fail to comply with the prescribed regimen. Under such circumstances, it seems somewhat inappropriate for a quality assessment method to reach an unfavorable finding.

Another factor besides the treatment regimen that affects the use of outcome measures is changes in the diagnostic method and its accuracy. This can be illustrated by the calculation and comparison of five-year survival rates for breast cancer from the 1960s with those from the 1980s. Over this 30-year period the survival rates have increased substantially. However, techniques are available today to detect this condition earlier and more accurately than ever before. Because earlier diagnosis increases the survival rate, it is likely that a significant amount of the reduction in mortality from breast cancer is due to earlier diagnosis rather than to better treatment. Thus, although much progress has been made, it would be misleading to assume that it is the sole result of more efficacious treatment.

A second limitation of outcome measures is that the data they require is not readily available from medical records. Patients must be interviewed (at some length if protocols such as the SIP are to be used) both at the onset of the treatment regimen and at its conclusion. This introduces the third limitation. Outcome measures are time-dependent. Consider, for example, a situation in which five-year survival rates are to be calculated for a pharmaceutical alternative to surgery. The clinical trials of the new drug therapy would have to run long enough to enroll a sufficient number of patients, who would then have to be followed up for five years. As a result, outcome measures are not conducive for use in situations where a reasonably rapid assessment of health care quality must be made.

As indicated above, the three methods of assessing the quality of health care focus on different aspects of the delivery process. They also rely on different indicators of that quality. Each has its own strengths and

340

*Quality Assurance,
the Medicalization
of Life, and the
Coming of the
Physician Surplus*

weaknesses. Despite these differences, there is some overlap between them. Moreover, it is becoming quite common for quality assessments to incorporate some combination of the three basic methods in order to minimize the limitations of any one of them. As a result, quality assessment is rapidly becoming a rather complex process that provides a more detailed evaluation of health care delivery.

Cost Containment and Quality Assurance

Although the need for cost containment has been well documented (see chapter 13), its potential effect on the quality of health care has received considerably less attention. This is a serious shortcoming that has only recently begun to be addressed (see Donabedian, Wheeler, and Wyszewianski, 1982; Fuchs, 1986a, 1986b; Wyszewianski, Wheeler, and Donabedian, 1982). At the heart of the problem lies the fact that most market-oriented cost containment proposals (see Enthoven, 1978; Feldstein, 1971; McClure, 1978; Pauly, 1968, 1980) focus on increasing the price consciousness of all those involved in the decision-making process. This includes patients, health care providers, third-party insurers, and employer groups.

According to Wyszewianski and colleagues (1982), this focus is further concentrated at the points where three decisions are made: "1) at the point of deciding what insurance to buy or which health care plan to enroll in, 2) at the point of selecting a provider from whom to receive care, and 3) at the point of deciding which services to utilize." The principal method for modifying price consciousness at these three points involves changing the ways in which the federal income tax structure treats employers' contributions toward health insurance premiums and employees' medical expenses. By reducing the subsidy effects for insurance and expenses, the market-oriented proposals expect to create more of an economist's ideal market for health care.

The intentions of the market-oriented proposals are admirable. Their implementation, however, is likely to alter the interaction between patient and practitioner in undesirable ways that will adversely affect the quality of health care. The probability of this occurring is increased by the marked absence of built-in quality assurance mechanisms. Indeed, this is one of the major concerns about the Prospective Payment System introduced during 1983 for Medicare beneficiaries. As indicated in chapter 13, there is growing evidence that Medicare patients are being discharged too early and that hospitals are reaching out to stimulate the demand for their most financially rewarding product lines.

Wyszewianski, Wheeler, and Donabedian, (1982) have been among the first to consider in detail the implications that the market-oriented cost containment proposals have for health care quality. They begin their analysis by identifying six important facts that have been well established in the literature on health care quality. These include the following observations: (1) both the provision of unnecessary services and the failure to provide necessary ones have been documented in various delivery systems; (2) unilateral emphasis on reducing unnecessary services often results in cutting necessary services as well; (3) the general quality of health care is so sufficiently low in the absolute sense that every opportunity ought to be taken to increase it; (4) all subgroups in the population do not receive the same quality of health care; (5) physician performance varies markedly from doctor to doctor; and (6) patient and provider assessments of health care quality do not always coincide. It is on these relationships that Wyszewianski and colleagues base their assessment of the cost containment proposals' implications for health care quality.

After methodically reviewing the market-oriented strategies, Wyszewianski and colleagues (1982) reach two important conclusions. The first is rather obvious. The overall effect will ultimately depend on which plan is adopted and exactly what its provisions include. At issue here are such fundamental components as (Wyszewianski et al., 1982)

the feasibility of cost-sharing provisions related to income; the development of effective mechanisms that pay as much attention to the non-provision of necessary care as to the provision of unnecessary care; the likelihood that consumers can and will become informed about the technical quality and the cost-effectiveness of the care available from different providers; and the extent to which people are induced to join HMOs, and the characteristics of the HMOs that will be available to them.

These components cluster around two themes. One is the ability to alter the health care delivery system in an effective manner, and the other is the ability to enhance consumer sophistication. As indicated in chapter 13, both of these are formidable tasks.

The second conclusion that Wyszewianski and colleagues (1982) reach is based on their view that enhancing consumer sophistication to the level necessary to assure health care quality is not feasible. Therefore, they favor those proposals that reflect less (or no) confidence in achieving consumer sovereignty. They argue that (Wyszewianski et al., 1982) "at the very least the market-oriented proposals must not damage quality on the average, nor make the benefits of quality more inequitably distributed than they are now. To make sure that this does not happen it is essential that all the best features of the current proposals be implemented simultaneously and as a whole. But beyond that, a constant vigilant watch over quality must be the necessary companion of competition in the market for medical care use." Inasmuch as the tradition of health care policy in the United States is most frequently described as something akin to "incrementalist tinkering" (see Lee and Benjamin, 1984), it is not likely that Wyszewianski and colleagues will get their way. Therefore, the tension between cost containment and quality assurance is likely to increase.

The Medicalization of Life

Up to this point we have focused on the good that medicine can, and does, do for patients, their families, and society in general. But sometimes we might be better off without it. The examples that most readily come to mind typically involve clinical iatrogenesis. Illich (1976) defines such doctor-induced injuries as follows:

In the most narrow sense, iatrogenic disease includes only illnesses that would not have come about if sound and professionally recommended treatment had *not* been applied. Within this definition a patient could sue his therapist if the latter, in the course of his management, failed to apply a recommended treatment that, in the physician's opinion, would have risked making him sick. In a more general and more widely accepted sense, clinical iatrogenic disease comprises all clinical conditions for which remedies, physicians, or hospitals are the pathogens, or "sickening" agents.

Although the incidence of clinical iatrogenesis, and the litigation resulting from it, has reached record levels, it is the nonclinical forms of iatrogenesis that have become the concern of many medical sociologists (see Carlson, 1975; Conrad and Schneider, 1980; Freidson, 1970a). After presenting an overview of the issues involved, we shall turn to an application of these concerns in the illustrative case of hyperactive children.

Social and Cultural Iatrogenesis: The Heart of the Medicalization Issue

Throughout this book we have chronicled the rise of American medicine and its special role in society (see Anderson, 1985; Starr, 1982). Concomitant with that rise to power has been the recognition of medicine as one of the two premier social control agencies in society (see Freidson, 1970a; Parsons, 1951). The concern of those who write about the medicalization of life is that the domain that falls under medicine's purview has expanded beyond its functional expertise (see Illich, 1976). Zola (1972) has concisely summarized this argument:

The theme . . . is that medicine is becoming a major institution of social control, nudging aside, if not incorporating, the more traditional institutions of religion and law. It is becoming the new repository of truth, the place where absolute and often final judgments are made by supposedly morally neutral and objective experts. And these judgments are made, not in the name of virtue or legitimacy, but in the name of health. Moreover, this is not occurring through the political power physicians hold or can influence, but is largely an insidious and often undramatic phenomenon accomplished by "medicalizing" much of daily living, by making medicine and the labels "healthy" and "ill" *relevant* to an ever increasing part of human existence.

In general, those who warn of the medicalization of life fear most its implications for the control of social deviance.

And this fear is no small matter. Even the most ardent countercritics of the medicalization thesis acknowledge its salience. For example, in criticizing the critics Fox (1977) writes that

casting persons in the sick role is regarded as a powerful, latent way for society to exact conformity and maintain the status quo. For it allows a semiapproved form of deviance to occur which siphons off potential for insurgent protest and which can be controlled through the supervision or, in some cases, the "enforced therapy" of the medical profession. Thus, however permissive and merciful it may be to expand the category of illness, these observers [those who raise the issue of medicalization] point out, there is always the danger that society will become a "therapeutic state" that excessively restricts the "right to be different" and the right to dissent. They feel that this danger may already have reached serious proportions in this society through its progressive medicalization.

Indeed, the countercritics recognize the seriousness of the issue as well as the deplorable nature of its consequences.

Where the countercritics (see Fox, 1977; Strong, 1979) disagree, however, is on what the current trend really is. In contrast to those who believe that medicalization is on the increase, the countercritics see a trend toward the demedicalization of American society. They cite as evidence for their position the patients' rights movement, the increase in consumerism (including the shift from referring to individuals in treatment as "patients" to "clients" or "consumers"), the recognition of the importance of self-care and "living right" in living longer and healthier lives, and the reidentification of medical problems as social ones (e.g., homosexuality). Perhaps the most controversial evidence mustered by the countercritics is their focus on the changing perspective on pregnancy. They see a shift away from its

being considered an illness and a rise in the use of midwives and natural childbirth methods. For the countercritics this represents a decline in medical responsibilities.

Illich (1976) has clarified, if not strengthened, the critic's view by identifying analogs of clinical iatrogenesis at the social and cultural level. These situations occur "when professional autonomy degenerates into a radical monopoly and people are rendered impotent to cope with their milieu." For Illich, the "radical monopoly" refers to the way in which the social order, especially in America, has come to be built around medicine as its focal point. The result has been a marked decline in the humanity of Homo sapiens.

According to Illich (1976), social iatrogenesis occurs whenever an individual's health is damaged by the adverse effects of the social organization of medicine within the total social milieu. (Note the striking similarity between this approach and Freidson's, 1970a, concern about the flaw of professional autonomy; see chapter 9.) Social iatrogenesis is defined as follows (Illich, 1976): "[It] designates a category of etiology that encompasses many forms. It obtains when medical bureaucracy creates ill-health by increasing stress, by multiplying disabling dependence, by generating new painful needs, by lowering levels of tolerance for discomfort and pain, by reducing the leeway that people are wont to concede to an individual when he suffers, and by abolishing even the right to self care." Thus, social iatrogenesis involves medicine's deprivation of individuals, families, and communities of their right to control their own bodily states and their larger social milieu.

Cultural iatrogenesis, however, is even more devastating. According to Illich (1976) it

sets in when the medical enterprise saps the will of the people to suffer their reality. It is a symptom of such iatrogenesis that the term "suffering" has become almost useless for designating a realistic response because it evokes superstition, sadomasochism, or the rich man's condescension to the lot of the poor. Professionally organized medicine has . . . undermined the ability of individuals to face their reality, to express their own values, and to accept inevitable and often irremediable pain and impairment, decline and death.

In essence, modern medicine has stripped away much of what was once human nature and a fundamentally expected part of human life. One telling example is the changing way in which death has come to be viewed (see chapter 8). It has progressed from a celebration of the life that went on before, to the all-out war against death by means of extraordinary and dehumanizing life-support systems.

These arguments, especially those dealing with cultural iatrogenesis, have been most effective. Indeed, even some of the most staunch countercritics have softened somewhat. Fox's (1977) recognition of the degree to which cultural iatrogenesis has been entrenched in American society is most telling. After rebuking most of the critics' arguments, she notes that

none of these trends implies that what we have called *cultural* demedicalization will take place. The shifts in emphasis from illness to health, from therapeutic to preventive medicine, and from the dominance and autonomy of the doctor to patient's rights and greater control of the medical profession do not alter the fact that health, illness, and medicine are central preoccupations in the society which have diffuse symbolic as well as practical meaning. All signs suggest that they will maintain the social, ethical, and existential significance they have acquired, even though by the year 2000 some structural aspects of the way that medicine and care are organized and delivered may have changed.

Thus, although the social organization of medicine may be modified in order to reduce its "radical monopoly," its dominant role in our culture may require the passage of several successive generations before it suffers any significant erosion.

The Hyperkinetic Impulse Disorder: An Example of the Medicalization of Life

Perhaps a clearer understanding of the general effects of social and cultural iatrogenesis can be gained by an examination of one specific instance of the medicalization of life. Therefore, let us consider the case of the hyperkinetic impulse disorder, or hyper-

activity. In a remarkably informative study Conrad (1976) addresses these issues by raising the following question: "How does deviant behavior become defined as a medical problem?" He then proceeds to document how hyperactivity evolved from a problem of family socialization and control into a specifically medical problem and disease entity.

Conrad (1976) begins by defining the medicalization of deviant behavior. For him it is relatively straightforward and involves the defining of deviant behavior as a medical problem, especially the labeling of certain behaviors as constituting an illness. Once these behaviors have been defined as an illness, it is then in the province of medicine to provide some type of treatment; this becomes a form of social control. Examples of this include defining alcoholism as a disease, drug addiction as a medical problem, and violence as a genetic or brain disorder. This is not a new function of the medical institution: psychiatry and public health have always been concerned with social behavior and functioning, and have traditionally functioned as agents of social control.

How hyperactivity came to be "discovered" as a clinical (medical) problem is a fascinating story.

As early as 1937 experimental research demonstrated that when amphetamines were administered to schoolchildren with behavioral disorders or learning disabilities, these children became more "normal" in their behavior. After terminating the experimental treatment, the children returned to their original behavioral patterns. Although research on childhood behavior disorders continued, it was not until 1957 that the "hyperkinetic impulse disorder" was described as a specific diagnosis in medical journals. And it was nearly 10 years later before there was general agreement that the underlying cause was "minimal brain dysfunction" (see Conrad, 1976).

The most important historical event in the discovery of hyperactivity, however, came not from medicine but from the pharmaceutical revolution (Conrad, 1976). In the 1950s a new drug named Ritalin was synthesized. It has many of the important qualities of amphetamines, but none of their

344

*Quality Assurance,
the Medicalization
of Life, and the
Coming of the
Physician Surplus*

side effects. Upon its approval by the Food and Drug Administration, Ritalin became the treatment of choice for hyperactive children. By the mid 1970s the diagnosis of hyperkinesis became fairly widespread, with an estimated prevalence rate of between 3 and 10 percent of all school-aged children. This has resulted in an interesting example of cohort differences. In the 1970s and 1980s school-aged children who suffered behavior problems were treated using medical regimens. In the 1950s and 1960s, however, these same behavioral problems were dealt with using disciplinary methods.

From a sociological standpoint, Conrad (1976) finds something else more interesting. He notes that

the treatment was available long before the disorder . . . was clearly conceptualized. . . . The social control mechanism (in this case pharmacological treatment) preceded the label (hyperkinesis) by 20 years. This presents an interesting problem for a sociological perspective: Do medical labels appear when medical social control mechanisms are available? In this case, an extremely cynical reading of the history of the development of medical control might be that the label was invented to facilitate the use of a particular social control mechanism, in this case psychoactive drugs.

It is the sociological exploration of the process of medicalizing deviant behavior that consumes most of Conrad's work. In the end, he postulates five conditions necessary for the medicalization of any deviant behavior.

The first condition is that the behavior in question must be defined as being deviant and as a problem for which some portion of society seeks a remedy. In the specific case of hyperactivity, restlessness, aggressiveness, and extreme activity were defined as deviant behavior in both the classroom and familial settings. In addition to defining these symptoms as a problem, teachers and parents felt a need for a way to cope with such deviant behavior outside of traditional obedience responses. The second condition is that existing or traditional forms of social control over the deviant behavior are neither effective nor acceptable. In the case of hyperactivity, the traditional training and socialization of children by parents and teachers was

felt to be both ineffective and no longer appropriate. Indeed, the corporeal punishment of children has come to be viewed as a violation of their individual rights. Accordingly, some new form of social control must be brought into play.

This leads to the third condition. A medical form of social control must be available. Herein lies the importance of discovering that when given certain amphetamines, hyperactive children could be "calmed down" to a "normal" state. The fourth condition for the medicalization of deviant behavior is that there must be some organic data that can be used to document the "true" cause of the deviant behavior. In the case of hyperactivity, the organic syndrome that medicine pointed to was "minimal brain dysfunction." The use of "minimal brain dysfunction" as the "true" culprit in hyperactivity underscores the generally ambiguous and equivocal nature of the "causes" involved in cases of the medicalization of deviant behavior.

The final condition for the medicalization of deviant behavior involves the willingness of the medical profession to accept the nonnormative acts as lying within its jurisdiction. With the case of hyperactivity, this was evidenced by the rapid acceptance among physicians of treating overactive children with Ritalin. As Conrad (1976) points out, this basically involved honoring the school's and parents' labeling of the children as hyperactive. More often than not, there was no serious additional questioning or examination for other underlying factors.

In consort with these five necessary conditions for the medicalization of deviant behavior, Conrad (1976) specifies two related contingencies: "(1) The greater the benefit to established institutions, the greater the likelihood of medicalization, and (2) The greater the acceptance of the proposed scientific explanation, the greater the likelihood of medicalization." With respect to hyperactivity, both the family and the school benefited considerably. This increased the speed with which hyperactivity was medicalized. When coupled with the fact that the "minimal brain dysfunction" syndrome is a very scientific sounding and documentable explanation, it is no wonder that the medicalization of hyperactivity occurred so rapidly.

The Coming of the Physician Surplus

Much has been made of the coming physician surplus (see Anderson, 1985; Graduate Medical Education National Advisory Committee, 1981; Light, 1984, 1985, 1986a, 1986b; Rushing, 1985; Starr, 1982). Indeed, in an August 15, 1986, editorial in the *Journal of the American Medical Association*, J. Alexander McMahon, a former president of the American Hospital Association, labeled the increase in the relative supply of physicians as *the most important* change in the health care industry during the past decade. As such, he ranks it ahead of Diagnostic Related Groups (DRGs), health maintenance organizations (HMOs), and the proliferation of sophisticated technologies. Although not everyone agrees with McMahon about the primal importance of the relative increase in the physician supply (see Hafferty, 1986), there is no disagreement that it is at least one of the key factors facing the health care delivery system today. Therefore, it seems appropriate to bring this book to an end by considering the coming of the physician surplus. To do this we shall first examine the conceptual issues involved in determining how many physicians are too many. Then we shall consider the implications of their increasing relative supply for individuals, the cost of health care, and other providers of health services.

How Many Physicians Are Too Many?

It would seem only logical that the first issue to be addressed in discussions of the coming of the physician surplus would be to reach some consensus on what constitutes a surplus. That, however, has not been the case. Rushing (1985) underscores this point when he writes, "Whether we are indeed entering a period of 'physician surplus' depends on one's perspective. If one views the current supply as ample for meeting the needs of society, the increase is a national

waste and would constitute a surplus or a glut." To be sure, the discussion of the future supply and distribution of physicians presented in chapter 3 assiduously avoided using the term *surplus*. Instead, that discussion focused on the increase in the relative supply of physicians, defined in terms of physician-to-population ratios. The reason for this aversion lies in the difficulty of determining how many physicians are enough and how many extra it takes before a surplus exists.

Many (e.g., Anderson, 1985; Starr, 1982) would simply point to the physician manpower requirements identified by the Graduate Medical Education National Advisory Committee (GMENAC) in 1981, which were discussed at some length in chapter 3 and presented in their entirety in Table 3-5. An informed discussion of the issues, however, must first consider the historical events that brought about the GMENAC report. This becomes self-evident upon the recognition that in the 1960s there was thought to be a physician shortage.

Two factors are believed to have resulted in the perception that there was a drastic physician shortage in the 1960s (Light, 1986b). The first of these was the result of the Hill-Burton Hospital Construction Act passed in the immediate post–World War II era. That act set a national goal of 4.5 hospital beds per 1,000 persons, a standard that exceeded the then-available supply in any state. It also committed nearly $4 billion in federal and over $9 billion in state and local government appropriations for the construction of new hospitals and the renovation of existing ones. According to Light, the Hill-Burton program also "set the stage for training mostly hospital-based specialists." As indicated in chapter 9, this resulted in a "specialty surplus" that did not alleviate the difficulty of finding a primary care physician (see Aiken, Lewis, Craig, Mendenhall, Blendon, and Rogers, 1979).

The second factor involved in the perceived physician shortage of the 1960s was the baby boom (Light, 1986b). Although medical school enrollments increased by more than 15 percent during the 1950s (see Table 9-5), their expansion was not sufficient to maintain the relative supply of physicians. Indeed, the number of patients per active physician actually increased from 706 in 1950 to 735 in 1960. Accordingly, there was a considerable push from both the health care industry and public policy-makers to rapidly expand medical education. As Table 9-5 indicates, this was accomplished by expanding class sizes as well as bringing a number of new medical schools on-line during the 1960s and 1970s.

The result of responding to the perceived shortage of physicians in the 1960s is the alleged surplus of 70,000 physicians by 1990 (see Table 3-5) and 144,700 physicians by 2000 (Graduate Medical Education National Advisory Committee, 1981). In polite terms one might say that this represents an overresponse. Light (1986b), however, suggests that it was far more than that. He notes that even in 1960 the physician-to-population ratio for the United States was almost 50 percent higher than that typically found in HMOs. Inasmuch as the quality of health care in HMOs is at least as good, if not better, than that found in more conventional delivery systems (see Wolinsky, 1980a), this suggests that the relative supply of physicians may have reached the "surplus threshold" three decades ago. At the very least, Light argues that a physician shortage did not exist.

Rushing (1985) is even less restrained. He notes that much of the current pressure for cost containment

is in large measure a result of policies implemented by the state and federal governments in the fifties, sixties and seventies (e.g., the federal Health Manpower Act of 1965). Future increases in the supply of physicians [beyond those shown in Table 3-5] have already been put in place by policy decisions of the past. The point here is not that policymakers are necessarily myopic . . . though the political process in American society probably does encourage a short-term rather than a long-term outlook. In any case, the results of past policy decisions with respect to physician manpower have contributed to an increase in society's expenditures for medical care about which policymakers are now making decisions and will continue to wrestle with in the future.

In essence, the current physician "surplus" is the result of two factors that have tradi-tionally been both most difficult to resolve and highly interrelated. One has been the failure to address head-on the most fundamental question of how many physicians are actually needed. The other has been the deviation of the health care industry from an economist's notion of an ideal marketplace. Although both of these difficulties have been discussed in detail in chapter 13, it bears repeating here that their resolution requires something akin to public utility regulation.

The Implications of Having Too Many Physicians

Regardless of whether one accepts the notion that a physician surplus exists, the marked increase in their relative supply clearly has important implications. It is likely to have a considerable effect on individuals, health care costs, and other health care providers. What is not exactly clear, however, is what the nature of those effects will be. In concluding this chapter we shall briefly consider the views of several leading medical sociologists about the impact on the health care delivery system of having too many physicians (see Hafferty, 1986; McKinlay, 1986; Light, 1986a, 1986b; Lorber, 1986; Rushing, 1985).

With regard to the consequences on physicians themselves, McKinlay (1986) continues to develop his "proletarianization" thesis (McKinlay, 1973, 1982; see also chapter 9). In today's political climate, however, he suggests that it might be more appropriate to refer to it as "corporatization." McKinlay sees three major outcomes from the physician surplus. The first involves the continued demystification of medical knowledge. In many ways this is similar to Haug's (1973, 1975, 1977; Haug and Lavin, 1978, 1981, 1983) view that the knowledge gap between patient and practitioner has been and continues to shrink. The second consequence that McKinlay sees involves the increasing accountability of physicians. As the competition for patients increases, providers are forced to be more responsive to their needs and desires. The third consequence is quite related. As competition increases, physician autonomy (with respect to both colleagues and clients) decreases. Proletarianization (including a dramatic decline in the relative status of physicians) is the inevitable result of these changes.

Lorber (1986) and Light (1986a), however, suggest that the broad brush strokes of McKinlay's (1986) proletarianization thesis neglect some important gender differences in the effects of the physician surplus on doctors. They believe that as the relative supply increases, women physicians will receive preferential consideration in hiring decisions within the more bureaucratic practice settings, such as HMOs. There are three reasons for this. First, women physicians have traditionally commanded less pay for the same amount and kind of work as their male counterparts (see Lorber, 1984; Wolinsky and Marder, 1985). This represents an opportunity for the organization to lower its fixed costs. Second, women physicians traditionally spend more time per patient than their male counterparts, and most of this additional time is believed to focus on the affective aspects of the patient-practitioner relationship. As a result, patient satisfaction is likely to be higher with women physicians. Finally, women physicians typically require fewer follow-up visits with their patients, partly due to the increased time spent gathering additional information during the initial visit. In delivery systems involving capitation-based reimbursement mechanisms this can be a very effective cost containment strategy. Therefore, both Lorber and Light see the effects of the physician surplus as less damaging for women physicians (aside from the moral issues associated with such corporate exploitation) than for their male counterparts.

When viewed from the patient's perspective, the marked increases in the relative supply of physicians suggests their (i.e., patients') enhanced market position. Although a buyers' market (in which terms are dictated to sellers) has not yet been achieved (see Light, 1986a; Rushing, 1985), it seems reasonably clear that ever-increasing attention is being given to issues related to consumer satisfaction. For example, both waiting room queues and the lead time necessary for scheduling routine office visits with phy-

sicians are at their lowest levels in decades (see Aday, Fleming, and Andersen, 1984; Wolinsky and Marder, 1985). Moreover, this newly found concern for the affective dimension of health care has not been limited to the ambulatory setting. It has become especially important with respect to the amenities associated with institutional-based care. Indeed, the 1980s have witnessed the emergence and rapid rise in importance of "guest services" within the organizational structure of hospitals (see Schulz and Johnson, 1983).

The effect of the increasing relative supply of physicians on health care expenditures has been addressed by a number of health economists (e.g., Feldstein, 1983; Pauly and Satterthwaite, 1980; Ramsey, 1980; see also chapter 13). They traditionally focus on the relatively cynical view that additional physicians (Newhouse, 1978) "merely create work for themselves by recommending needless operations, performing more tests, and advising consumers to return for unnecessary observations." Rushing (1985) has recently examined the relationship between the supply of physicians and health care expenditures from a more sociological perspective. He believes that there are four reasons behind the strong positive relationship between the two (which yields a product-moment correlation coefficient of .88).

The first reason is a variation on Durkheim's (1933) classic notion of "dynamic density." Rushing (1985) notes that the necessary precursor for health care expenditures involves patient-practitioner interaction. If the number of practitioners is increased, then the probability of such interaction, and its resultant costs, is also increased. The second reason is somewhat more complex. Rushing suggests that concomitant with the relative increase in the supply of physicians will be a decrease in the pressures they face to move on to the next patient. Therefore, more time is likely to be spent with each patient. This will probably result in the patient's presentation of more symptoms, prompting more probing and subsequent testing by the physician. The consequence is additional expenditures for laboratory tests, their interpretation, and

348

*Quality Assurance,
the Medicalization
of Life, and the
Coming of the
Physician Surplus*

the ultimate reporting of the results to the patient in a subsequent visit.

A third reason for the positive relationship between physician supply and health care expenditures involves expectations. Rushing (1985) notes that patients expect certain things when they visit their physicians. These expectations include the identification and definition of medical needs, and the prescription of regimens to treat them (see chapters 5 and 7 for discussions of the expectations commonly associated between patient and practitioner). Therefore, an increase in the relative supply of physicians represents (Rushing, 1985) "a structural force which provides physicians with more opportunities to do what they are expected to do."

The final factor is a combination of the first three. A considerable amount of patient-practitioner interaction occurs during follow-up visits (see Eisenberg, 1986). Because the amount of initial contact with physicians increases with their relative supply, it follows that the number of follow-up visits is likely to increase as well. Indeed, Rushing (1985) notes that "there is an escalating number of physician-patient contacts as the supply of physicians increases. Consequently, more services are rendered and more charges are to be paid." From the sociological perspective, Rushing argues that it simply does not matter whether the increase in health care expenditures results from supply or demand pressures. Regardless of which is the culprit, "the volume of services increases as the supply of physicians increases."

The policy implications of Rushing's (1985) subsequent analysis are most telling. He believes that it is "questionable" whether recent policy initiatives (including DRGs) will have any appreciable effect on reducing health care expenditures. The reason for this is that those initiatives focus on *unit* costs. Although they may be effective at containing the costs of individual units of health care, Rushing points out that the increasing relative supply of physicians will simply increase the aggregate *volume* of health services delivered (see chapter 13). The end result will be a continued escalation of health care expenditures. Therefore,

Rushing (1985) argues that "it will take organizational and financial changes that represent major departures from the current organization and financing of medical care before upward pressures on expenditures begin to be contained." One of the more promising departures would involve increasing emphasis on person-year capitation reimbursement methods. As indicated in chapter 13, these are most effective at systemwide cost containment. Unfortunately, less than 10 percent of the American public currently receives their health care under such arrangements (such as in HMOs).

The effect of the increasing relative supply of physicians on alternative and assistant practitioners has received the least attention from medical sociologists. Perhaps the most thoughtful considerations have come from Light (1985, 1986b). He suggests that registered nurses may well suffer the most. The reason for this is that they bear the brunt of the effect from both the physician and hospital surpluses. As hospitals are forced to contain costs in the face of ever less-advantageous reimbursements under programs like DRGs, their response has been to focus on reducing labor costs, which effectively means reducing nurse-patient ratios. At the same time, the increasingly technological nature of institutional-based medicine has intensified the specialization movement within nursing. The result may be differentially fewer opportunities for general (i.e., medical-surgical) nurses than for nurse specialists and clinicians.

Similarly, the increasing relative supply of physicians bodes poorly for nursing. One physician response to the resulting competition has been to regain many of the functions (such as the taking of medical histories, blood pressures, and so on) previously delegated to nursing. If this trend continues, nursing's role will become less sophisticated, increasing the likelihood of substituting cheaper labor inputs (nurses' aides and practical nurses) for registered nurses. Similarly, physicians' renewed interest in the delivery of public health and home health care (including the once extinct house call) may encroach on nurses' employment opportunities outside the hospital.

As suggested in chapter 10, the increasing relative supply of physicians may be in the process of fundamentally altering the role of physician extenders. It is reasonably well established that about three fourths of most ambulatory care procedures can be delegated to physician extenders without suffering any decline in the quality of care delivered (see Light, 1985). Moreover, patient satisfaction with them, especially with nurse practitioners, usually exceeds that associated with physicians. Because physician extenders are paid only a fraction of physicians' salaries, they represent a most attractive alternative to more corporatized delivery systems, such as HMOs, and other large-scale buyers of health services (Light, 1986b). As a result, nurse practitioners, nurse midwives, and physicians' assistants are likely to find increasing opportunities in HMOs, hospitals (especially as replacements for medical residents serving as house staff), and industry (as substitutes for company doctors).

Summary

In this chapter we have examined three of the most interesting and pressing issues facing the health care delivery system today. The first section focused on quality assurance. It began by drawing an analogy between quality assurance and the reporter's six guiding questions (i.e., who, what, where, when, why, and how). After considering the difficulties involved in reaching consensus on what constitutes appropriate standards (let alone their operationalization), we turned to the three basic approaches to quality assessment (structural, process, and outcome methods). Each has its own strengths and weaknesses. Structural and process methods are easier to use, but both involve questionable presumptions. The former assumes that if the right organizational features are in place, the outcome will be quality health care. Similarly, the latter assumes that if the right algorithms are followed in treating patients, the outcome will be quality health care. Outcome methods avoid these tenuous assumptions but introduce two other limitations. They assume that no other factors affect the outcome (such as patient noncompliance), and they are both time- and patient-dependent.

The discussion of quality assurance concluded with a consideration of the potential impact on it of the more popular market-oriented cost containment proposals. These programs unilaterally concentrate on increasing the price consciousness of patients, providers, third-party insurers, and employer groups. Although their intent is admirable, they will likely have an adverse effect of the quality of health care because none of them has built-in assurance mechanisms. Therefore, constant vigilance will be necessary if the current absolute level of health care quality is to be maintained.

The second section focused on the medicalization of life. After defining clinical iatrogenesis as doctor-induced injuries, we turned to the more complex issues of social and cultural iatrogenesis. The primary concern here is whether medicine has expropriated the social control functions traditionally associated with the legal, religious, and familial institutions. Both the critics of the health care industry and their (the critics') critics believe that this was once the case. The countercritics, however, believe that demedicalization has been taking place over the past decade or two. As evidence they cite the patients' rights movement, the increase in consumerism and self-care, and the reidentification of previously medical problems as social ones (e.g., homosexuality).

We then considered the hyperkinetic impulse disorder as an example of the medicalization of life. The evidence in this case suggests that the development of an effective medical treatment (psychotropic drugs) resulted in the medicalization of what had previously been only nonnormative behavior. Perhaps more importantly, the hyperactivity example underscores the willingness of the existing social institutions to be relieved of their social control responsibilities. After all, it was the parents and school personnel who went to their doctors seeking a diagnosis of the children's hyperkinetic impulse disorders, and not vice versa.

In the final section we focused on the coming of the physician surplus. We began with a review of two related issues. These

350

*Quality Assurance,
the Medicalization
of Life, and the
Coming of the
Physician Surplus*

were the difficulties in deciding how many physicians are too many and how there came to be too many physicians. The implications of having too many doctors on physicians, patients, health care costs, and other health care providers were then considered. Because the physician surplus is a relatively recent development (and comes almost immediately on the heels of three decades of shortages), its implications are not yet entirely clear. There seems to be general agreement, however, that physicians' relative social and economic advantages are on the decline.

References

Aday, Lu Ann, and Ronald Andersen. 1974. "A Framework for the Study of Access to Medical Care." *Health Services Research* 9:208–20.

Aday, Lu Ann, and Ronald Andersen. 1975. *Access to Medical Care*. Ann Arbor, MI: Health Administration Press.

Aday, Lu Ann, and Ronald Andersen. 1981. "Equity of Access to Medical Care: A Conceptual and Empirical Overview." *Medical Care* 19(December Suppl.):4–27.

Aday, Lu Ann, Ronald Andersen, and Gretchen V. Fleming. 1980. *Health Care in the U.S.: Equitable for Whom?* Beverly Hills, CA: Sage Publications.

Aday, Lu Ann, and Robert Eichhorn. 1972. *The Utilization of Health Services: Indices and Correlates*. DHEW Publication No. 73–3003. Washington, D.C.: U.S. Government Printing Office.

Aday, Lu Ann, Gretchen V. Fleming, and Ronald Andersen. 1984. *Access to Medical Care in the U.S.: Who Has It, Who Doesn't*. Chicago: Pluribus Press.

Aiken, Linda H., Charles E. Lewis, J. Craig, Robert C. Mendenhall, Robert J. Blendon, and David E. Rogers. 1979. "The Contribution of Specialists to the Delivery of Primary Care: A New Perspective." *New England Journal of Medicine* 300:1363–70.

Aiken, Linda H., and David Mechanic, eds. 1986. *Applications of Social Science to Clinical Medicine and Health Policy*. New Brunswick, NJ: Rutgers University Press.

Albrecht, Gary L., and Judith A. Levy. 1982. "The Professionalization of Osteopathy: Adaptation in the Medical Marketplace." *Research in the Sociology of Health Care* 2:161–206.

Alexander, Jeffrey, James Anderson, and Bonnie Lewis. 1985. "Toward an Empirical Classification of Hospitals in Multihospital Systems." *Medical Care* 23:913–32.

Alexander, Jeffrey, Michael Morrisey, and Stephen Shortell. 1986. "Effects of Competition, Regulation, and Corporatization on Hospital-Physician Relationships." *Journal of Health and Social Behavior* 27:220–35.

Alexander, Jeffrey, and Mary Fennell. 1986. "Patterns of Decision Making in Multihospital Systems." *Journal of Health and Social Behavior* 27:14–27.

Alford, Robert. 1975. *Health Care Politics: Interest*

Group Barriers to Reform. Chicago: University of Chicago Press.

American Hospital Association. 1986a. *AHA Guide, 1986 Edition.* Chicago: Author.

American Hospital Association. 1986b. *Hospital Statistics, 1986 Edition.* Chicago: Author.

American Medical Association, National Commission on the Cost of Medical Care. 1978. *National Commission on the Cost of Medical Care, 1976–1977,* 3 vols. Chicago: American Medical Association.

American Nurses' Association. 1985. *Facts About Nursing, 1984–1985.* Kansas City: Author.

American Nurses' Association, Committee on Nursing. 1965. "First Position on Education for Nursing." *American Journal of Nursing* 65:106–11.

American Osteopathic Association. 1982. *What Is a D.O.? What Is an M.D.?* Chicago: Author.

American Osteopathic Association. 1983. *Osteopathic Medicine.* Chicago: Author.

American Osteopathic Association. 1984. *You Probably Think All Doctors Are M.D.s. If So, You're Wrong!* Chicago: Author.

American Psychiatric Association. 1980. *Diagnostic and Statistical Manual of Mental Disorders,* 3rd ed. Washington, DC: Author.

American Red Cross Association. 1985. *What You Should Know About Giving Blood.* Chicago: Author.

Andersen, Ronald. 1968. *A Behavioral Model of Families' Use of Health Services.* Chicago: Center for Health Administration Studies.

Andersen, Ronald, and Odin Anderson. 1967. *A Decade of Health Services.* Chicago: University of Chicago Press.

Andersen, Ronald, and Odin Anderson. 1979. "Trends in the Use of Health Services." In Howard Freeman, Sol Levine, and Leo Reeder, eds., *Handbook of Medical Sociology,* 3rd ed. Englewood Cliffs, NJ: Prentice-Hall.

Andersen, Ronald, Joanna Kravits, and Odin Anderson. 1975. *Equity in Health Services.* Cambridge, MA: Ballinger.

Andersen, Ronald, Joanna Kravits, and Odin Anderson. 1976. *Two Decades of Health Services.* Cambridge, MA: Ballinger.

Andersen, Ronald, and John Newman. 1973. "Societal and Individual Determinants of Medical Care Utilization in the United States." *Milbank Memorial Fund Quarterly* 51:95–124.

Anderson, Odin W. 1985. *Health Services in the United States: A Growth Enterprise Since 1875.* Ann Arbor, MI: Health Administration Press.

Anderson, Odin W., and Norman Gevitz. 1983. "The General Hospital: A Social and Historical Perspective." In David Mechanic, ed., *Handbook of Health, Health Care, and the Health Professions.* New York: Free Press.

Anderson, Odin, and Milvoy Seacat. 1958. "Behavioral Science Research in the Health Field: A Statement of Problems and Priorities." *Social Problems* 6:268–71.

Antonovsky, Aaron. 1972. "Social Class, Life Expectancy, and Overall Mortality." In E. G. Jaco, ed., *Patients, Physicians, and Illness,* rev. ed. New York: Free Press.

Antonovsky, Aaron M. 1979. *Health, Stress, and Coping.* San Francisco: Jossey-Bass.

Arluke, Arnold. 1987. "Sick Role Concepts." In D. S. Gochman, ed., *Health Behavior: Emerging Research Perspectives.* New York: Plenum Publishing Company.

Arluke, Arnold, Louanne Kennedy, and Ronald C. Kessler. 1979. "Re-Examining the Sick Role Concept: An Empirical Assessment." *Journal of Health and Social Behavior* 20:30–36.

Arms, Suzanne. 1977. *Immaculate Deception.* New York: Bantam.

Arrington, Barbara. 1985. *The Effect of Multi-Institutional Affiliation and Arrangements on Selected Measures of Hospital Performance.* Unpublished doctoral thesis, St. Louis University Medical Center.

Atchenbaum, W. Andrew. 1985. "Societal Perceptions of Aging and the Aged." In Robert Binstock and Ethel Shanas, eds., *Handbook of Aging and the Social Sciences,* 2nd ed. New York: Van Nostrand Reinhold.

Atchley, Robert C. 1985. *Social Forces and Aging,* 4th ed. Belmont, CA: Wadsworth.

Atkinson, Paul. 1981. *The Clinical Experience: The Construction and Reconstruction of Medical Reality.* Westmead, England: Gower.

Badgley, Robin F., ed. 1976. "Social Science and Medicine in Canada." [Special Issue.] *Social Science and Medicine* 10:1–68.

Bakwin, H. 1945. "Pseudodoxia Pediatrica." *New England Journal of Medicine* 232:691–97.

Bandura, Albert. 1969. *Principles of Behavior Modification.* New York: Holt, Rinehart, and Winston.

Barnhart, C. L., ed. 1965. *The American College Dictionary.* New York: Random House.

Barrett, Diana. 1979. "Multihospital Systems: The Process of Development." *Health Care Management Review* 4(3):49–59.

Barry, J. 1968. "General and Comparative Study of the Psychokinetic Effect on a Fungus Culture." *Journal of Parapsychology* 32:237–43.

Bates, Barbara. 1972. "Nurse-Physician Dyad: Collegial or Competitive?" In *Three Challenges to the Nursing Profession.* Kansas City: American Nurses' Association.

Bates, Erica. 1983. *Health Systems and Public Scrutiny: Australia, Britain, and the United States*. New York: St. Martin's Press.

Bauer, W. W., and Warren E. Schaller. 1965. *Your Health Today*. New York: Harper and Row.

Bayes, Marjorie. 1968. "Maternity Care in the World." In *Report of a Macy Conference: The Midwife in the United States*. New York: Josiah Macy, Jr. Foundation.

Becker, E. Lovell. 1986. *International Dictionary of Medicine and Biology*. New York: Wiley.

Becker, Ernest. 1973. *The Denial of Death*. New York: Free Press.

Becker, Ernest. 1975. *Escape From Evil*. New York: Free Press.

Becker, Howard, Blanche Geer, Everett Hughes, and Anselm Strauss. 1961. *Boys in White*. Chicago: University of Chicago Press.

Becker, Marshall. 1974. *The Health Belief Model and Personal Health Behavior*. San Francisco: Society for Public Health Education.

Becker, Marshall, Don Haefner, Stan Kasl, John Kirscht, Lois Maiman, and Irwin Rosenstock. 1977. "Selected Psychosocial Models and Correlates of Individual Health-Related Behaviors." *Medical Care* 15(May Suppl.):27–46.

Becker, Marshall, and Lois Maiman. 1983. "Models of Health-Related Behavior." In David Mechanic, ed., *Handbook of Health, Health Care, and the Health Professions*. New York: Free Press.

Becker, Marshall, Lois Maiman, John Kirscht, Don Haefner, and Robert Drachman. 1977. "The Health Belief Model and Prediction of Dietary Compliance: A Field Experiment." *Journal of Health and Social Behavior* 18:348–66.

Beiser, Morton. 1974. "Components and Correlates of Mental Well-Being." *Journal of Health and Social Behavior* 15:320–27.

Beiser, Morton, Jacob J. Feldman, and C. J. Egelhoff. 1972. "Assets and Affects: A Study of Positive Mental Health." *Archives of General Psychiatry* 27:545–59.

Bender, George A. 1965. *Great Moments in Medicine*. Detroit: Parke-Davis.

Benedict, Ruth. 1934. *Patterns of Culture*. New York: Houghton Mifflin.

Benor, Daniel J. 1984. "Psychic Healing." In J. Warren Salmon, ed., *Alternative Medicines*. New York: Tavistock.

Berg, Robert L. 1973. *Health Status Indexes*. Chicago: Hospital Research and Education Trust.

Berger, Peter L., and Thomas Luckmann. 1966. *The Social Construction of Reality*. Garden City, N.Y.: Doubleday.

Bergner, Marilynn. 1985. "Measurement of Health Status." *Medical Care* 23:696–704.

Bergner, Marilynn, Ruth A. Bobbitt, William Carter, and Betty S. Gilson. 1981. "The Sickness Impact Profile: Development and Final Revision of a Health Status Measure." *Medical Care* 19:787–805.

Bergner, Marlynn, Ruth A. Bobbitt, and Alice Krenel. 1976. "The Sickness Impact Profile: Conceptual Formulation and Methodological Development of a Health Status Index." *International Journal of Health Services* 6:393–415.

Berkanovic, Emil, and Carol Telesky. 1982. "Social Networks, Beliefs, and the Decision to Seek Medical Care: An Analysis of Congruent and Incongruent Patterns." *Medical Care* 20:1018–26.

Berkanovic, Emil, and Carol Telesky. 1985. "Health Orientations and Responses to Symptoms." Unpublished manuscript.

Berkanovic, Emil, Carol Telesky, and Sharon Reeder. 1981. "Structural and Social Psychological Factors in the Decision to Seek Medical Care for Symptoms." *Medical Care* 19:693–709.

Berki, Sylvester, and B. Kobashigawa. 1976. "Socioeconomic and Need Determinants of Ambulatory Care Use: Path Analysis of the 1970 Health Interview Survey." *Medical Care* 14:405–17.

Berki, Sylvester, J. N. Lepkowski, and Leon Wyszewianski. 1986. *High-Volume and Low-Volume Users of Health Services, United States, 1980*. DHHS Publication No. 86–20402. Washington, DC: U.S. Government Printing Office.

Berki, Sylvester, Leon Wyszewianski, Richard Lichtenstein, Phyllis Gimotty, Joyce Bowlyow, Elise Papke, Tina Smith, Stephen Crane, and Judith Bromberg. 1985. "Health Insurance Coverage of the Unemployed." *Medical Care* 23:847–54.

Berkman, Lisa F., and Lester Breslow. 1983. *Health and Ways of Living: The Alameda County Study*. New York: Oxford University Press.

Berkman, Paul R. 1971. "Measurement of Mental Health in a General Population Survey." *American Journal of Epidemiology* 94:105–11.

Berry, Ralph, and Roger Feldman. 1983. "Economics and Health Services Research." In Thomas Choi and Jay N. Greenberg, eds., *Social Science Approaches to Health Services Research*. Ann Arbor, MI: Health Administration Press.

Bice, Thomas. 1984. "Health Services Planning and Regulation." In Stephen Williams and Paul Torrens, eds., *Introduction to Health Services*, 2nd ed. New York: Wiley.

Billings, John S. 1879. In Henry Buck, ed., *Treatise on Hygiene and Public Health*. New York: Wood.

Binstock, Robert L. 1985. "The Oldest Old: A Fresh Perspective or Compassionate Ageism Revisited." *Milbank Memorial Fund Quarterly* 63:420–51.

Binstock, Robert, and Ethel Shanas, eds. 1985. *Handbook of Aging and the Social Sciences*, 2nd ed. New York: Van Nostrand Reinhold.

Birren, James E. 1968. "Psychological Aspects of Aging: Intellectual Functioning." *The Gerontologist* 8:16–19.

Birren, James E., and K. Warner Schaie, eds. 1985. *Handbook of the Psychology of Aging*, 2nd ed. New York: Van Nostrand Reinhold.

Bloom, Samuel. 1963a. *The Doctor and His Patient*. New York: Free Press.

Bloom, Samuel W. 1963b. "The Process of Becoming a Physician." *Annals of the American Academy of Political and Social Science* 346: 77–87.

Bloom, Samuel. 1965. "The Sociology of Medical Education: Some Comments on the State of the Field." *Milbank Memorial Fund Quarterly* 43:143–84.

Bloom, Samuel W. 1973. *Power and Dissent in the Medical School*. New York: Free Press.

Bloom, Samuel W. 1979. "Socialization for the Physician's Role: A Review of Some Contributions of Research to Theory." In E. C. Shapiro and L. M. Loenstein, eds., *Becoming a Physician: Development of Values and Attitudes in Medicine*. Cambridge, MA: Ballinger.

Bordley, James, and A. McGehee Harvey. 1976. *Two Centuries of American Medicine*. New York: Oxford University Press.

Bosk, Charles A. 1979. *Forgive and Remember*. Chicago: University of Chicago Press.

Botwinick, Jack. 1985. *Aging and Behavior*, 3rd ed. New York: Springer.

Bradburn, Norman M. 1969. *The Structure of Psychological Well-Being*. Chicago: Aldine.

Bradburn, Norman M., and David Caplovitz. 1965. *Reports on Happiness*. Chicago: Aldine.

Bramwell, Susan T., Minoru Masuda, N. N. Wagner, and Thomas H. Holmes. 1975. "Psychosocial Factors in Athletic Injuries." *Journal of Human Stress* 1(3):6–20.

Brenner, Berthold. 1970. *Social Factors in Mental Well-Being at Adolescence*. Unpublished Ph.D. thesis, American University, Washington, D.C.

Brierly, J. B., J. H. Adams, and D. I. Graham.

1971. "Neocortical Death After Cardiac Arrest." *Lancet* 2:560–65.

British Voluntary Euthanasia Society. 1935. *How To Die With Dignity*. London: British Voluntary Euthanasia Society.

Brook, Robert, Allison Davies-Avery, Sheldon Greenfield, L. Jeff Harris, Tova Lelah, Nancy Solomon, and John Ware, Jr. 1977. "Assessing the Quality of Medical Care Using Outcome Measures: An Overview of the Method." *Medical Care* 15(9, suppl.):1–65.

Brook, Robert, John Ware, Jr., Allison Davies-Avery, Anita L. Stewart, Cathy A. Donald, and S. A. Johnson. 1979. "Overview of Adult Health Status Measures Fielded in RAND's Health Insurance Study." *Medical Care* 17(7, suppl.):1–53.

Brooks, Edward F., and Susan L. Johnson. 1986. "Nurse Practitioner and Physician Assistant Satellite Health Centers: The Pending Demise of an Organizational Form?" *Medical Care* 24:881–90.

Brown, George W. 1974. "Meaning, Measurement, and Stress of Life Events." In B. Dohrenwend and B. Dohrenwend, eds., *Stressful Life Events: Their Nature and Effects*. New York: Wiley.

Bruhn, John G., Bill U. Phillips, and Paula L. Levine. 1985. *Medical Sociology: An Annotated Bibliography*. Houston: Garland Publishing.

Bucher, Rue, and Joan Stelling. 1977. *Becoming Professional*. Beverly Hills, CA: Sage.

Bullough, Bonnie, and Vernon Bullough. 1969. *The Emergence of Modern Nursing*, 2nd ed. New York: Macmillan.

Bush, Warren W. 1978. *In the Matter of Karen Ann Quinlan*. New York: National Broadcasting Corporation.

Butler, Robert N. 1975. *Why Survive: Being Old in America*. New York: Harper & Row.

Butler, Robert N. 1982. "An Overview of Research on Aging and the Status of Gerontology Today." *Milbank Memorial Fund Quarterly* 61:351–61.

Cape, Ronald, Rodney Coe, and Isadore Rossman, eds. 1983. *Fundamentals of Geriatric Medicine*. New York: Raven Press.

Caplan, Arthur. 1981. *Concepts of Health and Disease: Interdisciplinary Perspectives*. Boston: Addison-Wesley.

Caplan, Robert. 1971. *Organizational Stress and Individual Strain: A Social-Psychological Study of Risk Factors in Coronary Heart Disease Among Administrators, Engineers, and Scientists*. Unpublished Ph.D. thesis. Ann Arbor: University of Michigan.

Caplan, Ronald Lee. 1984. "Chiropractic." In

J. Warren Salmon, ed., *Alternative Medicines*. New York: Tavistock.

Carlson, Rick J. 1975. *The End of Medicine*. New York: Wiley.

Carlton, Charles, and Ron Miller. 1971. "Kisch's Health Status Proxy: Two Suggested Improvements." *Health Services Research* 6:184–86.

Carr-Saunders, A. M., and P. A. Wilson. 1933. *The Professions*. London: Oxford University Press.

Cavan, Ruth, Ernest Burgess, Robert Havighurst, and Herbert Goldhamer. 1949. *Personal Adjustment to Old Age*. Chicago: Science Research Associates.

Cecchi, Robert. 1986. "Living with AIDS: When the System Fails." *American Journal of Nursing* 86:45, 47.

Chen, Martin K. 1976. "Health Status Indexes: Work in Progress." [Special Issue.] *Health Services Research* 11:330–528.

Christman, Luther P., and Michael A. Counte. 1982. *Hospital Organization and Health Care Delivery*. Boulder, CO: Westview Press.

Clark, Leon H. 1977. *Mortality American Style: A Tale of Two States*. Washington, DC: Population Reference Bureau.

Claus, Lisabeth M. 1983. "The Development of Medical Sociology in Europe." *Social Science and Medicine* 17:1591–97.

Cleary, Paul, and Ronald Kessler. 1982. "The Estimation and Interpretation of Modifier Effects." *Journal of Health and Social Behavior* 23:159–69.

Cleland, Virginia. 1971. "Sex Discrimination: Nursing's Most Pervasive Problem." *American Journal of Nursing* 71:1542–47.

Clendening, Logan. 1960. *Sourcebook of Medical History*. New York: Dover.

Cockerham, William C. 1981. *Sociology of Mental Disorders*. New York: Prentice-Hall.

Cockerham, William. 1983. "The State of Medical Sociology in the United States, Great Britain, West Germany, and Austria: Applied vs. Pure Theory." *Social Science and Medicine* 17:1513–27.

Cockerham, William C. 1986. *Medical Sociology*, 3rd ed. Englewood Cliffs, NJ: Prentice-Hall.

Coe, Rodney M. 1978. *Sociology of Medicine*, 2nd ed. New York: McGraw-Hill.

Coe, Rodney. 1983. "Social Epidemiology of Diseases of Aging." In Hans T. Blumenthal, ed., *Handbook of Diseases of Aging*. New York: Van Nostrand Reinhold.

Coe, Rodney M. 1987. "Communication and Medical Outcomes: Analysis of Conversations Between Doctors and Elderly Patients." In Russell Ward and Sheldon Tobin, eds., *Health in Aging: Sociological Issues and Policy Directions*. Beverly Hills, CA: Sage.

Coe, Rodney, and Leonard Fichtenbaum. 1972. "Utilization of Physician Assistants: Some Implications for Medical Practice." *Medical Care* 10:497–504.

Coe, Rodney M., and Christine Prendergast. 1985. "The Formation of Coalitions: Interactive Strategies in Triads." *Sociology of Health and Illness* 7:236–47.

Coe, Rodney M., Christine Prendergast, and George Psathas. 1984. "Strategies for Obtaining Compliance with Medical Regimens." *Journal of the American Geriatrics Society* 32:589–93.

Cogan, Morris. 1953. "Toward a Definition of Profession." *Harvard Educational Review* 23:33–50.

Cohen, Raquel E. 1973. "The Collaborative Co-Professional: Development of a New Mental Health Role." *Hospital and Community Psychiatry* 24:242–44.

Cohen, Sheldon, Tom Kamarck, and Robin Mermelstein. 1983. "A Global Measure of Perceived Stress." *Journal of Health and Social Behavior* 24:385–96.

Cohen, Sheldon, and S. Leonard Syme, eds. 1985. *Social Support and Health*. New York: Academic Press.

Cole, Stephen, and Robert Lejeune. 1972. "Illness and the Legitimation of Failure." *American Sociological Review* 37:347–56.

Committee on Certification in Medical Sociology. 1986. *Guidelines for the Certification Process in Medical Sociology*. Washington, DC: American Sociological Association.

Comstock, G. W., and K. J. Helsing. 1975. "Symptoms of Depression in Two Communities." *Psychological Medicine* 6:551–63.

Conrad, Peter. 1976. *Identifying Hyperactive Children*. Lexington, MA: Lexington Books.

Conrad, Peter, and Joseph Schneider. 1980. *Deviance and Medicalization*. Saint Louis, MO: C. V. Mosby.

Cooley, Thomas. 1964. *Human Nature and the Social Order*. New York: Schocken.

Coser, Rose L. 1979. *Training and Ambiguity: Learning Through Doing in a Medical Hospital*. New York: Free Press.

Cottrell, Leonard. 1942. "The Adjustment of the Individual to His Age and Sex Roles." *American Sociological Review* 7:617–20.

Coulter, Harris L. 1982. *Divided Legacy: A History of the Schism in Medical Thought*, Vol. 3. Richmond, CA: North Atlantic Books.

Coulter, Harris L. 1984. "Homeopathy." In J. Warren Salmon, ed., *Alternative Medicines*. New York: Tavistock.

Croog, Sydney, and Donna VerSteeg. 1972. "The Hospital as a Social System." In Howard Freeman, Sol Levine, and Leo Reeder, eds., *Handbook of Medical Sociology*, 2nd ed. Englewood Cliffs, NJ: Prentice-Hall.

Cruikshank, Brenda, Toni Clow, and Brenda Seals. 1986. "Pediatric Nurse Practitioner Functions in the Outpatient Clinics of a Tertiary Care Center." *Medical Care* 24:340–49.

Cumming, Elaine. 1963. "Further Thoughts on the Theory of Disengagement." *International Social Science Journal* 15:377–93.

Cumming, Elaine, Lois Dean, and David Newell. 1960. "Disengagement: A Tentative Theory of Aging." *Sociometry* 23:23–37.

Cumming, Elaine, and William Henry. 1961. *Growing Old*. New York: Basic Books.

Cummings, K. Michael, Marshall Becker, and Marla Maile. 1980. "Bringing the Models Together: An Empirical Approach to Combining Variables Used to Explain Health Actions." *Journal of Behavioral Medicine* 3:123–45.

Curran, James W., W. Meade Morgan, Ann M. Hardy, Harold W. Jaffe, William W. Darrow, and Walter R. Dowdle. 1985. "The Epidemiology of AIDS: Current Status and Future Prospects." *Science* 229:1352–57.

Dachelet, Christy. 1978. "Nursing's Bid for Increased Status." *Nursing Forum* 17:18–45.

Davis, Fred. 1966. "Problems and Issues in Collegiate Nursing Education." In Fred Davis, ed., *The Nursing Profession*. New York: Wiley.

Davis, Fred. 1972. *Illness, Interaction, and the Self*. Belmont, CA: Wadsworth.

Davis, Fred, and Virginia Olesen. 1967. "Initiation into a Women's Profession: Identity Problems in the Status Transition of Coed to Nurse." *Sociometry* 26:84–101.

Davis, Karen, and Diane Rowland. 1983. "Uninsured and Underserved: Inequities in Health Care in the United States." *Milbank Memorial Fund Quarterly* 61:149–76.

Dawber, T. R., G. F. Meadors, and F. E. Moore. 1951. "Epidemiological Approaches to Heart Disease." *American Journal of Public Health* 41:279–86.

Denton, John. 1978. *Medical Sociology*. New York: Houghton Mifflin.

Denzin, Norman. 1968. "The Self-Fulfilling Prophecy and Patient-Therapist Interaction." In Stephen Spitzer and Norman Denzin, eds., *The Mental Patient: Studies in the Sociology of Deviance*. New York: McGraw Hill.

Department of Health, Education, and Welfare. 1974. *How Medical Students Finance Their Education*. Washington, DC: U.S. Government Printing Office.

Department of Health, Education, and Welfare.

1975. *Medical Care Expenditures, Prices, and Costs: Background Book*. Washington, DC: U.S. Government Printing Office.

Department of Health and Human Services. 1985. *Health, United States, 1984*. DHHS Publication No. 85–1232. Washington, DC: U.S. Government Printing Office.

Department of Health and Human Services. 1986. *Utilization of Short-Stay Hospitals by Diagnosis-Related Groups, United States, 1980–84*. DHHS Publication No. 86–1748. Washington, DC: U.S. Government Printing Office.

Department of Health and Human Services. 1987. *Health, United States, 1986*. DHHS Publication No. 87–1232. Washington, DC: U.S. Government Printing Office.

DeVries, Raymond G. 1982. "Midwifery and the problem of licensure." *Research in the Sociology of Health Care* 2:77–120.

de Tourngay, Rita. 1971. "Two Views on the Latest Health Manpower Issue: Extending the Nurse's Role Does Not Make Her a Physician's Assistant." *American Journal of Nursing* 71:974–77.

Dohrenwend, Barbara. 1973. "Social Status and Stressful Life Events." *Journal of Personality and Social Psychology* 28:225–35.

Dohrenwend, Barbara, and Bruce Dohrenwend. 1981. *Stressful Life Events and Their Context*. New Brunswick, NJ: Rutgers University Press.

Dohrenwend, Bruce. 1975. "Sociocultural and Social-Psychological Factors in the Genesis of Mental Disorders." *Journal of Health and Social Behavior* 16:365–92.

Dohrenwend, Bruce, and Barbara Dohrenwend. 1974a. "Psychiatric Disorders in Urban Settings." In S. Arieti, ed., *Handbook of Psychiatry*. New York: Basic Books.

Dohrenwend, Bruce, and Barbara Dohrenwend. 1974b. *Stressful Life Events: Their Nature and Effects*. New York: Wiley.

Dohrenwend, Bruce, and Barbara Dohrenwend. 1976. "Sex Differences and Psychiatric Disorder." *American Journal of Sociology* 81:1447–54.

Donabedian, Avedis. 1980. *The Definition of Quality and Approaches to Its Measurement*. Ann Arbor, MI: Health Administration Press.

Donabedian, Avedis. 1981. *The Criteria and Standards of Quality*. Ann Arbor, MI: Health Administration Press.

Donabedian, Avedis, John R. C. Wheeler, and Leon Wyszewianski. 1982. "Quality, Cost, and Health: An Integrative Model." *Medical Care* 20:975–92.

Donnison, Jean. 1977. *Midwives and Medical Men*. London: Heinemann.

Dorland, William A. 1985. *Dorland's Illustrated Medical Dictionary*, 26th ed. Philadelphia: W. B. Saunders.

Dorn, H. F. 1959. "Tobacco Consumption and Mortality from Cancer and Other Diseases." *Public Health Reports* 74:581–93.

Dubos, Rene. 1959. *Mirage of Health*. New York: Doubleday.

Duff, Raymond, and August Hollingshead. 1968. *Sickness and Society*. New York: Harper & Row.

Durkheim, Emile. 1933. *The Division of Labor in Society*. New York: Macmillan.

Durkheim, Emile. 1956. *The Division of Labor in Society*. New York: Free Press.

Durkheim, Emile. 1957. *Professional Ethics and Civic Morals*. Glencoe, IL: Free Press.

Eaton, William W. 1980. *The Sociology of Mental Disorders*. New York: Praeger.

Eaton, William W., and Larry G. Kessler. 1981. "Rates of Symptoms of Depression in a National Sample." *American Journal of Epidemiology* 114:528–32.

Eaton, William W., and Larry G. Kessler, eds. 1985. *Epidemiological Field Methods in Psychiatry: The NIMH Epidemiological Catchment Area Program*. New York: Academic Press.

Ehrenreich, Barbara, and John Ehrenreich. 1970. *The American Health Empire: Power, Profits, and Politics*. New York: Random House.

Eisenberg, John M. 1986. *Doctors' Decisions and the Cost of Medical Care*. Ann Arbor, MI: Health Administration Press.

Elinson, Jack. 1976. "Sociomedical Health Indicators." [Special issue.] *International Journal of Health Services* 6:1–225.

Elinson, Jack. 1985. "The End of Medicine and the End of Medical Sociology?" *Journal of Health and Social Behavior* 26:268–75.

Enthoven, Alain C. 1978. "Consumer-Choice Health Plan: A National Health-Insurance Proposal Based on Regulated Competition in the Private Sector." *New England Journal of Medicine* 298:709–20.

Epstein, R. H. 1965. "The Epidemiology of Coronary Heart Disease: A Review." *Journal of Chronic Diseases* 18:735–74.

Ermann, Dan, and Jon Gabel. 1984. "Multihospital Systems: Issues and Empirical Findings." *Health Affairs* 3:50–64.

Ermann, Dan, and Jon Gabel. 1985. "The Changing Face of American Health Care: Multihospital Systems, Emergency Centers, and Surgery Centers." *Medical Care* 23:401–20.

Ernst, Richard L., and Donald Yett. 1985. *Physician Location and Specialty Choice*. Ann Arbor, MI: Health Administration Press.

Fanshel, S., and J. W. Bush. 1970. "A Health-Status Index and Its Application to Health Service Outcomes." *Operations Research* 18:1021–66.

Faris, Robert, and Warren H. Dunham. 1939. *Mental Disorders in Urban Areas*. Chicago: University of Chicago Press.

Farley, Pamela J. 1985. "Who Are the Underinsured?" *Milbank Memorial Fund Quarterly* 63:476–503.

Fazio, A. F. 1977. *A Concurrent Validation Study of the NCHS General Well-being Schedule*. DHEW Publication No. 78–1347. Washington, DC: U.S. Government Printing Office.

Feifel, Herman, ed. 1977. *New Meanings of Death*. New York: McGraw Hill.

Feldstein, Martin. 1971. "A New Approach to National Health Insurance." *The Public Interest* 23:93–105.

Feldstein, Paul J. 1983. *Health Care Economics*, 2nd ed. New York: Wiley.

Fetter, Robert B., Soon Youngsoo, James L. Freeman, and John Thompson. 1980. "Case Mix Definition by Diagnostic Related Groups." *Medical Care* 18(2, suppl.):1–136.

Finch, Caleb E., and Edward L. Schneider, eds. 1985. *Handbook of the Biology of Aging*, 2nd ed. New York: Van Nostrand Reinhold.

Finney, John W., Roger C. Mitchell, Ruth C. Cronkite, and Rudolph H. Moos. 1984. "Methodological Issues in Estimating Main and Interaction Effects: Examples from the Coping/Social Support and Stress Field." *Journal of Health and Social Behavior* 25:85–98.

Fischer, David Hackett. 1978. *Growing Old in America*, expanded ed. Oxford, England: Oxford University Press.

Flexner, Abraham. 1910. *Medical Education in the United States and Canada*. New York: Carnegie Foundation for the Advancement of Teaching.

Flood, Ann B., and Richard Scott. 1978. "Professional Power and Professional Effectiveness: Quality of Surgical Care in Hospitals." *Journal of Health and Social Behavior* 19:240–53.

Flook, Evelyn, and Paul Sanazaro, eds. 1973. *Health Services Research and R&D in Perspective*. Ann Arbor, MI: Health Administration Press.

Forsyth, Gordon. 1973. "United Kingdom." In J. Douglas Wilson and G. McLachlan, eds., *Health Service Prospects: An International Survey*. Boston: Little, Brown.

Foster, George M. 1975. "Medical Anthropology: Some Contrasts with Medical Sociology." *Social Science and Medicine* 9:427–32.

Fox, Renee C. 1977. "The Medicalization and Demedicalization of American Society." In John Knowles, ed., *Doing Better and Feeling Worse:*

Health in the United States. New York: Basic Books.

Fox, Renee C. 1979. *Essays in Medical Sociology.* New York: Wiley.

Fox, Renee C. 1984. "It's the Same, but Different: A Sociological Perspective on the Case of the Utah Artificial Heart." In Margery W. Shaw, ed., *After Barney Clark: Reflections on the Utah Artificial Heart.* Austin: University of Texas Press.

Fox, Renee C. 1985. "Reflections and Opportunities in the Sociology of Medicine." *Journal of Health and Social Behavior* 26:6–14.

Frankenberg, Ronald. 1974. "Functionalism and After? Theory and Developments in Social Science Applied to the Health Field." *International Journal of Health Services* 3:411–27.

Freeman, Howard, Sol Levine, and Leo Reeder. 1972. "Present Status of Medical Sociology." In Howard Freeman, Sol Levine, and Leo Reeder, eds., *Handbook of Medical Sociology,* 2nd ed. Englewood Cliffs, NJ: Prentice-Hall.

Freeman, Howard, and Leo Reeder. 1957. "Medical Sociology: A Review of the Literature." *American Sociological Review* 22:73–81.

Freidson, Eliot. 1963. *The Hospital in Modern Society.* Glencoe, IL: Free Press.

Freidson, Eliot. 1970a. *Profession of Medicine: A Study in the Sociology of Applied Knowledge.* New York: Harper & Row.

Freidson, Eliot. 1970b. *Professional Dominance.* New York: Atherton.

Freidson, Eliot. 1980. *Doctoring Together: A Study of Professional Control.* Chicago: University of Chicago Press.

Freidson, Eliot. 1983. "The Theory of Professions: State of the Art." In R. Dingwall and P. Lewis, eds., *The Sociology of Professions: Lawyers, Doctors, and Others.* London: Macmillan.

Freidson, Eliot. 1984. "The Changing Nature of Professional Control." *Annual Review of Sociology* 10:1–20.

Freidson, Eliot. 1985. "The Reorganization of the Medical Profession." *Medical Care Review* 42:11–35.

Freidson, Eliot. 1986. "The Medical Profession in Transition." In Linda Aiken and David Mechanic, eds., *Applications of Social Science to Clinical Medicine and Health Policy.* New Brunswick, NJ: Rutgers University Press.

Freidson, Eliot, and Buford Rhea. 1963. "Processes of Control in a Company of Equals." *Social Problems* 11:119–31.

Freidson, Eliot, and Buford Rhea. 1965. "Knowledge and Judgment in Professional Evaluations." *Administrative Science Quarterly* 10:107–24.

Freud, Sigmund. 1953–1966. *Standard Edition of the Complete Works of Sigmund Freud.* London: Hogarth.

Fuchs, Victor. 1974. *Who Shall Live? Health Economics and Social Change.* New York: Basic Books.

Fuchs, Victor. 1986a. "Paying the Piper, Calling the Tune: Implications of Changes in Reimbursement." *Frontiers of Health Services Management* 2:4–27.

Fuchs, Victor. 1986b. "Has Cost Containment Gone Too Far?" *Milbank Memorial Fund Quarterly* 64:479–88.

Funch, Donna P., and James R. Marshall. 1984. "Measuring Life Stress: Factors Affecting Fall-Off in the Reporting of Life Events." *Journal of Health and Social Behavior* 25:453–64.

Gairola, G. A. 1982. "Physician Assistant Graduates: Factors Related to Rural-Urban Practice Location." *Journal of Community Health* 8:23–35.

Gaitz, C. M., and J. Scott. 1972. "Age and Measurement of Mental Health." *Journal of Health and Social Behavior* 13:55–67.

Gallagher, Eugene B. 1976. "Lines of Reconstruction and Extension in the Parsonian Sociology of Illness." *Social Science and Medicine* 10:207–18.

Garceau, Oliver. 1961. *The Political Life of the American Medical Association.* Hamden, CT: Anchor Books.

Geersten, Reed, M. Klauber, M. Rindflesh, Robert Kane, and Robert Gray. 1975. "A Re-Examination of Suchman's Views on Social Factors in Health Care Utilization." *Journal of Health and Social Behavior* 16:226–37.

Geiger, H. Jack. 1975. "The Causes of Dehumanization in Health Care and Prospects for Humanization." In Jan Howard and Anselm Strauss, eds., *Humanizing Health Care.* New York: Wiley.

Georgopoulos, Basil, and Floyd Mann. 1962. *The Community General Hospital.* New York: Wiley.

Georgopoulos, Basil, and Floyd Mann. 1972. "The Hospital as an Organization." In E. Gartly Jaco, ed., *Patients, Physicians, and Illness,* 2nd ed. New York: Free Press.

Gersten, Joanne, Thomas Langner, Jeanne Eisenberg, and Ora Simpcha-Fagan. 1977. "An Evaluation of the Etiologic Role of Stressful Life Change Events in Psychological Disorders." *Journal of Health and Social Behavior* 18:228–44.

Gibbons, Russell. 1980. "The Rise of the Chiropractic Establishment, 1897–1980." In *Who's Who in Chiropractic,* Vol. 2. Littleton, CO: International Publishing.

Gibson, Geoffrey. 1972. "Theory vs. Application at the ASA: A View of the Issues." *Health Services Research* 7:243–53.

Gilson, Betty S., James J. Gilson, Marilynn Bergner, Ruth A. Bobbitt, and William Carter. 1975. "The Sickness Impact Profile: Development of an Outcome Measure of Health Care." *American Journal of Public Health* 65: 1304–16.

Glaser, Barney, and Anselm Strauss. 1966. *Awareness of Dying.* Chicago: Aldine.

Glaser, Barney, and Anselm Strauss. 1967. *The Discovery of Grounded Theory.* Chicago: Aldine.

Glaser, Barney, and Anselm Strauss. 1968. *Time for Dying.* Chicago: Aldine.

Glaser, William A. 1986. "Payment Systems and Their Effects." In Linda Aiken and David Mechanic, eds., *Applications of Social Science to Clinical Medicine and Health Policy.* New Brunswick, NJ: Rutgers University Press.

Goffman, Erving. 1961. *Asylums.* New York: Anchor Books.

Goffman, Erving. 1963. *Stigma.* New York: Anchor Books.

Gold, Margaret. 1977. "A Crisis of Identity: The Case of Medical Sociology." *Journal of Health and Social Behavior* 18:160–68.

Gonda, Thomas A., and John E. Ruark. 1984. *Dying Dignified: The Health Professional's Guide.* New York: Addison-Wesley.

Goode, William. 1960. "Encroachment, Charlatanism, and the Emerging Profession: Psychology, Sociology, and Medicine." *American Sociological Review* 25:902–14.

Gordon, Gerald. 1966. *Role Theory and Illness.* New Haven, CT: Yale University Press.

Goss, Mary E. W. 1961. "Influence and Authority Among Physicians in an Outpatient Clinic." *American Sociological Review* 26:39–50.

Goss, Mary E. W. 1963. "Patterns of Bureaucracy Among Hospital Staff Physicians." In Eliot Freidson, ed., *The Hospital in Modern Society.* Glencoe, IL: Free Press.

Grad, B. 1965. "PK Effects on Fermentation of Yeast." *Proceedings of the Parapsychological Association* 2:15–16.

Grad, B. 1967. "The Biological Effects of the 'Laying on of Hands' on Animals and Plants: Implications for Biology." *Journal of the American Society for Psychical Research* 61:286–305.

Graduate Medical Education National Advisory Committee. 1981. *Report of the Graduate Medical Education National Advisory Committee: Executive Summary.* Washington, DC: U.S. Government Printing Office.

Graham, Saxon. 1968. "Cancer of Lung Related to Smoking Behavior." *Cancer* 21:30–53.

Graham, Saxon. 1972. "Cancer, Culture, and Social Structure." In E. G. Jaco, ed., *Patients, Physicians, and Illness,* rev. ed. New York: Free Press.

Graham, Saxon, S. Crouch, M. L. Levin, and F. G. Back. 1963. "Variations in Amounts of Tobacco Tar Retrieved from Selected Models of Smoking Behavior Simulated by Smoking Machine." *Cancer Research* 23:1025–30.

Graham, Saxon, M. Levin, and A. Lilienfeld. 1960. "The Socioeconomic Distribution of Cancer at Various Sites in Buffalo, New York: 1948–1952." *Cancer* 13:180.

Greenblatt, Howard N. 1975. *Measurement of Social Well-Being in a General Population Survey.* Berkeley: California State Department of Health.

Greenfield, Sheldon, Charles Lewis, and Sidney Kaplan. 1975. "Peer Review by Criteria Mapping: Criteria for Diabetes Mellitus. The Use of Decision-Making in Chart Audit." *Annals of Internal Medicine* 83:761–70.

Gregory, Samuel. 1974. "Man-Midwifery Exposed and Corrected." In C. Rosenberg and C. Smith-Rosenberg, eds., *The Male Midwife and the Female Doctor.* New York: Arno Press.

Grusky, Oscar, and Melvin Pollner, eds. 1981. *The Sociology of Mental Illness: Basic Studies.* New York: Holt, Rinehart, and Winston.

Gulack, Robert. 1983. "What a Nurse Means When She Says: I'm a Professional." *RN Magazine* 46(9):29–35.

Gurin, Gerald, Joseph Veroff, and Sheila Field. 1960. *Americans View Their Mental Health.* New York: Basic Books.

Habenstein, Robert, and Edward Christ. 1955. *Professionalizer, Traditionalizer, and Utilizer.* Columbia, MO: University of Missouri Press.

Hafferty, Frederick W. 1986. "Impact of the Physician Surplus on the Organization and Delivery of Medical Care." Paper presented at the annual meeting of the American Sociological Association, August, New York.

Haig, T. H. Brian, David A. Scott, and Louise I. Wickett. 1986. "The Rational Zero Point for an Illness Index with Ratio Properties." *Medical Care* 24:113–24.

Hall, Oswald. 1948. "The Stages of a Medical Career." *American Journal of Sociology* 53: 227–36.

Hammond, E. Cuyler, and Daniel Horn. 1958. "Smoking and Death Rates: Report on Forty-Four Months of Follow-Up." *Journal of the American Medical Association* 166:1154–1308.

Harkey, John, David Miles, and William Rushing. 1976. "The Relation Between Social Class and Functional Status: A New Look at the Drift

Hypothesis." *Journal of Health and Social Behavior* 17:194–204.

Harris, Daniel. 1975. "An Elaboration of the Relationship Between General Hospital Bed Supply and General Hospital Utilization." *Journal of Health and Social Behavior* 16:163–72.

Harvard Medical School, Ad Hoc Committee. 1968. "A Definition of Irreversible Coma: Report of the Ad Hoc Committee of the Harvard Medical School to Examine the Issue of Brain Death." *Journal of the American Medical Association* 205:337–40.

Haug, Marie. 1973. "Deprofessionalization: An Alternative Hypothesis for the Future." *Sociological Review Monographs* 20:195–211.

Haug, Marie. 1975. "The Deprofessionalization of Everyone?" *Sociological Focus* 3:197–213.

Haug, Marie. 1977. "Computer Technology and the Obsolescence of the Concept of the Profession." In M. Haug and J. Dofny, eds., *Work and Technology*. Beverly Hills, CA: Sage.

Haug, Marie. 1979. "Doctor-Patient Relationships and the Older Patient." *Journal of Gerontology* 35:852–60.

Haug, Marie, and Bebe Lavin. 1978. "Method of Payment for Medical Care and Public Attitudes Toward Physician Authority." *Journal of Health and Social Behavior* 19:279–91.

Haug, Marie, and Bebe Lavin. 1981. "Practitioner or Patient: Who's in Charge." *Journal of Health and Social Behavior* 22:212–29.

Haug, Marie, and Bebe Lavin. 1983. *Consumerism in Medicine: Challenging Physician Authority.* Beverly Hills, CA: Sage.

Havighurst, Robert, and Ruth Albrecht. 1953. *Older People.* New York: Longmans, Green.

Havlicek, Penny L. 1985. *Medical Groups in the U.S.* Chicago: American Medical Association.

Hayes-Bautista, David. 1976a. "Modifying the Treatment: Patient Compliance, Patient Control, and Medical Care." *Social Science and Medicine* 10:233–38.

Hayes-Bautista, David. 1976b. "Termination of the Patient-Practitioner Relationship: Divorce, Patient Style." *Journal of Health and Social Behavior* 17:12–22.

Heidt, P. 1979. *An Investigation of the Effect of Therapeutic Touch on the Anxiety of Hospitalized Patients.* Unpublished doctoral thesis, New York University.

Henry, Jules. 1954. "The Formal Structure of a Psychiatric Hospital." *Psychiatry* 17:139–51.

Hetherington, Robert, and E. Hopkins. 1969. "Symptom Sensitivity: Its Cultural and Social Correlates." *Health Services Research* 4:63–75.

Hiatt, Wilma. 1961. "Associate Degree Programs in California." *American Journal of Nursing* 61:62–68.

Hogstel, Mildred. 1977. "Associate Degree and Baccalaureate Graduates: Do They Function Differently?" *American Journal of Nursing* 77:1598–1600.

Holbrook, Stewart. 1979. *The Golden Age of Quackery.* New York: Macmillan.

Hollingshead, August, and Frederick Redlich. 1958. *Social Class and Mental Illness.* New York: Wiley.

Holmes, Thomas H., and Richard H. Rahe. 1967. "The Social Readjustment Rating Scale." *Journal of Psychosomatic Research* 11:213–18.

Homans, George. 1959. *The Social Group.* New York: Free Press.

Horn, Susan D. 1983. "Measuring Severity of Illness: Comparisons Across Institutions." *American Journal of Public Health* 73:25–31.

Horn, Susan D., Mary S. Sharkey, and David A. Bertram. 1983. "Measuring Severity of Illness: Homogeneous Case Mix Groups." *Medical Care* 21:14–30.

Horn, Susan D., and Paul D. Sharkey. 1983. "Measuring Severity of Illness to Predict Patient Resource Use Within DRGs." *Inquiry* 20:314–21.

Hough, Richard, Diane Fairbank, and Alma Garcia. 1976. "Problems in the Ratio Measurement of Life Stress." *Journal of Health and Social Behavior* 17:70–82.

House, James H. 1974. "Occupational Stress and Coronary Heart Disease: A Review and Theoretical Integration." *Journal of Health and Social Behavior* 15:17–21.

Huber, Bettina. 1984. "A[merican] S[ociological] A[ssociation] Council Discusses Certification and Licensure Issues." *ASA Footnotes* March, pp. 2–6.

Hughes, Everett, Helen Hughes, and Irwin Deutscher. 1948. *Twenty Thousand Nurses Tell Their Story.* Philadelphia: J. P. Lippincott.

Hulka, Barbara, Leo Kupper, John Cassel, and Frank Mayo. 1971. "A Method for Measuring Physicians' Awareness of Patients' Concerns." *HSMHA Health Reports* 86:741–53.

Hulka, Barbara S., and John R. Wheat. 1985. "Patterns of Utilization: The Patient Perspective." *Medical Care* 23:438–60.

Hull, F. M. 1972. "How Well Does the General Practitioner Know His Patients?" *Practitioner* 208:688–91.

Humphrey, Derek. 1984. *Let Me Die Before I Wake: Hemlock's Book of Self-Deliverance.* Los Angeles: Grove Press.

Ibrahim, Michel A. 1983. "An Epidemiologic Perspective in Health Services Research." In T. Choi and J. N. Greenberg, eds., *Social Science Approaches to Health Services Research.* Ann Arbor, MI: Health Administration Press.

Illich, Ivan. 1976. *Medical Nemesis: The Expropriation of Our Health*. New York: Pantheon.

Inui, Thomas S., and William B. Carter. 1985. "Problems and Prospects for Health Services Research on Provider-Patient Communication." *Medical Care* 23:521–38.

Jaco, E. Gartley. 1958. "Areas for Research in Medical Sociology." *Sociology and Social Research* 42:441–44.

Jago, John D. 1975. "'Hal'—Old Word, New Task: Reflecting on the Words 'Health' and 'Medical'." *Social Science and Medicine* 9:1–6.

Jameson, Eric. 1961. *The Natural History of Quackery*. Springfield, IL: Charles C. Thomas.

Jenkins, C. David. 1971. "Psychologic and Social Precursors of Coronary Disease." *New England Journal of Medicine* 284:244–55, 307–17.

Jenkins, C. David, R. H. Rosenman, and Meyer Friedman. 1967. "Development of Objective Psychological Test for the Determination of Coronary-Prone Behavior Pattern." *Journal of Chronic Diseases* 20:371–79.

Johnson, Amos N. 1968. "Comments." In *Report of a Macy Conference: The Midwife in the United States*. New York: Josiah Macy, Jr., Foundation.

Johnson, D. McIntyre, and Nancy Dodds, eds. 1957. *The Plea for the Silent*. London: Christopher Johnson.

Johnson, Malcolm. 1975. "Medical Sociology and Sociological Theory." *Social Science and Medicine* 9:227–32.

Judge, Richard D., and George D. Zuidema. 1974. *Methods of Clinical Examination: A Physiological Approach*. Boston: Little, Brown.

Kadushin, Charles. 1958. "Individual Decisions to Undertake Psychotherapy." *Administrative Science Quarterly* 3:379–411.

Kansas, The State of. 1970. *Kansas Statutes*. Chapter 77, Section 202.

Kaplan, Howard B. 1983a. "Psychological Distress in Sociological Context: Toward a General Theory of Psychosocial Stress." In H. B. Kaplan, ed. *Psychosocial Stress: Trends in Theory and Research*. New York: Academic Press.

Kaplan, Howard B. 1983b. *Psychosocial Stress: Trends in Theory and Research*. New York: Academic Press.

Kaplan, Robert M., J. W. Bush, and Charles C. Berry. 1976. "Health Status: Types of Validity and the Index of Well-Being." *Health Services Research* 11:478–507.

Kart, Cary S. 1985. *The Realities of Aging: An Introduction to Gerontology*, 2nd ed. Boston: Allyn & Bacon.

Kart, Cary S., and Barbara Manard, eds. 1976. *Aging in America*. Port Washington, NY: Alfred Publishing.

Kasper, Judith A., David C. Walden, and Gail R. Wilensky. 1978. *Who Are the Uninsured?* National Medical Care Expenditures Survey, Data Preview No. 1. Hyattsville, MD: National Center for Health Services Research.

Kassebaum, George C., and Barbara O. Baumann. 1965. "Dimensions of the Sick Role in Chronic Illness." *Journal of Health and Human Behavior* 6:16–27.

Kelley, Lucie. 1974. "Nursing Practice Acts." *American Journal of Nursing* 74:1310–19.

Kelman, Sander. 1975. "The Social Nature of the Definition Problem in Health." *International Journal of Health Services* 5:625–42.

Kendall, Patricia. 1963. "Medical Sociology in the United States." *Social Science Information* 2:1–13.

Kendall, Patricia, and Robert Merton. 1958. "Medical Education as a Social Process." In E. Gartley Jaco, ed., *Patients, Physicians, and Illness*. New York: Free Press.

Kendall, Patricia, and George Reader. 1972. "Contributions of Sociology to Medicine." In Howard Freeman, Sol Levine, and Leo Reeder, eds., *Handbook of Medical Sociology*, 2nd ed. New York: Prentice-Hall.

Kesey, Ken. 1962. *One Flew Over the Cuckoo's Nest*. New York: Viking.

Kessler, Ronald. 1983. "Methodological Issues in the Study of Psychosocial Stress." In H. B. Kaplan, ed., *Psychosocial Stress: Trends in Theory and Research*. New York: Academic Press.

Kessler, Ronald C., and James A. McRae. 1981. "Trends in the Relationship Between Sex and Psychological Distress: 1957–1976." *American Sociological Review* 46:443–52.

Kisch, Arnold, Joel Kovner, Leonna Harris, and George Kline. 1969. "A New Proxy Measure for Health Status." *Health Services Research* 4:184–86.

Knowles, John. 1968. *Views of Education and Medical Care*. Cambridge, MA: Harvard University Press.

Kohn, Melvin. 1974. "Social Class and Schizophrenia: A Critical Review and Reformulation." In Paul Roman and Harvey Trice, eds., *Explorations in Psychiatric Sociology*. Philadelphia: F. A. Davis.

Korsch, B. M., E. K. Gozzi, and V. Francis. 1968. "Gaps in Doctor-Patient Communication: Doctor-Patient Interaction and Satisfaction." *Pediatrics* 42:855–58.

Krause, Eliott A. 1977. *Power and Illness: The Political Sociology of Health and Medical Care*. New York: Elsevier.

Kubler-Ross, Elisabeth. 1968. *On Death and Dying*. New York: Macmillan.

Lamb, Karen. 1973. "Freedom for Our Sisters, Freedom for Ourselves: Nursing Confronts Social Change." *Nursing Forum* 12:328–52.

Lanese, M. M. 1973. "Quick Quack Quiz." *The Physical Educator* December, pp. 217–18.

Langner, Thomas. 1962. "A 22-Item Screening Score of Psychiatric Symptoms Indicating Impairment." *Journal of Health and Human Behavior* 3:269–76.

Law, Donald. 1975. *Guide to Alternative Medicine*. New York: Hippocrene Books.

Lawrence, P. S. 1958. "Chronic Illness and Socioeconomic Status." In E. G. Jaco, ed., *Patients, Physicians, and Illness*. New York: Free Press.

Lawrence, Robert, Gordon DeFriese, Samuel Putnam, Glen Pickard, Bruce Cyr, and Sarah Whiteside. 1977. "Physician Receptivity to Nurse Practitioners: A Study of the Correlates of the Delegation of Clinical Responsibility." *Medical Care* 15:298–310.

Lee, Anthony, and Ronni Sandroff. 1984. "1984 and Beyond: What's Ahead for Nursing." *RN Magazine* 47(1):26–29.

Lee, Anthony, and Ronni Sandroff. 1984. "1984 and Beyond: What's Ahead for Nursing." *RN Magazine* 47(1):26–29.

Lee, Philip R., and A. E. Benjamin. 1984. "Health Policy and the Politics of Care." In Stephen Williams and Paul Torrens, eds., *Introduction to Health Services*, 2nd ed. New York: Wiley.

Leifer, Ronald. 1969. *In the Name of Mental Health*. New York: Science House.

Leighton, Alexander H. 1959. *My Name Is Legion*. New York: Basic Books.

Leighton, Alexander H., Dorothy Leighton, and R. A. Danely. 1966. "Validity in Mental Health Surveys." *Canadian Psychiatric Association Journal* 11:167–78.

Lemert, Edwin M. 1951. *Social Pathology*. New York: McGraw-Hill.

Lemert, Edwin M. 1964. "Social Structure, Social Control, and Deviation." In M. Clinard, ed., *Anomie and Deviant Behavior*. New York: Free Press.

Lennon, Bruce, Vern Bengston, and James Peterson. 1972. "An Exploration of the Activity Theory of Aging: Activity Types and Life Satisfaction Among In-Movers to a Retirement Community." *Journal of Gerontology* 27:511–13.

LeShan, L. 1974. *The Medium, the Mystic and the Physicist: Toward a General Theory of the Paranormal*. New York: Ballantine.

Levine, Eugene. 1977. "What Do We Know About Nurse Practitioners?" *American Journal of Nursing* 77:1799–1803.

Levine, Sol, and Martin A. Kozloff. 1978. "The Sick Role: Assessment and Overview." *Annual Review of Sociology* 4:317–43.

Levine, Sol, and James R. Sorenson. 1983. "Medical Sociology and Health Administration." *Journal of Health Administration Education* 1:343–82.

Levinson, D. J. 1967. "Medical Education and the Theory of Adult Education." *Journal of Health and Social Behavior* 8:253–65.

Levit, K. R., D. R. Waldo, and L. M. Davidoff. 1985. "National Health Expenditures, 1984." *Health Care Financing Review* 7:1–35.

Lewin, Kurt. 1951. *Field Theory in Social Science*. New York: Harper & Row.

Lewis, David. 1975. *The Physician's Assistant Concept*. Unpublished doctoral thesis, Duke University, Durham, NC.

Liang, Jersey. 1986. "Self-Reported Physical Health Among Aged Adults." *Journal of Gerontology* 41:248–60.

Light, Donald. 1980. *Becoming Psychiatrists: The Professional Transformation of Self*. New York: Norton.

Light, Donald W. 1984. "Growing Physician Supply: Implications for Hospitals and Doctors." Unpublished manuscript, Leonard Davis Institute of Health Economics.

Light, Donald W. 1985. "Physician Surplus and the Future of Physician Extenders: GMENAC in an Era of Cost-Containment." Unpublished manuscript, Leonard Davis Institute of Health Economics.

Light, Donald W. 1986a. "Organizational Consequences of a Physician Surplus: An Overview." Paper presented at the annual meeting of the American Sociological Association, August, New York.

Light, Donald W. 1986b. "Surplus Versus Cost Containment: The Changing Context for Health Providers." In Linda Aiken and David Mechanic, eds., *Applications of Social Science to Clinical Medicine and Health Policy*. New Brunswick, NJ: Rutgers University Press.

Lilienfeld, Abraham M. 1980. *Foundations of Epidemiology*. New York: Oxford University Press.

Lin, Nan. 1986. "Modeling the Effects of Social Support." In N. Lin, A. Dean, and W. Ensel, eds., *Social Support, Life Events, and Depression*. New York: Academic Press.

Lin, Nan, Alfred Dean, and Walter Ensel. 1986. *Social Support, Life Events, and Depression*. New York: Academic Press.

Lin, Nan, Mary Woelfel, and Stephen C. Light. 1986. "Buffering the Impact of the Most Important Life Event." In N. Lin, A. Dean, and W. Ensel, eds., *Social Support, Life Events, and Depression*. New York: Academic Press.

Lindemann, E. 1944. "Symptoms and Management of Acute Grief." *American Journal of Psychiatry* 101:141–49.

Litman, Theodore. 1976. *The Sociology of Medicine and Health Care: A Research Bibliography*. San Francisco: Boyd and Fraser.

Litoff, Judy B. 1978. *American Midwives: 1860 to the Present*. Westport, CT: Greenwood Press.

Lodewick, L., and A. D. G. Gunn. 1982. *The Physical Examination: An Atlas for General Practice*. Lancaster, England: M. T. P. Press.

Loehr, F. 1969. *The Power of Prayer on Plants*. New York: Signet Books.

LoGerfo, James P., and Robert H. Brook. 1984. "The Quality of Health Care." In Stephen Williams and Paul Torrens, eds., *Introduction to Health Services*, 2nd ed. New York: Wiley.

Lorber, Judith. 1975a. "Good Patients and Problem Patients: Conformity and Deviance in a General Hospital." *Journal of Health and Social Behavior* 16:213–25.

Lorber, Judith. 1975b. "Women and Medical Sociology: Invisible Professionals and Ubiquitous Patients." *Sociological Inquiry* 45:75–105.

Lorber, Judith. 1984. *Women Physicians: Careers, Status, and Power*. New York: Tavistock Publications.

Lorber, Judith. 1986. "A Welcome in a Crowded Field: Where Will the New Women Physicians Fit In?" Paper presented at the annual meeting of the American Sociological Association, August, New York.

Luft, Harold. 1981. *Health Maintenance Organizations: Dimensions of Performance*. New York: Wiley.

Lysaught, Jerome. 1973. *From Abstract Into Action*. New York: McGraw-Hill.

Maddox, George. 1962. "Some Correlates of Differences in Self-Assessment Among the Elderly." *Journal of Gerontology* 17:180–85.

Maddox, George. 1964. "Self-Assessment of Health Status: A Longitudinal Study of Elderly Subjects." *Journal of Chronic Diseases* 17:449–60.

Mangus, A. R. 1955. "Medical Sociology: Study of the Social Components of Illness and Health." *Sociology and Social Research* 49:158–64.

Marcus, Alfred, and Lori Crane. 1986. "Telephone Surveys in Public Health Research." *Medical Care* 24:97–112.

Marcus, Alfred, and Teresa Seeman. 1981a. "Sex Differences in Health Status: A Re-Examination of the Nurturant Role Hypothesis." *American Sociological Review* 46:119–23.

Marcus, Alfred, and Teresa Seeman. 1981b. "Sex Differences in Reports of Illness and Disability: A Preliminary Test of the 'Fixed-Role Obligations' Hypothesis." *Journal of Health and Social Behavior* 22:174–82.

Marcus, Alfred, and Judith Siegel. 1982. "Sex Differences in the Use of Physician Services: A Preliminary Test of the Fixed Role Hypothesis." *Journal of Health and Social Behavior* 23:186–97.

Marmor, Theodore R., and Andrew B. Dunham. 1983. "Political Science and Health." In Thomas Choi and Jay N. Greenberg, eds., *Social Science Approaches to Health Services Research*. Ann Arbor, MI: Health Administration Press.

Marshall, James, David Gregorio, and Debra Walsh. 1982. "Sex Differences in Illness Behavior: Care Seeking Among Cancer Patients." *Journal of Health and Social Behavior* 23:197–204.

Mattera, Marianne Dekker. 1985. "Nursing Pay: Who's Doing Best Now?" *RN Magazine* 48(11): 32–39.

Mattera, Marianne Dekker. 1986. "Job Security: Will Things Get Any Worse?" *RN Magazine* 49(6):36–41.

Matthews, Karen A., and David G. Glass. 1981. "Type A Behavior, Stressful Life Events, and Coronary Heart Disease." In B. Dohrenwend and B. Dohrenwend, eds., *Stressful Life Events and Their Contexts*. New Brunswick, NJ: Rutgers University Press.

Mauksch, Hans. 1972. "Nursing: Churning for Change." In Howard Freeman, Sol Levine, and Leo Reeder, eds., *Handbook of Medical Sociology*, 2nd ed. Englewood Cliffs, NJ: Prentice-Hall.

McClanahan, Sarah S., and Jennifer L. Glass. 1985. "A Note on the Trend in Sex Differences in Psychological Distress." *Journal of Health and Social Behavior* 26:328–35.

McClure, Walter. 1978. "On Broadening the Definition of and Removing Regulatory Barriers to a Competitive Health Care System." *Journal of Health Politics, Policy and Law* 3:303–27.

McIntire, Charles. 1894. "The Importance of the Study of Medical Sociology." *Bulletin of the American Academy of Medicine* 1:425–34.

McKinlay, John B. 1972. "Some Approaches and Problems in the Study of the Use of Services: An Overview." *Journal of Health and Social Behavior* 13:115–52.

McKinlay, John B. 1973. "On the Professional Regulation of Change." *Sociological Review Monographs* 20:61–84.

McKinlay, John B. 1982. "Toward the Proletarianization of Physicians." In C. Derber, ed., *Professionals as Workers: Mental Labor in Advanced Capitalism*. Boston: G. K. Hall.

McKinlay, John B. 1986. "Proletarianization and the Social Transformation of Doctoring." Paper presented at the annual meeting of the American Sociological Association, August, New York.

McKinlay, John, and Sonja McKinlay. 1977. "The Questionable Contribution of Medical Measures to the Decline of Mortality in the United States in the Twentieth Century." *Milbank Memorial Fund Quarterly* 55:405–28.

Mead, George. 1934. *Mind, Self, and Society*. Chicago: University of Chicago Press.

Mechanic, David. 1962. "The Concept of Illness Behavior." *Journal of Chronic Diseases* 15: 189–94.

Mechanic, David. 1964. "The Influence of Mothers on Their Children's Health Attitudes and Behavior." *Pediatrics* 33:444–53.

Mechanic, David. 1966a. "Response Factors in the Study of Illness: The Study of Illness Behavior." *Social Psychiatry* 1:11–20.

Mechanic, David. 1966b. "The Sociology of Medicine: Viewpoints and Perspectives. *Journal of Health and Human Behavior* 7:237–47.

Mechanic, David. 1968. *Medical Sociology: A Selective View*. New York: Free Press.

Mechanic, David. 1972. "Social Psychological Factors Affecting the Presentation of Bodily Complaints." *New England Journal of Medicine* 286:1132–39.

Mechanic, David. 1975. "The Organization of Medical Practice and Practice Orientations Among Physicians in Prepaid and Nonprepaid Primary Care Settings." *Medical Care* 13: 189–204.

Mechanic, David. 1976a. *The Growth of Bureaucratic Medicine*. New York: Wiley.

Mechanic, David. 1976b. "Stress, Illness, and Illness Behavior." *Journal of Human Stress* 2:2–6.

Mechanic, David. 1978. *Medical Sociology: A Comprehensive Text*, 2nd ed. New York: Free Press.

Mechanic, David. 1979a. "Correlates of Psychological Distress Among Young Adults: A Theoretical Hypothesis and Results from a 16-Year Follow-Up Study." *Archives of General Psychiatry* 36:1233–39.

Mechanic, David. 1979b. "Development of Psychological Distress Among Young Adults." *Archives of General Psychiatry* 36:1233–39.

Mechanic, David. 1979c. "The Stability of Health and Illness Behavior: Results from a 16-Year Follow-Up." *American Journal of Public Health* 69:1142–45.

Mechanic, David. 1980. "The Experience and Reporting of Common Physical Complaints." *Journal of Health and Social Behavior* 21: 146–55.

Mechanic, David. 1983. "The Experience and Expression of Distress: The Study of Illness Behavior and Medical Utilization." In David Mechanic, ed., *Handbook of Health, Health Care, and the Health Professions*. New York: Free Press.

Mechanic, David. 1985. "Cost Containment and the Quality of Medical Care: Rationing Strategies in an Era of Constrained Resources." *Milbank Memorial Fund Quarterly* 63: 453–75.

Mechanic, David. 1987. "Epilogue: A Look to the Future." In Marcia Ory and Kathleen Bond, eds., *Aging and Health Care: Social Science and Policy Perspectives*. New York: Tavistock Publications.

Mechanic, David, and Sol Levine, eds. 1977. "Issues in Promoting Health: Committee Reports of the Medical Sociology Section of the American Sociological Association." *Medical Care* 15(Suppl. to Issue 5):1–101.

Mechanic, David, and Edmund H. Volkart. 1961. "Stress, Illness Behavior, and the Sick Role." *American Sociological Review* 25:51–58.

Medalia, Nahum Z. 1964. "Foreword: The Environmental Health Challenge to Medical Sociology." *Journal of Health and Human Behavior* 5:131–32.

Merenstein, Joel, Harvey Wolfe, and Kathleen Barker. 1974. "The Use of Nurse Practitioners in a General Office." *Medical Care* 12: 437–44.

Merrill, J. C., and R. J. Wasserman. 1985. "Growth in National Expenditures: Additional Analyses." *Health Affairs* 4:91–98.

Merton, Robert K. 1957. *Social Theory and Social Structure*. New York: Free Press.

Merton, Robert, George Reader, and Patricia Kendall, eds. 1957. *The Student Physician: Introductory Studies in the Sociology of Medical Education*. Cambridge, MA: Harvard University Press.

Meyer, Genevieve, and Mabel Hoffman. 1964. "Nurses' Inner Values and Their Behavior at Work." *Nursing Research* 13:244–49.

Miller, Dorothy. 1971. "Worlds that Fail." In Samuel Wallace, ed., *Total Institutions*. Chicago: Aldine.

Miller, R. 1980. *Study of Absent Psychic Healing in Hypertension*. Los Angeles: Holmes Research Foundation.

Millman, Marcia. 1977. *The Unkindest Cut: Life in the Backrooms of Medicine*. New York: William Morrow.

Mishler, E. G. 1984. *The Discourse of Medicine: Dialectics of Medical Interviews*. Norwood, MA: Ablex.

Mitchell, Wayne. 1975. "Medical Student Career Choice: A Conceptualization." *Social Science and Medicine* 9:641–53.

Monteiro, Lois. 1973. "After Heart Attack: Behavioral Expectations for the Cardiac." *Social Science and Medicine* 7:555–65.

Moody, Ralph. 1975. *Life After Life*. Atlanta: Mockingbird Books.

Moody, Ralph. 1976. *Reflections on Life After Life*. Atlanta: Mockingbird Books.

Moriyama, Iwao, Dean Krueger, and Jeremiah Stamler. 1971. *Cardiovascular Diseases in the United States*. Cambridge, MA: Harvard University Press.

Morlock, Laura, Jeffrey Alexander, and Heidi Hunter. 1985. "Formal Relationships Among Governing Boards, CEOs, and Medical Staffs in Independent and System Hospitals." *Medical Care* 23:1193–1213.

Mosely, Ray R., and Fredric D. Wolinsky. 1986. "The Use of Proxies in Health Surveys: Substantive and Policy Implications." *Medical Care* 24:496–510.

Mumford, Emily. 1970. *Interns: From Student to Physician*. Cambridge, MA: Harvard University Press.

Myers, George C. 1985. "Aging and Worldwide Population Change." In Robert H. Binstock and Ethel Shanas, eds., *Handbook of Aging and the Social Sciences*, 2nd ed. New York: Van Nostrand Reinhold.

Myers, Jerome K., Jacob J. Lindenthal, and Max P. Pepper. 1974. "Social Class, Life Events, and Psychiatric Symptoms." In B. Dohrenwend and B. Dohrenwend, eds., *Stressful Life Events: Their Nature and Effects*. New York: Wiley.

Nash, C. B. 1982. "Psychokinetic Control of Bacterial Growth." *Journal of the Society for Psychical Research* 51:217–21.

Nathanson, Constance. 1975. "Illness and the Feminine Role: A Theoretical Review." *Social Science and Medicine* 9:57–62.

National Center for Health Statistics. 1985a. *Charting the Nation's Health: Trends Since 1960*. DHHS Publication No. 85–1251. Washington, DC: U.S. Government Printing Office.

National Center for Health Statistics. 1985b. *Vital Statistics of the United States, 1982: Life Tables*. DHHS Publication No. 85–1104.

Washington, DC: U.S. Government Printing Office.

National Center for Health Statistics. 1986. *Detailed Diagnoses and Procedures for Patients Discharged From Short-Stay Hospitals, United States, 1984*. DHHS Publication No. 86–1747. Washington, DC: U.S. Government Printing Office.

Nelson, E. C., A. R. Jacobs, and D. G. Johnson. 1974. "Patients' Acceptance of the Physicians' Assistants." *Journal of the American Medical Association* 228:63–68.

Nesselroade, John, and Erich Labouvie. 1985. "Experimental Design in Research on Aging." In James Birren and K. Warner Schaie, eds., *Handbook of the Psychology of Aging*, 2nd ed. New York: Van Nostrand Reinhold.

Neugarten, Bernice. 1971. "Grow Old with Me. The Best Is Yet to Be." *Psychology Today* 5(12):45–48.

Newhouse, J. P., A. P. Williams, and B. W. Bennett. 1982. "Where Have All the Doctors Gone?" *Journal of the American Medical Association* 247:2392–97.

Newhouse, Joseph. 1978. *The Economics of Medical Care: A Policy Perspective*. Reading, MA: Addison-Wesley.

Nightingale, Florence. 1914. *Florence Nightingale to Her Nurses*. New York: Macmillan.

Nuttbrock, Larry, and James Kosberg. 1980. "Images of the Physician and Help-Seeking Behavior of the Elderly: A Multivariate Analysis." *Journal of Gerontology* 35:241–48.

Oakley, D. A. 1971. "Instrumental Learning in Neocordicate Rabbits." *Nature* 233:185–87.

Office of Health Research, Statistics, and Technology. 1981. *Health, United States, 1980*. DHHS Publication No. 81–1232. Washington, DC: U.S. Government Printing Office.

Office of Health Research, Statistics, and Technology. 1985. *Health, United States, 1984*. DHHS Publication No. 85–1232. Washington, DC: U.S. Government Printing Office.

Olesen, Virginia L. 1975. "Convergences and Divergences: Anthropology and Sociology in Health Care." *Social Science and Medicine* 9:421–25.

Olesen, Virginia, and Elvi Whittaker. 1968. *The Silent Dialogue*. San Francisco: Jossey-Bass.

Olmstead, A. G., and M. A. Paget. 1969. "Some Theoretical Issues in Professional Socialization." *Journal of Medical Education* 44:663–69.

Onetto, B., and G. H. Elguin. 1966. "Psychokinesis in Experimental Tumorgenesis." *Journal of Parapsychology* 30:220.

Otis, G. 1975. *Medical Specialty Selection: A Re-*

366

References

view. DHEW Publication No. HRA–75–8. Washington, DC: U.S. Government Printing Office.

Palmer, Daniel David. 1910. *The Chiropractor's Adjuster: A Textbook of the Science, Art, and Philosophy of Chiropractic for Students and Practitioners*. Portland: Portland Printing House.

Parsons, Talcott. 1951. *The Social System*. New York: Free Press.

Parsons, Talcott. 1972. "Definitions of Health and Illness in Light of American Values and Social Structure." In E. G. Jaco, ed., *Patients, Physicians, and Illness*, 2d ed. New York: Free Press.

Parsons, Talcott. 1975. "The Sick Role and the Role of the Physician Reconsidered." *Milbank Memorial Fund Quarterly* 53:257–78.

Parsons, Talcott, and Renee Fox. 1952. "Illness, Therapy, and the Modern Urban American Family." *Journal of Social Issues* 8:31–44.

Patrick, Donald L., J. W. Bush, and Milton W. Chen. 1973. "Toward an Operational Definition of Health." *Journal of Health and Social Behavior* 14:6–23.

Pattison, E. Mansell. 1969. "Help in the Dying Process." *Voices* 5:6–14.

Pattison, E. Mansell. 1977. *The Experience of Dying*. New York: Basic Books.

Paul, John R. 1966. *Clinical Epidemiology*. Chicago: University of Chicago Press.

Pauly, Mark V. 1968. "The Economics of Moral Hazard: A Comment." *American Economic Review* 58:531.

Pauly, Mark V. 1980. "Overinsurance: The Conceptual Issues." In Mark Pauly, ed., *National Health Insurance: What Now, What Later, What Never?* Washington, DC: American Enterprise Institute.

Pauly, Mark V., and Mark A. Satterthwaite. 1980. "The Effects of Provider Supply on Price." In *The Target Income Hypothesis*. DHEW Publication No. 80–27. Washington, DC: U.S. Government Printing Office.

Paykel, Eugene S. 1978. "Contributions of Life Events to Psychiatric Illness." *Psychological Medicine* 8:245–53.

Peabody, Barbara. 1986. "Living with AIDS: A Mother's Perspective." *American Journal of Nursing* 86:46–47.

Pearlin, Leonard I., Morton A. Lieberman, Elizabeth G. Menaghan, and Joseph T. Mullan. 1981. "The Stress Process." *Journal of Health and Social Behavior* 22:337–56.

Pearlin, Leonard I., and Carmi Schooler. 1978. "The Structure of Coping." *Journal of Health and Social Behavior* 19:2–21.

Pearsall, Marion. 1963. *Medical Behavioral Science: A Selected Bibliography*. Lexington: University of Kentucky Press.

Pellegrino, Edmund. 1964. "Ethical Implications in Changing Practice." *American Journal of Nursing* 64:110–12.

Perrow, Charles. 1963. "Goals and Power Structures: A Historical Case Study." In Eliot Freidson, ed., *The Hospital in Modern Society*. Glencoe, IL: Free Press.

Perry, Henry. 1976. *Physician Assistants: An Empirical Analysis of Their General Characteristics, Job Performance, and Job Satisfaction*. Unpublished doctoral thesis, Duke University, Durham, NC.

Perry, Henry. 1977. "Physician Assistants: An Overview of the Emerging Health Profession." *Medical Care* 15:982–90.

Perry, Henry, and B. Breitner. 1982. *Physician's Assistants*. New York: Human Sciences Press.

Perry, Henry, and E. L. Redmond. 1980. *Physician Assistants: Their Contribution to Health Care*. New York: Appleton-Century-Crofts.

Pflanz, Manfred. 1974. "A Critique of Anglo-American Medical Sociology." *International Journal of Health Services* 4:565–74.

Pflanz, Manfred. 1975. "Relations Between Social Scientists, Physicians and Medical Organizations in Health Research." *Social Science and Medicine* 9:7–13.

Phillips, Bernard S. 1957. "A Role Theory Approach to Adjustment in Old Age." *American Sociological Review* 22:212–17.

Phillips, Derek L. 1967. "Social Participation and Happiness." *American Journal of Sociology* 72:479–88.

Pott, Sir Percival. 1775. *The Chirurgical Works of Percival Pott*. London: Hanes, Clark, and Collins.

Presidential Commission for the Study of Ethical Problems in Medicine and Biomedical and Behavioral Research. 1981. "Report of the Presidential Commission for the Study of Ethical Problems in Medicine and Biomedical and Behavioral Research." *Journal of the American Medical Association* 246:2184–6.

Preston, Ronald Phillip. 1979. *The Dilemmas of Care: Social and Nursing Adaptations to the Deformed, the Disabled, and the Aged*. New York: Elsevier.

Prevention Research Center. 1986. *The Prevention Index '86*. Emmaus, PA: Rodale Press.

Psathas, George. 1968. "The Fate of Idealism in Nursing School." *Journal of Health and Social Behavior* 9:52–64.

Public Health Service. 1976. *Longitudinal Study of Nurse Practitioners, Phase I*. DHEW Publication No. HRA 76–43. Washington, DC: U.S. Government Printing Office.

Querido, A. 1963. *The Efficiency of Medical Care*.

Leiden, The Netherlands: H. E. Stenfret Kroese.

Quinn, J. 1982. *An Investigation of the Effect of Therapeutic Touch Without Physical Contact on State Anxiety of Hospitalized Cardiovascular Patients*. Unpublished doctoral thesis, New York University.

Rachels, James. 1986. *The End of Life: Euthanasia and Morality*. Oxford, England: Oxford University Press.

Radloff, L. S. 1977. "The CES-D Scale: A Self-Report Depression Scale for Research in the General Population." *Journal of Applied Psychological Measures* 1:385–401.

Rahe, Richard H., M. Romo, L. Bennett, and P. Silaten. 1974. "Recent Life Changes, Myocardial Infarction and Abrupt Coronary Death." *Archives of Internal Medicine* 133:221–28.

Ramsey, James B. 1980. "An Analysis of Competing Hypotheses of the Demand for and Supply of Physician Services." In *The Target Income Hypothesis*. DHEW Publication No. 80–27. Washington, DC: U.S. Government Printing Office.

Raus, Elmer, and Madonna Raus. 1974. *Manual of History Taking, Physical Examination, and Record Keeping*. Philadelphia: J. B. Lippincott.

Rayack, Elton. 1967. *Professional Power and American Medicine*. Cleveland: World Publishing.

Reiss, Albert, with Otis Dudley Duncan, Paul K. Hatt, and C. C. North. 1961. *Occupation and Social Status*. Glencoe, IL: Free Press.

Relman, Arnold. 1980. "The New Medical Industrial Complex." *New England Journal of Medicine* 303:963–70.

Renne, K. S. 1974. "Measurement of Social Health in a General Population Survey." *Social Science Research* 3:25–34.

Reynolds, Jeff W., William A. Rushing, and David L. Miles. 1974. "The Validation of a Function Status Index." *Journal of Health and Social Behavior* 15:271–88.

Rice, Dorothy, and Jacob Feldman. 1983. "Living Longer in the United States: Demographic Changes and Health Needs of the Elderly." *Milbank Memorial Fund Quarterly* 61:362–96.

Richardson, William C. 1984. "Financing Health Services." In Stephan J. Williams and Paul R. Torrens, eds., *Introduction to Health Services*, 2nd ed. New York: Wiley.

Ricks, David F., and Barbara S. Dohrenwend, eds. 1983. *The Origins of Psychopathology: Problems in Research and Public Policy*. Cambridge, England: Cambridge University Press.

Riley, Matilda White. 1971. "Social Gerontology and the Age Stratification of Society." *The Gerontologist* 11:79–87.

Riley, Matilda White. 1987. "On the Significance of Age in Sociology." *American Sociological Review* 52:1–14.

Robert Wood Johnson Foundation. 1986. *Program for Demonstration and Research on Health Care Costs, 1987*. Princeton, NJ: Author.

Roberts, Joan, and Thetis Group. 1973. "The Women's Movement and Nursing." *Nursing Forum* 12:302–22.

Roemer, Milton. 1961. "Bed Supply and Hospital Utilization." *Hospitals* 48:51–56.

Roemer, Milton, and Ray Elling. 1963. "Sociological Research on Medical Care." *Journal of Health and Human Behavior* 4:49–68.

Rogers, Paul. 1976. "Introduction." In *A Discursive Dictionary of Health Care*. Washington, DC: U.S. Government Printing Office.

Rose, Arnold. 1965. "The Subculture of Aging: A Framework for Research in Social Gerontology." In Arnold Rose and Warren Peterson, eds., *Older People and Their Social World*. Philadelphia: F. A. Davis.

Rosen, George. 1963. "The Hospital: A Historical Case Study." In Eliot Freidson, ed., *The Hospital in Modern Society*. Glencoe, IL: Free Press.

Rosenhan, David. 1973. "On Being Sane in Insane Places." *Science* 179(Jan. 19):250–58.

Rosenstock, Irwin. 1960. "What Research in Motivation Suggests for Public Health." *American Journal of Public Health* 50:295–302.

Rosow, Irving. 1985. "Status and Role Change Throughout the Life Cycle." In Robert Binstock and Ethel Shanas, eds., *Handbook of Aging and the Social Sciences*, 2nd ed. New York: Van Nostrand Reinhold.

Ross, Catherine, and John Mirowsky. 1979. "A Comparison of Life-Event-Weighting Schemes: Change, Undesirability, and Effect-Proportional Indices. *Journal of Health and Social Behavior* 20:166–77.

Rotter, J. B. 1966. *Generalized Expectancies for Internal Versus External Control of Reinforcement*. Psychological Monographs No. 80. Washington, DC: American Psychological Association.

Rousch, Robert E. 1979. "The Development of Midwifery—Male and Female, Yesterday and Today." *Journal of Nurse-Midwifery* 24:27–37.

Ruch, Libby O. 1977. "A Multidimensional Analysis of the Concept of Life Change." *Journal of Health and Social Behavior* 18:71–83.

Rushing, William. 1975. *Community, Physicians, and Inequality*. Lexington, MA: D. C. Heath.

Rushing, William. 1984. "Social Factors in the

Rise of Hospital Costs." *Research in the Sociology of Health Care* 3:27–114.

Rushing, William. 1985. "The Supply of Physicians and Expenditures for Health Services with Implications for the Coming Physician Surplus." *Journal of Health and Social Behavior* 26:297–311.

Sadler, Alfred, Blair Sadler, and Ann Blessa. 1972. *The Physician's Assistant Today and Tomorrow*. New Haven, CT: Yale University Press.

Sales, S. M. 1969. "Organizational Roles as a Risk Factor in Coronary Heart Disease." *Administrative Science Quarterly* 14:325–36.

Salloway, Jeffrey C. 1982. *Health Care Delivery Systems*. Boulder, CO: Westview Publishing.

Saunders, Cicely, and Mary Baines. 1983. *Living with Dying: The Management of Terminal Disease*. Oxford, England: Oxford University Press.

Saunders, Lyle, and Gordon Hewes. 1969. "Folk Medicine and Medical Practice." In L. R. Lynch, ed., *Cross-Cultural Approach to Health Behavior*. Rutherford, NJ: Fairleigh Dickinson University Press.

Schaie, K. Warner, and Christopher Hertzog. 1985. "Measurement in the Psychology of Adulthood and Aging." In James Birren and K. Warner Schaie, eds., *Handbook of the Psychology of Aging*, 2nd ed. New York: Van Nostrand Reinhold.

Schaller, Warren E., and Charles R. Carroll. 1976. *Health, Quackery and the Consumer*. Philadelphia: W. B. Saunders.

Scheff, Thomas. 1964. "The Societal Reaction to Deviance: Ascriptive Elements in the Psychiatric Screening of Mental Patients in a Midwestern State." *Social Problems* 11:401–13.

Scheff, Thomas. 1966. *Being Mentally Ill*. Chicago: Aldine.

Scheff, Thomas. 1974. "The Labelling Theory of Mental Illness." *American Sociological Review* 39:444–52.

Scheff, Thomas. 1975. *Labelling Madness*. Englewood Cliffs, NJ: Prentice-Hall.

Scheff, Thomas. 1984. *Being Mentally Ill: A Sociological Theory*, 2nd ed. New York: Aldine.

Schlotfeldt, Rozella. 1974. "On the Professional Status of Nursing." *Nursing Forum* 8:16–31.

Schneider, Joseph, and Peter Conrad. 1983. *Having Epilepsy: The Experience and Control of Illness*. Philadelphia: Temple University Press.

Schneller, Eugene. 1974. *A Comprehensive Bibliography on Physicians' Assistants*. Durham, NC: Health Care Systems.

Schneller, Eugene. 1975. "A Content Analysis of the Literature on the P.A.: A Method for Studying Occupations and Professions." Paper presented to the annual meeting of the American Sociological Association, August, Atlanta.

Schneller, Eugene. 1978. *The Physicians' Assistant: A Sociological Analysis of an Emerging Profession*. Boston: D. C. Heath.

Schramm, Carl J. 1983. "A Legal Perspective on Health Care Services." In Thomas Choi and Jay N. Greenberg, eds., *Social Science Approaches to Health Services Research*. Ann Arbor, MI: Health Administration Press.

Schulman, Sam. 1972. "Mother Surrogate: After a Decade." In E. Gartly Jaco, ed., *Patients, Physicians, and Illness*, 2nd ed. New York: Free Press.

Schulz, Robert. 1985. *The Economics of Aging*, 3rd ed. Belmont, CA: Wadsworth.

Schulz, Rockwell, and Alton C. Johnson. 1983. *Management of Hospitals*, 2nd ed. New York: McGraw-Hill.

Secretary's Task Force. 1985. *Report of the Secretary's Task Force on Black and Minority Health*. DHHS Publication No. 85–0–487–637 (QL3). Washington, DC: U.S. Government Printing Office.

Segall, Alexander. 1976a. "The Sick Role Concept: Understanding Social Behavior." *Journal of Health and Social Behavior* 17:163–70.

Segall, Alexander. 1976b. "Sociocultural Variation in Sick Role Behavior Expectations." *Social Science and Medicine* 10:47–51.

Segall, Alexander. 1987. "Cultural Factors in Sick Role Expectations." In D. S. Gochman, ed., *Health Behavior: Emerging Research Perspectives*. New York: Plenum.

Selye, Hans. 1956. *The Stress of Life*. New York: McGraw-Hill.

Shaw, Margery W. 1984. *After Barney Clark: Reflections on the Utah Artificial Heart*. Austin: University of Texas Press.

Shortell, Stephen, and James P. LoGerfo. 1981. "Hospital Medical Staff Organization and Quality of Care: Results for Myocardial Infarction and Appendectomy." *Medical Care* 19:1041–56.

Siegmann, Athilia E., and Jack Elinson. 1977. "Newer Sociomedical Health Indicators: Implications for Evaluation of Health Services." *Medical Care* 15(5, Suppl.):84–92.

Sigerist, Henry B. 1951. *A History of Medicine: Volume I: Primitive and Archaic Medicine*. London: Oxford University Press.

Sigerist, Henry B. 1960. *On the History of Medicine*. New York: M.D. Publications.

Silverman, D., R. Masland, and M. G. Saunders. 1969. "EEG and Cerebral Death: The Neurologist's View." *Electroencephalographic Clinical Neurophysiology* 27:549.

Simmons, Ozzie, and Emil Berkanovic. 1972. "Social Research in Health and Medicine: A Bibliography." In Howard Freeman, Sol Levine, and Leo Reeder, eds., *Handbook of Medical Sociology*, 2nd ed. New York: Prentice-Hall.

Smith, Harvey. 1955. "Two Lines of Authority Are One Too Many." *Modern Hospital* 85: 48–52.

Smoyak, Shirley. 1974. "Co-Equal Status for Nurses and Physicians." *American Medical News*, February 11.

Snell, F. W. 1980. "PK Influence on Malignant Cell Growth." *Research Letter, University of Ultrecht* 10:19–27.

Snow, Sir John. 1855. *On the Mode of Communication of Cholera*. London: Churchill.

Solfvin, G. F. 1982. "Psi Expectancy Effects in Psychic Healing Studies with Maleria Mice." *European Journal of Parapsychology* 4:160–97.

Soules, H. Maxine. 1978. "Professional Advancement and Salary Differentials Among Baccalaureate, Diploma, and Associate Degree Nurses." *Nursing Forum* 17:184–202.

Sousa, Marion. 1976. *Childbirth at Home*. Englewood Cliffs, NJ: Prentice-Hall.

Spitzer, Robert, and Paul Wilson. 1975. "Nosology and the Official Psychiatric Nomenclature." In A. Freedman, H. Kaplan, and B. Sadlock, eds., *Comprehensive Textbook of Psychiatry*. Baltimore, MD: Williams & Wilkins.

Srole, Leo. 1975. "Measurement and Classification in Sociopsychiatric Epidemiology: Midtown Manhattan Study (1954) and Midtown Manhattan Restudy (1974)." *Journal of Health and Social Behavior* 16:347–64.

Srole, Leo, Thomas Langner, S. T. Michael, M. K. Opler, and Thomas Rennie. 1962. *Mental Health in the Metropolis: The Midtown Manhattan Study*. New York: McGraw Hill.

Starkweather, David. 1971. "Health Care Facility Mergers: Some Conceptualizations." *Medical Care* 11:468–87.

Starr, Paul. 1982. *The Social Transformation of American Medicine: The Rise of a Sovereign Profession and the Making of a Vast Industry*. New York: Basic Books.

Stedman, Thomas L. 1982. *Stedman's Illustrated Medical Dictionary*, 24th ed. Baltimore, MD: Williams & Wilkins.

Stein, Leonard. 1967. "The Doctor-Nurse Game." *Archives of General Psychiatry* 16:669–702.

Stevens, Rosemary. 1971. *American Medicine in the Public Interest*. New Haven: Yale University Press.

Stevens, Rosemary. 1983. "Comparisons in Health Care: Britain as Contrast to the United States." In David Mechanic, ed., *Handbook of Health, Health Care, and the Health Professions*. New York: Free Press.

Stewart, Anita L., John E. Ware, Jr., and Robert B. Brook. 1977a. "The Meaning of Health: Understanding Functional Limitations." *Medical Care* 15:939–52.

Stewart, Anita L., John E. Ware, Jr., and Robert Brook. 1977b. *A Study of the Reliability, Validity, and Precision of Scales to Measure Functional Limitations Due to Poor Health*. Publication No. 5660. Santa Monica, CA: The Rand Corporation.

Stewart, Anita L., John E. Ware, Jr., and Robert H. Brook. 1981. "Advances in the Measurement of Functional Status: Construction of Aggregate Indices." *Medical Care* 19:473–88.

Stewart, Anita L., John. E. Ware Jr., and Sharon Johnston. 1975. *Construction of Scales Measuring Health and Health-Related Concepts from the Dayton Medical History Questionnaire*. Draft Working Paper. Santa Monica, CA: The Rand Corporation.

Stewart, Moira, and Carol Buck. 1977. "Physicians' Knowledge of and Response to Patients' Problems." *Medical Care* 15:578–85.

Still, Andrew T. 1908. *Autobiography of A. T. Still*. Kirksville, MO: A. T. Still Publications.

Straus, Robert. 1955. "The Development of a Social Science Teaching and Research Program in a Medical Center." Paper presented to the American Sociological Society.

Straus, Robert. 1957. "The Nature and Status of Medical Sociology." *American Sociological Review* 22:200–4.

Straus, Robert. 1959. "A Department of Behavioral Science." *Journal of Medical Education* 34:662–66.

Straus, Robert. 1963. "A Role for Behavioral Science in a University-Based Medical Center." *Annals of the American Academy of Political and Social Sciences* 346:99–108.

Strauss, Anselm, Shizuko Fagerhaugh, Barbara Suczek, and Carolyn Wiener. 1985. *The Social Organization of Medical Work*. Chicago: University of Chicago Press.

Strong, Peter M. 1979. "Sociological Imperialism and the Profession of Medicine: A Critical Examination of the Thesis of Medical Imperialism." *Social Science and Medicine* 13A:199–215.

Suchman, Edward. 1965a. "Social Patterns of Illness and Medical Care." *Journal of Health and Human Behavior* 6:2–16.

Suchman, Edward. 1965b. "Stages of Illness and Medical Care." *Journal of Health and Human Behavior* 6:114–28.

Suchman, Edward. 1967. "The Survey Method

Applied to Public Health and Medicine." In C. Y. Glock, ed., *Survey Research in the Social Sciences*. New York: Russell Sage.

Sullivan, Daniel. 1966. *Conceptual Problems in Developing an Index of Health*. DHEW Publication No. 66–1000. Washington, DC: U.S. Government Printing Office.

Surgeon General's Report, The. 1984. *The Health Consequences of Smoking*. DHHS Publication No. 84–50205. Washington, DC: U.S. Government Printing Office.

Susser, Mervyn. 1974a. "A Critical Review of Sociology in Health." [Special Issue.] *International Journal of Health Services* 4:403–578.

Susser, Mervyn. 1974b. "Ethical Components in the Definition of Health." *International Journal of Health Services* 4:539–48.

Susser, Mervyn. 1974c. "Introduction to the Theme: A Critical Review of Sociology in Health." *International Journal of Health Services* 4:407–9.

Suzman, Richard, and Matilda Riley. 1985. "Introducing the 'Oldest Old.'" *Milbank Memorial Fund Quarterly* 63:177–86.

Szasz, Thomas. 1960. "The Myth of Mental Illness." *American Psychologist* 15:113–18.

Szasz, Thomas. 1961. *The Myth of Mental Illness: Foundations of a Theory of Personal Conduct*. New York: Dell.

Szasz, Thomas. 1970. *The Manufacture of Madness*. New York: Dell.

Szasz, Thomas. 1974. *The Myth of Mental Illness*, rev. ed. New York: Harper & Row.

Szasz, Thomas, and Marc Hollender. 1956. "A Contribution to the Philosophy of Medicine: The Basic Models of the Doctor-Patient Relationship." *Journal of the American Medical Association* 97:585–88.

Tagliacozzo, Daisy, and Hans Mauksch. 1972. "The Patient's View of the Patient's Role." In E. Gartly Jaco, ed., *Patients, Physicians, and Illness*, 2nd ed. New York: Free Press.

Task Force on Death and Dying of the Institute of Society, Ethics, and the Life Sciences. 1972. "Refinements in the Criteria for the Determination of Death." *Journal of the American Medical Association* 221:48–53.

Tausig, Mark. 1986. "Measuring Life Events." In N. Lin, A. Dean, and W. Ensel, eds., *Social Supports, Life Events, and Depression*. New York: Academic Books.

Taylor, D. Garth, Lu Ann Aday, and Ronald Andersen. 1975. "A Social Indicator of Access to Medical Care." *Journal of Health and Social Behavior* 16:39–49.

Theorell, Tores, E. Lind, and B. Flonderus. 1975.

"The Relationship of Disturbing Life Changes and Emotions to the Early Development of Myocardial Infarction and Other Serious Illnesses." *Journal of Epidemiology* 4:281–93.

Thoits, Peggy. 1982. "Conceptual, Methodological, and Theoretical Problems in Studying Social Support as a Buffer Against Life Stress." *Journal of Health and Social Behavior* 23:145–59.

Thomas, Elizabeth, and Kaoru Yamamoto. 1975. "Attitudes Toward Age: An Exploration of School-Age Children." *International Journal of Aging and Development* 6:29–40.

Thomas, William I., and Florian Znaniecki. 1918. *The Polish Peasant in Europe and America*. New York: Gorham.

Thomson, William R. 1984. *Black's Medical Dictionary*, 24th ed. London: Adams and Charles Black.

Tomajan, Karen L. 1986. "Taking the Terror Out of Challenge Exams." *RN Magazine* 49(1):32–34.

Torrens, Paul. 1978. *The American Health Care Delivery System: Issues and Problems*. Saint Louis: C. V. Mosby.

Turnbull, Richard, ed. 1985. *Terminal Care*. New York: Hemisphere Publishing Corporation.

Twaddle, Andrew. 1974. "The Concept of Health Status." *Social Science and Medicine* 8:29–38.

Twaddle, Andrew, and Richard Hessler. 1977. *An Introduction to the Sociology of Health*. Saint Louis: C. V. Mosby.

Tyson, K. W., and J. C. Merrill. 1984. "Health Care Institutions: Survival in a Changing Environment." *Journal of Medical Education* 59:773–81.

Verbrugge, Lois M. 1983. "Demography and Health Services Research." In Thomas Choi and Jay N. Greenberg, eds., *Social Science Approaches to Health Services Research*. Ann Arbor, MI: Health Administration Press.

Verbrugge, Lois M. 1985. "Gender and Health: An Update on Hypotheses and Evidence." *Journal of Health and Social Behavior* 26:156–82.

Verbrugge, Lois. 1986. "From Sneezes to Adieu: Stages of Health for Men and Women." *Social Science and Medicine* 20:683–98.

Veroff, Joseph, Elizabeth Douvan, and R. Kulka. 1981. *The Inner Americans: A Self-Portrait From 1957 to 1976*. New York: Basic Books.

Veroff, Joseph, Gerald Gurin, and Sheila Field. 1962. "Dimensions of Subjective Assessment." *Journal of Abnormal and Social Psychology* 54:192–205.

VerSteeg, Donna, and Sydney Croog. 1979. "Hospitals and Related Health Care Delivery Set-

tings." In Howard Freeman, Sol Levine, and Leo Reeder, eds., *Handbook of Medical Sociology*, 3rd ed. Englewood Cliffs, NJ: Prentice-Hall.

Viseltear, Arthur J. 1977. "Book Review of *A Discursive Dictionary of Health Care*." *Medical Care* 15:446–49.

Waldron, Ingrid. 1976. "Why Do Women Live Longer than Men?" *Social Science and Medicine* 10:349–62.

Wan, Thomas. 1987. "Models of Health Care Utilization by Older People." In Marcia Ory and Kathleen Bond, eds., *Aging and Health Care: Social Science and Policy Perspectives*. New York: Tavistock Publications.

Wan, Thomas, and Scott Soifer. 1974. "Determinants of Physician Utilization: A Causal Analysis." *Journal of Health and Social Behavior* 15:100–8.

Wardwell, Walter I. 1979. "Limited and Marginal Practitioners." In Howard Freeman, Sol Levine, and Leo Reeder, eds., *Handbook of Medical Sociology*, 3rd ed. Englewood Cliffs, NJ: Prentice-Hall.

Wardwell, Walter I. 1980. "The Future of Chiropractic." *New England Journal of Medicine* 302(Mar. 20):688–90.

Wardwell, Walter I. 1982. "Chiropractors: Challengers of Medical Domination." *Research in the Sociology of Health Care* 2:207–50.

Wardwell, Walter I. 1983. "The State of Medical Sociology: A Review Essay." *The Sociological Quarterly* 23:563–71.

Ware, John E., Jr., Robert Brook, Allyson R. Davies, and Kathleen N. Lohr. 1981. "Choosing Measures of Health Status for Individuals in General Populations." *American Journal of Public Health* 71:620–25.

Ware, John E., Jr., Susan A. Johnston, Allyson Davies Avery. 1979. *Conceptualization and Measurement of Health for Adults in the Health Insurance Study. III. Mental Health*. Santa Monica, CA: The Rand Corporation.

Waters, Scott, and Jean Arbeiter. 1985. "Nurse Practitioners: How Are They Doing Now?" *RN Magazine* 48(10):38–43.

Watkins, G. K., A. M. Watkins, and R. A. Wells. 1973. "Further Studies on the Resuscitation of Anesthetized Mice." In W. G. Roll, R. L. Morris, and J. D. Morris, eds., *Research in Parapsychology, 1972*. Metuchen, NJ: Scarecrow Press.

Wax, Murray. 1970. In O. VonMering and L. Kasden, eds., *Anthropology and the Behavioral and Health Sciences*. Pittsburgh: University of Pittsburgh Press.

Weber, Max. 1968. *Economy and Society*. New York: Bedminster Press.

Weisman, A. D. 1980. "Thanatology." In Berton Kaplan, ed., *Comprehensive Textbook of Psychiatry*. Baltimore, MD: Williams & Wilkins.

Weissman, Myrna M., Diane Sholomskas, Margaret Pottenger, Brigette Prusoff, and Ben Z. Locke. 1977. "Assessing Depressive Symptoms in Five Psychiatric Populations: A Validation Study." *American Journal of Epidemiology* 106:203–14.

Wellin, Edward, and Milvoy Seacat. 1962. "Social Science in the Health Field: A Review of Research." *American Journal of Public Health* 52:1465–72.

West, Candace. 1984. *Routine Complications: Troubles with Talk Between Doctors and Patients*. Bloomington: Indiana University Press.

Weston, Jerry L. 1980. "Distribution of Nurse Practitioner and Physician Assistants: Implications of Legal Constraints and Reimbursement." *Public Health Reports* 95:253–71.

Weston, Jerry L. 1984. "Ambiguities Limit the Role of Nurse Practitioners and Physician Assistants." *American Journal of Public Health* 74:6–7.

Wheaton, Blair. 1980. "The Sociogenesis of Psychological Disorder: An Attributional Theory." *Journal of Health and Social Behavior* 21:100–23.

Wheaton, Blair. 1983. "Uses and Abuses of the Langner Index: A Re-Examination of Findings on Psychological and Psychophysiological Distress." In David Mechanic, ed., *Symptoms, Illness Behavior, and Help-Seeking*. New York: Prodist.

Wheaton, Blair. 1985. "Models for the Stress-Buffering Functions of Coping Resources." *Journal of Health and Social Behavior* 26:352–64.

Wilensky, Gail R., Pamela J. Farley, and Amy K. Taylor. 1984. "Variations in Health Insurance Coverage: Benefits vs. Premiums." *Milbank Memorial Fund Quarterly* 62:53–81.

Wilensky, Gail R., and David C. Walden. 1981. "Minorities, Poverty, and the Uninsured." Paper presented at the annual meeting of the American Public Health Association, November, Los Angeles.

Wilensky, Harold. 1964. "The Professionalization of Everyone." *American Journal of Sociology* 70:137–58.

Williams, A. P., W. B. Schwartz, and J. P. Newhouse. 1983. "How Many Miles to the Doctor?" *New England Journal of Medicine* 309:958–62.

Wilson, Robert N. 1970. *The Sociology of Health: An Introduction*. New York: Random House.

Wilson, Robert N., and Samuel Bloom. 1972. "Patient-Practitioner Relationships." In Howard Freeman, Sol Levine, and Leo Reeder, eds., *Handbook of Medical Sociology*, 2nd ed. Englewood Cliffs, NJ: Prentice-Hall.

Wing, Steve, Kenneth Manton, Eric Stallard, Curtis Hames, and H. A. Tyroler. 1985. "The Black/White Mortality Crossover: Investigation in a Community-Based Study." *Journal of Gerontology* 40:78–84.

Wolinsky, Fredric D. 1976. "Health Service Utilization and Attitudes Toward Health Maintenance Organizations: A Theoretical and Methodological Discussion." *Journal of Health and Social Behavior* 17:221–36.

Wolinsky, Fredric D. 1978. "Assessing the Effects of Predisposing, Enabling, and Illness-Morbidity Characteristics on Health Service Utilization." *Journal of Health and Social Behavior* 19:384–96.

Wolinsky, Fredric D. 1980a. "The Performance of Health Maintenance Organizations: An Analytic Review." *Milbank Memorial Fund Quarterly* 58:537–82.

Wolinsky, Fredric D. 1980b. *The Sociology of Health: Principles, Professions, and Issues.* Boston: Little, Brown.

Wolinsky, Fredric D. 1987. "Sick Role Legitimization." In D. S. Gochman, ed., *Health Behavior: Emerging Research Perspectives.* New York: Plenum Publishing.

Wolinsky, Fredric D., and Rodney M. Coe. 1984. "Physician and Hospital Utilization Among Elderly Adults: An Analysis of the Health Interview Survey." *Journal of Gerontology* 39:334–41.

Wolinsky, Fredric D., Rodney M. Coe, Douglas K. Miller, John M. Prendergast, Myra J. Creel, and M. Noel Chavez. 1983. "Health Services Utilization Among the Noninstitutionalized Elderly." *Journal of Health and Social Behavior* 24:325–36.

Wolinsky, Fredric D., Rodney M. Coe, and Ray R. Mosely. 1987. "The Use of Health Services by Elderly Americans: Implications from a Regression-Based Cohort Analysis." In Russell Ward and Sheldon Tobin, eds., *Health in Aging: Sociological Issues and Policy Directions.* Beverly Hills, CA: Sage.

Wolinsky, Fredric D., and William D. Marder. 1985. *The Organization of Medical Practice and the Practice of Medicine.* Ann Arbor, MI: Health Administration Press.

Wolinsky, Fredric D., and Steven R. Steiber. 1982. "Salient Issues in Choosing a New Doctor." *Social Science and Medicine* 16:759–67.

Wolinsky, Fredric D., and Sally R. Wolinsky. 1981a. "Background, Attitudinal, and Behavioural Patterns of Individuals Occupying Eight Discrete Health States." *Sociology of Health and Illness* 3:31–48.

Wolinsky, Fredric D., and Sally R. Wolinsky. 1981b. "Expecting Sick Role Legitimation and Getting It." *Journal of Health and Social Behavior* 22:229–42.

Wolinsky, Fredric D., and Marty E. Zusman. 1980. "Toward Comprehensive Health Status Measures." *The Sociological Quarterly* 21:607–21.

World Health Organization. 1958. *The World Health Organization: A Report on the First Ten Years.* Geneva, Switzerland: Author.

Wyszewianski, Leon, John R. C. Wheeler, and Avedis Donabedian. 1982. "Market-Oriented Cost-Containment Strategies and Quality of Care." *Milbank Memorial Fund Quarterly* 60:518–50.

Young, James C. 1981. *Medical Choice in a Mexican Village.* New Brunswick, NJ: Rutgers University Press.

Zborowski, Mark. 1952. "Cultural Components in Responses to Pain." *Journal of Social Issues* 8:16–30.

Zola, Irving K. 1962. *Sociocultural Factors in the Seeking of Medical Care.* Unpublished Ph.D. thesis, Harvard University.

Zola, Irving K. 1964. "Illness Behavior of the Working Class." In Arthur Shostak and William Gomberg, eds., *Blue Collar World.* Englewood Cliffs, NJ: Prentice-Hall.

Zola, Irving K. 1966. "Culture and Symptoms: An Analysis of Patients Presenting Complaints." *American Sociological Review* 31:615–30.

Zola, Irving K. 1972. "Medicine as an Institution of Social Control." *Sociological Review Monographs* 20:487–504.

Zuckerman, Howard. 1979. "Multi-Institutional Hospital Systems." *Inquiry* 16:289–302.

Zuckerman, Howard. 1981. "Multi-Institutional Systems: Adaptive Strategy for Growth, Survival." *Hospital Progress* 62:43–47.

Zusy, Mary Lloyd. 1986. "RN to BSN: Fitting the Pieces Together." *American Journal of Nursing* 86:394–97.

Index